DIVERS

AND U.S. FOREIGN POLICY

DIVERSITY

AND U.S. FOREIGN POLICY

a Reader

ERNEST J. WILSON III

ROUTLEDGE New York • London

Published in 2004 by
Routledge
270 Madison Avenue
New York, NY 10016
www.routledge-ny.com

Published in Great Britain by
Routledge
2 Park Square
Milton Park, Abingdon
Oxon OX14 4RN U.K.
www.routledge.co.uk

Routledge is an imprint of the Taylor & Francis Group.

© 2004 by Taylor & Francis Books, Inc.

Routledge is an imprint of the Taylor and Francis Group.

Printed in the United States of America on acid-free paper.
10 9 8 7 6 5 4 3 2 1

Library of Congress Cataloging-in-Publication Data

    Diversity and U.S. foreign policy : a reader / edited by Ernest J. Wilson, III.
      p. cm.
    Includes bibliographic references (p.) and index.
      ISBN 0-415-92857-5 (hc : alk. paper) — ISBN 0-415-92884-2 (pb : alk. paper)
      1. United States—Foreign relations—1989– 2. Multiculturalism—United States.
    3. Pluralism (Social sciences)—United States. I. Wilson, Ernest J., III
    E895.D59 2004
    327.73'0089—dc22

                                      2003023609

Contents

Part 3

Acknowledgments

The ideas about multiculturalism and international affairs explored in this volume were inspired by more than twenty-five years working in a variety of national and international institutions and universities. As a professor, I teach and write on these issues regularly. As a practitioner, I have observed ethnic and racial dynamics at close hand while serving as a senior staff member of the National Security Council at the White House, as a Congressional aid, in nonprofits such as the Council on Foreign Relations, and in private bodies such as the Global Information Infrastructure Commission.

This volume owes a great deal to individuals and institutions who provided unique opportunities to develop my ideas in supportive and challenging environments. Tom Rowe at the University of Denver and his International Career Advancement Program hosts each year a weeklong seminar in Aspen, Colorado, where these ideas are taken seriously and discussed by international affairs professionals. His vision and commitment helped inspire this volume. Abe Lowenthal, the founder of the Pacific Council on International Policy, held a national conference of Latinos, Asian Americans, and African Americans that prompted some of the work in this collection, and he has been a welcome part of the conversation since then. The Council on Foreign Relations wrestles regularly with these issues, and Council President Les Gelb has supported several initiatives at that body in which I have participated. The minority fellowship programs for college juniors interested in international affairs, under their various names, let me interact with some of the best and brightest young people in our country at the policy schools of the universities of Michigan and Maryland. The late William Diaz was an early leader and supporter of these programs at the Ford Foundation. For its part, the Congressional Black Caucus consistently takes on these tough issues at its annual forum, and there I have been privileged to work with Congressmen Sanford Bishop, Charles Diggs, Bill Gray, Mickey Leland, and Don Payne.

Others who informed the shape of this project include Goler Butcher, George Dalley, Rudolpho de la Garza, I. M. Destler, Lauri Fitz-Pegado, Will Itoh, Ed Perkins, Susan Rice, Peter Romero, Elliott Skinner, Shibley Telhami, and the members of the long-standing "foreign affairs Sunday brunch."

Of all these experiences, working as a senior advisor on President Clinton's 1992 national security and foreign affairs transition team helping select Cabinet and sub-Cabinet appointees was the best lesson imaginable to learn how the mix of technical expertise, substantive experience, political commitments, campaign support, gender, and ethnicity intersect at the highest levels of the foreign policy community. To that team, I extend my heartfelt thanks.

Research assistance is gratefully acknowledged from Bidisha Biswas, Tanja Owe, Neha Sahgal, and Delgreco Wilson. Finally, the following people read portions of this manuscript and made useful suggestions: Eric Henderson, Eric Liu, Miroslav Nincic, and Borany Penh. These colleagues and friends made this volume better than it would otherwise be; any errors of fact or judgment are my own.

Preface

This book is designed for readers interested in the multiple intersections of multiculturalism and foreign affairs. It can be read with value by students of international relations who wish to understand how the design and conduct of U.S. foreign policy is being shaped by ethnicity. It also can benefit those whose main interest is multiculturalism, and who wish to see how these forces play themselves out in the international arena.

The selection of materials for this volume reflects the editor's belief that the dividing line between the foreign and domestic has thinned over recent decades, and what was once "foreign" has become much more "domestic," and vice versa. It also reflects the reality that the United States is now experiencing one of the greatest influx of immigrants in its history, paralleling the great waves of new Americans that came to our shores at the turn of the last century. These newer immigrants, however, come from different countries with different cultures, and of course the global context of these two massive shifts is very different. The intersection of these elements—globalization, multiculturalism, and foreign affairs—is the subject of this volume.

The opening essay in this book, "Framing the Discussion of Diversity, Globalization, and U.S. International Affairs," grapples with the leading themes that emerge from this edited volume, and defines the meaning of the key terms—globalization, multiculturalism, and foreign affairs. It identifies the drivers of change that propel these phenomena toward their multiple intersections. The essay then analyzes several unique aspects of minority groups' views of foreign affairs—suggesting that these elements may create stronger U.S. international relations with the world. The essay also points to the current debate over the implications of domestic diversity and the conduct of U.S. international affairs.

I call the framework that unites these elements "Double Diversity," and the readings were selected to reflect this framework. The final reading analyzes this concept. Double Diversity begins with the notion that a great challenge and opportunity for America is integrating growing domestic diversity with increasing international diversity. In both, the position of people of color has become critically important. Internationally, few meetings of the World Trade Organization (WTO), the World Bank, or the United Nations occur without representation of countries once absent from these deliberations, for example, China, India, and Brazil. These three alone today represent more than a third of the world's population. By some accounts, China is the second largest economy in the world after the United States, and Brazil is easily the eighth largest. At home, America is becoming more brown, yellow, and black, as more people come to the United States from Africa, Asia, and Latin America. The way these two forces, external and internal, will interact cannot be predicted, and their combination suggests significant risks and opportunities that may hurt or help America. The terrorist attacks of 2001 force us to reflect on these issues, and they elevate multiculturalism to an issue of national security.

This volume contains material that was carefully selected from sources as varied as newspaper editorials, conference reports, and articles in scholarly journals. In making these selections I was guided by the following criteria:

Inclusion of a wide range of opinions, voices, and forms, to demonstrate the diversity of views on diversity and international affairs.

- Clear, sharp expressions of distinctive arguments.
- A mix of very contemporary and older classic pieces (such as Clough's "Wise Men" chapter).
- A wide definition of diversity and its attendant issues including gender, religious, and ideological diversity. Racial diversity is an important component, but not the only component, of diversity.

Implicit in these criteria is that there is not a uniform, politically correct "line" in this volume. This is certainly true in partisan left–right, conservative–liberal, nationalist–internationalist terms. However, underlying these views is the core contention that principled arguments derived from diverse life experiences are valuable, indeed imperative, for the design and conduct of American foreign policy in the world of the twenty-first century.

Introduction

Framing the Discussion of Globalization,
Diversity, and U.S. International Affairs

ERNEST J. WILSON III

NEW TIMES, NEW OPPORTUNITIES, NEW CONSTRAINTS

The new millennium presents a host of new challenges to the women and men charged with managing our international relations. Whether a brand manager for a multinational corporation, a relief worker with the Red Cross, an assembly line mechanic, an ambassador, or an educator, Americans today simultaneously confront a changed international order and a very different domestic order as well. And in this era of globalization, one of the most complex challenges facing those who care about international affairs is understanding and acting responsibly upon the shifting realities of culture, ethnicity, and race. Some commentators raise race and culture to central positions in their conception and conduct of foreign affairs, and the definition of the national interest.[1] Other intellectuals from Japan to Afghanistan to Singapore also insist upon the uniqueness of their own culture and its distinctiveness in the international community.[2] Some elements in the major communities of faith demand that the faithful conduct their foreign policies in accordance with the tenants of their religions, which they define as inseparable from their national cultures, whether Christianity, Judaism, Hinduism, or Islam. These views of a culture-based foreign policy are being articulated at a historical moment when the salience of culture, ethnicity, and race seems to be on the rise publicly.[3] From Bosnia to Rwanda, cultural and ethnic ties exert strong pulls on the conduct of domestic and regional politics, not always with positive consequences for nations, their peoples, or their global partners.[4] These new politicized assertions of identity express themselves in a variety of ways.

One horrific expression of the global intersections of race, religion, and power occurred in September 2001, with the terrorist assaults on the symbols and substance of America's global power. The external and perverse expressions of a culturally heterogeneous world crashed onto American soil with a viciousness that none had really anticipated. Americans learned that the boiling cauldrons of ethno-political resentment abroad could flow over violently into their own daily lives, and that the short- and medium-term responses were all problematic. Double Diversity can have a violent face as well.

In the United States from the 1970s on we have seen the rise of new attitudes, ideologies, and public actions that fall under the broad rubric of multiculturalism, and the reactions against multiculturalism.[5] In this essay I will ask: *Is multiculturalism and ethnic diversity affecting U.S. foreign policy, and, if so, is it a good or a bad thing? Is multiculturalism a big deal or just a minor development for U.S. international relations?*

1

I will show that the answers to these questions hinge in part on how one interprets the past experience of many minorities as among the most excluded elements of American society, typically occupying the bottom positions of the social pyramid. Curiously, it may be that the perspectives they bring to important issues like international development, intercultural communications, and globalization, gained through past exclusion and marginalization, may in fact help the country, as a whole, design better roadmaps to a more peaceful and cooperative global future. With the tragic terrorist incursions into the political and commercial centers of the country, the stakes are much higher for all Americans to find better ways to enhance our security and our engagement with the racial mosaics of the developing world.

Although the questions outlined above deal mainly with the conditions of the United States, they must be answered within the context of parallel conditions and concerns in other countries, developed and underdeveloped alike. Multiculturalism is itself a global phenomenon. If one has any doubt, one need only look at the efforts of German intellectuals, politicians, and officials to come to grips with their Turkish population's increase amid Germany's relatively homogeneous population, or France's efforts to craft a balanced policy toward Muslim North Africans in France, while simultaneously conducting a balanced foreign policy with North African governments. China's leaders also have tried desperately to deal with their own internal diversity in new ways, especially among the restive and poor western provinces abutting Tajikistan, Kurdistan, and other unstable Trans-Caucus countries. Malaysia struggles mightily to maintain its superlative economic growth and regional strategic position, a feat for which ethnic cooperation is both the prerequisite and the consequence. Each of these situations touches upon profound matters of foreign affairs.

In each case, unsuccessful multicultural relations can affect a country's ties with immediate neighbors, with overseas diasporas, with distant nations that send immigrants, and with the global community as a whole. Some of the consequences are direct—think of the regional impact of Yugoslavia's failed multicultural experiment. Other impacts are more indirect—certainly the U.S. domestic intercommunal violence in the 1960s tarnished its international image as pictures of police dogs attacking black demonstrators in Selma flashed around the world. A 1967 volume argued that "As a leading world power professing an official creed of equality, justice, and fair play, the United States has found that hostility and tension among its own ethnic groups are exploited more effectively than anything else as propaganda weapons by our political and economic rivals in the struggle for retaining or attaining power among the uncommitted blocs."[6] The complaints of immigrants from China, Burma, or South Africa about human rights violation because of their culture, religion, or race have been enough to add new elements of strain into bilateral relations with important countries. Multiculturalism and the politicization of ethnic diversity should be a concern to all Americans who care about foreign affairs.

Because this book operates at the intersections of three hugely important issues that are themselves quite complex—globalization, multiculturalism, and international affairs—and whose multiple intersections are even more complicated and at times contradictory, let me briefly define each.

GLOBALIZATION

Globalization refers to the accelerating speed, scope, and depth of international transactions. Trans-border movements are occurring faster and across more countries and sectors than before, and the measurements of globalization have become increasingly important to understand.[7]At the same time, these transactions of culture or economy are felt more deeply, whether through videotapes and VCRs, through one's reliance on distant markets, or access to new kinds of medicines.[8] Beyond quantitative increases, the term "globalization" also captures qualitative features of today's world, especially the degree to which its constituent parts are more closely interconnected than in the past, such that a change in one part of the global system is likely to provoke changes in another. Political developments in Iran or Iraq can spread quickly to Europe and North America. Cultural developments in the United States spread rapidly beyond.

Beyond the increased systemic links among actors horizontally across countries is the simultaneous link across levels of social action, such that, more and more, globalization reaches down to individual women and men and the communities in which they live.

MULTICULTURALISM

In its simplest terms, multiculturalism is equivalent to ethnic or cultural diversity. It indicates a society constituted of distinctive cultures or subcultures that occupy the same national borders. A multicultural society typically has a number of such groups, not simply one or two and issues of mutual accommodation and respect, as well as conflict, political jockeying, and attempts to seize scarce resources for one's own people are prevalent. Multiculturalism is a feature of developed societies such as the United States and Canada, as well as developing ones like Malaysia and Nigeria; it may be a relatively apolitical phenomenon, or it may be heavily politicized.

A second meaning of multiculturalism, sometimes explicitly stated and sometimes implicit, is growing (or at least more visible) ethnic assertiveness among non-Western or nonwhite groups. The interpretation is sometimes given by critics that "multicultural" means exclusionary and chauvinist on the part of those who make political claims in its name. Critics of multiculturalism as policy include the noted historian Arthur M. Schlesinger Jr.[9] Manning Marable, the scholar of African American history and politics, offers a more nuanced interpretation by identifying several quite distinct expressions of "multiculturalism."[10] He finds liberal "melting pot" interpretations of ethnic diversity, multinational corporate multiculturalism—emphasizing diversity of employment and multicultural capitalist markets; radical democratic multiculturalism that challenges the current distribution of power in prevailing institutions and systems; and the more ethnonationalist and chauvinist expressions of multiculturalism.[11] Whether a country exhibits one or the other—or more likely a mix of "multiculturalisms"—is a matter of empirical investigation.

INTERNATIONAL AFFAIRS

A generation or two ago we might take "international affairs" to be equivalent to a government's foreign policy. Few would make that claim today. "International affairs" refers to the full range of purposive human activities that transcend a nation's borders, whether conducted by private companies, nongovernmental organizations (NGOs), government agencies, or other actors. These activities can involve trade and commerce as well as church activities; they encompass tourism and terrorism equally. At some point, the term "international affairs" loops back through "globalization" as the boundaries between international and national, between foreign and domestic, dissolve; some analysts refer both to the "glocal," that is, the global in the local, and to "intermestic," that is, international and domestic affairs.[12]

A FRAMEWORK OF DOUBLE DIVERSITY

One way to frame the intersection of multiculturalism, globalization, and international affairs and to put it more centrally into our analysis of multiculturalism is through what I have termed "Double Diversity." Double Diversity refers to the multifaceted and open-ended intersections between two important aspects of modern life—one mainly domestic, the other international. The domestic half of Double Diversity is the growing ethnic plurality of American society as it becomes more black, brown and yellow. The United States is now more ethnically heterogeneous and plural; for example, "minorities" now constitute a majority of California's population. Since the roots of foreign policy always lie deep within domestic sources in all countries, this demographic shift matters.[13] The second element of Double Diversity is the increase of heterogeneity in the international system. Power in the international system also has become more plural and less homogeneous in many respects, such that nonwhite, non-Western actors are much more engaged with the conduct of consequential international affairs than they were in the recent past; no longer are the important international meetings as monocultural as they once were. Instead, decisive participation and governance of the international system has become more ethnically and culturally diverse. This reflects not just an increase in absolute or even relative numbers of people of color, but the creation of strong middle classes and their concomitant political mobilization in Brazil, South Africa, Taiwan, and other newly industrializing countries. Thus, Double Diversity describes the intersection between the twin phenomena of politically mobilized diversity "out there" and politically mobilized diversity "in here."

The intersections between domestic and foreign diversity occur in every field of activity. Commercially, Americans with roots in Asia, Africa, and Latin America are more engaged than ever before with their ancestral communities through trade, made easier by the growth of digital communications. Politically, U.S. groups lobby with federal and state governments for better relations with their traditional homelands, and also may lobby foreign governments to increase freedom and openness in their home societies. This volume's essay on Double Diversity spells out a few possible future scenarios—foreign and domestic intersections may be utopian and positive, or they may be negative, conflictual, and dystopian. The horrific bombings in 2001 of New York and Washington, D.C., demonstrate the negative consequences of trends in multicultural globalization that will have nasty and long-lasting consequences. By contrast, the growing commercial, community, and political ties among African Americans or Indian Americans with their traditional homelands has certainly improved America's overall linkages with those regions.

DRIVERS OF CHANGE

The arrival of Double Diversity has been driven by underlying domestic and international fundamentals that will continue to drive this issue in the future, and they are shaping minority attitudes and activities in foreign affairs. These are some of the same fundamentals driving other aspects of modern life, lest we think that multiculturalism and ethnic diversity are autonomous trends independent of other social forces.

Rising Ethnic Shares of the Total U.S. Population

The most obvious starting point for understanding multiculturalism and international affairs is the growing number of immigrants from non-Western nations crossing into the United States. Starting from a modern low of 4.7 percent in 1970, the percentage of foreign-born Americans reached 10.4 percent by the year 2000. The largest national deliverers of new Americans are no longer western or southern Europe, they are Mexico (27 percent of the immigrant population), China/Taiwan (4.9), the Philippines (4.3), India (3.5), Cuba (3.4), Vietnam (3.0), El Salvador (2.7), Korea (2.5), the Dominican Republic (2.4), and Canada (2.4).

Growth of the Middle Class

A second driver of change, of equal or greater importance as the growth of sheer numbers, is what might be called the embourgeoisification of some American ethnics. Ethnic communities are becoming more middle class and economically diversified. The share of doctors, lawyers, professional managers, successful entrepreneurs, and white-collar workers in general expanded substantially between 1950 and 2000, especially within historically agricultural and working-class communities, such as Mexican Americans and African Americans. In most countries, foreign affairs is largely a middle class preoccupation. There are important exceptions, including the international politics of labor unions, or the international politics of farmers concerned about policies they view as hurting or helping them. But while important, these remain exceptions. Typically, when communities and nations become more middle class, they also become more interested in "postmaterialist" issues, things beyond the daily struggles to keep food on the table, pay the rent, and send their kids to school.[14] Once able to meet basic needs, individuals are able and more likely to respond to wider opportunities in their environment, and tend to engage other issues beyond survival; they become more educated, more likely to become politically active, and more likely to get involved in foreign affairs. Yet it is also the case that, while the middle classes are growing, the overall economic situation for excluded minorities is not improving, according to the Rand Corporation. The Rand Corporation reported in 2001 that, in 1996, black "family income stagnated between 1970 and 1993, though there were signs of increases between 1993 and 1996. Latino family income decreased in the 1990s. . . . In contrast, Asian Americans . . . have the highest median family income of any group."[15] The post-2001 recession has not helped. The black and brown middle class grows, but they still sit atop populations that remain relatively poor.

Expansion of the Political Class

For multiculturalism to affect international affairs, it must act through a medium. One important medium for translating latent ethnic attitudes into purposeful action is the political maneuvering of politicians and senior civil servants who are minorities. To the degree that substantial numbers of Latinos, Asian Americans, and African Americans influence foreign affairs, it will be achieved in part through their politicians and senior policymakers. The number of minorities in elite foreign policy organizations such as the Council on Foreign Relations has increased, as has their political assertiveness in demanding activities more directly relevant to their particular interests.[16]

CHANGE DRIVERS ABROAD

Economic Development

Some change drivers include broad international trends. Double Diversity begins with an increasingly integrated world in which developments in other countries influence our perception and performance of international affairs.

An important driver of change has been the accelerated economic growth of the emerging markets of Asia, Latin America, and parts of Africa.[17] With growth rates hitting high single or double digits for years, many of the newly industrializing countries (NICs) now carry more clout with their international trading partners and more generally in the world system. As domestic ethnic groups have become more middle class, so too have the populations of many developing countries. These populations have more disposable income and attention to "invest" in foreign affairs, whether in the form of state-to-state diplomatic initiatives, international meetings and efforts to influence the "rules of the game," or nontraditional activities such as diaspora outreach. Countries such as China, India, Ghana, and Mexico have become much more sophisticated about reaching out to their own diasporas, for their own purposes. China and Mexico, for example, have special senior-level agencies charged with improving ties to their overseas populations. These diasporas are, as I suggest later, more sophisticated about sending home moneys to the motherland both to support their families and for investment. The growth of big middle classes in big countries can make big differences for the ambitions and actions of their diasporas. The fact that India has an English-speaking middle class of 250 million people—larger than the population of much of Western Europe—is no small consequence for their ties to the United States. Of course, the world's poor nations are important for immigration and for other factors as well, as Broad and Cavanagh,[18] among others, have demonstrated.

Political Development

Professor Sam Huntington of Harvard University has described the successive waves of democratization that have swept around the world, including the most recent flood in the decade of the 1990s that pushed dozens of countries from the nondemocratic to the democratic column.[19] This latest tide has been accompanied by the expansion of civil society actors, that is clubs, associations, and other bodies operating between the citizen and state power.[20] The spread of democratic practices and norms has had several impacts on international relations between less developed countries and the United States. Some of these NGOs have become actively engaged with their counterparts in the region or in other continents, one result being a more diverse, transparent, and international network of associations interacting regularly with their U.S. counterparts. Furthermore, the democratically elected heads of developing countries are more likely to permit these newly mobilized groups to operate unmediated with their international counterparts. In the past, dictators feared and repressed domestic organizations with direct international ties for fear they would undercut the ruler's own local—and international—authority.

Another issue worth mentioning is the removal of an old familiar driver of change—the Cold War. The competition between the U.S.S.R. and the U.S. was the single preeminent determinant of big power politics, and the spillover impact upon Africa, Asia, and Latin America is incalculable. That once-powerful determinant has been eliminated, and its absence provides new opportunities for other forces to gain greater sway, including economic globalization.

Globalization

The nature of the international system itself has changed in a few fundamental ways through the process of globalization. As defined earlier, globalization provides the broad framework within which these other variables operate. The speed, scope, and depth of all international transactions have expanded to unprecedented levels. Whether seen in economics or culture, cross-border transactions now constitute major concerns of people in international affairs around the world. Globalization is associated with immigration trends and increased flows of finance and knowledge that also propel forward the movement of people around the globe.

Finally, the deepening and extension of Double Diversity and the globalization of multiculturalism has received a big boost from the diffusion of new information technologies such as the Internet.[21] Diasporas from across the developing world use these new tools for a variety of purposes, the effect of which is to link them together into global social networks. For example, the government of Morocco has sponsored Web sites linking overseas Moroccans with one another and with Morocco. Overseas Ghanaians have recently launched a new Web site and listserv to link their diaspora. Chinese at home and abroad carry on intercontinental dialogues through a variety of bulletin boards and chat rooms.[22] The links between information technology (IT) and diasporas is reciprocal. Immigrants from India and China constitute a substantial part the managerial workforce of Silicon Valley.[23] As Indians in America have become more and more successful, they have come to constitute an extremely important source of investment capital for Mumbai, Bangalore, and other subcontinent cities.[24] Along with their money, these individuals also send back their ideas and their entrepreneurial energies, after having made it big in California. So extensive is this circulation of money, ideas, and people between the United States, India, China, and a handful of other developing countries that some observers now refer to it as the "brain gain" rather than the former "brain drain."[25] In the process, the locus of "globalization" shifts from being mainly something created by the West and imposed on the rest—into a mobile creation, regenerated at countless sites around the world.

SO WHAT?

If there is general agreement that these trends are occurring, there is far less agreement on their precise significance for multiculturalism and international affairs, or, indeed, multiculturalism's own contribution to advancing or undercutting U.S. interests. Some argue that these changes are important; others say they are unimportant. Some insist the changes are good, others say they are bad. Huntington concludes that the growth of non-Western or nonwhite ethnic assertiveness is a large and important trend that operates within the United States and abroad. He concludes that the new ethnic assertiveness is a big issue and a bad issue—it will have deleterious effects for American policy abroad.[26] For Huntington and others, American foreign policy should be managed by a disinterested, relatively homogeneous elite that will not bring its own ethnic brief to the design of foreign policy. Its members should be driven by a common vision of America's *national* interest, not subnational special pleading. Having too many minorities in the foreign policy–making apparatus risks reducing the common vision and enhancing the leverage of those who might hijack U.S. policy through special ethnic pleading. Huntington raises the question of the demographics of the U.S. foreign service and the relationship between personnel decisions and substantive policy outcomes. Other interpretations critical of multiculturalism, especially in the popular press, sometimes claim that Asians, Latinos, and others fall prey to "divided loyalty," as was argued in the case of California scientist Wen Ho Lee.[27]

A different answer to a slightly different question is offered by James Lindsay of the Council on Foreign Relations in his new work on the demographics of U.S. foreign policy.[28] Lindsay agrees that immigration-driven ethnic diversity has risen to levels not seen in the United States since the 1890–1915 period, with an important distinction that the source is no longer Europe but Latin America and Asia. He recognizes that the immigration upsurge is creating new conditions mainly within the domestic policy arena. He concludes that the foreign policy–related changes are *not* very significant for the substance of U.S. policy because the structure and content of minority views on foreign policy are not substantially different from those of the majority population.

In the main, Lindsay is correct. Most minorities define domestic issues as their first priority.[29] Even immigrants tend to view domestic U.S. policies on health care, education, and crime as their top priorities, just as do white Americans. Most minorities share the view that international cooperation is good, and that America should protect and advance its national interests through a mixture of engaged diplomacy and robust defense. Most minorities do not believe we should radically alter our European foreign policies. Most minorities agree that foreign policy is adequately conducted by experts. This is Lindsay's story—when it comes to foreign affairs, minority Americans are on the whole just like other Americans, only with different accents and countries of origin. Certainly this interpretation is consistent with some of the results found by the Tomas Rivera Policy Institute.[30]

A third school of analysis encompasses intellectuals such as Elliott Skinner, Ronald Walters, Brenda Gayle Plummer, and Ron Takaki, who argue that differences between minorities and majorities are indeed significant and tell an important but underexamined piece of American history. For these writers, race has always borne directly on the design and conduct of U.S. foreign policy.[31] Unlike writers like Lindsay, whose purpose is to emphasize *commonality and shared attitudes,* and whose conclusions suggest the effectiveness of American assimilation, these writers seek out the *distinctiveness* of hyphenated-Americans' worldview. They hearken back to intellectuals such as W. E. B. Du Bois, typically writing from "inside" their respective communities. For them, the history of colored people's exclusion from their proper place in international affairs perfectly parallels their exclusion from effective participation in the domestic arena. People of color, they argue, also bring different elements to the international affairs table. Most often the authors point to specific differences over concrete policy issues such as immigration, and general attitudes toward Africa, Asia, and Latin America. At other times, they make broader general claims about the attitudes, political capacities, and international interests of each group.

There is some merit in each of these three positions, although each is flawed. Huntington exaggerates the downside risks of multiculturalism and refuses to consider seriously the potential positive contributions that new international affairs recruits can bring, especially after 9-11 and given the broader trends toward greater involvement of civil society in policy consultations. He also conjures up an excessively positive picture of the "good old days" of harmonious American foreign policymaking. The definition of the "true" national interest has been fought over from the early 1800s, when the Federalists and anti-Federalists fought duels over these issues and Virginians conflicted with New Englanders over the meaning of America. American political pluralism has always ensured contention over foreign policy. Huntington is correct in saying that a shared common vision of American national interest, and indeed of America itself, is required to conduct effective international affairs. Africa for the African Americans, Asia for the Asian Americans, Ireland for the Irish Americans is a foolish basis from which to conduct a coherent foreign policy. Shared values and common views of the national interest are important for foreign policy, and they do not emerge automatically. They must be constructed through consultation and leadership.

Both Huntington and Lindsay show too little knowledge of the internal political dynamics of the ethnic communities and the ways their politicians and leaders have historically engaged international issues in the Caribbean, Africa, or Asia. Lindsay also plays down the political divisiveness and contention of real world politics between the white majorities of both parties in Congress and the Congressional Black Caucus and the Latino Caucus, particularly as the latter groups have fought to advance American interests in Africa and Latin America.

The intellectuals who write from within their own ethnic communities capture well the internal dynamics of those groups, and they point out how the absence of alternative voices has led to policies that harm developing countries, as occurred in the Cold War (one thinks of U.S. policies toward Central Africa and Central America). They are less interested in the broader sweep of international affairs that do not bear directly on concerns they view as central to minorities, nor do they propose full definitions of the national interest encompassing national security, economic stability, environmental policies, and so forth.[32]

Missing from many approaches toward foreign affairs is politics as it is actually practiced. If we flip the question around and start with politics rather than ignoring it, we should ask who are the most active groups consistently in support of Africa, the Caribbean, or Cuba. If we ask what interests typically mobilize in support of Israel or the Palestinians, or for that matter Ireland and Greece, we return to the hard-headed realities of pluralist American politics. It is invariable that those nation's diasporas are the most easily and frequently mobilized on foreign policy. The author has worked on congressional foreign affairs committees and in the White House as a foreign affairs advisor. Everywhere, whether in meetings, debriefings, congressional committees, or White House lunches, advisors are aware of diaspora concerns. Senior policymakers rarely make major decisions about Cuba, Ireland, Israel, or Poland without consistently interacting with each country's mobilized diaspora. Ethnic activists certainly do not dictate or determine policies; they are simply one among a wide range of potentially relevant interests to which policymakers attend; business, labor, or religious groups are others.

Many argue that given their absolute size and resources, some groups articulating ethnic interests are actually underperforming in translating their latent power to foreign policy leverage. Leaders of the small collections of foreign affairs experts in these communities constantly complain of their inabilities to mobilize greater support among their ethnic brothers and sisters. These complaints are echoed by policy makers inside government agencies and NGOs who bemoan the inconsistency of many minority activists to do the political heavy lifting necessary to effect policy change.[33] Certainly there have been some notable successes by minorities in international affairs: the success of the anti-apartheid supporters who lobbied for the 1988 Anti-Apartheid Act (even overriding a presidential veto); the successful passage of the Africa Growth and Opportunity Act; and the leadership of the Congressional Black Caucus in getting higher appropriations for foreign aid for Africa are a few examples.[34] And one can perhaps point to the appointment of one of the first Asian American career ambassadors, William Itoh, or the first Latino Assistant Secretary responsible for Latin America, Peter Romero. One also could point to successes in the nonprofit sector where ethnic mobilization successfully shaped a foreign policy or nongovernmental initiative. Nonetheless, these episodes are not consistent, nor, for the most part, are they central to the protection of America's national interest. They represent good opportunities to be seized to advance the United States and potentially help other regions. It remains to be seen whether the described substantive trends will lead to greater inclusion for people of color in international affairs, and if the issues that most concern them are addressed.

To evaluate accurately the intersections of multiculturalism and foreign affairs, we will need to wait a few years. Then we will see whether ethnics are overly powerful or insufficiently effective. There is always a substantial time lag between the latent power of an ethnic group in international affairs, represented by its aggregate income or congressional representation, and its real world influence.

FACTORS SHAPING FOREIGN POLICY VIEWS OF MINORITIES

Before turning directly to the attitudes that minorities hold about international affairs, we need first to consider the societal factors that shape these attitudes. Individual beliefs about international affairs derive from a whole raft of variables. The recent fascinating work by

Steve Kull, *Misreading the Public: The Myth of a New Isolationism,* and others on citizens' views of foreign affairs, demonstrates the ways different factors interact with one another.[35]

I argue there are at least four clear conditions that have traditionally distinguished the typical nonwhite citizen, foreign policy advocate, and policy official from their white counterparts. They include their positions at the bottom of the social pyramid; their status as institutional outsiders; and their links back to their culture of origin in a developing region—Africa, Latin America, or Asia. Attitudes also are shaped by the economic and geopolitical status of their ethnic homeland.

SHAPING MINORITY VIEWS OF FOREIGN POLICY

1. *Links of Culture, Language, and Religion.* People of color in the United States typically maintain cultural links, sometimes of language and religion, that tie them back to their original communities. These links vary from one group to another, and certainly one individual to another, in the degree to which they are immediate and experienced, or distant and intellectual. For example, Latino and Asian Americans are more likely to have directly experienced their country of origins than most African Americans. Caribbean Americans know their country and towns of origins, as do the more recent black neodiaspora,[36] but the majority of the black community do not. But whether the ties are directly experienced or reconstituted from interpretation and recovered family history, these ties shape the new communities in which they live in interesting ways.[37] Possessing these kinds of community ties is likely to affect individual attitudes, values, and behaviors toward international affairs.

2. *Being at the Bottom.* People of color are on the whole poorer than whites, both in income and in wealth. In wealth, the disparities are particularly stark, with the average white owning more than ten times the wealth of the average black person. Individuals of color come from poorer countries, and they are poorer in the United States. Relative to whites, they are disproportionately at the bottom of the American social pyramid. Whites are further advantaged through greater access to elite secondary schooling, Ivy League colleges, and elite professional experiences that together reinforce birth circumstances. Social science tells us that the view from the bottom is not the same as the view from the top, and this may influence one's view of international affairs.

3. *Being on the Outside.* African Americans, Asian Americans, and Latinos traditionally have been excluded from the leading institutions responsible for the design and conduct of foreign affairs. Past policies of explicit, legally mandated racial discrimination as well as implicit institutional practices have kept the middle and upper ranks of international institutions virtually devoid of color: the State Department, the U.S. Treasury, the Defense Department, the Red Cross, the *New York Times,* Texaco, United Fruits, the Ford Motor Company, and private foundations.[38] Being systematically excluded from particular institutions may affect inherent attitudes toward these institutions. As former Council on Foreign Relations Senior Fellow Michael Clough describes, the view from the top of the "wise old men" is also partial and distorting in its own way.[39]

4. *Homeland Status.* Minority attitudes toward foreign affairs certainly reflect their outsider/bottom status in the United States but also reflect the economic and political status of their homeland. Chinese American attitudes about foreign policies toward China[40] will differ in part from Central American immigrants' attitudes about U.S. policies toward El Salvador in important ways. The concerns of Americans of Haitian

descent will be issues of foreign assistance, of the risks of dangerous and forced immigration, and the absence of democracy among the poorest nations in the Western Hemisphere. Korean Americans will have other specific priorities. All other things being equal, Chinese Americans, Mexican Americans, and Jewish Americans will have more leverage than other Americans because the U.S. national interest is deeply implicated in China, Mexico, and Israel. It is not the case for Haiti in the Caribbean or Botswana in Africa.

The degree to which this same cluster of attitudes and preferences will sustain itself in the future as the structural and institutional conditions evolve remains unclear. But as Goodman and others demonstrate, diversification rates among the upper ranks of the U.S. foreign service, among private sector elites with international responsibilities, and among NGO officials is so low that these conditions will persist for the foreseeable future.

DISTINCTIVE MINORITY VIEWS ON INTERNATIONAL AFFAIRS

These sociological and institutional conditions of minority life in America may have affected the attitudes and preferences of citizens, activists, and officials of color toward international affairs in a variety of ways. It is certainly the case that not every minority individual interested in international affairs will hold these beliefs—many will not. Circumstantial evidence from national fellowship programs suggests minority students are starting to study regions and languages outside their regions of origin. Also some whites will hold these beliefs in whole or part.[41]

My argument is that out of one hundred foreign policy elites of color interviewed, it is likely that the sample will show more of these attitudes than a similar sample of their white counterparts. Those attitudes include:

1. *Redefining Places of Importance.* Survey data and informal observations suggest that minorities are disproportionately interested in their communities of origins—African American organizations seek to pay special attention to African countries, Jewish American groups give pride of place to Israel, Mexican Americans to U.S. ties to Mexico. This does not mean that individuals of talent from one background are not professionally engaged and highly expert on other regions—quite the contrary. But in the tradition of American pluralism we would expect to find such preferences made manifest in the political and social arena, and we do. One possible consequence of this process is that as more minorities get engaged with foreign affairs, the attention paid to these areas may start to receive greater attention by senior corporate, government, and NGO officials, and there will be relatively less time devoted to traditional areas of U.S. concern—especially Europe. In this respect, the role of the Congressional Black Caucus in redirecting more high-level attention and material resources to Africa should not be minimized.

2. *Redefining Subject Areas as Important.* Foreign policy has traditionally made a distinction between "high policy" areas and "low." High policy had the greatest status in the agenda of senior policymakers, and included official bilateral diplomacy with other great powers, arms control, armed forces structures, military missions, and other national security matters. "Low" policy included trade, the environment, immigration, cultural matters, and so forth. A variety of forces have conspired to knock holes in the once thick wall dividing "high" from "low." Some foreign policy surveys with attentive elites and others from communities of color indicate they believe that more

attention should be devoted to matters that more directly influence the parts of the world where their communities of origin are located—human rights, social justice, immigration, trade through small- and medium-sized enterprises, and foreign assistance. Polling data show that Latino elites more than their white counterparts believe there is too much attention paid to some of the more traditional national security subjects.[42]

3. *Who Are the Relevant Policy Elites?* Given the institutional outsider status of foreign policy experts who are minorities, and their closeness to heretofore excluded groups, broader consultations with NGOs, community groups, and others from nonminority communities may ensue. When serving abroad it may lead individuals from communities of color to get out beyond the gated, guarded compounds of the "official community" to meet local people on their own terms. Such minorities are likely to be more sympathetic to multiculturalism. Their linguistic and cultural skills may even give them an advantage when working in their own countries of ethnic origin, or when working in other overseas postings. They also are more likely to be critical of the inherent institutional structures of foreign affairs agencies, because such institutions have practiced de jure and de facto exclusion. The several highly contentious discrimination law suits by black foreign service officers against the State Department make this point clearly.

4. *Different Normative Expectations.* Arguably, individuals from communities of color may be more disposed toward normative positions tilting toward the underdog, and may be more likely to listen seriously to their concerns. Because they are from poor and excluded communities in which their opinions were deliberately ignored or discounted, they may be more open to other discounted views.

Survey research data suggest that differences between whites and African Americans can be significant across a whole array of policy and political attitudes, and these differences can be quite visible and politically consequent. Sometimes the differences are just at the margins as Lindsay points out. But in the senior councils of international affairs, margins make a difference. There are differences in substance, process, and probably style that are not irrelevant to the design and conduct of America's foreign affairs. Marginal differences can be politically significant and important for policy.

CONCLUSION

Let me close by pointing to a curious convergence. If the unique historical experiences and social status of people of color in the United States have created within them a unique set of values and policy priorities, then these values and priorities seem particularly well suited for the post–Cold War international environment at the start of the twenty-first century. This is certainly a strong implication of Clough, who sees the shift away from the old East Coast elite to a more inclusive, truly national group of foreign policy influentials as positive.[43] Greater sensitivity to nontraditional issues such as human rights or trade, greater attention to nontraditional countries outside the European heartland, greater attention to engaging with nontraditional elites in foreign countries (and at home), and normative sensitivities to the plight of the underdog are certainly positive and adaptive American attitudes as we confront the increasingly global, nontraditional issues of the twenty-first century. Indeed, when balanced with other more traditional notions of state craft and national security, they may represent a favorable rebalancing of priorities for U.S. foreign policy. They are insufficient to stand on their own as a complete package of foreign policy norms, but they are excellent ingredients for the reconstruction of American international relations.

In a very sensitive treatment of these issues, Yossi Shain argues persuasively that, as African Americans and other excluded groups integrate through U.S. society and its political system, their attitudes toward foreign affairs change with their societal position. He writes, "The transformation of the African American and Arab American foreign lobbies from outsiders seeking to penetrate the American system into insiders helping to shape its course or being mobilized in its service is testimony to the positive value of including ethnicity in U.S. foreign policy."[44]

In a recent book, the former *Wall Street Journal* correspondent G. Pascal Zachary insists that, in today's integrated world, multicultural societies such as the United States actually enjoy a significant competitive advantage over mainly monocultural societies such as Japan or Germany.[45]

Whereas these trends in minority attitudes and the experience of minority foreign policy engagement are suggestive, they are insufficient to allow us to conclude that multiculturalism is yet a major force in U.S. foreign policy. With a few exceptions of episodes in U.S. policy toward Africa or South Asia, there is little evidence to support the claims of Huntington or Takaki that multiculturalism has had a major impact on U.S. international affairs. Indeed, an argument can be made that the *absence* of adequate sensitivities in the conduct of U.S. foreign policy toward developing regions, especially during the Cold War, has yielded unhappy outcomes for U.S. policy toward Central Africa or Central America.

At the same time that we are witnessing an upsurge in African American, Asian American, and Latino interest in international affairs, there also is a broader rethinking of the most basic elements of American foreign policy taking place in leading universities, by think tanks and NGOs, and within the departments of Defense and State and the White House. These across-the-board reassessments of defense and national security policy are occasioned by the compelling salience of the change drivers identified earlier—the end of the Cold War, the acceleration of economic globalization, the information revolution, and, more recently, the terrorist attacks of September 2001. Will the traditional thinking about foreign relations intersect with ethnicity's positive elements to forge a new national interest? Whatever the outcome, the cross fertilization will not happen automatically. It requires leadership and vision among experts in every group to create the epistemic community needed to develop new policy paradigms. America would benefit from such a collaboration.

NOTES

1. Samuel Huntington, "The Erosion of American National Interest," *Foreign Affairs* (September/October 1997), pp. 28–49.
2. Kishore Madhubani, "The Dangers of Decadence: What the Rest Can Teach the West," *Foreign Affairs* (September/October 1993), vol. 72, no. 4, pp. 10–14.
3. Richard J. Payne, *The Clash With Distant Cultures Values, Interests and Force in American Foreign Policy* (Albany: State University of New York Press, 1995); "Culture and Diplomacy," *Correspondence* (Winter 2000/2001), no. 7, p. 1.
4. Ted Robert Gurr, Monty G. Marshall, and Deepa Khosla, *Peace and Conflict 2001: A Global Survey of Armed Conflicts, Self-Determination Movements and Democracy* (College Park, Md.: Center for International Development and Conflict Management, University of Maryland, 2001).
5. Paul Berman (ed.) *Debating PC* (New York: Laurel, 1992).
6. Milton L. Barron, *Minorities in a Changing World* (New York: Knopf, 1967), p. 4.
7. A. T. Kearney Company and Carnegie Endowment for International Peace, "Measuring Globalization," *Foreign Policy* (January/February 2001), 122, p. 56.
8. Anthony Giddens, *Runaway World: How Globalization is Reshaping Our Lives* (London: Profile Books, 1999).
9. Arthur M. Schlesinger, *The Disuniting of America* (New York: Norton, 1992); William J. Bennett, *The Devaluing of America* (New York: Summit Books, 1992).

10. Manning Marable, "Black Studies, Multiculturalism and the Future of American Education," in *Beyond Black and White: Rethinking Race in American Politics and Society* (New York: Verso, 1995), pp. 117–130.

11. Ibid.

12. Victor D. Cha (2000). "Globalization and the Study of International Security," *Journal of Peace Research,* 37(3), pp. 391–403.

13. Charles W. Kegley, Jr., and Eugene R. Wittkopf, *The Domestic Sources of American Foreign Policy* (New York: St. Martin's Press, 1988).

14. Ronald Inglehart, *Modernization and PostModernization* (Princeton, N.J.: Princeton University Press, 1997).

15. Rand Corp., "America Becoming: The Growing Complexity of America's Racial Mosaic," RB-5050, 2001, p. 3.

16. Council for Foreign Relations, *Member Directory: Project for Diversity in International Affairs* (New York: Council for Foreign Relations, 1997).

17. David Dollar and Aart Kraay, "Spreading the Wealth," *Foreign Affairs* (January/February 2002), 81 (1).

18. Robin Broad and John Cavanagh, "Don't Neglect the Impoverished South," *Foreign Policy* (Winter 1995–1996), no. 101, pp. 18–36.

19. Samuel P. Huntington, *The Third Wave: Democratization in the Late Twentieth Century* (Norman: University of Oklahoma Press, 1991).

20. Robert Pinkney, *Democracy in the Third World* (Boulder, Col.: Lynne Rienner Publishers, 1994).

21. Ernest J. Wilson III, *The Information Revolution in Developing Countries* (Boston, Mass.: MIT Press, 2002).

22. Guobin Yang, "The Global Construction of Online Public Forums: A Comparative Study of Three Chinese-language Electronic Bulletin Systems in China and the United States." Paper Presented at the Program of Information Technology, International Cooperation, and Global Security, Social Science Research Council, University of California at Berkeley, July 2001.

23. AnnaLee Saxenian, "The Bangalore Boom: From Brain Drain to Brain Circulation." Revised Paper Prepared for Working Group on Equity, Diversity, and Information Technology, National Institute of Advanced Study, Bangalore, India, Dec. 3–4, 1999. http://www.sims.berkeley.edu/~anno/papers/bangalore_boom.html.

24. Ibid.

25. Ibid.

26. Samuel Huntington, "The Erosion of American National Interest," *Foreign Affairs* (September/October 1997), pp. 28–49.

27. Eric Liu, "Fear of a Yellow Planet," in *The Accidental Asian: Notes of a Native Speaker* (New York: Vintage Books, 1998), pp. 115–144; Robert Wright, "Slanted: Racial Prejudice is Part of What Fueled the Clinton Campaign Scandal," *Slate* (January 1, 1997), retrieved from http://www.slate.com.

28. James Lindsay, "Getting Uncle Sam's Ear: Will Ethnic Lobbies Cramp America's Foreign Policy Style?," *Brookings Review* (September 10, 2001), pp. 37–40.

29. Rodolfo de la Garza, Miguel Baraona, Manuel Orozco, Harry P. Panchon, and Adrian D. Pantoja, *Family Ties and Ethnic Lobbies: Latino Relations with Latin America* (June 1998), The Tomas Rivera Policy Institute, pp. 1–8.

30. Ibid.

31. Elliott P. Skinner, "African American Perspectives on Foreign Policy," in Ralph C. Gomes and Linda Faye Williams (eds.), *From Exclusion to Inclusion: The Long Struggle for African American Political Power* (New York: Greenwood Press, 1992), pp. 173–185; Brenda Gayle Plummer, *Window on Freedom: Race, Civil Rights, and Foreign Affairs, 1945–1988* (University of North Carolina, 2003); Ronald Takaki, *A Different Mirror: A History of Multicultural America* (Boston: Little, Brown & Co., 1993); Ronald Walters, "The African Growth and Opportunity Act: Changing Foreign Policy Priorities Toward Africa in a Conservative Political Culture," in Charles P. Henry (ed.), *Foreign Policy and the Black (Inter)National Interest* (Albany: State University of New York Press, 2000), pp. 17–36.

32. See Charles Henry for an example of one writer who directly references some of the efforts to remedy these shortcomings.

33. See some of the comments in Council on Foreign Relations, Redefining the National Interest, New York: Council on Foreign Relations, 1997; Pacific Council on International Policy, "Advancing the International Interests of African Americans, Asian Americans and Latinos." Workshop Report. http://www.pacific-council.org/public/publications/allreports/allreports.asp#workshop. Los Angeles, 1998.

34. Ronald Walters, op. cit.

35. Charles W. Kegley, Jr., and Eugene R. Wittkopf (eds.), *The Future of American Foreign Policy.* (New York: St. Martin's Press, 1992); Steve Kull and I. M. Destler, *Misreading the Public: The Myth of a New Isolationism* (Washington, D.C.: Brookings Institution Press, 1999).

36. James L. Matory, *Sex and the Empire That Is No More: Gender and the Politics of Metaphor in Oyo Yoruba Religion.* (Minneapolis: University of Minnesota Press, 1994).

37. Robert D. Kaplan, "Travels into America's Future," *Atlantic Monthly* (August 1998), retrieved from http://www.theatlantic.com.

38. Allan E. Goodman, "Diversity in U.S. Foreign Policy Making: The Dilemma Endures," Prepared for the Workshop on Advancing the International Interest of African Americans, Asian-Americans and Latinos, March 20–21, 1998, pp. 1–5; Bruce Shapiro, "A House Divided: Racism at the State Department," *The Nation* (February 12, 1996), p. 11.

39. Michael Clough, "Grass-Roots Policymaking: Say Goodbye to the 'Wise Men,'" *Foreign Affairs* (January/February 1994), pp. 2–8; Bernard Johns, "Ethnocentricism Distorts Foreign Policy," *Focus* (November–December 1985), vol. 13, nos. 11–12.

40. Eric Liu, op. cit.; Robert Wright, op. cit.

41. Steve Kull and I. M. Destler, op. cit.

42. Rodolfo de la Garza, Miguel Baraona, Manuel Orozco, Harry P. Panchon, and Adrian D. Pantoja, op. cit.

43. Michael Clough, op. cit.; Bernard Johns, op. cit.

44. Yossi Shain, "Multicultural Foreign Policy," *Foreign Policy* (Fall 1995), no. 100, pp. 85–86.

45. G. Pascal Zachary, *The Diversity Advantage* (Boulder, Col.: Westview Press, 2003).

Part 1

Section 1

Growing Demographic Diversity
in U.S. Society

The major issue in Section One is the emergence of new patterns of domestic demography, political mobilization, and economic clout among minority groups in the United States as immigration from Third World countries has soared. A central element of globalization is the accelerated movement of people, goods, services, and money across national borders. One consequence is that most industrial nations are now much more demographically diverse than they were only a generation ago. The United States is a particularly prominent example of growing diversity, and the authors in this section analyze the country's changing demographic dynamics. In the United States, the 1980s and 1990s saw the greatest rates of inward migration since 1890–1915. The addition of millions of new Americans in such a compressed period of time has altered the demographic and racial face of American society. Immigration has created new employment opportunities and new political dynamics, each with its own strengths and stresses. This huge horizontal movement has been accompanied by some upward mobility as well, as people of color enter for the first time the senior ranks of business, government, and the professional world, though still in very modest numbers. The raw demographics that Johnston describes find their more literary expression in essayist Robert Kaplan's unique view of the new American melting pot that many cities on the West Coast have become, from Vancouver to Seattle to Los Angeles. In Kaplan's view, some of these cities are becoming "Asianized cit(ies) of the Pacific Rim." According to one of Kaplan's respondents, the cultural mix of Asians and WASPs is "the most potent in the history of capitalism."

1

Global Workforce 2000

The New World Labor Market

WILLIAM B. JOHNSTON

March–April 1991

For more than a century, companies have moved manufacturing operations to take advantage of cheap labor. Now human capital, once considered to be the most stationary factor in production, increasingly flows across national borders as easily as cars, computer chips, and corporate bonds. Just as managers speak of world markets for products, technology, and capital, they must now think in terms of a world market for labor.

The movement of people from one country to another is, of course, not new. In previous centuries, Irish stonemasons helped build U.S. canals, and Chinese laborers constructed North America's transcontinental railroads. In the 1970s and 1980s, it was common to find Indian engineers writing software in Silicon Valley, Turks cleaning hotel rooms in Berlin, and Algerians assembling cars in France. During the 1990s, the world's workforce will become even more mobile, and employers will increasingly reach across borders to find the skills they need. These movements of workers will be driven by the growing gap between the world's supplies of labor and the demands for it. While much of the world's skilled and unskilled human resources are being produced in the developing world, most of the well-paid jobs are being generated in the cities of the industrialized world. This mismatch has several important implications for the 1990s.

- It will trigger massive relocations of people, including immigrants, temporary workers, retirees, and visitors. The greatest relocations will involve young, well-educated workers flocking to the cities of the developed world.
- It will lead some industrialized nations to reconsider their protectionist immigration policies, as they come to rely on and compete for foreign-born workers.
- It may boost the fortunes of nations with "surplus" human capital. Specifically, it could help well-educated but economically underdeveloped countries such as the Philippines, Egypt, Cuba, Poland, and Hungary.
- It will compel labor-short, immigrant-poor nations like Japan to improve labor productivity dramatically to avoid slower economic growth.
- It will lead to a gradual standardization of labor practices among industrialized countries. By the end of the century, European standards of vacation time (five weeks) will be common in the United States. The forty-hour work week will have been accepted in Japan. And world standards governing workplace safety and employee rights will emerge.

Several factors will cause the flows of workers across international borders to accelerate in the coming decade. First, jet airplanes have yet to make their greatest impact. Between 1960 and 1988, the real cost of international travel dropped nearly 60 percent; during the same period, the number of foreigners entering the United States on business rose by 2,800 percent. Just as the automobile triggered suburbanization, which took decades to play out, so will jumbo jets shape the labor market over many years. Second, the barriers that governments place on immigration and emigration are breaking down. By the end of the 1980s, the nations of Eastern Europe had abandoned the restrictions on the rights of their citizens to leave. At the same time, most Western European nations were negotiating the abolition of *all* limits on people's movements within the boundaries of the European Community, and the United States, Canada, and even Japan began to liberalize their immigration policies. Third, these disappearing barriers come at a time when employers in the aging, slow-growing, industrialized nations are hungry for talent, while the developing world is educating more workers than it can productively employ.

These factors make it almost inevitable that more workers will cross national borders during the 1990s. Exactly where workers move to and from will greatly influence the fates of countries and companies. And even though those movements of people are not entirely predictable, the patterns already being established send strong signals about what is to come.

THE CHANGING WORLD LABOR FORCE

The developments of the next decade are rooted in today's demographics, particularly those having to do with the size and character of various countries' work forces. In some areas of the world, for instance, women have not yet been absorbed in large numbers and represent a huge untapped resource; elsewhere the absorption process is nearly complete. Such national differences are a good starting point for understanding what the globalization of labor will look like and how it will affect individual nations and companies.

Although looming labor shortages have dominated discussion in many industrialized nations, the world workforce is growing fast. From 1985 to 2000, the work force is expected to grow by some six hundred million people, or 27 percent (that compares with 36 percent growth between 1970 and 1985). The growth will take place unevenly. The vast majority of the new workers—570 million of the 600 million workers—will join the workforces of the developing countries. In countries like Pakistan and Mexico, for example, the workforce will grow at about 3 percent a year. In contrast, growth rates in the United States, Canada, and Spain will be closer to 1 percent a year, Japan's workforce will grow just 0.5 percent, and Germany's workforce (including the Eastern sector) will actually decline. (See Exhibit 1.)

The much greater growth in the developing world stems primarily from historically higher birthrates. But in many nations, the effects of higher fertility are magnified by the entrance of women into the workforce. Not only will more young people who were born in the 1970s enter the workforce in the 1990s but also millions of women in industrializing nations are beginning to leave home for paid jobs. Moreover, the workforce in the developing world is also better and better educated. The developing countries are producing a growing share of the world's high school and college graduates.

When these demographic differences are combined with different rates of economic growth, they are likely to lead to major redefinitions of labor markets. Nations that have slow-growing workforces but rapid growth in service sector jobs (namely Japan, Germany, and the United States) will become magnets for immigrants, even if their public policies

The World Work Force Is Growing Rapidly (in millions)

Country or Region	Labor Force 1970	Labor Force 1985	Labor Force 2000	Labor Force Annual Growth Rate 1985-2000
World*	1,596.8	2,163.6	2,752.5	1.6%
OECD*	307.0	372.4	401.3	0.5%
United States	84.9	122.1	141.1	1.0
Japan	51.5	59.6	64.3	0.5
Germany	35.5	38.9	37.2	-0.3
United Kingdom	25.3	28.2	29.1	0.2
France	21.4	23.9	25.8	0.5
Italy	20.9	23.5	24.2	0.2
Spain	13.0	14.0	15.7	0.8
Canada	8.5	12.7	14.6	0.9
Australia	5.6	7.4	8.9	1.3
Sweden	3.9	4.4	4.6	0.3
Developing Regions*	1,119.9	1,595.8	2,137.7	2.1%
China	428.3	617.9	761.2	1.4
India	223.9	293.2	383.2	1.8
Indonesia	45.6	63.4	87.7	2.2
Brazil	31.5	49.6	67.8	2.1
Pakistan	19.3	29.8	45.2	2.8
Thailand	17.9	26.7	34.5	1.7
Mexico	14.5	26.1	40.6	3.0
Turkey	16.1	21.4	28.8	2.0
Philippines	13.7	19.9	28.6	2.4
South Korea	11.4	16.8	22.3	1.9
USSR	117.2	143.3	155.0	0.5%

*Totals include some countries not listed in table.
Sources: For OECD nations except Germany: OECD, Department of Economics and Statistics, Labor Force Statistics, 1967-1987; U.S. Bureau of Labor Statistics; The World Bank, World Development Report, 1987. For developing nations and Germany: International Labour Office, Economically Active Population, 1950-2025; The World Bank, World Development Report, 1990.

Exhibit 1

seek to discourage them. Nations whose educational systems produce prospective workers faster than their economies can absorb them (Argentina, Poland, or the Philippines) will export people.

Beyond these differences in growth rates, the workforces of various nations differ enormously in makeup and capabilities. It is precisely differences like these in age, gender, and education that give us the best clues about what to expect in the 1990s.

Women will enter the workforce in great numbers, especially in the developing countries, where relatively few women have been absorbed to date. The trend toward women leaving home-based employment and entering the paid workforce is an often overlooked demographic reality of industrialization. As cooking and cleaning technologies ease the burden at home, agricultural jobs disappear, and other jobs (especially in services) proliferate, women tend to be employed in the economy. Their output is suddenly counted in government statistics, causing GNP to rise. (See Exhibit 2.)

More than half of all women between the ages of fifteen and sixty-four now work outside the home, and women comprise one-third of the world's workforce. But the shift from home-based employment has occurred unevenly around the world. The developed

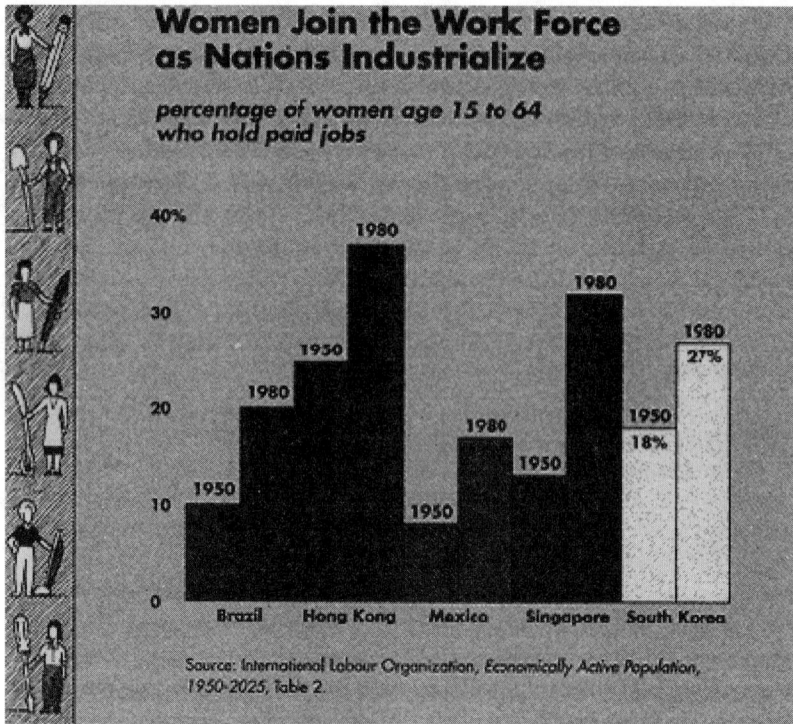

Women Join the Work Force as Nations Industrialize

percentage of women age 15 to 64 who hold paid jobs

Source: International Labour Organization, *Economically Active Population, 1950-2025,* Table 2.

Exhibit 2

nations have absorbed many more women into the labor force than the developing regions: 59 percent for the former, 49 percent for the latter. (See Exhibit 3.)

More telling than the distinction between the developed and developing worlds, though, are the differences in female labor force participation by country. Largely because of religious customs and social expectations, some developed countries have relatively few women in the workforce, and a small number of developing nations have high rates of female participation. The fact that women are entering the workforce is old news in Sweden, for instance, where four-fifths of working-age women hold jobs, or in the United States, where two-thirds are employed. Even in Japan, which is sometimes characterized as a nation in which most women stay home to help educate their children, about 58 percent of women hold paid jobs. Yet highly industrialized countries such as Spain, Italy, and Germany have fairly low rates of female participation. And for ideological reasons, China, with one of the lowest GNPs per capita of any nation, has female participation rates that are among the world's highest.

The degree of female labor force participation has tremendous implications for the economy. Although a large expansion of the workforce cannot guarantee economic growth (Ethiopia and Bangladesh both expanded their workforces rapidly in the 1970s and 1980s but barely increased their GNP per capita), in many cases, rapid workforce growth stimulates and reinforces economic growth. If other conditions are favorable, countries with many women ready to join the workforce can look forward to rapid economic expansion.

Among the developed nations, Spain, Italy, and Germany could show great gains. If their economies become constrained by scarce labor, economic pressures may well overpower social forces that have so far kept women from working. In developing countries

Women Hold More Than One-Third of the World's Jobs

Country or Region	Working Women 1985 or 1987* (in millions)	Female Share of Work Force (percentage of total work force)	Female Labor Force Participation (percentage of all females age 15 to 64)
World†	790.1	36.5%	51.3%
Developed Regions‡	156.5	40.9%	58.6%
United States	53.9	44.1	66.0
Japan	24.3	39.9	57.8
Germany	11.1	39.3	51.3
United Kingdom	11.7	41.4	62.6
France	10.2	42.5	55.2
Italy	8.9	36.9	43.4
Spain	4.8	32.6	37.5
Canada	5.7	43.2	65.4
Australia	3.1	39.7	54.1
Sweden	2.1	48.0	79.4
Developing Regions‡	554.2	34.7%	48.6%
China	267.2	43.2	75.5
India	76.8	26.2	32.3
Indonesia	19.8	31.3	38.0
Brazil	13.5	27.2	32.2
Pakistan	3.4	11.4	12.1
Thailand	12.2	45.9	74.8
Mexico	7.1	27.0	31.1
Turkey	7.3	34.0	47.4
Philippines	6.4	32.1	39.2
South Korea	5.7	34.0	42.2
USSR (1985)	69.2	48.3%	72.6%

*For developed regions, 1987 figures were used; for developing regions, 1985 figures.
†Totals include some countries not listed in table.
‡Developed and developing regions as defined by the International Labour Office.
Source: International Labour Office, *Economically Active Population, 1950-2025,* Table 2.

Exhibit 3

where religious customs and social expectations are subject to change, there is the potential for rapid expansion of the workforce with parallel surges in the economy.

Women are unlikely to have much effect in many other countries—Sweden, the United States, Canada, the United Kingdom, and Japan, all of which have few women left to add to their workforces. They may be able to redeploy women to more productive jobs, but the economic gains will likely be modest. Also, countries that maintain their current low utilization of women will have a hard time progressing rapidly. It is hard to imagine Pakistan, for example, a largely Moslem country where 11 percent of women work, joining the ranks of the industrialized nations without absorbing more of its women into the paid workforce.

As more women enter the workforce worldwide, their presence will change working conditions and industrial patterns in predictable ways. The demand for services such as fast food, day care, home cleaners, and nursing homes will boom, following the now-familiar pattern in the United States and parts of Europe. Child rearing and care for the disabled will be increasingly institutionalized. And because women who work tend to have more demands on them at home than men do, they are likely to demand more time away from their jobs. It is plausible, for example, that some industrialized nations will adopt a work week of 35 hours or less by the end of the 1990s in response to these time pressures.

The average age of the world's workforce will rise, especially in the developed countries. As a result of slower birthrates and longer lifespans, the world population and labor force are aging. The average age of the world's workers will climb by more than a year, to about thirty-five, during the 1990s.

But here again it is important to distinguish between the developed and the developing countries. The population of the industrialized nations is much older. Young people represent a small and shrinking fraction of the labor force, while the proportion of retirees over sixty-five is climbing. By 2000, fewer than 40 percent of workers in countries such as the United States, Japan, Germany, and the United Kingdom will be under age thirty-four, compared with 59 percent in Pakistan, 55 percent in Thailand, and 53 percent in China. (See Exhibit 4.)

The age distribution of a country's workforce affects its mobility, flexibility, and energy. Older workers are less likely to relocate or to learn new skills than are younger people. Countries and companies that are staffed with older workers may have greater difficulty adapting to new technologies or changes in markets compared with those staffed with younger workers.

By 2000, workers in most developing nations will be young, relatively recently educated, and arguably more adaptable compared with those in the industrialized world. Very young nations that are rapidly industrializing, such as Mexico and China, may find that the youth and flexibility of their workforces give them an advantage relative to their industrialized competitors with older workforces, particularly over those in heavy manufacturing industries, where shrinkage has left factories staffed mostly with workers who are in their forties and fifties.

Most industrialized nations will have 15 percent or more of their populations over age sixty-five by the year 2000, compared with less than 5 percent for most developing nations. The challenge that industrialized nations may face in preserving their competitive positions as their workforces age may be stiffened by the high costs of older workers and older societies. Older workers typically have higher wages because of seniority systems, and their pension and health care costs escalate sharply during the later years of their work lives.

As more workers in industrialized nations retire toward the close of the century, national health and pension taxes in these nations may rise as well. Unless these rising costs are offset by productivity gains, employers and nations that have older workforces may lose their competitive leadership in industries with standardized production technologies. This could be especially challenging for Japan, where the aging of the population is proceeding even more rapidly than in other industrialized nations.

One silver lining to this cloud of higher costs may be the higher rates of personal saving that come with older populations. As workers age, they tend to save a bigger chunk of their paychecks. This could increase the capital available for investment in industrialized countries and give them more money to buy productivity-enhancing equipment. (Of course, in a world of mobile capital, these funds could just as easily flow to the developing nations if economic conditions were more promising there.)

Country or Region	Share of Work Force Under Age 34		Share of Population Over Age 65		Labor Force Participation of Workers Over Age 65
	1985	2000	1985	2000	1985
World¹	57.1%	51.7%	5.9%	6.8%	32.8%
Developed Regions†	46.9%	40.7%	11.2%	13.3%	9.0%
United States	50.4	39.5	12.3	12.9	10.3
Japan	33.8	33.9	11.1	15.8	26.0
Germany	45.7	37.4	14.2	16.0	3.2
United Kingdom	43.6	38.8	15.5	15.4	4.6
France	47.0	41.5	13.6	15.6	3.0
Italy	48.0	44.6	14.0	16.7	3.9
Spain	49.9	49.0	9.1	11.5	3.8
Canada	50.9	39.7	11.1	13.1	7.1
Australia	50.7	44.4	10.7	11.6	5.1
Sweden	38.7	36.3	16.9	17.2	5.4
Developing Regions†	60.7%	54.9%	4.2%	5.1%	26.3%
China	63.7	53.3	5.5	7.3	16.0
India	55.6	52.0	3.4	4.1	40.1
Indonesia	55.7	52.7	2.8	4.2	38.3
Brazil	62.5	42.1	4.0	4.9	17.7
Pakistan	63.3	59.2	4.1	3.9	33.7
Thailand	62.8	55.2	3.9	5.2	27.2
Mexico	61.4	51.9	4.1	4.9	42.1
Turkey	59.6	54.4	4.3	5.2	10.9
Philippines	59.2	54.8	3.3	3.8	44.8
South Korea	54.7	44.3	4.5	5.9	26.5
USSR	50.2%	42.9%	9.3%	11.9%	4.4%

¹Trends include some countries not listed in table.
†Developed and developing regions as defined by the International Labour Office.
Sources: International Labour Office, Economically Active Population 1950-2025 and Yearbook of Labour Statistics, 1986.

Exhibit 4

Wealth could be redistributed in another way, too. As the number of retirees in industrialized countries rises, more of them are likely to cross national borders as tourists or immigrants. Traditionally, few retirees have settled outside their home countries. But cross-border retirements and travel are likely to burgeon in the 1990s: Japanese retiring to Hawaii, Americans receiving Social Security checks in Mexico, and English pensioners sunning themselves on the coast of Spain. As Algerians, Turks, and Mexicans return home bringing retirement checks with them, these flows could mirror the movements of young workers.

People worldwide will be increasingly well educated. The developing countries will produce a growing share of the world's high school and college graduates. Educational trends are hard to track because school and college systems differ so much from country to country and because the linkage between years of school and work skills is indirect and hard to document. Even the national data on years of education are often incomplete.

Still, the data reveal important developments. Based on the numbers of high school and college graduates, the world's workforce is becoming better educated. In the decade and a half between 1970 and 1986, world high school enrollments grew by some 120 million students, or more than 76 percent. College enrollments more than doubled during the period—from twenty-six million to fifty-eight million. This trend is likely to continue, as

Developed Countries Send More of Their Young to School

Country or Region	Percentage of Age Group in High School* 1986	Percentage of Age Group in College* 1986
OECD†	93.0%	39.0%
United States	95.0	59.0
Japan	96.0	29.0
Germany	72.0	30.0
United Kingdom	85.0	22.0
France	95.0	30.0
Italy	76.0	25.0
Spain	98.0	32.0
Canada	103.0	55.0
Australia	96.0	29.0
Sweden	83.0	37.0
Developing Regions†	40.0%	7.0%
China	42.0	2.0
India	35.0	9.0
Indonesia	41.0	7.0
Brazil	36.0	11.0
Pakistan	18.0	5.0
Thailand	29.0	20.0
Mexico	55.0	16.0
Egypt	66.0	21.0
Turkey	44.0	10.0
Philippines	68.0	38.0
South Korea	95.0	33.0
USSR	99.0%	22.0%

*Ratio of those enrolled to total school-age population. For high school, population base is typically age 13 to 17. For college population, age 20 to 24 is used. Gross enrollment level can exceed 100% if people from outside these ages are enrolled.

†Totals include some countries not listed in table.

Sources: United Nations Educational, Scientific, and Cultural Organization (UNESCO), Statistical Yearbook, 1988; U.S. Department of Education, National Center For Education Statistics, Digest of Education Statistics, 1989.

Exhibit 5

nations and individuals increasingly recognize the economic value of education. By the year 2000, it is likely that high school enrollment could grow by another 60 percent, reaching nearly 450 million, while college attendance could double again to top 115 million.

Today, higher percentages of children in industrialized nations attend high school and college. (See Exhibit 5.) Most of them educate nearly all children through high school and typically further educate about one-third of college-age youths. (Germany and Italy are notable exceptions; only three-quarters of children between ages twelve and seventeen go to secondary school.) Most of the developing nations have less than half their young people in high school, and they seldom place more than one-fifth in college (although South Korea, Argentina, and the Philippines enroll more than one-third in college). (See Exhibit 6.)

But an important shift is under way: The developing world is producing a rapidly increasing share of the world's skilled human capital. This trend has been underway for some time and will accelerate through the turn of the century. In the decade and a half between 1970 and 1986, the United States, Canada, Europe, the Soviet Union, and Japan saw their share of world high school enrollees shrink from 44 percent to 30 percent. If current trends continue, their share is expected to drop to only 21 percent by the year 2000. (See Exhibit 7.)

U.S. high school students made up 9 percent of world enrollees in 1970 but only 5 percent in 1986. Not only is their relative number shrinking but also U.S. students are performing worse relative to the rest of the world. International standardized tests suggest that high school students from many other nations are now better prepared, at least in mathematics and science. (See Exhibit 8.) In tests given to high school students worldwide during the mid-1980s, for instance, U.S. seniors ranked thirteenth among thirteen nations in biology, twelfth in chemistry, and tenth in physics. The U.S. performance looks even weaker considering that only small fractions of American students took the tests, while greater percentages of non-U.S. students did.

The developed world is also losing ground when it comes to higher education. Between 1970 and 1985, the share of the world's college students from the United States, Canada,

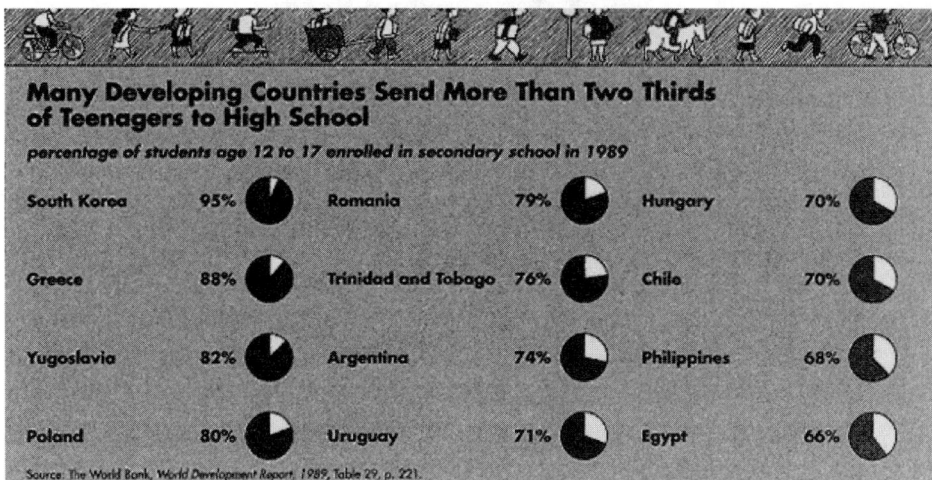

Many Developing Countries Send More Than Two Thirds of Teenagers to High School

percentage of students age 12 to 17 enrolled in secondary school in 1989

South Korea	95%	Romania	79%	Hungary	70%
Greece	88%	Trinidad and Tobago	76%	Chile	70%
Yugoslavia	82%	Argentina	74%	Philippines	68%
Poland	80%	Uruguay	71%	Egypt	66%

Source: The World Bank, World Development Report, 1989, Table 29, p. 221.

Exhibit 6

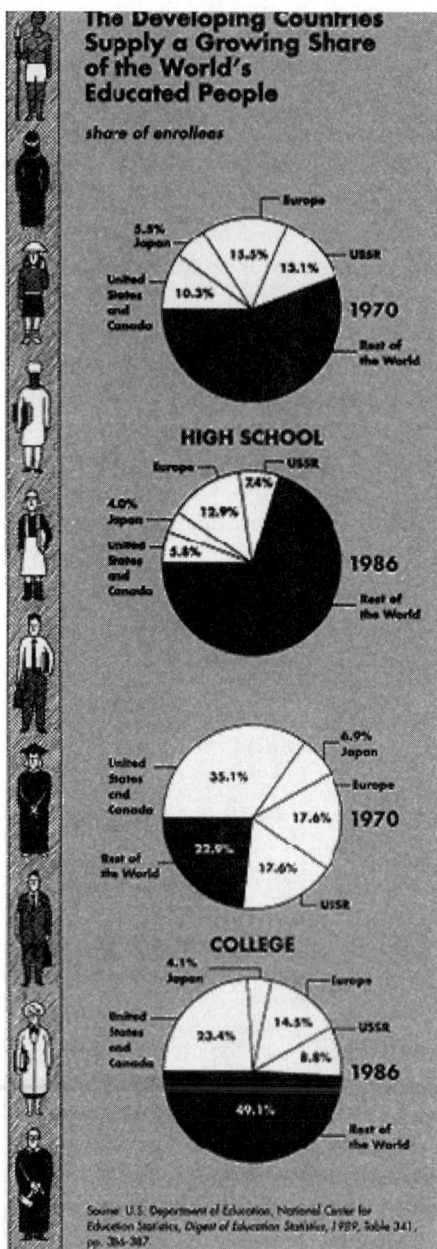

The Developing Countries Supply a Growing Share of the World's Educated People

share of enrollees

HIGH SCHOOL — 1970: Europe 15.5%, USSR 13.1%, Japan 5.5%, United States and Canada 10.3%, Rest of the World

HIGH SCHOOL — 1986: USSR 7.4%, Europe 12.9%, Japan 4.0%, United States and Canada 5.8%, Rest of the World

COLLEGE — 1970: Japan 6.9%, Europe 17.6%, USSR 17.6%, United States and Canada 35.1%, Rest of the World 22.9%

COLLEGE — 1986: Japan 4.1%, Europe 14.5%, USSR 8.8%, United States and Canada 23.4%, Rest of the World 49.1%

Source: U.S. Department of Education, National Center for Education Statistics, *Digest of Education Statistics, 1989*, Table 341, pp. 386–387

Exhibit 7

High School Students in Other Countries Outperform Americans in Science science test scores*			
Country or Region	Biology	Chemistry	Physics
Singapore	66.8	66.1	54.9
England	63.4	69.5	58.3
Hungary	59.7	47.7	56.5
Poland	56.9	44.6	51.5
Norway	54.8	41.9	52.8
Finland	51.9	33.3	37.9
Hong Kong	50.8	64.4	59.3
Sweden	48.5	40.0	44.6
Australia	48.2	46.6	48.5
Japan	46.2	51.9	56.1
Canada	45.9	46.6	48.5
Italy	42.3	38.0	28.0
United States	37.9	37.7	45.5

*Scores normalized to a mean of 50, with a standard deviation of 10.
■ Developing countries.

Source: U.S. Department of Education, Digest of Education Statistics, 1989, Table 348, p. 391.

Exhibit 8

Europe, the Soviet Union, and Japan dropped from 77 percent to 51 percent. The share of college students in the developing world leaped from 23 percent to 49 percent, and these figures may be understatements because many students in Western universities are citizens of other countries and will return home when they graduate. By the year 2000, students from developing nations will make up three-fifths of all students.

It's true that in absolute numbers, the United States, the Soviet Union, and Japan are still the leading producers of college graduates of all kinds, but a growing number of the world's college graduates originate outside the traditionally highly educated countries. Four of the next six greatest sources of college graduates are developing countries: Brazil, China, the Philippines, and South Korea. Differences in the numbers of graduates are especially intriguing when sorted by discipline. China and Brazil rank third and fifth in numbers of science graduates, followed by Japan. For engineering graduates, Brazil, China, Mexico, Korea, and the Philippines all place ahead of France and the United Kingdom. (See Exhibit 9.)

What makes the rising levels of education in developing countries especially significant is the link between education and economic growth. Those developing nations that educate large proportions of their young have achieved above average rates of growth and higher standards of living. Among the forty-two nations labeled by the World Bank as ''low income,'' only one, Sri Lanka, sends more than half of its high school-age children to school. Among those labeled "upper middle" or "high income" (excluding the oil producers), all but two send more than 60 percent of teenagers to school. Only Brazil and Portugal send fewer teenagers to school.

Much of the World's Scientific Brain Power Comes from Developing Countries

thousands of college graduates in 1986

Country or Region	Total College Graduates	Scientists	Engineers	Ph.D.s
United States	979.5	180.7	77.1	394.3
USSR	839.5	61.7	352.3	na*
Japan	378.7	33.5	74.5	23.5
Brazil	244.6	34.1	20.0	8.9
China	227.7	44.7	72.7	14.2
Philippines†	212.0	26.3	23.4	na*
Germany	172.5	35.4	30.2	22.3
France	164.4	30.6	15.0	53.9
South Korea	155.0	16.9	21.9	20.7
United Kingdom	132.7	31.4	17.0	37.4
Canada	118.9	21.1	8.4	19.8
Mexico	112.8	20.4	25.3	8.0
Egypt	101.0	11.4	9.3	10.4

*Not available.
†Estimated.

■ Developing countries.

Source: United Nations Educational, Scientific, and Cultural Organization (UNESCO), *Statistical Yearbook, 1988*, Tables 3-10; pp. 3-306.

Exhibit 9

THE PRESSURES TO EMIGRATE

The link between the education levels of the workforce and economic performance argues that some well-educated, middle-income nations may be poised for rapid growth in the 1990s. In Eastern Europe, for example, Poland, Hungary, and Czechoslovakia are especially well positioned for development because of their relatively well-educated workforces coupled with their relationships with other European countries. The Philippines, Egypt, Argentina, Peru, Cuba, and Mexico also have huge growth potential because they, too, have relatively well-educated workforces. But their fragile political and economic infrastructures and sometimes foolish economic policies make their development far less certain.

The tentative economic prospects of these well-educated nations illustrate the risks and opportunities facing countries whose educational systems outperform their economies. During the 1990s, workers who have acquired skills in school will be extremely valuable in the world labor markets. And if job opportunities are lacking in their native lands, better jobs will probably be only a plane ride away. Countries that fail to find a formula for growth can expect to become exporters of people. In Eastern Europe, for example, if the postcommunist rebuilding process stretches on for many years, hundreds of thousands— if not millions—of Poles, Czechs, and Hungarians will seek better opportunities in Western Europe or the United States. Similarly, if South America cannot find ways to restore investor confidence, the northward flow of economic refugees will accelerate.

Although most governments in industrial nations will resist these movements of people for social and political reasons, employers in the developed world are likely to find ways around government barriers.

The combination of slow workforce growth, fewer women left to enter the workforce, earlier retirements, and a shrinking share of high school and college graduates virtually guarantees that many industrialized nations will face labor shortages at various points during the economic cycles of the 1990s. When they do, a growing array of occupations and labor markets will become internationalized.

Not all workers are equally likely to emigrate—or equally likely to be welcomed elsewhere. The image of the labor force as a large pool of similar workers competing for jobs is inexact. There are actually many smaller labor pools, each defined by occupational skills. Patterns of immigration will vary, depending on the conditions of markets that are defined by specific skills.

Typically, unskilled workers—janitors, dishwashers, or laborers—are recruited locally. At higher skill levels, companies often search across states or regions. Among college graduates, national labor markets are more common: New York banks interview MBAs from San Francisco; Midwestern manufacturers hire engineers from both coasts. At the highest skill levels, the labor market has been international for many years. Bell Laboratories physicists, for example, come from universities in England or India as well as from Princeton or MIT. At Schering-Plough's research labs, the first language of biochemists is as likely to be Hindi, Japanese, or German as it is English.

When labor markets tighten and become even more specialized, however, many employers will expand the geography of their recruitment efforts. Recent trends in nursing and software design suggest the emerging patterns of the 1990s. As the shortage of nurses at U.S. hospitals became acute during the 1970s and 1980s, health care providers began to recruit in ever-widening circles. What was once a local labor market became regional, then national, and finally international. By the end of the 1980s, it was routine for New York hospitals to advertise in Dublin and Manila for skilled nurses. Similarly, in systems development, the shortage of engineers led rapidly growing companies to look to universities in England, India, and China to fill some of their U.S. job openings.

Government policies and corporate needs are likely to focus most on the immigration of younger, higher skilled workers filling specific occupational shortages. But while such flows of higher skilled workers will predominate, even unskilled jobs may become more internationalized in the 1990s. Indeed, during the 1970s and 1980s, some of the largest international movements of workers were relatively low-skilled workers immigrating to take jobs natives didn't want: Turks to Germany, Algerians to France, Mexicans to the United States. Although these movements of low-skilled workers generate explosive social and political tensions, the economic realities of the 1990s argue that the numbers will grow.

GAINS FROM TRADE IN PEOPLE

The globalization of labor is good for the world. It allows human capital to be deployed where it can be used most productively. Countries that recognize it as a positive trend and facilitate the flow of people will benefit most.

When workers move to a developed country, they become more productive because an established economic infrastructure can make better use of their time. (See Exhibit 10.) A street corner vendor of tacos in Mexico City would be lucky to gross $50 for a day's work, while the same worker at a Taco Bell in Los Angeles might sell ten to fifty times as much in a day. The higher output translates into higher wages. Even at minimum wage, the new Taco Bell employee will earn ten times his or her former daily income.

For highly skilled workers, the effects are magnified. An engineer once relegated to clerical work in Bangkok may design a new computer system when employed by a Boston electronics company. A Filipino nurse can go from poverty to middle class by taking a job at a hospital in Atlanta. The positive impacts of immigration are visible in robust economies of Southern California and South Florida.

Immigration will be especially good for advanced nations with high levels of capital per worker but constrained labor. In particular, immigration may boost the economies of the United States, Canada, Germany, and other European nations.

The United States is likely to fare particularly well for a number of reasons. For one thing, its wages are among the world's highest, so they attract top talent. Also, political barriers have always been low, and opportunities for immigrants to advance are great. Furthermore, its higher education system draws a large number of students from around the world. In 1987, U.S. universities granted to foreigners some 51 percent of doctorates in engineering, 48 percent in mathematics, 32 percent in business, and 29 percent in physical sciences. Many of these graduates return home, but many stay. Either way, they stimulate the U.S. economy—by enhancing trade relationships or by increasing the U.S. supply of human capital.

Australia, New Zealand, and some European nations—notably, Germany—are also likely to gain from the international flow of people. Historically, political and cultural obstacles have constrained emigration to Europe. But language and political barriers are weakening (English and German are becoming the languages of business), and the integration of formerly communist states in Eastern Europe into the Organization for Economic Cooperation and Development (OECD) trading regime suggests that Europe will increasingly welcome people who want to cross its borders. During the summer of 1990, for example, five nations in Western Europe agreed that they would eliminate all restrictions on the rights of their citizens to live and work anywhere within their five borders. In Germany, there has been a sharp political backlash against the guest worker program that allowed many Turkish workers into the country during the 1970s. Germany remains committed to preserving its ethnic identity and plans to tighten restrictions on immigration by non-Germans, but it continues to accept thousands of German-speaking people from Russia, Poland, and other East European countries. These workers are likely to strengthen the German economy during the 1990s.

Although the politics of accepting more foreigners are unfavorable in virtually every industrialized nation (and may grow worse during the coming recession), the demographic and economic trends will create pressures in most nations to accept greater flows of people. Only Japan is likely to reject increased immigration, regardless of its looming labor shortages. Japan's enormous language and cultural barriers and its commitment to preserving its racial homogeneity virtually rule out the acceptance of many foreign workers. For the foreseeable future, Japanese economic growth will depend on native Japanese human resources. This may pose a stiff challenge for Japan, because its workforce is among the oldest in the world and its workforce growth rate is among the lowest. One opportunity for Japan to pursue may lie in its female labor force: Although a high proportion of Japanese women have paid jobs, many are underemployed and therefore not as productive as they could be. This also may be true for many—if not all—developed economies, but it seems to be especially true of Japan.

Leaders of developing nations often express concern that mass migration of their young people will harm their economies, but there is little evidence to support these fears. The

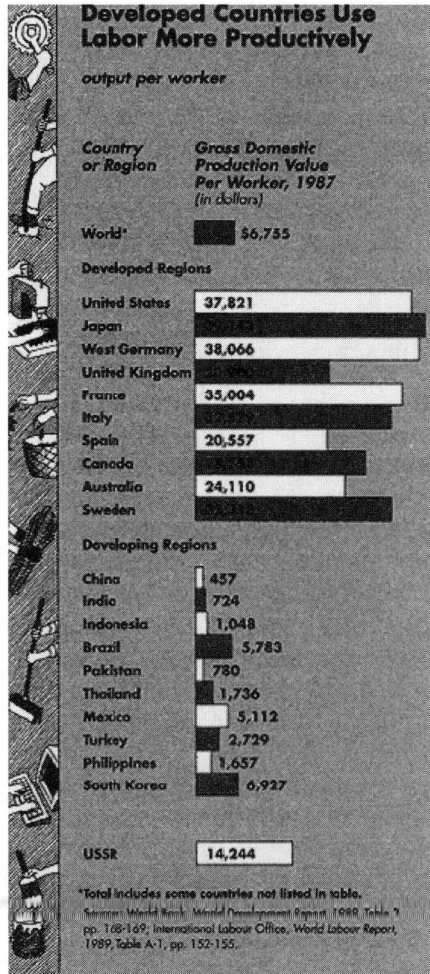

Developed Countries Use Labor More Productively

output per worker

Country or Region	Gross Domestic Production Value Per Worker, 1987 (in dollars)
World*	$6,755
Developed Regions	
United States	37,821
Japan	
West Germany	38,066
United Kingdom	
France	35,004
Italy	
Spain	20,557
Canada	
Australia	24,110
Sweden	
Developing Regions	
China	457
India	724
Indonesia	1,048
Brazil	5,783
Pakistan	780
Thailand	1,736
Mexico	5,112
Turkey	2,729
Philippines	1,657
South Korea	6,927
USSR	14,244

*Total includes some countries not listed in table.

Sources: World Bank, World Development Report, 1989, Table 1, pp. 168-169; International Labour Office, World Labour Report, 1989, Table A-1, pp. 152-155.

Exhibit 10

large numbers of Korean, Taiwanese, and Chinese scientists and engineers who have emigrated to the United States do not seem to have had any appreciable impact on the economies at home. Indeed, many immigrants have returned home at some point in their careers, and the cross-fertilization seems to have boosted both economies. Nor have larger movements of less skilled workers harmed the economies left behind. Actually, the earnings sent home from Mexicans in the United States, Turkish guest workers in Germany, Algerians in France, and Egyptians throughout the Middle East have stimulated growth in labor-exporting countries.

A demonstration of the gains from trade in people occurred in Kuwait in 1990, when the gains were suddenly extinguished. When Iraq invaded, Kuwait's economy ground to an immediate and almost complete halt. Kuwait could no longer export oil, the occupying military force looted many businesses but, most important, the Asian and Middle Eastern workers who had made up two-thirds of the workforce left for home. Hospitals lacked doctors and nurses, buses had no drivers, stores had no clerks. In the space of a few weeks, most of Kuwait's economy disappeared. Kuwait was not the only country to suffer. The huge repatriation of hundreds of thousands of Pakistani, Filipino, and Egyptian workers was equally traumatic for those nations. Not only did these workers and their families return to economies with few jobs available but their foreign earnings (a great part of which had been sent home from Kuwait) also were suddenly missing from the local economy. The gains from trade in people had been lost, and both the sending and the receiving nations were poorer because of it.

The developing countries can thrive despite massive emigration. The real test of whether they will realize their economic potential is how well they can combine their human capital with financial backing, sensible economic policies, and a sound business infrastructure. As always, they must win investors' confidence if they are to make any real progress.

FROM GLOBALIZATION TO STANDARDIZATION

The globalization of labor is inevitable. The economic benefits from applying human resources most productively are too great to be resisted. At least some countries will lower the barriers to immigration, and at least some workers will be drawn by the opportunity to apply their training and improve their lives. But more likely, many countries will make immigration easier, and many workers will travel the globe. By the turn of the century, developing countries that have educated their young and adopted market-oriented policies will have advanced faster than those that have not. Developed countries that have accepted or sought foreign workers will be stronger for having done so. As the benefits become more obvious, the movement of workers will become freer.

The world will be changed as a result. As labor gradually becomes international, some national differences will fade. Needs and concerns will become more universal, and personnel policies and practices will standardize. As developing nations absorb women into the workforce, for example, they are likely to share the industrialized world's concern about child care and demand for conveniences.

Two forces will drive workplace standardization: companies responding to global labor markets and governments negotiating trade agreements. For a global corporation, the notion of a single set of workplace standards will eventually become as irresistible as the idea of a single language for conducting business. Vacation policies that are established in Germany to attract top scientists will be hard to rescind when the employees are relocated to New Jersey; flexible hours of work that make sense in California will sooner or later become the norm in Madrid; health care deductibles and pension contributions designed for one nation will be modified so that workers in all nations enjoy the same treatment. Typical of most innovations in corporate personnel practices, the benefits of most importance to high-wage, highly valued employees (who will be the most often recruited internationally) will be standardized first.

Government efforts to harmonize workplace standards will accelerate these market-based responses. Currently, for example, officials from most European Community (EC) countries are seeking to draft a single set of rules to govern workplaces throughout Europe, beginning in 1992. These will cover such things as wage and hour standards, employment rights, and worker safety. Although the comprehensive European process is not likely to be repeated elsewhere, standardized working conditions and reciprocal work rules may become an element in many trade negotiations in the 1990s, particularly those relating to services. If Mexican and U.S. truck drivers were to be freely employed by companies on both sides of the border, for example, a U.S.-Mexico free trade agreement would need to cover driver licensing standards, hours of work, and fringe benefits.

Like the process of globalization of product and financial markets, the globalization of labor will be uneven and uncertain. Governments will play a greater role in world labor markets than in other markets, and governments often will be motivated by factors other than economic gain.

But for companies and countries that accept the trends, the 1990s and beyond can be a time of great opportunity. For countries seeking to maximize economic growth, strategies that develop and attract human capital can become powerful policy tools. For companies prepared to operate globally, willingness to compete for human resources on a worldwide basis can be a source of competitive advantage.

2

Travels into America's Future

ROBERT D. KAPLAN

SOUTHERN CALIFORNIA AND THE PACIFIC NORTHWEST

Imagine a land in which the dominant culture is an internationalized one, at every level; in which the political units that really matter are confederations of city-states; in which loyalty is an economic concept, when it is not obsolete; in which "the United States" exists chiefly to provide military protection. That is the land our correspondent glimpses, and it is no longer beyond the horizon.

Sandstone cliffs, a peacock-blue ocean, and an endless bar of cream-colored sand filled my first view of greater Los Angeles as I drove south from the Santa Barbara airport on the Pacific Coast Highway and entered Los Angeles County. With the ten-thousand-foot-high San Gabriel Mountains stepping down to the sea, L.A. appeared too beautiful to be real.

From north to south, greater Los Angeles spans close to a hundred miles of seacoast. I stopped at Santa Monica, a city of ninety thousand on the northwest edge of Los Angeles. After checking into a hotel, I looked at a map and saw that the Third Street pedestrian promenade was only half a mile away.

My decision to walk there was a mistake I did not repeat in Los Angeles. The scrawny palms provided no shade on the sun-blasted asphalt. Except for a bag lady, a woman pushing her child in a pram, and a young man with tattoos who passed me at high speed on Rollerblades, the street was empty for that half mile—a half mile that took me past the Civic Center and Auditorium, where the Academy Awards ceremony used to be held; the Art Deco town hall; and the Rand Corporation. Rather than people I saw only cars and enormous parking lots.

Cars could not enter Third Street, which was roped off for pedestrians, led with food and jewelry carts, and packed with shops and restaurants. The result was hordes of people strolling—whereas just across the street and all the way back to my hotel there had been almost none. The crowd here was young, heavily Asian, and fiercely middle class, dressed, like the crowds I have seen in Brazilian cities, in fashionable leisure and beachwear. I sat down at an outdoor Thai-Chinese restaurant for an early dinner. The manager was Japanese, the hostess Iranian, and the other help Mexican. The Iranian hostess, who wore many rings and had mint-green fingernails, was telling a friend that as a graduation present her father was going to drive her cross-country to see Elvis's grave, at Graceland. On the sidewalk beside my table a large crowd watched a black youth tap dance to Brazilian music. The globalized architecture of the shops and office façades was familiar from the upmarket malls I had seen in the Midwest. Also on Third Street I saw more homeless people than I had ever seen in a similar-sized area in New York City or Washington, D.C. They were doing crossword puzzles, talking to themselves, and trying to enter the restrooms of expensive restaurants before waiters caught them. They were overwhelmingly white and male. I saw one man with long gray hair wearing an Army jacket and a woolen hat despite the 80° temperature. He banged his hand against a bench and shouted disconnectedly. People moved away. The homeless barely threaten the panorama of prosperity secured in Santa Monica by a burgeoning multimedia and software industry, which the well-dressed, thirtyish crowd reflected.

Over the next few days I drove through the suburban San Fernando Valley bordering Santa Monica to the north, which is equally prosperous. Unlike Santa Monica, the San Fernando Valley is part of the City of Los Angeles. Its business and political leaders want to secede. With 1.3 million inhabitants, the San Fernando Valley would constitute the nation's sixth largest urban area, and one of its richest. This is not white flight—40 percent of the valley's residents are Latino or Asian. Among the white population, Jews are the largest ethnic group. These people want to duplicate the prosperity of incorporated posturban dynamos in northern Los Angeles such as Burbank—now the home of the Walt Disney Company, Warner Brothers, and NBC—and Glendale, 45 percent of whose population is foreign-born Latinos, Asians, and Armenians. Joel Kotkin, a Los Angeles-based urban-affairs specialist, calls the secessionist trend that has already Balkanized St. Louis and other American cities the "urban confederacy movement." Unlike the original secessionists, these activists will win, he thinks, because cities are now too big to work—they can function only as a league of smaller, incorporated pieces.

A third of all U.S.-born middle-class Latinos and more than a quarter of all U.S.-born middle-class Asians in the five-county greater Los Angeles region marry someone of another race. Even the notion of white versus black is losing relevance here, with Latinos constituting 38 percent of the Los Angeles County population and Asians and blacks 11 percent each. The racial polarization that divides Washington, D.C., for example, where white suburbs surround what is, in effect, a black urban homeland, is little apparent in L.A. Even within the Los Angeles city limits, blacks make up only 14 percent of the population, whereas they make up 29 percent in New York City. For ten days I drove throughout greater Los Angeles, stopping often to walk in different neighborhoods. Media images of the L.A. riots and the O. J. Simpson trial had prepared me for a city as divided as Washington. But in L.A., where more than eighty languages are spoken, that's not what I found.

Zaheer Virji is a twenty-seven-year-old ethnic-Indian immigrant from the East African nation of Tanzania. He wore a blue-velvet baseball cap, a white T-shirt, jeans, and running shoes when I met him and his American wife in a Santa Monica hotel lobby. Virji's family, which imports goods from Hong Kong to Tanzania, is part of a merchant community from the Indian subcontinent that forms the middle class in Tanzania, along with several other African countries. Virji remembers the times when police thugs under the control of the former Tanzanian President Julius Nyerere harassed his relatives and arrested his uncle. He told me that race relations are "so much better" in southern California than in Africa, where Indians and Africans completely stereotype each other: "I came here to escape not just Africans but Indians, too." (The name Virji is an alias.) He went first to England and then to Canada, where there are large Indian communities. But he didn't feel free. "In those places the community is what is happening. Here in the U.S., it's you that is happening. There is less of system here, fewer laws to restrict you."

Virji came to the United States six years ago, and has no college degree or green card—yet. In the six months before we spoke, he had earned more by investing in the stock market than his wife had made at her job—a reflection not only of his skill but also of an economy in which stocks and other assets have risen but wages have not. With this money, along with funds from his family in Tanzania, he was looking to buy a business: a flower shop, a gas station, whatever he could get the best deal on. He was using a broker; if the business was a gas station, he told me, he would need to know about underground tanks and environmental regulations. He wanted to go into partnership with the current owner for a three-year transition period, to secure part of his investment if the business did not turn out as advertised. Ten years from now, he explained, he wants to be the owner of a small business with able employees, so that he can spend his time investing the profits in the stock market.

Los Angeles is full of Asian and Latino immigrants creating their own civilization, just as European immigrants did a hundred years ago. Because these new immigrants bring different historical and cultural experiences, and because they are integrating into American society under more-advanced technological conditions than did immigrants in the past, they will further reduce the distance between America and the rest of the world.

I went east from Santa Monica across the City of Los Angeles to the suburbs of Monterey Park and San Gabriel. As I drove, I saw a sprawling metropolis in transition. The official, ceremonial downtown, composed of the convention center, courts, government offices, and the Los Angeles Times building, looked less vibrant than the new, pedestrian-packed downtowns I saw on the way—Westwood and Beverly Hills, a contiguous area marked by the office buildings of City National Bank, Occidental Petroleum, and others; a Korean church; a Mexican-American real estate agency; and one of the largest schools in the country that teaches English to foreigners. Several real estate agents told me that the 1992 riots in heavily black South Central Los Angeles had quickened the exodus of corporations toward the wealthier western part of the city.

I passed through West Hollywood, an area of gays, elderly Jews, and Russian immigrants; Koreatown; and the "Banana Republic," a neighborhood populated by Central American immigrants. The notorious Watts and South Central neighborhoods were one-story encampments of poor blacks encroached upon by the Latino immigrants who make up two thirds of the population of those areas. Upwardly mobile blacks are moving from here to the Moreno Valley and other inexpensive suburbs in an eastern area of greater Los Angeles called the Inland Empire. Watts and South Central are, in ethnic and racial terms, being annexed to Mexican East Los Angeles. Demographers say that in coming years Latinos will dilute the presence of blacks in Los Angeles, as they have already done in Miami. Latinos are now the majority of the region's industrial work force. The number of Latino- and Asian-owned businesses in Los Angeles County has increased from 70,000 to 220,000 since the early 1980s, whereas the number of black-owned businesses has remained static at 20,000.

I parked in East Los Angeles and walked about a mile past small stores selling furniture and other household goods. I noticed many bridal shops, suggestive of strong family patterns, and many pedestrians, too. Los Angeles, I had begun to realize, was very much a vibrant pedestrian city—in parts. One part I had seen was the largest garment district in North America, whose narrow alleys are packed with Latinos, Asians, and Middle Easterners, a throwback to early-twentieth-century New York. This vast confederation teems with successful commercial and residential areas like the Third Street Promenade and East Los Angeles. But you need a car to travel between them.

From the "Mexico" of East Los Angeles I crossed into "Asia": Monterey Park and San Gabriel, once gray and run-down and now booming with glittering banks, supported by Hong Kong Chinese and Chinese American immigrant money, and many new malls, among them San Gabriel Square.

At this mall, which is decorated with Spanish colonnades, I entered the 99 Ranch Market, part of a California Chinese supermarket chain. At first it seemed like any other enormous American supermarket, with dozens of aisles and too much air conditioning. But nearly every product in the store was an Asian specialty item, either imported or grown in the Los Angeles area. Chinese food stores are common in the nation's various Chinatowns, and so, increasingly, are supermarkets like this one. But never before had I seen forty aisles, each a hundred yards long, devoted to noodles, pork, taro, tofu, pea sprouts, dried shrimp, soybean paste, spicy bean cabbage, dried seaweed, rice spirits, and also Thai, Korean, and Japanese items. Next door was a Chinese restaurant with an over-abundance of employees and an absence of Western cutlery or Caucasian customers. Women crossed the red floor pushing food trolleys filled with saucers of chicken feet and other dishes.

An all-new Asian American civilization is forming here, and flourishing, too. Pacific Rim cultures that were antagonistic for centuries are cooperating in the California market-place. Traditionally nations rise and fall; but at the 99 Ranch Supermarket I wondered if America might escape that fate by shedding its skin as a nation to reveal an international civilization.

I visited another pan-Asian supermarket, this one to the south—in Cerritos, once a dairy farming district but now a planned, incorporated community 45 percent of whose inhab-itants are Asian. The checkout counters are manned by Latinos, and the customers are mainly Chinese. A few blocks away I called on Vincent Diau, a forty-four-year-old who emigrated from Taiwan in 1981. Although ethnic Chinese account for only 2.7 percent of Los Angeles County's population, one in five home buyers in the county is Chinese, and such top Los Angeles hotels as the Beverly Wilshire and the Los Angeles Biltmore are Chinese-owned. Diau wore expensive glasses and casual clothes; there were two cars in his driveway and new appliances in his house. Everything was in perfect order, almost as though nobody lived there, although Diau and his Chinese American wife, Alice, a school-teacher, share the house with their two children. The children's academic awards were framed near a violin and a piano, and their schedule for music lessons and other after-school activities was posted on a wall beside charts of the English alphabet and Chinese characters. The Diaus own a computer, as do 72 percent of Chinese Americans; 53 percent of Chinese American families are linked to the Internet, in contrast to 11 percent of all families. (Forty percent of Asian American adults hold college degrees—almost twice the percentage of Caucasians.)

Diau told me, "I moved to Cerritos for the same reason that many Chinese and Korean immigrants have—because Whitney High School is one of the best public high schools in the state." Diau has law and political science degrees from universities in Taiwan, and a law degree from Tulane; he is a consultant on Asia with the Hughes Corporation. People complain about the American legal system, he told me, but compared with those in Asia it is straightforward: "If you have discipline and determination and a strategic goal, this country is simple; only the language and alphabet are hard." Because Americans are clear and informal, "you can cut through issues quickly," he said. "In Taiwan everyone wants to control you: there is so much social pressure. Here, among people who are not Chinese, I can truly be myself." Diau told me that he mixes with all kinds of people—Latinos, Middle Easterners, Indians—but unfortunately not with blacks. This was less choice than adher-ence to tradition, he explained. Chinese families favor intermarriage with Caucasians but not with blacks. "I hope that changes," he said.

Why, I asked myself, worry about "the Asian threat"? The best way to contain Asian dynamism is to absorb it—which is exactly what the United States is doing.

As I drove through greater Los Angeles, the term "city-state" was foremost in my mind, not because L.A. is similar to ancient Athens or Sparta but because of the very size and eye-popping variety of this thriving urban confederation, with its hinterland of oil refineries and agricultural valleys. Santa Monica has the ambiance of a beach resort, East Los Angeles is like Mexico, Monterey Park is like Asia, and Cerritos is an Asian Levittown for the 1990s. Except for the prevalence of home-security systems, the winding streets near Dodger Stadium, north of downtown, have almost a rustic, Southern European aspect, with their vine-covered houses and steep hills. Going from one township to another, I often felt as if I had journeyed far and wide. The freeway system makes this compression of distance possible, and climate abets the system's expansion: Because Los Angeles gets little rain or frost, road surfaces are cheap and easy to maintain.

"I'm middle-class," Gregory Rodriguez, a researcher who lives on a steep street near Dodger Stadium, told me when I visited him. "But there are also working-class and poor people a block away, and some wealthy entrepreneurs: Jews, Anglos, Mexicans, Chinese, you name it. It's an Old World neighborhood of immigrants, like neighborhoods in Manhattan." I sought out Rodriguez, a thirty-one-year-old third-generation Mexican American, to learn more about ethnicity in southern California, and particularly about the culture of "Latinos"—a word Rodriguez prefers to "Hispanics," which he calls "cold and generic." " 'Hispanic' is a term people in the East use," he said, "but here no one does." Had I relied merely on my East Coast impressions, the figures Rodriguez presented would have startled me. In the Northeast, "Hispanics" are often Puerto Ricans and Dominicans, who have not assimilated as successfully as Mexicans; yet, nationwide, Mexicans account for 60 percent of all Latinos.

According to the U.S. Census Bureau, Rodriguez told me, 55 percent of Latinos are bilingual in English and Spanish. In greater Los Angeles, four times as many U.S.-born Latinos are in the middle class as live in poverty. A quarter of all middle-class families in southern California are Latinos, and in economic performance U.S.-born Latinos living in greater Los Angeles are not far behind whites and Asians: about half of U.S.-born Latinos here are in the middle class, whereas 58 percent of white or Asian households are. Among black households in the area, 38 percent are in the middle class; the national average is 26 percent. Perhaps the most telling distinction among Latinos, Asians, and blacks is in the percentage that are government employees in an increasingly entrepreneurial economy. Whereas 28 percent of middle-class blacks in greater Los Angeles work for the federal, state, or municipal government, only about 14 percent of middle-class Asians and 10 percent of middle-class Latinos do.

Rodriguez used his own term, "mestizo-ization," for a dual perspective prevalent among Latinos: they maintain a firm belief in some degree of bilingualism while welcoming U.S. citizenship and often intermarrying. David E. Hayes-Bautista, a medical sociologist at the University of California at Los Angeles, told me that the Latino experience suggests that "being American simply means buying a house with a mortgage and getting ahead—there is no agreement anymore on culture, only on economics." Seventy-five years ago, D. H. Lawrence called America a homeland "of the pocket" and not "of the blood."

Immigrant dynamism coupled with Asian as well as Latino mestizo-ization are the central facts of late-twentieth-century Los Angeles. And the reality is richer still, as Indian immigrants buy up Artesia, next to Cerritos, and Iranian immigrants, after buying many properties in Beverly Hills, buy now in nearby Westwood. "South Central is no longer a burnt-out core, and that is partly because of Latino immigrants," Rodriguez said. "Because Latinos came in at the bottom, a pool of home buyers existed for upwardly mobile blacks who needed to sell their properties and escape South Central and Watts for racially mixed, middle-class areas. Leftists talk of blacks being 'displaced,' but that disparages the very blacks who have succeeded. Is it 'displacement' to climb your way out of the ghetto?"

ORANGE COUNTY: AMONG THE WORLD'S BIGGEST ECONOMIES

Orange County, which forms the southern part of greater Los Angeles, is—along with Westchester, Marin, and Dade—among the few counties in America that are household names. Orange County is America's most fully evolved urban pod, in which alliances are based on technology rather than geography and classic definitions of city and suburb no longer apply. Perhaps the county—larger and less dense than the largest cities but smaller than the smallest states—will replace the city as the civic center of the future. Already the western Kansas City suburbs, which I had visited earlier, are called Johnson County, and the prosperous Maryland suburbs of Washington, D.C., are called Montgomery County.

Orange County—"a major airport in search of a city"—stands for what everybody hates about the suburbs, with their crass affluence and neither-nor landscape. It is often described as 782 square miles of dull residential streets, malls, and office parks without a downtown. And it is notorious for the 1994 bankruptcy of its treasury, the result of trying to fund its operations not through high taxes but through risky investments. I was prepared to hate Orange County. I came away respecting it, more intrigued than I had been by many "exotic" and "romantic" cities.

Parts of Orange County are beautiful, and the county works. If it were a state, its economy would be roughly equal to Arizona's; if it were a country, its economy would rank among the top thirty or so in the world. About a third of the firms in the county are involved in international trade, and they run the gamut of high-technology products. Orange County is now what Johnson County and other suburban pods I visited in the Midwest could become: a multiracial world trade center linked to overseas cities by direct flights—say, between Omaha and Beijing and Kansas City and Paris. (Since the late 1980s, the export sectors of many local economies in America have grown dramatically; from 1987 to 1995 by 200 percent in California, 250 percent in Utah, and 375 percent in Idaho.)

The received impression that Orange County's 2.6 million residents are "white bread" is false. Almost a quarter of the county's population is Latino, two and a half times the national average; 11 percent is Asian, nearly three times the national average. Only 2 percent of the population is black—one-sixth the national average.

Another false perception of Orange County is that there is no there there. In fact there are many theres there. The county comprises twenty-eight separate municipalities, many with their own centers. The term "suburb" does not properly describe this advanced, polycentric urban pod. Because these centers do not resemble traditional downtowns, they are overlooked by people whose eyes have yet to adjust to the postindustrial age.

I drove first to Newport Beach, one of Orange County's municipalities, to see Dennis Macheski, a real estate consultant who worked in a well-appointed two-story office complex beside the Pacific. "The myth that people in places like Orange County spend an inordinate amount of time in their cars is wrong," Macheski began. "The average commute in the United States is twenty-two minutes. In southern California it is twenty-five minutes—almost the average. That's because almost everyone in the area works close to home. The jobs are no longer in the city—they're right here, in postsuburbia, or whatever you want to call it. Even in the Inland Empire, whose suburbs are the least developed and attractive, seventy percent of the residents work locally. Nobody in the suburbs needs to drive more than thirty minutes to a great restaurant or a theater." In fact, established post-suburban regions like Orange County and northern New Jersey rank high nationally on availability of cultural venues. "We're no longer a suburb. Affluent New York City bedroom communities average fifteen hundred persons per square mile. Orange County's average density is six thousand. So we're far more urban in many respects than parts of New York."

"Tell me about the future of greater Los Angeles and the United States in terms of real-estate patterns," I said.

"Fifteen years hence we will be bigger. Nothing will stop us. Instead of fifteen million in greater Los Angeles we'll be eighteen million. Two-thirds of the new people will be in outlying areas as the urban region spreads farther. The same will be true for Las Vegas, Phoenix, Portland, Sacramento, cities in Colorado, and elsewhere. Two-thirds will be home-owners, but only one-quarter will be married with children. There will be more and more nontraditional families and singles.

"The number who work at home and telecommute may double, from 2 to 3 percent of homeowners to 6 percent. But so what? It's still just 6 percent. Because media people travel in the same circles as telecommuters, they exaggerate their importance, but in the real estate business we know that most people—no matter what wonders technology brings—want to be reasonably close to the action in urban regions.

"Otherwise the two big immigrations will continue, because the economy requires highly educated Asians to work in high tech, and low-skilled Latinos to be the housekeepers and gardeners, among other jobs, for the high-tech people. These are the people who will largely account for the increased growth of urban regions across America. In greater Los Angeles the black population grows at one percent a year, but the Asian-Latino population grows at three percent. Even in California politicians have proved that they lack the will and the ability to stop immigration. Proposition 187 [an effort to deny benefits to nonci-tizens] was directed against the poor—nobody thought the worse of Asians or middle-class Latinos. The result, of course, was merely to encourage more Latinos to apply for citizen-ship. Corporations will determine immigration; if they need highly skilled workers in defense and software industries, they will recruit them in one form or another from Asia and other places."

As I had been told over and over again by businesspeople and other experts, it is far more cost-efficient to import the rest of the world's talent than to train citizens at home, especially when weak or nonexistent national education standards and insufficient tax revenues have been the ruination of many local schools. For the low-skilled worker, U.S. citizenship confers less advantage than it used to, because those with higher skills will get the well-paying jobs anyway and become citizens in the process.

Macheski's analysis does not contradict Gregory Rodriguez's. The housekeepers and gardeners Macheski referred to are first-generation Mexican American; the skilled Latino middle-class workers Rodriguez documents are usually second- or third-generation.

Before you leave Newport Beach, go see the Fashion Island Mall," Macheski suggested.

"But I've seen malls before," I told him.

"See this one—it's really affluent and evolved. Believe me, it's worth it."

It was. From Macheski's office I drove past two more office campuses and then into a large parking lot. I ascended a wide stairway and entered the mall—an outdoor labyrinth of crowded pedestrian streets punctuated with large clay pots full of bright-red geraniums, and storefronts that mixed neoclassical and baroque styles with red-tiled roofs. There was a fountain shooting pellets of ice, and jewelry carts made of hand-tooled wood painted in rich earthen shades standing in the middle of a sidewalk that was laid with brilliant tiles. The geometric sweep of marble, sea-green wrought iron, and terra-cotta partially obscured by bougainvillea vines made for a brilliant mixture of late-twentieth-century abstractions and nineteenth-century intimacy and rusticity; I was as impressed as I had been when I saw the great squares of medieval Bukhara and Samarkand. I stood in an atrium made of pink and cream stone, veined marble, terra-cotta, what looked like malachite, and chrome alloys. Here postmodernism, the architectural style characterized by eclectic juxtapositions, was fully articulated. Malls in affluent pods of the Midwest may soon look like this.

Of course, the year-round warmth of southern California helps: it allows for the outdoor setting, and for the flowers that soften industrial aspects of the architecture. Still, I thought about what Joel Garreau suggests in *Edge City: Life on the New Frontier* (1991): a beautiful urban setting like Venice once seemed crass, too, to sophisticated people of the age; malls and office parks are only early phases of an architecture that might become equally lovely as it develops. Are the souks of Damascus or Fez truly more beautiful than the Fashion Island Mall? Not to me. But the Damascus and Fez souks do have one feature they share with ancient and medieval marketplaces and not with this one: they bustle with activity and chatter. The shoppers at Fashion Island Mall, unlike the less wealthy crowd at Santa Monica's Third Street Promenade, were quiet. Conversations were so few as to be memorable. I recall a group of men and women in business attire at a café table with open account books and spreadsheets, talking softly about a building plan. Otherwise, smooth elevator music was all I heard.

Alladi Venkatesh, of the Graduate School of Management at the University of California at Irvine, describes the Nordstrom's at nearby South Coast Plaza as "both a shopping complex and a fantasy land," where a shopper can try on a pair of Italian shoes while a live pianist plays Chopin. I saw similar scenes at Fashion Island Mall. The pursuit of style, whether in art, architecture, or the flesh (and physical comfort and high fashion are now much more widely available than in the past), may be the ultimate goal of the good life. But its side effect is social fragmentation: The threatening and unsightly poor are kept out of sight, and, as usual, people choose to live in exclusive residential areas.

Libertarianism—the politics of many Orange County residents—is the ideological companion of such fragmentation, favoring individual choice on such social issues as abortion and marijuana use along with fiscal conservatism and tax cuts. Libertarians say, "Leave me alone to live my life and don't bother me with paying to help less-fortunate citizens." Fashion Island Mall suggested how the urban pods I saw in western St. Louis and western Omaha could one day be as aesthetically agreeable as they were already economically efficient. But I wondered whether the new urban civilization evinced by this mall could also foster traditional patriotism or civic virtue.

Near the airport in Irvine, in another office park, was the *Orange County Business Journal*. When I had phoned for an appointment, the editor, Rick Reiff, offered to take me to lunch. I assumed he preferred to talk over lunch rather than in his office. I was wrong. Reiff took me to lunch to show me what really goes on in Orange County.

Reiff, who won a Pulitzer Prize for local reporting in Akron, Ohio, has run the editorial side of the *Business Journal* since 1990. He wore a blazer and a stylish collarless shirt without a tie. He drove me from his own office park to one just like it, where he led me to a restaurant, Bistango, next to a Japanese bank. Inside, amid sculptures, tinted glass, metal alloys, spotlights, canopies, and a black see-through pyramid stacked with expensive bottles of wine that reached almost to the ceiling, I heard the hum of conversation that had been absent at the Fashion Island Mall. The men and women who crowded the tables wore flashy ties and dazzling jewelry. I saw brown and yellow faces everywhere, and noticed many more cups of coffee and glasses of iced tea than alcoholic drinks. "That's because real business is occurring here," Reiff said, in his warm and rough Chicago accent, as we sat down to eat. "Millions of dollars are being transacted all around you." During the country's extraordinary urban growth of the 1880s, Rudyard Kipling observed that in America "men were babbling about money, town lots, and again money."

"Where's the power?" John Gunther always asked in his travelogue of mid-twentieth-century America, *Inside U.S.A.* In the late 1940s, the answer was often the local party machine. In the late 1990s, power was here, in this restaurant, dispersed among many more people, who were much less accountable. The issue was simply profit, disconnected from political promises or even geography. Orange County was merely a home base for the headquarters of global corporations, which could be moved in an instant—for example, in response to a tax increase.

"What kind of business is being transacted?" I asked.

"Biomedical, pharmaceutical, a little genetic engineering, international investment, precision manufacturing, apparel, computer chips, and all kinds of software multimedia," Reiff told me. "Global trade and workforces are everything for us. Orange County is roughly one percent of the U.S. population, but it has three percent of Fortune 500 companies. Every time there is a conflation of the publishing and multimedia industries, power shifts slightly to California from New York, because the future will favor multimedia over mere books."

Later, back at Reiff's office, I leafed through recent editions of the *Business Journal.* There were stories about this group of Iranians or that group of Taiwanese or Pakistanis or Mexicans from Sonora buying this or that technology company. Some years ago, the Polish journalist Ryzsard Kapuscinski, seeing Vietnamese, Cambodian, Laotian, and Mexican faces in an Orange County computer factory owned by a Pakistani and two Chinese, wrote that the culture of the southern California workforce is "a mix of Hispanic-Catholic family values and Asian-Confucian group loyalty," with hiring done through family networks. One quarter of science degree holders in the United States were born abroad, with Indians and Chinese predominating.

"Mexico has become both our cheap labor force and our export platform," Reiff went on. "Companies that are moving factories to Mexico would have left the U.S. anyway—and gone to Malaysia, for instance. The nation-state cannot keep them here if cheap, competent labor exists abroad. With NAFTA [the North American Free Trade Agreement], at least we can keep much of the work in North America."

I asked about Orange County's credit collapse in 1994, after officials had made bad investments with public money. "A blip on the screen—in historical terms just a rainy day," Reiff said. "Roads are still being paved. No police have been fired. What I'm saying is that the Orange County phenomenon is intact. Imagine the effect on Cleveland, for instance, if it lost two billion dollars in bad investments, the way Orange County did. If in twenty years all this glitter around you fades, historians will look back on the 1980s and 1990s here as a golden age, with the credit crash a minor theme."

Reiff continued, "I'm originally a city kid. I played baseball in the alleys in Chicago. I know what is urban and suburban, and this"—his eyes wandered around the room—"is neither; it's something new."

Reiff told me that the reason there are so many malls is that "with 'income tax' a dirty word, the only way for municipalities to raise revenue is through sales taxes, so they encourage mall building; some of these malls will go bust."

"Will this place fight for its country?" I asked. "Are these people loyal to anything except themselves?"

"Loyalty is a problem," Reiff said. "Only about half the baseball fans in Orange County root for the California Angels [whose stadium is in Anaheim, a county municipality]. I root for the Chicago White Sox. So many people here are from somewhere else, whether the U.S. or the world. People came here to make money and enjoy the good life. In the future patriotism will be more purely and transparently economic. Perhaps patriotism will survive in the form of prestige, if America remains the world economic leader."

After I left Reiff, I drove through Santa Ana, Garden Grove, and Anaheim, ending up in the northeasternmost township of Orange County: Yorba Linda, birthplace of Richard Nixon. The little wooden house that Nixon's father, Francis, built in 1912 with materials from a mail-order catalogue still stands. The President and his wife, Pat, are buried a few steps away. The memorial, which includes a museum and a library, was packed with visitors. The multiracial crowd at the site, like the people I saw on the streets of Yorba Linda, appeared to represent Nixon's "silent majority." Yorba Linda is the original, sepia-toned California—Iowa in the Sunbelt. The Latinos and Asians here looked wholesome and self-assured; they looked American, lacking the worldly flair of their compatriots at Bistango.

From Yorba Linda I headed southwest, back through Anaheim and Garden Grove, into the heavily Vietnamese Orange County municipality of Westminster. Amid miles of one-story tract homes, I pulled into a shingle-and-Sheetrock strip mall named Saigon Plaza to look for a place to eat dinner. I entered a run-down café where men were playing cards and listening to Vietnamese music. The atmosphere was thick with the smoke of unfiltered cigarettes. I felt that I was in Southeast Asia. Then somebody switched off the Vietnamese music and put on the NBA playoffs.

CANADA: THE WILD CARD

Whereas in southern California I focused on how the transformation of the city was changing the face of America, in the Pacific Northwest I focused on the idea of nationhood itself.

Dismissing Canada as irrelevant, boring, or a joke comes easily to Americans, and occasionally to Canadians as well. The Canadian novelist Mordecai Richler says that Canada is "not so much a country as a continental suburb, where Little Leaguers govern ineffectually, desperate for American approval." Canada has a population one ninth that of the United States (twenty-nine million as opposed to 261 million). Canada did not have to struggle for independence from Britain—Britain approved confederation in 1867, forcing disparate provinces to unite as a way to contain the United States after the reconsolidation of the Union. Whereas the United States represented the most daring political experiment since Athenian democracy (one that would succeed beyond imagining), Canada never had a clear-cut historical mission—except, perhaps, providing for its own survival. Polls show that Canada's sense of identity rests heavily on the country's social service institutions, including national health care, and even those are deteriorating.

Yet, to ignore Canada's fate is to miss the point of North American history. Military events in Canada may have set the stage for American independence in the first place. Had the French held on to Canada through the eighteenth century, they might well have constrained the thirteen colonies to retain a protective bond with Britain. The nineteenth-century historian Francis Parkman wrote, "So long as an active and enterprising enemy threatened [the colonists'] borders, they could not break with the mother-country, because they needed her help . . . [thus] there would have been no Revolutionary War; and for a long time, no independence." But, as it happened, the French and Indian War, part of a worldwide struggle among the European powers called the Seven Years' War, ended in 1763 with a British victory over French forces in Canada, which encouraged France's withdrawal from North America, obviating the English-speaking colonies' dependence on Britain.

During the War of 1812, New England actually debated secession and a closer link to British North America, and this threat hastened the rise of American nationalism under President Andrew Jackson. The relationship is still symbiotic—the dissolution of Canada would affect the United States more than any imaginable crisis overseas.

Moreover, Canada, which along with Switzerland is already among the most decentralized countries in the postindustrial world, is split by a blood-and-soil linguistic nationalism that threatens to dismember it. When I asked the president of one of America's most powerful international corporations what was the most important issue the Washington foreign policy elite was ignoring, he responded, "The eventual breakup of the Canadian federation and its effect" on our own nationhood.

Although Canada is the largest country in the Western Hemisphere, stretching to the polar ice cap, the habitable part of it looks like Chile laid on its side. Almost all Canadians live within a hundred miles of the U.S. border, so it is reasonable to imagine that they might merge politically with the rest of North America's temperate-zone population. In Canada's early days, before bridges and motorized boats, the Saint Lawrence River and the Great Lakes formed enough of a natural boundary for an Atlantic-oriented nation to take root. Even west of the Great Lakes, along the arbitrary border formed by the Forty-ninth Parallel, the fact that the fur trade was so much more important to the people north of that line than to those south of it made for some semblance of an organic division. But with expressways and ferries now crossing the waters, and the inexorable merging of the two countries' economies (four-fifths of Canada's export trade and two-thirds of its import trade are with the United States), Canada is increasingly like the northern United States.

However, as the frigid tundra keeps Canada's population from spreading northward, America's loud materialism, unruly style, and social problems keep Canadians from straying south. That hundred-mile-wide belt of population from the Atlantic to the Pacific has evolved as a subtly distinctive community, one that many citizens want to preserve. English and French Canadians might not mind separating from each other, but immigrants from throughout the world may demand Canada's continued existence. For them, Canada provides unlimited freedom and economic opportunity while offering protection from the ruthless laissez-faire capitalism of the United States.

The psychological importance for Canadians of their country's style and separate evolution should not be underestimated. Canadian resentment of the United States is clear in the way that Canadians smugly disapprove of those who attempt great endeavors. Indeed, says the Canadian writer Margaret Atwood, "Canadian rebellions have never become revolutions precisely because they have never received popular support. 'Prophets' here don't get very far against the civil service." Canada never had a Wild West, because Canadians love law and order—the Mounties are a national symbol. Canada's society prefers collective heroes, like the builders of the transcontinental railroad, over individual ones.

Not a stimulating place, perhaps, but one different enough that parts of English Canada are not eager to merge with parts of the United States; they would do so only if the Canadian federation fractured first. Such a dissolution may be as likely to begin in Canada's westernmost province, British Columbia, as in Francophone Quebec.

British Columbia and its urban dynamo, Vancouver, which is linked more closely to the Pacific Rim than to most of the rest of Canada, are animating North American regionalism. Strengthened by NAFTA, regionalism may yet undo the current divisions of sovereignty, which have their origins in the 1763 Treaty of Paris. Margaret Ormsby, a local historian, writes that "British Columbia was in, but not of, Canada." Canada did not grow westward in the same organic manner as the United States. British Columbia joined the

Canadian federation only in 1871, four years after the British forced the other provinces to unite. Out here, Ormsby writes, the Canadian Union was based not on "sentiment" but on "material advantage." The economic benefits of the transcontinental Canadian Pacific Railway in effect bribed British Columbia to join Canada. Even so, the British part of Columbia, which in 1846 split from the part that became the state of Washington, retained strong cultural and economic links to a region whose center was San Francisco. Today British Columbia's economy is separate, and the highway to Seattle and Portland and the air routes across the Pacific matter more than links to the rest of Canada. The province exports an amazing 40 percent of its goods to the Pacific Rim, and 50 percent to the United States; 80 percent of exports from Canada as a whole go to the United States. It is the only Canadian province that would surely do better, not worse, were the country to disintegrate. "Canada ends at the Rockies" is an expression I heard repeatedly.

This is not to say that British Columbia identifies with the United States. When I crossed the border at Osoyoos, the differences between the two countries were what I first noticed. Not only were the money, the measurement units, the shapes of the signs, the construction materials, and the flag (with the soft imagery of the maple leaf replacing the overtly political stars and bars) different in Canada but so were the accents, which were sharper and vaguely British. "Schedule," for instance, was pronounced without the c. But compared with the Third World–First World division I saw on the Mexican border, these differences were trivial.

I set out for Vancouver, a leisurely day's journey. Halfway there I reached Manning Provincial Park—across the border from North Cascades National Park. Manning Park marks the beginning of the Cascade Range, a north-south line of powder-white volcanoes and glaciers, tinted blue and garlanded by cold rain forests, which more than any other geographical feature—to say nothing of any state or national border—defines the Pacific Northwest. It is a magical frontier, breathtaking even when seen from the air. To fly from the eastern United States to Portland, Oregon, and see the "Ring of Fire"—the glacier-mantled peaks of Mount Baker, Mount Rainier, Mount Hood, and Mount St. Helens soaring over brooding, cathedral-dark forests—is to arrive in a distinct place, or almost nation.

I met Pacific mists, sparkling snow, moist and glistening spruce and fir forests, tumbling streams, and silvery lakes, beside one of which I watched an Indian immigrant family fishing for rainbow trout. The parents spoke in the accents of the subcontinent, the children in the hard-edged English of Pacific Canada. Harlequin ducks and gray-and-white belted kingfishers flipped off the water.

Farther west, close to Vancouver, the Fraser River was choked with massive logs, chained together and about to be dispatched, perhaps to the Far East. Vancouver appeared rather suddenly—a lesson in how compact the cities of the Pacific Northwest are compared with others on the continent. Here, even for urbanites, nature is close by.

Vancouver and "Cascadia"

It was late afternoon when I arrived in Vancouver and checked into a bed-and-breakfast in a residential neighborhood with flame-red hawthorn trees. Traffic islands at each crossing slowed cars. The cost of parking downtown was exorbitant, so I rode the bus. As in Portland and elsewhere in the Pacific Northwest, the nearby glaciers and volcanoes, visible from many an urban street, have led to a preoccupation with conservation, which has in turn generated penalties for automobile use.

The bus heading downtown was clamorous with conversation and filled with well-dressed people—so different from buses in many parts of the United States, whose riders are mostly silent and poor. (Portland buses, I would discover, are like Vancouver's.) Like the bus, the shiny stone benches on rose-bedecked Robson Street were filled not with the poor and homeless but with well-dressed people, talking. The only cell phone I saw belonged to a man with a New York accent who was telling someone that he would "be home in three days." There were many benches, and also a profusion of cafés, buzzing and crowded, set against buildings made of glass, marble, unusual metals, and polymers. As at the Fashion Island Mall, the trees and flowers that were planted beside new buildings in the 1970s and 1980s, and constant architectural refinements, have made for fine urban landscapes. But unlike the Fashion Island Mall, Vancouver had a true urban life. Even in newspaper-and-candy stores knots of people were talking by the counters.

Many of the faces were Asian. A third of greater Vancouver's 1.81 million people are Asian, with Chinese alone making up nearly 20 percent of the population. Asian immigrants account for much of the population growth of 2.5 percent a year. One local joke had it that "the Japanese want to buy Vancouver, but the Chinese won't sell it." I saw many signs in Punjabi, Hindi, Farsi, Arabic, and Khmer—but almost none in French, an official Canadian language. In the schools here, Mandarin is spoken more commonly than French. Vancouver, with its glitzy, visually lively high-rise condominiums, is becoming an Asianized city on the Pacific Rim of North America, dedicated to global materialism; a real East-West hybrid culture is emerging here.

The next morning I visited Warren Gill, an urban geographer and the executive director of the Harbour Centre campus of Simon Fraser University, an institution founded in 1965 and named for a nineteenth-century Vermont-born explorer and Northwest fur trader. The campus consisted of a single building with green and blue glass interiors. Finished in 1989, the building conjured for me "the future"—that is, it made me aware of transition and change. As the Ringstrasse in turn-of-the-century Vienna illustrates, social and economic change, often revealed through architecture, precedes political change. What the architecture here revealed was the abstract and urban character of our collective future, and the emergence of the city-state.

"There, you see it all—isn't it great?" Gill said. He waved his hand toward his office window, indicating the panorama of the Burrard Inlet, a belt of blue water crowded with seaplanes and set against the snow-capped peaks of the Coast Range, with Vancouver's bustling harbor, heliport, and nexus of railroad tracks in the foreground. "With a dynamic and highly educated population and strategic transport links," Gill said, "this is all you need to be sovereign in the phase of history we are entering. Cities and their environs provide garbage collection, schools, and even your neighborhood—but they get the least of your taxes. The bulk of your tax money still goes to the state or province and the federal government, and what do they do for you? Isn't it antiquated? But that will change. In the coming decades your tax money will increasingly go to the place you really care about." Gill's tone was enthusiastic and consciously provocative. "Though I guess we should all pay taxes to that Information Age military you are creating in Washington, D.C. They'll in effect sell us the protection we will need against terrorists and other bad people. You see, we don't need you [he meant America], and we certainly don't need Canada. What we need is your military!"

I didn't try to interrupt.

"The miracle is that Canada has lasted as long as it has. It makes no sense. Oh, yes, I'm fond of Canada. Canada is something you're fond of, like a drunken old uncle. And I'm proud to be a Canadian. We all are, in the sense that Canada is more aesthetically pleasing than the United States. It's cleaner and less unruly. But the nation-state is gone in Vancouver."

Gill called Vancouver "a beautiful setting in search of a city." He said, "Did you know that after L.A., Vancouver has one of the biggest entertainment industries in North America—seven hundred million dollars a year in revenue. Hollywood makes *The X-Files* here. The Canadian dollar is cheap, and we're in the same time zone as Los Angeles, so Hollywood finds us useful, especially since Vancouver looks like anywhere: It's a generic, modern-postmodern global place. But it's still not a real city in the sense of true creativity and economic dynamism—yet. It's not L.A. or New York."

Vancouver, as Gill and others told me, began as a real estate venture in the 1880s once the Canadian Pacific Railway was in place, and it is still very much a boom-and-bust town, floating now on a real estate bubble created by the Hong Kong Chinese, who in the 1980s and 1990s bought $2 billion worth of local real estate. In addition to real estate and the money that immigration brings—on average, each Asian immigrant will, over a lifetime, pay $30,000 more in taxes than he or she will use in the form of social services—there are the Hollywood-run movie industry, a cruise ship industry, and North America's closest air and sea links to Asia. Vancouver is one of the largest bulk-shipping ports on the continent, shipping out coal, sulfur, potash, natural gas, wheat, and timber products. But this economy, powered by real estate and natural resources, lacks the self-sustaining entrepreneurial and creative spirit of Seattle or Portland, San Francisco or Los Angeles. There are relatively few software and multimedia companies here, for instance. Most are scared away by the high taxes necessary to support the social-welfare system.

The frontier, though, has always produced more commerce and trade than books and art. "The distinctive element of the West Coast, from Alaska to Baja, is newness," Gill told me. "Many of these places have been built not to last. There are streets in my neighborhood that have been three different things in my lifetime. At the moment the element of newness has to do with race. Interracialness is walking down the street, arm in arm. Without the Asians we'd be a narrow-minded English town. In Portland they look to Vancouver to see the outer, Pacific world—not to California or even to Seattle." Asians "are in the process of re-WASPing us," Gill explained. "Through their driven work ethic they are allowing us to rediscover our Calvinistic WASP roots. In the twenty-first century hundreds of millions of Chinese and other Asians will become middle-class, tying themselves closer to North America. That will change Vancouver and the Pacific Northwest more than any development in North America itself."

Gordon Price, a member of the Vancouver City Council, picked up on that idea when we met in his apartment, in Vancouver's West End. "The Asian-British—that is to say, Asian-WASP—cultural mix," he told me, "is the most potent in the history of capitalism," notwithstanding the current Asian economic turmoil that has followed decades of economic growth. "Hong Kong and Singapore have represented the combination of British engineering, accounting, honest bureaucracy, and meritocratic government with Asian economic aggression. And it will work its magic here." Here we may be seeing something else, too: the erotization of race. As one Vancouverite told me, a walk down the street to see who's holding hands will show that whites find Asians, particularly Asian women, highly desirable.

Price took me to the city library, a multistory maze of concrete and glass designed by the world-renowned Israeli-Canadian architect Moshe Safdie. From nearby designer shops and espresso cafés one can look into the library and see people studying. Many of them are Asian. "Vancouver is attracting the young of the world's most dynamic middlemen minorities," Price told me. "If this happens across North America, the continent will rule the world's economy. Look at these Asian kids—many of them are sent here to study by their families. For them, Vancouver must be like Paris in the twenties—an earlier, modern capitalist culture, compared with the overnight glitz of the rest of the Pacific Rim."

What struck me was the urbanity, the roar of many conversations, and the crowded cafés and walkways. Safdie's glass-wall design, which encourages people to look at one another, contributes to this, but the library seems to celebrate what is apparent everywhere in the city. Vancouver is a rebuke to Orange County, downtown St. Louis, and most other places in the United States, where the automobile rules and often the only people on sidewalk benches are homeless. The sea and the mountains and the international border prevent sprawl, and the Canadian social welfare system prevents widespread poverty. The other part of the explanation for Vancouver's urbanity is a unified elite of investors and urban planners.

Paraphrasing Jane Jacobs, the classic writer on urbanism, Price told me, "People have confused overcrowding with high density. High density is actually desirable, because it means lively, safe, convenient, and interesting places in which to live." From 1956 to 1972 Price's West End neighborhood, for example, which had been overcrowded, transformed itself into a high-density area. Its population increased by about half, and the number of apartments quintupled: spacious one-bedroom apartments replaced teeming tenements. The West End now has the liveliness and sophisticated feel of Manhattan's Upper West Side. The ostensible reason for the neighborhood's success is that big businessmen took risks and built apartment blocks, while small tradesmen opened shops. Hong Kong Chinese culture, comfortable with high density, helped, too. But business and culture operated within a framework of deliberate planning choices. In the United States in 1956, the same year that the West End was rezoned for taller apartment buildings, President Eisenhower signed the Federal-Aid Highway Act, which created the interstates. Consultants from Los Angeles advised Vancouver to build a freeway-and-tunnel system through the city.

Vancouver citizens rejected that advice. The nineteenth-century grid pattern of narrow streets laid down by British engineers remained intact, and parks and benches, a profusion of cafés, and an explosion of tall residential buildings all followed.

"The automobile is the perfect metaphor for pure democracy," Warren Gill told me, "and pure individual freedom just does not work in an urban setting. The more urban the environment, the more controls you will need to make it work. Imagine how much more vibrant and crime-free Washington, D.C., would be with more planning but without the Beltway. Imagine how if Washington had prohibited a beltway, it would have had to build a whole new layer of public transport within the city, keeping many more people on the streets at all hours."

Vancouver, of course, is not perfect. More and more affluence on display means more iron bars, break-ins, and private security. "You're in a gated community right now, though it doesn't look like one," Price told me, referring to the electronic entry system of his West End apartment block. "Much of North America, metaphorically speaking, is becoming a privatized, gated community where the only urban reality that many well-off kids see is through the sensationalism of local TV news."

Still, Vancouver has something special—a cohesiveness evinced by the never-empty streets and the interracial couples. People would fight for this, I thought. No one would fight for Orange County. Put another way, an America of Orange Counties might for a time be a thriving continental archipelago of rising real estate values, but without the spirit of patriotism that grows out of communal affection.

Alan F. J. Artibise is the founder of the Cascadia Planning Group, an organization that assumes, without proclaiming it, the eventual breakup of Canada. Artibise, who is from Canada's heartland province of Manitoba, is a former president of the Association for Canadian Studies and a planning professor at the University of British Columbia. He has served on numerous planning commissions. His short gray hair is receding, and his voice is soft. His expensively furnished office overlooks the harbor. There is nothing radical or even vaguely counterestablishment about him.

For years, "Cascadia," formerly a geographic term for the Cascade Mountain region stretching from central Oregon to British Columbia, has been a trendy political concept in the Pacific Northwest. A 1975 novel, *Ecotopia,* by Ernest Callenbach, envisioned an independent nation in the Pacific Northwest; it has sold 650,000 copies. Cascadia is united by its wet, rather drowsy climate, which may account in part for the profusion of coffee bars and bookstores, and its unique ecology—a temperate rain forest boasting some of the world's largest firs, cedars, spruces, and hemlocks. Temperate rain forests are found only in slivers of coastal terrain in Japan, Chile, Scandinavia, New Zealand, and a few other places. In 1989, sixty legislators from both sides of the border formed the Pacific Northwest Economic Region; business leaders from both sides formed a group called Pacific Corridor Enterprise. More organizations, including Artibise's, followed.

What has emerged is nothing less than a strategic alliance of the business elite from Portland to Vancouver along "Portcouver," an urban corridor linked by the "I-5 Main Street" (Interstate 5 and Highway 99) and eventually to be connected by high-speed rail. (Passenger trains between Eugene, Oregon, and Vancouver already operate at 90 percent of capacity.) Cascadia would constitute a giant high-tech trading bloc, with major bulk-shipping ports in Portland and Vancouver and a container-shipping port in the Seattle-Tacoma area. Artibise said, "Cascadia is more talked about in Oregon and Washington than it is here. Because of the fragility of the Canadian federation, people are more sensitive on this side of the border—they know how possible Cascadia really is. If Quebec goes, all it would take is one skilled politician to take us out of the federation. It could happen very quickly. Though they rarely admit it, many British Columbians would probably be relieved if Quebec seceded." An unnerving one in three Canadians favors the use of force to seize Quebec's English and Native areas should the province leave. "All my students have been to Seattle and Portland, but never to Toronto," Artibise told me. "However, more sovereignty for British Columbia is not the answer. The province does even less for Vancouver than Ottawa does."

PORTLAND: ORANGE COUNTY NORTH?

Portland has perhaps the most architecturally pleasing and meticulously planned downtown of any major city in the United States. The city has been lionized by liberal national magazines, while its Metro 2040 Plan—designed to extend a vital city center and prevent sprawl—has been attacked by conservative free-marketeers. In three visits to Portland, I realized that although the view of liberal urban planners is the wiser one here, the conservative vision of unlimited growth is likely to triumph almost everywhere else on the continent. Beyond mere good design, culture and geography have made the cities of the Pacific Northwest more exceptional than local planners admit.

With its neat trolley lanes, geometric parks, rustic flowerpots beside polymer-and-glass buildings, crowded sidewalk benches, and cafés with modish awnings that hang from sandblasted stone and marble façades, Portland exudes a stagy perfection. "View corridors" regulated by municipal ordinances keep new construction from blocking the vistas from downtown of the Cascades and, in particular, Mount Hood. People speak in clipped accents similar to those in British Columbia. I even saw them wait in single file to cross the street at red lights. Eighty-nine percent of the population in the metro area is white. The percentage of minorities is less than half the national average, although the percentage of Asians is more than 1.5 times the national average. Portland—like Minneapolis, to which it is often compared—has the political and cultural atmosphere of a Scandinavian country, where almost everyone shares a background and values, and trusts the centralizing and controlling force of local government to preserve these things.

Not only was Portland, with its Florentine and Gothic façades, built before the car, unlike most of Los Angeles, but it was built even before the arrival of the transcontinental railroad. Abutting the city on three sides, the natural environment of mountains and rivers is ever-present in Portland and essential to its economy. Maintaining this pristine landscape is politically acceptable. Carl Abbott, an urban affairs expert, described the city's liberal environmental politics as "status quo conservatism," because it seeks to preserve the past rather than create a future.

Ethan Seltzer, the director of the Institute of Portland Metropolitan Studies, told me, "The whole point of our development plan is not to screw up our pastoral landscape, which is central to local history and culture. We seek a mythic, Native adaptation to place. The Natives burned the fields in the Willamette Valley once a year to keep the forest from encroaching; we must do something analogous to keep the suburbs from encroaching any more on the natural environment. And the only way to preserve the Cascade landscape while making economic use of it is to shift the economy further from agriculture and logging to high tech."

The Cascade landscape keeps Portland's new high-tech economy competitive, by providing cheap Columbia River water power for washing silicon, and the natural beauty attracts people with university degrees. High-tech products have already surpassed timber as Oregon's chief export. Twenty percent of Portland's economy is based on foreign trade, and that figure, along with high-tech production and the population of the metropolitan area, is expected to rise dramatically. By 2010, the four-county region that includes Portland and a portion of Washington just over the Columbia River will have some 1.9 million inhabitants, whereas last year [1997] it had 1.6 million.

The policy mechanism by which this rapid population growth can be accommodated is the "urban growth boundary," which delineates a belt around the metropolitan area and ultimately forces developers inside it to build higher-density neighborhoods, as in Vancouver's West End. Such a plan requires a regional government. "To preserve the environment," Seltzer told me, "we are making a transition away from city hall toward the urban region. In any case, very few urbanites in North America live their lives in one jurisdiction anymore. They live in one municipality and work in another; it's especially true with two-career couples."

This is another reason why, although the urban federation may be the future, traditional cities are fading. Manhattan, the twentieth century's premier urban location, has in recent years generated relatively few new businesses despite an impressive drop in crime and a popular Republican mayor, Rudolph Giuliani. Corporations appear to prefer posturban pods such as western Omaha. It is unclear whether Manhattan has made an authentic comeback as a twenty-first-century global meeting place or, in the words of one historian, is experiencing a beautiful Venetian sunset.

But the fading of the traditional city is not necessarily a social disaster, because all it may mean eventually is that instead of one downtown there will be many within a sprawling urban region, each performing the same socially unifying functions as the old downtowns.

Even the Orange County real estate expert Dennis Macheski said that despite our increasing ability to work at home by means of the computer, most people will want social venues close by. It is our very humanity—our need for others—that will help us through these troubling transitions. Denver, for instance, which I recently visited, now has three thriving downtowns—Cherry Creek, "LoDo," and downtown Denver—as it transforms itself into an urban confederation.

Seltzer and others told me that even if Metro 2040 succeeds—even if suburban sprawl in the Willamette Valley, to the south, is contained, and well-educated migrants move into high-density townhouses and "bungarows"—Portland will change dramatically in other ways. "The early settlers here recreated the New England village," Seltzer explained. "Since then we've been good at space arrangement and streetscapes. Our next challenge is to get along with each other." The white population is aging, and twenty years hence Portland will be like greater L.A. in terms of ethnicity.

The Pacific Northwest is, statistically, one of the last Caucasian bastions in the United States. Even the city of Seattle, which in 1993 elected a black mayor, Norm Rice, for a second term, has a minority population of only 15 percent—well below the national average of 25 percent. Washington and Oregon have among the lowest percentages of African-Americans in the country (3.1 percent and 1.6 percent of the population, respectively). Racism has a long history in Oregon. The state banned black immigration in 1849, to avoid the slavery question, and real estate agents redlined the northeastern part of Portland after World War II, to keep blacks away from well-off whites. Given the emphasis on high tech, what is likely to happen—and what people here admit only reluctantly—is that few blacks will migrate to the Pacific Northwest but many Asians will. In effect, economic factors will enforce racial segregation, nudging Seattle and Portland in Vancouver's direction as they trade more with the Pacific Rim.

But, although Portland will become more Asian, its urban layout will come to more closely resemble that of Orange County, as Portland grows because of the semiconductor boom, and decentralized workplaces and production centers increase the role of the car. Moreover, a recent statewide tax revolt may indicate what Metro 2040 can and cannot spend to ensure aesthetic zoning. The revolt also widened the chasm between a generally conservative state and a liberal urban area federation in the making. Similarly, the distance between Portland and Washington, D.C., continues to grow, as is made clear by vocal criticism of Department of Housing and Urban Development regulations—"designed for East Coast cities," in the words of a local expert, and "forced on us."

As I contemplated the future of Cascadia, I recalled once more that during the War of 1812, New England debated seceding from the United States. Future secessions of regions and posturban pods will be more likely to succeed, because they won't have to be acknowledged. Our subtle new regionalism will be largely invisible. Meanwhile, the two forms of urban confederation under this refined continental imperialism—the Portland form and the Orange County form—will compete for ascendancy. Hybrid forms will emerge, perhaps even within Portland and Orange County themselves, but the Orange County model will dominate.

As a number of experts told me, we cannot ultimately control these social and economic forces. The whole New World—all of the United States, certainly—has been one big subdivision marketed for most of our history to Europeans. American cities have been built and humanized not by idealists but by tacky carpetbaggers and get-rich-quick guys. The twist has been that in some places, like Portland, this greed has had to conform to existing cultural expectations. In many other places in America the communal culture is too thin for that.

Comparing the United States to Rome, Henry Adams wrote in 1906, "The climax of empire could be seen approaching, year after year, as though Sulla were a President or McKinley a Consul. Nothing annoyed Americans more than to be told this simple and obvious—in no way unpleasant—truth." Perhaps Adams was wrong only in his timing; the climax may come sometime in the early twenty-first century, a minor detail in the long span of history. Adams's belief that the end of American empire was "in no way unpleasant" dovetails with the gist of what people told me in my travels, from Rick Reiff, the gregarious journalistic booster of Orange County, to Ethan Seltzer, who wants to preserve the New England qualities of Portland. They all believe that the federal power structure is waning. The massive ministry buildings of Washington, D.C., with their oxen armies of bureaucrats, are the products of the Industrial Age, when American society reached a level of sheer size and complexity that demanded such institutions. This leaden federal colossus must somehow slowly evolve into a new, light-frame structure of mere imperial oversight—for the sake of defense, conservation, and the rationing of water and other natural resources. The evolution may allow for a political silver age, although not another golden one.

3

The New Face of America

Blended Races Making a True Melting Pot

MARIA PUENTE AND MARTIN KASINDORF

In the future, lots of us will be like Mariah Carey. Or Soledad O'Brien. Or Tiger Woods.

There's no guarantee we'll look that good, of course, or sing that well, let alone be able to drive a golf ball 350 yards. But in the next century more Americans are going to be black, white, and Hispanic, like the singer Carey and the TV news anchor O'Brien. Or black, white, American Indian, and Asian, like the golfer Tiger Woods.

As a new millennium looms, America is set to become more a nation of blended races and ethnic groups than it has ever been. Or at least that's the picture that emerges from the population projections made for the next century by the U.S. Census Bureau, by officials in individual states and by demographers like Barry Edmonston of Portland State University in Oregon and Jeff Passel of the Urban Institute, a Washington, D.C., think tank.

By 2050, Passel and Edmonston's calculations suggest, the percentage of the U.S. population that claims mixed ancestry—meaning some combination of black, white, Hispanic, and Asian—will likely triple, to 21 percent.

Within some groups, the rates will be even higher. Among Asian Americans, the percentage able to claim some other ancestry in addition to Asian is expected to reach 36 percent; for Native Americans 89 percent; for whites 21 percent; for blacks 14 percent; and for Hispanics 45 percent.

This means that millions more Americans will be of mixed racial and ethnic background. "So, them are us and us is them," quips Harry Pachon, president of the West Coast branch of the Tomas Rivera Policy Institute, a think tank in Claremont, California.

Furthermore, the Census Bureau says the Hispanic population is going to be huge— about 17 percent of the total population by 2025, about 25 percent of the total population by 2050—fueled both by higher fertility rates among Hispanics and continuing immigration from Latin America. Over the last two decades, immigrants from Latin America have made up about 40 percent of the total 19.4 million legal immigrants. Only three major metropolitan areas have dominant or substantial Hispanic populations today—Miami, San Antonio, and Los Angeles. But, in the next century, the list will include many more, including some in surprising places—such as Jersey City, New Jersey; Yakima, Washington; and Orange County, California.

The growing number of Hispanics will help fuel the already soaring intermarriage rate. Demographers say up to 30 percent of Hispanics and Asians marry outside their race or ethnic group now. Passel says his calculations suggest that up to 57 percent of third-generation Hispanics—the grandchildren of immigrants—marry a non-Hispanic.

"Growing up on Long Island, there was never any question that we were different," says O'Brien, thirty-two, a rising NBC correspondent and MSNBC anchor. Her mother is Cuban and black, and her father is Australian and Irish. "When I get on the subway in New York today, most of the people look like me—they're a mix of some kind."

In the future, more American communities are going to look like the New York City subways.

"The United States is once again on the eve of large ethnic transformations," says Passel. "This current phase (of change) has already involved social and political disturbances, and raises new questions about who are 'Americans.'"

Such transformations are not new, says Raul Yzaguirre, president of the National Council of La Raza, a Hispanic advocacy and civil rights organization. "It doesn't mean a fundamental change in America," he says. "It's a natural part of our evolution as a nation."

LOOKING LIKE FLORIDA

The Census Bureau's computers are on the second floor of Federal Office Building No. 3 in Suitland, Maryland. The machines collect and sift data, analyze decades of trends in births, deaths, and immigration, and then project those trends into the future. Every couple of years they spit out snapshots, somewhat fuzzy, of what the United States will look like demographically in ten, twenty, or even fifty years.

From these, demographers can get an idea of population growth, racial and ethnic breakdown, the spread of age groups, even the places where most people will live.

Predicting demographic change is notoriously tricky—many have been wrong before. "It's hard to get historical distance while you're in the middle of demographic change," says Jorge del Pinal, a Census Bureau demographer.

Next year's [2000] census is expected to provide loads of data on the nation's current demographic picture, including the number of Americans who consider themselves of mixed ancestry.

On the 2000 census form, Americans for the first time will be able to pick more than one race and ethnic category to describe themselves. This is the result of pressure from parents of biracial children who don't want their kids to have to choose one part of their ancestry over another. Current figures show that about 7 percent of the population could claim multiple ancestry.

In any case, the results the Census Bureau computers are spitting out these days may surprise, delight, or even alarm many Americans. Here are some of the projections:

- The total population of the country is projected to grow to 335 million by 2025, a 23 percent increase over the 1999 population. The population will be less Caucasian: 62 percent, compared to 72 percent in 1999. The growth rate of the white population will be only 6 percent, compared with much higher rates for Asians, Hispanics, and blacks.
- The largest minority group by 2005 will be people of Hispanic origin, who can be of any race. By 2025, there will be nearly sixty million Hispanics, about 17 percent of the total population, compared to thirty million, or 11 percent, in 1999.
- The black population will grow about 31 percent, but it will remain stable as a percentage of the population: 13 percent in 2025 compared with 12 percent in 1999.
- The fastest growth rate will be among people of Asian and Pacific Island descent—102 percent, from about ten million people in 1999 to nearly twenty-one million in 2025. But they will remain a relatively small group as a percentage of the total population, at about 6 percent.

- Native Americans—American Indians, Eskimos, Aleuts—will be the group that changes the least as a percentage of the population: They will be 0.8 percent in 2025, compared to 0.7 percent in 1999.
- The age distribution of the population will shift dramatically by 2025. More people will be very young (21 percent increase in the number of people fourteen or younger). Fewer people will be middle-aged (4 percent drop in the number of people age thirty-five to forty-nine). And more people will be very old (14 percent increase in the number of people over eighty and a 315 percent increase in the number of people one hundred or more).

"By 2020, the rest of the nation will look like Florida does now," says Peter Morrison, consultant demographer for California's Rand Corp.

- Age differences are even more marked when comparing different groups. The median age of the white population in 2025 is projected to be 42.7 years; by contrast, the median age for the Hispanic population is projected to be 29.4. Because there will be more Hispanics in 2025, their relative youth will act as a counterweight to the aging of the overall population.
- The shift of population away from the Northeast and Midwest toward the South and the West will accelerate. In 1995, 57 percent of the population lived in the South and West; by 2025, 62 percent of Americans will live in those regions.
- These population shifts will be particularly obvious in individual states. States such as New York, Pennsylvania, Ohio, Michigan, and Iowa are projected to grow less than 10 percent each by 2025. States such as Arizona, New Mexico, Utah, Nevada, Texas, Idaho, and Florida are projected to grow 45 percent or more each. California is projected to grow 56 percent, the largest jump, to 49.2 million people. West Virginia will grow only 1 percent.

Florida will become No. 3 in population after California and Texas, pushing New York to fourth place. Georgia will have more people than New Jersey—almost ten million—and North Carolina will be close behind.

Meanwhile, Americans can catch a glimpse of what the demographic future might be like by studying California, where change is already obvious. For instance, the shrinking of the white population is already noticeable in California, where sometime next year whites will cease to be the majority, slipping under 50 percent to become merely a plurality, says state demographer Linda Gage.

This kind of change can be tracked in unusual ways. For example, according to the Internet research firm Acxiom DataQuick, the top four surnames among 1997 Los Angeles County homebuyers were Garcia, Hernandez, Martinez, and Gonzales.

In fact, Hispanics will surpass non-Hispanic whites to become the single largest ethnic group in California by 2030. By 2040, Latinos, as they are usually called in California, will be nearly a majority in that state, totaling 28 million out of a state population of 58.7 million.

The city of Los Angeles, population 3.5 million now, is currently more than 50 percent Latino. In fact, after the 2000 census, "I would be surprised if it's not over 60 percent," says Vivian Dosh of the Southern California Association of Governments.

Meanwhile, the black population of Los Angeles County is expected to decline in numbers. Even now, says Joe Hicks, executive director of the Los Angeles City Human Relations Commission, many blacks are moving out of the city into distant Moreno Valley or Palmdale, or heading back to the Deep South.

Even in Orange County, a traditional fortress of white conservatives, Hispanics will become a plurality by 2030 and a near majority by 2040, according to state projections. In San Diego County, Hispanics will pass whites by 2040 to take the plurality.

In northern California, where the Asian population is heavily concentrated, more change is well under way. In Silicon Valley's Santa Clara County, where Asians now outnumber Latinos as the biggest minority, both these groups will climb fast.

By 2020, whites will be outnumbered by both Asian-Pacific Islanders and Hispanics, with nobody having a majority at least through 2040.

RACE, ETHNIC MIXING

But the most intriguing demographic trend may be the accelerating rates of race and ethnic mixing. It's a trend that varies from group to group. For example, blacks are the least likely to marry outside their race, while American Indians are the most likely to: about 60 percent, by various estimates.

"The black-white line is the most difficult to cross," says Passel. "About 10 percent of blacks are married to non-blacks, but that's up a huge amount in the last thirty years, from 1 percent or 2 percent."

What effect will blended Americans have on the social, cultural, and political landscape? Suppose Hispanic and Asian immigrants and their children assimilate in the same manner as Italian, Polish, or Irish immigrants in the past. Will most of the descendants of Hispanic immigrants lose Spanish just as, say, Italian immigrants lost Italian?

According to several studies, that is already happening. Will people identify as "Hispanic" or "Asian" if they are only part Hispanic or Asian and speak only English? What will it mean to be "Hispanic" or "Asian" in a world where significant portions of the population can claim the label?

No one can answer these questions with any certainty. But all this mixing suggests that the traditional definition of "assimilation into the American mainstream"—meaning to lose one's ethnic and racial identity in the process of becoming more Anglo—may lose its meaning.

"Assimilation has always been more of a confluence of different factors, and it's going to be more so in the future," says the Census Bureau's del Pinal. "Just look at the influence of Hispanic immigrants on popular culture now: Nachos have become one of the most popular food snacks. People drink lime with their beer. Salsa is everywhere. The future is going to be a big mixing of cultural influences like that."

THE IRISH EXAMPLE

There are always lessons from the past to remember, too: Once upon a time in America, Irish immigrants were considered a separate, nonwhite "race." Most Americans believed the Irish could never be assimilated, would forever remain alien, poor, uneducated, and criminal. Signs saying, "No Irish Need Apply" were common. Few Americans regarded marriage to an Irish immigrant with anything but horror.

Today, the Irish are considered indisputably white, solidly middle-class, educated, and upstanding, and so assimilated that no one thinks twice about it.

In fact, so many people claimed to be Irish in the 1980 census that demographers concluded the number could not be accounted for by immigration and fertility. "Most of the growth of the Irish Americans must have resulted from intermarriage and the children of intermarriage choosing to claim Irish ancestry," says the Urban Institute's Passel.

In other words, now everybody's Irish because it doesn't matter anymore.

Section 2

Political and Economic Diversity in the Global System

Section Two discusses the parallel processes of demographic changes, political mobilization, and economic increases in Third World nations as they gain greater economic and political influence. Large and influential countries such as China, Brazil, and India not only send many immigrants abroad but also exercise their own growing economic, political, and military clout in new ways. They seek greater influence in international bodies such as the Security Council of the United Nations, the World Bank, and the WTO. And as the 2001 terrorist attacks on the United States remind us, even the behavior of poor countries can have consequences for Americans, and we ignore them at our peril. The selections in this section address these shifting dynamics. Robin Broad and John Cavanaugh remind us that the global South is important to the America's strategic and economic interests; we ignore them at our peril. The growing sense of self confidence among countries of the South is expressed by Kishore Mahbubani, Singapore's ambassador to the United Nations, who, while admiring the real accomplishments of the West, also chides Westerners for their own cultural short-sightedness and their failure to take seriously the growing diversity among important international actors. Now more than ever, Americans are reminded that political developments in Third World countries have consequences for Americans. The nuclear standoff between India and Pakistan, the military muscle-flexing of China over Taiwan and the terrorist havens of Ben Laden are three troubling examples. Even though developing countries may not be important militarily, small countries such as Rwanda, Sierra Leone, and the Congo attract American foreign affairs experts because of the risks of fleeing refugees, civil war, national genocide, and terror strikes that may draw America into the region or put America on alert at home.

4

Don't Neglect the Impoverished South

ROBIN BROAD AND JOHN CAVANAGH

For four and a half decades, the Cold War offered Americans a prism through which to view the three-quarters of humanity who live in the impoverished countries of Latin America, Africa, and Asia. The United States fought or funded wars and covert operations in dozens of these countries—including Cuba, the Dominican Republic, Guatemala, Iran, Korea, Nicaragua, and Vietnam—with the stated goal of preventing the spread of Soviet-backed communism. Shaped to meet this goal, U.S. economic and military policies toward the so-called Third World, or South, were relatively simple and straightforward.

Today, a half decade into the confusing post–Cold War era and more than halfway through President Bill Clinton's first term, the Third World still erupts into the forefront of U.S. foreign policy with alarming regularity. The administration and media tend to categorize these episodes into one of three oversimplified images. The first and dominant one can be termed "the Rwanda image," and includes countries where, the media tells us, everything is falling apart, and people kill one another in large numbers. Bosnia in 1993, Haiti in 1994, or Somalia in 1993 fit the bill. A second image, promoted by beleaguered defense contractors and Pentagon hawks, paints certain volatile Third World nations and the former Soviet Union as emerging security threats equal to that posed by Moscow at the height of the Cold War. Here, North Korea and Iraq stand out, each with leaders easily caricatured by the media as Hollywood villains. Finally, there is the much newer image of a financially tattered Mexico and the fear that other nations may plunge rapidly into similar crises; tens of billions of dollars of short-term speculative capital race around the globe, abandoning yesterday's favorite "emerging market" for promises of quick returns elsewhere.

Content to respond to crises in these three categories, the Clinton administration has yet to forge an overarching policy framework that addresses the deep and changing problems of the South, which comprises approximately 150 countries. In fact, aside from attention to some crisis spots, the administration forfeited its chance to craft a new North-South policy agenda, preferring instead one that places in the foreground only a handful of these countries. And this policy is being managed not by the State Department or Treasury Department, but by the Commerce Department, which has singled out ten promising "big emerging markets" for U.S. exports and investments.

When pressed to articulate themes or values that underlie U.S. policy toward these countries and the rest of the South, Clinton administration officials unite around the rhetoric of markets and democracy: Freer markets, through pacts such as NAFTA, will, they claim,

63

bring both growth and greater democracy. Remarkably, the positions of most Republican leaders in Congress differ only slightly in substance from this agenda. They support the free-trade agenda and the notion that U.S. foreign policy should support U.S. business. A vocal minority who are more protectionist includes the powerful chairman of the Senate Foreign Relations Committee, Jesse Helms (R-NC). Despite his dramatic overstatements and misstatements that seek to distance him from the Democrats, Helms's attack on Clinton's North-South agenda has concentrated on one issue: cutting U.S. aid drastically (much of which, he likes to say, is "going down foreign rat-holes").

Thus, Washington is poised to continue neglecting the South, except in response to crisis-based chaos or through free-trade agreements and business promotion aimed at a few Third World countries. This lack of a broader North-South economic agenda, however, may well turn out to be one of the great blunders of the Clinton administration. The danger of neglect lies beneath the facile surface images of the Third World reality: a deteriorating living standard for the poorest 2.5 billion people in the world, widening inequalities in almost every nation on earth, and employment and environmental crises that beg global initiatives.

The Clinton administration and the Republican Congress face three immediate opportunities to address these larger problems—opportunities that should be seized to frame a more comprehensive policy toward the South. First, the administration has begun considering the expansion of NAFTA to include the Caribbean Basin, Chile, and the rest of Latin America. Second, Congress is debating new criteria for giving U.S. aid to poor countries. And, finally, the Mexico debacle initiated a propitious international deliberation on fundamental reform of the world's leading multilateral institutions—the World Bank and the International Monetary Fund (IMF)—to meet the new financial crises of the twenty-first century.

What is required to seize these opportunities is a deeper understanding of the new dynamics between North and South and a more comprehensive policy agenda. Unfortunately, Clinton's narrow policies are based on three deeply flawed assumptions (also shared by most Republican leaders) about the nature of the changes in the global economy. The first incorrect assumption is that free trade and the promotion of U.S. business interests overseas are good for U.S. workers and communities. Commerce Secretary Ron Brown is the clearest articulator of this view, and he supports it with planeloads of corporate CEOs on trips to such "big emerging markets" as Brazil, China, and Indonesia. These trips and the two major free-trade agreements completed under Clinton—NAFTA and a new round of the General Agreement on Tariffs and Trade (GATT)—have offered tens of billions of dollars in new business overseas to the United States' largest firms. As the former deputy director of policy planning at the State Department, John Stremlau, wrote in the Winter 1994–1995 issue of *Foreign Policy,* the administration's big-emerging-markets program "should create millions of new and better-paying jobs for Americans, spur domestic productivity, ease adjustment to technological change, restrain inflation, [and] reduce trade and fiscal deficits."

The second flawed assumption of U.S. policy is that free trade and increased U.S. engagement in the ten biggest emerging markets will not only help these economies but will also enhance growth in other Southern countries. Jumping on the big-emerging-markets bandwagon, American CEOs echo administration claims that U.S. policies are leading to the growth of huge middle classes—in countries such as China, India, and Indonesia—that will drive the world economy in the twenty-first century.

A third assumption is that the economic gap between rich and poor countries is now narrowing—a trend that the administration claims is aided by free trade and attention to the ten Third World countries with big emerging markets. Indeed, there is a widespread perception among U.S. policymakers that the Third World debt crisis that widened the gap during the 1980s has ended, that new capital is flowing into the Third World, and that the gap is beginning to close. These perceptions are reinforced by World Bank projections that over the next decade Third World countries will actually grow faster than richer countries, thus catching up.

A careful analysis of social and economic data from the United Nations, the World Bank, the IMF, and other sources, offers a shockingly different picture of trends in the global economy and the gap between rich and poor countries. There are two ways to measure what is happening economically between North and South. The first is to measure which is growing faster, and therefore whether the gap between them is growing or shrinking. The second is to measure financial resource flows between the two.

On the first issue the picture is clear: The North-South gap widened dramatically in the decade after 1982 as the Third World debt crisis drained financial resources from poor countries to rich banks. Between 1985 and 1992, Southern nations paid some $280 billion more in debt service to Northern creditors than they received in new private loans and government aid. GNP per capita rose an average of only 1 percent in the South in the 1980s (in sub-Saharan Africa, it fell 1.2 percent), while it rose 2.3 percent in the North.

Situating the "lost decade" of the 1980s within a longer time period reveals no drastic change: In 1960, per capita GDP in the South stood at 18 percent of the average of Northern nations; by 1990, it had fallen only slightly to 17 percent. In other words, the North–South gap remained fairly constant.

However, such aggregate figures camouflage a complex reality: For a small group of countries, primarily Asian big emerging markets such as China, Hong Kong, Singapore, South Korea, and Taiwan, the gap with the North has been closing. But—and here is the rub—for most of the rest, the gap has been slowly widening. In sub-Saharan Africa, the picture is even worse. Not only has the gap expanded significantly but, for many of these countries, per capita GNP has continued to fall.

Likewise, a look at various resource flows between North and South reveals a reality out of sync with prevailing assumptions. Despite the perception of an easing of the debt crisis, the overall Third World debt stock continues to swell by almost $100 billion each year (it reached $1.9 trillion in 1994). Southern debt service still exceeds new lending, and the net outflow remains particularly crushing in Africa. Whereas it is true that a series of debt reschedulings and the accumulation of arrears by many debtors have reduced the net negative financial transfer from South to North over the last few years, the flows remain negative.

Part of the reason some analysts argue that the debt crisis is no longer a problem is that, since the early 1990s, these outflows of debt repayments have been matched by increased inflows of foreign capital. Here, too, however, a deeper look at disaggregated figures reinforces the disconcerting reality.

According to World Bank figures, roughly half of the new foreign direct investment by global corporations in the South in 1992 quickly left those countries as profits. In addition, investment flows primarily to only ten to twelve Third World countries that are viewed as new profit centers by Northern corporations and investors. More than 70 percent of investment flows in 1991 and 1992 went to just ten of the so-called emerging markets: Mexico, followed by China, Malaysia, Argentina, Thailand, Brazil, Indonesia, Venezuela, South Korea, and Turkey.

There is another problem with these capital flows. Several of these countries (Brazil, India, Mexico, South Korea, and Taiwan) have attracted substantial short-term flows by opening their stock markets to foreigners and by issuing billions of dollars in bonds. Between 1991 and 1993 alone, foreign direct investment as a share of all private capital flows into poor countries fell from 65 to 44 percent as these more speculative flows increased. Recent events in Mexico provide an indication of the fickleness of these new investment flows: During the last week of 1994, an estimated $10 billion in short-term funds fled the country.

In addition, Third World countries have been hurt by the declining buying power of their exports vis-à-vis their imports. Southern nations have long pointed out the general tendency of the prices of their primary product exports to rise more slowly than the prices of manufactured goods imports. This "terms of trade" decline was particularly sharp between 1985 and 1993 when the real prices of primary commodities fell 30 percent. This translates into billions of dollars.

The 3.5 percent decline in the purchasing power of Africa's 1993 exports, for example, cost the continent some $3 billion. The inescapable conclusion is that the North-South economic gap is narrowing for about a dozen countries but continues to widen for well over one hundred others. Hence, without a major shift in policy, the world of the twenty-first century will be one of economic apartheid. There will be two dozen richer nations, a dozen or so poorer nations that have begun to close the gap with the rich, and approximately 140 poor nations slipping further behind.

GLOBALIZATION OF NORTH AND SOUTH

What about the administration's assumption that policies promoting U.S. business are good for overseas as well as domestic markets—that free markets and globalization raise standards of living across the board in both North and South? Here, too, the Clinton administration has missed a fundamental new reality of the global economy. As U.S. firms have shifted from local to national and now global markets over the past half century, a new division of winners and losers has emerged in all countries. A recent book, *Global Dreams: Imperial Corporations and the New World Order,* written by one of the authors [John Cavanagh] and Institute for Policy Studies co-founder Richard Barnet, chronicles how powerful U.S. firms and their counterparts from England, France, Germany, and Japan are integrating only about one-third of humanity (most of those in the rich countries plus the elite of poor countries) into complex chains of production, shopping, culture, and finance.

Although there are enclaves in every country that are linked to these global economic webs, others are left out. Wal-Mart is spreading its superstores throughout the Western Hemisphere; millions in Latin America, however, are too poor to enjoy anything but glimpses of luxury. Citibank customers can access automated teller machines (ATMs) throughout the world; the vast majority of people nevertheless borrow from the loan shark down the road. Ford Motor Company pieces together its new "global car" in Kansas City from parts made all over the globe, while executives in Detroit worry about who will be able to afford it.

Thus, whereas on one level the North-South gap is becoming more pronounced for the vast majority of Third World countries, on another level these global chains blur distinctions between geographical North and South. These processes create another North-South divide between the roughly one-third of humanity who comprise a "global North" of beneficiaries in every country and the two-thirds of humanity from the slums of New York to the favelas of Rio who are not hooked into the new global menu of producing, consuming, and borrowing opportunities in the "global South."

In contrast with the Pollyanna-ish assumptions of the Clinton administration, globalization, accelerated by the administration's new free-trade and investment agreements, has deepened three intractable problems that now plague almost every nation on earth including the United States: income inequalities, job losses, and environmental damage.

INCOME INEQUALITIES

The major adverse consequence of quickening global economic integration has been widening income disparity within almost all nations as the wealthier strata cash in on the opportunities of globalization, while millions of other citizens are hurt, marginalized, or left behind. Years ago, the economist Simon Kuznets hypothesized that as economies develop there is initially a growth-equity tradeoff, that is, income inequalities rise as nations enter the early stages of economic growth and fall in more mature economies. Today, however, the inequalities are growing everywhere—to such an extent that in late 1994 the *Economist* acknowledged that "it is no coincidence that the biggest increases in income inequalities have occurred in economies ... where free-market economic policies have been pursued most zealously" and that "it is a combination of lightly regulated labour markets and global economic forces that has done much more ... to favour the rich over the poor."

One sees this in the perverse widening of the gap between rich and poor within nations and across the globe. Thirty years ago, the income of the richest fifth of the world's population combined was thirty times greater than that of the poorest fifth. Today, the income gap is more than sixty times greater. Over this period the income of the richest 20 percent grew from 70 to 85 percent of the total world income, while the global share of the poorest 20 percent fell from 2.3 to 1.4 percent.

The number of billionaires grew dramatically over the past seven years, coinciding with the spread of free-market policies around the world. Between 1987 and 1994, the number more than doubled from 145 to 358. According to our calculations, those 358 billionaires are collectively worth some $762 billion, which is about the combined income of the world's poorest 2.5 billion people.

(There are no figures for the combined wealth of the world's poor but, because most have little wealth beyond income, their wealth total would not be much higher than their income total.) At the bottom, 2.5 billion people—approximately 45 percent of the world's population—eke out an existence using just under 4 percent of the world's GNP. At the top, 358 individuals own the same percentage.

The impact of free-market policies on this concentration of wealth has been particularly pronounced in Mexico, a country that essentially began its free-market opening in 1986 and that, until the peso debacle of December 1994, often was presented as the model of these policies' success. In 1987, there was just one billionaire in Mexico. By 1994, there were twenty-four who accounted for $44.1 billion in collective wealth. This exceeded the total income of the poorest 40 percent of Mexican households. As a result, the twenty-four wealthiest people are richer than the poorest thirty-three million people in Mexico.

JOB LOSSES

With the exception of a few East Asian economies, every nation—North and South—is grappling with high or rising unemployment, and many, including the United States, are suffering from deteriorating working conditions for a sizable share of the workforce. Worldwide, more than eight hundred million people are unemployed or seriously underemployed, with tens of millions more falling into this situation each year. Technology has combined with globalization in a devastating manner to spawn this crisis of work. Unlike previous industrial revolutions, the two most important technological innovations in recent decades—information/computers and biotechnology—destroy more jobs than they create.

At the same time, rapid strides in transportation and communications technologies allow increasing numbers of jobs to be sent to countries other than the United States.

Whereas a generation ago, firms shifted only apparel and consumer electronics jobs overseas, today they can move virtually the entire range of manufacturing and agricultural tasks (and a number of service jobs as well) to China, Mexico, or a range of other countries.

As corporations and governments alike strive to compete globally by cutting costs, the move to slash jobs accelerates. Fortune 500 firms have cut approximately four hundred thousand jobs a year for the past fifteen years. As many as one-third of U.S. workers are swimming in a global labor pool; their jobs can be moved elsewhere, and this fact confers on their global corporate employers enhanced power to bargain down wages and working conditions. U.S. car companies, for example, can attain roughly equivalent levels of productivity and quality at their Mexican plants today as in their U.S. plants. The denial of basic worker rights in Mexico, however, severely hampers Mexican workers' efforts to negotiate improvements in their working conditions, and their wages remain a fraction of those of U.S. autoworkers. The credible threat of moving more production to Mexico gives the U.S. companies bargaining chips against their U.S. workers when wages and benefits are set. Overall Mexican productivity climbed by at least 24 percent during the boom years from 1987 to 1992, while wages rose only 13 percent; this gap has increased even more since the peso crisis of late 1994. Likewise, according to the U.S. International Trade Commission, Brazilian workers were 59 percent as productive in 1986 as U.S. workers but earned 17 percent of the average U.S. wage. Even in Bangladesh, shirtmakers are about 60 percent as productive as their American counterparts but earn only 3 to 5 percent of a U.S. salary. In the South, roughly thirty-eight million people enter stagnating job markets each year.

Markets for Third World products are expanding quite slowly in the rich countries, and biotechnology innovations that create synthetic substitutes for everything from vanilla to cocoa and coffee threaten to eliminate the livelihood of millions of Third World agricultural workers. As in the United States, real wages have fallen in most of Latin America and parts of Asia since the early 1980s—a shock that hits women particularly hard as they earn 30 to 40 percent less than men doing the same jobs.

As job pressures grow across the South, many people leave for Europe and North America, where job markets are also tight. Violent acts of xenophobia and racism in the North are some of the ugliest manifestations of this current era of inequality and joblessness.

ENVIRONMENTAL DAMAGE

Just as jobs and working conditions become bargaining chips for firms in a deregulated global economy, so, too, do environmental standards. If the Mexican government can attract foreign firms by ignoring violations of environmental laws, it will do so, and, arguably, it must do so or lose investment. The same logic fuels the Republican party's crusade to eliminate a wide range of environmental and other regulations in the United States.

Another pressure on the environment in the South is the constant admonition by the World Bank and the IMF to increase exports. Because most of the world's minerals, timber, fish, and land are in the South, exports tend to be natural-resource intensive. The depletion of these resources hurts yields for millions of small farmers and fishers. The frenzy to ship more goods overseas accelerates environmental degradation and thus diminishes the real, long-term wealth of Southern nations.

By contrast, as Southern countries have rightly pointed out, most of the world's consumption, greenhouse gas emissions, ozone-depleting chemical emissions, and industrial pollution occur in the North. The heaviest burden for global environmental action rests there. But the creation of a "global North" in the South through the big-emerging-markets strategy also spreads environmental havoc. Following annual economic growth rates averaging 10 percent since 1978, China's commercial sector consumes more than one billion tons of coal annually.

Thus, China produces nearly 11 percent of the world's carbon dioxide emissions. If this rate of climb continues, the impact on global warming will be catastrophic. In India, increased consumption will exacerbate a situation in which scale already exceeds carrying capacity: 16 percent of the world's population is degrading just 2.3 percent of the world's land resources and 1.7 percent of its forest stock. And, to compensate for falling oil revenues, Indonesia is tearing down the world's second largest tropical rain forest, becoming the world's largest exporter of processed wood products.

COMPARATIVE DISADVANTAGE

The North–South reality of the mid-1990s hardly matches the soothing scenario suggested by the Clinton administration. Rather, we find the ominous combination of a growing gap between the majority of the Southern and Northern countries as well as the existence of a privileged minority in a "global North" and a marginalized majority in a "global South." Indeed, our analysis suggests three sets of problems that demand attention:

Most of the "global South"—some 45 percent of humanity who reside mainly in the 140 poorest countries of the Third World is locked in poverty and left behind as the richer strata grow.

Roughly 20 percent of the world's population—who are at the upper end of the two-thirds in the "global South," mainly in the big emerging markets—is beginning to enter the global consuming class in a fashion that threatens the environment and exacerbates social tensions.

An increasing number of workers among the top one-third, or "global North," of the world is experiencing falling incomes and an erosion of worker rights and standards.

Thus far, U.S. policy has largely ignored the bottom 45 percent, concentrated on the middle 20 percent in the big emerging markets, and exacerbated the tensions within the top third. The challenge for U.S. policymakers is to focus on this new global picture with a two-tiered set of policies—one aimed at the forsaken 45 percent primarily in Southern countries and the other focused on the growing inequalities and the job and environmental crises mainly in the big emerging markets and the richer countries of the North. The seeds of what has to change in terms of aid, debt, trade, and investment policies have, in most cases, already been planted. And, as was suggested earlier, the administration has ready venues to change course in the current policy debates on NAFTA expansion, aid reform, and World Bank and IMF restructuring.

THE BOTTOM 45 PERCENT

The main U.S. policy arena addressing the problems of the world's poor is the debate over aid. Helms is achieving deep cuts in aid but wrongly asserts that most poor countries are "foreign rat-holes" and are, hence, undeserving of assistance. Virtually all countries in the world now pursue the same basic package of market-opening, privatizing, government-trimming, export-driven policies. Although it is true that there is more corruption and inefficiency in some countries than in others, this is as true for favored countries that are at the center of U.S. policy (e.g., Mexico) as for the 140 neglected countries (e.g., Zaire).

At the same time, anyone who has studied development projects and policies on the ground cannot help but acknowledge the truth in some of Helms's criticisms.

Much U.S., World Bank, and other aid either fails to ease poverty or is conditioned on the recipient nation adopting policies that deepen social and environmental pain. More of the same aid is not the way to close the gap. The key is to make less aid more effective. The current obsession in Washington with restructuring aid agencies will be misplaced if it does not focus on the quality of aid. Any restructuring must learn from a growing number of aid experiments throughout the world that channel small amounts of funds directly to entities run by local citizen groups with guidelines that stress sustainability, participation, and equity.

Although it would be a good step to redirect more aid in this manner, a great deal more needs to be done outside the realm of aid to stop the hemorrhage of resource flows from the bottom 140 countries to the North. The most fruitful avenue is to try to close the gap by taking less money out of the South rather than by getting more money in. Here the focus needs to shift back to debt. The place to begin is with the roughly 17 percent of Third World debt owed to the World Bank and the IMF—with far higher percentages owed by the poorest African nations. The World Bank and the IMF could readily use their reserves ($17 billion and $40 billion, respectively) to cancel much of the outstanding debt owed to them by the poorest countries. The World Bank could likewise write off loans to other countries for projects and programs that have failed by its own economic criteria and/or have had severe adverse effects on local populations and the environment. (A World Bank study found that in fiscal year 1991 more than one-third of its projects were "unsatisfactory at completion" in meeting a minimum economic rate of return.)

As governments debate World Bank restructuring, it is important to note that there are alternatives to the World Bank's formula of excessive dependence on exports and capital inflows. If the goal is to prevent nations from falling into debt again, then debt reduction can be conditioned on policies that encourage productive investment, provide assistance to small entrepreneurs and farmers, and encourage less indebted economies. One alternative worth considering, proposed by a number of Mexican economists, is the adoption of policies for the World Bank and Mexico that reestablish land rights for the poor, steer access to affordable credit to small farmers and entrepreneurs, and restrict inflows of short-term speculative investment.

Economic reformers in Mexico and elsewhere also push for effective systems of fair taxation, while acknowledging how difficult that goal is because most tax systems are poorly enforced. Most critics of the World Bank model acknowledge the need to maintain smaller export sectors to finance vital imports of capital goods but place greater emphasis on production for the domestic market, as was done in South Korea and Taiwan in their early years of industrialization.

The World Bank and the Agency for International Development also should be restrained from pressing dozens of countries into simultaneous export binges on everything from cut flowers to coffee; the impact of so many countries exporting the same products inevitably will be to depress world prices. And these institutions should nurture the small but growing movement that is stimulating trade in goods produced under conditions that respect worker rights and the environment and recognize the deep discrimination that frequently exists against female producers. "Fair trade" entrepreneurs, who are particularly strong in Europe and are spreading in North America, are now responsible for hundreds of millions of dollars of trade in coffee, textiles, and other products and are developing new notions of what constitutes socially and environmentally responsible trade.

Not surprisingly, the agenda suggested for the bottom 45 percent draws from a more traditional set of remedies on how to shrink the North–South gap. However, attacking the trio of problems outlined for the global North and South—the inequities, joblessness, and environmental degradation—demands that these be implemented in conjunction with a newer set of policy instruments.

THE BIG EMERGING MARKETS AND ANXIETY AT THE TOP

Rather than quickening the pace to compete in an increasingly deregulated global economy, the United States can lead in calling for new rules to temper economic integration's socially and environmentally destructive effect upon unequal nations. It is important to recall that the United States rose to this same challenge on a national level in the 1930s when large firms were integrating the U.S. national economy and, in the process, playing rich unionized states off poor nonunion states. A strong trade union movement created the momentum for Franklin Roosevelt's administration to set new national rules for minimum wages, maximum hours of work, and decent health and safety standards.

In the 1990s, this same dynamic now occurs on a global stage, upon which global corporations play workers and environmental standards against one another to bargain richer countries down to the standards of the poorer ones. Free-trade agreements that accelerate integration without explicitly safeguarding labor and environmental rights and standards are only deepening global job and environmental crises. Therefore, internationally recognized standards on worker rights (including freedom of association, the right to collective bargaining, and a ban on discrimination based on gender or race) and the environment, which have been hammered out by member governments of the International Labor Organization (ILO) and various international environmental treaties, need to be grafted onto new trade agreements so that firms benefiting from lower tariffs would be obligated to respect those rights and standards.

The first steps in this direction have already been taken. Since 1984, U.S. trade law has conditioned the granting of "trade preferences" to a developing country's respect for internationally recognized worker rights. Threats by the U.S. government to withdraw trade preferences have led to important reforms in a number of countries. For instance, in response to looming U.S. sanctions, El Salvador has worked with the ILO to adopt a more comprehensive labor code. The government of Sri Lanka reacted to similar pressure by agreeing to open its garment industry to collective bargaining. Indonesia announced a 29 percent increase in its minimum wage in 1994 after the United States threatened to remove trade preferences. Building on this U.S. trade law, NAFTA's negotiators crafted side agreements that threaten minor sanctions to encourage enforcement of a small number of labor rights and environmental standards.

In addition to social clauses on trade agreements, global corporations should be held to codes of conduct that require compliance with these rights and standards. A number of U.S. firms, including Levi Strauss and Sears, have taken a step toward comprehensive corporate codes by agreeing to voluntary codes for the firms with which they subcontract in the Third World. New corporate codes and socially responsible trade and investment agreements would not solve all the world's job, environmental, and inequality problems, but they could be implemented in the short term and would help reverse the negative dynamic we now face. In the long term, such policies would be more effective if supplemented with strong national policies to address the job and environmental problems jointly.

Even with the best codes of conduct and social clauses on trade agreements, increased trade is likely to continue to be based on the unsustainable exploitation of natural resources. This creates two challenges: first, to raise standards of living in the big emerging markets and other Southern nations without exceeding the Earth's environmental limits, and, second, to get Northern societies to acknowledge the costs to the environment of their already high standards of living. Across the board, nations—and individuals—need to acknowledge the environmental costs of economic decisions.

One way to reduce trade in natural resources (such as virgin timber) and the use of resource-intensive products (such as cars) is for governments to adopt accounting systems that factor in the real costs of natural-resource depletion and environmental degradation. In fact, technical work on "environmental accounting" is already quite advanced, as seen in the World Resources Institute's work in Costa Rica, Indonesia, and other developing countries. Even the U.S. Commerce Department has begun recalculations for a "green GDP." In this regard, the World Bank and the IMF should be required to adopt a system of "shadow pricing" that accounts for environmental costs in their projects and programs. This would be an important step in the direction of seeing "green GDPs" become the conceptual framework across the globe.

ENLIGHTENED SELF-INTEREST

For the next year [1997], the Republican Congress will reinforce the Clinton administration's hesitancy to embrace a number of these proposals. Yet, there is an impetus for a shift in policy regarding the poorer majority of the world. In the tough debate over NAFTA, citizens' groups—trade unions, environmental groups, organizations of small farmers, consumer activists, religious groups, women's groups, and others—emerged in Canada, Mexico, and the United States to press for safeguards on labor, the environment, and agriculture. Although only small gains were realized in the final agreement, the democratization of the debate over international economic policy continued during the recent GATT deliberation and is likely to characterize the next debates over integration in the Americas and Asia. Similar citizen coalitions throughout the world have likewise gathered momentum for reform of the World Bank and the IMF. In other words, segments of civil society seem ahead of U.S. policymakers in comprehending that the widening inequalities within nations and between North and South pose crucial challenges that are in our enlightened self-interest to meet. Working conditions in a number of Third World countries have an increasing impact on working conditions in the United States. Growing inequalities in the South are increasing the flow of people, drugs, and environmental problems into the North. The rapid rise of the rich and the emergence of a middle class in the big emerging markets increase instability and tension vis-à-vis the vast numbers of people left behind—witness the growing labor unrest in China, Indonesia, and Mexico, as well as the continuing rebellion in Mexico's Chiapas state. Although the Clinton administration can continue to respond belatedly to crises and fall back on its faulty assumptions about the North-South economic reality, the attendant problems of the post–Cold War global economy will inevitably become clearer as an increasing number of people in the North and South are hurt. There is no way to get around the need for a fundamental rethinking of the North-South agenda. The question is simply whether the United States will take the lead in resolving these problems or will instead wait and be led.

5

The Dangers of Decadence

What the Rest Can Teach the West

KISHORE MAHBUBANI

In key Western capitals there is a deep sense of unease about the future. The confidence that the West would remain a dominant force in the twenty-first century, as it has for the past four or five centuries, is giving way to a sense of foreboding that forces such as the emergence of fundamentalist Islam, the rise of East Asia, and the collapse of Russia and Eastern Europe could pose real threats to the West. A siege mentality is developing. Within these troubled walls, Samuel P. Huntington's essay "The Clash of Civilizations?" is bound to resonate.

It will therefore come as a great surprise to many Westerners to learn that the rest of the world fears the West even more than the West fears it, especially the threat posed by a wounded West.

Huntington is right: Power is shifting among civilizations. But when the tectonic plates of world history move in a dramatic fashion, as they do now, perceptions of these changes depend on where one stands. The key purpose of this essay is to sensitize Western audiences to the perceptions of the rest of the world.

The retreat of the West is not universally welcomed. There is still no substitute for Western leadership, especially American leadership. Sudden withdrawals of American support from Middle Eastern or Pacific allies, albeit unlikely, could trigger massive changes that no one would relish. Western retreat could be as damaging as Western domination. By any historical standard, the recent epoch of Western domination, especially under American leadership, has been remarkably benign. One dreads to think what the world would have looked like if either Nazi Germany or Stalinist Russia had triumphed in what have been called the "Western civil wars" of the twentieth century. Paradoxically, the benign nature of Western domination may be the source of many problems. Today most Western policymakers, who are children of this era, cannot conceive of the possibility that their own words and deeds could lead to evil, not good. The Western media aggravate this genuine blindness. Most Western journalists travel overseas with Western assumptions. They cannot understand how the West could be seen as anything but benevolent. CNN is not the solution. The same visual images transmitted simultaneously into living rooms across the globe can trigger opposing perceptions. Western living rooms applaud when cruise missiles strike Baghdad. Most living outside see that the West will deliver swift retribution to nonwhite Iraqis or Somalis but not to white Serbians, a dangerous signal by any standard.

THE ASIAN HORDES

Huntington discusses the challenge posed by Islamic and Confucian civilizations. Since the bombing of the World Trade Center, Americans have begun to absorb European paranoia about Islam, perceived as a force of darkness hovering over a virtuous Christian civilization. It is ironic that the West should increasingly fear Islam when daily the Muslims are reminded of their own weakness. "Islam has bloody borders," Huntington says. But in all conflicts between Muslims and pro-Western forces, the Muslims are losing, and losing badly, whether they be Azeris, Palestinians, Iraqis, Iranians, or Bosnian Muslims. With so much disunity, the Islamic world is not about to coalesce into a single force. Oddly, for all this paranoia, the West seems to be almost deliberately pursuing a course designed to aggravate the Islamic world. The West protests the reversal of democracy in Myanmar, Peru, or Nigeria, but not in Algeria. These double standards hurt. Bosnia has wreaked incalculable damage. The dramatic passivity of powerful European nations as genocide is committed on their doorstep has torn away the thin veil of moral authority that the West had spun around itself as a legacy of its recent benign era. Few can believe that the West would have remained equally passive if Muslim artillery shells had been raining down on Christian populations in Sarajevo or Srebrenica.

Western behavior toward China has been equally puzzling. In the 1970s, the West developed a love affair with a China ruled by a regime that had committed gross atrocities during the Great Leap Forward and the Cultural Revolution. But when Mao Zedong's disastrous rule was followed by a far more benign Deng Xiaoping era, the West punished China for what by its historical standards was a minor crackdown: the Tiananmen incident.

Unfortunately, Tiananmen has become a contemporary Western legend, created by live telecasts of the crackdown. Beijing erred badly in its excessive use of firearms, but it did not err in its decision to crack down. Failure to quash the student rebellion could have led to political disintegration and chaos, a perennial Chinese nightmare. Western policymakers concede this in private. They also are aware of the dishonesty of some Western journalists: dining with student dissidents and even egging them on before reporting on their purported "hunger strike." No major Western journal has exposed such dishonesty or developed the political courage to say that China had virtually no choice in Tiananmen. Instead, sanctions were imposed, threatening China's modernization.

Asians see that Western public opinion—deified in Western democracy—can produce irrational consequences. They watch with trepidation as Western policies on China lurch to and fro, threatening the otherwise smooth progress of East Asia.

Few in the West are aware that the West is responsible for aggravating turbulence among the more than two billion people living in Islamic and Chinese civilizations. Instead, conjuring up images of the two Asian hordes that Western minds fear most—two forces that invaded Europe, the Muslims and the Mongols-Huntington posits a Confucian-Islamic connection against the West. American arms sales to Saudi Arabia do not suggest a natural Christian-Islamic connection. Neither should Chinese arms sales to Iran. Both are opportunistic moves, based not on natural empathy or civilizational alliances. The real tragedy of suggesting a Confucian-Islamic connection is that it obscures the fundamentally different nature of the challenge posed by these forces. The Islamic world will have great difficulty modernizing. Until then its turbulence will spill over into the West. East Asia, including China, is poised to achieve parity with the West. The simple truth is that East and Southeast Asia feel more comfortable with the West.

This failure to develop a viable strategy to deal with Islam or China reveals a fatal flaw in the West: an inability to come to terms with the shifts in the relative weights of civilizations that Huntington well documents. Two key sentences in Huntington's essay, when put side by side, illustrate the nature of the problem: First, "In the politics of civilizations, the peoples and governments of non-Western civilization no longer remain the objects of history as targets of Western colonization but join the West as movers and shapers of history," and, second, "The West in effect is using international institutions, military power and economic resources to run the world in ways that will maintain Western predominance, protect Western interests and promote Western political and economic values." This combination is a prescription for disaster.

Simple arithmetic demonstrates Western folly. The West has eight hundred million people; the rest make up almost four to seven billion. In the national arena, no Western society would accept a situation in which 15 percent of its population legislated for the remaining 85 percent. But this is what the West is trying to do globally. Tragically, the West is turning its back on the Third World just when it can finally help the West out of its economic doldrums. The developing world's dollar output increased in 1992 more than that of North America, the European Community, and Japan put together. Two-thirds of the increase in U.S. exports has gone to the developing world. Instead of encouraging this global momentum by completing the Uruguay Round, the West is doing the opposite. It is trying to create barriers, not remove them. French Prime Minister Edouard Balladur tried to justify this move by saying bluntly in Washington that the "question now is how to organize to protect ourselves from countries whose different values enable them to undercut us."

THE WEST'S OWN UNDOING

Huntington fails to ask one obvious question: If other civilizations have been around for centuries, why are they posing a challenge only now? A sincere attempt to answer this question reveals a fatal flaw that has recently developed in the Western mind: An inability to conceive that the West may have developed structural weaknesses in its core value systems and institutions. This flaw explains, in part, the recent rush to embrace the assumption that history has ended with the triumph of the Western ideal: Individual freedom and democracy would always guarantee that Western civilization would stay ahead of the pack.

Only hubris can explain why so many Western societies are trying to defy the economic laws of gravity. Budgetary discipline is disappearing. Expensive social programs and pork-barrel projects multiply with little heed to costs. The West's low savings and investment rates lead to declining competitiveness vis-à-vis East Asia. The work ethic is eroding, while politicians delude workers into believing that they can retain high wages despite becoming internationally uncompetitive. Leadership is lacking. Any politician who states hard truths is immediately voted out. Americans freely admit that many of their economic problems arise from the inherent gridlock of American democracy. While the rest of the world is puzzled by these fiscal follies, American politicians and journalists travel around the world preaching the virtues of democracy. It makes for a curious sight.

The hero worship is given to the idea of individual freedom. Much good has come from this idea. Slavery ended. Universal franchise followed. But freedom does not only solve problems; it can also cause them. The United States has undertaken a massive social experiment, tearing down social institution after social institution that restrained the individual. The results have been disastrous. Since 1960, the U.S. population has increased 41 percent, while violent crime has risen by 560 percent, single-mother births by 419 percent, divorce rates by 300 percent, and the percentage of children living in single-parent homes by 300 percent. This is massive social decay. Many a society shudders at the prospects of this happening on its shores. But instead of traveling overseas with humility, Americans confidently preach the virtues of unfettered individual freedom, blithely ignoring the visible social consequences.

The West is still the repository of the greatest assets and achievements of human civilization. Many Western values explain the spectacular advance of mankind: the belief in scientific inquiry, the search for rational solutions, and the willingness to challenge assumptions. But a belief that a society is practicing these values can lead to a unique blindness: The inability to realize that some of the values that come with this package may be harmful. Western values do not form a seamless web. Some are good. Some are bad. But one has to stand outside the West to see this clearly, and to see how the West is bringing about its relative decline by its own hand. Huntington, too, is blind to this.

Section 3

The Changing Face
of America's International Affairs

Who are the people who conduct U.S. international affairs today? Does this group reflect the new ethnic or gender diversity described in Section Two? And what difference does it make if the policymaking elite do or do not reflect these trends?

Allan Goodman, former Dean at Georgetown University and current head of the Institute for International Education, describes his extensive review of minorities in the senior ranks of the American foreign service, finding very low numbers and other disappointing trends. He argues that this de facto continuing segregation imposes hardships on the conduct of U.S. international affairs. It makes the U.S. government less representative in its dealings with other nations, and cuts off the foreign service and other professions from attracting talented candidates from diverse backgrounds. Goodman interprets this as a failure of American democracy to live up to its full potential. Bruce Shapiro recounts discriminatory practices that led black State Department officers to file a lawsuit against the State Department. Although we lack the same hard evidence of diversity in the international activities of the private sector, media, foundations, and think tanks, preliminary investigations by this author suggest the picture is equally dispiriting.[1]

Despite the currently low personnel figures, Michael Clough, former Senior Fellow at the Council on Foreign Relations in New York, claims we are witnessing the passing of an era. Passing away is the unquestioned authority of a traditional foreign policy elite mainly domiciled on the East Coast and mainly educated at the Ivies, based in business and law. Clough claims they are now giving way, slowly but inexorably, to more "grassroots" oriented leaders from different professions and different sections of the country. The author sees this evolution as quite positive and a much-needed improvement in the making of U.S. foreign affairs.

Smith Hempstone,[2] a former U.S. Ambassador to Kenya, claims that appointing too many women and minorities to international posts hurts American policy. Based on his experience in Africa, he argues that appointing black ambassadors and other foreign service officers to Africa runs the risk of damaging America's standing, as local leaders don't want to have blacks or women assigned to their country because they think they're being sent second-rate professionals.

NOTES

1. Ernest Wilson (New York, 1997), *Diversity in International Institutions*. Report to the Council on Foreign Relations.
2. Hempstone Smith (1997). *Rogue Ambassador: An African Memoir*. Sewanee, TN: University of the South Press.

6

Grassroots Policymaking

Say Good-Bye to the "Wise Men"

MICHAEL CLOUGH

Many pundits blame President Clinton's inexperience or indecision for the current crisis in American foreign policy. But the roots of the dilemma lie far deeper. They run to the collapse of America's postwar policymaking system—a collapse that not even the most sage and resolute leadership or the discovery of some new strategic formula could have averted. The problem, and the answer, is that the American people are in the process of reclaiming foreign policy from the "Wise Men" who have so assiduously guarded it for the past fifty years.

Over the last half-century, America has undergone a technological and demographic transformation. Increased mobility has forged new centers of culture, fashion, wealth, and power. A communications revolution has rewired the nation's nerve system with computers, faxes, and fiber-optic cables. Immigration approaches levels not seen since the turn of the century, and Americans travel and live abroad in numbers scarcely imaginable years ago. Such changes integrate Americans in new ways, with each other as well as with the rest of the world. But they also diversify and divide us as they slowly erode the lingering vestiges of our Mayflower roots.

This globalization of American society has made the idea of national interest more elusive. While America's politics has always intruded on its foreign policy, today a fresh constellation of domestic forces creates its own global policy. Making sense of American foreign policy requires a fuller understanding of the new domestic politics that now shapes America's relations abroad. Foremost among these pressures are the regionalization of global policymaking, the impact of ethnicity on American foreign policy, and the rise of powerful global issue groups.

THE ESTABLISHMENT DECLINES

For nearly five decades, the complexion and outlook of American foreign policymakers remained constant. In the view of the small, cohesive club of academics, diplomats, financiers, lawyers, and politicians that ascended to power during World War II—men such as Dean Acheson, Clark Clifford, George Kennan, John McCloy, and Paul Nitze—this was as it should be. National security and the national interest, they argued, must transcend the special interests and passions of the people who make up America. They believed that domestic politics should stop at the water's edge—and that foreign policy should be guided by bipartisan consensus. This separation of policy into foreign and domestic spheres rationalized and legitimized the emergence of the close community of experts that shepherded American foreign policy throughout the Cold War years.

After 1941, the Northeast played a dominant role in shaping foreign policy. But this was not always the case. For most of our nation's history, the influence of the more industrial and Anglophile Northeast was counterbalanced by other regions. In the controversy surrounding the French revolution, for example, opposition to the antirevolutionary views of Eastern opinion leaders such as John Adams, Alexander Hamilton, and Gouverneur Morris came from Thomas Jefferson and the South's other agrarian populists. Likewise, in the great debates over war and neutrality in the first half of this century, opposition to Eastern internationalist calls issued mostly from isolationists and populists from the Midwest and West.

How was this small band of Atlantic-minded internationalists able to triumph? What enabled them in the postwar period to subdue the isolationist impulses of the hinterland and turn the nation of "no entangling alliances" into both the world's policeman and its banker?

For the most part, the answer is—twofold: fear and prosperity. The dangers of the postwar world—the threat of Soviet expansion and the haunting memory of global depression—convinced the public that it was necessary for the United States to assume the mantle of world leadership, and the rapid growth and productivity of America's postwar economy convinced them that they could. It also helped that Eastern internationalists had gained great authority once it was clear that they were right about America's need to enter World War II. In contrast, many of the most prominent Midwestern opinion leaders on international affairs—such as Senators William Borah of Idaho and Gerald Nye of North Dakota—were discredited. By taking the lead both in mobilizing the nation for war and in preparing it for the peace that followed, the Eastern internationalists were able to shape and staff the burgeoning foreign policy institutions created in the late 1940s. Most important, this newly ascendant coterie fashioned the overarching consensus on containment and free trade that emerged as America's guiding international outlook. The preeminence of the East was reinforced by other postwar developments. The *New York Times* and, to a lesser extent, *Time* magazine emerged as the leading national sources of news and commentary on international affairs. The original big three national television networks all chose New York as the site of their headquarters, and hence their evening news shows. A small number of well-endowed foundations and influential foreign policy institutes also were based in New York and Washington. And a handful of Eastern seaboard universities played a critical role in training and employing America's new foreign policy cafés.

Together, these developments meant that the most reliable, the fastest, and often the only way to become a player in the domestic and foreign affairs has become national foreign policy debate was to locate oneself along the Harvard-Manhattan-Foggy Bottom corridor. This reality greatly contributed to the homogeneity of discourse on international issues that characterized the Cold War years. As long as the Cold War endured and nuclear Armageddon seemed only a missile away, the public was willing to tolerate such an undemocratic foreign policymaking system. But in the eyes of most Americans the world is no longer so menacing—messy, bloody, and sometimes shockingly brutal, yes, but a threat to our security and peace, no. With the Soviet Union residing in the dustbin of history and the United States reigning as the world's largest debtor, the twin logic of national security and the national interest is neither clear nor compelling. Without a clear and present danger, the public is no longer willing to trust the experts to make the right decisions when it comes to the lives of their sons and daughters, especially when the experts themselves are so deeply divided. The result is that the wall separating foreign affairs from domestic influences has come crumbling down. The old foreign policy establishment, already weakened and divided by its defeat in Vietnam, is losing both its bearings and its sway. And the old foreign policy-making system, no longer insulated by fear and prosperity, is more susceptible to societal pressures. As the muddled debate over intervention in Bosnia and Somalia attests, this rupture has left the ship of state dangerously adrift in a sea of geopolitical confusion. The idea of a separation between domestic and foreign affairs has become untenable.

GLOBAL POLICY IS LOCAL

The globalization of American society has greatly increased the incentives for individuals in all parts of the country as well as local, state, and regional institutions to become more involved in world affairs. As the world becomes increasingly interconnected, developments abroad matter more for local communities. War in Central America causes greater burdens on southern California's social services; drug feuds in Columbia lead to assassinations in New York; unrest in Russia affects port traffic in Seattle; and economic development in Mexico throws Americans out of work in Detroit.

At the same time, opportunities for local, state, and regional actors to influence global policy also have grown. Many state and local institutions are establishing direct links with counterparts around the world through technical assistance and exchange programs. Foundations and entrepreneurs are creating new regionally based foreign policy communities to provide the kind of leadership in world affairs that the Eastern establishment once monopolized. Almost every major university in the country now has some kind of international affairs degree program. The news media are also more diverse; CNN is based in Atlanta, and plans for new cable channels are being hatched across the country.

The East's privileged place in foreign affairs has eroded. New York no longer dominates the nation's economic relationships with the rest of the world, and the share of trade that flows through Eastern seaboard ports has shrunk dramatically. From southern California to the Great Lakes, and from the Pacific Northwest to the Texas border and southern Florida, regions are developing their own economic interests and orientations, and creating the trade offices and other institutions necessary to pursue them. In short, regionalization has not only lessened Eastern influence over the foreign policy-making process but also helped spawn a new process of global policymaking with sources of power far beyond the Washington beltway.

NEW VOICES, NEW ACCENTS

As America becomes more diverse, the economic, social, and political incentives for individuals to emphasize their ethnic identities are increasing. In the 1980s, for example, African Americans, motivated in part by the model of Jewish American support for Israel, largely succeeded in laying claim to U.S. policy, toward Africa—especially toward South Africa. More recently, Mexican American groups have begun to play a critical part in the NAFTA debate and in the formulation of U.S. policy toward Mexico generally. Similarly, a growing Chinese American community has played an increasingly significant role in policy toward China, and the American cousins of embattled East European nationalities have begun to mobilize as well.

This trend is reinforced by the economic advantage that can accrue to ethnic groups that serve as a bridgehead for potentially prosperous countries such as China and Mexico. More and more foreign countries are beginning to see their ethnic brethren in the United States as natural allies in campaigns to develop more favorable bilateral relationships. This web of societal ties linking American ethnic communities with their homelands is certain to thicken as the information revolution increases the ease and affordability of reaching out and touching previously distant kith and kin. Concentration of ethnic groups in particular geographic areas heightens the impact of the regionalization of foreign affairs. For example, Asian Americans constitute roughly 3 percent of the U.S. population but nearly 10 percent of the population of southern California and 15 percent of the San Francisco Bay area. Similarly, Hispanics account for roughly 9 percent of the national population, but they comprise one-third of southern Californians, one-third of south Floridians, and one-quarter of Texans. The more localized foreign policy becomes, the more likely that ethnic ties will influence the debate, especially as more blacks, Hispanics, and Asians are elected to local and state political offices.

The results are likely to vary. In some foreign policy areas, such as Africa, ethnic and racial considerations are likely to play a dominant role as long as high costs or risks are not involved. In most other areas, they will be increasingly important factors in a complex and changing equation, one in which ethnic organizations may not only attempt to influence U.S. foreign policy but also to develop their own global policies. If the United States today had a set of broadly recognized "national" interests and a clear global strategy, the impact of ethnicity on foreign policy would be less significant. At present, however, there is little prospect of either anytime soon.

THE GRASS ROOTS GROW

The final factor contributing to the breakdown of the old foreign policy consensus is the emergence of powerful, activist groups organized around individual issues such as human rights, the environment, humanitarian relief, and women's rights. These global issue group differ from traditional interest groups in that their principal goal is to change policies and living conditions beyond our borders rather than to promote and protect the economic interests or welfare of their American members. In most other respects, including origins, scope, size, resources, effectiveness, and commitment, they vary widely.

Once again, this phenomenon is not entirely new. For example, the International Committee of the Red Cross, the peace movement, and the international women's movement date back to the turn of the century. Beyond the peace movement, however, the number and influence of foreign policy issue groups in America had been limited. The turning point occurred in the 1970s with the creation in Washington of a number of well-staffed offices focused on particular issues. Today, these groups are increasingly attracting the best and brightest of young college graduates interested in world affairs.

During the Cold War, most of these issue groups were, by necessity, oppositional. Because there was little chance that the foreign policy establishment would give their objectives equal weight with the need to contain communism, they focused on exposing the effects of Washington's policies and, wherever possible, limiting governmental prerogatives. But government has begun to embrace many of the goals these groups have long sought to promote, thus presenting their leaders with a dramatically different set of strategic choices.

Their most important new challenge is to find ways to merge myriad single issue pressures into a coherent whole and to do so in an environment of shrinking resources. The tradeoffs involved no longer pit geopolitics against human rights or development. Instead, they pit environment versus development versus economic reform, and so on. Many participants in this emerging debate have sought to mute these conflicts by embracing concepts, such as sustainable development, that suggest that everything good can go together—and it may, but only in the long run. But for now, easy compromises and easy money are scarce. Moreover, it is very difficult, both intellectually and politically, for single issue groups to adjust their rhetoric in the ways necessary for a grand synthesis to emerge. One of the greatest strengths of the leadership of these groups has been their ability to persuade both funders and constituents that their particular issue deserves priority. Softening such claims could mean losing support.

The issue-group picture is also growing more complex. At first, it was dominated by a few national organizations such as Amnesty International and Human Rights Watch. In the 1980s, however, grassroots organizations sprang up across the country. Today, groups of varying size and character literally number in the hundreds. In addition, more and more groups are deemphasizing foreign policy advocacy and concentrating on their own global policy initiatives. This shift is most evident in areas such as South Africa, Eastern Europe, and the former Soviet Union, where the reasons to lobby Washington are rapidly declining and the opportunities for direct action abroad are rapidly increasing. The result is a whole new set of cleavages and complications.

SYNTHESIS OR STRUGGLE?

The breakdown of the old foreign policy system extends beyond the security realm to economics. Protectionism is nothing new. What is new is that environmentalists, human rights activists, labor leaders, and regional political leaders seem to be merging in a popular coalition that rejects free trade as the organizing principal of the global economy. This development is amply demonstrated by the stalled Uruguay round of the Geneva Agreement on Tariffs and Trade, as well as the long NAFTA debate. When the economy was growing and good jobs at rising wages were plentiful, such criticism fell on deaf ears. But what is true in good times is often false in bad, and for many Americans the good times seem over. A new and highly uncertain era has begun. It is possible that the heirs of the Wise Men will succeed in diversifying the foreign policy establishment and in enlisting these new forces under the banner of a new grand strategy such as "enlargement." But that is unlikely. The latest generation of Wise Men does not have enough public authority or institutional clout to forge a new consensus from the top down without a threat as clear and compelling as the Red menace. Nor are its leaders sufficiently nimble or creative to put out the prairie fire of independent global policy-making that is raging across the country.

These new domestic forces could well lead to the balkanization of the foreign policy-making process, with different communities and groups seeking to control different issues and policies. At best, such a development would create a system of separate policymaking domains organized around an implicit set of rules for resource allocation and conflict resolution between them. More likely, balkanization would cause a bitter and prolonged domestic struggle over America's role in the world, undermining its ability to lead in the era now dawning.

Only a radically redesigned foreign policymaking system, one fashioned to meet the global challenges of the twenty-first century in the same way that the national security apparatus was created to face the Cold War, would make a synthesis of these competing interests possible. Only an open, decentralized, and collaborative system, which encouraged the initiatives of regional actors, ethnic groups, and global issue groups, would restore public confidence that America's involvement in world affairs is still consistent with their own values and would improve the security and welfare of all.

7

Diversity in U.S. Foreign Policymaking

The Dilemma Endures

ALLAN E. GOODMAN

More than a half century ago, Gunnar Myrdal published the most troubling book yet about America and the subject of this conference [Workshop on Advancing the International Interests of African-Americans, Asian Americans, and Latinos, March 20–21, 1998, Los Angeles]. Entitled *An American Dilemma,* the study demonstrated the persistence of racial prejudice in American life and its impact on our institutions of governance, as well as the determination on the part of those disadvantaged to struggle to become more equal. That the societal and institutional practices that had prevented Americans of color from living in equality had not produced greater alienation was seen by social scientists of the time as allowing an interval—during which old practices would die out—between the end of World War II and the achievement of equality for all those who fought in it.

It is clear now that Myrdal thought the problem was going to be tougher. This is why, I think, he chose to characterize it as a dilemma because that class of problem in logic tends to resist quick solution and is very hard to resolve even over time. Some dilemmas only get resolved by fundamental changes in values. Race has turned out to engage America in "continuously struggling for its soul," as Myrdal predicted that it would. Unfortunately, the outcome of that struggle is still not clear.

For a country looked to as the paramount leader in a multicultural world, the United States has yet to come to terms with its own diversity. Race also continues to define who governs. American governmental institutions today remain remarkably resistant to embracing the contributions that persons of color can make to the policies and processes, which shape our future.

The latest data on the employment of minorities in the U.S. government indicate that persons of color account for slightly more than 30 percent of the federal workforce. However, the representation of minorities in government is largely confined to the lowest levels of the career services. At the middle and especially the top salary and responsibility grades, in fact, most government agencies report that they have consistently failed to accomplish equal employment opportunity recruitment goals and that the numbers of persons of color promoted into the middle and top ranks is declining. For FY 1996, the Equal Employment Opportunity Commission (EEOC) noted that "Women, all minority groups, and people with disabilities continued to be represented in Senior Pay Level positions at rates well below their representation in the Federal work force" and that "The average white collar grade for whites was one to two grades higher than the average white collar grade for minorities, as it has *been since 1982*."[1] Hispanics and Native Americans actually decreased in their representation in the Senior Executive Service and the Senior Foreign Service between FY 1995 and FY 1996.

Government-wide, and across all agencies (except for those in the Intelligence Community) and departments with five hundred or more employees, the percent of black males in the federal workforce actually declined over the ten-year period, 1987–1996. And, during this decade, in the agencies and departments with a special role to play in foreign policy decisionmaking and implementation, the representation of blacks declined at the Agency for International Development, the Departments of Commerce, Defense, State, and Treasury. Until FY 1995, the proportion of these agencies' and departments' workforces represented by Hispanic and Asian American officials remained essentially stagnant.[2]

This workshop is designed to address the challenge of changing this picture and what it portends about diversity in governance. In an environment of growing doubts about the constitutionality and also the effectiveness of affirmative action, the weapon of choice has so far proved to be equal employment opportunity suits and class actions. Complaints before the EEOC are all-time record numbers, especially from federal workers, and for the first half of the 1990s, were up more than 55 percent.[3] And several class action suits and complaints initiated by foreign service officers at the Department of State and the U.S. Information Agency and intelligence officers at the CIA have now led to settlements and resolution procedures that are beginning to grant minorities and women the promotions and assignments that will enable more to reach positions involving foreign policy formulation, decisionmaking, and implementation.[4]

All of this has come at tremendous and continuing cost to minorities, professionally and psychologically. Because change has had to come through the courts, minorities feel that their white counterparts now regard their advancement as due less to their abilities than to their willingness to hire aggressive civil rights lawyers and the liberal penchant of the federal judges in the District of Columbia, where most class action suits are brought against the U.S. Government.[5] The view is that minorities are less qualified for public service persists, despite consistent and considerable evidence that the supply of qualified minorities for public service is increasing. Minorities also think that the personnel system as a whole is far less flexible for a person of color than it is for white officers; to wit, the perceived regularity with which nonminority officers are granted career extensions and other types of temporary and special assignments to enhance operational effectiveness. There is also a widespread perception that minority officers are held to a much higher standard when it comes to such matters as certifying language proficiency than are their white counterparts. As a result, minority officers regard the personnel system as insensitive to their capabilities and needs, unforgiving of mistakes (compared to the treatment received by white officers who are perceived to be protected by a culture that considers their mistakes as learning experiences), and unwilling to take any steps that would provide opportunities to qualified minorities for the sake of increasing the diversity of viewpoints about the conduct of U.S. foreign policy. At the policy-setting level, interviews with minority officials suggest that they so frequently find themselves the only person of color at a decisionmaking meeting, that they routinely feel as if they are not intended to have a real role at such meetings and that their contributions, in any case, will not be welcomed.

The net effect of these perceptions is enormous personal stress, degradation, and shaken confidence on a daily basis as well as a tendency to conclude early on that the chances for advancement are poor and for senior responsibility nil. Minority Foreign Service Officers, especially those with more than a decade of service, thus uniformly perceive the U.S. government to have lost ground in the quest for diversity. They also do not think that the need for enhancing diversity is a prominent issue in debates over and policy planning about the future consolidation of the foreign affairs agencies. Ranged against this, the requirement that annual efficiency reports for all senior executives contain a section on what they did specifically to assure equal employment opportunity and accomplish agency and departmental affirmative action goals is seen as having had little effect on changing the ways in which leaders get identified and who gets promoted.

Although there is a clear and compelling national need to broaden the intellectual base of foreign policy that has to deal with a complex, multicultural world and a need to strengthen U.S. representational effectiveness abroad, there is no clear means at hand to do this. There is also declining interest on the part of young persons of color to enter the foreign affairs agencies as more is becoming known about the glass ceilings and glass walls that prevent minorities from receiving the kinds of assignments and awards that would enable them to advance to senior levels and meetings at which policy is made or to serve as leaders of embassies and U.S. missions abroad in which major foreign policy initiatives are to be carried out.

A key element to changing this situation will, thus, continue to be the willingness of minorities to file complaints against supervisors and systems that take promotion, assignment, and award decisions resulting in the persistent underrepresentation of specific groups of persons. More has so far been accomplished in this way than by any other means, including the appointment by the president of women and minorities to top leadership positions. Knowing when the results of selection panels are producing effects that suggest equal employment opportunity may not exist at a particular agency, however, is not something that is easy to do. This is because the government itself, and the foreign affairs agencies in particular, does not tend to report workforce demographics accurately or in a timely fashion.

Although the Central Personnel Data File, on which virtually all equal employment reporting is based, is updated monthly, the standard forms used for personnel actions within the federal system come in batches that can be as much as a year behind and often mix career services when it comes to the foreign affairs agencies (e.g., minority civil service personnel tend to be counted as foreign service officers (FSOs) when they occupy foreign service positions and vice versa). Moreover, the "annual accomplishment reports" that federal agencies are required to submit to the EEOC tend to be based on separate data provided to EEOC offices within particular agencies by human resource bureaus. Often there are several sets of books with different data about the racial composition of an agency's workforce and almost none of this data is filed or reported in ways that allow for the tracking of trends much beyond two years. In studies I did in 1996 and 1997 of two foreign affairs agencies (the Department of State and the U.S. Information Agency), not a single senior policy official was able to recall in interviews the existing level of diversity, recent trends, specific problems cited in the most recent annual accomplishment report submitted to the EEOC, or rate of progress made in achieving a career diplomatic service representative of American society (as called for in the Foreign Service Act of 1980).

This experience leads me to think that information is a key element to raising consciousness about recent trends within and across agencies and that accurate information about diversity is still not getting to selection panels. One specific step that would improve knowledge of what is going on would be to develop a single, integrated, and relational database system for all the career services feeding into the foreign affairs agencies and departments and build in to that data base the capacity to monitor EEOC progress specifically. The resulting report should be disseminated widely and well before promotion panels meet. The background and career history material that selection panels receive about officers

being considered for promotions and assignments also needs to be made both more transparent to the candidate, and they should be given a chance to review their files before the
material in them is provided to selection panels. The panels themselves need to be config-
ured to assure that every one has a person of color included among its members. And
agencies should aim to refresh and broaden the segments of society tapped as public
members for selection panels.

The purpose of these measures is to highlight the extraordinary effort that is still
required to be sure that the talents and interests of all groups in American society are taken
into fuller account in deciding on foreign policies and international priorities. The aim is
to achieve a foreign affairs community of professionals in which no meeting to formulate
a policy or decide on an implementing strategy would be considered complete or likely to
be successful if all the participants looked like me. Over time, adopting such an operational perspective would assure that the special assets minority Americans can bring to
formulating and shaping U.S. foreign policy will emerge because it is in the national interest
and not because it is what a judge has had to order.

A final word about whether or not U.S. foreign policy would be substantially or even
marginally different if greater diversity existed in the foreign affairs agencies and career
services. There is no research yet done (at least to my knowledge) that could confirm the
hypothesis that, when persons of color reach top leadership and decisionmaking positions,
their policies and policy preferences are substantially different than what a white person
might prefer or do. A close reading of the career of General Colin Powell does not suggest
to me that his command decisions were fundamentally different than those made by other
general officers in his cohort. The late Ron Brown's foreign policy activism as Secretary of
Commerce and his global reaching out, similarly, cannot be proved to be a direct function
of his color or even of his life experience. In my government service, I also observed that
the courses of action advocated by Ambassadors Andrew Young and Donald McHenry
with respect to such issues as opening and maintaining a dialogue with the PLO
[Palestinian Liberation Organization] or in taking a hard-headed line in the so-called
North–South Dialogue were grounded in no special considerations other than what would
be in the American interest.

In short, I do not expect that greater diversity will automatically or even necessarily
transform what America does in world affairs. But I cannot help think that U.S. actions
would be better received abroad and our options more effectively evaluated at home if the
councils of those who decide and command were certain to include the most diverse array
of talented Americans possible.

NOTES

1. Equal Employment Opportunity Commission, Office of Federal Operations, *Annual Report on the Employment of Minorities, Women and People with Disabilities in the Federal Government* (Washington, D.C.:
U.S. Government Printing Office, 1997), p. ii. Emphasis added. Ibid., p. 7.
2. Cf. Table 1–8, Ibid., pp. 28–45.
3. K. C. Swanson, "The Discrimination Complaint Process Is a Bureaucratic Maze that Often Punishes the
Innocent and Lets the Guilty Go Free," *Government Executive* (November 1996). p. 46.
4. For a review, see Karen Krebsbach, "Affirmative Action vs. Diversity," *Foreign Service Journal* (August
1996), p. 7, and Francine Modderno, "The Issue of Race, Ethnicity," Ibid. (November 1996), pp. 20–27.
5. See the research summarized in Philip E. Crewson and James F. Guyot, "Sartor Resartus: A Comparative
Analysis of Public and Private Sector Entrant Quality Reanalyzed," *American Journal of Political Science*
41 (July 1997), pp. 1057–1065.

8

The FSO of Tomorrow

MADELINE K. ALBRIGHT

This an edited excerpt of Secretary of State Madeleine K Albright's keynote address at the fiftieth anniversary of the Foreign Service Institute (FSI) on April 9, 1997.

The fundamental purpose of America's foreign policy is to protect our citizens, our territory, and our friends. As we look ahead, and we know that increasingly, this will require an effective response to problems that extend far beyond our borders. To function successfully in this diverse, fast-paced, and rapidly changing environment, we will need women and men trained to deal with the world not as it was, but as it is, and as it will become.

We will need people who can find the needle of information that counts amid the haystack of data that do not. We will need people who can function in partnership with those from elsewhere in our government, in other governments, and from the private sector. We will need people who can think and act globally—because that is what the American interests require. We must try to improve our record of recruiting qualified women and minorities.

Here at FSI, we will need more focused training in issues such as trade, climate change, refugee law, and information management, while maintaining a high standard on cultural studies and language skills. I have asked Deputy Secretary [of State Strobe] Talbott to develop a strategy that will help ensure that FSOs with backgrounds in global issues reach senior levels. While so doing, we cannot and will not ignore the more traditional aspects of diplomacy. We will maintain our focus on key alliances and relationships around the world.

But we also know that, in the future, our FSOs and other professionals will be asked to range far from the bargaining tables and communication centers of our largest embassies. They will be asked to promote a mix of economic, agricultural, and social policies that will ensure greater food security in Africa. They will be visited in factories to ensure that intellectual property and copyright restrictions are being respected. They will be working with public and private sector representatives who are striving to stabilize population growth, prevent complex humanitarian emergencies, and care for the new international homeless-displaced persons and refugees.

And they will be helping to establish police training programs, negotiate extradition agreements, and review bank secrecy laws to combat international crime wherever and in whatever form it appears.

Now there is a theory that advances in information technology have made the State Department obsolete. The State Department personnel are proving every day that the human factor still counts.

Consider what Ambassador [William Lacy] Swing and his team have done to promote human rights in Haiti, what Ambassador [Donald K.] Steinberg has done for the cause of peace in Angola, and what Ambassador [Richard] Holbrooke did in Dayton. We could not claim to be the indispensable country if we did not have indispensable diplomats applying their skills, their contacts, and their dedication every day. Nor have I ever seen a peace process that could be managed by e-mail from Washington.

The same is true for the management of our most effective assistance programs, from fighting desertification in Mali to supporting a regional coalition to save the Aral sea.

And I doubt that the Americans and others who found themselves trapped in Albania a few weeks ago would have traded Ambassador [Marisa] Lino and her country team for CNN's Christiane Annanpour.

Today, the greatest danger to America is not some foreign enemy; it is the possibility that we will ignore the example of the generation that founded FSI; that we will turn inward; neglect the military and diplomatic resources that keep us strong; and forget the fundamental lesson of this century, which is that problems abroad, if left unattended, will all too often come home to America.

9

A House Divided

Racism at the State Department

BRUCE SHAPIRO

One morning in March 1994, telex machines in U.S. State Department offices around the world ignited with a decidedly undiplomatic cable from W. Lewis Anselem, political counselor in the embassy to Bolivia. Anselem's incendiary subject was not U.S. policy toward Bolivia or any other nation. Rather, it was an attack on affirmative action within the ranks of the State Department. Anselem derided "diversity" programs as "contradictory, deceptive, condescending in the extreme." He called dark-skinned State Department workers "unscrupulous race and ethnic jumpers" trying to "con" their way to the top. Attempting to correct racial and gender imbalance, he said, is "repugnant and potentially dangerous."

Anselem (who in an earlier posting had helped cover up Guatemalan military involvement in the rape and torture of Sister Dianna Ortiz; see Allan Nairn, "Murder as Policy," April 24, 1995) was not mounting a rogue attack on affirmative action. Shortly before that cable made the rounds at Foggy Bottom, Secretary of State Warren Christopher had received a more polite letter from Tex Harris, president of the American Foreign Service Association, the professional organization of career State officers, asking him to suspend "diversity" efforts. "A continuation of these actions can only engender further resistance by officers who feel disadvantaged by them," Harris wrote.

The State Department—long a bastion of prep-school patronage where change has come harder and slower than in any other Cabinet-level department—is in the midst of an internal war over racism in its ranks, particularly in the four-thousand-member Foreign Service. The struggle has evolved over decades, but now, thanks in part to decidedly mixed signals from the Clinton White House and Christopher, it has reached a higher and probably decisive pitch. At the same time, a class-action discrimination suit brought a decade ago by black FSOs appears on the verge of a settlement that ironically may leave many of those who sued angry and embittered. The outcome of the battle is likely to influence not only the face of the Foreign Service but the face of foreign policy for years to come.

I am sitting with Walter Thomas and Raymond Robinson in the quiet, expansive bar of the Channel Inn, overlooking a boat basin in the southwest quadrant of Washington, D.C. At this late lunch hour the bar's patrons are all, like Robinson and Thomas, middle-aged African American professionals. The inflexible emotional armor of the careful bureaucrat sets the restaurant's temper. Thomas and Robinson, like everyone else in the room, scarcely raise their voices above a murmur. Yet they are recounting a daily racial humiliation in the workplace that belies that atmosphere of restraint: years spent being shuffled from one low-authority assignment to another while white peers are escorted by patrons up the power track. Fabricated charges of incompetence or malingering by white managers. Outright ostracism at social functions. And finally, retribution for speaking out against such abuses—retribution wrapped in the coded language of negative job evaluations.

Thomas and Robinson joined State during the Carter Administration. Foreign Service officers of any background are rarely combative by nature ("You join the State Department to be part of the establishment, not fight it," Thomas says), and it was only after years of battling for fair treatment within the boundaries of State that in 1986 they went to court, filing a lawsuit that now includes thirty named plaintiffs and seeks compensation for roughly three hundred black present and former Foreign Service officers. After a decade of on-again, off-again negotiations and hearings, they are profoundly worried that this lawsuit is about to be settled out from under them.

To opponents like W. Lewis Anselem, *Thomas v. Christopher*—it started as *Thomas v. Shultz*—is the source of much of today's racial acrimony at State. Since its establishment in the nineteenth century, State reflected an idea of diplomacy born in the imperial courts of Europe as well as Brahmin patronage. Although there was the occasional African American or woman—from Frederick Douglass as Ambassador to Haiti to Shirley Temple Black at the United Nations—State remained the original Old Boys Club. In 1989, a General Accounting Office study found that the eight Ivy League colleges provided more than 40 percent of all senior Foreign Service personnel, and an even higher percentage of nominees to ambassador and other posts requiring Senate confirmation.

The whiteness of State first attracted congressional scrutiny in 1962 with a House labor subcommittee hearing. With the civil rights movement raging at home and the Soviet Union allied with national liberation movements in several African countries, it seemed like a good idea to add a few black faces to represent the United States abroad. At the same time, a growing number of African Americans were graduating from the nation's elite universities, and some looked to State for careers. And finally, the Civil Rights Act of 1964 forced at least token efforts at integration by government agencies.

The handful of black officials who joined the department from those early years through the mid-1970s faced undisguised hostility from many quarters. Terence Todman, born on St. Thomas, joined the Foreign Service in the early 1960s and went on to attain the highest rank of any African American career diplomat—indeed, the highest possible rank in the Foreign Service. He was repeatedly told early in his career that his "accent was not sufficiently American," which he chose to ignore. Ulric Haynes Jr., who joined the Foreign Service in 1963 and served on Lyndon Johnson's National Security Council staff, arrived in 1977 at a July 4 party at the U.S. Embassy in Algeria where he had just been named Ambassador to overhear two diplomats' spouses discussing him: "Have you seen what Washington sent?" Even those white officials who claimed to want change resisted efforts to broaden the department's hiring pool. Todman remembers pressing the director general of the Foreign Service in the late 1960s to hire more minorities and women. "He was really at a loss. Finally he said: 'I'll tell you what. I have a Negro friend who has a son who is going to Yale next year. Maybe we can talk to him about coming on board eventually.'"

When black officials like Todman survived, they found themselves ghettoized: posted, whatever their real expertise, to countries of sub-Saharan Africa or the Caribbean. The explanations varied. Sometimes blacks were told that European racism would make it hard for them to be effective there; sometimes, that black staffing would arouse sympathy in African countries. The result was the same: complete exclusion of African Americans from the State Department's power tracks and policy-making circles. "I am by training an

Arabist," Todman says. "But I was assigned to Togo. Then Guinea. Getting out of Africa was impossible if you were black." In Todman's case, that took a career-risking act of bureaucratic disobedience: After Guinea in the 1970s, he simply refused further African postings. "I kept reminding them that I was qualified to serve anywhere. I will not go back to Africa. If that meant finding a new job, so be it."

In 1973, isolated and embattled, a handful of African American Foreign Service officers began meeting weekly under the innocuous-sounding title of the Thursday Luncheon Group (T.L.G.), at first simply to provide mutual support but then to conceive strategies for improving the situation. The founders of T.L.G., William Davis and Roburt Dumas, recall opposition not only from white officers but from what Davis calls the "B. B.s," or black blockers, who enjoyed their roles as "the F. and O.," the first and only blacks to hold certain high positions. T.L.G. quietly pressed the case for affirmative action, for more varied postings. And its members privately raised more than $2 million to fund minority-recruitment fellowships designed to provide entry-level positions for African Americans and other minorities.

THE BRIEF INTERREGNUM

Jimmy Carter was elected president in 1976, and, through Secretary of State Cyrus Vance, that year turned out to be the great watershed for blacks in the Foreign Service. Vance made shaking up the system a clear priority. He ordered a study that called State an "elitist, self-satisfied, walled-in barony populated by smug white males, an old-boy system in which women and minorities cannot possibly hope to be treated with equity in promotions and senior level responsibilities." He promoted African Americans and women within the bureaucracy to some of its highest offices, including such highly visible posts as Deputy Secretary of State for Inter-American Affairs. He aggressively recruited middle-grade minority officials from outside the department's ranks.

Perhaps most impressive, Vance took blacks out of the diplomatic ghetto. He named fifteen ambassadors—sending Terence Todman, for instance, first to Spain and then to Denmark. Ulric Haynes went to Algeria, others to Romania, East Germany, and Malaysia. "Cy Vance simply ignored channels and went directly to the president," Todman recalls today. "And he would ask the assistant secretaries what was happening with affirmative action and insisted on follow-up. The bureaucracy couldn't believe it." Haynes, who after his stint in Algeria advised Deputy Secretary of State Warren Christopher during the Iranian hostage crisis and is today executive dean of Hofstra University's business school, recalls the Carter Administration as "a time of real decency for blacks at State. And that was practically revolutionary."

It was in this hopeful environment that many young African Americans like Raymond Robinson and Walter Thomas joined the Foreign Service. In Thomas's case, the job was especially welcome. He had arrived at State after years in the Peace Corps that ended after he filed a discrimination complaint against a supervisor. An equal opportunity investigation had found in his favor, but Thomas found the atmosphere in the Peace Corps so poisoned he decided to head to State.

Thomas's hopes for an end to discrimination were quickly dashed. First, when the State Department's security people found out he had filed an equal opportunity complaint at the Peace Corps, he was suddenly required to submit to a psychiatric examination—even though he had already passed a physical and been recommended for clearance. ("I guess I should have got the message," he says now with wry anger. "If you file a discrimination complaint you must be crazy.") So blatant was the racial bias that the department's psychiatrist refused to cooperate. Congressman Joe Moakley, who represented Thomas's home district, went so far as to vent his outrage over the case in the *Congressional Record*. "Mr. Thomas pursued all the avenues of appeal Congress has opened to protect federal employees from racism. Yet men in the Department of State, who consider those who fight for their rights troublemakers, have devised a covert system for thwarting the will of Congress and the president."

A few years later, posted as a consular official in Antigua, Thomas was faced with a supervisor who wanted to replace him with a white crony. First, Thomas found himself assigned to housing far inferior to that of his white colleagues. Then the supervisor wrote a harsh evaluation of Thomas, accusing him of mishandling embassy affairs that the mission's reputation was damaged all over the island. Thomas decided not to take the evaluation sitting down. He rounded up letters from a host of Antigua officials—the small island's Interior Minister, its bishop, business leaders—defending his record and denying any knowledge of the problems described in the evaluation. With these in hand, he sought a hearing with State's equal opportunity office, which found in his favor. Today, Thomas insists on providing backup documentation for these stories. "It's happened so often I know I run the risk of sounding paranoid."

But, although he fought back, by the mid-1980s Thomas's clock at State was ticking down. The Foreign Service, like the military's officer corps, works on an "up or out" system: Those passed over for promotion are not just denied raises, they are "selected out," or forced to retire. And promotion, in turn, rides on evaluations by the very white supervisors who most want to preserve the status quo. "I have seen the pattern over and over again," Todman says. "There is a fine art to these evaluations. Those of black officers are routinely couched in carefully negative language—not too negative, mind you, lest there seem an ulterior motive. But the signals are there."

The Reagan/Bush years were difficult for the prospects of blacks at State. The number of African American ambassadors fell from fifteen to five. Aside from the controversial appointment of Edward Perkins as Ambassador to apartheid South Africa (a job Todman had refused because he felt he could not defend Reagan's South Africa policy), all were to postings for which "marginal" is a generous adjective: Mauritius, the Seychelles, Sierra Leone. Even Clarence Thomas, as head of the EEOC, wrote a 1987 report highly critical of the State Department's affirmative action efforts.

In 1989 an investigation by the House Subcommittee on the Civil Service found that minorities in the Foreign Service were denied tenure at a radically higher rate than whites, with black men "selected out" at roughly six times the rate of whites. Subcommittee chairman Gerry Sikorski declared the State Department "dramatically out of compliance" with civil rights laws. Secretary of State George Shultz did fire off a thirty-two-point affirmative action policy cable in 1986. But according to a report released last September by the General Accounting Office, the percentage of African Americans in the Foreign Service's crucial middle ranks—tenured officials poised for promotion to senior positions—declined between 1984 and 1992.

In this atmosphere, Thomas, Robinson, and other black FSOs finally despaired of change from within the department. In 1986 they went to the Lawyers Committee for Civil Rights, whose legal director, Joseph Sellers, has handled dozens of high-profile discrimination cases. Sellers, in turn, convinced one of the nation's most prestigious law firms, Akin, Grump, Strauss, Hauer, and Feld—among whose partners are well-connected influence-peddlers of both parties—to provide the legal legwork. Evenutally, twenty-nine others signed on to the suit, which claimed the State Department systematically discriminated in employment, assignment, and promotion. And they asked the federal courts to make it a class action on behalf of some three hundred present and former African American Foreign Service officers denied pay and promotion over a generation.

Knowing that discrimination exists and proving it are two different things. That's particularly true at an agency like State, in which the entire culture of the Foreign Service is one of educated obfuscation. (Indeed, in 1972 a female officer named Alison Palmer filed a sex-discrimination suit against the department. By 1976 she had won but State refused to change its policies; she and other women filed a second suit, finally resolved only two years ago.) Despite the occasional Anselem memo or Thomas investigation, the department's record on race has hinged on the former nuances of a bureaucratic system.

The linchpin for the State's institutional apartheid is the division of all jobs in the Foreign Service into broad categories of jobs called "cones." There is the "political" cone, the "economic" cone, the "administrative" cone, and the "consular" cone. Officers are assigned to cones after entering the Foreign Service and then rarely change through their entire careers. The department's higher policy-making ranks are drawn almost entirely from the political and economic categories; those in the consular and administrative cones are treated, essentially, as career paper-pushers. Repeated congressional investigations through the 1980s proved conclusively that African Americans and women were assigned in radically disproportionate numbers to the consular and administrative cones—assignments having nothing to do with their objective qualifications. Even more controversial is the matter of promotions—particularly given the State Department's "up or out" policy. A statistical analysis by the plaintiffs in the Thomas case shows that whites are promoted at a rate six times higher than African Americans, which means that dozens of black officers lost their jobs because they were not promoted.

One thing is certain: This tradition of discrimination has persisted more stubbornly at State than at any other federal department. The September G.A.O. report looked at the four departments with the poorest records on minority and female employment—State, Interior, the Navy, and Agriculture. In several key categories, State showed the least improvement over the past decade. Terence Todman says State's officials managed to evade affirmative action for so long in part by covering up the depth of the problem. "We are talking here about people who have a long track record of cooking the books to avoid the necessity of change." And he adds that the department's own equal opportunity office "has never had rank or status or authority." The G.A.O. report suggested a similar conclusion when it pointed out in a footnote that State has not kept figures—which every other department requires—for minority representation in "key jobs," an important measure of progress.

State's resistance to change earned harsh criticism from Federal Judge Stanley Sporkin, who is presiding in the Thomas discrimination case. "The arrogance of your office is beyond belief," he boomed at State Department lawyers two years ago. "Eight years is unbelievable. It's a disgrace, absolute disgrace. . . . You reject every type of proposal, everything, and it just isn't right." Sporkin has urged the department to settle the case.

A SIGNAL TO THE WORLD

The Clinton Administration seemed to promise a revival of Carter-era hope for blacks at State. Clifton Wharton, former chancellor of the State University of New York, was named Warren Christopher's top deputy. George Moose, a career Foreign Service officer, became Assistant Secretary of State for African Affairs, while an attorney, Conrad Harper, was named the department's legal adviser. Mario Baeza, a black Cuban-American, was named Assistant Secretary of State for Inter-American Affairs.

However, by the middle of last year, the atmosphere had soured. Christopher made Wharton a scapegoat for early policy failures in Bosnia and elsewhere. Clinton dropped the Baeza nomination after pressure from the Miami Cuban lobby. Moose was reportedly cut out of key decisions on Somalia. Symbolically, Clinton has retreated to the pre-Carter days: All but one of his fifteen appointments of African American ambassadors have been to sub-Saharan or Caribbean nations.

To some black State alumni, the Administration's lack of respect was crystallized last May when invitations went out to the department's first-ever reception honoring black ambassadors, named for Frederick Douglass. It was held not in one of State's elegant diplomatic reception rooms but in the public "exhibit hall," which led Ulric Haynes to write tartly to Christopher that attending meant "allowing myself to be used as just another 'exhibit' to cover up a problem that cries out for an immediate and permanent solution."

Ironically, these failures occur at a time when within State itself officials like Harper and Under Secretary for Management Richard Moose (no relation to George) have raised the hackles of white officers with blunt declarations of the need for greater diversity. "It just doesn't do to walk into a bureau and to see no one or only one person who looks like me," Harper told State's in-house employee magazine in early 1994. Christopher is "deeply committed to diversity," Harper told me. Starting last year Moose began hiring Foreign Service officers who had never taken the department's qualifying exam, which white candidates have historically passed in numbers vastly disproportionate to blacks. The department established a minority fellowship program modeled on the Reserve Office Training Corps (R.O.T.C.)—full-tuition scholarships in return for ten years in the Foreign Service. It was such efforts that roused the ire of Anselem and other white officers—including one David Catlin Pierce, who in 1994 filed a still-pending reverse-discrimination claim after he was passed over for a succession of jobs. Is such resistance simple racism? Tex Harris of the American Foreign Service Association explains it this way: "We are absolutely not talking about racism here. What we are talking about are contradictory standards that are quite destructive of morale."

Whether because of that effort or because of Judge Sporkin's angry prodding, in the spring of 1994 State's lawyers suddenly seemed ready to settle the Thomas case. "For the first time in a decade, they asked us what we wanted," recalls attorney Joe Sellers. "And then they came back with probably 85 percent of what we could have got at trial, which would have taken years longer."

But when Walter Thomas and the case's original plaintiffs took a look at the proposed deal early last year, they were stunned. It would offer pay raises to some black officers currently in the department whose promotions had been delayed but only token sums to people like Thomas who had been selected out years ago when they failed to be promoted at all. Any who wanted to have their jobs reinstated would have to apply before a personnel board. "I just felt the breath go out of me," Thomas says today. Raymond Robinson is more coldly analytic. "In a very real way, this settlement would reward those officers who slept with the department while leaving those who fought back with little."

The group of thirty plaintiffs voted by a two-to-one margin to reject the settlement—producing an awkward dispute between them and the lawyers. Their sense of betrayal by Sellers and Akin, Gump was only heightened earlier this year when similar divisions emerged among women Sellers represented at the CIA. There, too, a settlement to a class-action discrimination suit seemed to leave the women who had originally signed on as plaintiffs out in the cold—so much so that several agents voiced their anger in press interviews. Thomas and others began wondering if Sellers, who had been prominently mentioned as a nominee for various Administration jobs, was settling the case out of self-interest—or if Akin, Gump's Clinton connections had led to a sellout.

The conflict burst into public view on July 11, when Sellers and the attorneys working with him went to Judge Sporkin and asked that he approve the settlement. When Thomas rose and spoke of his concerns, Sporkin raised an eyebrow. "How can you speak in favor of it if your clients don't want it?" he asked the lawyers.

Sellers himself finds the conflict "sad and unfortunate. Thomas and the others took an enormous amount of risk. They want full vindication, and that is understandable. But it is hard to imagine a scenario in which they would get more than this." And he points out that while the 1991 Civil Rights Act allows for compensatory damages, the Supreme Court in 1994 refused to award such damages in cases predating that law.

The settlement is probably more a civil rights tragedy than conscious sellout. Nothing in the canons of ethics would prevent Sellers from staying with the case while being considered for an Administration job—and as he points out, at the height of that consideration in 1993 he won the largest settlement ever against a government agency, $4 million from the Labor Department. It is not unusual for large class-action settlements to be in the interests of the larger group but to leave original plaintiffs behind to some extent. Even Judge Sporkin warned Walter Thomas against "falling in love with your case." Negotiations, in any event, continue—now among three sides.

On one level, the story of discrimination at the State Department is a matter of individual careers shattered, like Walter Thomas's, or left in frustrating limbo, like Raymond Robinson's, who over the past five years has been shuffled between a variety of temporary administrative jobs at Foggy Bottom. On another, it is the story of a whole cluster of ambitious African American professionals.

It also has broader implications for foreign policy. "The marginalization of African Americans in the Foreign Service," says Ulric Haynes, "is part and parcel of this country's problems in dealing with dark-skinned people around the world." Randall Robinson, president of TransAfrica, an advocacy group for African and Caribbean issues, sees the issue in stark terms. "When you treat Africa or the Caribbean as a ghetto for your least-desired employees," he points out, "you are also in a sense pushing whole countries and peoples to the margins of consciousness." Such marginalization can lead to foreign policy disasters. Somalia is one example; the execution of Ken Saro-Wiwa in Nigeria, which caught the Clinton Administration off guard, is another.

Terence Todman puts the implications of State's historic institutional racism this way: "When you create a ghetto that is so visible, it actually raised credibility questions in other countries when you talk about human rights. And when State ranks both employees and countries on the basis of color, it is ignoring the fact that color is generally not the dominant factor in politics around the world. This makes for bad policy."

Section 4

The Politics of Multiculturalism in International Affairs

Shain and Uslaner both point out that the policies and strategies of foreign affairs flow from people other than elites within the State Department or the corporate sector. They also flow from interest groups beyond the Washington, D.C. Beltway that, in the classic American pattern, seek to influence institutional outcomes they judge to be important for their own group. These authors point to the channels, the motives, and the consequences of these pressures.

Not surprisingly, in diverse multicultural societies, ethnic groups, like other groups based on occupation, geography, or ideology, organize to make their views on foreign affairs known. Shain makes the telling point that minority groups such as African Americans and Arab Americans are experiencing a process of social inclusion, moving from the periphery of American politics to greater integration. This process results in a movement from protest activities to greater participation in the design and conduct of foreign affairs from within the halls of Congress, the Commerce Department, and the State Department.

On the other hand, Huntington is skeptical about the benefits of the policy of diversity promotion. He criticizes what he sees as the "balkanization" of American foreign policy through the appointment of too many minorities to responsibilities in their regions of ethnic origin, and the leverage that region-specific lobbies impose on policy coherence.

10

The Erosion of American National Interest

The Disintegration of Identity

SAMUEL P. HUNTINGTON

The years since the end of the Cold War have seen intense, wide-ranging, and confused debates about American national interests. Much of this confusion stems from the complexity of the post–Cold War world. The new environment has been variously interpreted as involving the end of history, bipolar conflict between rich and poor countries, movement back to a future of traditional power politics, the proliferation of ethnic conflict verging on anarchy, the clash of civilizations, and conflicting trends toward integration and fragmentation. The new world is all these things, and hence there is good reason for uncertainty about American interests in it. Yet that is not the only source of confusion. Efforts to define national interest presuppose agreement on the nature of the country whose interests are to be defined. National interest derives from national identity. We have to know who we are before we can know what our interests are.

Historically, American identity has had two primary components: culture and creed. The first has been the values and institutions of the original settlers, who were Northern European, primarily British, and Christian, primarily Protestant. This culture included, most importantly, the English language and traditions concerning relations between church and state and the place of the individual in society. Over the course of three centuries, black people were slowly and only partially assimilated into this culture. Immigrants from Western, Southern, and Eastern Europe were more fully assimilated, and the original culture evolved and was modified but not fundamentally altered as a result. In *The Next American Nation,* Michael Lind captures the broad outlines of this evolution when he argues that American culture developed through three phases: Anglo-America (1789–1861), Euro-America (1875–1957), and Multicultural America (1972–present). The cultural definition of national identity assumes that, while the culture may change, it has a basic continuity.

The second component of American identity has been a set of universal ideas and principles articulated in the founding documents by American leaders: liberty, equality, democracy, constitutionalism, liberalism, limited government, private enterprise. These constitute what Gunnar Myrdal termed the American Creed, and the popular consensus on them has been commented on by foreign observers from Crevecoeur and Tocqueville down to the present. This identity was neatly summed up by Richard Hofstadter: "It has been our fate as a nation not to have ideologies but to be one."

These dual sources of identity are, of course, closely related. The creed was a product of the culture. Now, however, the end of the Cold War and social, intellectual, and demographic changes in American society have brought into question the validity and relevance of both traditional components of American identity. Without a sure sense of national identity, Americans have become unable to define their national interests, and as a result subnational commercial interests and transnational and nonnational ethnic interests have come to dominate foreign policy.

LOSS OF THE OTHER

The most profound question concerning the American role in the post–Cold War world was improbably posed by Rabbit Angstrom, the harried central character of John Updike's novels: "Without the Cold War, what's the point of being an American?" If being an American means being committed to the principles of liberty, democracy, individualism, and private property, and if there is no evil empire out there threatening those principles, what indeed does it mean to be an American, and what becomes of American national interests?

From the start, Americans have constructed their creedal identity in contrast to an undesirable "other." America's opponents are always defined as liberty's opponents. At the time of independence, Americans could not distinguish themselves culturally from Britain; hence they had to do so politically. Britain embodied tyranny, aristocracy, oppression; America, democracy, equality, republicanism. Until the end of the nineteenth century, the United States defined itself in opposition to Europe. Europe was the past: backward, unfree, unequal, characterized by feudalism, monarchy, imperialism. The United States, in contrast, was the future: progressive, free, equal, republican. In the twentieth century, the United States emerged on the world scene and increasingly saw itself not as the antithesis of Europe but rather as the leader of European American civilization against upstart challengers to that civilization, imperial and then Nazi Germany.

After World War II, the United States defined itself as the leader of the democratic free world against the Soviet Union and world communism. During the Cold War, the United States pursued many foreign policy goals, but its one overriding national purpose was to contain and defeat communism. When other goals and interests clashed with this purpose, they were usually subordinated to it. For forty years, virtually all the great American initiatives in foreign policy, as well as many in domestic policy, were justified by this overriding priority: the Greek-Turkish aid program, the Marshall Plan, NATO, the Korean War, nuclear weapons and strategic missiles, foreign aid, intelligence operations, reduction of trade barriers, the space program, the Alliance for Progress, military alliances with Japan and Korea, support for Israel, overseas military deployments, an unprecedentedly large military establishment, the Vietnam War, the openings to China, and support for the Afghan mujahideen and other anticommunist insurgencies. If there is no Cold War, the rationale for major programs and initiatives like these disappears.

As the Cold War wound down in the late 1980s, Gorbachev's adviser Georgiy Arbatov commented: "We are doing something really terrible to you—we are depriving you of an enemy." Psychologists generally agree that individuals and groups define their identity by differentiating themselves from and placing themselves in opposition to others.[1] While wars at times may have a divisive effect on society, a common enemy can often help to promote identity and cohesion among people. The weakening or absence of a common enemy can do just the reverse. Abraham Lincoln commented on this effect in his Lyceum speech in 1837 when he argued that the American Revolution and its aftermath had directed enmity outward: "The jealousy, envy, avarice incident to our nature, and so common to a state of peace, prosperity, and conscious strength, were for a time in a great measure smothered and rendered inactive, while the deep-rooted principles of hate, and the powerful motive of revenge, instead of being turned against each other, were directed exclusively against the British nation." Hence, he said, "the basest principles of our nature" were either dormant or "the active agents in the advancement of the noblest of causes—that of establishing and maintaining civil and religious liberty." But, he warned, "this state of feeling must fade, is fading, has faded, with the circumstances that produced it." He spoke, of course, as the nation was starting to disintegrate. As the heritage of World War II and the Cold War fades, America may be faced with a comparable dynamic.

The Cold War fostered a common identity between American people and government. Its end is likely to weaken or at least alter that identity. One possible consequence is the rising opposition to the federal government, which is, after all, the principal institutional manifestation of American national identity and unity. Would nationalist fanatics bomb federal buildings and attack federal agents if the federal government was still defending the country against a serious foreign threat? Would the militia movement be as strong as it is today? In the past, comparable bombing attacks were usually the work of foreigners who saw the United States as their enemy, and the first response of many people to the Oklahoma City bombing was to assume that it was the work of a "new enemy," Muslim terrorists. That response could reflect a psychological need to believe that such an act must have been carried out by an external enemy. Ironically, the bombing may have been in part the result of the absence of such an enemy.

Georg Simmel, Lewis A. Coser, and other scholars have shown that in some ways and circumstances the existence of an enemy may have positive consequences for group cohesion, morale, and achievement. World War II and the Cold War were responsible for much American economic, technological, and social progress, and the perceived economic challenge from Japan in the 1980s generated public and private efforts to increase American productivity and competitiveness. At present, thanks to the extent to which democracy and market economies have been embraced throughout the world, the United States lacks any single country or threat against which it can convincingly counterpose itself. Saddam Hussein simply does not suffice as a foil. Islamic fundamentalism is too diffuse and too remote geographically. China is too problematic and its potential dangers too distant in the future.

Given the domestic forces pushing toward heterogeneity, diversity, multiculturalism, and ethnic and racial division, however, the United States, perhaps more than most countries, may need an opposing other to maintain its unity. Two millennia ago in 84 B.C., after the Romans had completed their conquest of the known world by defeating the armies of Mithradates, Sulla posed the question: "Now the universe offers us no more enemies, what may be the fate of the Republic?" The answer came quickly; the republic collapsed a few years later. It is unlikely that a similar fate awaits the United States, yet to what extent will the American Creed retain its appeal, command support, and stay vibrant in the absence of competing ideologies? The end of history, the global victory of democracy, if it occurs, could be a most traumatic and unsettling event for America.

IDEOLOGIES OF DIVERSITY

The disintegrative effects of the end of the Cold War have been reinforced by the interaction of two trends in American society: changes in the scope and sources of immigration and the rise of the cult of multiculturalism.

Immigration, legal and illegal, has increased dramatically since the immigration laws were changed in 1965. Recent immigration is overwhelmingly from Latin America and

Asia. Coupled with the high birthrates of some immigrant groups, it is changing the racial, religious, and ethnic makeup of the United States. By the middle of the next century, according to the Census Bureau, non-Hispanic whites will have dropped from more than three-quarters of the population to only slightly more than half, and one-quarter of Americans will be Hispanic, 14 percent black, and 8 percent of Asian and Pacific heritage. The religious balance is also shifting, with Muslims already reportedly outnumbering Episcopalians.

In the past, assimilation, American style, in Peter Salins's phrase, involved an implicit contract in which immigrants were welcomed as equal members of the national community and urged to become citizens, provided they accepted English as the national language and committed themselves to the principles of the American Creed and the Protestant work ethic.[2] In return, immigrants could be as ethnic as they wished in their homes and local communities. At times, particularly during the great waves of Irish immigration in the 1840s and 1850s and of the Southern and Eastern European immigration at the turn of the century, immigrants were discriminated against and simultaneously subjected to major programs of "Americanization" to incorporate them into the national culture and society. Overall, however, assimilation American style worked well. Immigration renewed American society; assimilation preserved American culture.

Past worries about the assimilation of immigrants have proved unfounded. Until recently immigrant groups came to America because they saw immigration as an opportunity to become American. To what extent now, however, do people come because they see it as an opportunity to remain themselves? Previously, immigrants felt discriminated against if they were not permitted to join the mainstream. Now it appears that some groups feel discriminated against if they are not allowed to remain apart from the mainstream.

The ideologies of multiculturalism and diversity reinforce and legitimate these trends. They deny the existence of a common culture in the United States, denounce assimilation, and promote the primacy of racial, ethnic, and other subnational cultural identities and groupings. They also question a central element in the American Creed by substituting for the rights of individuals the rights of groups, defined largely in terms of race, ethnicity, gender, and sexual preference. These goals were manifested in a variety of statutes that followed the civil rights acts of the 1960s, and in the 1990s, the Clinton administration made the encouragement of diversity one of its major goals.

The contrast with the past is striking. The Founding Fathers saw diversity as a reality and a problem: hence the national motto, e pluribus unum. Later political leaders, also fearful of the dangers of racial, sectional, ethnic, economic, and cultural diversity (which, indeed, produced the biggest war of the century between 1815 and), responded to the need to bring us together, and made the promotion of national unity their central responsibility. "The one absolutely certain way of bringing this nation to ruin, of preventing all possibility of its continuing as a nation at all," warned Theodore Roosevelt, "would be to permit it to become a tangle of squabbling nationalities."[3] Bill Clinton, in contrast, is almost certainly the first president to promote the diversity rather than the unity of the country he leads. This promotion of ethnic and racial identities means that recent immigrants are not subject to the same pressures and inducements as previous immigrants to integrate themselves into American culture. As a result, ethnic identities are becoming more meaningful and appear to be increasing in relevance compared with national identity.

If the United States becomes truly multicultural, American identity and unity will depend on a continuing consensus on political ideology. Americans have thought of their commitment to universal values such as liberty and equality as a great source of national strength. That ideology, Myrdal observed, has been "the cement in the structure of this great and disparate nation." Without an underlying common culture, however, these principles are a fragile basis for national unity. As theories of cognitive dissonance suggest, people can change their ideas and beliefs relatively quickly and easily in response to a changed external environment. Throughout the formerly communist world, elites have redefined themselves as devoted democrats, free marketeers, or fervent nationalists.

For most countries, ideology bears little relation to national identity. China has survived the collapse of many dynasties and will survive the collapse of communism. Absent communism, China will still be China. Britain, France, Japan, Germany, and other countries have survived various dominant ideologies in their history. But could the United States survive the end of its political ideology? The fate of the Soviet Union offers a sobering example for Americans. The United States and the Soviet Union were very different, but they also resembled each other in that neither was a nation-state in the classic sense of the term. In considerable measure, each defined itself in terms of an ideology, which, as the Soviet example suggests, is likely to be a much more fragile basis for unity than a national culture richly grounded in history. If multiculturalism prevails and if the consensus on liberal democracy disintegrates, the United States could join the Soviet Union on the ash heap of history.

IN SEARCH OF NATIONAL INTERESTS

A national interest is a public good of concern to all or most Americans; a vital national interest is one that they are willing to expend blood and treasure to defend. National interests usually combine security and material concerns, on the one hand, and moral and ethical concerns, on the other. Military action against Saddam Hussein was seen as a vital national interest because he threatened reliable and inexpensive access to Persian Gulf oil and because he was a rapacious dictator who had blatantly invaded and annexed another country. During the Cold War the Soviet Union and communism were perceived as threats to both American security and American values; a happy coincidence existed between the demands of power politics and the demands of morality. Hence broad public support buttressed government efforts to defeat communism and thus, in Walter Lippmann's terms, to maintain a balance between capabilities and commitments. That balance was often tenuous and arguably got skewed in the 1970s. With the end of the Cold War, however, the danger of a "Lippmann gap" vanished, and instead the United States appears to have a Lippmann surplus. Now the need is not to find the power to serve American purposes but, rather, to find purposes for the use of American power.

This need has led the American foreign policy establishment to search frantically for new purposes that would justify a continuing U.S. role in world affairs comparable to that in the Cold War. The Commission on America's National Interests put the problem this way in 1996: "After four decades of unusual single-mindedness in containing Soviet Communist expansion, we have seen five years of ad hoc fits and starts. If it continues, this drift will threaten our values, our fortunes, and indeed our lives."[4]

The commission identified five vital national interests: prevent attacks on the United States with weapons of mass destruction; prevent the emergence of hostile hegemons in Europe or Asia and of hostile powers on U.S. borders or in control of the seas; prevent the collapse of the global systems for trade, financial markets, energy supplies, and the environment; and ensure the survival of U.S. allies.

What, however, are the threats to these interests? Nuclear terrorism against the United States could be a near-term threat, and the emergence of China as an East Asian hegemon could be a longer-term one. Apart from these, however, it is hard to see any major looming challenges to the commission's vital *interests*. New threats will undoubtedly arise, but given the scarcity of current ones, campaigns to arouse *interest* in *foreign affairs* and support for major *foreign* policy initiatives now fall on deaf ears. The administration's call for the "enlargement" of democracy does not resonate with the public and is belied by the administration's own actions. Arguments from neoconservatives for big increases in defense spending have the same air of unreality that arguments for the abolition of nuclear weapons had during the Cold War.

The argument is frequently made that *American* "leadership" is needed to deal with world problems. Often it is. The call for leadership, however, begs the question of leadership to do what, and rests on the assumption that the world's problems are America's problems. Often they are not. The fact that things are going wrong in many places in the world is unfortunate, but it does not mean that the United States has either an *interest* in or the responsibility for correcting them. The *National Interests* Commission said that presidential leadership is necessary to create a consensus on *national interests*. In some measure, however, a consensus already exists that *American national interests* do not warrant extensive *American* involvement in most problems in most of the world. The *foreign* policy establishment is asking the president to make a case for a cause that simply will not sell. The most striking feature of the search for *national interests* has been its failure to generate purposes that command anything remotely resembling broad support and to which people are willing to commit significant resources.

COMMERCIALISM AND ETHNICITY

The lack of national interests that command widespread support does not imply a return to isolationism. America remains involved in the world, but its involvement is now directed at commercial and ethnic interests rather than national interests. Economic and ethnic particularism define the current American role in the world. The institutions and capabilities—political, military, economic, intelligence—created to serve a grand national purpose in the Cold War are now being suborned and redirected to serve narrow subnational, transnational, and even nonnational purposes. Increasingly people are arguing that these are precisely the interests foreign policy should serve.

The Clinton administration has given priority to "commercial diplomacy," making the promotion of American exports a primary foreign policy objective. It has been successful in bringing access to some foreign markets for American products. Commercial achievements have become a primary criterion for judging the performance of American ambassadors. President Clinton may well be spending more time promoting American sales abroad than doing anything else in foreign affairs. If so, that would be a dramatic sign of the redirection of American foreign policy. In case after case, country after country, the dictates of commercialism have prevailed over other purposes including human rights, democracy, alliance relationships, maintaining the balance of power, technology export controls, and other strategic and political considerations described by one administration official as "stratocrap and globaloney."[5] "Many in the administration, Congress, and the broader foreign policy community," a former senior official in the Clinton Commerce Department argued in these pages [*Foreign Affairs* journal], "still believe that commercial policy is a tool of foreign policy, when it should more often be the other way around—the United States should use all its foreign policy levers to achieve commercial goals." The funds devoted to promoting commercial goals should be greatly increased; the personnel working on these goals should be upgraded and professionalized; the agencies concerned with export promotion need to be strengthened and reorganized. Landing the contract is the name of the game in foreign policy.

Or at least it is the name of one game. The other game is the promotion of ethnic interests. While economic interests are usually subnational, ethnic interests are generally transnational or nonnational. The promotion of particular businesses and industries may not involve a broad public good, as does a general reduction in trade barriers, but it does promote the interests of some Americans. Ethnic groups promote the interests of people and entities outside the United States. Boeing has an interest in aircraft sales and the Polish American Congress in help for Poland, but the former benefits residents of Seattle, the latter residents of the Eastern Europe.

The growing role of ethnic groups in shaping American foreign policy is reinforced by the waves of recent immigration and by the arguments for diversity and multiculturalism. In addition, the greater wealth of ethnic communities and the dramatic improvements in communications and transportation now make it much easier for ethnic groups to remain in touch with their home countries. As a result, these groups are being transformed from cultural communities within the boundaries of a state into diasporas that transcend these boundaries. State-based diasporas, that is, trans-state cultural communities that control at least one state, are increasingly important and increasingly identify with the interests of their homeland. "Full assimilation into their host societies," a leading expert, Gabriel Sheffer, has observed in Survival, "has become unfashionable among both established and incipient state-based diasporas ... many diasporal communities neither confront overwhelming pressure to assimilate nor feel any marked advantage in assimilating into their host societies or even obtaining citizenship there." Because the United States is the premier immigrant country in the world, it is most affected by the shifts from assimilation to diversity and from ethnic group to diaspora.

During the Cold War, immigrants and refugees from communist countries usually vigorously opposed, for political and ideological reasons, the governments of their home countries and actively supported American anticommunist policies against them. Now, diasporas in the United States support their home governments. Products of the Cold War, Cuban Americans ardently support U.S. anti-Castro policies. Chinese Americans, by contrast, overwhelmingly pressure the United States to adopt favorable policies toward China. Culture has supplanted ideology in shaping attitudes in diaspora populations.

Diasporas provide many benefits to their home countries. Economically prosperous diasporas furnish major financial support to the homeland, Jewish Americans, for instance, contributing up to $1 billion a year to Israel. Armenian Americans send enough to earn Armenia the sobriquet of "the Israel of the Caucasus." Diasporas supply expertise, military recruits, and on occasion political leadership to the homeland. They often pressure their home governments to adopt more nationalist and assertive policies toward neighboring countries. Recent cases in the United States show that they can be a source of spies used to gather information for their homeland governments.

Most important, diasporas can influence the actions and policies of their host country and coopt its resources and influence to serve the interests of their homeland. Ethnic groups have played active roles in politics throughout American history. Now, ethnic diaspora groups proliferate, are more active, and have greater self-consciousness, legitimacy, and political clout. In recent years, diasporas have had a major impact on American policy toward Greece and Turkey, the Caucasus, the recognition of Macedonia, support for Croatia, sanctions against South Africa, aid for black Africa, intervention in Haiti, NATO expansion, sanctions against Cuba, the controversy in Northern Ireland, and the relations between Israel and its neighbors. Diaspora-based policies may at times coincide with broader national interests, as could arguably be the case with NATO expansion, but they are also often pursued at the expense of broader interests and American relations with long-standing allies. Overall, as James R. Schlesinger observed in a 1997 lecture at the Center for Strategic and International Studies, the United States has "less of a foreign policy in a traditional sense of a great power than we have the stapling together of a series of goals put forth by domestic constituency groups.... The result is that American foreign policy is incoherent. It is scarcely what one would expect from the leading world power."

Schlesinger had to recognize, however, that multiculturalism and heightened ethnic consciousness have caused many political leaders to believe this is "the appropriate way to make foreign policy." In the scholarly community, some argue that diasporas can help promote American values in their home countries and hence "the participation of ethnic diasporas in shaping U.S. foreign policy is a truly positive phenomenon."[6] The validity of diaspora interests was a central theme at a May 1996 conference on "Defining the National Interest: Minorities and U.S. Foreign Policy in the 21st Century." Conference participants attacked the Cold War definition of national interest and what was described as "the traditional policy community's apparent animosity toward the very idea of minority involvement in international affairs." Conferees explored "the experiences of Jewish-Americans and Cuban-Americans and sought to extract lessons from the way these two groups succeeded in influencing foreign policy while others failed." The sponsorship of this conference by the New York Council on Foreign Relations, once the capstone institution of the foreign policy establishment, was the ultimate symbol of the triumph of diaspora interests over national interests in American foreign policy.

The displacement of national interests by commercial and ethnic interests reflects the domesticization of foreign policy. Domestic politics and interests have always inevitably and appropriately influenced foreign policy. Now, however, previous assumptions that the foreign and domestic policymaking processes differ from each other for important reasons no longer hold. For an understanding of American foreign policy, it is necessary to study not the interests of the American state in a world of competing states but, rather, the play of economic and ethnic interests in American domestic politics. At least in recent years, the latter has been a superb predictor of foreign policy stands. Foreign policy, in the sense of actions consciously designed to promote the interests of the United States as a collective entity in relation to similar collective entities, is slowly but steadily disappearing.

THE PUSH AND PULL OF *AMERICAN* POWER

A decade after the end of the Cold War, a paradox exists with respect to American power. On the one hand, the United States is the only superpower in the world. It has the largest economy and the highest levels of prosperity. Its political and economic principles are increasingly endorsed throughout the world. It spends more on defense than all the other major powers combined and has the only military force capable of acting effectively in almost every part of the world. It is far ahead of any other country in technology and appears certain to retain that lead in the foreseeable future. American popular culture and consumer products have swept the world, permeating the most distant and resistant societies. American economic, ideological, military, technological, and cultural primacy, in short, is overwhelming.

American influence, on the other hand, falls far short of that. Countries large and small, rich and poor, friendly and antagonistic, democratic and authoritarian, all seem able to resist the blandishments and threats of American policymakers. On issues of protectionism, sanctions, intervention, human rights, proliferation of weapons of mass destruction, peacekeeping, and others, officials of foreign governments listen politely to American demands and entreaties, perhaps express general agreement with the ideas advanced, and then quietly go their own way. This tendency "to follow their own counsels," Jonathan Clarke observed in Foreign Policy in 1996, "includes both great and small nations. Defying intense American pressure in 1994, tiny Singapore proceeded to cane an American teenager. Bankrupt, isolated Cuba has successfully changed American immigration policy. Poland has defied American requests not to proceed with an arms deal with Iran. Jordan has resisted American pressure to break off commercial links with Iraq.... China has rebuffed American demands on human rights." The United States has been unable to achieve its goals on trade policy with China and Japan, unable to induce Russia to restrain arms and technology transfers to China and Iran, unable to get rid of Saddam Hussein, Castro, and Qaddafi, unable to pressure Israelis and Palestinians to be more accommodating with each other, unable to induce Serbs, Croats, and Muslims to cooperate meaningfully in Bosnia, unable to secure significant economic reform in Japan. The United States still clearly is able to veto any major international action, but its ability to induce other countries to act in the way it thinks they should act is hardly commensurate with its image as the "world's only superpower."

What explains this apparent gap between the extent of American power and the ineffectiveness of American influence? In part, the gap is a result of comparing the resources of a country with the strength of its government. Historically the United States has been a strong country with a weak government.[7] Apart from the military, most of the resources cited as evidence of American power are not easily subject to the control of the American government. Although its economy is the largest in the world, national government revenues are a smaller proportion of GNP (19.7 percent in 1993) than in all but two (Japan, Switzerland) of twenty-four high income countries. Similarly, the demands of the American government are not strengthened by the popularity of *Baywatch* and rap music. During the Cold War, major technological advances were in large part a product of the Department of Defense and its requirements. Now the military establishment is increasingly dependent on technological developments in the private sector. Antigovernmentalism is a pervasive theme in the American Creed and is not easily overcome in the absence of a foreign enemy. The impetus to balance the budget leads to major cutbacks in key elements of foreign affairs spending.

A second related explanation for the gap between resources and influence stems from the changing nature of American power. The United States is and will remain a global hegemon. The nature of that dominant role, however, is changing, as it changed for other hegemonic states. In their first phase, the influence of hegemons stems from their power to expend resources. They deploy military force, economic investment, loans, bribes, diplomats, and bureaucrats into other countries and often bring those territories and populations under their direct or indirect rule. American expansion in the 1950s and 1960s did not expand American rule but did produce an American military, political, and economic presence in large areas of the world. In the second phase of hegemony, the power to expend is replaced by the power to attract. By the 1970s, American hegemony began to move into this phase with the outward push in the first phase of hegemonic power giving way to the inward pull characteristic of the second phase, a process that also occurred in the evolution of Rome, Byzantium, Britain, and other hegemonic powers.

In the 1990s the United States still exports food, technology, ideas, culture, and military power. It is, however, importing people, capital, and goods. It has become the largest debtor in the world. It typically takes in more immigrants than all the other countries in the world combined. Farm laborers and Nobel Prize–winners alike want to move to the United States. Elites everywhere want to send their children to American universities. Most of all, businesses want access to the American market. American popular culture, as Josef

Joffe has observed, "is unique; its power comes from pull, not push." American power, in short, has become in Joseph S. Nye's term, the "soft power" to attract rather than the hard power to compel.

The power to attract depends on the willingness of foreigners to find it in their interest to send their money, goods, and children to the United States. It is, however, still power, and the typical form of power for a second-phase hegemon. This became strikingly clear in the Persian Gulf crisis. The fact that the American secretary of state had to go around the world engaging in "tin cup diplomacy," collecting money to pay for the war, was frequently cited as compelling evidence of American decline. In fact, it was imperial behavior of a classic sort: the collection of tribute by the imperial power from its satellites and dependents. The ability to impose and collect an unanticipated levy of more than $50 billion from other countries in a few months was an extraordinary exercise of second-phase hegemonic power. In the late 1940s the United States exercised its power in the Marshall Plan by giving large sums of money to its allies. In the 1990s the United States exercised its power by collecting comparable amounts of money from its allies.

In the past, the flow of money and people out of the United States far surpassed the flow into the United States. Increasingly, however, the gap has narrowed, as other countries have developed their resources and have found it desirable to send money and people to the United States. Although the United States was previously the world's biggest creditor, by 1997 its net foreign debt was more than $1 trillion and was increasing at an annual rate of 15 to 20 percent, with Japan owning almost $300 billion and China more than $50 billion in U.S. treasury bonds.

Between 1963 and 1967, the outflow of foreign direct investment from the United States was more than ten times the inflow to the United States ($24.5 billion versus $2.1 billion). During the late 1970s and 1980s, however, the inflow increased dramatically and by the early 1990s exceeded the outflow ($198.3 billion in versus $168.9 billion out for 1989–1993.) In the early 1960s, the number of Americans going abroad far exceeded the number of foreigners coming to the United States, an average of 6.1 million foreigners arriving each year between 1960 and 1964. By 1990–1994, the inflows and outflows were equal, an average of 44.2 million Americans going abroad each year versus 44.1 million foreigners coming to the United States.

During its first phase as a hegemonic power, the United States expended billions of dollars each year attempting to influence government decisions, elections, and political outcomes in other countries. These efforts clearly exceeded those of any other government, except possibly the Soviet Union, and almost certainly exceeded the total resources expended by foreign governments to influence American politics. Now this balance has changed dramatically, and the shoe is on the other foot. American activities designed to influence foreign governments have either stopped or been greatly reduced. Foreign aid is down and is concentrated on a few countries. Covert intervention is rare, and the money spent trying to influence elections and other outcomes in foreign countries is only a vestige of what it once was. The efforts of foreign institutions to influence American decision-making, in contrast, have increased significantly. The United States has thus become less of an actor and more of an arena.

Foreign governments and corporations now expend enormous resources on public relations and lobbying in the United States, with those from Japan, for instance, reportedly reaching $150 million a year. The governments of other foreign countries that have spent huge amounts to influence U.S. governmental decision making reportedly include those of Saudi Arabia, Canada, South Korea, Taiwan, Mexico, Israel, Germany, the Philippines, and more recently China. Foreign governments make a point of recruiting former U.S.

government officials to help them in these efforts. They have also gradually learned that the place to concentrate their attention is not on the relatively powerless State Department but on America's extraordinarily powerful legislature.[8]

Over the years, foreign influence on American elections has undoubtedly increased. Registered foreign agents make individual contributions to candidates, with Senator John Kerry (D-Mass.), for instance, receiving $44,200 from them for his 1996 campaign, even though he refused funds from domestic PACS [political action committees]. Foreign influence has contributed to the defeat for reelection of several representatives whose policies went against the interests of those governments. The 1996 senatorial election in South Dakota was a contest between Indians and Pakistanis as well as between Republicans and Democrats, with the defeat of Larry Pressler producing elation in Islamabad and dejection in New Delhi. In the coming years, as their numbers, wealth, and political savvy increase, Arabs are likely to fight it out with Jews in elections across the country. The China connection of John Huang and his associates and the millions of dollars they siphoned to the Democratic Party is only the latest and most publicized example of the expenditures of foreign resources to influence American politics.

American politics attracts foreign money because the decisions of its government have an impact on people and interests in every other country. The power to attract resources is thus a result of the power to expend them, and the resource inflow is aimed at affecting the direction of the resource outflow.

There are, however, obvious qualifications to the power to ingest. Elites in other countries have to see it in their interest to provide money and resources to the United States. It is hardly surprising that some allied leaders were heard muttering about "taxation without representation" during the Gulf War collection. And those who invest in capital facilities in the United States obviously expect to exercise some influence in American politics. In addition, the principal collective good the United States provided other countries during the Cold War, protection against the Soviet Union, has disappeared, and the United States may become increasingly unable to continue to provide other collective goods, such as an open world economy and access to the American market. What happens then if the United States levies tribute to support an American-led effort to provide a collective good and no one pays? Or, in a question asked in the 1980s, what happens if the Japanese and Saudis stop buying U.S. government obligations? By the end of the Cold War, the United States had gradually lost much of its power to expend resources. It entered the post–Cold War era with substantial power to attract but this too can fade. The United States may then continue to believe that like Glendower it "can call spirits from the vasty deep." The relevant question, however, will be that put by Hotspur: "Why, so can I, or so can any man;/But will they come when you do call for them?"

PARTICULARISM VERSUS RESTRAINT

American foreign policy is becoming a foreign policy of particularism increasingly devoted to the promotion abroad of highly specific commercial and ethnic interests. The institutions, resources, and influence generated to serve national interests in the Cold War are being redirected to serve these interests. These developments may have been furthered by the almost exclusive concern of the Clinton administration with domestic politics, but their roots lie in broader changes in the external and internal context of the United States and changing conceptions of American national identity.

The likelihood that these contextual factors will shift in the near future seems remote. Conceivably China could become a new enemy. Certainly, important groups in China think of the United States as their new enemy. A China threat sufficient to generate a new sense of national identity and purpose in the United States, however, is not imminent, and how serious that threat is judged to be will depend on the extent to which the Americans view Chinese hegemony in East Asia as damaging to American interests. Reviving a stronger sense of national identity also would require countering the cults of diversity and multiculturalism within the United States. It would probably involve limiting immigration along the lines proposed by the Jordan Commission and developing new public and private Americanization programs to counter the factors enhancing diaspora loyalties and to promote the assimilation of immigrants. These developments may well occur, but given the extent to which, in Nathan Glazer's phase, "we are all multiculturalists now," it will be a while before the recent denationalizing trends are reversed.

The replacement of particularism would require the American public to become committed to new national interests that would take priority over and lead to the subordination of commercial and ethnic concerns. At present, as polls show, majorities of the American public are unwilling to support the commitment of significant resources to the defense of American allies, the protection of small nations against aggression, the promotion of human rights and democracy, or economic and social development in the Third World.[9] As a result, the articulation of these and other broad goals by administration officials produces little follow-through, and with rare exceptions the calls of establishment figures for American leadership generate no effective action. Unable to deliver on its broad promises, American foreign policy becomes one of rhetoric and retreat, with the active energies of the administration concentrated on the advancement of particularistic concerns. Foreign governments have learned not to take seriously administration statements of its general policy goals and to take very seriously administration actions devoted to commercial and ethnic interests.

The alternative to particularism is thus not promulgation of a "grand design," "coherent strategy," or "foreign policy vision." It is a policy of restraint and reconstitution aimed at limiting the diversion of American resources to the service of particularistic subnational, transnational, and nonnational interests. The national interest is national restraint, and that appears to be the only national interest the American people are willing to support at this time in their history. Hence, instead of formulating unrealistic schemes for grand endeavors abroad, foreign policy elites might well devote their energies to designing plans for lowering American involvement in the world in ways that will safeguard possible future national interests.

At some point in the future, the combination of security threat and moral challenge will require Americans once again to commit major resources to the defense of national interests. The de novo mobilization of those resources from a low base, experience suggests, is likely to be easier than the redirection of resources that have been committed to entrenched particularistic interests. A more restrained role now could facilitate America's assumption of a more positive role in the future when the time comes for it to renew its national identity and to pursue national purposes for which Americans are willing to pledge their lives, their fortunes, and their national honor.

NOTES

1. See Vamik D. Volkan, *The Need to Have Enemies and Allies: From Clinical Practice to International Relationships* (Northvale, N.J.: Aronson, 1994); and Jonathan Mercer, "Anarchy and Identity," *International Organization* (Spring 1996), pp. 237–268.
2. Peter D. Salins, *Assimilation, American Style* (New York: Basic Books, 1996), pp. 6–7.

3. Quoted in Arthur M. Schlesinger Jr., *The Disuniting of America: Reflections on a Multicultural Society* (New York: W.W. Norton, 1992), p. 118.
4. *America's National Interests, A Report from the Commission on America's National Interests* (Cambridge, Mass.: Center for Science and International Affairs, John F. Kennedy School of Government, Harvard University, 1996), p. 1.
5. Lawrence F. Kaplan, "The Selling of American Foreign Policy," *The Weekly Standard* (April 23, 1997), pp. 19–22.
6. Yossi Shain, "Multicultural Foreign Policy," *Foreign Policy* (Fall 1995), p. 87.
7. For an explanation that links the structure of the American state to its foreign policy, see Fareed Zakaria, *From Wealth to Power: The Unusual Origins of America's World Role* (Princeton, N.J.: Princeton University Press, 1998).
8. Allan Gotlieb, Canada's ambassador in Washington during most of the 1980s, entertainingly describes how he learned this lesson in *I'll Be With You in a Minute, Mr. Ambassador: The Education of a Canadian Diplomat in Washington* (Toronto: University of Toronto Press, 1991).
9. See John E. Reilly, ed., *American Public Opinion and U.S. Foreign Policy, 1994* (Chicago: Chicago Council on Foreign Relations, 1995); and Arthur M. Schlesinger Jr., "Back to the Womb? Isolationism's Renewed Threat," *Foreign Affairs* (July/August 1995), pp. 2–8.

11

Multicultural Foreign Policy

YOSSI SHAIN

A decade has passed since *Foreign Policy* published three essays that introduced its readers to the international agenda of America's "new ethnic voices" and their influence on U.S. foreign affairs. The essays included an analysis of "Black American Demands" and an explication by two Arab American officials of "Arab American Grievances."[1] In light of the dramatic transformations world politics has undergone over the past ten years, it is time to reevaluate the international and domestic effects of ethnicity in American foreign policy. Such an examination is particularly important today when the United States is searching for a new sense of purpose in its foreign relations, and multiculturalism has heightened concerns over the nature of the American identity.

Scholars, journalists, and political practitioners increasingly recognize the ability of American ethnic groups to influence U.S. foreign policy. Yet very little has been said about how such influence bears on America's national interest abroad, on ethnic relations inside the United States, and on American civic culture in general. Do ethnic voices threaten to Balkanize U.S. foreign policy, or are they constructive? What is the relationship between an ethnic group gaining an effective voice in U.S. foreign policy and its adoption of American political ideals? What function do ethnic lobbies serve in America's global role as the champion of democratic ideals? And does ethnic commitment to ancestral countries impede U.S. domestic cohesion and encourage subnational loyalties?

Undoubtedly, many ethnic groups have undergone a major transformation, changing from outsiders who struggle to penetrate the U.S. foreign policy system to insiders who act in its service as exporters of American ideals. In fact, as the United States continues to concede a role to its ethnic groups in the formulation of foreign policy, it may recast them not only as marketers of the American creed abroad but also as America's own moral compass. Ethnic influences may thus help to keep U.S. foreign policy true to Wilsonianism at a time when neoisolationism is on the rise. The role of ethnicity in foreign affairs has already begun to show its effect on ethnic relations inside America, with some surprising results that should lessen fears about multiculturalism.

This argument is underscored by tracing the evolution of the African and Arab American diasporas in the last decade. The term diaspora, as opposed to ethnicity, accentuates the bond between Americans and their countries of origin. U.S. diasporas are Americans who maintain some affinity—be it cultural, religious, racial, or national—with their ancestral lands or their dispersed kinfolk elsewhere. The homeland may be a person's actual native country, or it may be a place that serves as a symbolic home, as Africa and the Caribbean are for many blacks in America and as Israel is for American Jews.

Diasporas in the United States have long been dedicated to political causes in their homeland. Some diasporas have been involved in the struggle for the political independence of their stateless nations. Others have taken an active role in securing the well-being of their independent home countries. U.S. diasporas also have devoted their efforts to the well-being of members of their dispersed kinfolk in other countries. Jewish Americans have been the driving force behind the transnational effort to liberate Jews in Syria, Ethiopia, and the former Soviet Union. The U.S. Armenian community has provided critical support to Armenians struggling for independence in Nagorno-Karabakh.

Other mobilized diasporas such as Cubans, Filipinos, Haitians, Koreans, and East Europeans have contributed to the weakening of dictatorial rule and the advent of democracy in their ancestral countries or symbolic homelands. The efforts of many Cuban Americans to unseat Fidel Castro generally have concurred with U.S. objectives. As a result, the Cuban American lobby has usually been well received in Washington, and its influence has grown. Other diasporic campaigns against authoritarian or communist home-governments that did not coincide with the U.S. Cold War design were ignored or even obstructed by the U.S. government, such as the Filipino American opposition to Ferdinand Marcos.

The American melting pot concept, which stresses assimilation into a Protestant Anglo-Saxon culture, has given way to a pluralist creed that recognizes ethnicity as integral to American life. Thus, immigrants are no longer required to give up their ethnic identity, language, or attachment to country of origin to become Americans. Hyphenation is well respected. Because they are less and less subjected to charges of disloyalty, ethnic officials and their constituencies are more inclined to reconstitute and strengthen their ties with their ancestral countries. In fact, many ethnic elites have discovered that by focusing on political causes in their homelands, they are better positioned to mobilize their communities for domestic empowerment in America. Moreover, efforts on behalf of ancestral countries are widely recognized as legitimate political practices, licensed and encouraged by the nature of the American party system and the power of each congressional representative.

By influencing state and local governments, diasporas also may have an impact on foreign policy. This was best demonstrated during the campaign by African Americans for comprehensive sanctions against South Africa. The federal government opposed trade sanctions against South Africa for many years, so activists persuaded institutions at the local level to divest. With ties to home countries reinforced by modern modes of transportation and communication, many home-governments (or their opposition) now make direct patriotic appeals to their diasporas, courting them to influence U.S. policy. For example, the Mexican government urged Mexican Americans to lobby Congress for passage of NAFTA.

DIASPORA POLITICS

Diaspora politics has been bolstered by the collapse of the Soviet Union, which resulted in a decline in the influence of traditional political elites, which dominated U.S. foreign affairs throughout the Cold War. In fact, the growing influence of diaspora politics on foreign policy has led many to question whether America's national interest is undermined by such partisan forces and whether the commitment of ethnic Americans to their ancestral countries impedes U.S. domestic cohesion by encouraging subnational loyalties. Some have wondered how far American leaders are willing to go in order to earn the support of the newly organized ethnic elements of the American electorate. Such concerns are compounded by the uncertainty regarding America's future international role. As U.S. strategic interests become less clear than they once were, and as U.S. decisionmakers appear unable to articulate or execute a coherent global strategy, foreign policy becomes more susceptible to pressures by diasporic lobbies.

Khachig Tololyan, editor of the journal *Diaspora,* recently dismissed the possibility that an ethnic group might become the decisive force in prompting American military intervention in its ancestral country: "Whether the issue is borders or regimes, the U.S. is likely to commit troops only when the foreign policy elites in government, business, the armed forces, the media and the academy are convinced that American national interests overlap or coincide with those of a specific ethnic group whose support for such a commitment would then be welcomed." Yet the political dynamic leading to U.S. intervention in Haiti in September 1994 demonstrated that such a broad consensus was not in place before (or after) President Bill Clinton committed American troops to reinstate Haiti's president-in-exile, Jean-Bertrand Aristide. In fact, U.S. intervention in Haiti is probably the most dramatic demonstration of the power of newly mobilized diasporas. Many observers assert that Clinton acted more in response to the organized elements of the African American electorate, primarily the Congressional Black Caucus and the African American international lobby TransAfrica, than to a broader national consensus. The episode that apparently tilted the balance toward an invasion was the hunger strike of TransAfrica's executive director Randall Robinson.

The potency of ethnicity and race in American society has alarmed many observers who caution against the tendency toward Balkanization. Critics of the growing "cult of ethnicity" in American education and civic culture are also rearticulating an old American anxiety that the devotion to ancestral homelands undermines national cohesiveness by exacerbating ethnic strains. They point to many instances of ethnic rivalries inside the United States that are prompted or fueled by diaspora relations with ancestral lands, such as the feuds between American Turks and Greeks, between blacks and Jews over such issues as Israel's relations with South Africa during apartheid and black support for the Palestinians, and between American Serbs and Croats. Another example is the tension between Cuban and African Americans in Miami, which grew primarily out of local struggles over economics and political power and was heightened in 1990, when Cubans in Miami snubbed visiting South African leader Nelson Mandela over his embrace of Castro. In retaliation, black leaders declared a tourism boycott that cost Miami's economy about $50 million.

Ethnic influences may help to keep U.S. foreign policy true to Wilsonianism at a time when neoisolationism is on the rise. According to Harvard professor Samuel Huntington, demographic trends indicate that ethnic conflicts in the United States will grow more common since "kin-country" loyalties run much deeper than liberal assimilationists are willing to admit. By 2050, whites are expected to lose their majority status in America, and as other groups grow in number so will both their cultural and political clout and, consequently, the likelihood of clashes among them. As a growing number of scholars and political observers point out, internal divisions also confuse U.S. external interests. Indeed, if America is becoming a multicultural society with powerful ethnic influences, one should expect to see strong ramifications in U.S. foreign affairs, including a redefinition of U.S. national interests.

Some political observers, such as Michael Clough, a senior fellow at the Council on Foreign Relations, have concluded that the reality of the growing number of ethnic groups creating their own foreign policy is at the core of Washington's failure to articulate a more coherent national interest. Others, however, reverse the causal order and argue that the exacerbation of U.S. domestic divisions is rooted in America's new international posture. Accordingly, America's loss of its Cold War enemies has undermined political leaders' ability to rally the nation around a unifying cause. In the absence of well-defined foreign policy challenges, Americans are turning inward to debate domestic problems. It is a process that encourages the flare-up of dormant culture wars and the renouncement of a common national identity. Many, therefore, worry that the fragmentation witnessed abroad is also affecting the United States.[2]

As a reexamination of the foreign policy roles of African and Arab Americans indicates, however, these fears are at least partially unfounded. African Americans, who since the mid-1980s have emerged as one of the strongest voices on U.S. policy toward Africa and the Caribbean, have been converted from outsiders trying to penetrate the system into mainstream foreign policy players. This metamorphosis, with all its advantages, also has brought new responsibilities and has already yielded dramatic changes in terms of African American international orientations. Whereas in his 1985 *Foreign Policy* article Kenneth Longmyer described the attitude of blacks toward U.S. foreign policy as essentially "noninterventionist," today the African American lobby is one of the leading forces behind U.S. interventionism. The lobby's new status also affects domestic alignments. It has strengthened the bond between mainstream blacks and whites while fracturing relations between black integrationists and black separatists. It has also eased tensions between blacks and Haitian immigrants as African American leaders have championed a return to democracy in Haiti.

Arab Americans also have recently gained a more respected voice in U.S. foreign policy. For decades the Arab American agenda was consumed by the Palestinian cause. Arab American organizations' support of Palestinian independence and of the PLO helped them build a domestic constituency. At the same time, however, it hindered their lobbying effectiveness because of the PLO's low standing in Washington. Yet, in the aftermath of the PLO-Israeli accords, mainstream Arab American organizations have been transformed from stigmatized "anti-Israel" ethnic lobbies into recognized promoters of peace. This new role has provided their officials with greater opportunities for domestic empowerment and with a voice in U.S. foreign affairs. The Middle East peace process has improved Arab American relations with American Jews. This new posture, however, has produced a crisis of identity and purpose.

Mainstream activists have felt pressured to assume a greater role in democratizing autocratic Arab regimes and have been forced to contend with the rise of Islamism among their diaspora kinfolk. Indeed, just as it seemed to reach its apex, the Arab American lobby finds itself in a deep crisis.

INTEGRATIONISTS VERSUS ISOLATIONISTS

Both African and Arab Americans have long been excluded from central roles in American politics and society. In order to confront their marginalization, members of the two communities face a choice between two strategies: isolationism or integrationism. Isolationists consider their culture, religion, or tradition as alien—and often superior—to American culture. They deliberately avoid acculturation, reject assimilation, and at times promote a cultural war against the dominance of European heritage in the United States.

Some even promote irredentism. In many respects, isolationists are the silent allies of Anglo-Saxon nativists, as they confirm the nativist position that membership in American society should be limited to those who are part of a particular Anglo-Saxon culture. Black Power separatists of the late 1960s advocated national liberation and rejected the civil rights movement's vision of a color-blind, integrated America. Their crusade was bolstered by the successful struggle for independence of African states and by the rise of Third World ideology. Conversion to Islam was a reaction to the perception of Christianity as "a slave religion." Yet by the early 1970s, black separatism was already waning, as more and more black leaders, including Martin Luther King Jr. and Roy Wilkins, the former executive director of the National Association for the Advancement of Colored People (NAACP), preached the gospel of power-sharing and pluralism and denounced Black Power as reverse racism. Moderate black leaders realized that only by playing an insiders' game and embracing the American electoral system and its democratic values could they hope to become equal participants in American society.

Isolationism was also a strong force in the Arab American community in the late 1960s. The ethnic identity of U.S. Arabs was mostly dormant until the 1967 Six-Day War. With no ideological core, political organization, or funding, Arab Americans—chiefly second- and third-generation Christians of Lebanese origin—retained little homeland affinity and remained politically inactive. The traumatic defeat of the Arabs in 1967, Israel's occupa- tion of the West Bank and Gaza, and the spread of anti-Arab sentiment in the United States, roused the Arab American community. As the Middle East conflict intensified and the U.S.-Israeli alliance grew stronger, Arab Americans began to organize. The first dias- pora organizers were mostly Palestinian American students and professors, who in 1967 established the Association of Arab American University Graduates (AAUG). The group preached against assimilation and soon discovered sympathizers in the Black Power move- ment. The black nationalists who dominated black political dialogue in the late 1960s characterized Israel as an extension of American imperialism and racism and condemned black leaders who supported the Zionist state as collaborators in the oppression of "our Palestinian brothers and sisters." The Black Panther Party, the Student Nonviolent Coor- dinating Committee, and the Nation of Islam (Black Muslims) all drew a parallel between Israeli treatment of Palestinians and South Africa's apartheid policy. They also denounced Zionism as racism and equated the exploitation of blacks in America with the mistreatment of Arabs by Israel. It was in this context that the civil rights alliance between blacks and Jews began to disintegrate. Arab American isolationists, like many black radicals, regarded the United States as an imperialist and racist country seeking to ominate the Arab world. Christians and Muslims alike immersed themselves in pan-Arab and Third World ideolo- gies that came to denote the struggle of the Palestinians. The Palestinian American scholar and PLO activist Edward Said provided the intellectual leadership when he explicated the notion of "orientalism." Said charged the West with an "unbending desire to discredit and thus debunk the Arabs as a people and as a society." Isolationists repudiated the United States in a manner that combined attacks on America's imperialist policies and its anti- Islamic bigotry.

By the early 1990s, however, the old Arab American Left had lost its allure. While some of its followers have remained hostile to the idea of becoming Americans and are irritated by the actions of Arab American integrationists, they are increasingly outnumbered by the moderate voices. Left-leaning isolationists are also outnumbered by the wave of Islamic revivalism. Even the AAUG has moved closer to the center: It has given greater attention to the issue of Arab dictatorial regimes and has denounced the mistreatment of women throughout the Arab world. In his 1994 address to the AAUG's annual convention, AAUG president Ziad Asali called upon his colleagues to reexamine their old convictions:

> It will not do to lay the blame solely on imperialism and Zionism to explain away the current state of disarray and degradation across the Arab world. It will not do

to formulate slogans and generalizations as a substitute for realistic strategies and thought out tactics.... The suppression of free expression across the Arab world adds an extra measure of responsibility on the shoulders of the Arab intellectuals in the West who are not encumbered by government or violent censorship.

Today, the isolationists among Arab Americans are mainly orthodox Muslims who reject, in principle, the idea of Muslims building a minority life in a non-Islamic country. While some of them may advocate the transformation of American society by attracting Americans to Islam through religious outreach (Da'awa), the militants consider the United States to be Islam's greatest enemy. Often led by exiled Muslim preachers (imams), Islamists tend to adopt a theology that construes their life in the United States as a transitional phase, a modern form of Hijra similar to the Prophet Muhammad's retreat to Medina, which marked the beginning of a Muslim community (umma), superseding a world of tribal kinship. Accordingly, the United States provides these exiles a temporary haven from which they can launch their campaign to return to a land conquered by so-called infidels. In recent years, there have been many reports about the growing number of militant Islamic groups that have established bases among Arab Americans.

In contrast to their isolationist kinfolk, the majority of African and Arab Americans seek integration. Although they may protest their exclusion, they still identify themselves as Americans. Even so, their political and intellectual elites encourage them to cling to ancestral identities. Yet, while they may resist assimilation into a dominant Anglo-Saxon culture, integrationists still endorse the vision of a pluralist democracy. They believe that American culture is dynamic, that it does not have a European essence, and that it may be utilized to address their own cultural affinities. In other words, although they reject the notion that every community in the United States has already achieved a cultural identity sufficient to enable it to blend into a multicultural society, integrationists still seek to achieve such an accommodation. Accordingly, they demand cultural and political recognition from mainstream U.S. institutions.

When it comes to foreign affairs, diaspora integrationists present their case in terms of "America's best national interest" and establish political lobbies to compete for their own interpretation of that interest. In the African American community, the integrationists' mode in foreign affairs is best represented by TransAfrica. From its inception, TransAfrica considered African American involvement in African and Caribbean affairs to be an additional mechanism for domestic empowerment. In the crusade to reverse America's posture toward South Africa, TransAfrica endeavored to apply Martin Luther King's domestic strategy of challenging Americans to live up to their democratic creed. When TransAfrica opened its foreign policy institute in Washington, D.C., in June 1993, Randall Robinson said: "This town produces policy as a result of a competition of policy ideas.... We have never competed evenly institutionally in the area of foreign affairs. That's why we wanted a fully fleshed out think tank to grind out the analysis that represents the interests of our community."

In the Arab American community, the integrationist organizations that focus on foreign affairs, and primarily on the Palestinian cause, have been the National Association of Arab Americans (NAAA), which endeavored to counter the impact of the American Israel Public Affairs Committee, the pro-Israel lobby; the Arab American Institute (AAI), which officially concentrates on empowering Arab Americans in the electoral system; and the American Arab Anti-Discrimination Committee (ADC), the initial goal of which has been to combat "anti-Arab racism." In their 1985 *Foreign Policy* article, David Sadd and Neal Lendenmann of the NAAA described their organization's goals in this way:

Arab Americans are deeply proud of their culture and heritage. They seek to promote the closest possible relations between the United States and the Arab world.... They are Americans first, last, and always. Their approach to lobbying, therefore, is to identify America's national interests in the Middle East and to promote those interests through advocacy and education.

Interestingly, all of the above groups, each of which has often expressed its resentment of Jewish American lobbying power, deliberately established themselves in the image of parallel Jewish groups. Yet while American Jewish organizations have been thriving by drawing on the energies and resources of their constituency, Arab American groups—which claim to speak on behalf of between two and three million Americans of Arab descent—have failed at grassroots mobilization. In 1995, the NAAA's staff was cut dramatically to three because its Arab benefactors slashed its funding. Khalil Jahshan, NAAA'S executive director, expressed agony, saying that "Arab-American organizations lack the cementing factors." Jahshan acknowledges that Arab American organizations failed to connect with their own constituency, and he concedes that the NAAA'S role in foreign affairs has ended: "When [Israeli prime minister Yitzhak] Rabin lobbies Washington for money for the PLO and when Arab governments ignore our existence, we must turn our energies [from foreign affairs] to the community."

For years, African and Arab Americans attributed their failure to affect U.S. external affairs to Jewish American hegemony over the public and institutional discourse in this field. The 1979 Andrew Young affair was a turning point in blacks' struggle to gain influence over U.S. foreign policy. Young, then the most influential African American in President Jimmy Carter's administration, was forced out of his post as ambassador to the United Nations after it was revealed that he negotiated with the PLO observer at the United Nations despite official U.S. policy barring such dialogue. The incident embellished the mythology of secret Jewish power and of black powerlessness. Young's removal was stamped as a form of Jewish racism that suggested that blacks were unqualified to participate in the realm of international diplomacy.

In a similar manner, Arab American activists have long argued that their exclusion radiates primarily from the Arab-Israeli conflict. It is a result, they claim, of associating them with Americans' twisted images of their Arab and Palestinian compatriots in the Middle East. These activists also held the pro-Israeli lobby responsible for the lack of access to the American political system. Thus, Arab American integrationists have drawn a direct link between their domestic empowerment and the ebbing of the Middle East conflict.

No to Apartheid, Yes to Palestinian Rights

Martin Weil wrote an article entitled "Can the Blacks Do for Africa What the Jews Did for Israel?" in the Summer 1974 issue of *Foreign Policy*. He predicted that sooner or later the United States would face a powerful black lobby that would challenge American policy in Africa. He further argued that to be successful, a black movement for reform of American policy toward Africa must be perceived as a vehicle for exporting American ideals. It must be an affirmation of black faith in the United States and a demonstration of black ability to manipulate the fine structure of American politics with the astuteness and finesse of previous practitioners. Blacks as blacks may identify with Africa, but it is only as Americans that they can change United States policy in Africa. If Afro-Americans ever gain leverage in foreign policy, it will be those black politicians who are most successful within the system who will do so—those who can command the respect of their black constituents and reassure white America at the same time.

Weil's projection began to come true in the mid-1970s with the sharp decline in black extremism. During the 1976 presidential campaign, blacks first made their mark on the Democratic party's platform by pushing the issue of independence for the white minority-ruled states of southern Africa. The establishment of TransAfrica in 1977 furthered the institutionalization of black political power in the U.S. foreign policy arena. The link between the black domestic agenda and the anti-apartheid struggle was reinforced during the Reagan administration, with many African American leaders believing that President Ronald Reagan was insensitive to civil rights issues in general and uncaring on apartheid in particular. Apartheid became a rallying cry for the rejuvenation of the political activism of the 1960s, as black Americans organized as insiders to set the American conscience back on track. As much as Reagan wanted to argue that support for the African National Congress (ANC) fortified communism, his administration's rhetoric rang hollow in the face of such clear violations of American ideals. The wave of protests, sit-ins, and voluntary arrests orchestrated by TransAfrica spread across the nation, helping to make apartheid a principal political concern for local governments, towns, media, and universities. The political momentum paved the way for an unprecedented coalition in the House and Senate, which approved sanctions against South Africa over Reagan's veto. The "domestication" of apartheid was complete; then Senate majority leader Bob Dole even acknowledged that the issue of sanctions had "now become a domestic civil rights issue."

The mobilization of the black community against apartheid coincided with a renewed search for black identity in the United States, which eventually manifested itself in the campaign to change the group appellation from "black" to "African American." The campaign for "African American" at that juncture represented a strong perception that integration and political power in the United States have much to do with an affiliation with a country and culture abroad. In late 1988, the Reverend Jesse Jackson declared: "Every ethnic group in this country has a reference to some land base, some historical, cultural base. African Americans have hit that level of cultural maturity." Ultimately, the identification with black South Africa emerged as one of the critical factors by which politicians' allegiance to domestic black causes was measured. By 1990, Arab American integrationists had already established high visibility in U.S. politics and media. They did so primarily by drawing upon Palestinian suffering during the intifada, and by rebuking the pro-Israeli lobby for what it called an abusive use of money to pressure Congress. Arab Americans made the Palestinian issue their ideological core, a cause portrayed as an extension of "America's most cherished ideals—Wilsonian self-determination, human rights, [and] freedom," as Gregory Orfalea, an Arab American activist and writer, said.

The AAI, for example, considered its most meaningful political accomplishment up to that point the breaking open of the debate on Palestinian rights and the Middle East peace process on the floor of the 1988 Democratic National Convention in Atlanta. In this debate, AAI president James Zogby announced: "Today we respond to the Palestinian people. We address . . . the violation of their basic human rights, the killings and the beatings, and agonizing expulsions, the daily humiliations of being a people without a state." The event was recognized by some Jewish American officials as "the Arab American intifada."

Regardless of their accomplishments, however, Arab Americans' entry into the American political arena remained circumscribed by events in the Middle East and by the negative publicity garnered by extreme elements in the diaspora. During the Persian Gulf war, Arab Americans were torn between their desire to express their American loyalty and their concern for Arabs abroad. The NAAA and the AAI moved uneasily between supporting U.S. intervention to restore Kuwait and requiring American "consistency" when it comes to Israel and the Palestinians.

Too often, as was evident in the immediate aftermath of the April 1995 bombing in Oklahoma City and in the wake of the February 1993 bombing of New York's World Trade Center by a small group of Islamists residing in the United States, the diaspora has been collectively held accountable for the repudiation of America in Arab and Muslim countries and for the terrorist activities of Islamists in the United States. This collective stain has frustrated the foreign policy efforts of Arab Americans even when their cause was consistent with American values; the U.S. failure to respond to the brutal assault on Bosnian Muslims demonstrates the inability of Arabs and Muslims in America to promote such a cause through the mechanisms of U.S. foreign policy.

Following the Gulf War, Arab American integrationists concluded that their domestic political empowerment could no longer remain in the sole service of Palestinian interests: They could not settle for a showdown with American Jews. In reality, some forms of Arab and Jewish American cooperation had already appeared in the 1980s, as more and more Israelis and American Jews called for a "two-state solution" to the Israeli-Palestinian conflict. Adopting the American jargon of opportunity and fair play, Zogby, a Lebanese Christian born in the United States, called in 1988 for reconciliation and cooperation with American Jews. "We do understand Jewish fears and the need for security felt so deeply by Israelis. Now I urge you to understand realities like Palestinian nationalism and the emergence of an Arab American political constituency." By 1991, the Jewish American habit of providing uncritical support for Israeli policies had begun to fade. The repercussions of the new geopolitical posture on U.S.-Israeli relations became apparent when President George Bush linked financial assistance to Israel with the halting of settlement practices in the West Bank and Gaza.

Caught between the Israeli government's expectation that it would use all its political influence in Congress to reverse the president's decision and the administration's position that such a showdown was equivalent to an act of disloyalty, the pro-Israeli lobby retreated. Indeed, in the 1992 election, Bush was supported by many Arab Americans who rewarded him despite their opposition to his policies in the Gulf.

After the signing of the Israeli-PLO accords on the White House lawn on September 13, 1993, Arab American integrationists expressed a huge sigh of relief. The AAI declared that the accords provide an opportunity for Arab Americans "to achieve full empowerment and assimilation into the mainstream of American culture and life." The ADC, which failed to endorse the accords, was soon marginalized. Ray Hanania, a leading ADC activist, recently wrote that the organization "was governed by a board consisting of old-fashioned thinking Arabs who had yet to understand what being an American is all about." Zogby's partnership with Jewish American leaders in the White House's "Builders for Peace" initiative—a joint venture aimed at developing the private sector economy in the West Bank and Gaza—is something of an American story of overcoming mistrust between two ethnic communities.

MARKETING THE AMERICAN CREED ABROAD

The African American anti-apartheid campaign largely parallels the Arab American crusade for Palestinian statehood. Both diasporas have built their foreign policy agendas around American ideals of democracy, pluralism, self-determination, and human rights.

Yet, in order to sustain their "democratic" reputation, they must now continually demonstrate their hostility to nondemocratic practices in their native countries or symbolic homelands. They also must be ready to challenge unequivocally their radical kinfolk inside the United States. Their responsibility to become "marketers" of the American creed abroad has been reinforced since the end of the Cold War by the greater emphasis on America's mission of spreading democracy and human rights abroad. This new posture marks a change from previous U.S. approval of "authoritarian" dictatorships friendly to the United States and opposed to communism. Thus, in recent years, one can observe symbiotic relationships between the makers of U.S. foreign policy and the roles assumed by U.S. diasporas. The more the diasporas are harnessed by the American government to promote democracy abroad, the more likely they are to improve their influence on U.S. foreign policy. In fact, because American policymakers may still try to retreat from their neo-Wilsonian pledge to traditional realism, as demonstrated by Clinton's friendly overtures toward China and his lengthy indecisiveness on Bosnia, diasporas may assume the role of a moral compass in U.S. foreign policy. Their pressure on policymakers to follow through on their commitment to promote democracy and human rights, even when such policies seem to hinder ad hoc strategic interests, are bound to create strains on U.S. relations with repressive regimes and to help ensure that oppressed groups cannot be ignored by U.S. policymakers.

During the Cold War, mainstream African Americans could vindicate their support of nondemocratic African governments as a way of countering U.S. "imperialist intervention" via authoritarian proxies. Arab American organizations could similarly overlook the autocratic quality of Arab regimes by focusing on Israeli violations of Palestinian national rights, a unifying cause that also bridged religious and national divisions within the diverse Arab American community.

However, with the collapse of communism, and with improving prospects for Palestinian statehood, the pretense and motivation for siding with or acquiescing to black or Arab transgressions disappeared. As a result, African American leaders have moved steadily to redefine their pro-Africa crusade along the democratic theme of urging the U.S. government to get serious about promoting democracy and human rights in Africa. In his testimony before the Senate Foreign Relations Committee in May 1991, TransAfrica's Robinson called for a new U.S. foreign policy in Africa "contingent on respect for human rights and progress toward political and economic reform." Bolstered by its striking success in influencing American policy on Haiti, TransAfrica recently launched a national campaign to restore democracy in Nigeria, urging the White House to take a more confrontational posture toward the military junta by refusing to buy Nigerian oil. This latest campaign is the first display of a strong African American protest against the abuses of a black African regime. The campaign has been applauded by some Nigerian opposition leaders, such as former foreign minister Bolaji Akinyemi. The Nigerian government and some Nigerian interest groups in the United States, however, charged Robinson with exploiting the Nigerian political tragedy to promote TransAfrica's fund-raising and warned that Robinson's crusade "will ultimately batter our national pride, and cause harm to the image of the black man," as one such group stated.

Similarly, with the unfolding of the peace process in the Middle East, Arab Americans began to speak about the need for democratic reforms in the Arab world. NAAA executive director Jahshan has written that "Palestinian chaotic democracy or 'the democracy of the guns' ... must be transformed into genuine democracy, in which basic and universal civil, human, and political rights are respected and protected." In January 1994, the AAI held a conference titled "Challenge '94: Making Democracy Work at Home and Abroad." Zogby warned that if the diaspora remains mute on the issue of spreading democracy into the Middle East, then it will compromise its political credibility:

> I feel deeply that this period requires a new way of thinking—a new paradigm. If the peace accords are to bear fruit then we must make every effort to begin to develop new priorities.... [While] we are committed to Palestinian statehood ... [and] are opposed to Israeli occupation of any Arab land ... we [also] want to see human rights and democracy in the Arab world.

More recently, Zogby has restrained his prodemocracy oratory. He is now calling for an Arab American alliance with pro-American Arab regimes, regardless of their internal practices. This position may still fall within the Clinton administration's foreign policy formula of "pragmatic Wilsonianism," to use Harvard professor Stanley Hoffmann's phrase, but it is unlikely to impress the many in the Arab American community who have heard allegations that the AAI has become dependent on Saudi money.

The transformation of the African and Arab American foreign lobbies from outsiders seeking to penetrate the American system into insiders helping to shape its course or being mobilized in its service is a testimony to the positive value of including ethnicity in U.S. foreign policy. The increasing involvement of these diasporas in foreign policy has already contributed to the decline of ethnic tensions inside the United States, especially between integrationist members of the two diasporas and moderates among American Jews.

Thus, one may consider the recent reconciliation between Jewish Americans and mainstream African American leaders on international matters as the first stage in the healing process. Jesse Jackson, whose rhetoric and deeds have long epitomized the shared nature of the internal and external rift between Jews and blacks, took it upon himself to become a domestic and international healer. Whereas in the past Jackson described Zionism as "a kind of poisonous weed," in a 1992 speech to the World Jewish Congress he identified it as a "liberation movement." Jackson also has called for the rebuilding of the civil rights alliance. He and other black leaders have expressed hope that the Middle East peace will bring peace between Jews and African Americans in the United States.

Thus, the dedication of diasporas to democratic causes abroad also may energize liberal discourse inside the United States in a manner that can temper the fear of American disunity. Just as the openness of American government to the influence of ethnicity has guided diasporic groups to champion the creed of democracy and human rights around the globe, it also forces them to be more committed to liberal pluralism domestically. As ethnic elites gradually find their way into the American mainstream via the diaspora channel, their affinity with isolationists and extreme multiculturalists in their own community becomes awkward. Many African American leaders, for example, have distanced themselves from extreme Afrocentrists and the anti-Semitic rhetoric of the Nation of Islam.

Zogby was among the signatories of the American Jewish Committee ads against the profanities of Louis Farrakhan's aide Khalid Abdul Muhammad: "We are Americans, whose diversity of faith, ethnicity and race unites us in a common campaign against bigotry." Edward Said seems to have undergone an intellectual metamorphosis as he called on the Arab American diaspora to capitalize on its freedom in the United States and to rescue the Arab culture from Arab leaders and governments: "It is now left to the Arab diaspora on its own to do for the Arabs what leaders and governments in the Arab world will not or cannot do for their people."

The damaging impact of ethnic influences in U.S. foreign affairs has been overstated. Ethnic involvement in U.S. foreign affairs may be seen as an important vehicle through which disenfranchised groups may win an entry ticket into American society and politics. Indeed, one of the signs that an ethnic group has achieved a respectable position in American life is its acquisition of a meaningful voice in U.S. foreign affairs. Yet, in order to obtain such a role, ethnic officials must first demonstrate their determination to advocate the principles of pluralism, democracy, and human rights abroad. In fact, in the aftermath of the Cold War and with the advent of a more unipolar, ideological world order that favors democracy and the free market economy, ethnic lobbies are likely to become mobilized diasporas. They are "commissioned" by American decisionmakers to export and safeguard American values abroad and are expected to become the moral conscience of new democracies or newly established states in their homelands. Such commissioning, in turn, further legitimates the ethnic voice in America's external affairs and enables diasporas to push American policymakers to adhere to America's neo-Wilsonian values of promoting democracy and openness around the globe, even when such policies seem to obstruct ad hoc strategic interests.

Finally, the new foreign policy role of ethnic groups is likely to reflect positively in American civic culture by reinforcing the values of democracy and pluralism at home. Contrary to conventional wisdom, diaspora politics has the potential to temper, rather than exacerbate, domestic ethnic conflicts, because it discourages tendencies toward Balkanization at home. In many ways, then, the participation of ethnic diasporas in shaping U.S. foreign policy is a truly positive phenomenon.

NOTES

1. See Kenneth Longmyer, "Black American Demands," and David J. Sadd and G. Neal Lendenmann, "Arab American Grievances," *Foreign Policy* (Fall 1985), no. 60.
2. See Bruce D. Porter, "Can American Democracy Survive?" *Commentary* (November 1993), pp. 37–40. See also Morris Dickstein, "After the Cold War: Culture as Politics, Politics as Culture," *Social Research* (Fall 1993), pp. 531–544.

12

All Politics Are Global

*Interest Groups and the Making of Foreign Policy**

ERIC M. USLANER

Interest groups are the stuff of domestic policymaking. Americans are used to speaking of diverse constituencies: butchers, bakers, candlestick makers, and so on. Members of Congress talk about their districts in terms of these interests. In the words of former Speaker Thomas P. O'Neill, "All politics is local." On foreign policy, we don't often think of a variety of interests within the United States. We see the world as "us" against "them." Especially in international crises, when the stakes are clear and our entire way of life might be threatened, the nation must speak with one voice, not many. There simply doesn't seem room for interest groups. Yet interest groups have long been active on foreign policy. Group activity has grown increasingly important in recent years as the world has become more interdependent. The new mantra has become "all politics is global."[1] Why has foreign policy been different from domestic policy, and how have things changed?

FOREIGN POLICY AND DOMESTIC POLICY

Interest groups have traditionally been less active on foreign policy than on domestic issues. First, the stakes are much higher in foreign policy. The entire world could be destroyed by nuclear weapons as a result of a decision that might take only minutes to make. Second, foreign policy decisions are often irreversible. Relations between nations change slowly. Unpopular domestic policies can be altered much more easily. Third, relations with foreign nations are not entirely within the control of American policymakers. Both domestic pressures and the attitude of the Chinese government precluded the establishment of diplomatic relations for more than three decades after the United States decided in 1949 not to recognize the regime. It was not until 1972 that President Richard Nixon visited China and 1979 that Beijing and Washington agreed to exchange ambassadors.

Fourth, foreign policy decisions, particularly in crises, need to be made quickly. During the Cuban missile crisis in 1962, President John F. Kennedy had to set national policy in just a few weeks as the threat of a nuclear confrontation with the Soviet Union loomed over the world. Domestic issues rarely get resolved so rapidly; government provision of medical care to the elderly remained just an interesting proposal on the legislative agenda for more than half a century. Expertise on foreign policy is much more centralized than on domestic policy. The goals of all Americans are posited to be the same: At the very least, the survival of a democratic way of life against a hostile power that is not committed to individual freedoms. If the nation does not speak with a single voice, our adversaries might think that we lack the resolve to defend ourselves.

Fifth, foreign policy issues are of less concern to most Americans than domestic policy. Citizens find events in the international arena far more remote than domestic affairs. Many members of Congress seek to highlight their role in domestic policy and to play down any interest they have in foreign policy. One member of the Senate Foreign Relations Committee said of his assignments:

> It's a political liability.... You have no constituency. In my reelection campaign last fall, the main thing they used against me was that because of my interest in foreign relations, I was more interested in what happened to the people of Abyssinia and Afghanistan than in what happened to the good people of my state.[2]

Only a small share—less than a quarter—of members of the House of Representatives consider themselves activists on foreign policy.[3] Most Americans are content to let the president make foreign policy and give virtually unchallenged support to the chief executive as long as crises do not appear to get out of hand.

Congress generally follows the president's lead, rarely overturning presidential initiatives in foreign policy. Partisan divisions have not traditionally disrupted international affairs the same way they affect most domestic issues.[4] Bickering over priorities is supposed to stop "at the water's edge," at each of the great oceans that long isolated the United States from the world's problems. Conflict over domestic policies was natural. On foreign policy there was but one interest—the national interest—behind which all Americans should—and generally did—unite.[5]

Groups that oppose a national consensus will be viewed with suspicion, especially if they could profit from a change in policy. Many Americans conjure up a diabolical picture of how private interests affect international politics for their own advantage, such as the 1970 attempt by International Telephone and Telegraph to rig an election in Chile to prevent the election of a Marxist president. Americans, always suspicious of the power of big oil, became even more hostile when the multinational energy giants tried to tilt U.S. foreign policy away from Israel and toward the Arabs following the 1967 and 1973 Middle East wars. Americans have ambivalent attitudes toward interest groups generally; a 1988 poll showed that 72 percent of Americans believed that big business had too much influence on American policy and 47 percent felt similarly about labor. A 1991 survey found that almost 60 percent of Americans believe that corporations do not strike a fair balance between profits and the public interest; 80 percent hold that business has too much power and 65 percent believe that business makes too much profit.[6] Groups with ties to foreign interests, whether they are primarily domestic or foreign, are viewed with particular suspicion.

INTEREST GROUPS AND FOREIGN POLICY

There has been a sharp rise in the number of groups participating in foreign policy since the 1970s, even as there are no firm numbers as to how many new actors there are. Why is foreign policy a more appropriate arena for interest group politics now than even twenty years ago? The principal reason is that in an interdependent world the traditional barriers between foreign and domestic politics have broken down. Most policies are now "intermestic."[7] The dramatic increase in oil prices in 1973–1974 (and again in 1979) changed our perception of energy policy. Before 1973, energy decisions were made strictly according to the domestic politics of specific fuels. Thereafter our attention shifted to the producing nations. President Jimmy Carter forbade grain sales to the Soviet Union following the nation's invasion of Afghanistan in 1979; Ronald Reagan made the unpopular embargo an issue in the 1980 elections and reversed the policy after his election. Domestic economic groups expanded their horizons to foreign policy as their international market share grew.

Foreign interests joined domestic ones in pressing their case. Foreign governments are among the new lobbyists. West Germany, Canada, France, Arab countries, Japan, China, and Mexico have mounted extensive efforts to sway American policies. These countries hire distinguished Americans who have served in the cabinet, in the Congress, and even in the vice presidency.[8] Japan alone spent up to $60 million in 1989 on lobbying, four times as much as in 1984. The government of Kuwait reportedly spent $10 million to drum up support for the Gulf War in 1990. Mexico hired at least thirty-three former U.S. government officials, including former Senator and Trade Representative Bill Brock, in a $28 million lobbying effort on behalf of the proposed NAFTA.[9]

A second reason is the decline of consensus on foreign policy. The Vietnam War changed the way Americans react to foreign policy. Support of the president's policies was no longer automatic. Various ideological interest groups sprang up to challenge some of the key assumptions behind our involvement in the war. The post–World War II era of bipartisanship in foreign policy had come to an end. From 1968 onward, parties increasingly took divergent stands on foreign policy in their platforms and in their votes on the floor of the House and Senate.[10]

The waning of a cohesive sense of national purpose gave rise to a greater number of interest groups on both foreign and domestic policy. The political universe expanded greatly from the late 1960s onward, as previously unheard voices—those of citizens groups—entered the fray. Interest groups concerned with foreign policy and national security most resembled organizations focusing on civil rights and civil liberties. Many were free of the taint of special interests seeking to profit from lobbying. Interest groups focusing on foreign policy were about equally divided between for-profit and not-for-profit organizations. Citizen groups in the 1980s were more interested in foreign policy than in any other issue area.[11]

These new interest groups came from sectors not traditionally associated with foreign policy. Church groups, which played an important role in war protest, branched out into concerns for nuclear disarmament, the conflicts in El Salvador and Nicaragua (some churches gave sanctuary to refugees from these countries), the ending of apartheid in South Africa, the establishment of a Palestinian state, and the Gulf War. Secular organizations formed for each of these policy areas as well. The New Christian Right chimed in on behalf of NAFTA, while several environmental organizations, most notably the Sierra Club, succeeded 1993 in blocking congressional consideration of the accord until the Environmental Protection Agency (EPA) prepared an environmental impact statement.[12] On energy, the environment, and agriculture, groups reflecting a dizzying array of complexity made policy formation on these intermestic issues very difficult.[13]

Some lobbying, especially that by churches and ethnic groups, is considered quite legitimate: Two-thirds of Americans believe it is legitimate for churches to engage in political activity.[14] Why are some types of group activity acceptable and other types held in disdain? The answer is little different from a distinction on domestic policy noted by E. E. Schattschneider between the National Association of Manufacturers (an umbrella organization of major firms) and the American League to Abolish Capital Punishment: "The members of the [latter] obviously do not expect to be hanged.[15] Although economic interests expect to gain something for themselves from lobbying, neither religious nor ethnic groups do. The United States is a nation of immigrants and many Americans have strong bonds with the countries of their heritage.

The rise of foreign policy interest groups is also tied to the more general increasing salience in foreign policy. The percentage of Americans who claim to be "very interested" in news stories about foreign policy has risen dramatically and now is about equal to the percentage claiming to be concerned with local and national news. In recent elections— 1992 excepted—candidate preference has been shaped by foreign policy issues as well as domestic concerns.[16] Finally, lobbying on foreign policy has spread for a very straightforward reason: It works.

ETHNIC GROUPS IN FOREIGN POLICY

Among the most prominent lobbies on foreign policy are those representing ethnic groups in the United States and their ties to the home country. Mohammed E. Ahrari has suggested four conditions for ethnic group success on foreign policy. First, the group must press for a policy in line with American strategic interests. Second, the group must be assimilated into American society, yet retain enough identification with the "old country" so that its foreign policy issue motivates people to take some political action. Groups that stand outside the mainstream of American life, Arab Americans for a complex of reasons discussed later and Mexicans because many are not citizens, cannot mobilize for political action. Yet something more is required: a high level of political activity. Fourth, groups should be politically unified.[17] To Ahrari's list we add several additional criteria. The group's policies should be backed by the larger public. The group should be sufficiently numerous to wield political influence. Finally, the group must be seen as pursuing a legitimate interest. Speaking on behalf of one's ethnic group is acceptable so long as others do not think you have divided loyalties or somehow will profit from your lobbying efforts.

American Jews are distinctive in their ability to affect foreign policy. They have established the most prominent and best-endowed lobby in Washington by fulfilling each of the conditions for an influential group. In recent years, some conditions have not been met and the pro-Israel lobby is no longer the dominant force it once was. Its rival in Washington, the pro-Arab lobby, has remained weak because it has failed to meet any of the conditions.

THE ISRAELI AND ARAB LOBBIES

The best-organized, best-funded, and most successful of the ethnic lobbies, indeed perhaps of all foreign policy lobbies, represents the interests of Israel. Jews, who dominate the pro-Israel lobby, comprise 2.7 percent of the American population. However, they are strongly motivated and highly organized in support of Israel. They seek to provide U.S. financial aid (both economic and military) to Israel and to deny it to those Arab nations in a state of war with Israel. And they have been very successful indeed: The lobby, since its inception in 1951, is believed to have lost on only four key decisions. In 1978 it failed to prevent the sale of F-15 fighter planes to Saudi Arabia and Egypt; in 1981 and 1986 it could not block arms sales to the Saudis;[18] and in 1991 it could not overcome President George Bush's opposition to loan guarantees to resettle Soviet Jews so long as Israel continued to build settlements in the West Bank and Gaza Strip. In 1992, when a new Israeli government pledged to stop the settlements, the loan guarantees went forward, although not through the efforts of the pro-Israel lobby.

Israel receives the largest amount of foreign aid from the United States, more than $3 billion a year. Only Egypt even approaches the Israeli aid figure. In 1985 Israel and the

United States signed a free-trade pact that would completely eliminate all tariff barriers between them by 1995. Israel annually benefits from large tax-exempt contributions from the American Jewish community, including some $500 million in direct charitable grants and a similar amount from the sale of Israeli government bonds.[19] No other foreign nation is so favored.

The Israeli lobby combines one organization devoted entirely to the cause of that country and a wide-ranging network of Jewish groups that provide support. The American Israel Public Affairs Committee (AIPAC), founded in 1951, has a staff of 150, an annual budget of $15 million, and fifty-five thousand members. It operates out of offices one block away from Capitol Hill as well as in other major cities.[20] The success of the Israeli lobby has been attributed to its political acumen. Sanford Ungar stated:

> In a moment of perceived crisis, it can put a carefully researched, well-documented statement of its views on the desk of every Senator and Congressman and appropriate committee staff within four hours of a decision to do so.[21]

The organization's close ties to many congressional staffers keep it well informed about issues affecting Israel on Capitol Hill. Its lobbying connections are so thorough that one observer maintained, "A mystique has grown up around the lobby to the point where it is viewed with admiration, envy, and sometimes, anger."[22] Activists can readily mobilize the network of Jewish organizations across the country to put pro-Israel pressure on members of Congress in their constituencies, even in areas with small Jewish populations. Even though liberals (and Democrats) tend to be somewhat more sympathetic to Israel than conservatives (and Republicans), the lobbyists are careful to maintain bipartisan support. AIPAC works together with other interest groups, particularly organized labor.[23] It blocked proposed arms sales to Jordan and Saudi Arabia in the late 1980s. In 1986 Secretary of State Shultz reportedly asked AIPAC what kind of arms and aid package the Reagan administration could get passed.[24] Among its recent activities was the organization of fifteen hundred "citizen lobbyists," armed with individualized computer printouts of their legislators' backgrounds, pressing for additional aid to Israel because of the damage it incurred in the Gulf War.[25]

The Arab lobbying effort has been singularly unsuccessful. There were no major Arab organizations operating at all before 1972, and a Washington presence did not begin until 1978. The oldest Arab group, the NAAA claims thirteen thousand members, a mailing list of eighty thousand names, most of whom are inactive, and a $500,000 annual budget funding a staff of twenty-five.[26] The NAAA seeks closer ties between the United States and the Arab world in political, military, and economic arenas. Despite its support for a weakening of the United States-Israel bond and creation of a Palestinian state, it recognizes the right of Israel to exist. A rival organization, the American Lebanese League, is harshly critical of the NAAA and views it as essentially anti-American.[27] Two newer organizations are the Arab American Anti-Discrimination Committee, with twenty-five thousand members, which fights negative stereotypes of Arab Americans, and the Arab American Committee. Only the NAAA lobbies in Washington; the AADC and the AAC are split by the personal animosities between the groups' founders.[28]

There have been some efforts to get American businesses with interests in the Middle East, especially oil companies, to do more lobbying and fund raising for the Arab cause, but they have not yielded much success to date. One analysis concludes: "Most Arab embassies throw impressive parties, but have little day-to-day contact with Congress, according to lawmakers and aides. Israel, by comparison, has a staff of congressional relations counselors who keep in touch with Capitol Hill."[29] Unlike AIPAC, the NAAA makes no pretense of being free from "mother country" direct influence. For example, advertisers in the business survey published by the NAAA are primarily Arab governments, the PLO, and firms doing business in the Persian Gulf. The Arab uprising in the West Bank and Gaza that began in 1987 has energized the Arab American community. NAAA now maintains a grassroots network organized by congressional district, patterned directly after AIPAC.[30]

A second major Arab organization, the American-Arab Anti-Discrimination Committee, was founded in 1980 on the model of the B'nai B'rith Anti-Defamation League, established some fifty years ago to combat discrimination against Jews. It does not lobby on legislation.

The heart of the difficulty of Arab American lobbying efforts is found in the existence of another group, the American Lebanese League, which claims ten thousand members and seeks a democratic and pro-Western Lebanon. It represents Christian forces in Lebanon, which have little in common with the Muslims and Druze of that country. Even a past president of NAAA admits the central hindrance to Arab lobbying in the United States:

> We can't represent the Arabs the way the Jewish lobby can represent Israel. The Israeli government has one policy to state, whereas we couldn't represent "the Arabs" even if we wanted to. They're as different as the Libyans and the Saudis are different, or as divided as the Christian and Moslem Lebanese.[31]

Inter-Arab divisiveness thus accounts for some, but not all, of the difficulties that these lobbying organizations confront.

Public opinion plays a much larger role. Americans have for a long time taken a much more sympathetic view toward Israel than toward the Arabs. Most polls show that Americans favor the Israeli position by better than a 3:1 margin. Occasionally, as during the Israeli invasion of Lebanon or the 1985 TWA hostage crisis, public support for Israel drops sharply, but it has generally rebounded. Even as the Arab uprising in the Israeli-occupied territories has sapped public support for Israel, there has been no appreciable increase in support for the Arab cause.[32]

The roots of the friendship between the United States and Israel include factors such as: (1) a common biblical heritage (most Arabs are Muslim, an unfamiliar religion to most Americans); (2) a shared European value system (most Arabs take their values from Islam, which is often sharply critical of the moral tenor of the West); (3) the democratic nature of Israel's political system (most Arab nations are monarchies or dictatorships); (4) Israel's role as an ally of the United States (most Arab countries have been seen as either unreliable friends or within the Soviet sphere of influence); and (5) the sympathy Americans extend toward Jews as victims (Arabs are portrayed as terrorists or exploiters of the American economy through their oil weapon).[33] The close connection of Arab American lobbying efforts to the Middle East does not help to overcome such difficulties.

The smaller Arab American population, two million to three million compared with almost six million Jews, further limits the political clout of Arab Americans. Even more critical, however, is the much greater political mobilization of American Jews, particularly in support of Israel. Jews have a very high rate of participation in politics, Arab Americans a rather low rate. Jews also are among the most generous campaign contributors in American politics: 60 percent of individual contributions to President Bill Clinton's 1992 campaign came from Jewish donors.[34] Arab Americans have not been very active in politics. Only a hundred thousand belong to any Arab American organization compared to two million Jews who are active in Jewish causes. Many Arab Americans, especially the older, native-born, shun politics. They are divided politically, with younger and more liberal Arab Americans voting Democratic and raising $750,000 for Jesse Jackson's 1988 race for the presidency. Older, more conservative Arab Americans identify with Republicans for their support for traditional social values. Democratic identifiers sometimes find their support unrequited: Arab Americans complained that the 1984 Democratic nominee returned their campaign contributions.[35]

While Arab groups are divided among themselves and have no common frame of reference, American Jews are united behind support of Israel. A 1982 survey of American Jews showed that 94 percent considered themselves either pro-Israel or very pro-Israel. Two-thirds often discuss Israel with friends and, by a 3–1 margin, reject the notion that support for Israel conflicts with one's attachment to the United States. Three-quarters of American Jews argue that they should not vote for a candidate who is unfriendly to Israel, and a third would be willing to contribute money to political candidates who supported Israel.[36]

Overall, the pro-Israel lobby prior to the late 1980s met all of the conditions identified as critical for a group to be successful. The Arab American lobby met none (see Table 12.1). Jews were well assimilated, had a high level of political activity, were homogeneous in their support of Israel, and had the support of public opinion. Israel was seen as a strategic asset by the American public and particularly by decisionmakers. Activity on behalf of Israel was perceived as legitimate by the American public; backers of AIPAC and other organizations did not stand to gain from their lobbying. They had to contribute their own money to participate. Although not numerous in comparison to many other groups, American Jews and other supporters of Israel were concentrated in key states that were important to presidential candidates (New York, California, Pennsylvania). Although Jews largely supported Democratic candidates, they were more likely than most other groups to shift their votes from one election to the next. In 1980, when they distrusted Jimmy Carter, they gave him just 42 percent of their vote; in 1992, when they distrusted George Bush, they gave his Democratic rival Bill Clinton almost twice Carter's percentage.

Table 12–1

Conditions for Foreign Policy Success by Ethnic Interest Groups: Pro-Israel and Arab American Groups

Conditions	Pro-Israel groups before 1987	Arab Americans	Pro-Israel groups after 1987
Group goals conform to U.S. strategic interests	+	−	•
Group well assimilated	+	−	+
High level of political activity	+	−	+
Group internally homogeneous	+	−	•
Group has support of public opinion	+	−	•
Group numerous with political clout	+	−	+
Group tactics legitimate	+	−	•

+ Condition met positively

− Condition not met (met negatively)

• Condition partially met

Arab Americans met none of the conditions. Until the Gulf War, few Americans saw any Arab nation except Egypt as a strategic ally of the United States; even after the war, many Americans harbored doubts about the reliability of most Arab nations as military partners. Many Arab Americans are not well assimilated into American society and politics; the community is neither homogeneous with respect to Middle East politics nor politically active. Arab Americans are more numerous than some other groups, but they are not strategically situated in states with large numbers of electoral votes. American public opinion has never been favorable to the Arab (or Palestinian) cause. The financing of Arab American organizations by Middle Eastern interests and the active pursuit of changes in U.S. policy by economic interests have served to weaken the legitimacy of the Arab American cause.

In 1987 the pro-Israel groups began to lose some of their clout. The Palestinian uprising against Israeli control of the West Bank and Gaza (the intifada) raised international consciousness about the Palestinian cause. The often-harsh Israeli attempts to quell it led to a drop in American public support for the Jewish state. They also led to conflicts within the Jewish community as to what Israel ought to do. One survey found that up to three-quarters of the leaders of major Jewish organizations favored direct talks between Israel and the PLO and similar shares backed some type of Palestinian homeland or state.[37]

AIPAC, on the other hand, became increasingly linked to the more hawkish right-wing government in Israel, which rejected the idea of "land for peace." When President Bush decided to withhold the $10 billion in loan guarantees for Israel, AIPAC decided to fight. Israel's opposition leader, Yitzhak Rabin, criticized AIPAC for interfering with the direct Washington-Jerusalem relationship. Bush also challenged the lobby, dramatically portraying himself as a lone statesman fighting "powerful political forces." Many more dovish Jewish organizations chose not to fight the president. AIPAC was battered in 1992–1993 when: (1) Rabin became prime minister promising to seek peace with the Palestinians and reiterating his criticism of the lobby; (2) the organization was accused of harassing Jewish peace groups and Arab American activists; and (3) the top officers of the organization were forced to resign for a variety of sins ranging from boasting about influence with the Clinton administration to uttering slurs against ultra-orthodox Jews and Israeli politicians. The collapse of AIPAC's governing structure reflected deeper tensions about the organization's loss of clout rather than simply a series of unrelated incidents.[38]

Some military leaders, politicians, and citizens no longer see Israel as an important strategic asset. In the Gulf War Bush saw Israel's treatment of the intifada as a barrier to cooperation with Arab states, reportedly calling Israel an "unruly partner and a nuisance." With the demise of the Soviet Union, Israel no longer was a strategic bulwark against countries allied with a hostile power.[39] Public opinion did not tilt toward the Arabs, but it became less supportive of Israel than it was in the 1970s and 1980s. By 1988, the public was almost equally divided over whether pro-Israel groups had too much influence or the right amount over U.S. foreign policy. Leading politicians, including the president, were willing to challenge AIPAC's role.[40] AIPAC's clout fell further in 1992 when several of its leaders, including Director Tom Dine, were forced to resign in internal power struggles over the direction of the organization.

The pro-Israel lobby was wounded, but not mortally. While the Arab Americans failed to meet any of the conditions shown in Table 12-1, even after 1987 the worst pro-Israel groups scored was a neutral rating. One senator who called AIPAC "ruthless" nevertheless admitted that "there's no countervailing sentiment."

The Arab American community has become more politically active in recent years. It was active in raising funds for Jesse Jackson's races for the presidency in 1984 and 1988.

Two NAAA leaders report that Arab Americans were the only ethnic group to provide Republican volunteers in every state for Reagan and that no ethnic group provided more volunteers than Arab Americans for the president's reelection campaign.[41] Arab Americans were highly visible in Jackson's 1988 campaign and unsuccessfully pressed the Democratic party to go on record in favor of a Palestinian state. Yet, James Zogby, head of the Arab American Anti-Discrimination Committee, admitted, "We don't make policy."[42]

The American Jewish community has become more heterogeneous about what Israel's strategy should be toward the Palestinians, but as the Gulf War indicated, if the fundamental interests of the Jewish state are at stake, the community closes ranks. When they perceive an American president as hostile to their interests—as they did with Bush—they form a cohesive voting bloc.

The few Arab Americans in Congress do not identify with their cause and do not caucus on Middle Eastern Issues.[43] The only Arab American senator, former Majority Leader George Mitchell (D-Maine), is a Lebanese Christian who received substantial support from pro-Israel political action committees. In contrast, Jewish members of Congress seek out committee assignments that focus on the Middle East. As of 1994, 20 percent of the members of the House Foreign Affairs Committee and 40 percent of that body's subcommittee on the Middle East were Jewish. The ranking minority member and the second- and third-ranking Democrats are Jewish.

OTHER ETHNIC INTEREST GROUPS

No foreign policy interest group, and certainly no ethnic group, has the reputation for influence that the pro-Israel forces have. Even a weakened AIPAC still sets the pace for two reasons. First, AIPAC is the model for most other successful groups. Second, other ethnic groups have been more divided over the best course of action for their countries of concern. The ethnic lobby that was poised to capture the role of "king of the Hill" from AIPAC, the Cuban American National Foundation (CANF), has been wrought with its own conflicts.

Latinos

Latinos now constitute almost 9 percent of all Americans, up from 6.4 percent in 1980. Yet they have little unity. Mexican Americans constitute 60 percent of all Latinos, but many are not American citizens and even those who are have ambivalent feelings toward Mexico. Until recently, Mexican leaders did not encourage intervention by Mexican Americans.[44]

The next largest group is Puerto Ricans. Yet they, too, are divided over the status of Puerto Rico, some favoring statehood, others continuation of the commonwealth status, and some independence. A 1985 meeting of the National Congress for Puerto Rican Rights could not reach a resolution over the issue of coordinating strategies with other Hispanic groups. Some Puerto Ricans resent other Latinos because on average Puerto Ricans earn less although they have had American citizenship longer.[45] Mexican Americans and Puerto Ricans are generally less well off than many other Americans. They overwhelmingly identify with the Democratic party.[46] For countries such as El Salvador and Nicaragua where American policy is more controversial, foreign policy lobbies are dominated by religious organizations, such as the Washington Office on Latin America, with few ties to the indigenous communities. These organizations largely focus on human rights issues. Some have influence on Capitol Hill, but their lobbying activities tend to concentrate more on legislators who are already committed to their cause.[47]

The third largest group, Cuban Americans, are much better off financially and vote heavily for Republican candidates. Cubans comprise just 5.3 percent of Latinos, yet they have established the second most potent ethnic lobby in the country. A small part of their success stems from modeling CANF upon AIPAC. Cuban Americans are generally strongly anticommunist. They helped to fund Lt. Col. Oliver L. North's legal expenses during the Iran-Contra affair and a lobbying effort to force Cuban troops from the African nation of Angola.[48]

CANF's leader, Jorge Mas Canosa, "may be the most significant individual lobbyist in the country."[49] The foundation lobbied successfully in 1990 for TV Marti, a direct broadcast station aimed at Cuba from the United States that has been effectively jammed by the Cuban government. State Department officials privately state that CANF has been responsible for maintaining the American hard line against Fidel Castro's regime. The federal government funds a resettlement program for Cuban refugees that CANF runs. Mas stood close to Bush when he signed the Cuban Democracy Act, strengthening sanctions against the Castro regime. CANF has one hundred directors, each of whom contribute $10,000. It claims fifty thousand donors. CANF contributed to fifty-six congressional campaigns in 1988 and to forty-eight in 1990, focusing largely on members of the House Foreign Affairs Committee. Overall, its Free Cuba Political Action Committee contributed $670,000 to congressional candidates from 1982 to 1992 and more than $1 million to presidential candidates in 1992 alone.[50] All three Cuban American representatives—two Republicans from Florida and a New Jersey Democrat—serve on the House Foreign Relations Committee, compared to just one other Latino member.

Yet CANF may have been proven too partisan for its own good. Although it has backed some Democrats in Congress, its partisanship has been overwhelmingly Republican. It believed that it held power over both parties and in early 1993 blocked a black Cuban American nominee of the Clinton administration for the post of chief policymaker on Latin America. That tilted the administration toward a more moderate line on Cuba. Clinton invited one hundred Cuban Americans to the White House for Cuban Independence Day, slighting CANF office holders. A new, more moderate Cuban American group, Cambio Cubano (Cuban Change), was founded, and the administration appeared more sympathetic to it when it did little to stop Congress from slashing funding in half for Radio Marti and from abolishing TV Marti.[51]

The fragmentation of the Latino community limits the unity and effectiveness (especially on foreign policy issues) of the Hispanic Caucus in the House of Representatives.[52] Not only is there tension among different groups of Latinos, but leaders of the Mexican American and Puerto Rican communities appear to be out of step ideologically with their more conservative constituencies.[53] Mexican Americans and Puerto Ricans are both numerous and concentrated in key states—Texas and California for the former and the Northeast for the latter—but they have low rates of participation. While Latin America is important strategically to the United States, it is not terribly salient to most non-Latinos. Latinos are not well integrated into American political culture: Most Mexican Americans and Puerto Ricans born in the continental United States identify themselves with their place of origin (usually their parents' place of birth) much more than as Americans; even native-born Cuban Americans are equally divided.[54] Cuban Americans are more united in their attitudes, very active politically, and constitute a powerful bloc in one of the nation's fastest growing states. They account for up to 10 percent of the Republican vote in Florida and have elected a Cuban American mayor of Miami. They have great political legitimacy and a compelling target in Castro's regime. Yet they have had limited success in isolating Castro and none at all in provoking direct confrontation with him. Americans may not like Castro, but they have not believed that his demise was imminent. Nor does Castro's rule appear very salient.[55] The collapse of the Soviet Union reduced the strategic threat of Cuba and opened up new opportunities for alternative Cuban American views; the election of a

Democratic president the CANF, opposed further weakened the clout of conservative forces within the community.

Greeks and Turks

Greek Americans were long considered second in power to the pro-Israel lobby. The American Hellenic Institute Public Affairs Committee (AHIPAC) is consciously modeled after AIPAC; the two groups often have worked together. AHIPAC lobbied successfully for an arms embargo on Turkey after its 1974 invasion of Cyprus and has pressed for a balance in foreign aid between the two states. The two million Greek Americans are very politically active and loyal to the Democratic party. In 1988 they raised more than 15 percent of Greek American Michael Dukakis's early campaign funds. In contrast, the Turkish American community of 180,000 is not well organized. Recently, it employed a Washington public relations firm to lobby the government, but Turkish Americans do not lobby. As one member of Congress stated, "I don't have any Turkish restaurants in my district."[56] Overall, in 1988 Greek Americans were advantaged over Turkish Americans on virtually every condition. They were more assimilated into American life, more active politically, more homogeneous and numerous, and—to the extent they were Christian rather than Muslim—had public opinion on their side. Each group claims strategic importance and, because the demands of each could be met through foreign aid, there was no fundamental clash. Greek American influence has waned as American foreign policy has shifted emphasis from Greece and Turkey to other trouble spots, especially after the fall of the Soviet Union limited the strategic value of both Greece and Turkey to the United States. In turn, the economic integration of Europe made both countries turn toward their own continent.

Eastern Europeans

Eastern Europeans have a long history of political activism in the United States. There are eight million Polish Americans and almost a million Lithuanians, Latvians, and Estonians. Several Midwestern states have large concentrations of Eastern Europeans, and both major political parties have recognized the importance of these groups by establishing divisions dealing with their affairs. Congress enacted a law in 1959 denoting the third week of July as Captive Nations Week, to be observed until the Soviet Union withdrew from Eastern Europe and the Baltic states.

These ethnic groups have little impact on foreign policy. They are not united among themselves and many worry that emphasizing their ethnicity would only stir negative emotions among other Americans. The lobbies are all understaffed and underfunded. They also pressed the government to sacrifice detente with the Soviet Union, a policy at odds with that of presidents of both parties. Especially as the policies initiated by Mikhail Gorbachev led to greater freedom within the Soviet Union and the liberation of eastern Europe, Bush did not want to jeopardize this new openness. The United States never accepted Soviet occupation of the Baltic states but refused to grant them recognition in 1989 and 1990 when Lithuania, Latvia, and Estonia declared independence. The ethnic lobbies favored such recognition, but the general public did not. After Lithuania, Latvia, and Estonia gained independence in 1991 the long-time alliances in the Baltic American community came apart as each ethnic group fought for a share of the decreasing American foreign-aid pie.[57] Neither the president nor Congress was willing to take any side in the many ethnic tensions emerging in eastern Europe, even as the small lobby of the seventy thousand Albanian Americans pressed for a resolution attacking discrimination against Albanians in the former Yugoslavia.[58] One of the least numerous groups in the United

States, Muslims from Bosnia Hercegovina, established the most unusual alliance in recent years. Muslim, Jewish, and Christian groups united to press the United States to intervene militarily to protect the Bosnian Muslims from attacks by Serbs and Croatians.[59]

Baltic Americans were never homogeneous, numerous enough, or sufficiently active to overcome the U.S. government belief that a united Soviet Union was more strategically important than a set of independent nations. When independence appeared imminent, public opinion among Americans failed Baltic Americans: 31 percent favored immediate recognition in March 1990, compared to 41 percent who favored bolstering the Soviet leader Mikhail Gorbachev.[60]

African Americans

African Americans, like Latinos, traditionally have been more concerned with domestic economic issues than with foreign policy concerns. Most black Americans cannot trace their roots to a specific African country. Until the 1960s, black participation in politics was restricted, both by law and by socioeconomic status. There were few blacks in Congress, especially on the foreign policy committees, or in the Foreign Service. Blacks contribute little money to campaigns and electorally they have been strongly tied to the Democratic party, thus cutting off lobbying activities to Republican presidents and legislators. Black activity on foreign policy heightened over the issue of the ending of the apartheid system of racial separation in South Africa. The Congressional Black Caucus and TransAfrica, a lobbying organization that in 1993 expanded its role to become a think tank dealing with foreign policy issues, are the two most prominent actors.

The South African issue united the black community. Whites also strongly opposed the South African regime. They responded in public opinion polls that giving black South Africans freedom was more important than keeping the country as a stable ally.[61] President Ronald Reagan ultimately agreed in 1985 to accept sanctions against the South African government; he was pushed in that direction by the weight of public opinion, a mobilized black community, and a supportive Congress. The Congressional Black Caucus, now with thirty-nine members, has taken firm stands on South Africa, sending U.S. troops to Somalia, and lifting the ban on Haitian immigrants infected with the AIDS virus. Four of the forty-five members of the House Foreign Affairs Committee are blacks; blacks have increasingly held key positions on foreign policy in the executive branch; and they are now more united on wider issues of Africa than ever before.[62] Although blacks are well assimilated into American politics and becoming more powerful, their overall level of activity remains lower than whites.[63] Their influence is further limited by the low salience of Africa and other black nations, especially as strategic concerns, to most Americans.

Asian Americans

Given the impressive lobbying efforts of Japan and Taiwan and the size of the Asian population—10 percent of the California population—one might expect considerable power from this group. Yet, they have not participated in politics in large numbers. Many recent immigrants are preoccupied with economic issues and eschew politics. They came from cultures without democratic traditions and have not placed adaptation at the top of their agenda. Older Japanese and other Asians who faced discrimination in earlier periods (especially during World War II) shy away from politics, in contrast to blacks, who have used politics to gain civil rights. The Asian American community, like the Hispanic community, is very diverse and there are few common bonds among Koreans, Indochinese, Japanese, and Chinese. There are tensions between Japanese Americans and Chinese Americans stemming from Japan's occupation of China during World War II. Vietnamese immigrants bear grudges against Cambodians, while Hindus and Moslems from South Asia have long-standing quarrels.[64]

Many recent Asian American immigrants still see themselves as "guests" in a strange land and are reluctant to get involved in politics. Others simply want to be left alone by the government, believing that self-reliance is the best course. Asian Americans constitute 3 percent of the population but 1 percent of the electorate. Those who do vote are among the most loyal Republican blocs in the population. They are attracted by the strong anti-communist positions of the GOP, as well as the party's emphasis on family values. Japanese Americans are an exception. They are overwhelmingly Democratic and have high rates of participation. Three of the five Asian Americans in Congress are of Japanese ancestry and all are Democrats. Only one Asian American, a nonvoting delegate from American Samoa, serves on the House Foreign Affairs Committee. Rep. Jay Kim (R-Calif.), the first Korean American elected to Congress, said: "I have no special agenda for Asian Americans."[65]

THE ELECTORAL CONNECTION IN FOREIGN POLICY

Most lobbyists concentrate on legislation in Washington, but tactics have been shifting increasingly toward the electoral arena. Interest groups use political action committees to channel contributions to candidates for Congress. If a sound presentation doesn't convince a legislator to accede to one's cause, the argument runs, perhaps a campaign contribution might.

Former Senator Charles McC. Mathias Jr. (R-Md.) worried that such tactics might make it difficult for the nation to speak with one voice on foreign policy, said:

> Factions among us lead the nation toward excessive foreign attachments or animosities. Even if the groups were balanced—if Turkish-Americans equaled Greek Americans or Arab Americans equaled Jewish–Americans—the result would not necessarily be a sound, cohesive foreign policy because the national interest is not simply the sum of our special interests and attachments.... Ethnic politics, carried as they often have been to excess, have proven harmful to the national interest.[66]

The strategies of pro-Israel groups usually have focused on placing intense constituency pressure on legislators who make either anti-Israel or pro-Arab statements. The most notable efforts occurred in Illinois in 1982 and 1984. Rep. Paul Findley (R) and Sen. Charles Percy (R), who chaired the Foreign Relations Committee, were strong critics of Israel. Jewish sources raised $685,000 to defeat Findley in 1982 and $322,000 to beat Percy two years later; a California donor contributed more than $1 million in "uncoordinated expenditures" against Percy. That same year, pro-Israeli groups targeted Senator Jesse Helms (R-N.C.), an even more strident critic of Israel, who upon reelection dramatically shifted to a pro-Israel position.

Pro-Israel political action committee (PAC) contributions rose from $2,450 in 1976 to $8.7 million in 1990—a higher figure than that for the largest domestic PAC, that of the realtors. Virtually every senator and most members of the House have received support from the more than eighty pro-Israel PACs. Senate Foreign Relations Committee members received $1.2 million from pro-Israel groups in 1990, more than twice as much from the second largest ideological PAC and 40 percent of *all* ideological political action committee contributions. Pro-Israel PACs have, like others, concentrated on incumbents; they also favor Democrats by more than two-to-one. Arab Americans are far behind: In 1986, they contributed just $70,000 to congressional candidates compared to $4.6 million from pro-Israel groups.[67]

The imbalance of resources between pro-Israel and pro-Arab groups is not the major reason for concern about the potential for campaign contributions to influence foreign policy. The nature of interest group participation in foreign policy may well change because of the heavy spending. What should the role of money in American politics be? Is political support to be given to the highest bidder? Even though ethnic lobbies do not stand to benefit financially from a foreign policy that suits their preferences, many Americans are simply so skeptical of the role of money in politics that they will worry that something is not right. Support for foreign policy initiatives might be open to the influence of campaign contributions. The victorious group might be viewed with suspicion by the larger public, much as large corporations are. The strategy of influencing policy by shaping the membership of Congress may thus backfire. The public and members of Congress may strongly disapprove of winning policy debates by threats.

Purely domestic issues have traditionally divided our parties, whereas foreign policy has been bipartisan. A strident electoral campaign by a foreign policy interest group might disrupt this pattern. Jewish groups give far more money to Democratic candidates than to Republicans. Might this endanger support for Israel among Republicans? Pro-Israeli groups recognized this problem in 1985 and 1986 when they gave 60 percent of their contributions to Republicans. This attracted the support of many Christian Right supporters in Congress, who disagree with American Jews on most other issues, especially prayer in schools. It did not prevent the emergence of partisanship on the Middle East. Secretary of State James Baker reportedly justified the Bush administration's strong criticism of Israel by noting that "[Jews] don't vote for us anyway."[68]

Some observers see this strategy as leading to a situation in which concern for Israel's security will be the only issue for American Jews; this will ultimately make political alliances between members of Congress and pro-Israeli forces into little more than contests for campaign contributions (not unlike some domestic political issues) rather than bonds based on long-term philosophical commitments.[69] As unsettling as this is for the Middle East, the problem is more widespread and even more ominous. Pro-Israel groups do not seek financial rewards for their campaign contributions. Nevertheless, such tactics might backfire. On the one hand, 61 percent of Americans believe it is acceptable for American Jews to contribute money to Israel. On the other, almost as many Americans hold that Israel has too much power in America as those who believe it has too little.[70]

Other PACs financed by foreign money, including American subsidiaries of Japanese firms and foreign car dealers, have more direct economic stakes and have used their clout to shape tax law in at least one state. As long as the money is raised exclusively in the United States, such practices are legal. As such strategies prove effective, they will become more widespread.

The bipartisan nature of our foreign policy is threatened by making international politics too much like domestic issues. We can afford to be contentious at home. The stakes are much greater abroad. Already Soviet leaders complain that negotiating with American presidents is difficult because our leaders cannot ensure that agreements reached will be approved by Congress. These problems could only increase if foreign policy issues became important in election campaigns marked by heavy expenditures and threats. What the correct policy ought to be becomes less important than which group can yell the loudest, and the volume is affected by the purchasing power of television advertising. Causes that have heretofore enjoyed widespread, bipartisan support among the public, such as support for Israel, might become objects of great conflict. The very groups that spawned this effort might ultimately regret such tactics.

NOTES

*The support of the General Research Board, University of Maryland—College Park, is gratefully acknowledged as is the assistance of Nalini Verma, Fred Augustyn, Rodger Payne, and Galen Wilkenson. The comments of Allan J. Cigler, Burdett A. Loomis, and George H. Quester are greatly appreciated.

1. "All Politics Is Global," *Wall Street Journal,* November 25, 1992, A12; E. J. Dionne "All Politics Is Now Global," *Washington Post,* July 13, 1993, A15.
2. Richard F. Fenno, Jr., *Congressmen in Committees* (Boston: Little, Brown, 1973), 141.
3. Eileen Burgin, "Representatives' Decisions on Participation in Foreign Policy Decisions," *Legislative Studies Quarterly* 16 (December 1991): 521–546.
4. See Aage R. Clausen, *How Congressmen Decide* (New York: St. Martin's Press, 1973).
5. Stephen Krasner, *Defending the National Interest* (Princeton: Princeton University Press, 1978).
6. Seymour Martin Lipset and William Schneider, *The Confidence Gap* (New York: Macmillan, 1983); CBS News Poll press release, October 23, 1988; and Times-Mirror Center for People and The Press, *The People, The Press, and Politics on the Eve of '92,* December 4, 1991 (Washington, D.C.: Times-Mirror Center for The People and The Press).
7. Bayless Manning, "The Congress, the Executive, and Intermestic Affairs: Three Proposals," *Foreign Affairs* (January 1977): 306–324.
8. David Osborne, "Lobbying for Japan, Inc.," *New York Times Magazine,* December 4, 1983, 133–139; and Robert Sherrill, review of Steven Emerson, *The American House of Saud, Washington Post Book World,* May 5, 1985, 4.
9. Clyde H. Farnsworth, "Japan's Loud Voice in Washington," *New York Times,* December 10, 1989, F1, F6; and Center for Public Integrity, *The Trading Game: Inside Lobbying for the North American Free Trade Agreement* (Washington, D.C.: Center for Public Integrity).
10. James M. McCormick, *American Foreign Policy and Process,* 2nd ed. (Itasca, Ill.: F.E. Peacock, 1992), 441–444; and McCormick and Eugene R. Wittkopf, "Bipartisanship, Partisanship, and Ideology in Congressional-Executive Foreign Policy Relations, 1947–1988," *Journal of Politics* 52 (November 1990): 1077–1100.
11. Jack L. Walker, *Mobilizing Interest Groups in America* (Ann Arbor: University of Michigan Press, 1991), 63, 71.
12. David S. Broder, "Christian Coalition, Shifting Tactics, to Lobby Against Clinton Budget," *Washington Post,* July 18, 1993, A7; and Peter Behr, "NAFTA Pact Jeopardized by Court," *Washington Post,* July 1, 1993, A1, A4.
13. On energy, see Eric M. Uslaner, *Shale Barrel Politics: Energy Politics and Legislative Leadership* (Stanford: Stanford University Press, 1989), esp. chaps. 5 and 6. On the three policy areas, see John Spanier and Eric M. Uslaner, *American Foreign Policy Making and the Democratic Dilemmas,* 6th ed. (New York: Macmillan, 1994), chap. 9.
14. Sixty-four percent uphold the right of religious organizations to endorse candidates. See Marjorie Hyer, "Tolerance Shows in Voter Poll," *Washington Post,* February 13, 1988, E18.
15. E. E. Schattschneider, *The Semisovereign People* (New York: Holt, Rinehart and Winston, 1960), 26.
16. John E. Rielly, *American Public Opinion and U.S. Foreign Policy* (Chicago: Chicago Council on Foreign Relations, 1991), 7–8; John H. Aldrich, John L. Sullivan, and Eugene Borgida, "Foreign Affairs and Issue Voting," *American Political Science Review,* 83 (January 1989): 123–142; Martin P. Wattenberg, *The Rise of Candidate Centered Politics: Presidential Elections of the 1980s* (Cambridge: Harvard University Press, 1991), 112–147; and Spanier and Uslaner, *American Foreign Polcy Making and the Democratic Dilemmas,* chap. 6.
17. Mohammed E. Ahrari, "Conclusion," in *Ethnic Groups and Foreign Policy,* ed. Mohammed E. Ahrari (New York: Greenwood Press, 1987), 155–158.
18. Thomas M. Franck and Edward Weisband, *Foreign Policy by Congress* (New York: Oxford University Press, 1979), 186; and Ben Bradlee, Jr., "Israel's Lobby," *Boston Globe Magazine,* April 29, 1984, 64.
19. Cheryl A. Rubenberg, "The Middle East Lobbies," *The Link* 17 (January-March 1984): 4.

20. Thomas L. Friedman, "A Pro-Israel Lobby Gives Itself a Headache," *New York Times*, November 8, 1992, E18.
21. Sanford J. Ungar, "Washington: Jewish and Arab Lobbyists," *Atlantic,* March 1978, 10.
22. Bradlee, "Israel's Lobby," 64.
23. Robert H. Trice, "Congress and the Arab-Israeli Conflict: Support for Israel in the U.S. Senate, 1970–1973," *Political Science Quarterly* 92 (Fall 1977): 443–463; and Robert Pear with Richard L. Berke, "Pro-Israel Group Exerts Quiet Might as It Rallies Supporters in Congress," *New York Times,* July 7, 1987, A8.
24. Hedrick Smith, *The Power Game: How, Washington Works* (New York: Random House, 1988), 222–228.
25. Lloyd Grove, "On the March for Israel," *Washington Post,* June 13, 1991, D10.
26. Bill Keller, "Supporters of Israel, Arabs Vie for Friends in Congress, at White House," *Congressional Quarterly Weekly Report,* August 25, 1981, 1527–1528; and David A. Dickson, "Pressure Politics and the Congressional Foreign Policy Process" (Paper presented at the annual meeting of the American Political Science Association, San Francisco, August-September 1990).
27. Keller, "Supporters of Israel," 1528.
28. Nora Boustany, "Arab American Lobby Is Struggling," *Washington Post,* April 6, 1990, A10.
29. Keller, "Supporters of Israel," 1528.
30. Rubenberg, "The Middle East Lobbies"; Keller, "Supporters Vie"; Steven L. Spiegel, *The Other Arab-Israeli Conflict* (Chicago: University of Chicago Press, 1985), 8; and David J. Saad and G. Neal Lendenmann, "Arab American Grievances," *Foreign Policy* (Fall 1985): 22.
31. Quoted in Spiegel, *The Other Arab-Israeli Conflict,* 8.
32. Spanier and Uslaner, *American Foreign Policy Making,* chap. 7.
33. Keller, "Supporters Vie," 1523.
34. Thomas L. Friedman, "Jewish Criticism on Clinton Picks," *New York Times,* January 5, 1993, All.
35. Boustany, "Arab American Lobby Is Struggling"; and Maralee Schwartz, "Parties Are Paying Greater Attention to Arab Americans," *Washington Post,* January 20, 1992, A10; Mae Ghalwash, "Arab Americans Face Voting Quandary," *Washington Post,* November 1, 1992, A12-A13; Peter Steinfels, "Despite Role on World Stage, Muslims Turn to the Personal," *New York Times,* May 7, 1993, A1, A13; and Robert A. Trice, *Interest Groups and the Foreign Policy Process* (Beverly Hills, Calif.: Sage Publications, 1976), 54–55.
36. Leon Hadar, "What Israel Means to U.S. Jewry," *Jerusalem Post,* international edition, June 19–25, 1982, 11; Bradlee, "Israel's Lobby," 8.
37. Peter Steinfels. "Survey of U.S. Jewish Leaders Finds Overwhelming Support for Israeli-P.L.O. Talks," *New York Times,* February 10, 1991, 11.
38. Thomas L. Friedman, "Uneasy Debate for Jews in U.S. on Loan Guarantees," *New York Times,* March 2, 1992, A1, A6; Friedman, "Israeli Loan Deal Is Linked by Baker to a Building Halt," *New York Times,* February 25, 1992. A1, A6; Robert Friedman, "The Wobbly Israel Lobby," *Washington Post,* November 1, 1992, C1, C4; and Robert S. Greenberger, "Head of Largest Pro-Israel Lobby Quits under Pressure in Flap Over Book Quote," *Wall Street Journal,* June 29, 1993, A4.
39. John M. Goshko, "Persian Gulf Crisis Drives U.S.-Israeli Relations to Historic Ebb," *Washington Post,* October 27, l990, A20; Clyde Haberman, "Israelis Worry If World's New Epoch Will Find Them Shunted Aside by U.S.," *New York Times,* August 3, 1992, A8.
40. Spanier and Uslaner, *American Foreign Policy Making and the Democratic Dilemmas,* chap. 7; and CBS News press release, October 23, 1988.
41. "Arab, Americans Take an Increased Political Role," *New York Times,* November 4, 1984, 74; and Saad and Lendenmann, "Arab American Grievances," 22.
42. Grove, "On the Move for Israel," D10; and Boustany, "Arab American Lobby Is Struggling."
43. Ungar, "Jewish and Arab Lobbists," 12.
44. Robert Reinhold, "Mexico Leaders Look North of the Border," *New York Times,* December 8, 1989, Al, A28.
45. Rodolfo O. de la Garza, "Chicanos and U.S. Foreign Policy: The Future of Chicano-Mexican Relations," *Western Political Quarterly* 23 (December 1980): 571–572; and Jesus Rangel, "Puerto Rican Need Discussed at Home," *New York Times,* June 3, 1985, B18.
46. Barbara Vobejda, "Asians, Hispanics Giving Nation More Diversity," *Washington Post,* June 12, 1992, A3; and Bernard Weinraub, "Wooing Cuban Americans in G.O.P.," *New York Times,* May 22, 1987, A14.
47. Bill Keller, "Interest Groups Focus on El Salvador Policy," *Congressional Quarterly Weekly Report,* April 24, 1982, 895–900.

48. Robert S. Greenberger, "Right-Wing Groups Join in Capitol Hill Crusade to Help Savimbi's Anti-Communists in Angola," *Wall Street Journal,* November 25, 1985, 58.

49. John Newhouse, "Socialism or Death," *The New Yorker,* April 27, 1992, 77.

50. Newhouse, "Socialism or Death," 76–81; Lee Hockstadter and William Booth, "Cuban Exiles Split on Life After Castro," *Washington Post,* March 10, 1992, Al, A14; Peter H. Stone, "Cuban Clout," *National Journal,* February 20, 1993, 449; and Larry Rohter, "A Rising Cuban American Leader: Statesman to Some, Bully to Others," *New York Times,* October 29, 1992, A18.

51. John M. Goshko, "Controversy Erupts on Latin America Post," *Washington Post,* January 23, 1993, A4; and Larry Rohter, "Moderate Cuban Voices Rise in U.S.," *New York Times,* June 27, 1993, A16.

52. David Rampe, "Power Panel in the Making: The Hispanic Caucus," *New York Times,* September 30, 1988, B5.

53. Robert Suro, "Hispanic Pragmatism Seen in Survey," *New York Times,* December 15, 1992, A20.

54. David Gonzalez, "What's the Problem with 'Hispanic'? Just Ask a 'Latino,' " *New York Times,* November 15, 1992, E6.

55. NBC News press release, October 4, 1991; and Yankelovich, Clancy, Shulman press release, September 10, 1992, which reported that only 37 percent of Americans believed that it mattered whether Castro remained in power (57 percent said it did not).

56. Thomas M. Franck and Edward Weisband, *Foreign Policy by Congress* (New York: Oxford University Press, 1979), 191–193.

57. Isabel Wilkerson, "A Battle Is Over for Baltic-Americans," *New York Times,* September 3, 1991, A9.

58. "The Albanians," *New York Times,* August 24, 1987, A14.

59. Amy E. Schwartz, "Brought Together by Bosnia," *Washington Post,* May 14, 1993, A31.

60. CBS News press release, April 5, 1990.

61. Kenneth Longniver, "Black American Demands," *Foreign Policy* (Fall, 1985): 3–18; Michael Beaubien, "Making Waves in Foreign Policy," *Black Enterprise,* April 1982, 37–42; and David Hoffman, "Americans Back S. Africa's Blacks," *Washington Post,* September 25, 1985.

62. Milton D. Morris, "African-Americans and the New World Order," *The Washington Quarterly* 15 (Autumn 1992): 19; and Keith B. Richburg, "Americans Bring an Agenda Out of Africa," *Washington Post,* May 30, 1993, A39.

63. Sidney Verba et al. "Citizen Activity: Who Participates? What Do They Say?," *American Political Science Review,* 87 (June 1993): 306.

64. Stanley Karnow "Apathetic Asian Americans?," *Washington Post,* November 29, 1992, C2.

65. Sonal Gandhi, "Asian American Political Behavior" (Student paper, Department of Government and Politics, University of Maryland, 1992); Karnow, "Apathetic Asian Americans?"; and "Asian Americans in Politics? Rarely," *New York Times,* June 3, 1993, A16.

66. Charles McC. Mathias, Jr., "Ethnic Groups and Foreign Policy," *Foreign Affairs* 59 (Summer 1981): 981.

67. Charles R. Babcock, "Israel's Backers Maximize Political Clout," *Washington Post,* September 26, 1991, A21; Barbara Levick-Segnatelli, "The Washington Political Action Committee: One Man Can Make a Difference," in *Risky Business,* ed. Robert Biersack, Paul Hernnson, and Clyde Wilcox (Armonk, N.Y.: M. E. Sharpe, 1994); Edward Roeder, "Pro-Israel Groups Know Money Talks in Congress," *Washington Times,* September 18, 1991, A7; and Richard H. Curtiss, Stealth PACs (Washington, D.C.: American Educational Trust, 1990).

68. Robert Kuttner, "Unholy Alliance," *The New Republic,* May 26, 1986, 19–25; Robert S. Greenberger, "Pro-Israel Lobby Faces Political Tug of War: Conservative Leadership vs. Liberal Constituents," *Wall Street Journal,* December 20, 1988, A16; and Haberman, "Israelis Worry."

69. See Robert Kuttner, "Unholy Alliance"; and Paul Taylor, "Pro-Israel PACs Giving More to GOP," *Washington Post,* November 4, 1985, Al, All.

70. Hyer, "Tolerance Shows in Voter Poll"; and CBS News press release, October 23, 1988.

13

Getting Uncle Sam's Ear

Will Ethnic Lobbies Cramp America's Foreign Policy Style?

JAMES M. LINDSAY

The daily schedule of any secretary of state or national security adviser attests to America's ethnic diversity. Interspersed with interminable staff meetings and appointments with visiting foreign dignitaries are sessions with domestic ethnic groups. It might be a breakfast talk with officials from the Cuban American National Foundation on U.S. policy toward Cuba, a luncheon address to members of the American Latvian Association on NATO expansion, or an evening speech to the American Jewish Committee on the Middle East peace process. In America, global politics is local politics—and local politics, often, is ethnic politics.

None of this is new, of course. Irish Americans lobbied nineteenth-century presidents to endorse Irish autonomy, and they joined with German Americans in pressing Woodrow Wilson to keep the United States out of World War I. Still, with the Soviet Union no longer around to give direction to U.S. foreign policy and with immigrants now arriving in America from every corner of the globe, ethnic lobbies are playing a more visible role in policymaking. In the eyes of critics, the United States has been worse off for it. Increasingly, some observers fear, American foreign policy will be driven—and often fragmented—by the pressures of small groups with intense interests.

September 11 appears to have tempered these fears, at least momentarily, by giving U.S. foreign policy a clear sense of direction for the first time since the Berlin Wall fell. Even so, ethnic lobbies will continue to shape American policy abroad. But the story of ethnic influence is more complicated, and more interesting, than it may at first appear. On balance, ethnic groups matter, but not nearly as much or as often as people might suspect. Within the ethnic universe, however, some groups will grow in influence, while others will decline. It is already possible, indeed, to glimpse who the winners and losers may be. And there is reason to think that U.S. foreign policy itself will, in the end, be among the winners.

NEW KIDS ON THE BLOCK

For a country that draws its citizens literally from around the globe, the United States is host to remarkably few ethnic foreign policy lobbies. One looks in vain, for example, for Dutch, French, Canadian, Italian, or Norwegian lobbies. And their absence cannot be explained by size or geographic dispersion. Each of these immigrant communities is far larger than those from, say, Greece or Cuba and is, like them, concentrated in a few U.S. states where they could make their electoral clout felt.

The truth is that ethnic groups weigh in on foreign policy matters only when conditions are right. Immigrants who came to the United States as political exiles (think Cubans) are much more likely to try to influence policy toward their ancestral homeland than those who came to find a better life (think French Canadians or Italians). Ethnics whose real or symbolic ancestral homelands are threatened by their neighbors (think Armenia, Greece, or Israel) are also more likely to lobby than those who come from countries that are secure (think Norway or Portugal). And it is no coincidence that prominent lobbies like Armenian Americans, Cuban Americans, Greek Americans, and Jewish Americans represent the most economically successful American ethnic groups. Impoverished ethnic groups are usually too focused on their own plight to worry about those they have left behind.

Economic hardship, together with the lack of either an exile mentality or a threat, explains why, Cuban Americans aside, Latino organizations usually sit on the sidelines of foreign policy. Groups such as the National Council of La Raza and the Mexican American Legal Defense and Educational Fund have concentrated their focus on the economy, civil rights, and immigration because those are the issues that matter to their members. Given the economic challenges facing the Hispanic community today and the relative security that most Latin American countries enjoy, foreign policy is not likely to galvanize Latinos any time soon.

What about other immigrant groups? One likely to be active in coming years is Indians. Not only does India face military threats—from both Pakistan and China—but Indian Americans are one of the most affluent ethnic groups in the United States. They have become active in politics, contributing an estimated $8 million to federal election campaigns over the past three elections. Congress has taken notice. The Congressional India Caucus, founded in 1993, now has more than 120 members, nearly double that of the Congressional Study Group on Germany.

The Chinese American community presents a different case. Historically, Chinese Americans, like Latinos, have been quiet on foreign policy. In their case, economics has not been a major barrier—Chinese Americans have prospered. Rather, what is lacking is a policy around which they can mobilize. China is not threatened, and unlike Cuban Americans, most Chinese Americans do not see themselves as political exiles and do not push for the overthrow of the communist government. Moreover, Chinese Americans are divided over whether to promote trade with China or to pressure Beijing to improve its human rights record.

Whether other Asian American groups will form significant foreign policy lobbies will depend to a considerable extent on how China behaves. A belligerent China will give Korean Americans, Vietnamese Americans, and Cambodian Americans reasons to mobilize. But if China is more pacific, U.S. relations with each of these countries will be more or less "normal," and the need to reshape U.S. policy to protect ethnic interests will decline.

WHO WINS, WHO LOSES?

Concerns that new ethnic lobbies will capture U.S. policy toward their ancestral homelands are longstanding. Yet just as their willingness to take on foreign policy is exaggerated, so too is their ability to get their way.

Consider the Jewish American lobby. No one doubts that it helps shape U.S. policy toward the Middle East. But it does not have an unbroken record of success. The United States sells high-tech weaponry to neighboring Arab states, pushes Israel to trade land for peace, and refuses to move the U.S. embassy from Tel Aviv to Jerusalem.

And the Jewish American lobby is in many ways an exception. Most other ethnic lobbies have far less impressive track records. The East European lobby failed in the 1950s and 1960s to persuade successive administrations to roll back Soviet gains in Eastern Europe, and while it pressed for NATO expansion during the 1990s, it was far from pivotal in the decision to expand. The Greek lobby had brief success in persuading Congress to impose an arms embargo on Turkey, and the Armenian lobby has made Armenia one of the highest per capita recipients of U.S. aid, but neither has disrupted close U.S. security ties with the Turkish government. The Serbian lobby had no impact on U.S. policy toward the Balkans in the 1990s. In short, ethnic lobbying does not translate automatically into policy influence.

So when are ethnic lobbies likely to get their way? That depends on both the characteristics of the lobby itself and the broader political context in which it operates. On the internal side of the ledger what matters is a community's size, commitment, unity, resources, and, most important, its political skill or ability to make effective use of the first four qualities. The Jewish American lobby scores high on all counts. By contrast, the Arab American lobby has been hobbled over the years by national and religious divisions.

The broader political factors that influence an ethnic lobby's effectiveness begin with whether it wants to preserve or to overturn the status quo. Preserving it is far easier—a lobby prevails if it wins at any step of the political process. For instance, cracks have developed in recent years in support for the four-decades-old embargo on Havana—a policy, by the way, that predates the rise of the Cuban American lobby—as Midwestern farmers have sought access to Cuba's market. Yet the embargo has remained essentially intact because the Cuban American lobby has maintained the support of House Republican leaders.

A second broad political factor is whether other powerful interests support or oppose an ethnic lobby's aims. The Jewish lobby succeeds partly because it is pushing on an open door—it advocates policies that most Americans favor on the merits. Israel is a stable, pro-Western democracy in a region where governments are often unstable, autocratic, and anti-American. Conversely, Armenian Americans cannot persuade Congress to criticize Turkey for refusing to apologize for the Armenian genocide during and after World War I because oil companies, defense contractors, and the U.S. military have joined to fend off a policy that jeopardizes their considerable interests in Ankara. Serbian Americans found almost no allies for their call for giving Belgrade a more sympathetic hearing.

Finally, events abroad matter. Castro's hatred of the United States has strengthened the hand of the Cuban American lobby. Had Havana sought a rapprochement with Washington, Cuban Americans might not have been able to fight off efforts to keep the Cuban embargo in place. The Greek lobby was most powerful in the 1970s when Turkey's invasion of Cyprus made it politically harder to defend pro-Turkish policies. The September 11 terrorist attacks and their aftermath may redefine the political terrain for both the Arab American and Jewish American lobbies. Much will depend on whether the lesson Americans draw from these events is that the United States has been too unquestioning in its support of Israel, or that America's Arab allies will not come to its aid in its hour of need, or that the Middle East is too dangerous to merit further U.S. engagement.

Which of the new ethnic lobbies look to be winners? One group likely to emerge as a political powerhouse is Indian Americans. Not only are they affluent and interested in India, but China's rising power and India's decision to move toward a market economy means their calls for a more "India friendly" foreign policy are likely to meet a receptive audience in Washington. Pakistani Americans no doubt will try to prevent a tilt toward India, and the war in Afghanistan has given Islamabad renewed geopolitical importance in

Washington. But Pakistani Americans will labor under two disadvantages—they are only one-tenth the size of the Indian American community, and Pakistan's military government maintains close ties to China. The potential for worsening U.S. relations with China is a major reason a Chinese American lobby is unlikely to be influential.

Again, Chinese Americans tend to favor engaging Beijing rather than isolating it. Should China act more aggressively, as its critics contend it will, Chinese Americans will find it hard to sustain a conciliatory policy toward Beijing. They (and their supporters) will find themselves vulnerable to politically damaging charges that they are aiding America's adversary—a charge that could resonate given that one out of four Americans harbors "very negative attitudes" toward Chinese Americans and one out of three doubts their loyalty to the United States. A more belligerent China would also strengthen the hand of other Asian ethnic groups that oppose demands for conciliatory policies. Conversely, if U.S.-Chinese relations follow a cooperative path in the years to come, the incentive for Chinese Americans to inject themselves into foreign policy debates will diminish.

What about the Latino lobby? Although Hispanic groups are likely to focus on domestic issues rather than foreign policy ones, the tremendous size of the Latino community means that a Hispanic lobby could be formidable when it does take up foreign policy issues. The open question is whether a Latino lobby can maintain a united political front. Issues that galvanize Salvadoran Americans may not arouse Cuban or Mexican Americans. Even within national groupings divisions may emerge. The once-solid Cuban American lobby now appears to be fracturing along generational lines, with younger Cuban Americans turning away from their parents' unforgiving hardline policies. Likewise, Mexican Americans could fracture along regional lines or, assuming that Mexico becomes a vibrant multiparty democracy, perhaps even along ideological lines.

It is also possible that some small ethnic communities may come to dominate U.S. policy toward their homeland. Somali American groups might carve out a powerful role on U.S. policy toward Mogadishu, or Hmong Americans might take control of policy toward Vientiane. But given the small number of voters such groups represent, their power will largely reflect the fact that no one else cares about U.S. relations with their ancestral homeland rather than any magical sway they might have over foreign policy.

Whom Will Ethnic Lobbies Represent?

Ethnic lobbies have passionate critics because of the lurking suspicion that they put the interests of their ancestral homeland before those of the United States. It is impossible to say whether this claim is true. The national interest and the best means for promoting it are not objective facts. Reasonable people can disagree over whether U.S. support for Israel is excessive, whether Washington should tilt toward Ankara or Athens, or whether NATO expansion makes sense. For that reason, the charge that an ethnic lobby puts its own interests ahead of the national interest can be (and have been) leveled against any lobby, be it the Cuban American National Foundation, the National Association of Manufacturers, or the AFL-CIO.

What is clear is that many foreign governments hope to use ethnic lobbies to influence U.S. policy. Visiting Armenian, Greek, Israeli, and Mexican officials routinely meet with fellow ethnics to enlist their support. Dominican President Fernandez Reyna once went so far as to encourage Dominicans in the United States to become U.S. citizens so they can vote, and presumably influence Washington's attitudes toward the Dominican Republic. At the same time, it is likely that some ethnic activists worry more about the interests of their ancestral homeland than about those of the United States.

Still, concerns that ethnic lobbies sacrifice U.S. interests can easily be overblown and usually are. To begin with, policies that benefit other countries do not necessarily harm the United States and may even help it. One need not belong to the American Israel Public Affairs Committee to believe that supporting Israel serves U.S. interests or be Lithuanian to favor expanding NATO. Nor do ethnic lobbies march lockstep with their fellow ethnics abroad.

During the 1980s, for instance, many Jewish groups had testy relations with Jerusalem because of intense disagreements over Israel's policies. On NAFTA and related issues, Mexican American groups have been more interested in how policies affect Mexicans living north of the border than south of it. Nor is there evidence that Chinese Americans have been particularly interested in doing Beijing's bidding.

Finally, the focus on where the loyalties of ethnic lobbies lie misses the contributions that they make to U.S. foreign policy. The transmission belt that enables ethnic lobbies to inject foreign perspectives into American politics also operates, perhaps even more strongly, in the opposite direction. As the political scientist Yossi Shain argues in *Marketing the American Creed Abroad,* ethnic lobbies are instrumental in disseminating American values and interests in their ancestral homelands. They frequently press ancestral governments to accommodate themselves to American political realities and hold them to American standards on everything from human rights to good governmental practices to economic policy. For that reason the consequence of America's growing Latino community may be as much the "Americanization" of Latin America (or parts of it) as it is the "Latinization" of America. Likewise, Arab Americans and Muslim Americans may play a crucial role in blunting anti-Americanism in the Arab and Islamic worlds.

None of this is to say that ethnic lobbies don't complicate the lives of policy makers. They do, at least when they oppose what an administration or Congress wants to do. (Often overlooked is that policy makers frequently find ethnic lobbies useful allies. The Clinton administration actively recruited Latino groups—which had been spectators— into lobbying for NAFTA's passage. It also used Eastern European groups to secure Senate approval of NATO expansion.) What it does say is that ethnic lobbies confront the same constraints that all interests groups do. And while the end of the Cold War means greater societal influence on foreign policy, that holds true for all interest groups, many of which have agendas at odds with those of ethnic lobbies. As a result, the appearance of new ethnic lobbies will undoubtedly change some policies; but, in the main, the end result of ethnic lobbying will be not so much to capture American foreign policy as to enrich it.

Part 2

Section 5

Hispanic Americans
and U.S. Foreign Policy

It is appropriate to start our discussion of the group-specific details of multicultur-alism and foreign affairs with the United States' Hispanic population. Perhaps more than any other, this population illustrates so many of the themes already identified in this volume. *Numerically,* they have just pulled into the number one position in minority population. The latest census found that the Latino population was even larger than anticipated, and at 35.3 million people they now constitute 13 percent of the American population. This is higher than the 34.6 million blacks who constitute 12.5 percent of the U.S. population.[1] Having moved beyond the traditional borders of California, New York, and the Southwest, Latinos are now the largest minority in twenty-three of the fifty states.[2] *Socially,* the Latino middle class is solidifying in places like Los Angeles and Chicago. The working classes in agriculture and services are being joined by Latinos moving into commerce and the professions. The *political class* has expanded dramatically, as mayors multiply beyond heavily Latino cities like Miami. Presidents Clinton and Bush made certain that Latinos were well represented in cabinet and subcabinet positions—including the first Latino appointed to be Assistant Secretary of Inter-American Affairs at the State Department. America's political leaders now recognize the linked nature of America's Latino populations and America's neigh-bors to the South. This was evident in President Bush's very visible efforts to court the American Latino vote at the same time that he sought compromise and cooperation with the new Mexican President Vicente Fox on issues of common concern such as immigration.

The Tomas Rivera Policy Institute also found that Latino elites share many of the mainstream values about U.S. foreign policy. They would, however, like more attention given to Latin America, and to issues like foreign assistance and foreign investment. And a sizable number of Latino elites believe that the United States puts too much emphasis on traditional "high politics" issues like arms control.

In terms of foreign policy effectiveness, the selections in this volume portray sharp differences between groups of Central and South American origin, and the "take no prisoners" battle plans of the Cuban Americans. Robbins shows decisively that the

Cuban community's successes were not automatic, but were the result of leadership and organizational skill coinciding with a major foreign policy interest of the United States—defeating communism, particularly in neighboring Cuba.

NOTES

1. Harry Pachon, "Seizing the Latino Moment," *Blueprint* (July/August 2001), p. 42.
2. Ibid.

14

The Keenest Recruits to the Dream

*Four Centuries After Spanish-Speakers Settled
in What Is Now the United States,
How Close Have Latinos Come
to Making Their Presence Felt?*

THE ECONOMIST

When Danny Villanueva became the first Latino to play in the National Football League (back in the mid-1960s, before his business acumen made him rich), players traveled in segregated buses. "Sometimes," he remembers, "I'd head for the white bus and the black guys would be hollering out the window, 'Hey, Taco! Taco, come ride with us!' And I'd ride with them. It got to be a joke. We'd head for the buses and I'd just stand there deciding which one to ride. The coach would say, "Okay! You guys on this bus, you guys on that bus; Villanueva, you take a cab."

In the polarized politics of race in America, Latinos have always been caught in the middle. At times they are accepted, at times abused; they have never been enslaved, yet have suffered segregation. Some Latinos are, in effect, native Americans, whose communities in the southwest go back to the sixteenth century. Far more came in, and still come in, as turn-of-the-century Europeans did: voluntarily, largely penniless, in pursuit of the American dream.

It is almost four hundred years to the day—April 30, 1598—since Don Juan de Onate's expedition waded across the Rio Grande, gave thanks, and claimed the lands to the north for Spain. It is also 150 years since the annexation of the Southwest after the Mexican American War, and the centenary of Puerto Rico's entry into the Union after the Spanish-American War. History, it seems, is asking the United States to reflect on its Spanish speakers. It is high time.

Latinos are the fastest-growing group in the country. There were around thirty million in the latest census, in 1990, about 15 percent of the population (not counting two to three million who were in America illegally). On current trends, the figure is expected to rise to ninety-six million by 2050; the Census Bureau predicts a 75 percent increase by 2015. Latinos immigrate, with or without papers, in far greater numbers than any other group. They have children younger and in far larger numbers than their counterparts. They live longer. And, increasingly, the future lies with them.

MANY-COLORED ENTERPRISE

Spanish-speaking Americans are as heterogeneous as the United States itself. They come in all shades of brown, white, black, and yellow. The breakdown is roughly 63 percent Mexicans, 12 percent Puerto Ricans, 8 percent Cubans, 12 percent Central Americans and "diverse" Latin Americans, and 5 percent Dominicans.

153

Each group brings with it a different history and different loyalties; all agree that the word "Latino," let alone "Hispanic," is unsatisfactory. Texans with Mexican ancestry call themselves Tejanos, other Americans with Mexican ancestry call themselves Chicanos; Hispanos are New Mexicans who trace their roots to Spain. Although Anglo-America would like to homogenize them, anything less like an ethnic lump is hard to imagine. It is language (and, to a lesser extent, Roman Catholicism and family values) that brings these people into a category that both black and white Americans can treat as "them."

Latino strength lies not just in how many there are, but in where they are. Apart from the Puerto Rican and Dominican pocket in the urban Northeast, they are concentrated in the West, the Southwest, and Florida. Latinos are expected to become the majority in America's two most dynamic states, Texas and California, by 2020. But many also are migrating to the heartland to do jobs, such as meatpacking, which blacks and whites are now reluctant to do; and to find, along the way, cheap houses and good schools. States with strong agro-processing industries, such as Iowa, have seen their Latino population double since 1987.

Even poor Latinos have middle-class aspirations. According to David Hayes Bautista, the head of the Center for the Study of Latino Health at the University of California at Los Angeles, Latinos have the highest rate of male participation in the labor force, the lowest use of public assistance and the highest rate of family formation. Latinos spend nearly twice as much as blacks on mortgages, and, although most arrive with no capital and take rock-bottom jobs, they are reaching the middle class in increasingly large numbers. In Los Angeles there are now around 450,000 middle-class Latino households, three times as many as in 1980.

The number of Latino-owned businesses, too, has almost doubled since 1993 in most states. In Los Angeles County they have grown from 57,000 in 1987 to 210,000 in 1997: much of California's recovery has been achieved by them. Overwhelmingly, immigrant Latinos work in the private sector. Only 3 percent of Latino immigrant men in Los Angeles worked for the government at the time of the 1990 census, against 18 percent of black men. Latinos have still not acquired the habit of looking to government either for welfare or for jobs.

According to Jeffrey Humphreys at the Selig Centre of the University of Georgia, the buying power of Latinos has risen 65 percent since 1990 to $348 billion today, or more than the GNP of Mexico. The buying power of California Latinos alone increases by $1 billion every six weeks. Because Latino consumers are concentrated in certain markets (California, Texas, New York, Florida, and Illinois, in order of importance), sophisticated Latino advertising agencies can aim precisely at them. Not only is the Latino market large and growing fast, it also has a reputation for brand loyalty that warms a corporate executive's heart. In short, there are big rewards to be had here.

THE STRUGGLE TO LEARN

There is, of course, another side. Immigrant Latinos are the most likely to live under the poverty line. Latinos may be less reliant on welfare generally, but 40 percent of the children on welfare in California are Latino. In the *colonias* of south Texas food stamps stave off malnutrition. Under the recent welfare reforms, legal immigrants will lose food stamps to the tune of $200–$300 a month.

Meanwhile more Latino immigrants, both legal and illegal, keep pushing in. The newer they are, the more eager they are to work for any pay, and they are so useful that employers rarely question their credentials. Every large border town has, loitering around the bus stations, recruiters for slaughterhouses or chicken-processing plants across the Midwest. A building foreman picking up workers in Houston confides that he seldom sees non-Latinos lining up for work.

"When I do see blacks or whites," he says, "I think of them as the last resort. Your Guatemalan is going to give you more value for money." They do so in the fields, too, where crops such as lettuce, tomatoes, and strawberries are picked almost exclusively by Latinos, most of them now legal immigrants, working for a pittance for sixteen hours a day.

Most of these workers eventually settle down; some remain as migrants, following the harvests from state to state, taking their children in and out of school. Yet even Latinos who stay put do not shine in the classroom. They lag behind both whites and blacks by almost every measure: higher dropout rates, lower test scores, fewer college graduates. "Our growth means nothing if we remain undereducated," says Antonia Hernandez, the head of the influential Mexican American Legal Defense Fund. "We Latinos have to become obsessed with education."

At present, that obsession is often focused in the wrong place: at university level. Both California and Texas, where Latinos account for a third of high school graduates, have struck down affirmative action—preference for minorities—in their universities; this year, far fewer Latinos will be going to the top-rank colleges in those states. This weakens one stepping-stone to economic success, as well as ensuring that the best and brightest Latinos will be lured away from the states where they have the best chance to advance in public life. Yet the key to Latino advancement lies not in the universities, but in the public school system; and that system, already dilapidated and short of cash, threatens to be over-whelmed by enrollments of Latino schoolchildren that will grow from 4.9 million in 1994 to 6.9 million in 2000.

Would these children be helped if they were taught in Spanish rather than English? The issue has been debated for years. Many Anglos suppose that Latinos do not want to learn English, and often they do not need to; by dint of market forces and grudging acceptance of history, Spanish has become as commonplace in Southwestern America as French in Canada.

Yet most polls say that over 90 percent of new immigrant Latinos want to learn English, and Latino parents want their children taught in English at school. They see it as the obvious route to a better life. They would rather not have to forget their Spanish; they want to be able to write checks in Spanish, and chat to each other in Spanish at the office. Yet they overwhelmingly want to have English as well. It is a key to their approach to the American enterprise.

POLITICAL AWAKENINGS

You might think such shifts in demography and culture would bring political change. So far, it has been slow to come. For all their numbers, Latinos have not yet swung a presidential election; in 1996, the only state where the outcome depended on their votes was Colorado. Years spent on the political margins have left them woefully underrepresented at every level of government. Nor have they had much luck. Henry Cisneros, the best-known Latino politician, left his job as secretary of housing and urban development under a cloud; the next-most-senior Latino, Federico Pena, the transport secretary, is leaving to spend more time with his family. There are now no Latinos left in Mr. Clinton's cabinet, which was meant to "look like America."

At state and city levels, however, the picture is more encouraging. There are more Latinos in elected office than ever before. In some counties of Texas and New Mexico almost every elected official is a Latino. Mr. Cisneros and Mr. Pena both rose to the cabinet after successful careers as mayors (Mr. Cisneros in San Antonio, Mr. Pena in Denver). A bigger breakthrough has been in California, where Antonio Villaraigosa has become the first Latino speaker of the state legislature. Texas has a Latino attorney general, Dan Morales, and a secretary of state, Al Gonzalez, who was raised in poverty by first-generation Mexican immigrants.

Mr. Gonzalez is that rarest of elephants, a Republican Latino. And thereby hangs a tale. Latinos, with their work ethic, their religion, and their love of family, might seem natural Republicans. But most of them dislike the party's hard line on immigration—and nowhere more than in California, where Governor Pete Wilson drove through Proposition 187, which cut off benefits to both legal and illegal immigrants.

This has pushed Latinos into unexpected political solidarity both in California and outside it. They have been galvanized both to vote, and to register to vote, in substantial numbers; and Republicans can no longer take comfort in the fact that Latinos have a miserable turnout at elections. In Texas alone, four hundred thousand new Latinos registered to vote in 1996. The political coming of age of the Latino middle class is, says Mr. Cisneros, "a genie that cannot be put back in the bottle."

This does not yet mean that Latinos have become a political unit. They vote all kinds of ways, and not necessarily for their own. In Odessa, a grimy oil town in west Texas where half the population is Latino, there is only one Latino on the six-member city council. "I don't care whether a politician is white, black, or brown," says Nicky Hernandez, a local car mechanic, "as long as he's down here in the neighborhood getting things done."

Conciliation goes further. Most Latinos prefer to walk away from abuse and confrontation. A Latino effort to imitate the black Million Man March was a humiliating failure. Latinos lack the leaders the black community has, and they are less clear about what offends them. When Taco Bell recently used a Spanish-speaking chihuahua called Dinky to advertise their burritos on television, some indignant Latinos demanded an apology; but more Latinos thought the dog rather cute. In these crazy times, almost any other minority in America would have united in outrage.

THE MARGIN OR THE CORE?

In some ways, Latinos are not yet fully absorbed into America. Their Catholicism, although it does not unite them politically, has other, subtler, effects: It gives them a sense of belonging to a larger world, and a certain resistance (at least for now) to American materialism. Their language keeps them close to the southern half of the continent, and new dual-nationality rules allow Mexican Americans to stay fully involved in Mexican politics. Latinos, although well involved in baseball, are almost absent from other mainstream American sports. Most of them prefer soccer, so much that Major League Soccer depends on them to stay afloat.

Latinos are largely absent from mainstream culture, too. Latino actors used to Anglicize their names, and Latinos are still stereotyped on screen (as blacks used to be) as dim-witted laborers. Public libraries carry few books on Latino culture. One large bookshop in Los Angeles has Jimmy Santiago Baca's award-winning poetry shelved with homosexual poets under "Minority Interests": ironically, it was Mr. Baca who wrote that Latinos had been "erased" from the American landscape.

Yet, for all that, the Latino internal market is exploding. Established publications such as *Hispanic* magazine (with one million readers) or *La Opinion*, an excellent Spanish-language daily in Los Angeles, have been joined by many other magazines aimed at Latinos, notably *People en Espanol* and *Latina*. Popular music performers who used to be concerned with breaking out of the Latino market now get rich from it. Spanish television networks—Univision, now headed by Mr. Cisneros, and its rival Telemundo—are hugely popular, acting as a filter for all things American in most Latino households. And all over the Southwest, the Latino radio stations have a stronger signal than the country music stations.

America tends to reduce its people's assorted origins to the flimsiest of tokens: a kilt, a leprechaun, a pizza. As the Latino population grows larger, it will also become more assimilated, particularly as Latinos have high rates of intermarriage with non-Latinos. Yet this is, after all, a very big chunk of the population, and one bolstered by the only language that is now a world rival to English. Spanish-speaking America is already the world's fifth-largest Hispanic nation. Within ten years, only Mexico will have more Spanish speakers.

Even if they can be digested, how strong will they become? Some Latinos like to think that, once they have come to run the Southwest and south Florida (which is not far off), it will be a short step to running the country. That is too blithe. Latinos will not punch their weight politically or economically for some time. If their education does not improve, most Latinos will be servicing rather than running twenty-first-century America. Even so, their eagerness for betterment, their readiness to do lowly jobs, and, above all, their refusal to choose between the white bus and the black will make them perhaps the most vital group in the whole American experiment.

15

Family Ties and Ethnic Lobbies

Latino Relations with Latin America

RODOLFO DE LA GARZA, MIGUEL BARAONA, MANUEL OROZCO,
HARRY P. PANCHON, AND ADRIAN D. PANTOJA

The increasing growth of the Latino population and its strong ties to Latin America are leading many to assess the potential impact this group may have in shaping the international priorities of the United States. This brief is part of a series of reports by the Tomas Rivera Policy Institute (TRPI) examining the impact Latinos have in shaping U.S.-Latin American relations. Our findings reveal that, while Latinos are not systematically attempting to influence the nation's foreign policy at the present time, the increased convergence of domestic and foreign policy concerns suggests that Latinos are likely to play an increasingly greater role in shaping the nation's international agenda.

RESEARCH QUESTIONS

This chapter addresses the following questions:

- How do governmental and nongovernmental elites in Latin America understand the role of U.S. Latinos (native-born and immigrants) in shaping relations and policies between home countries and the United States? What impact do U.S. Latinos have in their countries of origin?
- What kinds of policies are implemented by Latin American governments toward Latino communities in the United States?
- Do links exist between U.S. Latino organizations and Latin American NGOs? If so, how strong and enduring are the linkages?
- In what ways are U.S. Latino organizations involved in foreign policymaking activities in the United States? Are Latino organizations able to influence policy decisions? If so, which actors are influential?

METHODOLOGY

In an effort to answer these and other questions, TRPI conducted close to 170 extensive person-to-person interviews with individuals in the United States and in the five countries under study. Interviewees included diplomatic officials in the United States, government and NGO representatives in Latin America, Latino elites in the United States, and U.S. Department of State Officials in Washington, D.C., and in U.S. embassies in the five selected Latin American countries. The interviews lasted from forty-five minutes to three hours and were structured around semi-open questionnaires. In addition, in collaboration with Public Agenda, TRPI implemented a mail survey targeting Latino leaders in the U.S. A total of 454 individuals of the 1,380 who were mailed a questionnaire responded. The latter effort resulted in the publication of *Here to Stay: The Domestic and International Priorities of Latino Leaders,* which was the first publication ensuing from *Reshaping the National Interest: Latinos and U.S. International Relations.*

MAJOR FINDINGS

Our interviews with Latino leaders and organizations support the findings of our previous report *Here to Stay* (Public Agenda and The Tomas Rivera Policy Institute, 1998). Despite widespread interest in international and home-country affairs, the overwhelming majority of Latino organization leaders are primarily focused on issues related to the well-being of Latinos within the United States.

It is clear that all Latin American governments examined in this study have increased their outreach efforts and interest toward their co-nationals in the United States. Mexico is unquestionably the most dramatic example of such a shift. The governments of El Salvador and the Dominican Republic are also making huge strides in the same direction, while the governments of Colombia and Guatemala remain detached.

Regardless of increased outreach efforts by Latin American governments, there are few examples of Latino lobbying or other types of direct involvement in foreign policy processes. When Latinos have engaged in foreign policy, they have done so either autonomously or at the request of U.S. government officials.

No single pattern describes how home-country societies view emigrants or how interested home-country governments are in developing relations with their emigrants. Instead, societal views vary from highly positive to negative and indifferent, while governmental interest ranges from intense and well developed to undeveloped and uncertain. Overall, the most positive and comprehensive relationships are those between the Dominican Republic and its emigrees. However, it is Salvadoran society and its government that give greatest priority to relations with emigrants. The least developed linkages are those involving Guatemala and Colombia. Finally, Mexico's relationship is the most complex, mixing elaborate governmental initiatives with negative societal ties.

U.S. LATINO-LATIN AMERICAN RELATIONS

Latin American Elites and U.S. Latinos

Our study indicates that the role that Latino diasporas may play in shaping relations and policies toward their respective country of origin is not only a function of their own perceptions and behaviors toward ancestral lands but also the result of how they are perceived by governments and societies in those countries. Moreover, there are enormous contrasts among the respective national cases, and in each of our cases perceptions and behaviors are in a state of flux. In some countries such as El Salvador, Colombia, and Guatemala, they are just beginning to take form, while in others such as Mexico and the Dominican Republic, they are evolving from well-established patterns.

Mexico

This country has a long, and oftentimes conflictive, history of emigration to the U.S. Several consecutive generations of emigrants and their descendants' form a complex multi-layered community. Because of the many factors that have generated chronic "migratory expulsion" toward the United States, and because of the rather uneasy history of binational relations between both countries, there is a tradition of relatively negative perceptions among Mexican urban elites and among middle and upper classes towards their emigrants and their descendants (de la Garza 1980). However, both the official discourse and the policies of the Mexican government toward its emigres in the U.S., has undergone dramatic changes over the past ten years (de la Garza 1997). This shift began with the opening of the Mexican economy in the mid-1980s and was consolidated with the approval of NAFTA.

Nonetheless, the lives of Mexicans in the United States and of Mexican Americans (i.e., U.S. citizens of Mexican origin) seemed to be of interest to most of our interviewees in Mexico City only to the extent that they could be used as examples of either general mistreatment or blatant discrimination by U.S. society. Little knowledge exists about the importance of financial flows (remittances) prompted by Mexico-U.S. emigration, and about other political, cultural, or social contributions that emigrants may have made in favor of their country of origin. In this sense, the contrast between the government's new perceptions/policies, and the general social receptivity and interest toward emigrants and their descendants is sharp today in Mexico. This is a situation most likely to change toward greater closeness and interest, but it is impossible at this point to predict exactly how fast and how deeply this process will unfold.

El Salvador

Salvadoran respondents described their emigrants in overwhelmingly positive terms. The universality of this sentiment is explained by several factors. First, the emigrants left for "good reasons" (i.e., because of the civil war and acute political conflict), and although the majority of emigrants are from rural and urban working classes, there also were many members of the middle classes and the intellectual and political elites that had to flee the country to save their lives in the 1980s (Taran 1990). Thus, it is not strictly a migration of "poor people" seeking for a better life.

The movement begun as a refugee crisis, and eventually evolved into a more conventional migratory flow. Second, as one of our interviewees in San Salvador said, "every family has a relative in the U.S., and no one would like it if their relatives or close friends were disparaged." Third, as remittances increased and became a major source of sustenance for families, the government, and the economy in general (Siri and Delgado 1995; De la Garza, Orozco, and Baraona 1997) emigrants were transformed into "social heroes." El Salvador has thus a very positive image of its emigrants in the United States at all levels and in all sectors of society.

Dominican Republic

Dominican society also has very positive but more diverse and balanced images of its emigrants. In part, this is because there is a greater variety of institutions with linkages to Dominican groups in the United States. Thus, respondents described emigrants in terms of the contributions they are making to U.S. literature, music, politics, and the academy. Respondents also referred to the opportunities that emigrants have created for themselves (Guarnizo 1994; and Goris-Rosario 1994) as entrepreneurs specializing in limousine services and bodegas (traditional neighborhood groceries). This overwhelmingly positive portrait is reinforced by the persona of the current national president, Leonel Fernandez Reyna, a vigorous, articulate, and charismatic man who was born in the Dominican Republic but raised and educated in the United States. To many, he is the embodiment of the emigrant.

Colombia

Although emigrants are not an important issue to Colombian society, our interviewees were able to categorize them into three groups, all of which are viewed positively. The largest category includes the typical migrant who left searching for better economic opportunities. A smaller but very important group consists of professionals, especially doctors, who have enjoyed great success in the United States (Gilbertson and Gurak 1992). A third group, and one that is unique to Colombia, consists of prisoners in the United States. Although small, this group has gained the most visibility in Colombia. The Colombian Congress approved legislation requiring the Secretary of Foreign Relations to maintain regular contact with these prisoners to ensure that their human and constitutional rights are respected.

Guatemala

Guatemalans have nebulous impressions of their emigrants. As one respondent noted, "Futbol and how players will be selected for the soccer world championship in France is more important than our emigrants." There are, nonetheless, two views. The more general and widespread image is positive, emphasizing the obstacles that migrants must overcome to improve their lives. Landowners and the more affluent segments of society, by contrast, are said to be indifferent or hostile toward migrants, who are seen as disproportionately drawn from the poorer ranks of society (i.e., uneducated Indians and mestizos).

Latin American Governments and U.S. Latinos

All the governments of the countries included in this study have considered establishing or already have well-institutionalized outreach efforts toward their nationals in the United States. Despite varying national approaches toward linking home countries with emigrant communities in the United States, the governments of all five countries have attempted to forge closer relationships in recent years. This is true even of Guatemala, which of all the countries we have studied maintains the weakest official outreach effort. What emerges very clearly from our study is that there is no institutionalized "Latino ethnic lobby" organized to serve the foreign interest of any Latin American government. The closest exception was in the case of NAFTA, where Latinos played a moderately active role in negotiations toward the approval of the treaty, but this was on behalf of U.S. and Mexican governmental interests. In this case, they acted more as facilitators of a consensual agreement between both governments, rather than activists lobbying in favor of a specific interest or policy of a Latin American government before U.S. higher authorities. There is also the case of a small group of Colombian Americans who launched a feeble attempt to obtain support for U.S. certification of Colombia's efforts against the drug trade. However, this particular effort was never officially endorsed by the Colombian government and therefore, any attempt on their part to constitute something similar to an "ethnic lobby" never developed.

Mexico

The Mexican government's emigrant outreach efforts are deeply institutionalized and multifaceted. Established during the Salinas regime (1988–1994), such efforts have grown under President Ernesto Zedillo's current administration. They include the Paisano program and the Program for Mexican Communities Living Abroad (Gonzalez Gutierrez 1997; de la Garza 1997). The former attempts to improve the treatment that returning migrants receive at the hands of Mexican officials by reducing corruption and abuse. The latter provides a wide range of services to Mexicans residing in the United States (including health, education, legal, and social services) and also helps them target remittances toward local development efforts in their communities of origin. Consuls also have helped arrange meetings between community leaders and visiting governmental representatives from Mexico. Moreover, many state and local officials from emigrant-sending cities and states meet with and provide services to emigrant groups.

Mexican officials recently have established close ties with virtually every noteworthy Mexican American organization in the United States. Officials began to reach out during the NAFTA debates, when the Mexican government systematically recruited Mexican American lobbyists to marshall Latino support (Velasco 1997). In 1994 and 1997, the Mexican government invited large numbers of Mexican American politicos, media representatives, and academics to "observe" elections. The latter marks a significant turning point in terms of a new modality of relations not only with Mexicans and Mexican Americans in the United States but also with the rest of the world. The gradual opening of the Mexican government, political system, economy, and society to external participation seems to be a new trend that will most probably be reinforced by both emerging domestic and international forces.

El Salvador

Salvadoran officials are in the process of institutionalizing linkages with emigrant communities. In fact, developing relationships with emigrants is one of three major priorities of the Ministry of Foreign Relations. Influenced by Mexico's program, the ministry is designing various programs to assist emigrants (e.g., literacy classes that can be taught from El Salvador using distance learning technology). Also, the Salvadoran Embassy in the United States has added the position of "Counselor for the Community," whose responsibilities include meeting with organized emigrant groups, helping emigrants organize, helping groups send money for specific community development projects, and teaching emigrants their rights in the United States.

Dominican Republic

Dominican officials also have developed close ties to emigrants. President Fernandez Reyna has made this a priority, and the foreign ministry has responded by hiring emigrants to staff consulates and offices promoting exports and tourism. This has, according to one official, raised the professional level of these offices. Dominican officials also have begun working with business leaders to mobilize emigrants around key issues. For example, Dominican officials and the business community argue that Dominican exports have suffered greatly because of NAFTA. Therefore, a major foreign policy goal is to persuade the U.S. Congress to pass legislation that would provide parity between Mexican and Dominican exports. The Dominican Ambassador to the United States met with emigrant leaders in Washington, D.C., and asked them to contact Congress about this issue. President Fernandez Reyna also has exhorted emigrants to become U.S. citizens so they can vote.

Nevertheless, a business leader noted that, "We could then identify the groups to develop a lobby. The problem now, however, is that while the nations leadership understands the importance of parity legislation, the people (emigrants) do not." Government officials in the Dominican Republic have also encouraged the efforts conducted by Dominican politicos in the United States to promote naturalization as a strategy to elect a Dominican to the U.S. Congress, who, in turn, would defend the interests of the Dominican Republic.

Colombia

In Colombia, outreach initiatives are limited to the absentee ballot for emigres. Colombian officials also have began discussions to establish contacts with emigrant organizations as a means to mobilize them in opposition to U.S. drug certification policies, a tactic that, according to a senior Colombian diplomat, U.S. embassy officials in Bogota have also recommended. Nonetheless, such efforts have yet to develop into a significant form of international partnership between emigrants and home country officials.

Guatemala

There is a hint of a new incipient official interest toward co-nationals in the U.S., but there is no visible outreach program so far.

U.S. Latino NGOs and Latin American NGOs

Latino NGOs in the United States

Our fieldwork findings indicate that relationships between Latino NGOs and Latin America are relatively few and recent. Pan-Latinos groups directed by native-born Hispanic elites are more likely to emphasize domestic concerns, despite the fact that the leaders of these organizations typically have extensive professional experience abroad. Most pan-Latino NGO respondents have traveled abroad to attend international meetings and conferences and have been to Latin America for similar reasons during the past five years. However, this involvement in international and Latin American affairs typically reflected the activities of specific individuals and not their respective organizations' agendas. In general, institutional relationships are weak and relatively recent.

Latin American NGOs

In line with worldwide trends over the past twenty years, the NGO sector in Latin America has emerged as an important factor in civic and political life (Salamon 1994). In several countries, NGOs have played a critical role in the transition to more democratic political systems (Bebbington and Thiele 1993). Most Latin American NGOs have received administrative advice and financial support from entities, usually other NGOs, outside of their home countries (Edwards and Hulme 1992). This external link was decisive in ensuring their survival in the hostile, authoritarian political environments characteristic of the 1970s and 1980s (Carroll 1987). Thus, it was no surprise that nearly 80 percent of our Latin American NGO interviewees indicated that their organizations maintained regular contact with foreign, predominantly mainstream, U.S. and European NGOs. However, though virtually all respondents indicated an interest in working with U.S. Latino NGOs, almost none had done so to any significant degree. In general, those who had established contacts with Latino NGOs in the United States tended to have sporadic or very limited relations.

Most respondents who reported relationships with U.S.-based NGOs explained that their interaction was "functionally" rather than "ethnically" oriented (e.g., women's groups tend to work with women's groups, rather than with Latina organizations). Moreover, when cross-national Latino linkages are established, they tend to follow national lines. For example, Dominican businessmen are primarily linked to Dominican business associations in New York rather than to Puerto Rican or Cuban organizations. However, this is not always the case. A few respondents from various countries indicated that they have been in contact with the National Council of La Raza (NCLR), a prominent pan-Latino advocacy organization that represents Latinos living in the United States. Such relationships are, however, the exception, and they have not yet resulted in substantive collaborations.

LATINOS AND U.S. FOREIGN POLICY

Our research shows that U.S.-based Latino NGOs have little involvement in foreign policy issues. Except for two or three major organizations, Latino NGOs have exerted almost no influence upon the making of the U.S. international agenda. U.S.-based Latino NGO representatives are generally concerned with domestic issues and issues defining relations between their home country and the United States, rather than expressing general concern with broader hemispheric developments. Neither pan-Latino nor country-specific organizations appear to engage in foreign policy debates. In fact, according to one Latino member of the U.S. Congress, U.S. Latinos have not lobbied senior U.S. government officials regarding Latin American issues. Instead, these activities are carried out by Latin American-based groups with ties to the United States or international organizations.

Interviews with U.S. State Department officials working with the five countries included in our study, confirm the congressman's observation. The one exception—among the countries included in this study—is one U.S.-based Colombian organization, which lobbied in favor of the congressional certification of Colombia's official antidrug efforts.

CONCLUSION

There is no way to know precisely when U.S. Latinos will make international issues a political priority or what specific issues will top their agenda. What does seem clear is that they will bring their own views to bear on these issues with increasing frequency. Furthermore, we may say that their influence is on the rise and that the United States will be affected in one way or another by the demographic, political, cultural, and economic emergence of Latinos. Their perspectives, moreover, will not be those of the home country nor a mere reflection of today's "mainstream" America, but will instead reflect their experiences as immigrants who, in becoming Americans, are transformed into ethnic minorities. As "new" Americans, they are as unlikely to echo home country interests as they are to see Latin America through the same lens that the traditional foreign policy establishment. Rather, they may well be expected to propose new initiatives that challenge their home-country governments, U.S. officials, or both. In other words, Latinos will join with other citizens to help shape the nation's priorities and define the national interest. Before we began this research, we had great expectations regarding the role of the "Third Sector" (NGOs) in terms both of shaping international policies and relations between the United States and Latin America.

So much has been written and said about the emergence of the "Third Sector" that we truly expected to uncover evidence of the rising prominence of NGOs. However, it must be clearly stated that we found almost no evidence that either U.S. Latino NGOs or Latin American NGOs are engaging in international relations and affairs, or networking in any significant manner with each other across national borders. They remain thoroughly committed to activities and issues that are primarily domestic, although their agendas may have some unintentional international consequences. U.S. Hispanic and Latin American chambers of commerce or trade offices seem to be the exception, and this seems to be mainly an artifact of strengthening links between business communities in the United States and Latin America.

Clearly, U.S. Latinos are much more engaged with domestic issues than with foreign policy. There is no evidence to suggest that Latino "ethnic lobbies" are becoming prominent in shaping the U.S. foreign agenda or in influencing international policies of their countries of origin. There is evidence, however, that Latinos may become crucial international players in those few instances in which their participation is sought simultaneously by the United States and their country of origin. These are cases in which Latinos are "being called upon" rather than taking the initiative themselves.

Thus, even though Latinos are not currently systematically attempting to influence the nation's foreign policy, the increased convergence of domestic and foreign policy concerns combined with the strong bonds that link them to Latin America suggest that Latinos are likely to play an increasingly important role in shaping the nation's international agenda. A major reason for this increased influence is the continual growth of the Hispanic population. Hispanics are projected to become the nation's largest minority by year 2010 and to make up 25 percent of the nation's population by the year 2050. This phenomenal growth is mainly a consequence of immigration, driven primarily by the political crises and economic decline that have plagued Latin America since the 1970s. Specifically, more than 50 percent of Mexican, Dominican, Central American, and South American immigrants to the United States arrived after 1980. Nearly 70 percent of Central Americans entered during the 1980s. The high growth rate is expected to continue well into the next century. This growing potential is why Latin American officials have initiated efforts to institutionalize their links to Hispanics.

Not only are they interested in strengthening existing cultural and economic ties, but they also hope to have Latinos become an "ethnic lobby" that will support them in their dealings with the U.S. government. Latin American governments, in sum, hope to have Latinos play the same role in U.S.-Latin American relations that the Irish, Greek, and Jewish immigrants have played regarding U.S. policy toward Ireland, Greece, and Israel. As of today, as we have noted, this is, at best and in our judgment, an unlikely reality.

REFERENCES

Aguayo, Sergio. 1991. "From The Shadows To Center Stage: Nongovernmental Organizations and Central American Refugee Assistance." Hemispheric Migration Project, Center for Immigration Policy and Refugee Assistance. Washington, D.C.: Georgetown University.

Bach, Robert L., and Doris Meissner. 1990. "America's Labor Market in the 1990s: What Role Should Immigration Play?" Washington, D.C.: Immigration Policy Project of the Carnegie Endowment for International Peace.

Bebbington, Anthony and Graham Thiele. 1993. *Nongovernmental Organizations and the State in Latin America*. London: Routledge.

Carroll, Thomas S. 1987. *Supporting Grassroots Organizations*. Chicago, IL: Lincoln Institute of Land Policy.

Castaneda, Jorge. 1994. *Three Challenges to U.S. Democracy: Accountability, Representativeness, and Intellectual Diversity*. Notre Dame, IN: University of Notre Dame.

Copula. 1995. "Actualidad Colombiana." (Julio). Chicago, IL: Adelante-Copula.

de la Garza, Rodolfo O. 1980. "Chicanos and U.S. Foreign Policy: The Future of Chicano-Mexican Relations." *Western Political Quarterly*. vol. 33, no. 4, pp. 571–582.

de la Garza, Rodolfo. 1997. "Foreign Policy Comes Home: The Domestic Consequences of the Program for Mexican Communities Living in Foreign Countries." In Rodolfo O. de la Garza and Jesus Velasco, eds., *Bridging the Border: Transforming Mexico-U.S. Relations*. Lanham, MD: Rowman & Littlefield.

de la Garza, Rodolfo, Manuel Orozco, and Miguel Baraona. 1997. *"Binational Impact of Latino Remittances."* Claremont, CA: The Tomas Rivera Policy Institute (TRPI).

Edwards, Michael, and David Hulme. 1992. *Making a Difference: NGOs and Development in a Changing World*. London: Earthscan Publications.

Gonzalez Gutierrez, Carlos. 1993. "The Mexican Diaspora in California: Limits and Possibilities for the Mexican Government." In Abraham F. Lowenthal and Katrina Burgess, eds., *Mexican-U.S.-Relations: Conflict and Convergence*. Stanford, CA: Stanford University Press.

———1995. "La Organización de los Migrantes Mexicanos en Los Angeles: La Lealtad de los Oriundos." *Politiea Exterior*. 46. Spring.

———. 1997. "Decentralized Diplomacy: The Role of Consular Offices in Mexico's Relation With Its Diaspora."

In Rodolfo O. de la Garza and Jesus Velasco, eds., *Bridging the Border: Transforming Mexico-U.S. Relations*. Lanham, Md.: Rowman & Littlefield.

Goris-Rosario, Anneris Altagracia. 1994. *"The Role of the Ethnic Community and the Workplace in the Integration of Immigrants: A Case Study of Dominicans in New York City."* Unpublished Thesis. Fordham University.

Guarnizo, Luis E. 1994. "Los Dominicanyorks: The Making of a Binational Society." *The Annals of the American Academy of Political and Social Science*. May, vol. 533, pp. 70–87.

Huntington, Samuel. 1996. "The West: Unique, Not Universal" in *Foreign Affairs* November/December, vol. 75, no. 6.

Huntington, Samuel. 1997. "The Erosion of American National Interests," *Foreign Affairs* September/October, pp. 28–49.

IEPRI. 1997. "Colombia: Una Nueva Sociedad en un Mundo Nuevo." Amilisis *Politico (Julio)*. Bogota, Colombia: Universidad Nacional de Colombia.

Matthews, Jessica T. 1997. "Power Shift." *Foreign Affairs*, 76 (1), Jan.–Feb., pp. 35–52.

Public Agenda and The Tomas Rivera Policy Institute. 1998. *Here to Stay: The Domestic and International Priorities of Latino Leaders*. Claremont, CA: The Tomas Rivera Policy Institute.

Salamon, Lester M. 1994. "The Rise of the Nonprofit Sector." *Foreign Affairs*, 73 (4), July–Aug., pp. 22–45.

Siri, Gabriel, and Pedro Abelardo Delgado.1995. Uso *Productivo de las Remesas Familiares en El Salvador*. San Salvador, El Salvador: FUSADES.

Smith, Robert. 1996. *Mixteca in New York; New York in Mixteca*. Report on the Americas. July, vol. 26, no. l. pp. 39–43.

Speart, Jessica. 1995. "The New Drug Mules." *The New York Times Magazine* (June 11), p. 44.

Taran, Patrick A. 1990. *Central American Refugees in the* U.S. Church World Service Immigration & Refugee Program. Ullman, Richard H. 1995. A Late Recovery (President Clinton's Foreign Policy). *Foreign Policy* (Winter), no. 101, pp. 76–80.

U.S. Bureau of the Census. 1980 *Census of Population*. Washington, D.C.: U.S. Government Printing Office.

U.S. Bureau of the Census. 1990 *Census of Population*. Washington, D.C.: U.S. Government Printing Office.

U.S. Bureau of the Census. *Current Population Survey: The Foreign-Born Population: 1994* (pp. 20–486). Washington, D.C.: U.S. Government Printing Office.

U.S. Department of Commerce, *Population Projections of the United States by Age, Sex, Race and Hispanic Origin: 1995–2050*. Washington, D.C.: U.S. Government Printing Office. February 1996.

Velasco, Jesus. 1997. "Selling Ideas, Buying Influence: Mexico and American Think Tanks in the Promotion of NAFTA." In Rodolfo O. de la Garza and Jesus Velasco, eds., *Bridging the Border: Transforming Mexico-U.S. Relations*. Lanham, MD: Rowman & Littlefield.

16

International Interests and Foreign Policy Priorities of Mexican Americans

PATRICIA HAMM

INTRODUCTION

Any discussion of the foreign policy and international interests, priorities, and activities of Mexican Americans must be prefaced with a caveat about the heterogeneous nature of the community. The cleavages that exist in the community—especially divisions of class, national origin, and length of residence in the United States—make it more challenging to discuss their foreign policy and international stakes. As I point out later, some issues divide its members along these cleavages, thus the task of reaching a consensus on issues, goals, and strategies to advance their interests is more difficult than when a community is monolithic.

MEXICAN AMERICAN INTERESTS

Most of the foreign policy and international interests and priorities of Mexican Americans overlap with those of the U.S.-Mexico bilateral relationship. They are characterized by their "intermestic" nature, diversity, and focused on Mexico. The issue basis for Mexican Americans includes international trade, immigration, U.S.-Mexico border, narcotics, and Mexican politics and development. I will not discuss the issues of immigration and narcotics in greater detail, because they are the topic of another panel.

Trade

At the top of the list of foreign policy priorities are U.S. trade policies, especially with Mexico, because they are closely linked to matters such as employment and business opportunities, which are of vital importance to Mexican Americans in California and the West. This is a new issue in the agenda of Mexican American elites. Before NAFTA, the issue of jobs was treated mostly as a domestic issue. Yet, increasing integration between the Mexican and the American economies, especially the expansion and liberalization of international commerce, has fundamental implications for Mexican Americans.

There are various reasons why Mexican Americans can be disproportionately affected by NAFTA or the expansion of the agreement to Latin America. First, most Mexican Americans live in California, the state most likely to be affected by the NAFTA due to its large trade volume with Mexico. Second, the Mexican American labor force, especially Mexican-born, is highly concentrated in low-skilled jobs, mainly in the manufacturing sector, which are likely to be the most negatively affected by job flight to Mexico. Third, there is a significant Mexican American business and professional community in the state who can greatly benefit from increased trade and investment opportunities in Mexico. Although this issue is divisive, because its impact is likely to translate into loses for some and gains for others, a common ground can be found in U.S. policies that contemplate mechanisms to compensate the losers.

Immigration

A second priority for Mexican Americans is immigration. This issue has been a traditional, yet divisive, concern for the community. The stakes for "old Californios" are not necessarily the same as for Mexican citizens from Oaxaca who migrated illegally at the end of the 1980s. More recently, however, the xenophobic backlashes that the community as a whole has suffered, especially in California, have reduced some differences. Therefore, because of its large component of recent immigrants, and to limit or prevent discriminatory measures, Mexican Americans have a large common stake in U.S. immigration policies that effectively, but fairly, regulate and limit immigration flows; foster safe and legal immigration; and speed naturalization processes.

U.S.-Mexico Border

Third on the list of priorities is the question of the border. The Southwest is the home of most of the population of Mexican origin, although border issues affect more directly those who live along the boundary line between Mexico and the United States. The lax Mexican environmental and urbanization regulations, the explosion of the "maquiladora" industry, and increased migrant populations have contributed to the worsening of the quality of life at the border. Given that the lives of the communities on both sides of the border are so intertwined, Mexican Americans on the San Diego side of the border would benefit greatly from improved infrastructure in Tijuana. Moreover, they also have a stake in solving pollution problems on both sides of the border. It is thus in the interest of Mexican Americans to foment U.S.-Mexico policies conducive to a prosperous and environmentally healthy border region. Although part of the traditional concern of Mexican Americans with border matters, the questions of the infrastructure and the environment in the U.S.-Mexico border have taken a new connotation since they were redefined as trade-related issues in the NAFTA side agreements.

Narcotics Trade

Fourth on the list of priorities, narcotics trade is a relatively new concern for Mexican Americans. They have a large stake in U.S. policies that reduce illegal drug flow into the United States, especially in California, because they are among the groups most directly and severely affected by high levels of consumption and drug-related criminal activity. Yet, in view of the results from several studies about the relative ineffectiveness of international efforts to stop drug trafficking, it is in their interest to push for a U.S. dual-track approach with a greater emphasis on domestic drug enforcement measures.

Mexican Politics and Development

The issues of democratization, development, the peace in Chiapas, and human rights in Mexico, are last in the list of priorities for Mexican Americans. These international or transnational issues are not so important compared to other matters, because the latter affect their everyday life in more direct and tangible ways. Nonetheless, the stakes for Mexican Americans are higher than for non-Mexican Americans because of their cultural, linguistic, material, and familial ties to Mexico. By harming their relatives, friends, or even properties in Mexico, events south of the border also have an effect, though indirect, on Mexican Americans—especially on first and second generations. As a result of the 1994 economic and financial crisis, many Mexican Americans felt compelled to increase their remittances to relatives in Mexico. Mexican American workers and business and investment entrepreneurs also stand to lose or benefit from Mexico's economic and political conditions. For these reasons, Mexican Americans have a stake in U.S. Mexican policies that assist Mexico to achieve sustainable development and overcome economic and financial crises. It is in their interest to ensure that U.S. (and IMF) policies—loans, debt relief, stabilization measures—contribute to these goals.

Moreover, their various ties to Mexico make it very difficult to dissociate the image of the diaspora from that of their ancestral homeland, and vice versa. Mexican Americans would have a better chance of being viewed positively in the United States when democracy, peace, and prosperity materialize in Mexico. At the same time, they have a stake in preventing that foreign policy processes serve as vehicles to denigrate Mexico. Each time U.S. politicians imbue their rhetoric with negative and stereotypical, often exaggerated and distorted, views about Mexico, they also indirectly tarnish the image of Mexican Americans in the United States.

Although it is related to the traditional factors pushing Mexican migration into the United States, the issue of Mexican politics and development is also a relatively recent concern. Since the late 1980s, the 1988 Mexican elections and the eruption of the conflict in Chiapas in 1994 have sparked a more active interest on Mexican events among Mexican Americans, especially those of the first generation.

MINORITY-SHARED INTERESTS

Mexican Americans share several interests with other ethnic minorities in California and the West. I will list some relevant ones. First, an issue of common concern among Mexican Americans, African Americans, and Central Americans is that they are all likely to disproportionately suffer the negative effects of NAFTA. Like those of Mexican Americans, the traditional low-skilled, low-wage jobs of these other groups are at stake, because they are similarly concentrated—although to different extents—in industries that are most likely to be hammered by increased international competition.

Second, although Mexican Americans have been the ones most severely affected by the current xenophobic climate in California, there are other minorities with a high stake in U.S. immigration policies. Other groups of Latin American, Asian, and Persian origin, among others, also suffer the consequences of detrimental immigration policies and the tensions and frictions that they often incite. The elimination of some social benefits for legal residents at the federal level and the passage of Proposition 187 are some examples of the discriminatory measures and postures that have hurt these groups.

Third, Mexican Americans share an interest in solving the drug problem with other ethnic minorities, especially African American and Central American families in Los Angeles. They all suffer from similar high consumption levels and the criminal activities that result from drug trafficking.

PROMOTION OF MEXICAN AMERICAN INTERESTS: THE LATINO CONSENSUS ON NAFTA

Several issues have sparked interest and foreign policy and transnational activity among Mexican American elites. They include their involvement in the passage of IRCA in 1986 and in the debates on fast-track authority to President Bush to negotiate the NAFTA, and to President Clinton vis-à-vis the expansion of the free trade agreement to Latin America. Yet none surpasses the campaign mounted by the Latino Consensus on NAFTA in terms of the levels of involvement, mobilization, sophistication, and effectiveness. The Latino Consensus formed in 1991 as a broad coalition of organizations including MALDEF [Mexican American Legal Defense and Education Fund], NCLR [National Council of La Raza], and the SVREP [Southwest Voter Registration Education Project], and many smaller organizations, local elected officials, and their allies in Congress. Its purpose was to mobilize the community in the Southwest and the Midwest, and lobby American and Mexican top negotiators to pay attention to their concerns about NAFTA. Backed by several Mexican American and non-Mexican American federal lawmakers—particularly California Representatives, they threatened to withhold their support for NAFTA unless at least two core conditions were met to ameliorate the impact of NAFTA on workers and the U.S.-Mexico border. They sought, and achieved, a commitment from the United States and Mexico to create a NADBank [Newspaper Audience Data Bank] and a NAFTA-TAA [North American Free Trade Agreement–Transitional Adjustment Assistance] program as part of the side agreements.

Effectiveness of the Latino Consensus on NAFTA

Considering the still relatively low economic and political clout of Mexican Americans at the national level, this effort was amazingly effective. The NADBank and the NAFTA-TAA can bring potential benefits not only to Mexican Americans but also to non-Mexican American environmentalists and workers, the borderlands, and California and the Southwest in general. Moreover, Mexican American activists and lawmakers also obtained other intangible, yet valuable gains, such as their long-held goal to see the community recognized as a legitimate and effective actor in U.S.-Mexican policy. In addition, the community was also recognized as a strategic actor in Mexico's internal and external politics. Most important, in the context of deep domestic cleavages over the NAFTA, the Latino Consensus was able to play a strategic role in the outcome of the NAFTA by delivering some crucial votes needed for its ratification in late 1993.

TECHNIQUES AND INSTRUMENTS

Several techniques and instruments contributed to the success of the Latino Consensus. Grassroots mobilizing and coalition building are among the most important strategies.

Grassroots Mobilizing Strategies

Ethnic mobilization turned out to be a useful foreign policy instrument for Mexican Americans. Mobilizing along class lines would have drawn them into the more confrontational position of the AFL-CIO, and would have precluded the benefits they derived thanks to their conditional stance. Moreover, it would have made it more difficult to use their ties to Mexico as a leverage to heighten the perception among Mexican and American top negotiators that their support was indispensable for the passage of NAFTA.

Community organizing was another crucial vehicle for success. Between 1992 and 1993, the Latino Consensus held many regional conferences throughout the Southwest and the Midwest, a summit in Washington, D.C., and various other meetings and workshops involving local, state, regional, and national groups. This campaign was designed to identify common foreign policy, international, and transnational interests, as well as to educate local activists and community leaders about the links between international and domestic issues, and their impact on the community. Thanks to this strategy, the Latino Consensus could identify common, narrow interests and clear and viable objectives. It also was able to generate grassroots pressure on targeted Latino community leaders and state and federal elected officials to adopt positions favorable to their interests.

Coalition Building Strategies

If Mexican Americans are to maximize their political leverage, they need to build political coalitions within and without the community. They need to involve Mexican American local, regional, and national organizations of various types. They also need to reach out to other Latino groups, as well as cross over ethnic, class, and sectoral lines. But they must base their alliances on narrow issues where they can reach a consensus, and follow clear and specific objectives. Otherwise, they run the risk of defections that can jeopardize the effectiveness of the coalition.

The coalition that different major Mexican American organizations like the NCLR, SVREP, and MALDEF built with other less prominent local and regional groups and membership-oriented associations contributed to the effectiveness of the Latino Consensus. Lacking a membership of their own, it would have been more difficult for the NCLR, MALDEF, and the SRVEP to portray themselves effectively as spokesmen of a community that national leaders and lawmakers had to contend with.

The most effective cross-over alliance that the Latino Consensus built with a non-Mexican American organization was with the moderate wing of the environmentalist movement. Congressman Torres and other coalition members presented the NADBank to the Clinton and Salinas administrations as a mechanism to solve the problem of funding environmental protection measures in the border. The moderate environmentalists obliged by endorsing the NADBank over other funding proposals. By supporting each other's interests concerning NAFTA, both factions gained. By contrast, the alliances that Mexican American entrepreneurs tried to build with Puerto Ricans, Cubans, and the U.S. Hispanic Chamber of Commerce, among others, fell apart or were ineffective—to a large extent because they had different priorities and objectives. Staunch opposition to the agreement from organized labor and African Americans also precluded feasible alliances with them.

Another asset to the Latino Consensus campaign was its participation in policy networking. This network involved various actors including Mexican American top leaders, scholars, and elected and appointed officials; non-Mexican American Representatives; American and Mexican negotiating team members and government officials; as well as policymakers from the Labor and Treasury Departments, among others. In this manner, the Latino Consensus could come up with specific policy proposals (NADBank and NAFTA-TAA); articulate its position in the appropriate forums; make itself indispensable for committees and negotiating teams from both Mexico and the United States as a useful source of technical information; and, even more crucial, garner support to make its proposals financially, legally, and politically viable. Policy networking, and the effectiveness of its NAFTA campaign in general, were possible largely because of the presence of savvy, sophisticated, and skilled political entrepreneurs in the ranks of the Latino Consensus.

If Mexican Americans are to become national, international, and transnational power players they must emphasize foreign policy, international, and transnational issues on their agenda. Foreign policy activity as a strategic instrument for (external and internal) political empowerment can lend credibility, visibility, legitimacy, experience, and leverage to groups with relatively low political and economic power like Mexican Americans. Actually, their ties to the ancestral homeland provide a ready-made opportunity for diasporas to play a role in U.S. relations with the home country, possibly with a higher potential for viability and success. The prestige, experience, and political muscle that the Latino Consensus derived from its involvement in U.S.-Mexico trade relations has already enhanced the capacity of its members and allies to mount other successful campaigns in the future. Indeed, their NAFTA involvement and success were facilitated by such ties and transnational interactions between Mexican Americans and Mexican top negotiators, government officials, opposition parties, and non-governmental groups. Mexicans in favor and against NAFTA eagerly sought their support and the opportunity to present their positions before Mexican Americans—elites and ordinary individuals.

To a large extent, these techniques and instruments contributed to the community's effectiveness by compensating for its deficiencies. Mostly, they compensated for the absence of a strong Mexican American presence in Washington and lobbying capability. They also counterbalanced the lack of a more substantial economic and electoral power proportional to their demographic might, both at the state and national level. To be sure, the Latino Consensus coalition was not able to get U.S. and Mexican top negotiators to incorporate its concerns into NAFTA itself, but in the parallel accords. This is a flaw that is now largely responsible for the poor implementation of the NADBank and the NAFTA-TAA program. But neither was the AFL-CIO able to compel Presidents Clinton and Salinas to renegotiate the agreement signed in 1992, despite its tremendous political and economic resources. The significance of this point is that while relatively low economic and electoral power is still a critical barrier to substantial political clout, it is not necessarily an insurmountable obstacle to the attainment of some success, sometimes, and under certain circumstances.

DISTINCTIVE MINORITY INTERESTS

One important interest that Mexican Americans share with African Americans and Asian Americans, which is not shared by the mainstream, is their stake in "democratizing" the definition of national interests. In other words, it is in their interest to incorporate their visions, perspectives, and priorities into the definition of what is or is not in the interest of the United States. Enriched in this manner, the agenda of national priorities would truly reflect the diverse make up of the American society. Historically the definition of the national interests has been dominated by the perspectives and priorities of the dominant ethnic group. This explains to a large extent the traditional emphasis on "good" relations with Great Britain and Western Europe, on the one hand, and, on the other, the often tense relations and sporadic, crisis-oriented attention to Latin America. Members of the foreign policy establishment often claim that the attempts of minority groups, especially ethnic, to influence policymaking reduce state capacity to protect or advance the national interest—as defined by them. Recently, there have been allegations that the so called "fragmentation" (a.k.a. ethnic and cultural diversity) of the American society hindered the ability of the United States to launch its military attack on Iraq, thus jeopardizing the U.S. national interest.

How can minorities put themselves in a position to "democratize" U.S. national interests? Obviously, political and economic power increases the chances of influencing foreign policymaking and the definition of national interests. Also, I already noted that foreign policy involvement itself increases these chances. Another crucial factor is the ability of the groups to frame and articulate their positions in ways that leave no doubt that the views they advocate, or the priorities they emphasize, are bound to benefit, or at least not jeopardize, the United States. One way of achieving this is to stress how their positions promote values cherished by the American people, regardless of ethnic origin. Some of these values include democracy, equality, and economic and religious freedom, among others. The case of Jewish Americans is the prototype of this kind of approach. In supporting the state of Israel, they have portrayed themselves as defenders of American values in a region dominated by authoritarian, non-Western, fundamentalist regimes. In their fight against apartheid, African Americans adopted a similar approach by portraying their efforts as a struggle for equality. Cuban Americans declare that they support the embargo to promote democracy and economic freedom in Cuba.

IMPLICATIONS FOR U.S. NATIONAL INTERESTS

A Mexican American majority in California could potentially have strong implications for the definition and the pursuit of U.S. national interests. The enormous economic, political, and demographic assets of the state of California place its residents and representatives in a position to wield great national influence. Once a majority in California, Mexican Americans would have a greater potential to influence foreign policy decisions as interest groups or as members of the policymaking establishment. From this position, they could potentially contribute to the "democratization" of U.S. national interests.

Mexican Americans could play a role similar to the one that Americans of Jewish and Cuban descent play in the definition of U.S. policies and interests in the Middle East and Cuba, respectively. This possibility is enhanced by the evidence that, despite their varied ties to the ancestral homeland, Mexican American elites stress their political loyalty to the United States as well as advocate values and perspectives that are congruent with American principles. There is sufficient evidence to show that when they engage in foreign policy activities, they do not seek to defend Mexico's interests, but their self-interest—a distinctively American value.

A demographically, economically, and politically powerful Mexican American community in California could improve the nature of U.S.-Mexico relations and help correct the harmful misperceptions that most foreign policymakers have about Mexico and its importance for the United States. Traditionally, U.S.-Canadian relations have been closer and more mutually respectful than U.S.-Mexico relations, because of cultural and linguistic affinities between their foreign policy establishments. When this large Mexican American minority becomes a majority in parts of the country, and plays a significant role in foreign policy-making circles, the Mexican culture, language, and polity will no longer be so foreign and incomprehensible to most policymakers. Hence, by narrowing the cultural and linguistic gaps that have hindered U.S.-Mexico relations, the differences that have separated them could potentially be reduced and lead to an enriched bilateral relationship, as well as to better relations with the rest of Latin America.

17

Dateline Washington

Cuban American Clout

CARLA ANNE ROBBINS

Fidel Castro has AIDS. No, wait a minute, it's cancer. Or a heart attack—at least those were some of the rumors that whipped through Miami's Cuban exile community. For years, Castro's opponents promoted such wishful thinking—believing that only an act of God would rid them of the tyrant. No longer. Moscow has severed Cuba's economic lifeline. Agricultural communes use oxen to plow fields. Cigars are rationed. And Castro's days look numbered.

The Bush administration, however, has not come up with a plan to stabilize post–Castro Cuba or even to speed Castro's departure. American policy toward Cuba—an economic embargo and diplomatic isolation—has not changed substantially since the Kennedy years. U.S. officials argue that changing anything now, softening trade sanctions or opening a dialogue, would only strengthen Castro at the very moment he is faltering. "Castro would use any move from Washington as proof that American resolve is weakening and that he can tough things out," argues one senior Bush administration official. "We cannot give him that hope."

But key human rights activists in Cuba, as well as a growing number of Castro's opponents in the United States and Europe, disagree. They believe that an overture from Washington might help promote constructive change. At the least, it would call Castro's bluff, exposing to the Cuban people that he, not the United States, is the real cause of their misery. It might even convince Castro's inner circle—the likeliest agents of change—to move against him. Right now, they do not know whether to expect a hero's welcome from Washington or Nuremberg-type trials. The most the Bush administration has offered is a pledge to drop the embargo if Castro chooses to hold free elections. That sort of all-or-nothing dare is unlikely to convince Castro or anyone else in Cuba to move.

The only new development in U.S. policy toward Cuba was a private warning given recently by American officials to Havana that a repeat of the 1980 Mariel refugee exodus— a serious danger if conditions on the island worsen—would be "considered an act of war." That is an improbable threat and a peculiar anachronism coming from an administration that advocates dialogue and constructive engagement with just about anyone else, even China's leaders after the Tiananmen Square massacre and Syria's Hafez al Asad.

High-pressure domestic politics is the key to understanding President George Bush's position on Cuba. The White House does not want to offend its longtime supporters, the Cuban American National Foundation—a millionaires' club of right-wing exiles with a hefty campaign war chest and the support of many South Florida voters—especially with upcoming elections. The Foundation and its chairman, Jorge Mas Canosa, vehemently oppose any change in American policy that does not punish and isolate Castro even more. Dialogue with Castro, they believe, is tantamount to sleeping with the enemy; and anyone who suggests it, including human rights leaders on the island, must be either a communist dupe or a traitor. In the face of such passion and political clout, the Bush administration, which tends to ignore crises until they explode, has decided to do nothing at all. "The Foundation has had a chilling effect on the debate," admits one administration official. "Any time anyone starts to think creatively about Cuba we're told: What do you want to do, lose South Florida for us?" The Bush administration claims at least one change in Cuba policy. It has worked hard to woo Moscow away from Castro and may have helped convince the former Soviet president Mikhail Gorbachev to stop subsidizing the Cuban economy—although economic necessity probably played a larger role. But neither Gorbachev nor the Russian president Boris Yeltsin have been willing to cut the cord as definitively as the Bush administration has asked. Despite Gorbachev's promise in the fall of 1991 to withdraw a Soviet combat training brigade from Cuba, twenty-four hundred troops remain. The Russians also have not shut down their "big ear" electronic eavesdropping station in Lourdes. "Whether or not Castro's in power, we have certain assets there we will not abandon," says a senior Russian official, "especially when other countries like Spain are spoiling to take them over."

When Yeltsin visited Bush in Washington in June 1992, he failed to sign on to an American-scripted joint statement urging Castro to hold free elections. Why he balked is a matter of debate. "Yeltsin was never serious from the start," insists one senior administration official, who says that the Russians never even asked to see a version of the statement until the last minute. But other sources blame White House hardliners who conspicuously removed a line from the statement denying any "aggressive intent" toward Castro—a minimum Yeltsin demand. "No aggressive intent" is the official policy of the Bush administration. But such a public reiteration would have infuriated the exile right.

While Bush fiddles, the exile lobby is developing its own policy on Cuba. The group has drafted a new constitution for the post-Castro era, commissioned supply-side wizard Arthur Laffer (Milton Friedman turned it down) to develop an economic blueprint, and pledged billions of dollars to buy state lands. More than thirty years after they left, Foundation leaders are laying the groundwork for a triumphant return to Cuba.

To those still living on the island, the exile leaders seem to have a clear American endorsement. News from the Foundation is lavishly broadcast to Cuba on the U.S. Information Agency's Radio Marti. A Foundation-conceived project cozily overseen by chairman Mas Canosa, who heads the Presidential Advisory Board on Broadcasting to Cuba, Radio Marti beams news, information, and entertainment to Cuba twenty-four hours a day. Supporters claim that the station's in-depth coverage of the Foundation is proportionate to the group's power and influence in the exile community. Critics charge, however, that the radio has become a propaganda arm for the Foundation—at a cost of $15 million a year to the American taxpayer. "Mas Canosa, his projects, his politics are presented as if they were American policy," claims Ernesto Betancourt, a former director of Radio Marti who says he was forced out of his job for opposing Mas Canosa. "If you were a Cuban listening to all that, what would you think?" Congressional investigators in the General Accounting Office issued a report in May 1992 criticizing Radio Marti's far less successful sister, TV Marti (it cannot be seen on the island because of Cuban government jamming), for a "lack of balance" and for promoting the Foundation's views too heavily.

In Washington, meanwhile, the lobby is pushing new legislation to tighten the thirty-year-old U.S. trade embargo. The embargo, as currently enforced, prohibits all direct trade and financial dealings with Cuba. The so-called Cuban Democracy Act, in its initial form, would also bar trade with Cuba by foreign subsidiaries of American corporations and deny U.S. aid, debt relief, or free-trade benefits to any countries assisting Cuba.

Congressional aides ridicule the bill privately as "a dog" and a "throwback to the 1960s." Its popularity, they say, is proof of the potency of the interest-group politics played by Mas Canosa and the Foundation. The legislation's author is New Jersey Democrat Robert Torricelli, the new chairman of the House Subcommittee on Western Hemisphere Affairs. Torricelli—who voted against funding for the Nicaraguan contras, a project also dear to the Foundation—attributes his animosity toward Castro and his enthusiasm for the bill to the 1962 Cuban missile crisis. "Fidel Castro almost destroyed everything that I value most in life," he says. Still, party politics and Torricelli's own political ambitions may have something to do with his position on Cuba as well. The Democratic leadership was clearly delighted in putting the administration "on the wrong side" of the Foundation. "Most of the Democrats backing [the bill were] hoping the White House [would] veto it," says one Democratic aide on Capitol Hill. And while Torricelli's Bergen County district has few Cuban Americans, the state of New Jersey has a large Cuban American constituency—85,000 strong, many in next-door Union City—a solid base of support if Torricelli decides to run for governor or the Senate. A prodigious fund-raiser, Torricelli is receiving large political contributions from the Foundation and its supporters.

Despite its close ties to the Foundation, the Bush administration originally opposed the bill. "The proposed legislation would remove the focus on Cuba and shift the burden to the United States," warned Principal Deputy Assistant Secretary of State for Inter-American Affairs Robert Gelbard in testimony before the House Foreign Affairs Committee. Officials worried that the bill's slash-and-burn tactics could play into Castro's hands, provoking a nationalist backlash in Cuba and giving him a further excuse for the island's disastrous economic situation. Officials also warned of the bill's high diplomatic cost. They were particularly concerned that the legislation's mandated sanctions on countries that give aid or provide favorable terms of trade to Cuba would prevent Washington from helping Russia and Eastern Europe. In addition, they said that the ban on foreign subsidiaries' trading with Cuba placed an unfair burden on American companies abroad and could strain Washington's foreign relations by imposing American laws extraterritorially. Furthermore, the legislation's requirement that Washington actively lobby its allies to adopt an embargo against Cuba, they said, could undermine America's international credibility. "Our attempts would be rejected," said Gelbard. "While many governments agree that Cuba should not receive aid, few want to impose an embargo against it."

The Bush administration clearly did not relish antagonizing the Foundation, and more often than not, its opposition was delivered in a whisper rather than a shout. Assistant Secretary of State for Inter-American Affairs Bernard Aronson—respected throughout Washington for his impeccable political instincts—chose not to testify against the bill, sending his able, but lower-profile, deputy instead.

Then presidential politics intervened. In April, the Bush administration got word that Democratic presidential candidate Bill Clinton planned to endorse the legislation. And Clinton did just that, declaring at a Little Havana fund-raiser, "I like it." "With those three words," wrote *Miami Herald* political editor Tom Fiedler, "Clinton may have done more for Democratic prospects among Cuban Americans than any previous Democrat." He also raised about $125,000 that evening. The White House was certainly worried. According to Fiedler, the news of Clinton's impending endorsement set off a panic. Bush interrupted his Kennebunkport weekend to announce that he was tightening the embargo by requiring that ships carrying Cuban goods obtain special licenses to enter U.S. ports—a clear attempt to steal the legislation's thunder. Then the White House began to negotiate a compromise.

The White House signed on after Torricelli agreed to soften the legislation—urging, rather than requiring, the president to impose sanctions on countries that aid Cuba, and urging, rather than requiring, the administration to lobby allies to sign on to the embargo.

But the ban on foreign subsidiary trade with Cuba stayed in—paving the way for future troubles with Canada, Great Britain, and other allies. As for concerns that the legislation could give Castro a political boost at home and strain American credibility abroad, those were forgotten as well. When Mas Canosa says jump, politicians lace up their sneakers.

THE FEUD

Visceral anti-Castroism is a fine American tradition—and a bipartisan one—that long predates the rise to influence of Mas Canosa and the Cuban American National Foundation. The idea for the 1961 Bay of Pigs invasion was authorized by President Dwight Eisenhower and implemented by President John Kennedy. For three decades, under both Democratic and Republican administrations, the United States has tried to overthrow Castro through conventional means—diplomatic and economic sanctions—and, for about a decade, through some very unconventional ones. Until 1972, the CIA trained and funded exiles for countless assassination attempts, infiltrations, and guerrilla raids on the island—all to no avail. In 1975, the Senate Select Committee on Intelligence, the so-called Church committee, detailed an embarrassing series of anti-Castro dirty tricks and buffoonery, from poison cigars and exploding sea shells to a depilatory shoe-spray intended to make his beard fall out. Nothing worked.

So why did successive administrations keep trying, and with such obvious fervor? Why are Americans so fanatically anti-Castro? Why is a new look at Cuba policy one of the last taboos in the new world order?

Castro is certainly a bad guy. He is a dictator, a communist, a human rights abuser, and an exporter of revolution. For those sins he deserves to be reviled by the United States, but so do countless other thugs with whom Washington has cut cozy deals over the years. Iraq's Saddam Hussein and Syria's Hafez al-Asad are only the most recent. What makes Castro different is that he committed all his sins in America's backyard. Violate the Monroe Doctrine and test U.S. containment policy, as Castro did, and the result is explosive.

But old prejudices fade with time. And by the mid-1970s, Washington—which had already opened up to "Red" China—seemed ready for some accommodation with Castro. In 1973 the United States signed an antihijacking agreement with Cuba, and by late 1974, aides to U.S. Secretary of State Henry Kissinger began secret talks with the Castro government. The following year, the United States voted to end the Organization of American States (OAS) sanctions against Cuba and softened its own embargo. Talks were suspended, however, when Cuba dispatched thousands of troops to Angola in the fall of 1975. Castro's revolutionary comrades in the Popular Movement for the Liberation of Angola were about to be swept aside by South African invaders.

Castro's decision showed either remarkable insensitivity or a fundamental lack of interest in improving relations with the United States. It gave credibility to hard-line arguments that negotiations with Cuba were pointless. However, the Ford administration must bear some of the blame as well. The United States also was deeply involved in Angola, sending about $30 million in covert aid to two separate guerrilla groups.

Jimmy Carter came to office with a new enthusiasm for normalizing relations with Havana and with a willingness to look the other way on Angola. In early 1977, the two sides began successful negotiations on fishing rights and maritime boundaries. The week of the signing ceremony, the Americans broached an even more significant subject: establishment of "interests sections," sort of subembassies, in Havana and Washington. A full diplomatic opening, complete with a dismantling of the embargo, appeared to be only months away. It was not. The White House first wanted to ensure passage of the Panama Canal treaties (another right-wing taboo). Then the Cubans, who clearly had not learned from their Angolan experience, sent troops to Ethiopia in December 1977—infuriating Carter and his hard-line national security adviser, Zbigniew Brzezinski. Havana tried to resurrect the process the following year by offering to release several thousand political prisoners. Knowing that human rights were dear to Carter's heart, the Cubans clearly hoped to wheedle the Americans back to the table. Talks were held and eventually thousands of prisoners were released, but Carter's enthusiasm for normalization had waned. Wayne Smith, former chief of the U.S. interests section in Havana, writes in his book *The Closest of Enemies* that the Carter administration was so angry about Ethiopia—and nervous about its right flank—that it did not even take credit for the prisoners' release. "The [National Security Council] instructed us to say ... that the U.S. government welcomed the release of these prisoners, but that we had not negotiated for it and did not know what had prompted it!"

With no luck in Washington, Castro tried another route: opening a dialogue with the exile community to discuss family visits to Cuba and the already negotiated prisoner release. The dialogue was truly revolutionary, although in ways that neither side ever imagined. The seventy-five exiles—businessmen, ministers, and academics—who accepted Castro's invitation to Havana were reviled as traitors in Miami. Two were murdered and many were threatened. But when Castro opened the doors to family visits, more than one hundred thousand exiles defied their community leaders and traveled home. As Raquel Raquero, then a thirty-eight-year-old secretary, told the *Miami Herald* at the time: "I have two children and my mother in Cuba, and besides I never gave up my country.... Pride doesn't exist. Sentiment does."

The hard-liners' worst fears, and Castro's hopes, however, failed to materialize. Whereas the visits changed the exile community's feelings about the United States—many exiles returned more committed to their adopted home—they did not build any sympathy for Castro or any desire for a diplomatic settlement. In Cuba, meanwhile, the return of the prodigal sons and daughters bearing suitcases full of gifts and offering tales of the good life ninety miles away created deep feelings of dissatisfaction. The 1980 Mariel refugee exodus, in which more than 125,000 Cubans escaped to Florida's shores, was proof of how unhappy Cubans had become with their lot. Mariel also contributed to Carter's defeat at the polls. His successor, Ronald Reagan, had no interest in reviving the negotiations.

LA CAUSA AND WASHINGTON

While they pursued their openings with Havana, both Gerald Ford and Jimmy Carter worried about conservative opposition. But by most accounts, neither administration was particularly concerned about the feelings of the Miami exile community. Before the appearance of the Foundation in the early 1980s, Cuban Americans simply had no organized voice in Washington.

Almost every one of the hundreds of thousands of Cubans who poured into Miami (today there are 1.1 million Cubans in the United States, more than half of them in South Florida) swore undying hatred for Castro and communism. But most were willing to cede leadership to Washington. The U.S. government, they believed, would someday take care of the tyrant. And while they called themselves exiles and were slower than other groups to apply for citizenship, they followed the route of the most successful immigrants: building businesses, educating their children, buying homes. The small number of activists who committed their lives to La Causa (the cause) also abdicated political leadership to the gringos, signing up for the Bay of Pigs invasion and staying on with the CIA long after their defeat. When Washington suspended its terrorist attacks on Cuba in 1972, some extremists continued to fight, although mainly against each other. Half a dozen exile leaders were killed in Miami turf-wars during the mid-1970s. In service of La Causa, Cuban terrorists blew up a Cubana airliner over Barbados, killing seventy-three people; rocketed a Polish freighter in the Port of Miami; and planted bombs at Miami International Airport and a host of government offices in Miami. They assassinated, among others, an exiled Chilean ambassador and his associate on Washington's embassy row. Their acts of futility made them heroes to many in their community but had no effect on Castro's rule or Washington's policies. Most important, the exile community made little effort to influence U.S. politics and policy through more conventional means. Naturally, any politician campaigning in South Florida—from a candidate for county clerk to presidential hopefuls—had to bash Castro on the stump. But it went no further than that.

Mas Canosa changed all that, bringing La Causa to Washington. The rise of the Cuban American National Foundation and its chairman is a genuine American success story. Mas Canosa fled to Miami in 1960, before he could finish law school. He joined the failed Bay of Pigs invasion, although his boat never made it ashore. He began working as a milkman and now owns a multimillion-dollar construction company. Through it all, Mas Canosa's militant anti-Castroism never wavered. Regardless of the political climate, dialogue and reconciliation with Castro have always been acts of treason for Mas Canosa. He declared in 1979: "The dialogue has helped define a lot of people who posed as anti-Castro leaders. The longer this dialogue lasts the more it will separate the good guys from the bad guys."

Reagan was clearly one of the good guys. Mas Canosa and his wealthy Miami colleagues had learned the costs of being out of the loop during the Ford and Carter years. Thus, when Reagan's first national security adviser, Richard Allen, suggested setting up a lobbying group along the lines of the powerful American Israel Public Affairs Committee, the Foundation was born.

Not everyone in the community shares the Foundation's hard-line approach. Polls consistently show that Cuban Americans want Castro out, but that they differ on the most effective means. "When you do the polling you find 90 percent of Cuban Americans say yes, they support a military invasion; 60 percent say they support negotiations, too," says University of Miami professor Enrique Baloyra, who heads the Cuban Social Democratic Coordination. "The logic is: 'You give me a freebie and I'll support it; if not I'll entertain other options.'" And within the community, a host of competing political groups have been organized in recent years. But the groups are small, poorly funded, and driven by philosophical and personal disagreements. Even those exiles and exile groups who challenge the Foundation's hard-line and advocate dialogue disagree on whether the talks should take place between Castro and the Cuban people, or between Castro and the United States. And those who oppose the Torricelli legislation also disagree on whether the United States should lift or soften the embargo or maintain the status quo.

But whatever their beliefs, most Cuban Americans are still too intimidated to speak out against the Foundation. The few who do dare to criticize Mas Canosa publicly have yet to promote their ideas in Washington. "Frankly, a lot of progressive people in Miami find it repulsive to give their money to a bunch of WASP congressmen," says Baloyra. "But it's a good idea and one worth looking at."

In just a decade, Mas Canosa has made Cuban Americans a serious political force in Washington with the Foundation as their official voice, at least in the eyes of the non-Cuban establishment. Bush's son Jeb, a Miami businessman, helped host the Foundation's annual meeting in 1991, and he is the Foundation's point man to the White House. The neoconservative icon Jeane Kirkpatrick and three U.S. senators—Florida's Bob Graham and Connie Mack and Connecticut's Joseph Lieberman—serve on its Blue Ribbon Commission. Reagan can be counted on for a cameo appearance. Its campaign chest is impressive. The Foundation's sixty-five directors each contribute $10,000 to the organization each year and pledge to make another $10,000 in political contributions per campaign. Its Free Cuba PAC made $114,000 in contributions during the 1989–1990 campaign cycle and intends to spend between $250,000 and $400,000 in 1991–1992, with both Democrats and Republicans benefiting from its largesse. As of June 1992, the Free Cuba PAC had already contributed a total of $55,750 to twenty-six congressional candidates. Not surprisingly, the biggest recipient was Torricelli, the Cuban Democracy Act sponsor, who had already "maxed out" with a $10,000 contribution from the PAC as well as receiving a maximum personal contribution of $2,000 from PAC president Domingo Moreira, $1,500 from Foundation chief Mas Canosa, and hefty donations from other Foundation directors and friends. Other major PAC recipients include Senator John Breaux (D-La., $5,000); retiring senator Kent Conrad (D-N.D., $5,000); Senator Arlen Specter (R-Penn., $3,400); Representative Dave McCurdy (D-Okla., $4,000); and Representative Stephen Solarz (D-N.Y., $5,000).

Money clearly talks in Washington, and the Foundation's clout on Capitol Hill is undeniable. Besides gaining funding for Radio Marti and TV Marti, it has successfully lobbied for U.S. aid for Jonas Savimbi's Angolan rebels and for the Nicaraguan contras. The Cuban Democracy Act is the new jewel in the Foundation's crown. And Bush's sudden turnaround is proof of the Foundation's lobbying muscle.

For all that, it is also possible to overstate the Foundation's influence. Bush has been known to defy powerful interest groups—most notably the pro-Israel lobby—even during an election year. But that defiance, say aides who know the president well, came after years of questioning, the trauma of the Persian Gulf War, and the president's personal conversion to the cause of the peace process. None of that has happened with respect to Castro, whose own intransigence also argues against any policy change. The only voices aggressively criticizing the current inertia—human rights activists in Cuba and some Castro opponents in Miami—are so far too weak to be taken seriously, no matter how noble their credentials or convincing their arguments.

For now, one question the administration is not asking itself is how fragile is its own political support in the Cuban American community—and how strong is the Foundation's. If Bush defied the Foundation, would he really lose the votes of intrinsically conservative Cuban Americans?

Since the fall of the Berlin Wall, Mas Canosa has gone international. In 1991, when the White House was still unsure of its own feelings about Yeltsin, a picture of Mas Canosa and the Russian leader appeared proudly on the cover of the Foundation's magazine. "Other exiles might not have talked to Yeltsin, because he was once a Communist," says one senior U.S. official admiringly. "Not Mas, he'd go to hell and talk to the devil if it would screw Fidel Castro."

MAS CANOSA'S BATTLES

But there is also a dark side to Mas Canosa that raises serious questions about his judgment, his plans for Cuba, and Washington's close identification with his cause. Mas Canosa drives a bullet-proof Mercedes and has accused competing exile leaders of plotting to kill him. (The FBI investigated but found no proof.) After a Miami City commissioner scuttled his plans for a $130 million real estate deal (one of Mas Canosa's partners was Jeane Kirkpatrick), Mas Canosa publicly challenged him to a duel with swords or revolvers; the commissioner suggested waterpistols instead. A court ordered him to pay his brother $1.2 million in libel damages after Mas Canosa sent out two scathing letters attacking him for setting up a competing business. By his own account, Mas Canosa convinced federal agents in 1989 to bash in the door of Ram Cernuda, a competing exile leader who favors dialogue with Castro, and to seize his collection of Cuban art on the grounds that it violated the trade embargo. The paintings were later returned and apologies issued. But an unrepentant Mas Canosa bragged on Miami radio: "In effect, we are responsible for this and other investigations that I hope will materialize. I'm going to continue to get an investigation of Cernuda and of twenty other Cernudas."

Mas Canosa declined to be interviewed for this article, his office first citing a prior agreement with CBS's 60 *Minutes,* then asking if any one of a list of his critics would also be quoted, and finally pleading a packed schedule. His fellow director and PAC chief, Miami businessman Domingo Moreira, however, made a reasoned presentation of the Foundation's views. His group has no quarrel with the Cuban people, only with Castro; the Foundation has no intention of kicking anyone out of their homes or off their land; they want a peaceful transition for Cuba. "What we want to take back is a lot of what we've learned about democratic processes, about tolerance. . . . Otherwise there isn't anything to go back to," he said.

But when Mas Canosa is rallying the faithful on Miami's Spanish-language radio stations, he projects a very different image. Pretty much anyone who disagrees with him ends up being tarred as "close to" or "sounding like" Castro, a tactic that has his critics calling him "The Next Fidel." When the *Miami Herald* challenged his views, he said the newspaper was run by "unscrupulous . . . people who chop off heads, destroy people, families, put people in jail." Earlier, when a group of Miami professors challenged his plans for a state-funded, "independent"—read Foundation-directed—Cuban research center at Florida International University, Mas Canosa accused them of being "close to Castro" despite their fondness for "McDonald's hamburgers and Burger King." Mas Canosa's supporters insist, however, that his pronouncements on Spanish-language radio should not be judged by American standards. "There is a passion, a form of political debate that just doesn't make sense to Americans," says Jose Cardenas, spokesman for the Foundation.

One case where the translation has clearly failed is Mas Canosa's battle with the *Miami Herald.* For years, the Foundation and its supporters have accused the *Herald* of being insensitive to Cuban Americans; and for years, *Herald* reporters have complained that the paper pandered to the Foundation. But when the editorial board criticized the Foundation's new Cuba legislation, Mas Canosa accused the paper of sounding like Granma, the official organ of the Cuban Communist party, and intimated that darker influences were at work in the newsroom. He demanded that parent-company Knight-Ridder's two top Cuban American executives resign. Publisher David Lawrence and the two executives received unsigned death threats. *Herald* newsboxes were smeared with excrement.

Mas Canosa blamed Castro agents for the threats, but the battle continued with the two sides trading blistering accusations on the *Herald* editorial pages. The Foundation bought billboards on sixty city buses in Miami declaring in Spanish and English: "I don't believe the *Herald.*" Mas Canosa also told Miami radio that he planned to take the crusade national, airing anti-*Herald* television ads and going to Wall Street, apparently for an assault on Knight-Ridder's stock. In recent months, passions have cooled somewhat.

Most disturbing of all is the uncertainty about what Mas Canosa and the Foundation really want for Cuba. The Foundation's pressure-cooker strategy advocating a tighter economic squeeze on a country where bread rations have already fallen to a single roll a day, while offering no option for dialogue or negotiation, could lead to a social explosion. How much will the Cuban people sacrifice and when will they snap? It is impossible to predict. There was almost no warning before Mariel, or any of the uprisings in Eastern Europe for that matter. For his part, Castro is not taking any chances. To head off possible trouble, he has added "rapid-reaction brigades" to his usual complement of neighborhood spy groups, and he has begun rounding up known opponents. With no avenue for dialogue, chances are that any popular uprising against the regime will be bloody.

As much as Americans want Castro to fall, social upheaval in Cuba would be disastrous for the United States. The suffering in Haiti and the outpouring of thousands of Haitian boat people has been a terrible tragedy, but the Bush administration has so far managed to shrug it off as not its responsibility. Cuba would be different. For one, the United States is legally committed to admitting Cuba's "political refugees" no matter what their reasons for fleeing, and no matter whether they number in the thousands or hundreds of thousands. And if Castro's troops turn their rifles on demonstrators, the powerful Cuba lobby and a million Cuban Americans will undoubtedly demand American military action, and the United States will probably have to comply. Given the long, inglorious history of American interventions in Cuba, even such a mission of mercy could easily backfire. It is a choice Americans should not have to make and the best argument for pursuing a negotiated settlement.

If Castro were about to throw in the towel or if the Cuban people were on the verge of their own "velvet revolution," then staying the current course, or even intensifying the pressure, would make sense. Why give up with the objective in sight? It might even be argued that the Foundation's bad-cop role—if carefully delineated from the interests of the United States—could actually reinforce the official strategy: Cut a deal now, or face the wrath of the Foundation later. Unfortunately, neither Castro nor the Cuban people appear ready to move, and Washington's close identification with the Foundation may, in fact, delay Castro's downfall.

Before the Fall 1991 Cuban Communist Party congress, Cuban officials hinted that their leader was considering new reforms: a reopening of private farmers' markets and a widening of the political debate to let off steam. Instead, Castro chose to go to the mattresses, dispatching rapid-reaction brigades to suppress any dissent. In November, after the poet Maria Elena Cruz Varela called for direct elections to Cuba's puppet National Assembly, she was dragged out of her apartment and forced to eat her political writings. She was then arrested, tried, and sentenced to two years in prison. In January 1992, a mob surrounded the home of human rights activist Elizardo Sanchez Santacruz, destroying his office and howling for his blood. Sanchez, who spent years in jail for opposing Castro, is also on the Foundation's enemy list because he advocates dialogue with the regime. It is impossible to know why Castro chose such a route. But it may well be that, having studied events in Eastern Europe, Castro has decided not to make the mistakes of his East European comrades, who lost power only after they loosened their iron grip.

The Cuban people are not about to follow the example of Eastern Europe either. For one, the building blocks of political dissent do not yet exist. There is no Solidarity in Cuba, no strong Catholic Church, no Lech Walesa or Vaclav Havel. Although there are more Cruzes and Sanchezes than ever before, the number of Cubans willing to speak out publicly against Castro is still in the dozens, rather than in the thousands.

Betancourt, formerly of Radio Marti, argues that the most important difference between Cuba and Eastern Europe is the role played by Gorbachev and the Soviet army. Eastern Europe's revolutions were in good part born in Moscow. While a cutback of Soviet aid helped create some of the prerevolutionary conditions, as it has in Cuba, far more significant was a lessening of Soviet-backed repression. First, Gorbachev urged glasnost on Eastern Europe's skeptical leaders. Then, he told them that the Soviet army and KGB-trained police would no longer keep them in power. "It was only then that in one country in Eastern Europe after another massive demonstration took place and the ante was raised from seeking moderate reforms to the complete dismantling of the Communist system," writes Betancourt in testimony he offered to Torricelli's subcommittee on the Cuban Democracy Act—but was never asked to deliver. Gorbachev urged political opening to Castro as well. But Castro never did depend on Soviet tanks, thousands of miles away across an ocean, to repress his people. The cutoff of Soviet aid, and indeed the disappearance of the Soviet state, has not changed that situation. The Cuban army and police are Castro's alone, and for now at least they continue to follow his orders.

Any serious challenge to Castro will most likely come from his own inner circle. The 1989 trial and execution of Angolan war hero General Arnaldo Ochoa Sanchez, who was accused of drug trafficking, is seen by some as a preemptive strike by Castro against a charismatic rival. Western diplomats in Havana report rumors of military-guarded arms shipments disappearing from Havana's docks, and conspiracy theories swirl through the exile community, with the army frequently cast as the protagonist.

The cutoff of Soviet aid has certainly made life tougher for long-pampered military officers and party leaders. U.S. officials and the Foundation argue that further economic pressure will only increase their desire for rebellion. Perhaps, but unremitting hostility from Washington and the lobby could also create a bunker mentality. Castro's inner circle may wonder why they should take the risk if the Yanqui colossus is not going to cooperate. Why take the chance if the Yanquis' Cuban government-in-exile (the Foundation) is going to put you on trial for treason? Certainly everything that the Cuban elite hears about the Foundation's plans, and their tacit endorsement by the U.S. government, suggests that their welcome would be less than cordial.

The Cuban people, meanwhile, share many of the same fears. For them the message from Miami is particularly disturbing. Mas Canosa says he can raise billions of dollars to privatize state lands, but to many Cubans that sounds as if he were planning to buy up the country. "People in Cuba are asking themselves what will follow Castro.... What happens to me if I don't have the money to buy a Hertz dealership?" says Elliot Abrams, a former assistant secretary of state under Reagan and a contra supporter whose anticommunist credentials are beyond reproach. "The answers coming out of Miami are not reassuring."

The Bush administration denies any such revanchist plans. Aronson, Abrams's successor, correctly told the Foundation in 1991 that "the United States has no blueprint for Cuba." That message, however, is drowned out by all the Foundation's plans and posturing and by the administration's cosseting of the Foundation.

One particularly embarrassing episode took place in January 1992. Several State Department officials told the *Miami Herald* that as a matter of standard antiterrorist policy, the administration had tipped off the Castro government to a series of attacks planned by Cuban exiles, including a plot to set off bombs at the 1991 Pan-American Games. All hell broke loose on Miami radio, with accusations of high-level betrayal and even communist infiltration at the State Department. The crisis shot all the way up to the White House and National Security Adviser Brent Scowcroft. Aronson phoned the *Herald* to deny that there was anything regular about the cooperation. "Our policy is to enforce the laws of the United States, including the neutrality law, but there's no ongoing policy of cooperating or collaborating with the Castro regime," he said. Meanwhile, Jeb Bush, the president's son, went on Miami radio to cool passions. When asked if enemy infiltrators in the State Department were responsible for the story, he damned the department with very faint praise. "I do not believe that the problem with the State Department in many cases is that they are traitors," said Bush, "but that they have their own agenda." The community in Miami may have been placated, but what message was sent to the people of Havana? That the United States actually did support terrorism?

Abrams, who argues for the continuation of the embargo, says that Washington cannot maintain such contradictory positions and must distance itself from Mas Canosa and the Foundation. The Bush administration "needs to make it clear that nobody will have a privileged position after Castro." The return of Mas Canosa and his friends is a fear that Castro constantly plays up. "What are they going to do with the houses the revolution has given to the people?" Castro asked in a recent speech. "Are they going to turn the child care centers into brothels?"

All of that implies a need for several changes in U.S. policy toward Cuba. First, the Bush administration and the U.S. Congress need to distinguish themselves from the Foundation and its policies. Washington needs to demonstrate to the Cuban people that the real obstacle to change is Castro and not the unremitting hostility of the United States. And it has to find a way to reassure Cubans, particularly those around Castro, that anyone who dares to move against the dictator will be received as a hero and not as a collaborator.

In essence, the United States needs to pursue some form of measured, constructive engagement. That does not mean dropping the embargo—at least not at first. However, it does require engaging Castro. Francis Bouchey of the conservative Council for Inter-American Security Foundation, believes the administration should "[lob] a succession of small 'reform balls' at Cuba," to call Castro's bluff and to encourage his opponents to step forward. He suggests that Bush could announce that American tourists will be permitted to visit the island if Castro allows the Cuban people into foreigner-only hotels and resorts. The point of the exercise, says Bouchey, is to make "clear to the Cuban people that neither the American people nor the Bush administration has hostile intentions toward them."

Those who argue that such a policy is a long shot, or that it could play into Castro's hands by marginally improving life on the island, must remember that the current pressure-cooker policy has even greater risks. "The gradual route, the route of dialogue, may not be satisfying for people who want Castro to fall today," says Baloyra. "But it is the most prudent way to go. You preach drastic and sudden change and you scare a hell of a lot of people in Cuba. You turn up the pressure and it all could explode in your face—with the very real risk of a U.S. invasion."

The Bush team, which has turned coalition building into a cottage industry, could lead an international effort to promote reform. How about an International Conference on Democracy in Cuba, with working groups and follow-on meetings; with the European Community, the Russians, and maybe even NATO all working together with no drain on the U.S. taxpayer unless Castro agrees to real reforms? James Baker and George Bush would be in their element. And Castro would be put on the spot. So far, all the State Department has come up with is an idea to spend $500,000 on an independent academic review of policy options toward Cuba, led, perhaps, by some of the same professors who challenged Mas Canosa's research center. Whether even that proposal will survive once the Foundation gets wind of it is doubtful.

18

Here To Stay

The Domestic and International
Priorities of Latino Leaders

THE TOMAS RIVERA POLICY INSTITUTE

Hispanics[1] are projected to become the nation's largest minority group in the year 2010 and to make up 25 percent of the nation's population by the year 2050. In a recent *Foreign Affairs* article, Samuel Huntington cautions about the effect of rising ethnic interests in the United States, and warns they will lead to fragmentation of national interest in our nation's foreign policy. But America, the old truism holds, is a nation of immigrants, and immigrant groups—from the Irish, to European Jews, to Germans, to Cubans—have historically sought to weigh in when America's foreign policy touched the nations they were close to. What might the nation expect from its Latino leaders?

This is a study of the views of 454 Hispanics who hold leadership positions in key institutions—including government, academia, business, media, the arts, and the nonprofit sector.[2] What issues absorb their attention, and what do they think lies in store for their community? Just how concerned and active are they regarding U.S.-Latin American relations? Are the interests of Latino leaders so tied to their countries of origin that they are blinded to U.S. interests or do they have a perspective that is more subtle? Is there a single "Hispanic" perspective toward Latin America or are the views of Latinos as disparate as the nations they come from?

Two organizations—Public Agenda and the Tomas Rivera Policy Institute—joined to answer these and other questions. Public Agenda is a nonprofit, nonpartisan research organization specializing in the analysis of public and leadership opinion on public policy issues. Its partner in this research, the Tomas Rivera Policy Institute, is an independent, nonprofit, nonadvocacy organization, conducting social, political, and economic policy action research on major issues relevant to all groups in the Latino community.

In addition to the survey, in-depth follow-up interviews were also conducted with about a dozen survey respondents; quotes from these conversations are used throughout the report to shed light on their thinking.

Finding One: Hispanic leaders expect the political and economic influence of their community to grow. But they are wary of a potential backlash in the United States and divisions within the Hispanic community itself.

GROWING CLOUT

Latino leaders are optimistic about the prospects for the U.S. Hispanic community, anticipating gains on the economic and social fronts. "We're living the impact now," said one leader, "in terms of culture, food, music, and the economy." Nearly eight in ten (77 percent) also believe economic opportunities for Latinos will increase in the near future as well. One leader said, "We'll gain more board of directors, where we are now a paltry few, and that will influence the direction of business."

Nor are the gains Hispanic leaders expect to see restricted to the economic realm: An overwhelming majority (87 percent) believes the influence of U.S. Hispanics on the political process will increase in the near future. "We're going to be the largest minority," predicted one leader, "we're going to become politicians, be more involved." Seven in ten (71 percent) think the United States will show greater concern and attentiveness toward Hispanic affairs in general.

Perhaps because they think these trends will lead to concrete consequences, nearly two-thirds (66 percent) of Latino leaders also believe the nation is headed toward a greater acceptance of Spanish as the second most important language in the United States.

MIXED BLESSINGS?

But along with these positive trends, Hispanic leaders see some serious problems and speak about impediments to progress for the U.S. Latino community. Perhaps most troubling to them is their expectation that anti-Latino sentiment in the United States is likely to grow— an expectation shared by 80 percent of the leaders responding to this survey. Indeed, some explicitly connect the growing influence of Hispanics to expectations of a backlash. "Clearly, we've already become a much more visible factor in politics and the economy," said one leader. "But with that comes another dimension of the problem: Many Americans of good will—not just white supremacists—will become very spooked. There will be more bigotry, rather than less."

Even the increased acceptance of the Spanish language has a downside, according to another leader: "I think Spanish will become the second language, but reluctantly ... what happened in Miami—where people were upset about all the Spanish language signs—will be happening a lot more." Perhaps this is why the state of race and ethnic relations in the U.S. is a pressing concern for Hispanic leaders: eight in ten (80 percent). Hispanic leaders believe improving race and ethnic relations ought to be a very important policy goal for the United States.

INTERNAL DIFFERENCES

Latino leaders point to the diversity among U.S. Hispanics as something that has in the past hindered the progress of their community. The many differences in identity and countries of origin, according to this view, have diluted Hispanic strength. "The diversity is incredible," said one leader interviewed, "the Tex-Mex, the New Mexican, the Louisiana, the Florida Hispanic, etc.—they're all very different groups." About six in ten (58 percent) leaders feel that the diversity of backgrounds and identities among U.S. Latinos has weakened their influence. Leaders of Mexican heritage are less likely than other leaders to think diversity has weakened the influence of the U.S. Hispanic community (49 percent vs. 65 percent).

The very question of what to name Hispanics/Latinos can be controversial in and of itself: "I have problems with the phrase 'Latin Americans'," said one leader, "and I've never been that keen on the phrase 'Hispanic' as an overall term. It's a term to fill a U.S. need to categorize and label a group of people the U.S. doesn't know what to do with or call. It assumes a homogeneity that is not there."

Latino leaders responding to this survey predict these differences within the Hispanic community in the United States will recede. Nearly two-thirds (64 percent) expect to see the "emergence of a more unified Hispanic/Latino identity among Latinos in the U.S. regardless of their country of origin."

Finding Two: Latino leaders are far more concerned about the well-being of the Hispanic community within the United States than they are about the state of U.S.-Latin American relations. Domestic issues—education, race relations, and economic growth—are their top priorities.

FOCUS ON THE HOME FRONT

It is the progress and well-being of the Hispanic community in the United States that most absorbs the attention of Latino leaders—not the state of U.S.-Latin American relations or foreign policy issues in general. Nearly nine in ten (87 percent) say U.S. Latinos should be most concerned with the well-being of the Latino community in the United States. Another three in four (75 percent) also say that "what happens to the Hispanic/Latino community in the U.S. is more important to me than the state of U.S. relations with Latin America." "Basically, we should cultivate our own garden" said one survey respondent in a follow-up interview. "We should be focused on the amelioration of conditions here in the U.S." Leaders born in the United States are more likely to focus on the U.S. Hispanic community rather than Latin America (81 percent); but even 64 percent of Hispanics born in Latin America concur. Interestingly, only a narrow majority (51 percent) of Hispanic leaders of Cuban origin agree that U.S. Latinos are more important to them than relations with Latinos outside the country.

Latino influentials clearly focus on the issues that are close to home, and domestic priorities such as education and the economy top their list of concerns. Rating the importance of a wide-ranging list of eighteen domestic and international policy objectives, including maintaining economic growth, improving education, combating international terrorism, and reducing our foreign trade deficit, Hispanic leaders choose domestic goals as their top five policy priorities for the United States.

EDUCATION IS THE TOP PRIORITY

Improving education is clearly highest on their agenda, with nearly all leaders—fully 95 percent—saying it is a very important goal. One Hispanic leader said, "Education is the key to the growth of the person and the community. Without education, we will be on the same treadmill of low income, poor jobs, and so on."

Other issues that occupy their top tier of concerns would no doubt also emerge in any survey conducted with the general American public. Maintaining economic growth is cited by three in four (76 percent) as a very important goal. Reducing crime and improving the U.S. environment are cited by six in ten as very important issues (61 percent and 60 percent, respectively). Historically, these same issues have been at the forefront of the American public's mind.

In the end, it is interesting that the only foreign policy objective to attract a high level of concern is a dramatic, high-stakes one—preventing the spread of nuclear weapons (62 percent say it is very important). Even a fairly innocuous and benevolent issue—improving the global environment—fails to rally overwhelming interest, with less than half of the leaders (46 percent) judging it to be very important. Other matters abroad are much less compelling: maintaining superior military power worldwide (20 percent), and defending our allies' security (8 percent), for example.

But since these leaders are clearly more concerned about domestic priorities and the well-being of the Hispanic community within the United States, the question naturally arises: How much do Hispanic leaders really care about foreign policy toward the region? And if they do care, what role do they see for themselves?

Finding Three: Hispanic leaders maintain strong bonds with Latin America. Most believe Hispanics should be more active and influential regarding U.S. policy toward Latin America, but also believe their agenda should not contradict official U.S. policy.

STAYING IN TOUCH

Hispanic leaders have hardly turned their backs to Latin America—in fact, as individuals they have a wide web of relations and points of contact with the region and routinely track what goes on there. Almost nine in ten (87 percent) Hispanic leaders closely follow current events in Latin America. Almost all (92 percent) have been to Latin America—and more than half of these (59 percent) have traveled there within the last twelve months.

What's more, their social contacts, friends, family, and peers at work reinforce and remind them of their connection to Latin America. More than half (52 percent) have participated in activities regarding U.S.-Latin American affairs ranging from writing letters to offering expert advice to participating in associations. More than seven in ten (74 percent) say at least some of their Latino colleagues at work or friends keep close track of events in Latin America, and 40 percent work for organizations that have extensive dealings in Latin America. Two-thirds (66 percent) have relatives in Latin America, and of these, 66 percent maintain regular contact with them. In the end—whether through personal ties or professional action or both—the relationship between Hispanic leaders and Latin America is a close one.

It is perhaps not surprising to note that leaders born in Latin America are more likely to follow events in the region very closely than those born in the United States (54 percent compared to 30 percent); to have relatives in Latin America (84 percent to 56 percent); and to stay in close touch with those relatives (82 percent to 51 percent, among those with relatives).

A BRIDGE TO LATIN AMERICA

Perhaps because of their extensive contacts and relations in the region, Hispanic leaders believe they can make a unique contribution to U.S. foreign policy toward the region, and that it is proper and appropriate for them to get involved in the shaping of policy. Fully seven in ten (70 percent) reject the view that "there is little reason for the Hispanic/Latino community in the U.S. to develop and pursue its own agenda on U.S. policy toward Latin America." Another eight in ten (79 percent) would like to see U.S. Hispanics increase their efforts to influence U.S. policy toward Latin America. "Latinos should get involved," remarked one leader, "because we know the region better than others, because we're from there. Our relatives live there, we speak the language." Another leader was equally upbeat about the possibility: "We could be a terrific bridge to Latin America for the U.S. and increasingly we will be. It's in the U.S. interest. Hispanics shouldn't be sheepish about getting involved."

NO LOOSE CANNONS

But Hispanic leaders do not believe that the involvement of ethnic groups has always worked to the benefit of the United States and perhaps for that reason prefer a moderate approach to their own involvement. Asked to assess the impact of such ethnic groups as

Irish, Jewish, or Cuban upon U.S. foreign policy, 20 percent believe they have tended to harm the U.S. national interest; 13 percent say they have benefited the national interest. The majority (54 percent) say such groups have had mixed effects. One leader interviewed expressed misgivings about the Cuban lobby and cited it as an example of what not to do: "It's a group that concentrates all their energies on one issue.... This one group has held U.S. policy towards Cuba hostage, and I don't think that should be the goal."

Most Hispanic leaders believe they have an obligation to work within the framework and bounds of official U.S. foreign policy. Forced to choose among three roles Hispanic organizations should play—from working independently regardless of U.S. policy, to working on behalf of U.S. policy, to working independently but not in contradiction— most Hispanic leaders choose the moderate course. Only one-fourth (26 percent) say U.S. Latino organizations should pursue their own objectives regardless of U.S. policy, and only one-fourth (24 percent) believe the opposite—that they are obligated to coordinate action with the government in support of U.S. goals in Latin America. The plurality (43 percent) believes it appropriate to independently pursue their own objectives in Latin America so long as they do not contradict U.S. foreign policy priorities or interests.

"We should influence it [foreign policy toward Latin America] but not monopolize it," said one leader. "At the end of the day we are just part of this greater community of the United States. Just because we know it better doesn't mean we have the right answers."

WHAT THE FUTURE WILL BRING

Many Latino leaders anticipate their influence on U.S.-Latin American relations will increasingly flow through informal and nontraditional links with Latin America. More than half (53 percent) expect to see closer interactions between Latin American governments and U.S. Latinos in the future. Some (42 percent) even believe that U.S. Hispanics are likely to have a growing influence on the domestic affairs of Latin America, although 56 percent say this is not likely to happen. Given the variety of points of contact and interaction between the U.S. Hispanic community and Latin America, it would seem Hispanic leaders have ample resources and opportunities to independently engage the region.

Finding Four: Although domestic affairs are their foremost concern, Latino leaders want the United States to be actively involved in the world, and particularly in Latin America. They believe U.S. policy toward Latin America should focus upon trade and development, and promoting democracy and human rights.

Hispanic leaders have distinct views on U.S. policy toward Latin America and offer some "do's and don'ts" to guide its actions.

STAY ACTIVE ...

Although Hispanic leaders are fundamentally concerned with domestic matters and the well-being of the U.S.-Hispanic community, they are hardly isolationists, sharing with other U.S. leaders surveyed in the past a global perspective and a proclivity toward an activist U.S. foreign policy. About nine in ten (89 percent) think it is better for the future of the United States to take an active part in world affairs rather than to stay out. Only 14 percent of Latino leaders responding to this survey say "keeping involvement abroad to a minimum" should be a top priority for U.S. foreign policy. In Public Agenda's 1995 study of the foreign policy views of a broad sample of U.S. leaders, 14 percent responded the same way. In a separate survey Gallup conducted of the foreign policy views of a broad sample of American leaders, 98 percent wanted the U.S. to take an active part in world affairs, as did 65 percent of the general public.

... ESPECIALLY IN LATIN AMERICA

Hispanic leaders want the United States to adopt an activist foreign policy, not only on the world scene but also in Latin America. Eighty-five percent say the United States should be paying more attention to its relations with Latin America. Hispanic leaders are convinced greater U.S. activity will have positive consequences for Latin America. Seven in ten (71 percent) leaders say that more U.S. activity in the region will be better for Latin America. "I think on the whole the U.S.-Latin American relationship has been beneficial," said one respondent.

To say the United States should maintain—and even enhance—its engagement in Latin American affairs is one thing, but toward what goals?

TWO PILLARS: TRADE AND DEMOCRACY

Hispanic leaders want two policy themes to drive U.S. objectives in Latin America: improvement in trade and development and strengthening of democracy and human rights. More than half (56 percent) of Latino leaders give top priority to increasing trade, economic growth, and development in its relations with Latin America. Asked to choose the one issue that deserves the highest priority from a list of seven—including limiting political instability, controlling drug trafficking, and protecting the environment—the plurality (44 percent) opt for trade and growth.

The focus on economic relations plays out in concrete terms: NAFTA is extremely popular among Hispanic leaders as a good pattern to replicate in U.S.-Latin American trade relations. Seven in ten (69 percent) say the United States should extend free trade with other Latin American countries on the NAFTA model. What's more, although support for the extension of NAFTA is, not surprisingly, highest among the business leaders surveyed (81 percent), the sentiment is shared by respondents working in the nonprofit, academic, media, and political sectors as well. Finally, 77 percent of Hispanic leaders think the future holds greater interdependence between U.S. and Latin American economies.

But Hispanic leaders do not want U.S-Latin American relations to be only about business: a little more than half (52 percent) also want support for democracy and human rights to be a central pillar of policy toward the region. "This is a democratic hemisphere," stated one leader, "so we need fair elections and the rule of law."

Some believe that democracy and economic growth are intertwined—that one trend will reinforce the other—and that both must therefore be pursued simultaneously. "[The United States] should favor pluralistic democracies and the liberalization of markets with less governmental control," said a Hispanic leader. "I think there's a very firm link between economic liberalism and limited constitutional governments. You can't have one without the other." Another leader echoed this feeling: "Just as it happened in Europe with the collapse of authoritarian regimes, it's clear that a free economy and democracy go hand-in-hand."

There is also a sense that Hispanic leaders should themselves try to move the United States toward tying regional trade with support for human rights. Fully 75 percent of Hispanic leaders surveyed say U.S. Latinos should push for linking trade and aid to advances in democracy and human rights in Latin America. "But there are limits," counseled one leader. "We shouldn't link trade completely to how pure the democracy is or how pure the economy is."

DRUGS OVERSHADOW RELATIONS

Are the priorities of U.S. Latinos in line with current U.S. policy toward the region? Latino leaders do not think so. More than four in ten (44 percent) leaders say that if they had to choose one issue that deserves highest priority in U.S.-Latin American relations, they would choose increasing trade, economic growth, and development. But only 22 percent believe this is what now gets highest priority from the United States. And, whereas another 28 percent of leaders would choose support for democracy and for human rights as their number one priority, only 4 percent believe this is currently what the United States focuses upon most.

Instead, the perception among the plurality of Hispanic leaders (41 percent) is that the predominate U.S. objective in Latin America is combating drug trafficking. And while this objective is important in the eyes of Hispanics, many also believe it overwhelms and obscures other important aspects of relations with Latin America. One leader said, "To a certain extent, the drug problem does overshadow our relations with some countries." Another said, "We shouldn't stop trying to deal with the drug crisis, but there's more to life than drugs. There's a need for U.S. involvement in the region that has nothing to do with drugs."

Latino leaders would also place less emphasis on illegal immigration. While only 12 percent believe this issue should be a top priority, 25 percent say it currently gets the most attention from the United States.

TO SOLVE ILLEGAL IMMIGRATION—MAKE DEALS

These differences may point to more than disagreements over emphasis: Hispanic leaders underscore trade and support for democracy because they see these as key to improving the conditions of the people living in Latin America and as key to stabilizing the area. In the words of one leader: "What better way to deal with illegal immigration than to trade, to make deals? Because what causes illegal immigration is economic need." Improve the situation of Latin Americans, Hispanic leaders suggest, and you will improve the illegal immigration and drug trafficking problems.

But several leaders questioned in the followup interviews thought U.S. strategy was incomplete and prone to dealing with symptoms—often in a heavy-handed manner. "Treat Latin America with the same degree of respect as Europe," said one leader. "How many Noriegas have we extricated from Germany, England? Whenever there was a communist in government, did we walk in with the military and just hunt them down? We did it in Chile, Panama, Grenada.... That is not an example for the development of democratic institutions."

A GAP BETWEEN HISPANIC LEADERS AND THE PUBLIC

Some interesting differences come to light when the priorities of Hispanic leaders are compared with those of the general American public. The general public seems to place a good deal more importance on stopping both illegal immigration and drugs than do Hispanic leaders. In a 1995 Gallup poll, 72 percent of the public said controlling and reducing illegal immigration should be a top priority; in a 1997 Pew study 42 percent said reducing illegal immigration should be a top priority. But, only 14 percent of the Latino leaders said it was very important to reduce illegal immigration.

And while the illegal drug issue troubles Latino leaders, the general public seems more concerned. In the Gallup poll, 85 percent of the public said that controlling the flow of illegal drugs should be a top priority for the United States; in the Pew poll, 67 percent of the public responded in this way. But 54 percent of Latino leaders responding to this survey said stopping the flow of illegal drugs should be a very important policy goal. In follow-up interviews, several suggested that immigration and illegal drugs are top public concerns because of media coverage. "That's what the public hears, because that's what the press tells them," one leader said. "But that doesn't mean that's all the public wants—they just don't know."

But while the views of Hispanic leaders may differ from the public, they are not so different from those of U.S. leaders overall. While 72 percent of the public want curbing illegal immigration to be a top priority, only 28 percent of a broad sample of American leaders surveyed by Gallup say this is a very important goal for the United States (compared to 14 percent of Hispanic leaders). And while 85 percent of the public think controlling drugs is a very important goal, only 57 percent of U.S. leaders agree (as do 54 percent of Hispanic leaders). Thus, the decreased emphasis Latino leaders place on these issues may be more a function of their status as leaders rather than because they are Hispanic.

Hispanic leaders also caution the United States to be wary of trying to cure internal political instability and unrest within Latin American nations. Only 12 percent feel the United States should give top priority to limiting civil unrest and political instability in Latin American countries. This reluctance may stem from lingering doubts about whether the U.S. can be an honest broker—in the words of one respondent, "Given the history of the U.S. in a country like Mexico and its attempts to limit [Mexican] autonomy." It also may be a function of the widely shared reluctance among the U.S. public and leadership about getting involved in civil conflicts. Only 43 percent of the public, for example, would approve the use of U.S. forces "if the Mexican government was about to fall because of revolution or civil war."

Finding Five: Latino leaders are ambivalent about U.S. involvement in the internal affairs of Latin American countries and counsel against military intervention in the area. They consistently prefer that the United States respond to regional crises with economic and political measures in cooperation with other countries in the area.

BE CAREFUL

Although most Hispanic leaders want more U.S. involvement in Latin America, they have reservations and caveats about just how that engagement occurs. As one leader cautioned, "[It] depends on the involvement. Memories are long in Latin America." The vast majority of Hispanic leaders (84 percent) believe the U.S. already has a lot of influence over what happens within Latin American countries. Yet, a little more than half (52 percent) nevertheless believe the United States should stay completely out of their domestic affairs.

DON'T GO IT ALONE

Hispanic leaders counsel the United States to act carefully in Latin America: to avoid military intervention in the region, and to pursue objectives multilaterally, in cooperation with other countries in the area.

The survey asked respondents how the United States should respond to six hypothetical crises in Latin America—for example, a democracy asks for U.S. help to resist a coup, or chaos in Mexico triggers a dramatic increase in illegal immigrants—given a range of options from staying out entirely, to responding with military means. In no scenario did a significant number of Latino leaders favor unilateral military action; and in no situation did Latino leaders favor the "stay out" option. In fact, in none of the six scenarios did a majority favor any military response, even one conducted in concert with other nations. Instead, majorities wanted the United States to respond with diplomatic and economic measures in all six hypothetical crises, either unilaterally or in cooperation with other Latin American countries. For example, one scenario depicts a situation in which "Fidel Castro dies, chaos and fighting break out in Cuba, and a flood of refugees begins to pour into Florida." Most Hispanic leaders (62 percent) would have the United States rely on diplomatic and economic actions (36 percent would do so only in cooperation with other Latin American countries, 26 percent would do so even if alone). In contrast, only 29 percent, would respond with military means (12 percent would do so only with regional cooperation; 16 percent even if alone).

Support for U.S. military intervention is highest when the scenario depicts a Latin American democracy requesting U.S. help as it tries to fight off a military coup—perhaps not surprising, because support for democracy and human rights is a top priority for Hispanic leaders. But even here support for a military response—either alone or multilaterally—only reaches 34 percent. Military intervention is justified, in the words of one respondent, "only if there's a direct threat—like Mexico invading the U.S."

GOING IT ALONE

Finally, the only two scenarios where majorities, including leaders of Mexican origin, support unilateral action—either military or diplomatic—involve Mexico. To deal with a "drug kingpin under indictment in U.S. court [who] is living openly in Mexico, where he is protected by corrupt officials and runs a massive operation smuggling drugs across the border," 42 percent believe the United States should respond with diplomatic and economic means, even if alone, and another 16 percent would respond with military means, even if alone. To deal with a dramatic increase in illegal immigrants crossing the Mexican border into the United States, 42 percent would respond with diplomatic and economic means, even if alone, and 14 percent would do so with military means, even if alone. Majorities of leaders of Mexican origin respond in similar fashion.

The reluctance of Hispanic leaders to support military action is interesting given that the United States has already relied upon the military to deal with the drug problem or illegal immigration. The exception is also interesting to note: In all six scenarios, Cuban respondents are more likely to support the use of U.S. military force, either alone or multilaterally. It may not be surprising to find 57 percent, of Cuban leaders—but only 24 percent of others—supporting a military response to the scenario in which "Fidel Castro dies, chaos and fighting break out in Cuba, and a flood of refugees begins to pour into Florida." But support for military intervention continues, for example, when 48 percent of Cubans—versus only 15 percent of other leaders—think the United States should respond militarily if major disturbances in Haiti "prompt massive immigration to the U.S."; and when 43 percent of Cubans—compared to only 23 percent of other leaders—support a military response against a U.S.-indicted drug kingpin living in Mexico under the protection of corrupt officials.

Finding Six: Most Latino leaders are focused on Latin America, and tend to believe Mexico is more important to U.S. interests than other areas of the world, such as Western Europe or Asia. This view may be driven by their continuing ties to Latin America and their sense that American foreign policy and media have given short shrift to the area.

Mexico Is the Centerpiece

When they look abroad, Hispanic leaders are far more likely to focus on Latin America than on other areas. By a 58 percent to 7 percent margin, they acknowledge they are personally more interested in events and developments in Latin America than in some other region of the world, although a third (34 percent) say they are equally interested in both. And within Latin America, Mexico is the focal point: six in ten (59 percent) say they follow developments and current events there very closely. Cuba is a distant second with 38 percent of Hispanic leaders saying they follow current events there very closely.

The strong connection that Latino leaders have to Latin America—and to Mexico especially—parallels their desire to put that area front and center of U.S. policy. When asked to rank eleven countries and regions in order of importance to the United States, more than half (57 percent) of Hispanic leaders placed Mexico either first or second. By contrast, only half as many (28 percent) gave Western Europe the same ranking. Other regions that have traditionally garnered substantial attention in U.S. policy are seen as top-ranking by even smaller percentages: Only about one fifth of Hispanic leaders give top rankings to Asia (23 percent), the Middle East (22 percent), and Canada (21 percent).

Balancing the Scales?

In follow-up interviews, leaders talked about the proximity of Mexico, its trade with the United States, and the crossover in population from there to explain why they thought Mexico was so important. "Mexico is the great Hispanic neighbor, the one that has the most clout," said one leader. "We have more investment in it than any other Hispanic country in the area—even before NAFTA." But there seemed to be another reason as well, a sense that there is currently an imbalance in U.S. foreign policy—an inattentiveness toward Latin America in general and Mexico, especially—that needs to be redressed. "Mexico is very important, it needs to be higher on America's priority list," one said. Another leader said: "I don't know what our policy is.... I'm not even sure we have a concerted policy effort towards Latin America."

Most leaders interviewed after the survey did not think the issue was a zero-sum game— they were not calling for a lessening of U.S. relations with Europe or Asia but simply saw a need to pay increased attention to Latin America. "Japan and China are the future, and Europe too, not just because of the past but for economic and other reasons," said one leader, "so it doesn't make sense to change our focus, but it makes tremendous sense to enlarge our focus to include Latin America." Another said, "Some reorientation toward South America is necessary, but I don't view it as a zero-sum game regarding attention to Europe."

One leader saw the issue in more blunt, realpolitik terms: "Is there a huge army in Latin America? Are there atom bombs? China has a huge population and the atom bomb. No country in Latin America competes with that. So our focus is a matter of practicality." But even he thought inadequate attention was being paid to Latin America.

Central America Is Not Iowa

There is a sense among Latino leaders that the United States has been too quick to gener-alize about Latin America, and that a more nuanced perspective is necessary. "Latin America is not just one country, each country is different," pointed out one leader, "the only thing that ties us is the language." About six in ten (62 percent) leaders say it is impossible to generalize about Latin America as a region because of differences in their economies, politics and problems, whereas only 36 percent instead say that there are enough common areas to make generalization possible.

But leaders often sense that such distinctions are lost on both the public and the nation's leaders: "Most Americans think Central America is Iowa," one said. "There is an ignorance, people don't pay attention, and this allows faulty policies. The lack of information results in missing some critical opportunities. And meanwhile, we've gone without an ambassador to Mexico for nearly two years!"

MEDIA COVERAGE

There are similar disappointments with media coverage of Latin America, a sense that there is not enough of it and that what little there is misleads or focuses on a narrow range of issues such as drugs or illegal immigration. Nearly seven in ten (68 percent) strongly agree with the statement that "the mass media do a poor job reporting on Latin America" (another 23 percent agree somewhat). Interestingly, 64 percent of the responding Latino leaders who work in the media also strongly agree. "I read things like the *Times* and the *Economist* and I couldn't tell you what our foreign policy toward Mexico was. The only way I can stay informed about Latin America is Univision." But some thought this merely reflected the poor quality of news coverage in the United States: "Basically, most American media coverage on politics, especially international politics, stinks. We're as ignorant about Latin Americans as we are about the Poles."

Yet despite their dissatisfaction with media coverage of Latin America, fully 69 percent rely heavily on English-language media for information about the region. The next most-used sources are Spanish-language television (50 percent rely on it heavily), Latino/Hispanic magazines and newsletters (49 percent), and Spanish-language newspapers (37 percent). A quarter (26 percent) rely heavily on Internet sites on Latin America.

Finding Seven: Hispanic leaders share with other U.S. leaders some top priorities such as preventing the spread of nuclear weapons, expanding trade, stopping the flow of illegal drugs, and improving the global environment. But Hispanic leaders demur when it comes to some traditional foreign policy priorities of other U.S. leaders, such as limiting conflict, defending our allies' security, and maintaining military superiority.

Compared to a broad sample of U.S. leaders surveyed by Public Agenda in 1995, Latino leaders share the foreign policy priorities of improving trade and business, promoting democracy and human rights, and protecting the environment." Latino leaders' top foreign policy goals also mirror those of U.S. leaders surveyed in 1995 by Gallup for the Chicago Council on Foreign Relations: preventing the spread of nuclear weapons, stopping illegal drugs, improving the global environment, combating world hunger, and protecting the jobs of American workers.

Consistent with their concerns about U.S. involvement in Latin America, Latino leaders are much less likely to support the realpolitik approach of limiting conflict in important regions, particularly in Latin America. About half (49 percent) of U.S. leaders in the 1995 Public Agenda study said limiting conflict in important areas should be a top priority." But only 12 percent of Latino leaders say limiting conflict should be a top priority for the U.S. in Latin America, and only 34 percent say this should be a top foreign policy priority in general. Latino leaders are also far less likely to support conflict-oriented foreign policy goals, such as defending our allies' security (1995 Gallup leaders: 60 percent vs. Latinos leaders: 8 percent), and maintaining superior military power (54 percent vs. 20 percent). The orientation toward a nonmilitary approach is illustrated in the six Latin American scenarios discussed earlier: In none was the use of force supported by a majority. Instead of the military solutions that have marked U.S. historical involvement in the region, Latino leaders prefer a focus on building mutual trade and democracy.

Notes

1. The terms "Hispanic" and "Latino" are used interchangeably throughout this report.
2. Methodology: This study reports the views of 454 Hispanic leaders who responded to a mail survey conducted in the fall and winter of 1997. The Tomas Rivera Policy Institute initially mailed letters from a database of approximately four thousand Hispanic leaders, requesting their involvement in the survey. Of these, 509 agreed to participate. The questionnaire was mailed at the end of September 1997 to those who had agreed to participate and to an additional 871 names from other lists of Hispanic leaders. Reminder postcards were then sent, followed by a second mailing of the same questionnaire. The fielding of the survey ended December 31, 1997.

   Recipients were asked to discard the survey if they were not of Latino/Hispanic descent. The questionnaire itself was in English, although recipients were offered the opportunity to complete it in Spanish. The sample participants were selected from various directories of Hispanic organizations in the U.S., in roughly six categories:

   - Nonprofit organizations, including community-based organizations, nongovernmental organizations, and others—mostly obtained from the *Hispanic Yearbook,* an annual directory of Hispanic organizations (16 percent of the sample)
   - Journalists drawn primarily from a list provided by the association of Hispanic journalists (25 percent)
   - Public officials at the federal, state, and local levels drawn from lists provided by the Congressional Hispanic Caucus and the National Association of Latino Elected and Appointed Officials (13 percent)
   - Business leaders, including members of the U.S. Hispanic Chamber of Commerce (10 percent)
   - Academics from various disciplines, including political science, history, and American studies, selected from various academic directories (22 percent)
   - Other fields—including members of the Hispanic Council on International Relations and the Council of Foreign Relations' Project for Diversity in International Affairs, as well as artists, religious leaders, and labor union leaders (14 percent).

   Following the survey, open-ended telephone interviews were conducted with a small number of respondents to give voice to the attitudes captured statistically through the survey. Public Agenda takes full responsibility for the research analysis in this study.

Section 6

Asian Americans and U.S. Foreign Policy

Section Six demonstrates how the internal complexity of communities of color and the implications for foreign affairs are reflected in the Asian American community experience. The Asian community is very diverse, in terms of origins, social structure, and recent experiences with international affairs. The experiences of the South Asians differ from those of the Vietnamese, for example, both in the reasons for emigration and their history in the United States. Yet commonalities exist.

Several highly publicized cases of charges of "divided loyalties" have come to the fore in recent years, as Robert Wright describes. Wright and others charge that the press makes insufficient effort to distinguish between Asian Americans and Asians. Phrases such as "Asian connection," "favor-hungry foreigners," "insidious networking," and "penetration by Asian interests" are phrases that writer Eric Liu points to in his book, *Accidental Asian*. His nuanced portrait of the pride and prejudice associated with being Chinese American in the era of the Asian miracle sensitively describes the ambivalent pulls and tugs that come with that status. Liu's publication is especially revealing, as he was an official on the National Security Council at the White House. In this volume, Arati Rao describes the fascinating internal differentiation and new communication patterns at work among the South Asian populations in the United States, where "[t]he most dramatic turn in South Asian life and politics in America is the younger generation's interest in collaboration, networking, and coalition-building." If the experiences of those from India, Pakistan, Sri Lanka, Bangladesh, and other nations of the region are particular, they still share many aspects with other communities of color. This includes both the goals individuals seek to achieve through their engagement with the American foreign policy system, and the ways they negotiate ties with ethnic homelands. As with Latinos, the Asians find, too, that their own cooptation into the foreign policy establishment is on the rise. The growth of Bangalore's IT sector, the explosion of Indian immigration, and the bold political engagement through channels such as TIE, India Alert, and Coalition Against Anti-Asian Violence demonstrate greater attention to politics. For all these reasons, the relative importance of South Asian countries for America's foreign policy agenda is rising.

19

Bridges Across Continents

South Asians in the United States

ARATI RAO

South Asians in the United States historically have played important roles in constructing the boundaries of outsider and insider, foreigner and citizen, sojourner and resident. Although the term "South Asian" denotes the geographical area south of the northern Himalayan mountain ranges, South Asian identity is a unifying political garb not easily worn by the extraordinarily diverse peoples from Bangladesh, Bhutan, India, the Maldives, Nepal, Pakistan, and Sri Lanka (U.S. Bureau of the Census 1990). Because this term has emerged only recently in response to political exigencies in American society, it is likely to become more prevalent as South Asian communities become increasingly politicized.

Recent immigrants, particularly South Asians who arrived after the 1965 Immigration Reform and Control Act, value the possibility of success in the workplace, the culturally central institutions of the family and the community, and the general public's response to their presence in the United States. Unlike the earlier farmer immigrants whose numbers and status were kept low by discriminatory legislation, the post-1965 immigrants from South Asia have achieved a relatively high degree of economic success which influences their participation in "high" politics, particularly in the campaigns of both major parties, fundraising, and lobbying for domestic programs as well as foreign policy affecting South Asia.

The 1980s, however, saw the emergence of other kinds of South Asian Americans: the American children born of post-1965 immigrants and less educated immigrants in low-paying service sector jobs. The young South Asian Americans contribute to a new configuration of class and immigrant history and practice are grassroots-oriented activism, which includes coalition building with other minority groups on the basis of shared oppression. The climate of hostility and violence in the United States against visibly different people, combined with anger against recent immigrant populations and envy of their economic success, has prompted vulnerable South Asian Americans to reassess political strategy in favor of broader coalitions with similarly targeted groups, particularly other Asian America communities, in organizations such as the New York-based Coalition Against Anti-Asian Violence (CAAV).

SOUTH ASIANS TODAY

Statistics from the Census Bureau (1990) show that South Asians constitute the economically most successful ethnic group in the United States today. Historically, however, the general impact of their presence on the larger American society has always outweighed

199

their numbers. From the early 1900s to the end of World War II, the total number of South Asians or East Indians, as they were called, rarely exceeded six thousand. In that period, they remained geographically concentrated in the western states, notably Washington and California. For much of that time, they remained a predominantly male working-class population in whose name a small group of educated urban Indians struggled for legal justice and social respect.

In the two decades following the 1965 Immigration Act, immigration numbers leaped dramatically, and census data from 1990 shows a national Indian immigrant population of about 815,000 and a Pakistani population of roughly 81,000. South Asians constitute roughly 11 percent of the total Asian population of 7,274,000 in the category of Asians and Pacific Islanders (Chandrasekhar 1982; Dutta 1982; Peterson 1985; Statistical Abstracts of the United States 1994). As many as 75 percent of the South Asians in the country today were born outside the United States. Given their numerically higher representation and concomitant greater presence in research data, I focus on Indian Americans in this chapter as a significant, although not exhaustive, example of South Asian experience. South Asians continue to experience the evil legacy of color-based hatred of the Other.

The frequent physical and verbal attacks on South Asians, their personal experience of the glass ceiling in the workplace, and their suffering at the hands of organized gang terrorism in states like New Jersey have caused many South Asians to rally around their group identity. The ambiguous nature of their self-identification—caught between cultures, countries, indeed, worlds—has given way to a confident use of economic status and organizational skills in political participation. The latest generation of South Asian Americans has taken innovative turns in coalition building and political participation, which suggest a radically new direction for future American citizens of South Asian origin, and call for a fresh understanding of politics itself.

Discrimination and Violence against South Asians

South Asians face multilevel discrimination in different contexts. The most articulate are among the professional classes, who continue to experience the glass ceiling. Some note that they can advance only where their merit is measured without prejudice, thus, the preponderance of Indians in technical rather than managerial or administrative positions. Strategies to combat white-collar discrimination take the form of lawsuits or formal complaints to professional associations and government authorities. Turbaned Sikh men remain vulnerable to the same religious and cultural discrimination that the early immigrants encountered. For example, a turban-wearing Sikh was fired four days after being hired by the New York City Transit Authority on account of the policy requiring hard hats to be worn by car inspectors. The fired employee's response was to file suit against the Transit Authority (*News India Times* 1995: 26).

Discriminatory treatment is not experienced by the professional classes alone (see Gibson 1988). In 1987, local anger against all Indians erupted in New Jersey when gangs, calling themselves "Dotbusters," systematically attacked South Asians. In a letter published in a local newspaper in Jersey City, home to about fifteen thousand Indians at the time, the Dotbusters wrote, "We will go to any extreme to get Indians to move out of Jersey City. If I'm walking down the street and I see a Hindu and the setting is right, I will just hit him or her. We plan some of our more extreme attacks such as breaking windows, breaking car windows, and crashing family parties. We use the phone book to look up the name Patel. Have you seen how many there are?" In September that year, a young man, Navroz Mody, was beaten to death by youths who chanted, "Hindu, Hindu" (Takaki 1989: 481).

Today, South Asians are increasingly verbally and physically harassed in public places. The attacks come from a variety of ethnic and racial groups. For example, in 1994, three teenagers accosted a twenty-five-year-old Indian immigrant in Queens, said that they "did not like Indian people," beat him up and burned his face with a cigarette. Local Indian and Pakistani merchants told a reporter that youths harassed them frequently "because we are different" (*New York Times* 1994: 43). In addition to personal attacks and stone throwing, South Asian places of worship continue to be targeted for vandalism and burglary (Fenton 1988). The perception of a common threat has real uniting power among otherwise disparate groups. The particular cultural practices that mark a South Asian for racist attack, such as physical appearance or clothing or religious accouterments, make it difficult to perceive one's predicament as grounds for coalition with other victims of harassment. This is a primary area in which coalition building can be more forcefully addressed; unfortunately, violence is a great leveler of distinction.

Conflicts and Coalitions

In the face of concrete discouragements to remaining in the United States, South Asians since the early part of this century have found ways to straddle both countries and, indeed, both continents: one country left behind with some idea of return after acquiring wealth in the United States; the other country itself unsure about rewarding nonwhite immigrants with citizenship and the right to belong. In occupying this liminal space in America, South Asians have had to retain both fictions, of sojourner and of citizen, awaiting the day when American law and society would change and give them full access to America. Because legal change occurred only thirty years ago with the 1965 Immigration Act, South Asians continue to bridge Asia and America in real and symbolic ways.

In material terms, South Asians participate fully in American economy and society. From this home base, they nurture family and business connections in their country of origin and often take their children back for holidays. In addition, fresh emigrants from South Asia continue to enter the United States under current immigration laws, furthering this pattern of connection between the old and new worlds, moving between Asia and America across the familiar bridges of departure, residence, and return.

In symbolic terms, however, the recent nature of their entry into America, along with the anti-immigrant and racist trends that target South Asian Americans, have encouraged the sense that one is not fully welcome, that one is assumed to have a home elsewhere to which one is expected to return, that one's enthusiastic embrace of the American Dream is no guarantee of acceptance. Discrimination in the workplace, ignorance in media portrayals, hatred on the streets, and unresponsiveness from government officialdom to complaints have resulted in the emerging awareness among Americans of South Asian descent that acceptance is not accorded on merit but has to be fought for.

Part of the American Dream for immigrant populations is the aspiration to attain the status of the social and economic elite: well-off whites. It is not until nonwhite immigrants encounter obstacles that they start the painful soul-searching: What does it take for a successful professional to understand that economic prosperity is no protection against hostility and anger? What are the costs and benefits of going against the current of complicity with hegemonic elites to form coalitions with non-South Asian communities? How can we confront our own racism, often imperceptibly sown already in our country of origin, but always encouraged to grow in the racially charged climate of the United States? There comes a point when tending one's own garden is not enough, when one is forced by political realities to look for common ground in the larger surrounding society.

Three levels of coalition must be addressed. First, the disparate groups from South Asia must construct a unity that they did not need or would never have considered in their home countries. Accordingly, a common bond now may be forged in the United States between an Indian and a Pakistani, neither of whom had had reason to travel to the other's country while residing in South Asia. In America, these equally advantaged and disadvantaged immigrant professionals look at American society through similar tenses, reify their cultural practices, and retain a keen interest in a South Asia to which they very likely will not retire (although they talk about it often).

Second, building on this first stage of a partially imposed, partially embraced, unifying "South Asianness," South Asians then can join the many ethnicities under the umbrella term "Asian" to generate political alliances with other Asian groups. Third, subsequently, they identify common issues with non-Asian minority groups, such as African Americans and Latinos. The last step has been taken by younger American-born South Asians who do not use the bridge across the continents with the frequency of their parents' generation: These Americans are here to stay. (The bridge may be used again by their own children, in the established pattern of returning to roots in alternating generations.) Their self-perception of their Americanness brooks no suggestion that they go back to where they came from: Their sights are set on the struggle for justice and respect from fellow Americans. Their youth and early awareness of discrimination and racism makes liaisons with other ethnic minorities more possible; their class diversity makes them more willing to seek alliances with others rather than rely on a fantasy of the invulnerability in wealth.

In order to understand the strains of politicization among South Asians, we first need to learn their unique history in the United States. Despite the small numbers and limited economic advancement of the first immigrant Indians in the early twentieth century (prior to Indian independence from British rule and the creation of Pakistan in 1947, they were generally known as Indians), their presence triggered serious debates in the United States, which shook key pillars of American society, notably the meaning of "American," the definition of citizenship, and concepts like freedom, democracy, pluralism, and assimilation. As shown later, the obstacles to acquiring a stable identity kept Indians apart from other Asian groups, as well as from the rest of America. Even the 1946 Luce-Celler Act, which revoked the 1923 denial of citizenship to Indians, did not mean much to South Asians until 1965.

EARLY HISTORY OF SOUTH ASIANS IN NORTH AMERICA

The South Asian presence in the United States has a long but forgotten history, with which even South Asians are not familiar. A colonial diary of 1790 reports the presence of a man from Madras in Salem, Massachusetts, and over half a century later, local sources write of six Indians attending the 1851 Fourth of July festivities in Salem. California in 1849 saw Indians in its Gold Rush as well as in its ports as visiting merchants. Not until the turn of the century did immigrants, most from the northern Indian agricultural region of Punjab, begin to arrive in North America, having been recruited to work in the lumber industries of British Columbia, Canada, and the Canadian Pacific Railway Lines.

Racist anger in local Canadian populations prompted exclusionary measures from the government. Indeed, when Indians who met all the onerous requirements of Canadian law arrived in Vancouver harbor in 1914 on the ship Komagata Maru, they were fired upon and not allowed to land. The Indians soon looked southward "hoping for a better reception, a less rigorous climate, more congenial employment and higher wages" (Chandrasekhar 1944: 141).

These Indians encountered in the United States racist profiles of Asians identified with Chinese immigrants. The racial exclusions of immigration law were reinforced by domestic laws on intergroup marriage, property ownership, land rights, legal personhood, and education. Still, they stayed, hoping to make money and return to India. In addition to racist legislation, they suffered racial attacks as early as 1907, when white workers invaded an Indian community in Bellingham, Washington, and drove seven hundred Indians across the border to Canada. This violence was, ironically, directed against a woefully small Indian presence: at this time the population of Indians in the United States did not exceed six thousand. As Chandrasekhar (1944: 138) observes, Indians were "a microscopic minority in the population." They seldom lived in communities exceeding thirty men, but their appearance and language marked them as different. Brown (1982: 41–47; see also Leonard 1982: 30) suggests that "the overwhelming majority" was Sikh, turbaned, and therefore easily targeted.

Despite popular rage, the law was not clear on the racial status of Indians. Their legal story is framed by the 1790 law reserving naturalization to one racial group: "any alien, being a free white person, who shall have resided within the limits and under the jurisdiction of the United States for the term of two years, may be admitted to become a citizen thereof" (Debates and Proceedings 1834). The impact of this law is inestimable: not until the mid-twentieth century did race lose its centrality in the criteria for immigration in the United States.

Are Indians "White?" The Supreme (Court) Challenge

South Asians constitute the only immigrant group whose very definition was questioned almost immediately after its arrival. Without doubt, the American government's reliance on the hopelessly indeterminate classification system arising out of late-nineteenth-century "scientific" classification of the world's "races" faced its most serious challenge from Indians (cf. Appiah 1992). It took three major Supreme Court decisions spread over three decades to decide the perplexing question: Were Indians "Caucasians" and therefore "white," and consequently free to become naturalized citizens under the 1790 law?

This ambiguity had two major consequences for Indians. First, the differences between and within communities in their native lands (such as caste, language, religion, and region) now were subsumed under an artificial and imposed unity of identity: Indian. This concept challenged legal race classifications of white as well as Asian and Oriental. Second, particular groups like the Indians learned to use this imposed unity to negotiate the boundaries of these categories in order to exempt themselves from the exclusionary principles. Thus, a dialectical process of Indians self-identification emerged over the decades, with the government's racial call receiving a reifying response from its targeted immigrant group. Accordingly, Indians used a variety of identity-based strategies at different historical moments, to gain recognition. They claimed a common Aryan ancestry with Europeans to claim "whiteness"; they retained Indianness but refused Asianness; they rebuffed race in favor of religion, caste, or ethnicity as their primary identification; they referred to international standards such as the Atlantic Charter to claim universal human rights over group differences.

The first two Supreme Court decisions on the question of Indian whiteness—*Balsara* in 1910 and *Mazumdar* in 1913—held that since Indians were scientifically classified as Caucasian in race, naturalization as whites was allowed (*U.S. v. Balsara*, 1910, 180 Fed. 694; see also *U.S. v. Akhay Kumar Mazunidar*, 1913, 207 Fed. 115). However, the 1923 *Thind* decision dramatically reversed this conclusion in a ruling that dismissed "Caucasian" as "a conventional word of much flexibility," and redefined "white" in terms of popular perception of skin color rather than scientific categorization (*U.S. v. Bhagat Singh Thind*, 1923, MI I I S 204–215).

As Helweg and Helweg (1990: 54) observe, "It was a time of complete confusion of biology, geography, and culture, and situations were interpreted to suit the mood of the public and authorities at the time." The Supreme Court's *Ozawa* decision in 1922 had relied on the synonymity of "Caucasian" and "white" in ruling against Japanese eligibility for citizenship. Thus, Ozawa buttressed the security of one Asian group (Indians) with the legal exclusion of another Asian group (Japanese) (*Takao Ozawa vs. United States*, 1922, 260 U.S. 178). The Thind decision the following year, however, taught Indians that all nonwhite groups, including themselves, were vulnerable to exclusion.

In the *Thind* opinion, Justice Sutherland (himself a naturalized American citizen via England and Canada) denied the scientific basis for "white persons" and rejected Mr. Bliagat Singh Thind's ethnological claim of historical common Aryan ancestry with Europeans because "the average man knows perfectly well that there are unmistakable differences between them today." Even the framers of the 1790 law had relied on "the words of familiar speech" to refer to those inimigrants who were "bone of their bone and flesh of their flesh." The law's reference to free white persons was "to be interpreted in accordance with the understanding of the common man."

The common man—and woman—had already expressed their understanding of racial distinctions in publications and action. Agnes Foster Buchanan asserted in 1908 that, unlike the "suppliant" Chinese and the "stealthy" Japanese laborers, the new "full-blooded Aryan" entrant from India was "a brother of our own race." And yet, because the frugal, family-less Indian men economically undercut white labor, Buchanan concluded by urging the State Department to inform Indians that "while the earth is large enough for us all, there is no one part of it that will comfortably accommodate both branches of the Aryan family" (1908: 308–313). Herman Scheffauer warried of the new peril to the United States, this "dark, mystic race" with a turbaned "face of finer features" which rose like a chimera out of the Pacific, bringing "a new and anxious question" (1910: 616–618).

In this charged climate, *Thind* had far-reaching consequences for Indians in the United States as well as for future immigrants. Finding the discrimination and exclusion unbearable, about three thousand Indians returned to India between 1920 and 1940. Along with Mr. Thind, scores of naturalized Indians had their citizenship retroactively revoked by the government with the approval of the Departments of State, Justice, and Labor. Although these revocations were successfully overturned in higher courts, the basic issue of eligibility remained unresolved.

The 1965 Immigration Act, with its benign view of family unification, was central to the emergence of the resident, and not sojourner, South Asian. Earlier, Indian immigrants had been belittled by white Americans because they had no families and lived in male communal housing, but there were reasons for this lonely life. Early Indian immigrants were overwhelmingly men. Many had mortgaged their Indian farms for the trip, believed they would return home to their wives and children after making their fortune. In any event, within a few years of their arrival, 1917 Immigration Act prohibited the entry of wives from home. Indian men who wished to marry white women became subject to antimiscegenation laws, particularly in California (where the laws remained on the books until 1950). At times, they traveled from California to get married in states like Arizona, where the laws were enforced in varying degrees. Some Indian men in California married Mexican women, over half of whom were immigrants themselves. According to one authority, there were fewer than thirty Indian women in California until 1930, when the Indian immigrant male-female ratio was calculated as 1,572 men per 100 women (Taylor and Vasey 1936: 291; see also Leonard 1982: 67).

Within weeks of *Thind*, the California state government began proceedings to nullify Indian land purchases under its 1913 Alien Land Law. During the Depression, Indians were turned away from federal relief programs because they were aliens ineligible for citizenship. Throughout, labor organizations such as the American Federation of Labor were at the forefront of opposition to changes in naturalization laws, testifying before Congress in tones of dire prophecy regarding the fate of white working-class America. The Indian working man, however, was caught in limbo: unable to return to India and not permitted to sink roots in America.

DEMOCRACY AND EXCLUSION

The small educated student body among the early immigrants used American notions of democracy and self-determination to further the cause of India's freedom from the British Raj, and to fight the exclusion of Indians from American citizenship. Their small numbers and colonial predicament focused the spotlight on their own situation; they did not look to forge alliances with other excluded groups. The United States government, however, responded readily to pressure from Britain by suppressing Indian publications and attacking Indian organizations for violating neutrality laws during World War I.

However, when the United States joined World War II, the Nazi ideology of racial hierarchies and annihilation generated compelling arguments for racial equality from the Indian communities in the country. Writing from his office in the Department of Oriental Studies at the University of Pennsylvania, Chandrasekhar (1944: 142) warned, "If the United States is to successfully combat such dangerous ideas, it can ill afford to practice racial discrimination in its relations with Asiatic countries. The immigration policy of this country now excludes nearly a quarter of the human race. America cannot afford to say that she wants the people of India to fight on her side and at the same time maintain that she will not have them among her immigrant groups."

The call to justice and fair play with which Chandrasekhar concluded his article was met by the government's pragmatic consideration of the war effort. The government eventually decided that the potential success of Japanese propaganda and military strategy in South Asia required a preemptive counterweight from America, and the support of Indians to the Allied cause was deemed important. The efforts of various Indian lobbies paid off with the favorable Luce-Celler Act a year after the war ended, which established a tiny annual immigration quota of 100 Indians. So even this did not significantly increase their numbers: over the following eighteen years, twelve thousand Indians entered the country. Still, as Hess (1982: 32) observes, "had not immigration and naturalization laws changed in 1946, the East Indian community would almost certainly have eroded significantly perhaps to the point of extinction."

By now, Indians in America had formed organizations and lobbying alliances among themselves. The first Asian to be elected to Congress was an Indian, Dalip Singh Saund, who came to the United States as a student in 1920 (Saund 1960). Elected president of the Indian Association of America in 1942, he directed war bond drives among Indians, hoping to earn the trust and confidence of patriotic white America. When President Truman signed the Luce-Celler Act in 1946, Saund applied for naturalization immediately. There were about fifteen hundred Indians in the United States at the time.

In November 1956, campaigning from the Twenty-ninth Congressional District, Saund won his Democratic seat in the U.S. House of Representatives.

In the Eighty-fifth Congress, the freshman congressman was appointed right away to the prestigious Foreign Affairs Committee, and promoted the United States foreign aid program to Asia in a tour of the Far East and Middle East in 1957. In India, he addressed a joint session of both houses of Parliament, an honor reserved usually for a visiting head of state. He served three terms in Congress until a stroke incapacitated him during his bid for a fourth term. He died in 1973. Among his survivors was his son, Dalip Singh Saund Jr., a veteran of the Korean War. Congressman Saund often used to say, "My guideposts were two of the most beloved men in history, Abraham Lincoln and Mahatma Gandhi."

The 1965 Immigration Act and After

Until 1965, South Asians received no encouragement to become "American." Although numerous interpretations continue to be generated as to what this term means, for South Asians the prerequisites for their Americanness were precisely those rights and privileges that were denied them, directly or by consequence of denials of rights to other similarly situated groups. Helweg and Helweg (1990: 57) see the same themes playing through Indian immigrant lives over the decades to the present day: "the fight for rights in the new country, continued concern for India, and the desire to excel in America."

The watershed 1965 Immigration Reform and Control Act abolished the national origins system in favor of hemispheric quotas, allowed all nationalities equal right to apply for immigration, and gave preferential treatment to professionals and relatives of U.S. citizens and residents. Great Britain, the traditional goal for immigrating South Asians, already had passed its restrictive and racism-informed 1962 Parliamentary Act: "America's doors were opening and Britain's were closing" (Helweg and Helweg 1990: 60). Highly educated and talented South Asians now left home—amid rancorous debates about the brain drain—to fulfill their economic and career ambitions in the United States. They brought their families and settled down as permanent residents in their new country.

South Asians also entered the United States from non-Asian countries. When Britain passed legal restrictions on nonwhite immigration in 1962, Asians from Kenya used their British passports to enter the United States under the immigration quota for Britain. Ten years later, President Amin of Uganda ordered a mass overnight expulsion of Asians from his country in August 1972. Some came to the United States, using their business skills to sink new economic roots, much as the characters do in Mira Nair's *Mississippi Masala,* a film that portrays the experiences of one Ugandan Indian family engaged in running a motel in small town America (cf. *Asian Week* 1986).

ECONOMIC PARTICIPATION AND MINORITY STATUS

Like other Asian groups, Indians made significant contributions to the national economy from the very start, working in the meanest farm and factory jobs without status or legitimacy in America. But after 1965, the arrival of many of India's educated and social elite signified a dramatic shift in the Indian experience. Economic success was not always immediate but very possible. The absence of the comfortable home and accepting environment left behind was now offset by professional and economic advancement—a tradeoff that continues to be reassessed ever since the hard times in the U.S. economy in the 1970s, which resulted in layoffs in industries such as aerospace, in which Indian engineers oten were the first to be let go.

As early as 1975, Indians sought economic help from civil rights legislation. A 1975 memo from the director of the Office of Federal Contract Compliance, which stated that persons of Indian descent were to be "regarded as white," generated differing views among Indian community leaders, who wished to publicize this racial discrimination but differed on how best to do it. The Association of Indians in America said to the U.S. Civil Rights Commission that year:

The language of the Civil Rights Act clearly intends to protect those individuals who might be disadvantaged on the basis of appearance. It is undeniable that Indians are different in appearance; they are equally dark skinned as other non-white individuals and are, therefore, subject to the same prejudices … .While it is commonly believed that the majority of Indians working in this country are well-educated and employed in jobs of a professional nature, their profiles are not at all unlike those of Korean and Japanese immigrants (Takaki 1989: 446–447).

In contrast, the India League of America in Chicago argued against claiming minority status with the warning: "If employers find it possible to fill some kind of minority 'quota' by reporting high-level Indo-American employees, while continuing to discriminate against the truly disadvantaged minorities, we may find many Americans turning against us" (quoted in Takaki 1989: 446–447).

In 1982, the National Association of Americans of Asian Indian Descent got the Small Business Administration to recognize them as a socially disadvantaged minority group. Although the fight for minority status raised the same complex issues, the community clearly recognized that this status now rendered them eligible to compete with other minority businesses for government contracts.

These instances reveal a fundamental ambivalence among even the most vocal and politically engaged Indians about their location in the United States. On the one hand, they have benefited from prior advantages as well as struggled to receive the fruits of hard work and commitment. On the other hand, their experiences of discrimination despite this success forces them to consider themselves as disadvantaged. The coexistence of these two perceptions has produced a sense of separateness from other groups in society, which often invite equally ambivalent responses from the society at large.

In 1980, changes in census categories testified to other anibivalences that generated another self-protective move. In 1976, the government sponsored a meeting between representatives of all Asian Americans and Pacific Islanders to discuss the 1980 Census categories. As a result of these deliberations, the census bureau agreed to add the category "Asian Indian" to the 1980 Census, thereby enabling Indians to move out of the "White/Caucasian" and "Other" categories. Here, the overwhelming numerical representation of Indians among all South Asian groups resulted in another paradox: the insistence on "Indian" rather than "South Asian" in an environment in which all South Asians are equally targeted for discrimination regardless of particular country of origin. The triumph of Indian lobbyists is one of nationalists lobbying for the simple majority rather than for a political principle: all the more regrettable in a situation in which political bridge building and strategic unity, rather than nationalism should have prevailed (cf. Dutta 1982: 77).

Rich Indians, Poor Indians

The model minority fantasy among nonminority groups obscures the reality that all societies, including immigrant groups, are riven with differences. Scholars of all backgrounds focus the spotlight on the most visible kinds of prosperity, leaving whole areas of their realities, particularly gender and class inequalities, in darkness. For example, Saran (1980) calls the post-1965 Indians "elite ethnics." Leonard (1982: 186) writes: "They are members of the most affluent, highly placed Asian immigrant group in the United States." A Center for Immigration Studies report released in Washington, D.C., in 1994 found Indian Americans the highest-paid group of immigrant professionals, in part because of the large numbers in the medical profession. Two-thirds of all Indian professionals had advanced degrees and over 90 percent had diplomas. The success of Indian professionals was heightened by the background statistics on other groups: Asian-born professionals had the highest median income, followed by white foreign-born, Chinese, and Japanese professionals. Mexicans were the lowest paid foreign-born professionals (Bouvier and Simcox 1994).

Yet, an unreleased study completed by the U.S. Commission on Civil Rights in the 1980s found that American-born Indians had the highest level of poverty, over 20 percent, five times higher than that for any other group (Helweg and Helweg 1990: 188–189). Other research data from 1990 shows that the increased success of mid- and upper-level professionals conceals low income as well as poverty levels.

The reader of Table 19-1 should keep in mind that precisely because the Asian Indian population does not exceed 800,000, the percentage of Indians living at the poverty level ought to be all the more avoidable. Similarly, the public perception of Indians as uniformly affluent, despite their small numbers, is more informative of the public's willingness to homogenize Indians, than any universal Indian prosperity.

Poverty in the Indian community can be explained on many grounds. Alongside the increase in nonprofessional immigrants following the 1965 Immigration Act, family reunification rules continue to bring persons who are not members of the professional classes. Furthermore, the increase in numbers of South Asians across America has resulted in increased exploitation of the underprivileged, outside the community as well as within. For example, restaurant workers, domestic workers, cleaning staff, and small business employees remain pitifully underpaid, ill-treated, without job benefits, and without hope of improvement of their condition (*India Today* 1995b: 76b–76c). Often, South Asians enter low-income areas of economic participation for lack of capital and alternatives. For example, almost half of the roughly 350 newsstands in New York City are licensed to Indians or Pakistanis. Many remain open twenty hours a day. The typical South Asian newsstand owner works twelve hours a day in all weather and takes home $450 a week; he and his co-workers (often family members of either sex) are under constant threat of mugging, robbery, and harassment (*India Today* 1994b: 68e). South Asians are increasingly visible as taxi drivers in New York City, as indicated by the Taxi and Limousine Commission's most recent survey of new applicants for licenses in 1992: 43 percent were South Asian. Counting South Asian cab drivers already on the job, Vivek Bald estimates in his film *Taxivala/Autobiography* that up to 60 percent of New York's taxi operators are South Asian.

Table 19–1 Household Income and Poverty Levels by Ethnicity, 1990

Ethnicity	Median Income	% Income Less Than $10,000	% Income Greater Than $10,000	Below Poverty*
Chinese	$37,600	15	19	14
Filipino	$43,000	6	18	7
Japanese	$42,800	9	19	7
Asian Indian	$43,000	8	22	10
Korean	$30,300	17	11	15
Vietnamese	$31,300	16	11	25
South Asian	$18,300	26	4	46
Other Asian	$32,000	15	12	17
Pacific Islander	$32,900	13	10	20

*Poverty rate is based on the proportion of the population that resides in a family with an income below the official poverty line.
Source: Compiled from 1990 1% Public Use Microdata Sample taken from Ong and Hee, 1994.

Changes in United States government regulations continue to shape afresh the smaller South Asian communities, particularly their economic condition. For example, the State Department in 1995 expanded quotas for countries that were not traditional immigrant sources, allotting Bangladesh 3,850 visas for 1995. In their turn, these new immigrants are bound to apply for visas for family members. However, their economic well-being depends on the responsiveness of the Bangladeshi community's resources as well as the U.S. economy to the needs of this increased population. In New York, the American Bangladesh Friendship Association complained that no Bangladeshi-owned businesses had received contracts from Republican Mayor Giuliani's administration, unlike the preceding Democratic administration. The association's president warned, "We don't need welfare and will not go on welfare, but unless someone steps in to help with job and language training and helps them settle in, things will be a big mess" (*New York Times* 1995).

POLITICAL PARTICIPATION

Those who entered the United States immediately after 1965 were already in possession of the qualities necessary for a certain degree of immediate economic success in the United States: education, professionalism, personal confidence, and a sense of social worth. Similar adult South Asians continue to enter and contribute to the United States as successful professionals. However, the hidden South Asians today include the poor as well as the American born, thereby throwing into confusion the erroneous popular belief that all South Asians are prosperous recent immigrants.

Like most people, South Asians are primarily interested in the well-being of their immediate circle of family and friends. Family plays a central role in South Asian cultures, encompassing a wider range of relatives than the dominant American notion of the nuclear family. However, the linguistic, regional, and religious affinities that gave the first post-1965 immigrants a sense of community and belonging in a strange land have given way to a complex and changing set of personal ties. The longer an immigrant group remains and the greater its sense of security, the looser become the traditional bonds of kinship and community. Thus, well-off Indians actively engage in political lobbying and participation at the highest levels. We also find poorer and more recent immigrants whose lack of language and economic advancement keeps them working for low wages among their own kind, or taking ill-paid jobs requiring little training or knowledge of English in the service sector, without participation or representation at any political level.

The politicization of South Asians may seem at first glance to be moving at a slow pace, but closer examination will show the giant strides they have taken in the three short decades since 1965. In the 1980s, President Reagan's reiteration of the model minority description of Asians drew the ire of South Asians. They joined forces with other Asian groups to demand recognition for their contributions and to publicize their experiences of far from model treatment from the larger society. By the 1988 elections, Indians also had learned the power of financial contributions to political candidates. In California and New York (states with the largest number of Indian residents), Indians contributed generously to the campaigns of Senator Alan Cranston (D) and Congressman Stephen Solarz (D).

Politics in countries of origin spill over into South Asians' politicking in America. In addition to the Sikh separatist movement's demand for their own state of Khalistan, the Indo-Pakistani conflict over the status of the Himalayan region of Kashmir, and Tamil separatism in Sri Lanka have energized South Asian groups to become more politically active. Many right-wing Hindu political parties in India, such as the Bharatiya Janata Party (BJP) and the Vishwa Hindu Parishad (VHP or World Hindu Council), have support among the Indian American community. Overseas Friends of the Bharatiya Janata Party (OFBJP), which has branches in almost every state in the United States, and the VHP of America, have sent money to buy bricks for a Hindu temple to be constructed on the site of the sixteenth-century Babri mosque in Ayodhya, India, after the mosque's demolition (*Business Today* 1993: 57–59). This demolition was undertaken by a mob in December 1992, sparking off rioting and significant loss of life all over India in an orgy of right-wing fanaticism from which the country will take a long time to recover.

Antifundamentalist groups of South Asian Americans undertook vigorous campaigning after the Ayodhya tragedy, such as the Coalition Against Communalism (CAC) and Concerned South Asians (CSA). These activists signify a radical change in South Asian Americans' understanding of themselves as South Asians and Americans, who can use their resources in the United States without relinquishing their connections with their ethnic country of origin. They use the Internet to engage in spirited debate about political projects, publish newsletters, and mount letter-writing and fund-raising campaigns. On university campuses, South Asians continue the work through study groups and conferences.

Since the 1988 presidential election, Indians have held important organizational and fundraising positions in both major political parties, even though one study reports that only 20 percent of Asian Indians were registered voters in 1988 (*India Today* 1989: 86–88). Today, South Asians themselves hold political office with the newfound security of permanent residence in America. For example, Joy Cherian, an Indian American, served as a commissioner on the U.S. Equal Employment Opportunity Commission under the Bush administration. Following the 1994 elections, Maryland governor-elect Parris Glendening put twelve Indian Americans on his transition team, including the treasurer of the Glendening for governor campaign. South Asian organizations in California like Coalition 2001 and Narika (for battered South Asian women) mounted an unsuccessful struggle against Proposition 187.

Indian Americans running for public office do not appeal to parochial constituencies. Their assimilation into the American mainstream is testified to by their constituencies, which tend to be white-dominated when they are not partly mixed. Although this indicates the candidate's desire to be judged on merit alone rather than on parochial loyalty, it does make political unity among Indian Americans themselves difficult. This must not be mistakenly viewed as Indian Americans' disinclination to to aggregate their community power through numbers. Rather, it is indicative of the pattern of dispersed settlement of Indian Americans, who do not congregate in particular parts of a city, or even a particular region of the country. True, there are a few states of predictably high concentration, but this is open to change whenever the economic demographics of the country change and immigrants seeking economic success move and settle accordingly. Where enclaves have arisen, as in Queens, New York, and New Jersey, South Asian immigrants rarely let community ties get in the way of economic advancement. By and large, the well-off majority is as mobile, if not more so, as most white Americans of their class and education levels (see Table 19-2).

Prosperous Indian Americans lobby Congress on issues important to India: expanded economic relations, separating human rights from trade issues, reviewing controls on export of technology, removing labor or environmental conditions from trade agreements, and containing regional nuclear proliferation. Recent lobbying on issues important to Indians in America has focused on the spouse reunification bill supported by Senator Ted Kennedy. Under current conditions, the wait for South Asians to join their spouses in America can be as long as ten years (*India Today* 1994a: 48b–48c). The dramatic gains of the 1965 Act have been sabotaged by bureaucratic delays and suspicion: a dreadfully hard blow to South Asians in America and the home country alike.

Table 19-2 Residence Patterns of Indians in the United States

State	1974–75	Percent	1980	1990 (Projected)
California	8,406	11	57,989	119,584
Florida			9,138	22,078
Illinois	8,622	11	35,711	74,876
Maryland	2,971	4	13,705	27,576
Massachusetts	2,249	3	8,387	17,886
Michigan	3,561	5	14,680	53,770
New Jersey	8,411	11	29,507	61,386
New York	15,471	20	60,511	135,272
Ohio	3,572	5	13,105	27,104
Pennsylvania	4,385	6	15,212	34,460
Texas	2,700	3	22,226	46,790
Virginia			8,483	18,092
Total	75,847	100	361,544	797,318

Note: Blanks denote no data available.
Source: Adapted from Helweg and Helweg, 1990, 265–226.

It is revealing that South Asian American lobbyists target congresspeople for their stand on issues pertaining to the home countries in South Asia, more than for their position on matters pertaining to South Asian Americans, the most politically involved of whom are affluent professionals. In early 1994, the Indian government hired a Washington lobbying firm to improve access to Capitol Hill (*New India Times* 1994: 1). Along with Indian American community organizations, the firm lobbied critics of India, like Dan Burton (Rep.-Ind.), Robert Toricelli (Dem.-N.J.), and Dana Rohrabacher (Rep.-Calif.), as well as supporters of India, like Sherrod Brown (Dem.-Ohio), Jim McDermott (Dem.-Wash.), and Bob Andrews (Dem.-N.J.).

Although Indian Americans lobbied vigorously for the nomination of Stephen Solarz to the post of ambassador to India, the Clinton administration took a year before it appointed a career diplomat to the post—a delay that the community took hard. However, South Asia does command a certain response from the administration. Energy Secretary Hazel O'Leary, Defense Secretary William Perry, and Treasury Secretary Lloyd Bentsen visited India and Pakistan in 1994 and 1995. Hillary Clinton's trip to the region around the same time with her daughter Chelsea was designed to focus attention on the status of women.

The economic prosperity of Indian Americans bridges many gaps in Indo-U.S. relations. Indians abroad repatriate hundreds of millions of dollars annually (Helweg and Helweg 1990: 213–216). In 1986, the currency restrictions to encourage nonresident Indians (NRIs) to invest in their home country and set up collaborative business and technological ventures. Over the past three years, the economic restructuring program of the World Bank in India has encouraged NRIs to extend their investments in India. Several Indian American corporate leaders accompanied Secretary of Commerce Ron Brown on his February 1995 trip to India, a mission that generated $7 billion in contracts, mostly in the power and energy fields.

Political participation has educated Indian Americans. The rejection earlier immigrants felt when they arrived in the United States has given way to legal acceptance and economic advancement. The ability to stay and rear families in the United States was acquired very recently. The legitimate stake in America had been withheld from them for so long that Indians are having to learn about America as they rear their children here. Many of the post-1965 South Asian immigrants retain the sojourner mentality toward America although most of them will not go back to their country of origin. Indians with children continue to take their families back to their home country to inculcate in the next generation a sense of roots and cultural continuity. Like many other immigrant groups, they reify their cultures and traditions in desperate attempts to indoctrinate the next generation, trying to slow down, if they cannot halt, the tide of inevitable Americanization. Many Indian parents apply traditional notions of family honor, respectability, culture, and gender roles to their American children, fearing for their future as products of uncertainty: neither fully accepted in America nor fully familiar with their country of origin. The struggle to hold on to both home fronts, which shaped earlier Indian immigrant experience, continues to structure the dreams and fears of the post-1965 communities.

Redefining Politics: The New Generation

The most dramatic turn in South Asian life and politics in America is the younger generation's interest in collaboration, networking, and coalition building. These young Americans, most of whose parents came after the 1965 Immigration Act, see their future in the United States. In their education, social life, career objectives, and personal goals, they differ from their parents' generation. This new generation is inextricably connected to the American world of popular culture, individualism, and social engagement in which they were reared. Although conflicts with the older generation do emerge in the home, this new generation exemplifies the incorporation of many cultures without losing a sense of personal cohesion and identity. They are not as bound by distinctions of ethnicity, subcaste, language, and region as the older genertion. They share American lives and American Culture with one another.

Whatever one's economic status, the transmission of traditional cultural beliefs and practices to one's children, who are not South Asian but American, has resulted in a complex relationship for both generations with their South Asian country of origin. Children generally acquire the characteristics of the communities in which they are reared. Accordingly, the few areas of high concentration of South Asians in areas such as Queens, New York, and parts of New Jersey, with shops, restaurants, and places of worship catering to their traditional practices, produce children who are in touch with their community practices. However, the larger American society in which these children also function has proven to be more powerful in its call than parental admonitions regarding dress, dating, and popular culture. When these children attain adulthood, their lives tend to take more cosmopolitan and American turns.

South Asians in the United States take advantage of their numbers (roughly one million) for quick communication and easy targeting of interested compatriots in organizing around socially relevant issues in local groups. Some groups have country-wide networks, such as India Alert, which disseminates human rights information and organizes letter-writing campaigns. Groups like South Asians Against AIDS (SAAA) in New York establish liaisons with similar groups in other countries, like Naaz of Great Britain. Others, like the Coalition Against AntiAsian Violence (CAAV) in New York, extend the boundaries of their political concerns to address a broad range of discriminatory treatment against Asians in America. Various groups address women's particular concerns, such as SAKHI (female friend) for South Asian Women and Manavi (woman) in the northeast, and Narika (woman) on the west coast. Gay rights groups have become active in pressing for their civil rights all over the country, including South Asian Lesbian and Gay Association (SALGA) in New York, Shamakarm in San Francisco, and Trikone (triangle) in San Jose, California.

The most important consequence of this grassroots mobilization among South Asian communities is that the "high" politics of the formal political arena of elections, fundraising, and campaign management is not the last word on political participation. This new, socially aware, and energetic political activism has expanded conventional understandings of political participation to include a wide range of concerns: issues of local interest in specific communities that are placed before local politicians—and city councils; immigration issues that affect South Asians regardless of their geographical location; political and economic issues in South Asian countries on which America can have an impact, such as Kashmir, and bilateral trade; and international issues such as AIDS, ill-treatment, and discrimination. This is inclusive politics, democratic in the most literal sense of the word.

Despite strenuous efforts, South Asians have only just begun to make an impact on national politics. Until now, their particular history of recent immigration and post-1965 economic success has kept what political engagement there is at the level of formal or high politics. Consequently, they entered the coalition game rather late and are still building common bases among their extremely diverse membership. The general public's emphasis on their professional advancement and economic prosperity obscures the complexity of South Asians' existence in America. South Asians and the larger society both forget that recognition does not occur in a vacuum; they and the larger society are mutually constitutive. Race-based views prevalent in society, intellectually bankrupt though they are, continue to block complete acceptance of their presence in America. The escalation of immigrant bashing in the country also has taken its toll on the community's hard-won sense of belonging. South Asian political activity only recently has begun moving away from a reactive mode to counterdiscriminatory treatment, toward an autonomous assertion of presence and political interest.

This newfound independence is now being pushed forward to the next stage: to find ways in which common ground can be established between South Asians and non-South Asian groups. As the first woman of color to be executive director of the National Gay and Lesbian Task Force, Indian-born Urvashi Vaid puts it regarding the gay movement today, "We are seeing the limits of identity-based politics. Identity is very important: I am an Indian and I am never going to disown that identity. But organising around identity has gotten us into single issue politics and we've not been able to come together to build an electoral majority" (*India Today*, 1995a: 68b–e).

Building that electoral majority remains the political goal for all minorities as they forge new lives in the United States. To this rethinking of political strategy must be added the emergence of a new sense of self. In the words of anthropologist James Clifford (1988: 10–11), identity is "mixed, relational, and inventive.... A sense of difference or distinctness can never be located solely in the continuity of a culture or tradition. Identity is conjunctural, not essential." For South Asians who cross and recross the bridging space between Asia and North America, their inventive engagement with the United States surely will, one day, convince the world and themselves that this is truly their home.

REFERENCES

Appiah, Kwame Anthony. 1992. *In my father's house.* New York: Oxford University Press.

Asian Week. 1986. Indians discuss assimilation. October 10.

Bouvier, Leon F., and David Simcox. 1994. *Foreign born professionals in the United States.* Washington, D.C.: Center for Immigration Studies.

Brown, Emily. 1982. Revolution in India: Made in America. *Population Review* 25, nos. 1–2: 41–47.

Buchanan, Agnes Foster. 1908. The West and the Hindu invasion. *Overland Monthly and Out West Magazine* 54, no. 4 (April): 308–313.

Business Today (New Delhi). 1993. The saffron vision 2000, July 22-August 6, 57–59.

Chandrasekhar, S. 1944. Indian immigration in America. *Far Eastern Survey* 13 (July 26): 15, 141.

———. 1982. Some statistics on Asian Indian immigrants to the United States of America. In *From India to*

America: A brief history of immigration, Problems of discrimination, admission and assimilation, edited by S. Chandrasekliar, 86–92. La Jolla, Calif.: Population Review.

Clifford, Jamies. 1988. *The predicament of culture.* Cambridge, Mass.: Harvard University Press.

Debates and Proceedings in the Congress of the United States, 1789–1791. 2 vols. Washington, D.C.: 1834 vol. 1, 998, 1284; vol. 2, 1148–1156, 1162, 2264.

Dutta, Manoranian. 1982. Asian Indian Americans: Search for an economic profile. In *From India to America: A brief history of immigration, Problems of discrimination, admission and assimilation,* edited by S. Chandrasekhar, 76–85. La Jolla, Calif.: Population Review.

Fenton, John Y. 1988. *Transplanting religious traditions: Asian Indians in America.* New York: Praeger.

Gibson, Margaret. 1988. *Accommodation without assimilation: Sikh immigrants in an American high school.* Ithaca, N.Y.: Cornell University Press.

Helweg, Arthur W., and Uslia M. Helweg. 1990. *An immigrant success story: East Indians in America.* Philadelphia: University of Pennsylvania Press.

Hess, Gary. 1982. The Asian Indian immigrants in the United States: The early phase, 1900–1965. *Population Review* 25: 32.

India Today. 1989. Indian Americans: The lobbying game. September 30, 86–88.

———. 1994a. Separated by law. August 15, 48b–c.

———. 1994b. Good morning, New York. September 30, 68e.

———. 1995a. Mainstream movers. January 15, 68b–e.

———. 1995b. Bonded in America, January 31, 76b–c.

Leonard, Karen. 1982. Marriage and family life among early Asian Indian immigrants. In *From India to America: A brief history of immigration, Problems of discrimination, admission and assimilation,* edited by S. Chandrasekhar, 67–75. La Jolla, Calif.: Population Review.

———. 1992. *Making ethnic choices: California's Punjab Mexican Americans.* Philadelphia: Temple University Press.

New York Times. 1994. Indian immigrant's face is burned with a cigarette. February 20.

———. 1995. A small melting pot, in danger of overflowing. January 22.

News India Times. 1994. Lobbying efforts cost $70,000 a month, December 16, 1.

———. 1995. Sikh files suit against MTA, January 6, 26.

Ong, Paul, and Suzanne J. Hee. 1994. Economic diversity. In *The state of Asian Pacific America: Economic diversity, issues, and policies,* edited by Paul Ong. Los Angeles: LEAP Asian Pacific American Public Policy Institute and UCLA Asian American Studies Center.

Peterson, William. 1985. Who's what: 1790–1980. *Wilson Quarterly* (Summer): 97–120.

Saran, Parniatma. 1980. New ethics: The case of the East Indians in New York City. In *Sourcebook on the new immigration,* edited by Roy Sinion Bryce-Laporte. New Brunswick, N.J.: Transaction Books.

Saund, Dalip S. 1960. *Congressman from India.* New York: Dutton.

Scheffauer, Herman. 1910. *The tide of turbans.* vol. 43 (June): 616–618.

Statistical Abstracts of the United States. 1994. Washington, D.C.: U.S. Department of Commerce, Economic and Statistics Administration, Bureau of the Census, Data User Sevices Division.

Takaki, Ronald. 1989. *Strangers from a different shore.* Boston: Little Brown.

Taylor, Paul S., and Torn Vasey. 1936. Historical background of California farm labor. *Rural Sociology* 1: 291.

U.S. Bureau of the Census. 1990. *1990 census of population, general population characteristics.* Washington, D.C.: Government Printing Office.

20

Slanted

Racial Prejudice Is Part of What Fueled the Clinton Campaign Scandal

ROBERT WRIGHT

The *New York Times* runs a lot of headlines about scandals, but rarely does it run a headline that is a scandal. On Saturday, December 28, it came pretty close. The headline over its lead Page One story read: "DEMOCRATS HOPED TO RAISE $7 MILLION FROM ASIANS IN U.S." On the inside page where the story continued, the headline was: "DEMOCRATS' GOAL: MILLIONS FROM ASIANS." Both headlines were wrong. The story was actually about a 1996 Democratic National Committee document outlining a plan to raise (as the lead paragraph put it) "$7 million from Asian-Americans."

Memo to the *New York Times:* "Asian-Americans" are American citizens of Asian ancestry. "Asians," in contrast, are Asians—citizens of some Asian nation. And "Asians in U.S." are citizens of some Asian nation who are visiting or residing in the United States. This is not nit-picking. It gets at the heart of the subtle, probably subconscious racial prejudice that has turned a legitimately medium sized scandal into a journalistic blockbuster.

Would a *Times* headline call Polish-Americans "East Europeans in U.S.?" (Or, in the jump headline, just "East Europeans?") And the headline was only half the problem with Saturday's story. The story itself was wrong-headed, implying that there's something inherently scandalous about Asian Americans giving money to a political campaign. In fact, the inaccurate headline was necessary to prevent the story from seeming absurd. Can you imagine the *Times* running—over its lead story—the headline "DEMOCRATS HOPED TO RAISE MILLIONS FROM U.S. JEWS?"

Political parties target ethnic groups for fund-raising all the time (as Jacob Weisberg recently showed in these pages [the pages of *The Earthling*]). They target Hispanics, they target Jews, they pass the hat at Polish-American dinners. To be sure, the Asian American fund-raising plan was, in retrospect, no ordinary plan. It went quite awry. Some of the projected $7 million—at least $1.2 million, according to the *Times*—wound up coming in the form of improper or illegal donations (which, of course, we already knew about). Foreign citizens or companies funneled money through domestic front men or front companies. And sometimes foreigners thus got to rub elbows with President Clinton. For all we know, they influenced policy.

But the truly scandalous stuff was old news by December 27. What that day's story added was news of the existence of this document outlining a plan to raise money from Americans of Asian descent. And that alone was considered worthy of the high-scandal treatment.

Leave aside this particular story, and consider the "campaign-gate" scandal as a whole. What if the same thing had happened with Europeans and Americans of European descent? It would be just as improper and/or illegal. But would we really be so worked up about it? Would William Safire write a column about it every fifteen minutes and use the loaded word "aliens" to describe European noncitizens? If Indonesian magnate James Riady looked like John Major, would *Newsweek* have put a huge, ominous, grainy black-and-white photo of him on its cover? ("Clinton's European connection" wouldn't pack quite the same punch as "Clinton's Asian connection"—the phrase that *Newsweek* put on its cover and Safire has used sixteen times in thirteen weeks.) Would the Times be billing minor investigative twists as lead stories?

Indeed, would its reporters even write stories like that Saturday's? The lead paragraph, which is supposed to crystallize the story's news value, is this: "A White House official and a leading fund-raiser for the Democratic National Committee helped devise a strategy to raise an unprecedented $7 million from Asian-Americans partly by offering rewards to the largest donors, including special access to the White House, the committee's records show." You mean Democrats actually offered White House visits to Americans who cough up big campaign dough? I'm shocked. Wait until the Republicans discover this tactic! The Friday after Christmas is a slow news day, but it's not that slow. And as for the "unprecedented" scale of the fund-raising goal: Virtually every dimension of Clinton's 1996 fund-raising was on an unprecedented scale, as we've long known.

There are some interesting nuggets in the *Times* story. But among them isn't the fact, repeated in the third paragraph, that fund-raisers told Asian American donors that "political contributions were the path to power." And among them isn't the fact, repeated (again) in the fourth paragraph, that "the quid pro quo promised" to Asian American donors was "in many cases a face-to-face meeting with the President." And, anyway, none of these nuggets is interesting enough to make this the day's main story. The only way to do that is to first file Asian Americans in the "alien" section of your brain. That's why the story's headline is so telling.

The funny thing about this scandal is that its root cause and its mitigating circumstance are one and the same. Its root cause is economic globalization—the fact that more and more foreign companies have an interest in U.S. policy. But globalization is also the reason that the scandal's premise—the illegality of contributions from "foreign" interests—is increasingly meaningless. Both the *Times* and the *Washington Post* (in its blockbuster-lite front-page story, the next day) cited already reported evidence that a $185,000 donation (since returned) may have originated ultimately with the C.P. Group. The C.P. Group is "a huge Thai conglomerate with interests in China and elsewhere in Asia" (the *Times*) and is "among the largest foreign investors in China" (the *Post*). But of course, Nike, Boeing, General Motors, Microsoft, IBM, and so on are also huge companies with interests in China and elsewhere in Asia. They, no less than Asian companies, at times have an interest in low U.S. tariffs, treating oppressive Asian dictators with kid gloves, and so on. Yet it is perfectly legal for them to lubricate such lobbying with big campaign donations.

Why no journalistic outrage about that? Well, for starters, try looking at a grainy newsweekly-sized photo of Lou Gerstner and see if it makes you remember Pearl Harbor. (By the way, neither the *Times* nor the *Post* noted that the ominous C.P. Group is involved in joint ventures with Ford and Nynex.)

You might think that, in an age of globalization and with the fate of the United States increasingly tied to the fate of other nations, the best newspaper in the United States would be careful not to run articles that needlessly feed xenophobia. Guess again. Six weeks ago a *Times* op-ed piece by the political scientist Lucian Pye explored the formidable mindset that governs China today. Current Chinese leaders have "distinctive characteristics" that give them "significant advantages" over the United States in foreign policy. They "see politics as exclusively combative contests, involving haggling, maneuvering, bargaining and manipulating. The winner is the master of the cleverest ploys and stratagems [*sic*]." Moreover, Chinese leaders are "quick to find fault in others" and try "always to appear bold and fearless." Finally ("in a holdover from classical Chinese political theory"), China's leaders "insist on claiming the moral high ground, because top leaders are supposed to be morally superior men." In short, China's "distinctive" edge lies in combative, Machiavellian, mud-slinging, blustery, self-righteous politicians. Gosh, why didn't we think of that?

These peculiar traits, Pye noted, aggravate another disturbing feature of modern China. It seems that the Chinese people vacillate "between craving foreign goods and giving vent to anti-foreign passions." In other respects, too, they evince a "prickly xenophobic nationalism." Imagine that.

Section 7

Jewish Americans and U.S. Foreign Policy

If there is a "model minority" in terms of success in international affairs, it is probably the Jewish supporters of Israel. As Ken Organski has argued, there are a number of geopolitical, cultural, historical, and other reasons why the United States would consistently back Israel, but there are also important elements of leadership and organization among Israel's supporters. This is effectively demonstrated in Bat-Ami Zucker's essay on the origins of the special relationship between the United States and Israel. This piece reminds us that, aside from the effective political lobbying that has gone into nurturing this critical relationship, there are underlying structural reasons for shared interests that may not obtain in other regions, such as Africa. The flipside of the picture is Arab American difficulties in making their concerns known, and influencing foreign policy organizations, whether governmental or nongovernmental. It is apparent from these readings that the structural features are important, as is an elite's capacity to focus on a single country (Israel, Armenia) rather than having to speak on behalf of an entire continent (Africa) or region (the Arab world).

21

The Genesis of the Special Relationship Between the United States and Israel, 1948–1973

BAT-AMI ZUCKER

Since the establishment of the State of Israel in 1948, a special relationship has developed between the United States, one of the largest and most powerful nations, and Israel, one of the smallest Middle Eastern countries. It's most obvious and profound expression has been America's continuing support for Israel's existence and safety. Despite occasional discord and contrasting trends among American policymakers, especially those who consider support for Israel to be a burden on American Middle Eastern policy, the fundamental sympathy and support for Israel has not diminished. Israel is perceived and discussed in favorable terms, and support for Israel enjoys wide appeal, bipartisan consensus, and acknowledgment by presidents and the Congress. The long-standing U.S.-Israeli relationship is unusual even among friendly nations. The fact that it has endured despite the absence of any formal arrangement, even at times when strategic logic dictated against strong support for Israel, suggests that strategic motives alone cannot fully explain the relationship between the two countries.

Various studies, both pro- and anti-Israel, offer explanations of America's decisions with regard to Israel that focus mainly on domestic political considerations.[1] This study will attempt to illustrate the unique pattern of the American-Israeli relationship as a bond that combines a range of factors, but is dominated and backed by sincere public sympathy and sentiment. Both domestic and international politics no doubt contribute their share, yet it is the widespread and established concern for Israel that developed in the United States after World War II that is the cornerstone for American support.

THE ORIGIN OF AMERICA'S PRO-ISRAEL POLICY

Our study focuses on the period from the establishment of Israel in 1948 to the Yom Kippur War in 1973. It is our belief that the special relationship between the two countries was formed and established then, when Israel's enemies were continuously threatening to destroy the state. This is not to say that U.S.-Israel relations have undergone major changes since 1973, although a different pattern has indeed developed now that peace initiatives have become the dominant element in U.S. Middle Eastern policy. Rather, it reflects the fact that America's relationship with Israel between 1948 and 1973 differed significantly not only from its relationships with other friendly countries during the same period but also from its relations with Israel since 1973.

What is of particular interest to us is an analysis of how and why U.S. policy toward Israel—only one of the small states in the Middle East with which the United States maintains friendly relations—has taken a completely different form from that followed elsewhere.

Although research shows that American attitudes to Israel are dominated by a sense of moral obligation, which in itself is somewhat unusual even among friendly nations, moral obligations have also been a factor in U.S. relations with other countries, albeit to a lesser degree. Only in the case of Israel, however, has a moral commitment to the safety of another country been articulated by every single American president since 1949. Furthermore, the notion that the American commitment to Israel is outside the realm of political debate has not only been reiterated by every administration, also been manifested in the bipartisan record as well as in the media.[2] In an exclusive interview published in *U.S. News and World Report*, Secretary of State Henry A. Kissinger described the U.S. commitment to Israel in these terms: "We have a historic commitment to the survival and the well-being of Israel. This is a basic national policy reaffirmed by every administration."[3]

Prior to that, at a 1967 meeting in Glassboro, New Jersey, when Soviet Premier Alexei Kosygin asked President Lyndon Johnson why Americans supported Israel against the Arab world, the latter simply replied: "Because we think it's right"—an argument rarely used in diplomatic circles.[4] A June 1967 *Washington Post* editorial expressed the same idea when it stated that "Israel's moral claims upon the Western world ... make it unthinkable for this country, or its allies, to permit the Jewish state to be destroyed."[5]

The humanitarian aspect of America's support for Israel is often referred to in administration statements. In discussing the bond between the United States and Israel, Deputy Secretary State Kenneth Rush told a Senate appropriations subcommittee on November 5, 1973, that "There is a strong humanitarian interest ... and in a very strong non-partisan way this country considers itself a friend of Israel who will help Israel in time of trouble and at other times."[6] And the unique nature of the commitment has been stressed as well; for example, by Under-Secretary of State Joseph Sisco, who said; "The United States has supported the security and well-being of Israel ... with a constancy rarely surpassed in the history of relations between nations."[7]

COLD WAR CONSIDERATIONS

The uniqueness of America's relationship with Israel has drawn much attention.[8] Even though the relationship has not been formalized, the countries are bound together by a bond that in practice has been as strong as any alliance, written or unwritten.[9] Fascinated by the tie between Israel and the United States, especially in view of the immense disparity "in size, in power, and international role between the two countries,"[10] many scholars have sought to examine its motivations.

In the 1950s, some argued that it was the policy of containment,[11] adopted shortly before Israel establishment, that led to America's friendly and supportive attitude, stressing that Israel, as a stable democracy, fit nicely into the American plan to prevent Soviet expansion in the Middle East.[12] However, this view fails to take into consideration the cruel fact that a state with a Jewish population of less than 2.5 million (at that time) could hardly be counted upon as a strategic asset in the face of the many large Arab states that criticized any and all American assistance to Israel as a menace to their own well-being. Moreover, in a period when courting the Arab countries was deemed necessary to bring them into the Western defense system, and when Europe was still totally dependent on these countries for its oil, it seemingly made more strategic sense to let Israel stand on its own.[13] Indeed, this is precisely what State Department specialists recommended, considering Israel a burden to the United States and an obstacle to friendly relations with the Arab countries.[14]

In view of the preceding analysis, one must conclude that there was, and still is, more behind the American-Israeli special relationship than strategic motives. Even Senator J. William Fulbright, a leading figure in pro-Arab circles, concluded in August 1970 that "America [was] tied to Israel less by strategic consideration than by bonds of culture and sentiment."[15] Yet there is no doubt that anti-Soviet objectives also played a role in the identification of American interests with Israel's, especially during the Johnson administration. The tendency of the United States to refrain from associating the Arab countries with the Western defense zone was already evident in the late 1950s. Keeping to the old objective of retaining America's position, U.S. policy, during the Kennedy and Johnson administrations, was to protect America's interests against Soviet expansion by cultivating friendly countries—Arab states as well as Israel—on an individual basis.[16] It was in this context, especially after the Six-Day War in June 1967, that Israel, politically stable, militarily powerful, and friendly, was deemed a valued asset in stabilizing the balance of power in the region. As Senator Henry Jackson said in 1971, "The Israelies are today in the frontline in resisting the historic imperial ambitions that lie behind Soviet policy.... They deserve our support because they are allied with the security interests of the United States in a vital region of the world."[17]

To sum up, it was not containment as such, but the broader global objectives of American foreign policy, especially in the Middle East, that facilitated U.S. support for Israel.[18] For, despite differences in tactics and occasional discord, support for Israel continued to be a central element of American Middle East policy and "a matter of concern for all Americans."[19]

The fact that the U.S. commitment to Israel continued even when strategic logic dictated against it leads us to conclude that the relationship between the two countries could be explained, as Senator Jackson put it, by "shared values, cultural affinities and a common ethical and religious heritage."[20]

ISRAEL AS A SISTER DEMOCRACY

First among the factors that contributed to widespread American sympathy and goodwill toward the State of Israel during the period from 1948 to 1973 are the common beliefs shared by the people of both countries. Israel's commitment to maintaining a democratic form of government—unique in the Middle East—guaranteed American support from the outset. In 1950, the *Washington Post* called Israel "an example of genuine democracy."[21] And in 1960, the *New York Times* described it as "an outpost of democratic government and haven for the oppressed."[22]

The *Congressional Record* of the late 1960s is replete with citations representing Israel as "the democratic oasis in a desert of dictators" and as a "solid bastion of freedom and democracy against the forces of aggression and totalitarianism."[23]

More than any other new nation born in this century, Israel has proved the indomitable strength of democracy. The miracle of Israel lies not alone in the flourishing democracy it has created in the Holy Land but also in its unique success in spreading the idea and practice of democracy ... to other lands, to emerging nations of Africa and Asia.[24]

In the decades following the establishing of Israel, the *New York Times* and the *Washington Post* competed in parading the new state as "the showplace of democracy" which had accomplished the impossible,[25] the *Times* even using phraseology similar to that in Lincoln's Gettysburg Address to express why America so closely identified with Israel, which was "conceived in idealism and born in fire."[26] A positive reaction to the small and distant state seemed to come naturally to the American public, as "the concepts of social justice and democracy upon which [Israel] was founded are among [America's] most cherished ancient traditions."[27]

ADMIRATION FOR A NATION OF PIONEERS

Similarities in the origins and history of the two countries further stimulated American understanding, sympathy, and nostalgia.[28] Much like the United States, "Israel is a nation of different peoples . . . endeavoring to build a new and just society."[29] Its pioneering spirit was often compared with that of the American pioneers, thereby evoking reminiscences of American's glorious past.[30] For Americans, dedicated to the idea of achievement and progress, Israel's accomplishments were seen as "little short of a miracle";[31] "If ever a desert has been made blossom like the rose, modern Israel it is."[32] Moreover, Israel's economic success was seen as an example of what could be attained "though determination, hard work, and application of modern technology."[33] Finally, the Israelis themselves were admired as young, gallant, and courageous, and were praised for their industriousness, determination, and sacrifice—an outcome of the "unconquerable strength of a pioneer spirit welling up from two thousand years of tragic history."[34]

CHRISTIAN SYMPATHY FOR ISRAEL

Reinforcing the effect of a common democratic heritage and pioneering background were America's religious and historical ties to the Old Testament, which facilitated the development of a natural kinship with the land of the Bible and people of the book. The link between the ancient Hebrews and the modern Israelis was played up repeatedly. Although many Americans were reluctant to identify the cause of religion with that of a state,[35] and it has always been difficult to establish anything like a consensus concerning Israel among American's Christians,[36] the absence of a united position on Israel does not mean that Americans do not have strong feelings regarding the security of the Jewish state.[37] Furthermore, for many, Israel's very existence is a proof for the realization of biblical prophecies. The vision of Israel as the land where the biblical happenings took place stimulates the American imagination. "The Bible stories," President Johnson reminisced at a B'nai B'rith meeting in 1968, "are woven into my childhood memories as the gallant struggle of modern Jews to be free of persecution."[38] Once the link between the Bible, the Holy Land, and Israel was established, "a profound bond" was erected between "the Jews of Israel and the Christians of America,"[39] the latter seeing "the hand of the Lord in the creation of Israel and . . . in bringing the Jews back to Israel."[40]

A poll in June 1967, when Israel was engaged in a war to prevent its extinction, indicated that support for Israel stemmed, among other reasons, from "sympathy for the 'little guy' fighting the 'big guy'."[41] Involved here was not only the traditional American concern for the underdog,[42] but the American attachment of the Bible as a source of moral and social justice. In this respect, the Puritan heritage, which identified the Old Testament with supreme good, can be said to have had an impact on American attitudes toward Israel.[43]

AMERICAN JEWS AND ISRAEL

If believing American Christians were emotionally affected by the vision of Israel as the land where biblical promises were fulfilled, this vision promoted a much deeper bond between American Jews and the new Jewish state. It should, however, be stressed at the outset the American Jewish attitude toward Israel—affectionate and consistently supportive as it has been—arose, for the most part, from the wellsprings of the Jewish experience in America. In this sense, it reflects an attitude similar to that of Christian Americans. Thus, although most American Jews do not seek to disassociate themselves from their Jewish identity, they primarily visualize themselves as Americans and act accordingly. Therefore, American Jewry's moral, political, and financial support for Israel reflects general American beliefs as well as an identification with Judaism and solidarity with the Jewish people. To most American Jews, this identification is "visceral, profound, overwhelmingly beyond fighting."[45] As Melvin Urofsky puts it, "American Jews have proved that they are also very much Americans, and their predominate value system is an amalgam of Jewish teachings and American democratic norms."[46] When administrations have considered adopting a less sympathetic attitude toward Israel, therefore, American Jews have opposed such changes "as Americans, as men and women dedicated to freedom, to democracy and humanity."[47] In sum, whether for religious or traditional cultural reasons, American Jews have given Israel and its well-being increasing attention since 1948.[48]

No doubt it is the sense of belonging to one family, of sharing a heritage of faith, history, and fate that has determined the American Jewish attitude toward Israel. Although American Jewry is a highly complex community composed of diverse groups and viewpoints, and its members often differ in regard to Israel, the American Jewish community has nevertheless evinced strong attachment to the Jewish state and acknowledged its sovereignty by helping to provide for Israel's financial as well as political needs.[49]

The fact that the American Jewish community was, and still is, "unified and motivated to work in Israel's behalf"[50] reflects Israel's having become "the crucial operative element in shaping organized Jewish life."[51] In this regard, American Jewry views relations between itself and Israel as similar to that of "partners ... [in] a real marriage between two highly strong individuals facing an unfriendly world together."[52] To follow the same image, American Jews indeed represent a strong partner in a marriage. After having succeeded in establishing their status as Americans in American society, they can now identify with Israel overtly without being accused of parochialism.[53] Their ability to profess their deep connection with and concern for Israel points to the democratic nature of American society as well as to their acceptance and acculturation. This has been manifested time and time again, for example, in the actions of the many Jewish members of Congress who have been willing and able to demonstrate their commitment to the survival and safety of the Jewish state by forming an "in-house lobby" for Israel,[54] taking leadership roles in resolutions supporting Israel and providing it with additional aid.[55]

Analyzing the American Jewish community after World War II, Jacob Neusner explains that "after four generations [in the United States], to be Jewish is a mode of being American, taken for granted by Jews among other Americans, and no longer problematical."[56] With their position in America established, Jews now felt safe and secure enough, in both their Jewishness and their Americanism, "to challenge major aspects of the United States' foreign policy, with regard both to the Middle East and Soviet Union."[57] Thus, when Richard Nixon and George McGovern tried to make aid to Israel a political issue during the 1972 presidential campaign,[58] the eight top national Jewish organizations banded together to deplore such appeals to American Jews, stressing that "Jews vote as individual

Americans ... according to their individual judgments," and have "a deep interest in the broad range of domestic and foreign policies involved in the present campaign."[58] An editorial in the *New York Times* confirmed the authenticity of this statement: "All studies indicate that the Middle East problem is only one of many entering into the voting decisions of Jewish Americans now and in the past."[59] Even fiery Prime Minister David Ben-Gurion, who was well known for feeling that all Jews belong to Israel, acknowledged that American Jews "have only one political attachment and that is to the United States of America."[60]

Nevertheless, given America's freedom and democratic political system, the Jewish community could openly express its loyalty to the State of Israel, "the national home of the entire Jewish people,"[61] whenever it deemed such expression necessary to Israel's security. Indeed it is the successful interrelation between Jewish and American beliefs that has allowed American Jews the unique position of being fully dedicated to and identified with America and its interests, both domestic and foreign, and at the same time to acknowledge their Jewishness by supporting Israel.[62] To those who cast doubt on the Americanism of Jews who support Israel, implying that this means a watered-down loyalty to the United States or a possible class between their American and their Jewish interests,[63] it must be pointed out that two sets of values operate on the American Jewish scene, one dealing with inner substance and the other with civic identification. Whereas in their support for Israel American Jews express their inner being and Jewish identity, which neither is nor should be defined in terms of civic loyalty, their attitude toward the United States has always evinced their political and social fidelity as citizens of that country. Indeed, it is the harmony between Jewishness and devotion to what America stands for that has motivated American Jews to involve themselves in American political life far beyond their proportion of the U.S. population. In other words, it is their feeling that in the United States they can participate on equal terms that gives them the sense of security to combine their civic loyalty with an overt declaration of their faith.

THE PRO-ISRAEL LOBBY

The pro-Israel lobby in Washington reflects both aspects of American Jewish life. As Hyman H. Bookbinder once put it: "What's good for American society is terribly important to the Jewish community."[64] Similarly, the American Israel Public Affairs Committee (AIPAC), a Washington lobby representing "the totality of Jewish influence in America,"[65] functions to aid Israeli interests within the broad parameters of the American political system," on the basis of American interests."[66] Indeed, almost all responsible American Jewish activists who engage in the support of Israel repeatedly underline that they are acting as Americans.

In this regard, AIPAC has always stressed that it is an American, not a Jewish lobby.[67] I. N. Kenen, who founded the American Zionist Council, which became AIPAC in 1954, was convinced from the start that in order to succeed, the organization would have to be "an American outfit, run by Americans with taxable—not tax-free—dollars."[68] Thus, while AIPAC engages in activities aimed at influencing presidents and members of Congress to provide for the safety of Israel its goals have always included the creation of a bridge between the Jewish communities of Israel and the United States and the promotion of friendly relations between the two countries.[69] Furthermore, despite its obvious concern for Israel, AIPAC does not follow the Israeli line, as its director, Morris Amitay, stressed in 1975 when he stated that his organization did not maintain any formal ties with the Israeli embassy.[70] Nonetheless, as a one-issue organization committed to the safety of Israel, AIPAC has pressed for the same things as the Israeli government.[71]

Given the fact that American Jews constitute an important interest group,[72] it was likely from the start that an energetic pro-Israel lobby would have a good chance of making itself heard and listened to. While Jews made up only about 3 percent of the general American population and 4 percent of the voting population during the period we are considering, their concentration in specific regions, their education, wealth, and unusually broad involvement in politics, and their strong feelings for Israel made the Jewish vote an important consideration for many policymakers, as it still is.[73] The centrality of the State of Israel in the American Jewish mind, together with the importance of the Jewish community in pressing for pro-Israel legislation, thereby add yet another dimension to the special relationship between the United States and Israel.

Although the Israel lobby has been credited with extraordinary successes and has acquired a reputation as a "highly organized and well-endowed association" that is "the most powerful, best-run, and effective foreign policy interest group in Washington,"[74] critics of the strong U.S. commitment to Israel have taken a less positive view of the lobby's influence.[75] Thus, Senator Fulbright, a chairman of the Senate Foreign Relations Committee and a long-time foe of the United States-Israel alliance, proclaimed that the lobby "can count on 75 to 80 votes on anything ... [in which it is] interested in the Senate."[76] More balanced appraisals describe the lobby as "neither insidious nor so overwhelmingly powerful."[77]

Although the exact role and the degree of success of the Israel lobby have always been disputed, there does seem to be agreement that whatever strength it has lies in its being in accord with the generally positive American attitude toward Israel.[78]

ISRAEL AND THE HOLOCAUST

Support for Israel between 1948 and 1973 was widespread in Congress, government, and the general populace, all of who favored Israel's "existence, integrity, and security." The positive American attitude toward Israel, together with the historical, cultural, and democratic similarities between the two countries, facilitated pro-Israel activities by non-Jewish Americans and enabled American Jews to achieve peace of mind and soul regarding their fellow Jews outside the United States. Moreover, the creation of the Jewish state led to increased identity with their own Jewishness. In addition to the crucial role Israel played in shaping and strengthening the self-identity of American Jews, its activity represented a total contrast to the horrors of the Holocaust, for "Israel stood, symbolically, as the redemption of the Holocaust; Israel made it possible to endure the memory of Auschwitz."[79]

This aspect of Israel's establishment led to two diametrically opposed attitudes toward the Jewish state. For some, Israel's democratic sovereignty and independence were a triumphant negation of the Holocaust, or as survivor and author Eli Weisel put it: "Behind the army of Israel stood another army of six million ghosts."[80] By contrast, and perhaps integrally connected with the first, was the view—especially on the eve of the Six-Day War and during the Yom Kippur War—that focused on Israel's possible destruction and the consequent fatal blow to both Jewishness and Jewish status in the United States.[81]

Among proponents of this latter view, "there was a widespread feeling that the lives of all Jews, that the fate of Judaism itself, hung in the balance. If Israel perished then Jews everywhere would perish ... because their faith could not survive a second onslaught."[82] Among those who held this view was Senator Rudy Boschwitz of Minnesota, the chairman of the Senate Foreign Relations Sub-Committee on the Middle East during the Six-Day

War. Born in Germany into a family that managed to escape in 1933, Boschwitz has always been aware of his responsibility as a Jew and as someone who could have been a victim of the Holocaust. This, he acknowledged, "has given me more of that so-called Holocaust mentality than most people would otherwise have had.... I have a great sense of the dangers facing Jews and Israel."[83]

As indicated earlier, these two attitudes combined to underscore the moral commitment to the security of Israel as a guarantee against a second Holocaust. For, "were Israel to be destroyed, then Hitler would be alive again, the final victory would be his."[84] This feeling is not limited to Jewish circles. The United States government has always emphasized its role in the establishment of Israel, and has sometimes expressed its responsibility and moral commitment to the Jewish survivors of the Nazi slaughter of six million Jews.[85] In the words of Adlai Stevenson in 1956, "Israel is the symbol ... of man's triumph over one of the darkest sorrows in human history—the attempt of Adolf Hitler to destroy a whole people."[86]

CONCLUSIONS

To sum up, it is the combination of American ideals and the aspirations of American Jews that has been largely responsible for the willingness of the U.S. government to respond to and cooperate with American Jewry. This parity of ideals and common interests has made possible an American policy toward Israel that generally reflects support of American Jewish concerns when Israel's enemies have continuously threatened to destroy the state. No less important in this regard is the fact that initiating, launching, or supporting Jewish and/or Israeli goals has often proved politically rewarding.[87]

Although some government officials and members of Congress have criticized the pressure put on the United States by interest groups in general and by the Israel lobby in particular, the majority of the American public believes in the justice and validity of Israel's cause. As Senator Charles McC. Mathias of Maryland has concluded: "... even if there were no Israel lobby, the American people would remain solidly committed to Israel's survival."[88]

Although the pro-Israel stance in Congress and in successive presidential administrations has no doubt come about because support for Israel combined the pursuit of U.S. national interests in the Middle East with electoral profit in the form of Jewish political support, it has been the sympathy, appreciation, admiration, and identification of the American public at large with Israel's democratic and moral values with its heritage and long-overdue homeland-that is really behind the special and unprecedented relationship between the two countries.

This study derives from my long-standing interest in the American-Israeli special relationship, particularly during the period from 1948 to the Yom Kippur War in October 1973. It is of historical interest because it sheds light on the events themselves and, even more, because it enables us to better understand the continuity of the unique relationship between Israel and the United States after 1973. Before the Yom Kippur War, this relationship flourished under constant Arab threats to destroy Israel; since then the political atmosphere in the Middle East has changed. Relations between the two countries are now dominated by a different set of priorities in which American peace initiatives have more than once conflicted with Israel's political orientation. However, the bond established during 1948 to 1973 has held despite the more open American criticism of Israel and the occasional tension between Washington and Jerusalem.

NOTES

1. See, for example, Bernard Reich, *The United States and Israel: Influence in the Special Relationship* (New York: Praeger, 1984); Edward B. Glick, *The Triangular Connection: America, Israel and American Jews* (London: George Allen & Unwin, 1982); Cheryl A. Rubenberg, *Israel and the American National Interest: A Critical Examination* (Chicago: University of Illinois Press, 1986).

2. With regard to the media, our examination focused on two representatives of the elite press, the *New York Times* and the *Washington Post* . They were singled out because they are considered the most prestigious and influential papers in the United States; so much so, in fact, that successive administrations have been sensitive to the views presented on their editorial pages. For the media's attitude, see, for example, *New York Times* editorials, February 26, 1956, September 10, 1968, and September 2, 1969; *Washington Post* editorial, "Israeli Shift," October 19, 1950.

3. *U.S. News and World Report*, June 23, 1975, p. 23.

4. Cited in Glick, *Triangular Connection*, p. 106.

5. Editorial "The Lessons of History," *Washington Post*, June 6, 1968.

6. Cited in "Evolution of United States Role in the Middle East," *Congressional Quarterly*, "The Middle East: U.S. Policy, Israel, Oil and the Arabs" (April 1974), p. 8.

7. An address to the American Academy of Political Science on April 11, 1969; *Department of State Release*, no. 78, p. 2.

8. See, for example, Robert F. Drinan, *Honor the Promise: America's Commitment to Israel* (New York: Doubleday, 1977). Even a pro-Arab analysis argues that "such a moral commitment to another state is unique in the annals of international relations and foreign policy"; Rubenberg, *Israel and the American National Interest*, p. 10.

9. James Lee Ray, *The Future of American-Israeli Relations: A Parting of the Ways?* (Lexington: University Press of Kentucky, 1985), p. 1.

10. Nadav Safran, Israel: *The Embattled Ally* (Cambridge, Mass.: Harvard University Press, 1978), pp. 332–333.

11. The term "containment" was popularized by Soviet affairs expert George Kennan, who served as minister-counselor in Moscow in 1944 and returned as ambassador to the U.S.S.R. in 1952. See George Kennan, *Memoirs, 1925–1950* (New York: Pantheon, 1967), pp. 361–367.

12. See, for example, the May 3, 1959, news release by Congressman Emanuel Celler (Celler Collection, Library of Congress, Manuscript Division, Subject File 504, "Israel—General, 1959–1960"): "Israel is the only democracy in the Middle East. The Administration must know that it can rely upon Israel and its army as its major bulwark in the Middle East."

13. See, for example, editorial *Washington Post*, February 21, 1956; John P. Roche, "Europe Fears U.S. Role in Israel Poses War Peril Involving NATO," *Washington Post*, June 17, 1970.

14. See also C.L. Sulzberger, "The Roots of Hell," *New York Times*, June 9, 1967: "Pragmatic American interests were clearly with the Arabs, who possessed vast petroleum deposits in which U.S. firms had invested fortunes."

15. Cited in J. Kraft, "The Prophet Fulbright," *Washington Post*, August 23, 1970.

16. Such an orientation was possible because of a change in the strategic global situation when the growing use of ballistic missiles reduced the necessity of foreign bases and the United States began seeking relations based on more substantial interests.

17. *Congressional Record* (hereafter CR), September 3, 1971, p. H-14867. See also Senator Henry Jackson's report in U.S., Congress, Senate, Committee on Armed Services, *The Middle East and American Security*, 91st Cong., 2nd sess., December 1970; statement by Senator Jackson, CR, March 23, 1971, pp. 53518–53519; Stephen S. Rosenfeld, "An Offensive View of Israel's Relations with U.S.," *Washington Post*, April 9, 1971.

18. In an address to the National Executive Council of the American Jewish Committee on October 28, 1973, Eugene V. Rostow argued that "the United States is supporting Israel in order to protect vital national interests of the U.S. and of its allies and friends in Europe, the Middle East and Asia." Typescript, p. 1. For a different opinion, see former Assistant Secretary of State Parker T. Hart, "The Go-Between: A Role that the U.S. Can No Longer Play," *New Middle East,* November 1972, pp. 7–10.

19. Senator Robert F. Kennedy's statement on the eve of the 1967 war, in Thomas Ronan, "Kennedy Urges Steps for Peace," *New York Times*, June 4, 1967.

20. Senator Jackson's report to the Committee on Armed Services.

21. Editorial, "Israeli Shift," *Washington Post*, October 19, 1950.

22. Editorial, "Ben-Gurion in Washington," *New York Times*, March 10, 1960.

23. Congressman Pucinsky, *CR*, April 23, 1969, p. 10139; Congressman Minish, *CR*, May 15, 1968, p. 13538; Senator Clark, ibid., p. 11541; See also a joint statement issued by several senators, *New York Times*, October 22, 1950.

24. *CR*, May 2, 1968, p. 11541. See also a joint statement issued by several senators, *New York Times*, October 22, 1950.

25. Editorial, "Israel at the Poles," *Washington Post*, August 1, 1951.

26. Editorial, "Israel's Tenth," *New York Times*, April 24, 1958.

27. Congressman Rodino, *CR*, May 11, 1970, p. 15001.

28. Senator Kefauver, *CR*, May 11, 1970, p. 14.

29. Congressman Wolff, *CR*, May 2, 1968, p. 11424.

30. See, for example, E. Morton Cutler, "The Founding of Two Nations: Israel and the United States," *Georgia Review* 8 (Summer 1954): 1–4; Abba Eban, "U.S. and Israel: Common Traditions," *American Zionist 5* (September 1953): 8–12. See also *New York Times*, May 14, 1950.

31. Congressman Morgan, *CR*, May 2, 1968, p. 11422; Congressman Farbstein, ibid., p. 11423.

32. John Chamberlain, "What Israel Has Done for the West," *Washington Post*, June 5, 1957.

33. Editorial "Israel's President," *Washington Post*, August 2, 1966.

34. Editorial "Israel's Tenth," *New York Times*, April 24, 1958.

35. John B. Orr, "Theological Perspectives on Arab-Israeli Conflict," in *The Middle East: Quest for an American Policy*, ed. Willard Berling (Albany: SUNY Press, 1973), p. 345.

36. The traditional organs of Christian political comment, *Christianity and Crisis, Christian Century, Christianity Today, Commonwealth Journal of Ecumenical Studies*, reflect the absence of a unified Christian approach. See, for example, Roger L. Shinn, "The Tragic Middle East," *Christianity and Crisis*, 29, no. 15 (September 15, 1969): 233–236.

37. Drinan, *Honor the Promise*, pp. 235–236.

38. *Weekly Compilation of Presidential Documents*, September 16, 1968, p. 1343.

39. Drinan, *Honor the Promise*, p. 3.

40. Alan R. Balboni, "A Study of the Efforts of American Zionists to Influence the Formation and Conduct of United States Foreign Policy during the Roosevelt, Truman, and Eisenhower Administrations" (Ph.D. diss., Brown University, 1973), p. 66. See also Congressman Friedel, *CR*, April 23, 1969, p. 10139.

41. *Washington Post*, June 12, 1967.

42. Senator Pearson's Statement, *CR*, November 5, 1971, p. 39583.

43. C.L. Sulzberger, "The Roots of Hell," *New York Times*, June 9, 1963: "There is [a] somewhat mystical bond that stems from Puritan ideas and Bible fundamentalism and which existed long before Zionism."

44. Eugene Borowitz describes the unique and free behavior of American Jews with regard to Israel as follows: "Instead of trying to hide their Jewishness, American Jews were now proud ... about their identity." See Eugene B. Borowitz, *A New Jewish Theology in the Making* (Philadelphia: Jewish Publication Society, 1968), p. 19. See also D. Elazar, "Building Jewish Citizenship in the Emerging Jewish Community," *Forum* 23 (Spring 1975): 8.

45. Roger Kahn, *The Passionate People: What It Means to Be a Jew in America* (New York: William Morrow, 1968), p. 52.

46. Melvin I. Urofsky, *We Are One: American Jewry and Israel* (Garden City, N.Y.: Anchor Press, 1978), p. 375.

47. Senator Herbert H. Lehman's statement before American Jewish leaders, *New York Times*, March 8, 1953.

48. See, for example, Norman Podhoretz, "Now, Instant Zionism," *New York Times Magazine,* February 3, 1974, p. 11; Arthur Hertzberg, "Israel and American Jewry," *Commentary* 44 (August 1967): 72: "The sense of belonging to a worldwide Jewish people of which Israel is the center ... seems to persist even among Jews who regard themselves as secularists or atheists."

49. Bernard Reich, *Quest for Peace: United States-Israel Relations and the Arab-Israeli Conflict* (New Brunswick, N.J.: Transaction Books, 1977), p. 369; Glick, *Triangular Connection*, p. 126.

50. Bernard Reich, *The United States and Israel: Influence in the Special Relationship* (New York: Praeger, 1984), p. 193–

51. Daniel Elazar, *Community and Polity: The Organizational Dynamics of American Jewry* (Philadelphia: Jewish Publication Society, 1976), p. 79.

52. Glick, *Triangular Connection*, p. 126.

53. Amy Stone and David Szonyi, "Jews in Congress," *Moment*, May-June 1976, pp. 31-32; Urofsky, *We Are One*, p. 72.

54. David M. Szonyi, "What Does Your Congressman Know About the Middle-East?" *Interchange 1* (February 1976): 1, 6.

55. Stone and Szonyi, "Jews in Congress," pp. 31-32.

56. Jacob Neusner, *American Judaism, Adventure in Modernity: An Anthological Essay* (New York: Ktav, 1978), pp. 3, 88; see also Congressman Farbstein's statement in *CR,* May 2, 1968, p. 11423.

57. Stephen D. Isaacs, *Jews and American Politics* (Garden City, N.Y.: Doubleday, 1971), pp. 241-245; Wolf Blitzer, *Between Washington and Jerusalem: A Reporter's Notebook* (New York: Oxford University Press, 1985), p. 133: "American Jews have risen in the political and economic structure of the country, they have begun to feel more comfortable with lobby openly."

58. Irving Speigel, "Campaigning on Israel Deplored by Jews," *New York Times,* September 2, 1972.

59. Editorial, "Israel and the Election," *New York Times,* September 2, 1972.

60. Cited in Peter Grose, *Israel in the Mind of America* (New York: Alfred A. Knopf, 1983), p. 305.

61. Bert Lockyer, chairman of the Zionist Executive, cited in W. T. Mallison, Jr., "The Legal Problems Concerning the Juridical Status and Political Activities of the Zionist Organization Jewish Agency: A Study in International and United States Law," *William and Mary Law Review,* Spring 1968, p. 563.

62. Reich, *U.S. and Israel,* p. 195. See also Orr, "Theological Perspectives," p. 345: "Israel is the answer to European Jewry's need for a haven for everyday life, but it is also an answer to Americans ... for a haven from the secular embrace of everyday life. That is to say, what is secular nationalism in Israel is piety in America."

63. Merrill Simun, *Middle East at the Brink* (Washington, D.C.: Center for International Security, 1982), p. 58; Blitzer, *Between Washington and Jerusalem,* p. 135.

64. Judy Gardner, "Israel Lobby: A Strong but Nebulous Force," *Congressional Quarterly 33* (April 30, 1975): 1872. Bookbinder, assistant director of the Office of Economic Opportunity between 1964 and 1967, was also a special assistant to Vice President Hubert H. Humphrey.

65. Bookbinder's definition of the Jewish lobby in Gardner, "Israel Lobby," p. 1873. Although there are several other national and umbrella Jewish organizations in the United States, notably the Conference of Presidents of Major American Jewish Organizations, that join together with AIPAC to form the major coordinating bodies in the lobbying efforts for Israel, AIPAC is the only officially registered domestic lobbying organization established for the purpose of influencing legislation regarding Israel and its security. Reich, *U.S. and Israel,* p. 199.

66. Statement by Morris J. Amitay, director of AIPAC, cited in Gardner, "Israel Lobby," p. 1872.

67. William J. Lanouthe, "The Many Faces of the Jewish Lobby in America," *National Journal* 19 (May 13, 1978): 748.

68. Ibid., p. 750.

69. Gardner, "Israel Lobby," p. 1872.

70. Interview in *Congressional Quarterly 33* (August 30, 1975).

71. Blitzer, *Between Washington and Jerusalem,* p. 147.

72. The term "interest group" has been defined as "any group that, on the basis of one or more shared attitudes, makes certain claims upon other groups in the society for the establishment, maintenance ... of forms of behavior that are implied by the shared attitudes," in David Truman, *The Governmental Process* (New York: Knopf, 1951), p. 33.

73. Reich, *Quest for Peace,* pp. 367-370.

74. Charles W. Yost, *The Conduct and Misconduct of Foreign Affairs* (New York: Random House, 1972), p. 41; David P. Calleo, "American Domestic Priorities and the Demands of Alliance," *Political Science Quarterly* 98 (Spring 1983): 6, 7.

75. "Israeli Lobby: Calling in the Congressional Votes," in *The Middle East: U.S. Policy, Israel, Oil and the Arabs, Congressional Quarterly,* April 1974, p. 54.

76. Cited in "The Israel Lobby: Instant Votes When Needed," *Congressional Quarterly Weekly Report* 31 (October 27, 1973): 2858. See also Seth P. Tillman, "United States Middle East Policy: Theory and Practice," *American-Arab Affairs* 4 (Spring 1983): 9-10.

77. Ray, *Future of American-Israeli Relations,* p. 32; see also Glick, *Triangular Connection,* p. 103 "It is at best an oversimplification and at worst an untrue to claim or believe that American Jew control or determine what the American government wants and does in the Middle East."

78. Reich, *Quest for Peace,* p. 372.

79. Ibid., pp. 374, 433-434; Gardner, "Israel Lobby," pp. 1873-1874; Hyman Bookbinder, "Ethnic Pressure and the Jewish Lobby: Myths and Facts," *Washington Letter,* September 1975, pp. 1-8. See also the Harris Survey articles that appeared in the *Washington Post* on June 11, July 10, and October 9, 1967; July 24, 1968; March 19, 1970, November 11 and December 23, 1973.

80. Urofsky, *We Are One,* p. 351.

81. Ibid., p. 359.

82. Podhoretz, "Now, Instant Zionism," p. 42: "The feeling was and is—that if Israel were to be annihilated, the Jews of America would also disappear."

83. Urofsky, *We Are One,* p. 351.

84. Cited in Blitzer, *Between Washington and Jerusalem,* p. 118.

85. Urofsky, *We Are One,* p. 351. See also Glick, *Triangular Connection,* p. 126: "Both Israel and the Jews of America carry . . . a shared fear of [the] repetition [of the Holocaust], and a shared determination that they must do everything in their combined power to prevent its ever happening again."

86. *New York Times,* October 24, 1956.

87. See, for example, J. Alsop, "Democrats and Jews," *Washington Post,* June 9, 1971.

88. Charles McC. Mathias, "Ethnic Groups and Foreign Policy," *Foreign Affairs* 59 (Summer 1981): 997.

Section 8

Arab Americans, Middle Eastern Americans, and U.S. Foreign Policy

It is still unclear what effect the September 11 events will have on the capacities of Arab Americans and Muslim Americans to leverage their respective positions in international relations. Arab Americans, for example, have become more visible and their views and customs given greater prominence in the American media. The op-ed piece included in this section points to steps that community itself can take to advance its foreign policy clout. But as countless commentators have reported, this community has also fallen victim to unprovoked physical attacks and verbal abuse, and accused of disloyalty. The post–September 11 dynamic underscores a troubling element of Double Diversity—the inherent utopian versus dystopian potential to provoke very powerful racialist sentiments. As we see in Section 11, the terrorist attacks have profoundly impacted all Americans, in ways which weigh upon the very definition of what it means to be a citizen, a loyal American, and to claim a legitimate, active voice in international affairs.

22

Local Politics Is Global, as Hill Turns to Armenia

STEVEN MUFSON

Rep. James E. Rogan (R-Calif.) doesn't pretend to be a foreign policy expert. A former state assemblyman and onetime deputy district attorney who made his name prosecuting rapists, gang murderers, and drug dealers, Rogan, forty-three, has traveled outside the United States only once in his lifetime. But this is an age when politics can be local and global at the same time. Thus Rogan has sided with Armenians in an eighty-five-year-old historical dispute that threatens to disrupt U.S. relations with Turkey, one of America's most staunch allies and a moderate, democratic bulwark against Islamic extremism.

Rogan's district in Southern California happens to be home to the largest concentration of Armenian Americans in the United States. Locked in a tight race for reelection, Rogan has been courting this voting block with help from House Speaker J. Dennis Hastert (R-Ill.), who agreed in August to push a resolution labeling as "genocide" the massacres of Armenians that took place under the Ottoman Empire from 1915 to 1923.

That resolution was passed by the House International Relations Committee last week and may come to a vote on the floor this week. But what began as a nod to a local constituency has turned into an international incident—and the latest example of the role Congress often plays when it seizes on one narrow facet of foreign policy.

The Turkish government, successor to the Ottoman Empire, objects to branding the killings as "genocide." Turkish President Ahmet Necdet Sezer called President Clinton last Monday to express "grave reservations" about the resolution. U.S. corporate lobbyists fear that it could endanger billions of dollars in defense contracts, and U.S. diplomats fret that Ankara might limit U.S. use of Incirlik Air Base in southern Turkey for patrolling the "no-fly" zone over northern Iraq. A letter signed by thirteen former U.S. Cabinet members and military commanders said adoption of the resolution "would deliver a severe blow to U.S. interests in the region."

The flap is a case study of the clout wielded by members of Congress who latch on to a single dimension of U.S. foreign policy with little regard to broader national interests. Often these members are motivated by a constituency, contributor, or personal passion. Such parochial interests are not new. But with the end of the Cold War, the breakdown of the congressional foreign policy establishment, and an administration that has been unable to forge a new foreign policy consensus, these lawmakers have stepped into a vacuum and acquired tremendous influence.

"The old adage that politics stops at the water's edge has long since gone by the boards," says former representative Lee H. Hamilton (D-Ind.). "Too many people place constituent interests above national interests. They don't see much difference between lobbying for highway funds and slanting foreign policy toward a particular interest group."

One former U.S. diplomat joked last week that politics still stops at the water's edge, only now it's the waters of the Bosporus.

STATESMANSHIP MISSED

A former U.S. ambassador to Saudi Arabia, Charles W. Freeman, Jr., laments what he calls "the franchising of foreign policy," with various interest groups dictating areas of policy. The American Israel Public Affairs Committee, or AIPAC, influences policy toward Israel. The Congressional Black Caucus often sways Haiti policy. Nonproliferation crusaders rule on North Korea. Farmers bend trade policy. Christian groups dominate discussion of Sudan, whose Muslim-dominated government is waging war on the largely Christian south. Cuban Americans resist any easing of sanctions on Havana.

Part of the problem is ideological. Without a Soviet foe, the foreign policy agenda has become diffuse, with congressional power now spread among committees on banking, finance, appropriations, judiciary, and the environment.

Part of the problem is institutional. Senior foreign policy specialists in Congress have departed, including senators Nancy Landon Kassebaum (R-Kan.), Robert J. Dole (R-Kan.), Sam Nunn (D-Ga.), and William S. Cohen (R-Me.). In 1999, first-term senators chaired all seven subcommittees of the Foreign Relations Committee. Many of them would have preferred other committee assignments.

Meanwhile, the Republican congressional leadership is isolationist and often uninterested in foreign policy. One exception was the effort by Senate Majority Leader Trent Lott (R-Miss.) to persuade the Clinton administration to sell to Taiwan destroyers built in a shipyard in his home state.

As a result, individuals can drive policy—even, as in Rogan's case, when they are junior lawmakers and do not sit on the foreign affairs committees. Rep. Frank Pallone Jr. (D-N.J.), whose district includes many Indian Americans, uses his position on the Commerce Committee to promote India's interests. Rep. Christopher H. Smith (R-N.J.), who was once director of the New Jersey Right to Life organization, uses his perch on the International Relations Committee to restrict funding for United Nations organizations he feels promote abortions worldwide. Rep. Ileana Ros-Lehtinen (R-Fla.), who also has a seat on International Relations, vociferously reflects the anti-Castro views of her Cuban American constituents.

"What we've lost in Congress are the statesmen," said William A. Reinsch, who has grappled with Congress as undersecretary of commerce for export administration. "People who tended to look at the bigger picture, who understood the broader range of U.S. interests and how at any given moment one would be more important than another, and who understood that presidents need flexibility."

ADROIT LOBBYING

The Armenian genocide resolution illustrates this clash of special and national interests, as well as the stakes involved.

Although the resolution is nonbinding and does not have a Senate counterpart, the International Relations Committee debated it for seven hours in two sessions before a throng of Armenian Americans, corporate lobbyists, defense contractors, human rights activists, and Turkish parliamentarians. Lines outside the hearing stretched down the hall of the Rayburn House Office Building.

"This is the most closely fought election in the House in fifty years," said a lobbyist for Turkey. "Control could hinge on the outcome of a single race. And the speaker has succumbed to the temptation to bring this resolution forward, unaware of the consequences to the country if it were to pass."

Although Hastert's support for Rogan was a catalyst, the resolution is also the product of years of political lobbying by Armenian Americans, who founded the Armenian Assembly of America as a grassroots organization in 1972. Today it has seven thousand individual and organizational members and a budget of $2.5 million. It grades members of Congress on votes concerning Armenia. On the genocide resolution, it has retained the lobbying services of former representative Susan Molinari (R-N.Y.).

Ross Vartian, executive director of the Armenian Assembly, says it has modeled itself on groups such as AIPAC, the tobacco lobby and the gun lobby. "You look at their methodologies," he said. "It's standard stuff. It's numbers and intensity and the quality of your argument."

The Armenian Assembly has also made allies with Greek Americans and human rights groups, longtime critics of Turkey. In Congress, Sen. Paul S. Sarbanes (D-Md.), a Greek American, has been a strong supporter.

The organization has chalked up a string of victories. Armenia, with just 3.4 million people, receives $102.4 million in aid from the United States. Moreover, Section 907 of the Freedom Support Act bars U.S. assistance to Azerbaijan, a strategically located oil producing country that has a long-running dispute with Armenia over the territory of Nagorno-Karabakh.

"Azerbaijan ends up becoming a very important location, and here we are with one and a half hands tied behind our backs," said one administration official.

For more than a decade, however, the Armenian Assembly has sought and failed to win passage of a genocide resolution. Few people deny that massacres took the lives of hundreds of thousands and perhaps as many as 1.5 million Armenian men, women, and children during and immediately after World War I. But some historians and Turkish officials say it resulted from forced relocations and widespread fighting in the region. They also say millions of Turks died in the same region over the same period.

Usually the Armenian Assembly has pushed its genocide resolution around April 24, the anniversary of an initial 1915 roundup of 235 Armenian intellectual and religious leaders who were later murdered. This year Armenian groups changed their timing to take advantage of the importance of Rogan's race to Republican efforts to keep control of the House.

Rogan's district boasts Armenian Boy Scout troops, churches and community groups; five Armenian newspapers; three Armenian-language cable TV stations; and more than twenty-one thousand Armenian American registered voters. Armenian organizations are trying to boost their rolls to twenty-five thousand, about 8 percent of the electorate.

Rogan has long wooed these voters. In September 1999, he made his first and only overseas trip, visiting Armenia for five days and stopping in Rome to meet the pope.

The resolution, which directs the president to use the word "genocide" in statements marking the event, "is not an issue of foreign policy," argues Rogan spokesman Jeffrey Solsby. "This is a moral issue.... It is our obligation to work with the Armenian community and their friends in Congress to make sure they are remembered and that this atrocity does not occur again on the face of the Earth."

Rogan's Democratic opponent, state Sen. Adam Schiff, does not intend to be outdone. Schiff has co-sponsored California legislation on the Armenian genocide, to prohibit Turkey from funding academic chairs in Ottoman studies, and to fund an Armenian film foundation to document the massacres. Two weeks ago, Gov. Gray Davis (D) signed legislation Schiff sponsored to remove the statute of limitations and enable Armenian families to file insurance claims for losses that occurred during the massacres.

"This is an issue I've been active on for several years," Schiff said in an interview. As for Rogan, Schiff charged, "how does he explain that in three and a half years he's never tried to bring this [genocide resolution] to a vote?"

REAL CONSEQUENCES

To many policymakers, the stakes seem higher than twenty-five thousand votes in Southern California.

In a letter to the House International Relations Committee, seven former top officials and six former military commanders—including former defense secretaries Frank Carlucci and William J. Perry and former chairman of the Joint Chiefs of Staff John Shalikashvili—urged members to consider "the real world consequences" of adopting the resolution.

The former officials noted that Turkey has helped combat terrorism, contributed to NATO forces in the Balkans, hosted U.S. and British forces enforcing the Iraqi no-fly zone and imposed sanctions on Saddam Hussein's government even though the sanctions have cost the Turkish economy billions of dollars.

American defense contractors also quietly support Turkey, which plans to spend $20 billion modernizing its armed forces over the next five years. Textron Inc. is trying to wrap up a sale of 145 attack helicopters for an estimated $4.5 billion.

A Russian diplomat said last week that tensions over the House resolution have revived Moscow's hope that Turkey might choose instead a Russian helicopter equipped with Israeli avionics.

Turkey has also deployed lobbyists, including former Republican representatives Bob Livingston (R-La.) and Gerald B. H. Solomon (R-N.Y.), each of whom gets $700,000 to represent Ankara, and former Democratic representative Stephen Solarz (D-N.Y.), who is being paid $400,000.

Turkey's parliament dispatched a delegation to attend last Tuesday's session of the International Relations Committee. One Turkish lawmaker told the committee that the massacres were "indisputable" but that there was no evidence their purpose was genocide.

Rep. Smith of New Jersey said the Turkish parliamentarian's denial "made our case" and showed the need for the resolution. Other committee members bristled at the thought that they should mute historical facts for the sake of strategic interests. One asked whether some future German government, in the name of strategic alliance, could insist that the U.S. Holocaust Memorial Museum be dismantled "brick by brick."

After the committee passed the resolution by a vote of twenty-four to eleven, Turkey announced that it would send an ambassador back to Baghdad for the first time since Iraq invaded Kuwait in 1990, but it did not link the move to the resolution. Separately, the leaders of Turkey's five major parties said they would bear in mind the resolution when Turkey's parliament decides whether to renew the U.S. mandate to use a Turkish base for flights over northern Iraq. The mandate expires December 30.

"What is most important for us is that the resolution should be stopped before it can overshadow the strategic partnership we have," Turkey's ambassador to Washington, Baki Ilkin, said in an interview. He contended that passing the resolution would be "a disservice to Armenia" because "Armenia needs Turkey more than Turkey needs Armenia." And he warned that "the fabric of our relations with the United States would inevitably be affected."

That, however, would be a matter for the next administration, and Congress, to deal with.

23

American Foreign Policy in the Middle East and Its Impact on the Identity of Arab Muslims in the United States

YVONNE YAZBECK HADDAD

Muslim identity in the United States has been influenced by the American environment in general and by individual and corporate experiences of immigrants in various American localities during the last hundred years; it is also conditioned by the distinctive self-perceptions that immigrants bring with them to the United States. This identity is clarified and molded daily by the treatment Muslims receive in their places of residence and employment,[2] in the school,[3] and by the courts.[4] It is altered and negotiated repeatedly as a result of the discrimination they experience as they deal with the images projected about them by the host society in literature,[5] the movies,[6] and the media.[7] And, in a very dramatic way, it has been shaped during the last four decades by the vagaries of American foreign policy in the Middle East and America's relations with Muslim countries throughout the world. And, in a very dramatic way, it has been shaped during the last four decades by the vagaries of American foreign policy in the Middle East and America's relations with Muslim countries throughout the world.[8]

The Muslim community in the United States comprises a variety of people from more than sixty nations who represent different linguistic, national, and racial backgrounds. They have emigrated in several waves, reflecting changes in American immigration policies as well as sociopolitical and economic upheavals overseas, and, like other immigrants, Muslims represent myriad interests and goals. Their immigration was initiated in an effort to enjoy the various benefits the United States provides: economic and social enhancement, political refuge, and religious freedom. Over the years they have shaped and reshaped their social and religious organizations to reflect the changing interests and growing concerns of the members of their community. A variety of factors impinge on the formation of their identity,[9] of which this study considers one particularly important aspect—the influence of American foreign policy in the Middle East. Although it is clear that this factor is increasingly significant in forging an American Muslim consciousness among the various ethnic and national groups that constitute the Muslim community in the United States, this study focuses on those persons who seem to be most immediately affected, the immigrants from Arab countries.

Immigration from the Arab world to the United States began around 1880 and has continued to the present. Each wave of immigrants has brought with it the distinctive identity fashioned by its generation. At the turn of the century, Muslims from Arab countries were identified as "Ottoman subjects." The colonial experience formed their identity in relation to specific nation-states; they were seen as Syrian, Lebanese, Palestinian, Jordanian, and so on. More recently, these immigrants have defined themselves first in relation to Arab nationalism, dominant in the postcolonial period, and then to the more recent phenomenon of Islamism.[10]

The immigrants also brought with them their home country's perception of the United States at the time of their emigration. Until the 1950s, America was for many both the land of opportunity, where "gold grows on trees," and a model of virtue. Its popularity was based, among other things, on President Wilson's espousal in 1919 of the right of subject peoples to self-determination. America was perceived as champion of a righteous world political order that endowed national communities with the right to independence and to free choice of their own form of government.[11]

AMERICAN FOREIGN POLICY IN THE MIDDLE EAST

The United States assumed an active role in Middle Eastern affairs some forty years ago. Vigilant against communist infiltration and anxious to fill what was considered a "vacuum" in the area, America, through the Truman Doctrine (1947), proclaimed its foreign policy to be one of containment. In assuming the leadership of the free world in the 1950s, the United States became entrenched in a cold war mentality that divided humanity into two camps, free nations and communist nations. Third world countries were increasingly seen as objects of manipulation and reduced to the level of potential puppets to be courted, bribed, pressured, cajoled, or manipulated as clients of the major powers. This mentality generally granted these nations no independent judgment, local interests, separate identity, or national pride unless it was somehow linked in subservient status to the United States or the Soviet Union. It insisted that nations must choose allegiance to one or the other of the two superpowers, doing their bidding and fulfilling their interests—a choice necessitated by the polarization of military strength.

Each succeeding U.S. administration has produced a new doctrine, which has generally been defined as consistent with previous policies and actions of the American government and as a continuing clarification of stated American values of democracy and freedom. However, such presidential doctrines have been perceived in the Middle East as increasingly inconsistent with these values, giving the impression of an erosion in America's support of them. The Muslim community has come to suspect that expedient justification of specific actions plays a major role in the development of succeeding policies.

The Truman Doctrine of 1947 promised U.S. support for free people who were resisting "attempted subjugation by armed minorities of by outside pressures." For many immigrants from the Arab world, this promise should have qualified the Palestinians for American support in resisting the foreign Jewish armed terrorist gangs such as the Haganah, Stern, and Irgun, which were trying to displace them. Consequently on May 5, 1948, when President Truman recognized the State of Israel even minutes after Ben Gurion declared its formation, Arab-Americans perceived this recognition to be without regard for the hopes or even the rights of the Arab people.[12] It shattered the image of American political values held not only by Arabs overseas but by the immigrant communities in this country.

Truman's recognition of Israel initiated forty years of American foreign policy in the Middle East and resulted in what Muslims believe to be an injustice inflicted on the Palestinian people, primarily to win an election. Truman is reported to have explained his action with the words, "I am sorry, gentleman, but I have to answer to hundreds of thousands who are anxious for the success of Zionism; I do not have hundreds of thousands of Arabs among my constituents."[13] The immigrants were also dismayed at the intense pressure the

American delegation to the United Nations applied to other countries to win support for the State of Israel.

America's recognition of Israel and its continuing support for that nation has been wrapped in ethical and ideological justifications. The language used to defend administration policy and actions in the Middle East is experienced by Arabs with intense disappointment as making subterfuge, duplicity, and hypocrisy. It is clear that since 1947 the stated American foreign policy objectives in the Middle East have continued to be governed by domestic considerations regardless of apparent conflicts with cherished American values.[14] There have been some exceptions from which Arab Muslims have drawn temporary hope. Eisenhower's willingness to apply American pressure to secure the withdrawal of Britain, France, and Israel from Sinai after the 1956 war became the hallmark by which Arabs judged the United States. "If we agree that armed attack can properly achieve the purposes of the assailant," he said on national television on February 20, 1957, "then I fear that we have turned back the clock of international order."[15] His stance was perceived as proof not only that America can influence policies in Israel, but also that, given a strong president, it can live up to its moral and ethical commitments and ideals of an international moral order regardless of partisan politics.

The war of 1967 can be seen as a watershed in Arab–American relations. It followed a period in which the Democratic administration of John Kennedy (the first American president to sell arms to Israel) promulgated the Kennedy Doctrine, which affirmed, "We will act promptly and decisively against any nation in the Middle East which attacks its neighbors." Lyndon Johnson, by sending American offensive weapons to Israel, shifted the policy of evenhandedness that Eisenhower had fostered. In the minds of many American Muslims, America's apparent willingness to abandon Eisenhower's principle that nations should not be allowed to hold on to territory acquired by war is the direct cause of present conditions in the Middle East. American acquiescence to Jewish pressure to allow Israel to retain those territories is seen increasingly as being directly linked to two persistent factors: government accountability to the Jewish lobby and Israeli intransigence.[16]

Successive American administrations since the 1967 war have placated Arabs over the rights of the Palestinians in the Occupied Territories while concurrently providing Israel with economic and military support to maintain the occupation. On December 9, 1969, Richard Nixon's secretary of state, William Rogers, stated that U.S. policy is to refuse to support changes in recognized political boundaries that are executed through conquest, other than minor ones agreed on for reasons of mutual security. "We do not support expansionism," he said. "We believe troops must be withdrawn as the resolution provides. We support Israel's security and the security of the Arab states as well. We are for a lasting peace that requires security for both."[17] In actuality, however, implementation of American foreign policy in the Middle East has deviated sharply from the Rogers Plan. The last two decades have been marked by frustration on the part of the Arabs and Muslims in America and the Middle East as they have tried to understand what is increasingly described as American "hypocrisy" in the Middle East. Nixon himself seems to have been aware of that hypocrisy when he wrote in his memoirs, "I knew that the Rogers Plan could never be implemented, but I believed it was important to let the Arab world know that the United States did not automatically dismiss its case regarding the occupied territories."[18]

The 1970s were marked by increased distress in Arab cities that precipitated attacks by the Palestinian Liberation Organization (PLO) against Israeli targets, resulting in increased anti-Arab sentiment in the United States. A scheme known as Operation Boulder placed

Arab-Americans under FBI surveillance and produced some rash statements from American leaders, including the public accusation by then Congressperson Gerald Ford that Arab-Americans were agents of Communist China.

Under the administration of Jimmy Carter the perceived double standard continued, culminating in the Camp David agreement. This accord, so highly acclaimed in the West, is perceived by Arabs as a wedge to divide the Arab world, isolate Egypt, and give Israel a free hand to rearrange the map of the Middle East.[19] Early in his tenure, President Carter in a public statement in Clinton, Massachusetts, appeared to affirm the right of the Palestinians to self-determination, saying that "There has to be a homeland provided for the Palestinian refugees who have suffered for many, many years."[20] After the Camp David agreement, however, Israel appears to have assumed the right to continue to establish Jewish settlements in the West Bank by appropriating Arab land. Carter, under strong and vocal pressure from the Israeli lobby, and to the intense disappointment of the American Muslim community, acquiesced.[21]

While other administrations were able to maintain some semblance of evenhandedness, however shallow, the Reagan administration rarely bothered to distance itself from Israel's interests.[22] Ronald Reagan came to the presidency during a period of heightened fear of "things Islamic." The fall of the Shah and the establishment of the Islamic Republic of Iran, coupled with the holding of American hostages for 444 days by Iranian students, were dramatically reported by an American press, which tended to blame Islam and Muslims for everything contrary to the interests of America. Reagan played on this fear during his administration to garner the support of the American people for his policies.[23] His tenure as president was a period of intense stress for the Muslim community in the United States.[24] Statements by members of his administration were seen as racist and derogatory to Arabs and Muslims, and the perception of an administration cast in a religious aura of Judeo-Christian righteousness set on stamping out Islam and Islamic fervor took root.

This perception was aggravated by media reports of the uncompromising militancy of the Iranian regime toward the United States. Having come to power by capitalizing on Carter's moral anguish and apparent indecision in dealing with Iran—which became a symbol of American impotence—Reagan began his presidency with what was perceived as a blatant diatribe against Islam and Muslims. In an interview with *Time* magazine in November 1980, he was quoted as saying that Muslims believe the way to heaven is to lose their lives fighting Christians and Jews. Objections of the Muslim American community to this statement went unheeded.[25] Successive statements and policies articulated during his administration did not dispel Muslim concern, but rather intensified them as the administration became increasingly embroiled in Israeli adventures in Lebanon, Iraq, Tunisia, and Iran. Toward the end of his administration, this involvement shifted Reagan's perception of the "Evil Empire" he felt heroically called upon to defeat from Communism to Islam.

It seems clear that when he assumed office, Reagan and his first Secretary of State, Alexander Haig, adopted the Israeli view of the Middle East. They announced that the cornerstone of U.S. foreign policy would shift from human rights concerns to combating terrorism. In the process, the United States cast an aura of approval over Israeli intervention and heavy-handed exploits in Lebanon. (The Israeli government had adopted the practice of referring to the Palestinians as terrorists with the result that all Israeli policies of destruction of homes, indiscriminate bombings, deportations, and abductions were legitimated as a means of response to terrorism.)

George Schultz, who succeeded Haig as secretary of state, was the strongest supporter of antiterrorism, and his most vigorous attacks on terrorist activities were usually staged before Zionist audiences. The Reagan administration appropriated the Likud policy of referring to Palestinians as terrorists rather than as people. Secretary Schultz announced that he favored the Israeli model of dealing with terrorists, leading to the establishment of the Jonathan Institute to combat terrorism with assistance from Zionist sources. The Israeli UN ambassador's book on terrorism was necessary reading for members of the administration. Even the deliberations of the members of the Reagan administration were determined by what the Israelis told them were legitimate questions to ask, answers to contemplate, and options to follow. Israel was cast as America's partner in being a target of terrorism. As a consequence, and with unfortunate ramifications for American Muslims, American pluralistic society was increasingly defined by the administration as Judeo-Christian.

The image of America as a nation that fears and hates Islam has been enhanced by a chain of events and cycle of American reactions, generally precipitated by intimate American involvement in the Israeli war in Lebanon. The following evidence can be cited:

- In 1982 massacres were committed at the refugee camps of Sabra and Shatila in which more than nine hundred Palestinian civilians were killed. The Muslim community worldwide was appalled by what one American Muslim termed "the conspiracy of silence" around these atrocities. Although it is argued that the role of the Israelis was probably limited to running interference while the Phalangists perpetrated the atrocities, the United States is held accountable not only because it was American arms, money, and political support that empowered Israelis to facilitate such actions, but more pointedly, because the United States had guaranteed the security of the civilian population of the camps against such atrocities. Furthermore, while the Kahan Commission (the 1983 Israeli High Commission) determined that several Israeli generals allowed the atrocities to take place, the American government accepted the credentials of one of these generals, General Amos Yaron, who was assigned as military attaché to the Israeli embassy despite protests of the Arab American Anti-Discrimination Committee.[26] The Canadian government, however, denied his credentials.

- In 1985 the Israeli air force bombed the PLO headquarters in Tunis, killing sixty-two people, mostly civilians. In commenting on the attack, President Reagan said that it was "justifiable." He later retracted his statement when American diplomats and the press reported international Muslim outrage and especially Tunisia's hostile reaction to America.

- When the hijacking of the cruise ship *Achille Lauro* resulted in the death of Leon Klinghoffer, an American Jew, President Reagan condemned the act repeatedly on television, in speeches, and in interviews. In his quest to punish the perpetrators, he went so far as to send the air force to intercept the plane carrying the hijackers to bring them to justice. However, when Alex Odeh, an Arab-America Christian, was killed a few days later by a bomb the FBI believes was planted by the Jewish Defense League, President Reagan was silent.[27] The alleged perpetrators escaped justice by taking refuge in a settlement in Israel. To date, the American government has not tried to extradite them, nor has any attempt been made to bring them to justice. Attacks on various mosques and Islamic institutions throughout the United States, including the bombing of the Houston mosque, were met with silence by the administration. This raised serious questions in the minds of American Muslims as to whether America in general and the American administration in particular base the value of human lives on the victim's religious or ethnic affiliation.

- Terrorist attacks on the Rome and Vienna airports on December 27, 1985, were condemned severely and repeatedly by President Reagan, especially because a six-year-old child was killed. When American air force attacked Azzizaya in Libya on April 15, 1986, Muammar Ghaddafi's adopted two-year-old daughter was killed. Secretary Schultz, asked on television what he thought America achieved by that act, responded, "We feel good about ourselves."
- The duplicity involved in what came to be known as the Irangate Affair is now well-known. Claiming to support Iraq and the security of the Arab Gulf nations, America's shipment of offensive weapons to the Khomeini regime in fact undermined that security.
- Hostility toward Palestinians is so evident in the U.S. Congress that some Arabs and Arab-Americans have begun to refer to the American legislative branch of government as "The Hostages on the Hill," a reference to their accountability to the Zionist pressure the American Israel Political Action Committee has repeatedly boasted about. It was a bill initiated by Congress that closed the PLO office in Washington.[28]
- In 1987, the Immigration and Naturalization Service initiated deportation proceedings against seven Palestinians and a Kenyan (popularly referred to as the LA 8) who were accused of minor visa violations but "treated as if they were criminal threats."[29] This attempt and the declassified FBI report that revealed the Reagan administration was renovating army camps in the South as a contingency plan for possible internment of Arabs and Iranians have increased the fear and alienation of the Muslim population.

THE DILEMMA OF THE MUSLIMS OF AMERICA

As these examples suggest, a major element in the experience of the Muslim community in the United States during the last forty years has been a rising sense of the hypocrisy of succeeding presidential administrations. Muslims feel they are living in a country that is hostile not only to their ethnic origins, but, increasingly, to Islam and Muslims in general. Their situation has been likened to being on a roller coaster on which they are forced to experience new heights of distortion and vilification.

Arab Muslims have become increasingly aware of the power of the Israeli lobby, which to them appears to have "hijacked" the American government and subverted it to Israeli interests. Other Americans who have experienced the power of the lobby share their view. To some Washington experts, it is quite evident that America is unable to execute an independent American foreign policy in the interest of the United States. Former Assistant Secretary of State Richard Murphy grumbled that American policy is controlled by Israel and its allies, whose approval is necessary before any action can be taken. Identifying Jordan as a friend in need of American assistance against outside aggression and terrorism, he acknowledged that this assistance can be provided only when we are able to persuade Israel that the security of Jordan is in Israel's interests.[30] Donald McHenry, former U.S. ambassador to the United Nations, expressed a similar opinion when he acknowledged that the Israeli lobby prevents the United States from freely pursuing its own national interests in the Middle East.[31]

American strategic goals in the Middle East are generally listed as maintaining access to Middle East oil, preserving the state of Israel, perpetuating good relations with pro-

Western Arab nations, maintaining peace and stability, and preventing Communist penetration of the area.[32] It is clear, however, that American foreign policy has had
contradictory results. Growing dissatisfaction with these policies and statements as well as
the apparent American distaste for independent Arab nationalist tendencies in the Middle
East have been perceived as being inconsistent with American ideals and values and undermining the independence of the Arab nations. They can be seen as the direct cause of
Marxist and socialist gains in the Arab world in the 1950s and the 1960s. America's uncritical support for Israel since the 1967 war and the growing disenchantment with the U.S.
administrations that have supported Israel's demands and policies with seeming disregard
for the human, political, and civil rights of the Palestinians have led to growing popular
support for radical Islamic ideologies hostile to the United States. Islamic militancy is
consistently described by its advocates as a response to Christian, Jewish, and atheistic
(Marxist) militancy.

American policies appear to be governed by a variety of considerations and principles,
which are increasingly perceived by Muslims worldwide as prejudiced against Arabs, Islam,
and Muslims. The proclaimed religious affinity between Israel and the United States based
on a heritage shared by Judaism and Christianity fails to acknowledge Islam as a moral
force in bringing about peace in the international order. Statements by American government officials, especially members of Congress, have revealed prejudice against "backward"
Palestinians who are to receive the benefits of Israel's sharing of Western enlightenment
and civilization. Israel continues to be depicted as the "underdog," a fledging nation fighting
against formidable odds. The massive infusion of American arms into Israel's arsenal is
defended as an attempt to maintain the balance of power in the region. And more recently,
some in the Department of Defense have been describing Israel as "the unsinkable aircraft
carrier," providing American troops with support facilities for possible future military
engagements in the area.

Israel's supporters[33] have increasingly presented Israel and the United States as inextricably bound together in a common destiny in the area. Israel is depicted as the incarnation
of American utopian ideas as well as the defender and maintainer of American values in
the Middle East. Arabs, however, wonder why Americans, who theoretically advocate separation of religion and state and tolerate varieties of religious expression under the umbrella
of pluralism, support Israel in its insistence on Jewish identity as a prerequisite for citizenship, denying the political and human rights of Muslims and Christians under its
occupation. Israel not only bans the return of Palestinian gentiles to their homeland, but
also restricts its Christian and Muslim citizens to specified living areas[34] and limits their
access to resources which are monopolized and confiscated by the state (such as education,
water, and land).[35]

The dilemma of Muslims living in the Arab world, Islam, and Muslims is being distorted
for political expediency by those in office. Arabs are repeatedly cast by members of the
Congress and administration as intransigent and bent on the destruction of Israel. Yet, in
many cases once out of office these same officials freely admit to the truth. For example,
in a joint article in the February 1983 *Readers Digest*, former Presidents Ford and Carter
wrote that "the Arab leaders have indicated a readiness ... to live in peace with Israel."
Deputy Secretary of State Kenneth W. Dam said on April 11, 1983: "Today Arab leaders
are talking about how—not whether—to make peace with Israel."[36] Even Syria, considered by Israel as the rejectionist state, has been acknowledged as willing to make peace.[37]
Officials who have been candid about the role of Israel in influencing U.S. policies include
former Secretary of State Cyrus Vance, former U.S. Ambassador to Syria Talcott Seelye,

and Willian Quandt, of the National Security Council in the Carter administration.[38] Arab-Americans continue to be dismayed that those in public office who have access to accurate information and could set the record straight fail to do so.

AMERICAN FOREIGN POLICY AND THE FORGING OF THE MUSLIM IDENTITY

Arab immigrants at the turn of the century experienced prejudice at the local level, and in some cases were subject to discriminatory immigration policies on the part of the U.S. government. However, because the United States at that time was not heavily involved in the Middle East, American foreign policy had little impact on their identity. With the growth of Zionism in the American Jewish community and its attendant influence on American policy, however, things changed drastically.

The reputed Zionist solicitation of funds in the 1940s with such slogans as "Pay a dollar, kill an Arab" evoked the natural anger of Arab immigrants as they sought to redress this negative propaganda. Their frustration was heightened by the awareness that Arab communities were small and scattered throughout the United States and that they lacked organizational structures to influence public policy. Their feelings of marginality were intensified as they recognized they had no input to shape American priorities, opinion, or foreign policy and insignificant access to the press to help correct the false reports being published about their heritage. In response, a few individuals became involved in gathering information, debating, and lecturing to anyone who would listen, trying to present a fair and undistorted image of the Arab people.

By the middle of the century, some efforts were being made to provide organization and structure to the Arab Islamic community in the United States. In 1952, under the leadership of the World War II veteran Abdullah Igram, they formed the Federation of Islamic Associations in the United States and Canada (FIA) to bring together more than twenty immigrant Muslim congregations to coordinate efforts to provide for the social, cultural, and religious needs of the community. Modeled on similar associations within American society, the FIA served both to provide a sanctioned context for young Muslim people to gather and to present Islam in its legitimate context as one of the several religions constituting the fabric of America. While some newspapers report Igram's appearance before several civic groups in Iowa to describe the Palestinian situation, the FIA in his time does not seem to have engaged in any significant efforts to raise Arab political consciousness.[39] What it did, however, was provide the bureaucratic structure to seek recognition of Islam as a religion by the U.S. armed services. The gesture by the Eisenhower administration to allow Muslims to declare their religion on their identification tag was seen by the Muslim community as an important step in the legitimation of Islam in the American context.

The 1956 war in the Middle East had an electrifying effect on immigrants from the Arab world. The Eisenhower administration's insistence on the withdrawal from Sinai of the occupation forces of Britain, France, and Israel and its condemnation of Israeli aggression in 1956 restored some of the community's confidence that America would live up to its stated ideals. America once again appeared eager to uphold international law and order.

The withdrawal of the tripartite forces was perceived as the final defeat of colonialist subjugation of the people of the area and confirmed Arab beliefs in America's devotion to fair play and justice. Gamal Abdul Nasser, whose position throughout the Arab world was enhanced as a result, became a hero for many Arab immigrants in the United States. They began to identify their Arab heritage with pride rather than to stress the regional or national identities with which they had previously associated themselves. Nasser's resistance to the West fostered the hope that Arabs really could withstand outside forces perceived as bent on destroying the people of the area. His "victory" inspired the new generation, who began to believe in the potential of the future, vindication of the Arab cause, and their emergence as full participants in the modern world. In short, it provided an identity of which to be proud.[40]

By the middle of the 1960s, Arab identity had become a badge of pride for Arabs overseas as well as for the recent immigrants. It superseded regional identification and became a sign of hope that unity under an ethnic and linguistic umbrella could be the key to belonging. The 1967 war and the biased reports it received in the American press heightened the immigrants' awareness of their marginality and inability to get fair coverage of the issues. It gave birth to several Arab American organizations. These included the National Association of Arab Americans, the Arab American Anti-Discrimination Committee, and the Association of Arab American University Graduates, Inc.[41] (This identity also coincided with American acceptance of the "hyphenated" ethnic identities as a consequence of the Black Power Movement in the United States.)[42]

In 1963, the Muslim Student Association (MSA) was formed on several American campuses, organized by a small group of foreign Muslim students disenchanted with Arab nationalism. The majority were from the Muslim Brotherhood, with a substantial number of Pakistanis who found Arab identity restrictive. The MSA had a very modest beginning, but its membership grew dramatically in the period after the 1967 war, and became especially strong after the war of 1973 in which the United States seemed not even to pretend to be evenhanded in its Middle East policy. It is during the early 1970s, for example, that Ismail al-Faruqi, a Palestinian immigrant noted for his writings on Arab nationalism, was converted to an Islamic identity and became one of the most important leaders of the movement and its most eloquent defender in the United States.

The fall of the Shah's regime has been a very important factor in heightening Islamic identity in the United States. The Shah was perceived as the enemy of the Arab people because of his role in providing Israel with oil. Furthermore, American foreign policy under Kissinger had empowered the Shah at Arab expense. Iran, Israel, and Turkey had been designated as the nations who were to act as surrogates to contain the Arabs, and the United States had allowed the Shah to acquire strategically located Arab islands in the Gulf. His removal from power fueled the belief that an organized Islam could provide the energy to mobilize the masses to remove corrupt rulers as well as Arab regimes perceived as lackeys of the United States and impotent before Israel.[43] This renewed hope in the power of Islam has been extremely significant in the thinking of many Muslims as they seek to define their role in the context of American society.

Several realities have been particularly important in recent years in determining Arab Muslim's sense of self-identification in America. One of these is the growth in the power of the Israeli lobby in the United States, which has had a profound impact on the American Muslim community.[44] American acquiescence in Israel's invasion of Lebanon and the inability of Arab regimes to do anything to protect Arab people from the long arm of the Israeli military has led to further erosion in the perception of America's evenhandedness. Arabs are aware that Israel is empowered by the infusion of $3 billion of U.S. taxpayers's money per year and the use of U.S. veto power in the United Nations. They see this as instrumental in Israel's ability to flout international laws and carry out its colonialist policies in the occupied territories with impunity. They believe that the 1982 invasion of Lebanon and its aftermath of deteriorating relations were possible because of the power of the Israeli lobby through its ability to influence American public opinion and the members of Congress.[45] This concern about the power of the lobby and about the apparent resulting disenfranchisement of Arab Americans has produced a variety of options for Muslim life in the United States. Some Muslims have abandoned any hope of setting the American government on an evenhanded course and have opted for a marginalized existence in terms of political involvement. Others have made the opposite choice, seeking as much input as possible in the American political process.

It is clear that American foreign policy has had a profound influence on Muslim identity and on the ways in which Muslims choose to participate in the American process. U.S. dealings in the Middle East over the last forty years appear to have alienated the majority of its Muslim citizens. The last decade has been a particularly difficult period for Muslims as they have tried to function in an atmosphere charged with hostility. As a result they have sought to frame their identity in a number of ways, their choices resulting in special sets of characteristics, perceptions, and attitudes.[46] In very general terms, they fall into two major groupings.

Some continue to see themselves first as Arab-Americans. Although Muslim, they are generally secularists who see religion as a personal matter between the individual and God. They emphasize an ethnic identity based on heritage and linguistic affinity, which includes Christians and Jews from Arab countries. Comprising the majority of Arab Muslims in America, they are of two general types. Some can be called American Muslims—that is, persons who are consciously both American citizens and members of the community of Islam and want to hold America accountable to its ideals and values. Others are what might be called the "unmosqued," nominally Muslim but finding their identity in ethnic or political organizations.

Arab Americans often have decided to reach out to other sectors of society and work together for a better America, a place where people outside the Judeo-Christian faith can feel at home, an America that will be transformed to live up to its potential and to its ideals. They include a large number of second-, third-, and fourth-generation American-born Muslims. Among them is Abdeen Jibara, president of the Arab American Anti-Discrimination Committee, whose leadership he shares with its founder, former U.S. Senator James Aburezk of Lebanese Christian background. This organization, which includes American Christians and Muslims of Arab background, has striven since the late 1970s to sensitize Americans to the presence of Arabs in their midst, to the prevalent racism against Arabs, and to the inconsistent policies of the American government in the Middle East.

Arab American Muslims take exception to the portrayal of Islam as having a different value system from the Judeo-Christian tradition of the dominant culture, as well as to the frequent accusation that it espouses violence. They are concerned that America itself is not living up to its ideals. This perception is well expressed in the following excerpts from a speech Queen Noor of Jordan delivered in the United States:

> We grow increasingly concerned about the widening gap between America's principled declarations and what we perceive as predominantly unhelpful American actions in the Middle East.... I see an America that promotes negotiations between Arabs and Israelites, but itself refuses to open a dialogue with the chosen representatives of the Palestinian people.... I see an America that tacitly recognizes the illegality of Israeli settlements in occupied Arab lands, but continues to increase its annual aid to Israel, thereby actively helping to perpetuate those very settlements.... I see an America that asks Jordan and the Palestinians and other Arabs to show moderation and boldness, while America's military aid to Israel is characterized by immodera-

tion in quantity as well as a distressing lack of resolve in applying the letter or spirit of the legal sanctions that govern the use of the weaponry it supplies.... I see an America that speaks of justice and peace in the Middle East, but helps perpetuate Israel's illegal practices by generous foreign aid.... I see an America that claims to value Arab moderation, but pursues policies of virtually unquestioning support for Israel.... I see an America that expects the Arabs to enter negotiations for peace without any preconditions, while America's own Middle East policy continues to reflect many of Israel's longstanding pre-conditions.... I believe it is time for the United States to ask itself the hard questions that others are asking throughout the Middle Eastand throughout much of the rest of the world: Why does this country that gave the world the concept of self-determination refuse to apply it to the Palestinians?[47]

A second category includes those who might be called Muslims in America, persons who identify themselves specifically as Muslims and are often alienated from American culture. They, too, fall into two general subtypes.

On the one hand, are persons whose feelings of alienation and distrust have led to a withdrawal from social and political life in America. Muslim Americans who have opted out of the political system emphasize the relationship of God to man as primary and do not try to influence the world around them. Caught in the tension between an idealized image of the home country, where brotherhood and community support abound, and the reality of the experience of an uncaring, and at times hostile, environment, these immigrants look to a reconstituted community with a coherent and harmonious purpose under the umbrella of Islam as a way of fitting into the context of American society. Theirs is an Islam that focuses all efforts in this life on the hope of recompense in the hereafter. Among these are groups such as the Tableeghi Jamaat, whose emphasis is primarily on spiritual matters.

The other kind of Muslims in America are those who see America's hostility toward Islam as a continuation of the Crusades. They are dedicated to transforming this reality. Their goal is to bring about peace and justice through the conversion of America to Islam. This identity has been appropriated by a growing number of Muslims during the last decade. In this view Islam is a unique order of life established by God for humanity, in which religion and politics must be intertwined to ensure justice and freedom. It provides special cohesiveness and support to a community going through atroubled period of perceived rejection, the object of hate and fear. Muslims who opt for this vision identify with a universal view of brotherhood that does not discriminate among human beings according to race, color, language, or national origin. The scope of this vision is universal; it seeks the conversion of the world. Separateness in the U.S. context is thus contained and experienced not as the result of rejection by the host culture but, rather, as a divine commission made necessary because America has deviated from a moral life devoted to God.

Muslims in America react to American distaste for Islam, to rampant prejudice, and to the perception of being ruled out of the system when national leaders call America a Judeo-Christian country. They affirm that Islam must prevail because America and Israel are scheming to destroy the Islamic faith and the Muslim people. Those who adhere to this identity generally despair of changing the status quo or reforming it. America, they believe, has been coopted by special interest groups, which has caused its deviation from the values and vision that previously merited God's blessing. Thus,

America needs not only salvation but also radical transformation that can restore it to its mission, to an America that lives in obedience to God and surrenders to His will, an America that dwells in Islam.

This perspective was well articulated in a sermon, delivered at the Islamic Center of Hartford, Connecticut, in the Fall of 1984, by Ibrahim Zaid al-Kilani, vice chairman of the Sharia College at the University of Jordan in Amman, then on a visit sponsored by the U.S. Information Agency.

Fellow Muslims, there is an open season on Muslims in the world. Muslims are targeted for slaughter in Lebanon, Palestine, the Philippines and India. And no one cares! You know, Americans are very sensitive people. They are compassionate; they do not like violence; they care for the oppressed. Today, we were in Boston where there was a huge demonstration against experimentation on mammals. They have Greenpeace; they put their lives on the line in order to protect the seals from being clubbed to death. They protest; they lobby; they march and they raise their voices. When it comes to the death of Muslims, they are silent, Their tax money, their airplanes, their tanks, and their bombs are employed to kill! Muslims. Ponder your fate. You as Muslims are treated as less than animals. Have you heard any outcry to stop the carriage? They dubbed west Beirut as "Muslim" Beirut and that gave the Israelis license to level it. They used fragmentation bombs, phosphorus bombs and even "vacuum" bombs to destroy Muslims. What has brought us to this fate? Why have the Christians and the Jews conspired to destroy us? Brothers and sisters, God has revealed to us in the Qur'an that our defeats are due to our faithlessness. As long as we forsake Islam, God will forsake us. As long as we pander after the friendship and approval of the West and ignore God's commandment to obedience and commitment, we shall be the target of elimination by the combined forces of the Judeo-Christian conspiracy.

What has become of the Muslims that we have now become the guinea pigs on which America tests its weapons? What has become of us as a nation that Muslim flesh is chosen for experimentation? Christian bombs are dropped by Jewish boys on Muslims in Beirut in order to determine the potency of phosphorus in burning flesh. Fragmentation bombs are exploded to dismember you, Who is there to defend you? Who will stand up for you? We have no leadership to thunder with your voice, no army to defend you. Why are we helpless? Why has God forsaken us?

The negative media portrayal of things Arab and Islamic has had its toll on the Muslim community in the United States. Muslims continue to wonder what the next chapter in their life in America will be as they struggle to define their future in an atmosphere of apparent continuing hostility toward Islam. Will the Muslims of North America survive as a vibrant religious community, able to participate fully and freely in its religious mosaic and to help define its future as a pluralistic society? The realization that the religion of Islam clearly is not appreciated by many in the United States may mean that some will feel that the only option for Muslims is a marginalized existence in this society, albeit one that is freely and consciously chosen. Whatever the alternative, American Muslims cherish the hope that their children will not so identify with Western culture that they abandon the faith, and that they will continue to espouse and live by the sacred values of their Islamic heritage.

NOTES

1. Yvonne Haddad, *A Century of Islam in America* [Occasional Paper No. 4, Islamic Affairs Program] (Washington, D.C.: The Middle East Institute, 1986).

2. Salim Khan, "A Brief History of Pakistanis in the Western United States," Master's thesis, California State University, Sacramento, 1981.

3. Ayad al-Qazzaz, "Images of the Arab in American Social Science Textbooks," and Sharon McIrvin Abu-Laban, "Stereotypes of Middle East Peoples: An Analysis of Church School Curricula," both in *Arabs in America: Myths and Realities*, ed. Baha Abu Laban and Faith Zeadey (Wilmette, 11: Medina University Press International, 1975); Samir Ahmad Jarrar, "Images of the Arabs in the United States Secondary Schools Social Studies Textbooks: A Content Analysis and Unit Development," Ph.D. Diss., Florida State University, 1976; W. Griswold et al. *The Image of Middle East in Secondary School Textbooks* (New York: Middle East Studies Association of North America, 1975); G. Perry, "Treatment of the Middle East in American High School Textbooks," *Journal of Palestine Studies* 4:3 (1975), 46–58; National Association of Arab-Americans, *Treatment of the Arab World and Islam in Washington Metropolitan Area Junior and Senior Textbooks* (Washington, D.C.: NAAA, 1980); Barbara Aswad, "Biases and Inaccuracies in Textbooks: Depictions of the Arab World," in *The Arab World and Arab-Americans: Understanding a Neglected Minority*, ed. Sameer Y. Abraham and Nabeel Abraham (Detroit: Wayne State University Center for Urban Studies, 1981).

4. Phillip K. Hitti, *The Syrians in America* (New York: Doran Press, 1924), p. 88.

5. Edward Said, *Orientalism* (New York: Pantheon, 1978); Janice Terry, "Arab Stereotypes in Popular Fiction," *Arab Perspectives*, April 1982; Janice Terry, "The Arab Israeli Conflict in Popular Literature," *American-Arab Affairs*, Fall 1982; Janice Terry, "Images of the Middle East in Contemporary Fiction," in Edmund Ghareeb, ed., *Split Vision: Portrayal of Arabs in the American Media* (Washington, D.C.: American-Arab Affairs Council, 1983), pp. 315–26.

6. "From 1984 to the present, a period of nearly two and one-half years, this writer has documented nineteen films that focus on Arab portrayals. The image of the Arab in most films parallels the image of the Jew in pre-Nazi Germany. The cinema of Nazi Germany offered viewers the Jews, as scapegoat." Jack J. Shaheen, "The Hollywood Arab: 1984–86," *Mideast Monitor*, reprinted and distributed by the Arab-American Anti-Discrimination Committee.

7. Mary C. McDavid, "Media Myths of the Middle East: The U.S. Press on the War in Lebanon," G. Neal Lendenmann, "Arab Stereotyping in Contemporary American Political Cartoons," Patricia A. Karl, "In the Middle of the Middle East: The Media and the U.S. Foreign Policy," and Jack G. Shaheen, "The Image of the Arab on American Television," all in Ghareeb, *Split Vision*.

8. Hatem I. Hussaini, "The Impact of the Arab-Israeli Conflict on Arab Communities in the United States," in *Settler Regimes in Africa and the Arab World*, ed. Ibrahim Abu-Lughod and Baha Abu Laban (Wilmette, Ill.: The Medina University Press International, 1974), pp. 201–22; Michael W. Suleiman, "The Effect of American Perceptions of Arabs on Middle East Issues," in Ghareeb, *Split Vision*.

9. Yvonne Haddad, *The Muslim Experience in the United States* (New York: Oxford University Press, forthcoming).

10. Yvonne Haddad, "Nationalist and Islamist Tendencies in Contemporary ArabAmerican Communities," in Hani Faris, ed., *Arab Nationalism and the Future of the Arab World* (Belmont Mass.: Association of Arab-American University Graduates, Inc., 1986), pp. 141–59.

11. Thus, when the General Syrian Congress in Damascus adopted a resolution expressing a desire to establish a constitutional monarchy based on democratic principles in 1919, it went on to say, "If, however, the peace conference should insist on establishing a mandate, we ask the United States of America to be the mandatory power, of a period not exceeding 20 years." Quoted in Mohammad T. Mehdi, *A Nation of Lions, Chained* (San Francisco: New World Press, 1962), p. 59.

12. Mehdi, *A Nation*, p. 35.

13. Public Papers of the Presidents of the United States, *Dwight D. Eisenhower, 1957* (Washington, D.C.: U.S. Government Printing Office, 1958), p. 151; cf. Mehdi, *A Nation, p.* 95.

14. Examples cited as evidence of this view can be gleaned from American political history concerning the region. They go back to President Roosevelt, who during the presidential campaign of 1944 sent a message to the Annual Conference of the Zionist Organization of America in which he promised that "if elected I shall help to bring about its [Israel's] realization." Shortly afterwards, as a follow-up to a meeting with King Abdul Aziz of Saudi Arabia, he wrote: "I assure you that I would take no action ... which might prove hostile to the Arab people." Seth P. Tillman, *The United States in the Middle East: Interests and Obstacles* (Bloomington: Indiana University Press, 1989), p. 15.

15. Eisenhower, Public Papers, p. 151.

16. When Henry Kissinger was unable to get any concessions from the Israelis, the Ford Administration declared a "reassessment" of its policy. More than three-fourths of the Senate objected, forcing Kissenger and Ford to withdraw their plans.

17. Quoted in A Select Chronology and Background Documents Relating to the Middle East, 2nd rev. ed., Committee on Foreign Relations, U.S. Senate, February 1957 (Washington, D.C.: U.S. Government Printing Office, 1975), pp. 249–250.

18. Richard Nixon, The Memoirs of Richard Nixon (New York: Gosset and Dunlap, 1978), p. 479.

19. See, for example, Naseer Aruri, "The United States and Israel: That Very Special Relationship," in Nasser Aruri, Fuad Moughrabi, and Joe Stork, Reagan and the Middle East (Belmont, Mass.: Association of Arab-American University Graduates, Inc., 1983), p. 1, where he writes: "What was achieved at Camp David in 1978 and in Washington the following year was at best a separate peace between Egypt and Israel-the fulfillment of a long-cherished Zionist dream."

20. Weekly Compilation of Presidential Documents, Jimmy Carter, 1977, 13, 12, March 21, 1977.

21. When Israel accelerated the establishment of settlements in the occupied territories, a matter not allowed under the Camp David agreement, the administration of incumbent Jimmy Carter supported the UN Security Council resolution calling for a halt to such illegal activities. Ambassador Charles Yost said the following: "The United States considers that the part of Jerusalem that came under the control of Israel in the June [1967] war, like other areas occupied by Israel, is occupied territory and hence subject to the provisions of international law governing the rights and obligations of an occupying power.... The occupier must maintain the occupied areas as intact and unaltered as possible, without interfering with the customary life of the area, and any changes must be necessitated by immediate needs of the occupation. I regret to say that the actions of Israel in the occupied portion of Jerusalem presents a different picture, one which gives rise to understandable concerns that the eventual disposition of East Jerusalem may be prejudiced, and the rights and activities of the population are already being affected and altered." This prompted Mayor Koch of New York City to express his fear that Carter would lose the New York State primary. Consequently, Carter carefully reiterated a U.S.-Israeli policy that included "an undivided Jerusalem." Even this apparently did not satisfy the Jewish leadership as Robert S. Strauss, his campaign manager, and Sol M. Linowitz, his special ambassador to the Middle East negotiations, informed him. It was only after he left office that Carter was candid about letting Sadat down on the issue of Jerusalem through this compromise.

22. Richard B. Strauss, a former member of the American Israel Public Affairs Committee, wrote that "U.S. Middle East Policy under President Ronald Reagan and Secretary Shultz has 'shifted so dramatically in favor of Israel' that it amounts to nothing less than a 'revolution'." Mr. Strauss quoted an unidentified former State Department official as saying, "We used to have a two-track policy. Now only Israel's interests are considered." Donald Neff, "Reagan Administration Called Most AntiArab and Pro-Israel in U.S. History," Middle East Times 4: 18 (May 18–24, 1986), 1 and 20. Neff also quotes one former U.S. diplomat who refused to be identified as saying, "There has never been an administration that has so completely supported Israel and so completely ignored America's interests in the Arab world."

23. Bob Woodward of the Washington Post broke the story that Larry Speaks, White House spokesman, misled the press with disinformation about Libya's role in international terrorism to justify the bombing of that nation.

24. The Arab-American Anti-Discrimination Committee accused the Reagan administration of "Arab-bashing" and documented a substantial rise in hate-violence directed against Arab-Americans and their institutions in the United States. "Beginning with the very night of the April 14 bombing [of Libya] a sharp increase in reports were received amounting to 28.6 percent of the annual calls. All these reports were directly attributable to the Libya bombing backlash. The total reports related to the pre- and post-Libya bombing attack amount to 38.1 percent of the overall reports received in 1986. Albert Mokhiber, 1986 ADC Annual Report on Political and Hate Violence (Washington, D.C.: ADC, April 1987), p. 25.

25. The Council of Masajid condemned the statement as a "slanderous travesty of and a fallacious distortion of the teachings of Islam." They cabled Reagan, saying "We consider this matter as transcending politics and a flagrant violation of Muslim rights as enshrined in the U.S. Constitution." "Mosque Council Condemns Reagan's Attack on Islam," Majallat al-Masajid 2: 2 (Feb. 1981), 17–18.

26. Three Palestinian women survivors of the massacre sued General Yaron under the Nuremberg Principles, drafted by the United Nations' International Law Commission, as being responsible for war crimes and crimes against humanity. The American court agreed with his defense lawyers that he could not be brought to trial because of diplomatic immunity. "Shatila Survivors Contest Yaron's Immunity Defense," ADC Times 8: 5 (July 1987), 3. See also Bob Tutt, "Lawsuit May Put Focus on Arab Plight," Houston

Chronicle, May 8, 1987, Section 1, p. 30; *ADC Newsletter* 5: 1 (June 1987), 1; *ADC Times* 8: 2 (Feb. 1987), 9.

27. Janice Terry, professor of Middle East history at Eastern Michigan University, spoke about the biased press reporting at a media panel during the Third National Convention of the Arab-American Anti-Discrimination Committee in 1987. "The terrorist murder of Arab-American Alex Odeh in October 1985 did not win the same kind of media attention as the terrorist murder of Leon Klinghoffer during the Achille Lauro incident; the terrorist attack against Palestinian students at the Hebron Islamic College in 1983 got far less press than the terrorist attack on an Istanbul synagogue in 1986. "The Media and Arab-Americans," *ADC Times* 8: 3 (April 1987), 10.

28. "ADC Out in Front to Stop Anti-PLO Bill," ADC Times 8: 5 (July 1987), 1.

29. "Mokhiber: ADC Goes to Court," ADC Newsletter 5: 1 (June 1987), 1. See also "New Hearing Due in L.A.; ADC v Meese going to Appelate Court," *ADC Times* 8: 5 (July 1987).

30. Murphy, "Current Political," p. 11.

31. Paul Findly, "The American Political Process and U.S. Middle East Policy," *American-Arab Affairs* 16 (Spring 1986), 5. Findly adds, "in respect to Middle East policy, our government is not a superpower—not even a minor power—in its capacity to fend off pressures by a lobby devoted to the interests of a foreign government" (p. 5).

32. Philip Groisser, *The United States and the Middle East* (Albany: State University of New York Press, 1982), p. 170.

33. See, for example, Nadav Safran, Israel: The Embattled Ally (Cambridge, Mass.: Harvard University Press, 1981); Groisser, The United States.

34. In 1972, the rights of the Christian inhabitants of Berem and Iqrit were confirmed by the Israeli High Court allowing them to return to their villages from which they were removed after 1948. The Israeli government destroyed all their homes. Golda Meir rejected the Court's decision because "the villagers were gentiles—Maronite and Greek (Melkite) Catholics. Their lands were now occupied by Jewish immigrants. Allowing the original residents to return and rebuild, she noted, would therefore be an erosion of Zionist values." Edwin M. Wright, *A Tale of Two Hamlets* (Cleveland: The Northeast Ohio Committee on Middle East Understanding, Inc., position paper No. 4, 1973), p. 1. See also Sabri Jiryis, *The Arabs in Israel* (New York: Monthly Review Press, 1976).

35. Not too long ago, a twenty-year Druze veteran of the Israeli Border Guards was denied the right to open a business in a village designated for Jewish residents, even though it had been an Arab village until the 1960s when it was expropriated by the state. Noam Chomsky, *The Fateful Triangle*, p. 159.

36. U.S. Department of State, Current Policy, No. 475 (April 11, 1983), 4. See also Harold H. Saunders, *The Middle East Problem in the 1980s* (Washington, D.C.: American Enterprise Institute, 1981), p. 9.

37. See Adeed Dawisha, "Comprehensive Peace in the Middle East and the Comprehension of Arab Politics," *Middle East Journal,* Winter 1983, p. 50; cf. Zeev Schiff, "Dealing With Syria," *Foreign Policy,* Summer 1984, p. 102; Robert G. Newmann, "Assad and the Future of the Middle East," *Foreign Affairs,* Winter 1983–84, p. 247.

38. Cyrus Vance, *Hard Choices: Critical Years in America's Foreign Policies* (New York: Simon and Schuster, 1983), p. 167; Talcott Seelye, *Christian Science Monitor,* April 9, 1983; William Quandt, "Reagan's Lebanon Policy," *Middle East Journal,* Spring 1984, p. 253.

39. Yvonne Y. Haddad, "The Muslim Experience in the United States," *The Link* 12: 4 (Sept.–Oct. 1979).

40. El-Kholy quotes a woman in Detroit who told a Jordanian official accompanying King Hussein in 1959 as saying, "Whenever a party is opened in the name of the Prophet, no one is particularly moved. If it is opened in the name of God, no one cares either. But the name of Gamal Abdul-Nasser electrifies the Hall." Abdo A. Elkholy, *The Arab Moslems,* p. 48. See also *An Islamic Lebanese Community,* pp. 37, 87; Said Muhammad Massoud, *I Fought as I Believed* (Montreal, 1976).

41. Edward Said, professor of English and comparative literature at Columbia University, said at the Third Annual Convention of the ADC, "It was a result of 1967 that for the first time, the Arab-American identity came to a crisis of collective selfknowledge. There would [be] no Arab-American organization had it not been for 1967. Quoted in "Said, Robinson, Conyers: Justice Knows No Borders," *ADC Time* 8: 3 (April 1987), 20.

42. Haddad, "Nationalist" pp. 141–59.

43. Yvonne Haddad, "The Impact of the Islamic Revolution in Iran on the Syrian Muslims of Montreal," in Earle Waugh Baha Abu-Laban and Regula Qureshi, eds., *The Muslim Community in North America* (Edmonton: The University of Alberta Press, 1983), pp. 165–81.

44. A visitor to the mosque in Houston will find it has a shelf with hundreds of copies of two books: the

Qur'an and They Dare Speak Out. The latter highlights some of the victories the Israeli lobby has won against any one seeking an independent policy for the United States.

45. For a report on the Hasbara Project whose supporters include key U.S. media executives who support the State of Israel and have used the American media to propagate Israeli interests, see Robert I. Freedman, "Selling Israel to America," *Mother Jones* 12: 11 (Feb./March 1987), 20ff.

46. For a typology of Muslim identity in the United States, see Yvonne Yazbeck Haddad and Adair T. Lummis, *Islamic Values in the United States* (New York: Oxford University Press, 1987), pp. 170–172.

47. Noor al-Hussein, "Peace Efforts: Principles Versus Practices," *American-Arab Affairs* 8 (Spring 1984), 2–3.

24

How to Define a Muslim American Agenda

MOHAMMED AYOOB

The terrorist attacks of September 11 must foster a fundamental rethinking about the American Muslim agenda. Muslim Americans, like other Americans, were horrified at the attacks on New York and Washington. Many are rightly distressed by the American public perception of a link between Islam and acts of terror. And many believe that this connection, and consequent religious profiling of Muslims, is the result primarily of the lack of knowledge among non-Muslim Americans of Islam.

While this is true, many American Muslims fail to recognize that the link between Islam and terrorism is also the result of extremist groups' appropriation of the Islamic idiom to legitimize their actions. Worse, such appropriations were rarely, if ever, denounced by mainstream American Muslim organizations before September 11.

Had responsible Muslim leaders in America been vigilant and forceful in condemning such extremism, the connection between terrorism and Islam would not have been so readily fixed in the public's mind. The Muslim community is now paying dearly for this failure.

Behind this silence lies a mind-set that needs to be drastically reshaped. Muslims, especially first-generation immigrants, need to define themselves as Muslim Americans with a focus on issues in this country.

Yet in many immigrant communities, political discourse is carried over from home countries and grounded in longstanding ethnic or national discontent. Political causes are labeled Islamic even when they have no connection to Islam.

This blurring of agendas increases the likelihood that Islam will be perceived as associated with foreign political causes and even terrorism. It is also divisive, because American Muslims are not homogeneous and different national and ethnic groups have different, often opposing positions on political issues. Changing the territorial status quo in Kashmir may be dear to many Pakistani Muslim hearts, but preserving the status quo is equally dear to most Indian Muslims opposed to another partition based on religion.

By the same token, some Iraqi and Arab Muslims may be agitated about the imposition of sanctions and no-fly zones on Iraq and the provision of safe havens to Kurds. However, many Kurdish Muslims would support the freeing of Kurdistan from Baghdad's yoke. Similarly, many Shiite Muslims welcome the no-fly zones that protect their compatriots in southern Iraq. Such issues have nothing to do with Islam itself and should not be portrayed as Islamic causes.

An agenda for the American Muslim community should instead focus on issues of religious and racial equality, civic and political rights, and the economic advancement of Muslims in this country.

It is worth pointing out that the concerns of African American Muslims who make up more than one-third of the Muslim population are not adequately reflected in the programs and activities of many Muslim organizations. African Americans form an important and growing constituency for Islam because of the strong commitment to social and racial equality in Islamic teachings. The future of Islam in America will be determined to a large extent by the capacity of Muslim institutions to address the needs and concerns of African American Muslims.

Unfortunately, the appropriation of the Muslim agenda by special-interest groups focused on politics abroad has made this shift late in coming. It is time that Islamic organizations in this country made efforts to separate their message from divisive foreign issues often peripheral to the community's real concerns. Those in the Muslim community who feel compelled to pursue national or ethnic agendas should be free to do so through separate national or ethnic associations and lobbies.

Muslim organizations need to think hard about how they can help correct the distorted image of Islam that many Americans, including many people of good will, now hold.

Merely blaming the misperception of others for one's plight is not enough.

25

Arab and Muslim America

A Snapshot

SHIBLEY TELHAMI

In a *New York Times* article appearing a week after the horror that befell America on September 11, a Muslim woman described her dilemma this way: "I am so used to thinking about myself as a New Yorker that it took me a few days to begin to see myself as a stranger might: a Muslim woman, an outsider, perhaps an enemy of the city. Before last week, I had thought of myself as a lawyer, a feminist, a wife, a sister, a friend, a woman on the street. Now I begin to see myself as a brown woman who bears a vague resemblance to the images of terrorists we see on television and in the newspapers. I can only imagine how much more difficult it is for men who look like Mohamed Atta or Osama bin Laden."

Excruciating moments like those the nation experienced last September test the identity of all Americans, but especially those whose identity may be caught in the middle. Many Arab and Muslim Americans lost loved ones and friends in the attacks in New York and Washington, and others had loved ones dispatched to Afghanistan as American soldiers to punish those who perpetrated the horror (Muslims are the largest minority religion in the U.S. armed forces). But many also had double fears for their own children. On the one hand, they shared the fears of all Americans about the new risks of terror; on the other, they were gripped by the haunting fear of their children being humiliated in school for who they are.

TWO PARTIALLY OVERLAPPING COMMUNITIES

There is much that's misunderstood about Arabs and Muslims in America. Although the two communities share a great deal, they differ significantly in their makeup. Most Arabs in America are not Muslim, and most Muslims are not Arabs. Most Arab Americans came from Lebanon and Syria, in several waves of immigration beginning at the outset of the twentieth century. Most Muslim Americans are African American or from South Asia. Many of the early Arab immigrants assimilated well in American society.

Arab American organizations are fond of highlighting prominent Americans of at least partial Arab descent: Ralph Nader, George Mitchell, John Sununu, Donna Shalala, Spencer Abraham, Bobby Rahal, Doug Flutie, Jacques Nasser, Paul Anka, Frank Zappa, Paula Abdul, among many others. Like other ethnic groups in America, Arabs and Muslims have produced many successful Americans whose ethnic background is merely an afterthought.

Arab Americans now number more than three million, Muslims roughly six million (though estimates range from three million to ten million). The income of Arab Americans is among the highest of any American ethnic group—second only to that of Jewish Americans. Arab Americans have become increasingly politicized over the years. According to a recent survey, proportionately more Arab Americans contribute to presidential candidates than any other ethnic group—and the groups surveyed included Asian Americans, Italian Americans, African Americans, Hispanic Americans, and Jewish Americans. Over the past decade especiallyArab American political clout has increased. Although Arab Americans were long shunned by political candidates, President Clinton became the first sitting president to speak at conferences of Arab-American organizations, and both President Clinton and President Bush have normalized ongoing consultations with Arab and Muslim American leaders. In the Fall 2000 election, presidential candidates sought the support of Arab Americans, not only for campaign contributions but also as swing voters in key states, especially Michigan. The September 11 tragedy, coming just as Arab American political clout was ascendant, has provided a real test for the community's role in American society and politics.

IMPACT OF SEPTEMBER 11

For Arab and Muslim leaders, the terrorist crisis has been like no other. It has forced them to contemplate profoundly their identity. Are they Arabs and Muslims living in America, or are they Americans with Arab and Muslim background? The answer came within hours after the terrorist attacks. Major Arab and Muslim organizations issued statements strongly condemning the attacks, refusing to allow their typical frustrations with issues of American policy in the Middle East to become linked to their rejection of the terror. Rarely have Arab and Muslim organizations in the United States been so assertive.

The enormity of the horror, the Middle Eastern background of the terrorists, and the terrorists' attempt to use religion to justify their acts have inevitably led to episodes of discrimination against Arabs and Muslims, as well as against those, such as Sikhs, who resemble them. But the support that both Arabs and Muslims received from thousands of people and organizations far outweighed the negative reaction. Arab and Muslim organizations were flooded with letters and calls of empathy from leaders and ordinary Americans, including many Jewish Americans, for most understood that at stake were the civil liberties of all Americans.

In large part, the public reaction was a product of quick decisions and statements by President Bush and members of his cabinet, members of Congress from both parties, and local political leaders. The president in particular acted quickly to make two central points that seem to have resonated with most of the public. The first was that the terrorists did not represent Islam and that Osama bin Laden must not be allowed to turn his terror into a conflict between Islam and the West. The second was that Muslim and Arab Americans are loyal Americans whose rights must be respected. Bush's early appearance at a Washington, D.C., mosque with Muslim American leaders underlined the message.

The message seems to have gotten through. Despite the fears that many Americans now associate with people of Middle Eastern background, a survey conducted in late October by Zogby International found that most Americans view the Muslim religion positively and that the vast majority of Arabs and Muslims approve of the president's handling of the crisis. (Among Arab Americans, 83 percent give President Bush a positive performance rating.) Moreover, 69 percent of Arab Americans support "an all-out war against countries which harbor or aid terrorists."

Certainly, the events of September 11 will intensify the debate within the Arab and Muslim communities in America about who they are and what their priorities should be. One thing is already clear. Although both communities have asserted their American identity as never before and although 65 percent of Arab Americans feel embarrassed because the attacks were apparently committed by people from Arab countries, their pride in their heritage has not diminished. The October survey found that 88 percent of Arab Americans are extremely proud of their heritage. So far, however, the terrorist attacks have not affected the priorities of the Arab public in America as might be expected, given the Arab American deep fear of discrimination.

Typically, Arab American organizations highlight such domestic issues as secret evidence and racial profiling and such foreign policy issues as Jerusalem, Iraq, and the Palestinian-Israeli conflict. While Arab Americans, like other minorities, are involved in all American issues and are divided as Democrats and Republicans, as groups they inevitably focus on issues about which they tend to agree. The situation is no different from that of American Jews, who are also diverse, but whose organizations largely focus on issues of common interest.

Given the fear of profiling that Arab Americans had even before September, one would expect this issue to have become central for most of them since September 11. And for many it certainly has. Arab American organizations, especially, have focused on it. But the findings of the Zogby poll among Arab Americans in October were surprising. Although 32 percent of Arab Americans reported having personally experienced discrimination in the past because of their ethnicity, and although 37 percent said they or their family members had experienced discrimination since September 11, 36 percent nevertheless supported profiling of Arab Americans, while 58 percent did not. Surprisingly, 54 percent of Arab Americans believed that law enforcement officials are justified in engaging in extra questioning and inspections of people with Middle Eastern accents or features.

Though their views on profiling have been mixed since September 11, Arab Americans have been considerably more unanimous on one subject—the need to resolve the Palestinian-Israeli dispute. Seventy-eight percent of those surveyed agreed that "a U.S. commitment to settle the Israeli-Palestinian dispute would help the president's efforts in the war against terrorism." Although most Arab Americans are Christian and mostly from Lebanon and Syria—and only a minority are Palestinians—their collective consciousness has been affected by the Palestinian issue in the same way that Arab consciousness in the Middle East has been affected. In a survey I commissioned in five Arab states (Lebanon, Syria, United Arab Emirates, Saudi Arabia, and Egypt) last spring, majorities in each country consistently ranked the Palestinian issue as "the single most important issue to them personally." The role of this issue in the collective consciousness of many Arabs and Muslims worldwide is akin to the role that Israel has come to play in contemporary Jewish identity.

Like all Americans since September 11, Arab and Muslim Americans are searching for solutions to terrorism. Like all Americans, they are also finding new meaning in aspects of their identity to which they might have given little thought a few short months ago.

Section 9

African Americans and U.S. Foreign Policy

The diversity within American ethnic groups is especially visible in the differences between the historical experiences described in Sections 5 to 9, and the social and structural niches they occupy. Unlike the small and focused U.S. Armenian community or the well-educated and more middle-class Jewish Americans, the African American community demonstrates its historical experience of entering at the bottom of American society, beginning as slave labor, then low-end wage labor. The African American community expresses the legacies of these experiences in their attitudes toward Africa and toward America. It was the great African American intellectual W.E.B. Du Bois, who wrote poignantly about the "two-ness" of being a despised minority and an American, and that the problem of the twentieth century was the problem of the "color line." Skinner reminds us that the attitudes and behaviors of African Americans in foreign policy are the products of a long, unique historical legacy dating back hundreds of years. As a former U.S. ambassador to an African country, Skinner is keenly aware of the ways in which the formulations of the meaning of race in America intersect with the definitions of the American national interest. He recognizes that while influence over the details of foreign policy is important, it is equally imperative to influence the discourse over the broader meaning of the "national interest." Walters shows how a variety of political, institutional, and economic trends converged in 2000 to create a rather new political struggle at the intersections of Double Diversity—the play of politics and ideology over legislation that would improve U.S./Africa trade relations. Although much of this volume concentrates on social structures, institutions, racial balances, class structures, and demographic features, Stanford describes the impact an individual, such as Jesse Jackson, can have on U.S. international relations. Her essay reminds us, too, that "citizen diplomacy" is very much a growing phenomenon in U.S. international relations, and must not be overlooked. This essay stirs to mind the successes of individuals such as Marcus Garvey and Jorge Mas Canosa, who used a variety of tactics, from creating new organizations and mobilizing nationalist sentiment, to reshaping how an ethnic group related to its original homeland, in order to affect foreign U.S. policy.

26

Citizen Diplomacy and Jesse Jackson

A Case Study for Influencing U.S. Foreign Policy Toward Southern Africa

KARIN L. STANFORD

INTRODUCTION

Since his dramatic bid for the presidency in 1984, impassioned attempts have been made to examine the implications of the Jesse Jackson phenomenon. One result has been a spirited discourse on Jackson's domestic agenda and his attempts to attract attention to his intended programs.[1] What has been neglected, however, is an in-depth examination of Jackson's foreign policy agenda and his international initiatives.[2] It is not implausible to agree, for example, that during the 1984 and 1988 presidential election campaigns, Jackson's international endeavors may have broadened the discussion of foreign policy in election forums to include such issues as apartheid in South Africa and Third World issues, which otherwise would have received less attention. In addition to, and perhaps even more important, is that Jackson's international activities focused attention on citizen diplomacy, a dimension of international relations that has been insufficiently studied.

This discussion is an assessment of Reverend Jesse Jackson's diplomatic effort in Southern Africa in 1986. The purpose is to link the abstract concept to an actual practice and to illuminate the motivation for his diplomatic activity, the strategy employed, and the effectiveness of the mission. The intent is to consider Jackson's international endeavor in Southern Africa using an analytical framework that is useful for understanding the global efforts of many U.S. private citizens. In addition, because Jackson was promoting the international concerns of many African Americans, it is befitting that the concerns and problems of African Americans in international politics be alluded to.

Citizen diplomacy is defined as the diplomatic efforts of private citizens in the international arena for the purposes of achieving a specific objective or accomplishing constituency goals. One of the most distinctive features of this type of diplomacy is that it operates outside of the existing national foreign policymaking system and may not be supportive of official policy.

Even though there are no universal norms with regard to citizen diplomacy, several themes remain constant. The citizen diplomat is often motivated by a strong desire to make issues, of morality salient in world affairs and is gravely concerned with peaceful conflict resolution. Citizen diplomats bypass the official foreign policymaking system usually after they have exhausted other measures for influence and when they perceive that policymakers are insensitive to their concerns. The most frequent concerns relate to issues of peace, war, hostages, business deals, disagreement with U.S. policy, feelings of nationalism, and/or ideological affinity.

Although its participants bypass official policymaking processes, similar to the U.S. democratic political system, citizen diplomacy also functions to favor established individuals. Thus, citizen diplomats are usually acclaimed in a specific field of endeavor and are frequently considered national leaders. This characteristic is perhaps the most essential for gaining the attention of policymakers and highlights the fact that those individuals who are not viewed as prominent or distinguished in a certain field of endeavor may find it very difficult to meet with high-ranking foreign officials, much less presidents of nations. Therefore, citizens without distinction in a given society are not likely to gain international infuence individually, but maybe as a member of a powerful interest group or by relegating their international activities to people-people contact. This implies that not all citizens will be able to engage in citzen diplomacy and therefore participation in the international arena for those citizens must be accessed through another point of entry.

The goals of citizen diplomats are most often to solve problems, develop preconditions for conflict resolution, facilitate agreements, maintain open communication between governments, and inform publics. When citizen diplomats enter the international arena they represent their own constituencies. Passing messages, negotiating, bargaining, conciliation, and exchanging information between U.S. officials or with foreign leaders are the methods most often used by citizen diplomats to accomplish goals and/or influence policy. The attempts to influence U.S. policy are most often directed at contacting foreign officals to persuade them to act in a fashion that will force a desired response from the U.S. government. Upon return, many citizen diplomats hold meetings with government officials to report on the mission and to offer suggestions on how to resolve the problem at hand.

The effectiveness of citizen diplomacy is dependent upon various factors, such as the prestige of the citizen diplomat, the willingness of nations to resolve disputes, the political advantages and/or vulnerability of the disputing parties involved, timeliness, and perhaps most importantly, the difficulty of the goal pursued. The least difficult task would be gathering information, while the most difficult is to change policy goals of U.S. policymakers.

Determining effectiveness is a difficult task. Concerns relate to the question of how one measures effectiveness considering that many variables can be attributed to outputs, and how does one measure influence in a situation where the individual is attempting to influence policy, when he or she has no official standing. The foremost questions are: Is influence only measured by policy change, or does having input and consideration in the decision-making process satisfy influence? Because effectiveness can have various meanings, there are grounds for arguing that if the goal was ultimately accomplished or the citizen diplomat is able to make a "meaningful" contribution to the output of a situation, then the effort should be considered effective.

THE SIGNIFICANCE OF CITIZEN DIPLOMACY

The importance of citizen diplomacy stems from a dilemma that has continually existed regarding the issue of democratic participation in foreign affairs. The quandary centers on whether or not there should be broad democratic participation in the formulation of U.S. foreign policy or should foreign policymaking be controlled by a small elite.[3] The dominant view is that on domestic issues, widespread participation is expected by the U.S. citizenry; however, on foreign policy issues the emphasis is on expertise, considering the high stakes involved, and thus usually the President and his key advisers dominate in those affairs. Hence, considering that the structure of foreign policymaking in the U.S. is concentrated in the hands of elites, and the fact that African Americans traditionally have been excluded from holding significant foreign policy positions,[4] the question one must ask is how can African Americans be influential in U.S. foreign policymaking?

In the attempt to understand African American input into U.S. foreign policy, the broader approach would be to conduct analyses of African American organizations that have endeavored to impact U.S. foreign policy. Specifically, one must seek to understand those that operate as interest group actors, such as TransAfrica (the African American Lobby for Africa and Caribbean). This is practical because such activities fit squarely into the pluralist model of democracy and are therefore sanctioned by the foreign-policymaking establishment. However, after researching the area, one will discover that often, many African Americans bypass U.S. foreign policy processes and the interest group model to engage in international activity on their own—for instance, W. E. B. Du Bois, Malcolm X, and Harry Haywood. This avenue, taken not only by many African Americans but also other private citizens, has not been fully appreciated in the mainstream literature. The failure to acknowledge the activities of these sometimes very important international actors and their accomplishments results in a deficiency of information in the field of democratic participation in foreign affairs.

The lack of appreciation for these ideas stem from conventional models of U.S. foreign policymaking that focuses on rational actors in bureaucracies. Bureaucracies themselves, and actors within the executive branch such as Graham T. Allison's Bureaucratic Model.[5] In addition, there are other models of power in foreign policymaking that usually see actors in hierarchical constructs consisting of several tiers, usually the President and key advisors; second, bureaucrats and advisers; third, political parties and interest groups; and forth, public opinion and the media.[6] Based upon this model, the active citizen would fit into the third circle of political parties and interest groups who are considered to play only a minor role in crisis situations.

However, the private citizen does engage in international activity that is different from that of interest groups or as participants in opinion surveys. In many instances, they actually bypass official avenues created for private citizens' participation and actually hold meetings with foreign officials themselves in an attempt to bring about action that will directly influence policy of the U.S. government and/or foreign entities. This type of activity often grants the private individual more force and flexibility than those participants in interest groups—not only because he or she engages in lobbying to influence political parties, congresspersons, and officials in the executive branch—but mainly because this actor places himself or herself alongside the executive branch in an attempt to negotiate resolutions.[7]

The citizen diplomacy of Jesse Jackson is one of the best cases for an examination of this subject because his efforts highlight many other significant issues. First, Jackson's efforts enabled an examination of one African American's attempt to influence U.S. foreign policy toward an area in Africa. Second, Jackson's efforts allowed for a discussion of citizen diplomacy in relation to the politics of presidential election campaigns.[8] Third, Jackson's efforts broadened the discussions of where citizen diplomacy is likely to take place. In the past, the plurality of citizen diplomacy was directed toward the Soviet Union as a reaction to the Cold War, while most other efforts have taken place during times of war. For instance, many private citizens such as Jane Fonda and Ramsey Clark traveled to Vietnam to hold talks with the Hanoi government in order to discuss issues that could help bring a resolution to that conflict. Jackson's energy was directed predominately toward economically depressed and crises-inflicted areas in the world. Thus, a more complete picture of U.S. foreign policy and its diversity emerges when examining Jackson's foreign policy agenda and his diplomatic efforts. And, finally, Jackson's efforts help to distinguish citizen diplomacy from ordinary interest group participation in international affairs and provides a line of demarcation between the actions of established interest groups, which utilize formal channels of influence, and private citizens and interest groups who bypass orthodox channels. It must be noted here that depending upon which individual case or context, Jackson may act solely as a private citizen and interchangeably as a representative of the Rainbow Coalition.[9] The purpose here, however, is not to determine when the Rainbow Coalition's concerns are the basis for his actions but to focus on the activity itself.

The Roots of Jesse Jackson's Internationalism

Perhaps the group that has received the most recognition for its efforts to influence the behavior of foreign nations on behalf of its people are members of the American Jewish community. An illustrative example of its citizen diplomacy can be found in the case of Israel Singer, the Secretary General of the World Jewish Council (ICJ), who traveled to the Soviet Union on several occasions to initiate talks with high level party officials to secure better treatment of the Jews living there.[10] Polish and Irish Americans also have received attention for their citizen diplomacy on behalf of the people in their native homelands.[11] By contrast, attempts by African Americans to influence policy toward Africa has often been perceived as futile—suggesting that the efforts of African Americans in the international arena cannot be taken seriously.[12] Because of the predominance of this perception, it is no wonder that the idea of African American citizen diplomacy has just begun to surface. If not for the international diplomacy of Jesse Jackson, the efforts of African Americans would be virtually absent in the discourse.[13]

Jackson's citizen diplomacy evolves out of a long tradition of efforts by African Americans to influence international affairs. Paradoxically, while African Americans were battling for full participation in American society, they were simultaneously repudiating the very system they were struggling to penetrate. Frequently, these denunciations occurred abroad and on occasion African American citizen diplomats sought the assistance of other nations to help them accomplish specific objectives inside the United States.

However, African Americans also sought to influence occurrences in other parts of the world. Beginning with the prominence of emigration schemes and activity throughout the nineteenth century, African Americans have initiated progressive efforts in the international arena. For instance, in 1890, George Washington Williams, a leading African American historian, traveled to the Congo on behalf of the U.S. Congress to investigate charges of Belgium brutality against the native population. In a report addressed to the King of the Belgiums, Williams presented evidence supporting the allegations that the Belgian government was engaged in the slave-trade. William's report persuaded Booker T. Washington to join the agitation for reform in the Congo. Washington became vice president of the Congo Reform Association and helped rally American public opinion against King Leopold's administration of the territory.[14]

In addition, from the nineteenth century onward, when African Americans were not even a generation out of slavery, they advocated a more humane and moral policy toward Africa and the black world. The Du Boisian Pan-African Movement was used as the structure for which to guide the discussions and address the relevant concerns. While promoting the idea that the problem of the twentieth century was "the color line," W. E. B. Du Bois posited that Pan-Africanism was the key to African liberation. Du Bois stressed that African Americans must recognize their oneness with all Africans and further postulated that the struggle for equality in the United States was tied directly to the fight for African independence. Considered the intellectual father of Pan-Africanism, Du Bois organized four meetings between 1919 and 1945. The Fifth Pan-African Congress, chaired by Du Bois, was attended by future African heads of states such as Kwame Nkrumah of Ghana and Jomo Kenyatta of Kenya, both of whom used the conference as a springboard for African independence movements.

Although the Du Boisian Pan-African Movement united black leaders intellectually, the masses of blacks on the continent and in the diaspora were not greatly inspired. It was Marcus Garvey's appeal to the masses using the slogan, "Africa for Africans at home and abroad," that ignited the masses in the African world. Through his organization, the Universal Negro Improvement Association (UNIA), founded in 1917, Garvey preached pride of self and heritage. He called for a return to Africa of which he named himself the provisional president, and the unity of all Africans under one great single body. The UNIA also advocated economic nationailsm and identified the problems of African Americans with the problems of colonialism in Africa.[15] The Garvey Movement, as it became known, eventually became the largest mass movement of African Americans. Garvey, perhaps more than anyone else, did much to energize African Americans about issues related to Africa.

The popularity and acceptance of Garvey's messages were demonstrated in 1935 when the Italian leader Mussolini launched a campaign to colonize Ethiopia. In response, African Americans boycotted Italian merchants and African American leaders made appeals to the federal government. In addition, citizen organizations were set up to aid Ethiopia and a delegation of African Americans attended the International Peace Campaign in Brussels in 1936.[16]

Notwithstanding the internal battle for equality and justice in which they were engaged, many African Americans continued to acknowledge that the question of color pervaded the formulation and execution of U.S. foreign policy and consistently fought to eliminate the inherent biases. For instance, in 1937, a year after the Italian invasion of Ethiopia, Max Yergen organized the Council on African Affairs (CAA), the first black-led group dedicated to influencing U.S. policy toward Africa. The CAA established close working relationships with African nationalists and labor leaders and lobbied the U.S. government on their behalf.[17]

The leadership of African American civil and human rights organizations also focused on African liberation. For instance, in 1969, the Congress of Racial Equality (CORE) announced its desire to assist the African liberation movements and established a chapter of its organization in Kenya after a visit by its leader Roy Innis.[18] "Martin Luther King, leader of the Southern Christian Leadership Conference (SCLC), decried the war in Vietnam and spoke out against the U.S. and Great Britain's policies that led to economic benefits for South Africa." Malcolm X, the former leading minister of the Nation of Islam, helped make the connection between the oppression of African Americans and the problems of Africa when he visited the continent in 1964. While there he spoke at a meeting of the Organization of African Unity (JOAU) and equated the racist practices of the United States with those of South Africa. Upon his return, he formed the Organization of Afro-American Unity, (OAAU) to champion the cause of Pan-Africanism throughout the world and to promote the worldwide liberation of African peoples.

As the freedom struggle within the United States progressed in the 1960s, African Americans who held more radical views began to take over the leadership of organizations, such as the Student Nonviolent Coordinating Committee (SNCC). Under the leadership of Stokley Carmichael, a delegation of SNCC leaders visited Africa. When they returned home, they instituted programs to help forge closer links between Africans and African Americans. These same activists began using colonial metaphors to explain the conditions of African-America and visited not only Africa and other nations of color but also socialist states.

African American scholars also began to place more emphasis on African Studies. This Pan-African spirit was evidenced in May 1970 at Howard University, where approximately two thousand people attended the second annual conference of the African Heritage Studies Association. With the objective of uniting all African people, faculty and students from the United States and Africa worked toward realizing that goal under the theme, "Africanism—Toward a New Definition."[20] Many of these scholars took on a more activist role in the fall of 1970 when President Richard Nixon refused to schedule a meeting with President Kenneth Kaunda of Zambia, while he was in New York to speak to the General Assembly of the U.N.[21] In addition to the foregoing, under the leadership of Dr. Elliot Skinner, former ambassador to Upper Volta, African American scholars formed an ad hoc committee of "Afro-Americans Concerned About U.S. Policy in Africa." They expressed their displeasure with U.S. policy toward Africa, and requested that, among other things, the U.S. president revise his policies and develop ones that were more meaningful.[22]

By the 1970s, African Americans began to focus more intently on the elimination of apartheid in South Africa. Pushing for sanctions against South Africa were scholars and student groups on college campuses, liberation support committees throughout the country, and African American members of Congress. Representative Charles Diggs of Detroit had become the Chair of the House Subcommittee on African Americans and an important spokesperson on African issues.[23]

Randall Robinson, a former staff aide to Diggs and a leader of student demonstrations on behalf of sanctions was instrumental in the founding of TransAfrica, the African American lobby for Africa and the Caribbean in 1978. TransAfrica mobilized the African American community to defeat efforts to lift sanctions against Rhodesia and persuaded African American leaders to support sanctions and rally voters in their districts. Through TransAfrica, and other organizations such as Africare, African Americans also addressed issues of relief for Africans who were victims of drought and famine. Many African Americans solicited resources to help famine victims and ultimately moved from relief to long-term development.

Along with its involvement in relief efforts, during the 1980s, African American political influence toward Africa was exerted primarily through the legislative branch. The Free South Africa Movement, which TransAfrica helped to establish soon after the 1984 elections, mobilized the public and lobbied Congress to pass the Comprehensive Anti-Apartheid Act of 1986.[24] In addition, the organization was in the forefront of the campaign to release the renowned South African political prisoner Nelson Mandela.[25]

Although the primary international concerns of most African Americans are mainly related to Africa, African Americans are concerned with pertinent issues in other parts of the world. International peace efforts, activism on behalf of socialism, and relief efforts to help other nations—such as Armenia, which had experienced a massive earthquake in 1990—also claimed the attention of African American organizations.[26]

In addition to the historical legacy of African American activism in the international arena, Jackson's international endeavors are also derived from other sources. First, well represented in Jackson's diplomacy are rudimentary elements of African American political culture, which is rooted in a religious ethos and a tradition of protest and direct action—that is, exemplified by his personal preoccupation with morality in foreign policy. Pan-African sentiments provide the ideological base for Reverend Jackson's focus on Africa, especially South Africa and his objective of establishing closer ties between African Americans and continental Africans. The example of international activism practiced by

Jackson's predecessor and mentor, the late Martin Luther King Jr., also bears some responsibility for influencing Jackson's diplomatic initiatives. And, finally, Jackson's boldness and audaciousness, which are necessary characteristics of citizen diplomats, are also conditions that facilitate his propensity to involve himself in international dilemmas.

CITIZEN DIPLOMACY AND THE JACKSON CAMPAIGN

It is important to discuss the Jackson Campaign because Jackson's citizen diplomacy in the 1980s took place within the context of Jackson's presidential bids. Thus, understanding the nature of the Jackson campaign, which at its core was an independent political movement within the confines of the Democratic Party, helps to comprehend how citizen diplomacy naturally arose within that setting. Primarily consisting of a constituency whose political philosophy and aspirations were considered left of center, Jackson supporters perceived that their policy positions were consistently neglected and, therefore, frequently participated in unconventional means of political expression. Although a large section of this constituency were organized into interest groups, many of them had relinquished the idea of projecting measurable influence into the U.S. two-party system.

Essentially, the Jackson campaign advocated a "new direction" for U.S. foreign policy and raised serious questions about whether or not decisions that exclude the concerns of a large segment of society are really reflective of the national interest. Therefore, Jackson attempted to address the international concerns of those he believed had been ignored. Eventually, the seemingly dormant views of Jackson's foreign affairs constituency were brought to the fore through the Jackson campaign. Indeed, the issues surrounding foreign affairs and international relations distinguished Jackson from both Republicans and moderate Democrats.

Jesse Jackson's foreign policy positions in 1984 can be attributed to several factors. First, as a consequence of the issues set forth by his ethnic constituency, Jackson focused on immigration issues and on anti-Arab sentiments that were a consequence of foreign affairs questions. He opposed the Reagan administration's policies toward the Republic of South Africa, which only served to buttress the apartheid regime against economic decline. To appease his Hispanic constituency, Jackson opposed the Simpson-Mazzoli immigration bill, refused to use the term illegal alien—referring instead to use "undocumented workers"—and denounced U.S. foreign policy in Central America.[27] In addition, many leaders of the organized peace movements in the United States played an active role in the Jackson campaign. Hence, Jackson made nuclear disarmament and a noninterventionist foreign policy a keystone to his presidential bid. He called for a 20–25 percent cut in the Pentagon budget, a bilateral nuclear freeze, and cancellation of all strategic defense initiatives including the ballistic missile defense system and antisatellite weapons. Jackson was endorsed by prominent peace organizations such as the Fellowship of Reconciliation and the Coalition for Nuclear Disarmament. Ultimately, the Jackson campaign advocated a more humanistic and moral foreign policy and in so doing offered standards of humanism and morality that contrasted with those professed, by President Reagan and mainstream Democrats.

Jackson's controversial foreign policy views also have been attributed to his numerous left-wing advisors.[28] Considered the strongest link between Jackson and the "radical left," was the Jackson campaign's chief foreign policy advisor Jack O'Dell, the former International Affairs Director for Operation Push and currently a key staff member of the Rainbow Coalition. O'Dell has a long history of involvement in the Civil Rights Movement, working alongside Martin Luther King Jr. on the staff of the Southern Christian

Leadership Conference, and is said to have a history of working on Marxist/Leninist causes and with pro-Soviet institutions.[29] Other prominent advisors on international issues included Mary Tate of the World Peace Council; attorney Ramsey Clark, noted for speaking out against numerous U.S. foreign policies and engaging in citizen diplomacy on his own; left-of-center academics and activists, such as Ronald Walters, a Ph.D. in international relations and an intellectual who has a history of activism on issues related to U.S. foreign policy and the concerns of the African American community; and Robert Borosage, former director of the progressive Institute for Policy Studies (IPS).

With regard to Jackson's personal concerns and perspective, he lacked "that knee-jerk anticommunism that has conditioned discourse on almost all aspects of U.S. foreign policy."[30] And, consistently reiterated that many of his views came from his understanding of the Third World. In fact, Jackson's approach to foreign policy was identified, with the perspective of many in the Third World and charged that the United States possessed a policy that viewed the Third World only in relation to superpower conflict. Jackson deplored this practice and advocated a new doctrine to guide U.S. relations with Africa, Latin America, Asia, and the Middle East. The Jackson Doctrine, highlighted in the 1988 campaign, was based on four principles: (1) support for international law; (2) self-determination; (3) human rights; and (4) the promotion of international economic justice and development.[31]

As a consequence of its deviation from mainstream opinion, the viability of the Jackson Campaign's foreign policy perspectives were scorned and often challenged as radical and without respectability. Accordingly, it became necessary to legitimize the Jackson approach to foreign policy by using the strategy and tactics with which many of the Jackson constituency were already familiar. Henceforth, the catalyst for Jackson's use of citizen diplomacy was similar to the motivation of his presidential election campaigns; the inability of the Jackson constituency to influence domestic and foreign policy within the confines of American pluralism.

CASE STUDY: SOUTHERN AFRICA

South Africa has always been a key issue on Jackson's international agenda. The importance is demonstrated by his mission to South Africa in 1979, to help bring international attention to the issue of apartheid in South Africa,[32] and the fact that Jackson succeeded in making the issues surrounding Southern Africa one of his most vocal initiatives during the 1984 presidential election campaign. For instance, during the debates, Jackson constantly reiterated that apartheid was an important issue to a large segment of the U.S. population and therefore should not be ignored.[33]

Motivation

The mission to Southern Africa in 1986 was conceived not only to underscore the fallacies of Reagan's policies and interest others in the issue of the Republic of South Africa's regional aggression, but also to highlight the necessity of passing the then-upcoming comprehensive sanctions bill, introduced in the House by Congressperson Ronald Dellums (D-Calif.). The mission also provided Jackson with the opportunity to sustain in the minds of U.S. voters his prowess on international issues, a crucial element for his impending 1988 presidential election bid.

The Reagan administration, which defined Southern Africa as a region in which the activity of the Soviet Union threatened vital interests, responded to the Pretoria regime's internal and regional aggression with a policy of "constructive engagement." That is, the

Reagan Administration toned down its criticism of South Africa, relaxed export restrictions, received South African military officials, moved toward normalizing nuclear cooperative relations, facilitated delay of a Namibia settlement, allowed the opening of new South African consulates in the United States, and publicly claimed South Africa to be a reliable friend and ally.[34] The purported logic of the Reagan policy was to "induce" South Africa to be cooperative in the dismantling of apartheid by offering positive incentives.

From its outset, Jackson strongly opposed Reagan's policy of constructive engagement toward South Africa, a position that he felt made the U.S. an active collaborator in maintaining the immoral apartheid system. The two other critical issues that brought into focus the differences between the Jackson and Reagan approaches in that region were Pretoria's continued illegal occupation of Namibia and U.S. refusal to recognize Angola. Namibia was important to South Africa because of its location: it borders South Africa from the north. The South African government, fearful of a government that it could not control that close to its borders, was determined to prevent the independence sought by the majority of the population in the country and thus occupied the territory and controlled it politically, socially, and economically. In addition, the Southwest African People's Organization (SWAPO), the major opponent to South Africa's occupation of Namibia, was backed miltarily and financially by the Soviet Union. So what U.S. action should be taken regarding Namibia was one issue dividing Reverend Jackson and the Reagan administration.

With regard to the second issue, the U.S. government held that the presence of thirty thousand Cuban troops in Angola and Angola's close ties with Moscow were major obstacles to establishing U.S.-Angolan diplomatic relations. Cuban troops had entered Angola in 1975 to assist the Popular Movement for the Liberation of Angola (MPLA) in its struggle for victory against two Western-supported armies. Angolan authorities contended that the Cubans were needed because of frequent South African attacks and to help combat rebels from the Total Union for the Liberation of Angola (UNITA). The South African government wanted, by contrast, the removal of the Cuban troops in order to enhance its sense of security, to weaken the MPLA and to strengthen UNITA—whom they wanted to take over governing Angola. Whereas, Jackson called for the immediate independence of Namibia and U.S. recognition of Angola, the Reagan Administration introduced the concept of linkage—that South Africa should leave Namibia only if the Cuban troops withdrew from Angola.

Hence, the overriding purpose of the mission was to help forge a comprehensive and humane U.S. policy for the Southern Africa region. The goals were related to fact-finding as well as seeking ways to persuade the United States and South Africa to modify their policies. Policy goals were to: build momentum for the passage of the 1986-Sanctions Bill; help improve relations between the United States and the Frontline States; persuade the United States to recognize Angola (only the United States and South Africa refused to recognize the legitimacy of Angola); put pressure on the United States to reverse its policy of supporting UNITA; and to forge closer relationships between Africans and African Americans.[35]

Mode

The 1986 mission was precipitated by the ongoing crisis inside the Southern region of Africa and U.S. response to the crisis. As Pretoria increased its attacks upon its neighbors, the Frontline States became more desperate to promote their cause internationally. The opportunity presented itself in 1986 at the U.N. International Seminar for Sanctions against South Africa held in Paris. Jesse Jackson, who had been invited as a major speaker, held a meeting with all the Foreign Ministers of African States in attendance. It was during that meeting that the invitation was extended by the foreign ministers to Jackson to visit Africa. The ministers believed that Jackson could popularize the notion of sanctions and bring attention to the problems in the region.[36]

In most cases of citizen diplomacy, the primary strategy is generally focused on fact-finding, negotiations, and exchanging information with foreign officials or insurgents. The attempts to influence U.S. policy are usually directed at contacting foreign officials or insurgents to persuade them to act in a fashion that would help force a desired response from the United States. The mode utilized by Jackson was not much different from the other cases, and in the Southern Africa mission, the strategy was twofold: fact-finding and negotiations. The negotiations were centered on persuading the Frontline States leaders to issue communiques stating their position on key issues and, when possible, to grant concessions that would increase the likelihood of bringing the United States to the negotiating table. The second part of the strategy was to return to the United States with information on pertinent issues in order to help increase the pressure on the United States to change its policies toward the region.

The seventeen-day, eight-nation tour to Nigeria, Congo, Angola, Botswana, Mozambique, Zambia, Tanzania, and Zimbabwe took place August 13–28, 1986. Hence, Jackson and his delegation met with the presidents of the six Frontline nations, key political leaders in Nigeria and the Congo, who were assisting financially and politically with the effort, and the leadership of African liberation organizations. The Jackson group was barred from entering South Africa.

In each of the eight countries visited, Jackson identified himself with African Blacks and pledged to support them in their fight against South Africa. He also presented himself as an advocate of an alternate U.S. foreign policy toward the region and offered himself as someone who could help African leaders take their message to the United States.

Effectiveness

In terms of effectiveness, as previously alluded to, Jackson had two sets of goals for each mission: fact-finding and policy goals. Of course, the fact-finding goals were the least difficult to achieve, because Jackson had gained the support of the host countries who helped facilitate the fact-finding endeavors. Thus, Jackson gained insight into the extent of South Africa's geoeconomic stronghold on the region and learned how Pretoria used it to reinforce its neighbors' dependence, and took that information home to the U.S. citizenry and officials. Upon his return, Jackson held a press conference at the National Press club to report on his findings. He also took the issues raised during his tour of Southern Africa to the State Department where he found the officials receptive but noncommittal.[37]

In his continuing effort to accomplish the goal of passing the Comprehensive Sanctions Bill, Jackson testified before the House Banking International Development Subcommittee. In his statement, Jackson referred to South Africa as an "octopus with tentacles" that was strangling neighboring black nations, and argued that the United States must provide economic and military aid to those countries.[38]

In August 1986 the Senate voted for a modified and limited version of the Sanctions Bill.[39] Although President Reagan vetoed it, on October 2, Congress overrode the president's veto. For the first time, official U.S. policy toward South Africa included substantive sanctions.[40]

However, with regard to the policy goals of improving relations between the United States and the Frontline States, persuading the United States to recognize Angola, and pressuring the United States to reverse its policy of supporting UNITA, Jackson was unsuccessful. First, Jackson's request for a meeting with President Reagan and Secretary of

State George Schultz was denied (although Jackson had held meetings with more junior State Department officials); and, second, Reagan declined to meet with the Frontline States leaders for scheduling reasons. Ultimately, Jackson was more effective at persuading foreign heads of states to temper their policies than he was in his efforts toward his home nation.

Despite those failures, other accomplishments of the trip were realized, including the establishment of closer relationships between African American leaders and African leaders. For instance, since 1986, Jackson and other prominent African Americans have hosted several of the African dignitaries in the United States, most notably President Kenneth Kaunda of Zambia, and Sam Nujoma (leader of SWAPO and, in 1990, president of Namibia). And now, when many African leaders travel to the United States, they "touch base" with African American leadership and often African Americans provide assistance in terms of political and economic contacts.[41]

It also is important to note that given the personal nature of citizen diplomacy, the basis for evaluating each mission should also include the nonsystemic, autonomous goals of the citizen diplomat, such as establishing personal or business relationships with international leadership. Although Jackson did not couch his efforts in terms of personal goals, it is clear that his intention was not just to be considered a key player in the international affairs of African people globally but also as a person capable of articulating the concerns of African Americans. Thus, he gained personal credibility in the region, which was evidenced by the signing of agreements by all six Frontline States leaders. In this regard, Jackson's missions and the publicity surrounding them gave him the credibility and legitimacy necessary to be perceived as someone who should be consulted on international affairs.

SUMMARY AND CONCLUSION

Overall, the motivation for the venture to Southern Africa was humanitarian and based upon concerns related to morality in U.S. policy. Primary policy interests centered on shifting U.S. policy away from assisting Pretoria to one that would ameliorate the conditions of blacks in Southern Africa. Personal interests that centered on sustaining support for Jackson's 1988 presidential bid and establishing relationships between Africans and African Americans also were strong motivating factors for diplomacy. The mode consisted mainly of factfinding and negotiations. Jackson's efforts were instrumental in providing to the United States public firsthand information on South African aggression within its borders and in the region, and was instrumental in providing additional information to Congress for decisionmaking on the 1986 Sanctions Bill.

With regard to the causes of success and failure, Jackson was able to enlist the support of African leaders generally and persuade the Frontline States leaders to sign communiques offering concessions because they were interested in establishing better relationships with U.S. policymakers. The United States, by contrast, was more interested in eliminating the Soviet presence in the region, which they believed was a prominent benefit of supporting the Pretoria regime, and therefore would not consider altering its policies.

Other issues were resolved as a result of this investigation. First, the central question of this case study was whether or not citizen diplomacy provides an alternate approach for private citizen participation in the international arena. As demonstrated by the efforts of Jesse Jackson in Southern Africa, private citizens are able to interact in a domain that has been primarily reserved for officials. Operating outside the existing national foreign-policymaking system, they travel abroad and meet with foreign officials themselves in order to achieve a specific objective or to influence policy. Thus, the value of this form of diplomacy relates to its function as an additional avenue for private citizen influence in international affairs, especially for those who have been excluded or ineffective in utilizing conventional strategies.

Engaging in citizen diplomacy is significant for other reasons. First, private citizens are able to obtain and provide U.S. citizens and governmental officials with information from foreign entities that they may not otherwise be privy to. Second, citizen diplomacy allows for the inclusion and the perspective of those individuals and groups whose ideas are considered out of the mainstream, and therefore broadens the debate in U.S. society on international questions. Third, it helps to make salient those international concerns of African Americans and other politically active ethnic groups. And, finally, although citizen diplomacy does not represent a significant challenge to the executive and legislative branches' authority over foreign affairs, the citizen diplomat can publicize within the United States and abroad the fallacies of a particular policy and can align himself or herself ideologically with a foreign nation or with international consensus which can embarrass an administration.

In certain instances, the citizen diplomat is able to achieve more laudable goals. For instance, in 1984 Jackson was able to negotiate the release of Lt. Robert Goodman, a downed-Navy pilot from Syria,[42] and in that same year he was able to negotiate the release of forty-eight prisoners from Castro in Cuba.[43] Although no such tangible accomplishments resulted from the Southern Africa venture, the importance of the mission is derived from the information provided on South African regional aggression to the American people and to Congress for additional ammunition in support of the Sanctions Bill, and for the other symbolic accomplishments alluded to. In addition, because of the publicity generated by the Jackson venture, Jackson was able to set forth his foreign policy approach and his views on Southern Africa internationally. Jackson was also able to promote the idea of an African American consensus on U.S. foreign policy, one that is promulgated by those who have been excluded from many of the benefits in American society and thus excluded from holding prominent positions in the foreign policy-making arena. Engaging in this process of citizen diplomacy can help promote and solidify the idea that there are many citizens in the U.S. democracy whose policy orientations are distinctive from U.S. foreign policy elites but, because of exclusion, they have had to create alternate mechanisms.

NOTES

1. For instance, see Sheila Collins, *The Rainbow Challenge: The Jackson Campaign and the Future of U.S. Politics* (New York: Monthly Review Press, 1986); Elizabeth O. Colton, *The Jackson Phenomenon: The Man, The Power, The Message* (New York: Doubleday, 1989); Thomas Landess and Richard Quinn, *Jesse Jackson and the Politics of Race* (Ottawa, Ill.: Jameson Books, 1985); Ernest R. House, *Jesse Jackson and the Politics of Charisma* (Boulder, Col.: Westview Press, 1988); Adolph L. Reed, Jr., *The Jesse Jackson Phenomenon* (New Haven, Conn.: Yale University Press, 1986); and Lucius J. Barker and Ronald W. Walters, Editors, *Jesse Jackson's 1984 Presidential Campaign* (Urbana: University of Illinois Press, 1989).

2. At this point, there are two scholarly articles that address Jesse Jackson in the international arena. They are Elliot P. Skinner, "The Jesse Jackson Campaign and U.S. Foreign Policy," and David A. Coolidge, Jr., "The Jesse Jackson Campaign and the Palestinian Question," both in Lorenzo Morris, ed., *The Social and Political Implications of the 1984 Jackson Presidential Campaign* (New York: Praeger Press, 1990).

3. John Spanier and Eric Uslander, *How American Foreign Policy is Made* (New York; CBS College Publishing, 1982): 5.

4. Except for a few individuals (such as General Colin Powell, the former Head of the Joint Chiefs of Staff) who have not demonstrated an interest in challenging the nature and direction of U.S. foreign policy.

5. Graham T. Allison, *Essence of Decisions: Explaining the Cuban Missile Crisis* (Boston: Little Brown Pub. Co., 1971).

6. See John Spanier and Eric Uslander, *How American Foreign Policy is Made*.

7. Note that citizen diplomacy parallels the interest group model. Both citizen diplomatic and interest group initiatives usually result from the concerns of a specific group of individuals. And both interest groups and citizen diplomats interact with other groups in society in order to gain support for their efforts. The differences are that interest groups emphasize the use of lobbies and the formation of PACs to increase their chances for policy influence, whereas citizen diplomats experience difficulty in obtaining assistance from powerful lobbies and PACs because of dominant biases in the prevailing political system. In addition, the U.S. foreign policy establishment (especially during the Reagan era) often refuses to acknowledge treat their concerns as legitimate. Hence, in order for their concerns to be addressed, an alternate approach is necessary.

8. Note that Jackson had engaged in citizen diplomacy before his mission to Southern Africa in 1986. For instance, in 1979 he traveled to the Middle East in order to help find the best possible solution to the problems between the PLO, other Arab nations, and Israel. The purpose was to return to Washington to submit his findings to the President. While there, Jackson advocated a mutual recognition policy between the PLO and Israel. In July 1979, he also traveled to South Africa at the invitation of South African church groups in order to bring attention to the problems of apartheid and U.S. complicity with that policy. No substantive changes resulted from his visit, but again, it brought attention to the problem of apartheid in the United States.

9. The Rainbow Coalition is a broad-based progressive U.S. political coalition, founded by Reverend Jesse Jackson, which cuts across the traditional dividing lines of race, religion, region, sex, and sexual orientation.

10. See Gale Warner and Michael Shuman, *Citizen Diplomacy: Pathfinders In Soviet-American Relations and How You Can Join Them* (New York: Continuum, 1987), 329, for a brief discussion of Singer's activities.

11. See Martin Weil, "Can Blacks Do For Africa What the Jews Did For Israel?" *Foreign Policy* (Summer 1974) for a discussion of the attempts by Polish and Irish U.S. citizens to influence U.S. policy toward their homelands.

12. See Martin Weil, "Can Blacks Do For Africa What the Jews Did For Israel?" 109, and Kenneth Longmeyer, "Black American Demands," *Foreign Policy* 60 (Fall 1985): 3–17.

13. For instance, in the discourse on private citizen's diplomacy, African Americans are virtually nonexistent. See Maureen R. Berman and Joseph E. Johnson, eds., *Unofficial Diplomacy* (New York: Columbia University Press, 1977); Gale Warner and Michael Shuman, *Citizen Diplomats: Pathfinders in Soviet-American Relations and How You Can Join Them* (New York: Continuum, 1987); Philip D. Stewart, "Informal Diplomacy: The Dartmouth Conference Experience" in *Private Diplomacy With The Soviet Union*, ed. David Newsom (Lanham: University Press of America, 1987); John W. McDonald and Diane Bendahmane, eds. *Conflict Resolution: Track Two Diplomacy* (Washington, D.C.: Foreign Service Institute, U.S. Department of State, 1987). However, in Curtis C. Simpson, III, "TheLogan Act of 1799: May It Rest In Peace," *California Western International Law Journal* 10 (Spring, 1980): 365–385, Jackson's efforts are briefly alluded to.

14. Edwin Dorn and Walter C. Carrington, *Africa In The Minds and Deeds of Black American Leaders* (Washington, D.C.: Joint Center for Political and Economic Studies, 1991): 10.

15. See Theodore G. Vincent, *Black Power and the Garvey Movement* (San Francisco: Ramparts Press, 1971), 13–30, for a discussion on Garvevism and the UNIA.

16. C. Eric Lincoln, "The Race Problem and International Relations," in *Racial Influences in American Foreign Policy*, ed. George W. Shepard (New York: Basic Books, Inc., 1970), 51.

17. Edwin Dorn and Walter C. Carrington, *Africa in the Minds and Deeds of Black American Leaders* 13.

18. Ibid., 210–211.

19. See Martin Luther King, Jr., *Where Do We Go From Here: Chaos or Community?* (New York: Harper & Row, 1967), 133–135, 173–174, 182–190.

20. Robert Weisbord, *Ebony Kinship* (Westport, Conn.: Greenwood Press, Inc. 1973), 208.

21. Ibid., 215.

22. Ibid., 216.

23. Edwin Dorn and Walter C. Carrington, *Africa In the Minds and Deeds of Black American Leaders* 15.

24. Comprehensive Anti-Apartheid Act. Oct. 2, 1986, 22 U.S.C. 5001–5116 (Supp. IV 1986).

25. Nelson Mandela was finally released from prison in February 1990.

26. *The Washington Post*, January 30, 1989, sec. a, p. 15, col. 1.

27. See Armando Guttierez. "The Jackson Campaign in the Hispanic Community: Problems and Prospects for a Black-Brown Coalition," in Barker and Walters, eds., *Jesse Jackson's 1984 Presidential Campaign*, 33.

28. See Harvey Klehr, *Far Left of Center: The American Radical Left Today* (New Brunswick: Transaction Books, 1985), and Arch Puddington, "Jesse Jackson, the Blacks and American Foreign Policy, *Commentary* 77 (April 1984): 19–27, especially page 26.

29. Harvey, Klehr, *Far Left of Center: The American Radical Left Today*, 172.

30. Elliot P. Skinner, "The Jesse Jackson Campaign and U.S. Foreign Policy," edited by Lorenzo Morris. *The Social and Political Implications of the 1984 Jackson Presidential Campaign* (New York: Praeger Press, 1990), 172.

31. Frank Clemente and Frank Watkins, *Keep Hope Alive: Jesse Jackson's 1988 Presidential Campaign* (Boston: South End Press, 1989), XIX.

32. Joseph Egelhot, "A 'delighted' Jackson Returns From South Africa." *Chicago Tribune*, August 3, 1979, sec. 1, p. 11, col. 3.

33. Walters, *The Issue Politics of the Jesse Jackson Campaign for President* 33. Also see Elliot Skinner. *Beyond Constructive Engagement: United States Foreign Policy Toward Africa* (New York: Paragon House Pub., 1986), ix-x, for a discussion of other presidential candidates' attempts to ignore the problem of South Africa during the debates. Also see Peter Dougnan's commentary, 237–248.

34. See Gwendolyn Carter, "United States Policies Toward South Africa and Namibia," in *Beyond Constructive Engagement*, ed. Elliot Skinner, 228–235, and TransAfrica, Washington, D.C., *United States Foreign Policy and the Black World: Proposals for a New Relationship*, Four Sets of Recommendations by Black National Organizations (May 1988), 5.

35. Ronald Walters, Ph.D., of Howard University, interview by author and Jackson Staff Memorandum July 31, 1986 on the mission to Southern Africa.

36. Interview with Ronald Walters, Ph.D., Professor of Political Science at Howard University, by author on March 5, 1992, Washington, D.C.

37. Joanne Omang, "Jackson, U.S. Aides Meet on African Summit Idea," *Washington Post*, September 10, 1986, p. A34.

38. See *Big Red News*, October 18, 1986, p. 30.

39. Comprehensive Anti-Apartheid Act. Oct. 2, 1986, 22 U.S.C. 5001–5116 (Supp. IV 1986).

40. Phyllis Johnson and David Martin, *Frontline Southern Africa: Destructive Engagement* (New York: Four Walls Eight Windows, 1988), 432.

41. Interview with Ronald Walters, Ph.D., of Howard University.

42. Ibid., 3.

43. Ibid., 1.

27

African American Perspectives on Foreign Policy

ELLIOTT P. SKINNER

African Americans must develop the mechanisms and build the institutions with which to play a larger role in the foreign policy of the United States, if this nation is to compete and prosper in the twenty-first century. When in his inaugural address on March 4, 1933, Franklin Delano Roosevelt lamented that one third of Americans were "[i]ll-fed, ill-housed, and ill-clothed," he was talking about the commonality of Americans whose livelihood had been threatened by the Great Depression. He later pledged that he was "determined to make every American citizen the subject of his country's interest and concern; and we will never regard any faithful, and law-abiding group within our borders as superfluous."[1] More than thirty years later, another president, Lyndon Baines Johnson, aware that Roosevelt's pledge had not been fulfilled, launched his "War on Poverty." He wished to draw America's attention to the need for equality among the nation's poor—this time, primarily its minorities.[2] Johnson did not "overcome" as he had vowed, because this nation's tragic foreign policy led to disaster in Southeast Asia. That one-third of the nation that suffered most when the United States squandered lives and treasure in Vietnam must help to direct a foreign policy that will protect them and the nation in the future.

That continuing travail of "one-third of the nation," if not soon addressed, could endanger the future of the United States. The reason for this urgency is that there have been fundamental changes in the structure of the world system over the past decades. Thanks in part to Roosevelt, this nation recovered from the Depression to become the arsenal of democracy during World War II. Like a giant the United States bestrode the world, and using its diplomacy and economic might, it sponsored the United Nations, the Bretton Woods Agreement, and the Marshall Plan; treated relatively benignly the Germans and Japanese; and refused to support old-fashioned colonialism, thereby contributing greatly to the world as it is now known. The one cloud on the horizon was the messianism of the Soviet Union and the beginning of the Cold War.

Starting with the tragic diplomatic and military failure in Vietnam, an event that marked the retreat of the West from Asia, there arose a nagging sense that the United States has lost its *elan vital*, and like ancient empires is on the road to decline. This doom was recently spelled out by James Laxer in his book, *Decline of the Super-Powers*, and a number of incidents appear to have created concern in America and in the world. "Over the quarter-century from 1960 to 1984, the United States fell behind its major competitors in the rate of growth in every single significant category of economic life. In the quarter-century that followed, its lead was lost, or was slipping away in the major sectors of the economy."[3] To complicate the matter, during the 1980s, the Ronald Reagan administration felt more at ease "asserting American power against a host of sinister foes—the Libyans, the Sandanistas, the Angolans, and sometimes the Soviet Union—than against America's capitalist competitors."[4]

Alvin and Heidi Toffler concluded that "the major powers of the world are vigorously pursuing master plans for survival in the new century. There is one notable exception, however."[5] What attracted their attention was not only "Project Perestroika" but Europe's "Project 1992," "Project Deng," and the activities of the Tigers or dragons of East Asia— South Korea, Singapore, and Taiwan, which with Japan make up what used to be called "Asia's Co-prosperity Sphere." The Tofflers did not mention the recently created Magrebean Arab Union, nor SADCC (Southern African Development Coordinating Council) or ECOWAS (Economic Community of West African States), nor did they stress that Gorbachev's glasnost and perestroika threaten to change the very rationale of American post–World War II politics and diplomacy. The Tofflers did mourn that:

> Americans, with good reason, are suspicious of master plans or industrial strategies but now face a world in which these are multiplying. Moreover, the absence of any American project, in turn, casts everyone else's project into high uncertainty. On the eve of the next century, outsiders increasingly see the United States as a "wild card" in the world system—a nation with immense muscle but little brain.... The 21st century has begun—everywhere but in Washington."[6]

ETHNICITY AND RACE IN THE U.S. RISE TO WORLD DOMINATION

Linked to the perception of the danger to the preeminence of the United States in the twenty-first century has been a series of statements about the possible cause for it. It has been said that the success of the United States engendered the sense of security that prevented it from modernizing its technological infrastructure. It also has been alleged that the propensity of this country's capitalists for seeking greater profits by shipping industries abroad has ruined America's ability to compete. American diplomacy also has been judged incapable of identifying or dealing with the course of tensions in the world system that even threatens the lives and safety of Americans. More serious have been statements about the weaknesses in American culture. And if the Japanese leader Yasuhiro Nakasone is to be believed, America's decline is linked to the presence within its boundaries of a racial potpourri of African Americans and Latinos, and lesser breeds.

It is truly ironic that the racial mix that now characterizes the United States, and will increasingly do so in the near future, is being given as one of the reasons for its problems. It is doubly ironic that this charge has come not from Europeans, but from the leader of a nation that has been a victim of racism—Japan. After all, it was the U.S. fear of a Japan that had defeated Russia in 1905, and thereby joined the ranks of the great imperialists, that raised the specter of the "yellow peril." Then, during 1907–1908, in complicated diplomatic maneuvers, President Theodore Roosevelt was able to persuade the Californians to stop discriminating against American-born Japanese, if Japan would accept a "gentleman's agreement" and halt the emigration of its people to the United States. That the Japanese never forgot that humiliation was demonstrated at Pearl Harbor in 1941; and, although defeated in World War II, Japan has risen, phoenix-like, from the infernos of Hiroshima and Nagasaki to challenge the world, not yet militarily, but economically and technologically.

Given the attempt of earlier generations of Americans to use diplomacy to control immigration to this country, Nakasone's brutal assertion that the United States is suffering the plight of being somewhat of a nation of mongrels leads to dealing with the question of why the United States became great and why it needs to chart a course that would ensure its future progress. The English, who finally conquered the area that became the United States, were as interested as the contemporary Japanese in building a homogeneous nation. Ignoring the Africans who had been introduced among them as bond servants and who had been transformed into slaves, the English treated as contemptible "boers" those Dutch and German farmers who arrived in their midst.

The Scot-Irish and the Irish received equally cold welcomes, and the Catholics, who, although of Western European origins, were subject to "Acts of Toleration."

In their efforts to build a new Jerusalem in America's green and fertile land, the English, like all the other Europeans in the Americas, felt that this was an impossible task without the labor of Africans. Black servants were brought to Jamestown, Virginia, in 1619, one year before the celebrated Pilgrim Fathers landed in Plymouth, Massachusetts. They proved so valuable that more than one hundred years later, in 1735, an agent of the colonists in Georgia, protesting an attempt to restrict the slave trade, declared: "In spite all Endeavors to disguise this Point, it is clear as Light itself, that Negroes are as essentially necessary to the Cultivation of Georgia, as Axes, Hoes, or any other Utensil of Agriculture."[7] Even though by this time most Africans in the British colonies were declared "slaves for life" and were increasingly being judged an unwelcome presence southern planters still needed and wanted them.

America had difficulty deciding whether to pay more for Negroes, who were held as important as axes and ploughs for their plantations, than for their more unfortunate cousins in Europe to come to this land. Adhering to the dictates of Adam Smith, Ricardo, and the early theorists of capitalism, Americans permitted market forces to dictate their own behavior and railed at the mercantilism forced upon them by a cruel homeland. The War of Independence enabled the colonists to separate from England and to build a United States of America that hopefully would avoid the broils from embattled Europe. Paradoxically, however, a nation created in liberty permitted slavery to persist and the "unwelcome" presence of Africans led to a Civil War in which many thousands of newly arrived emigrants died, not to mention some of the flowers of North and South. That war preserved the Union but left the country with a legacy of racism and discrimination that has persisted to this day.

The United States, which sent its people West to conquer the lands of the Native peoples and crossed the Pacific to fulfill its manifest destiny, continued to welcome the huddled white masses of Europe yearning to breathe free, but it soon became clear that the elite groups in the nation feared for the very character of the nation. This was perhaps inevitable, given the changing demographic profile of the country. Initially a society of Englishmen whose values impregnated the emerging nation, the United States soon became a "nation of immigrants." Whereas between 1861 and 1870, 87.7 percent of the migrants came from northwestern Europe, by the turn of the century a concentrated wave of some 70.8 percent of the migrants came from southeastern Europe. Moreover, this flood came as the United States was emerging as a world power; and at a time when liberal revolutionary movements were affecting Europe, and when racial theories asserting the superiority of Anglo-Saxon people were abroad in the land.

Concern for American values revived the antiforeign feelings of the "Know-Nothing" movement of the 1850s, raising concern for future American homogeneity and culture. In reaction, the Congress passed an immigration law in 1924 with a "national origin" quota designed to favor white Anglo-Saxon and northern European immigrants. However, this was too late to change the demography of the country and its ethnic complexity. By 1976, the bicentennial year, nearly fifty million representatives of almost all nations of the world had settled in the United States.

ETHNICITY, RACE, AND U.S. FOREIGN POLICY

Despite America's success with immigrants, the nation's leaders have always been ambivalent about the role that ethnicity and race should play in national life, especially in foreign policy. A number of the founding fathers were deeply concerned that factionalism might hurt the emerging nation. In Federalist Paper Number 10, James Madison warned against combinations of citizens who, "united and actuated by some common impulse of passion or of interest," might be adverse to the rights of other citizens, or to "the permanent and aggregated interests of the community."[8] George Washington in his farewell address cautioned that the primary allegiance of all Americans should be to the nation. He urged: "Citizens by birth or choice of a common country, that country has a right to concentrate your affections. The name of America, which belongs to you in your national capacity, must always exalt the just pride of patriotism more than any appellation derived from local discriminations."[9] Washington primarily feared the possibility of conflict because of ethnic concentrations within the United States. He felt that it was only in union that Americans could experience that "security from external danger, a less frequent interruption of their peace by foreign nations, and what is of inestimable value, they must derive from union an exemption from those broils and wars between themselves which so frequently afflict neighboring countries."[10]

President Theodore Roosevelt was particularly hostile to the attempts of ethnic groups (often referred to as "the hyphenates") to influence American foreign policy. In a speech in 1895 he inveighed against the particularisms of "the hyphenated Americans—the German-American, the Irish-American, or the Native-American."[11] He warned that unless all of these groups considered themselves "American, pure and simple" then the future of the nation would be impaired. Woodrow Wilson attributed the propensity of many American ethnic groups to seek the interests of their ancestral lands to the fact that "only part of them has come over" from the old countries.[12]

Ethnicity was viewed as an important factor in American foreign policy in the years prior to, during, and after World War II. When the United States entered World War II, the editors of influential *Fortune* magazine warned that "There is dynamite on our shores." They thought that while some immigrant European groups unqualifiedly supported the war, others somewhat reluctantly supported it, and others submitted to the war effort with traces of subversive defiance. The editors wondered whether the United States could transform this mélange into a "working model of political warfare."[13] There was apparently less question of the potential disloyalty of Japanese Americans; as noted in "Restricting in the 1990s: Opportunities and Risks for African Americans," by Walter Hill (in *From Exclusion to Inclusion*), they were systematically rounded up and incarcerated in concentration camps.

Given the contemporary unraveling of the Soviet Bloc, it is instructive to note that Polish Americans exerted a great deal of pressure on President Franklin Roosevelt during his negotiations with the Soviet Union on the projected postwar boundaries between the U.S.S.R. and Poland. They thought that the settlement at Yalta made a mockery of the Atlantic Charter, and urged representatives and senators not to ratify the agreement. When Dwight Eisenhower came to office, many citizens of central European origin wished the United States to "liberate" their ancestral lands. It is, however, generally admitted that while these groups failed in their effort "to force the government to do something it did not want to do, on occasion they have been able to sabotage steps that Washington would have liked to undertake."[14] George F. Kennan, America's brilliant Ambassador to the Soviet Union, remarked bitterly in his Memoirs that Croatian Americans "never failed to oppose any move to better American-Yugoslav relations or to take advantage of ally opportunity to make trouble between the two countries."[15] The most recent attack on the efforts of minorities in the United States to influence foreign policy was that of Senator Charles McC. Mathias Jr. of Maryland. He lamented "ethnic politics, carried as they often have been to excess, have proven harmful to the nation." Mathias updated George Washington's concern that factionalism, in this case ethnicity, can generate both unnecessary animosities among Americans and create among them illusions of common interests with outsiders, where in fact none exist. He expressed alarm at the attempts of U.S. ethnic groups to put pressure on both the domestic and foreign policymaking institutions of the United States to adopt measures in favor of their lands of origin. This included: Afro-Americans lobbying on behalf of Africa, Caribbean people on behalf of the people of the Caribbean basis; Greeks lobbying both the president and Congress against granting arms to Turkey, a NATO ally; Jewish groups promoting the cause of Israel; Mexican Americans and Italian Americans supporting immigration policies to benefit the areas from which their ancestors came; and Polish Americans and some central and northeastern Europeans attempting to enlist the aid of the United States against Soviet activities and presence in their ancestral homes. The Senator did not suggest that the ethnic advocacy of Americans was unpatriotic. He did stress, however, that the administration's "resistance to the pressures of a particular group in itself signals neither a sellout nor even a lack of sympathy with a foreign country or case, but rather a sincere conviction about the national interest of the United States."[16]

Senator Mathias's concern that racial and ethnic advocacy on behalf of their ancestral lands might not be in the national interest should be examined theoretically and practically. Some scholars believe that it is true that ethnicity has played an important role in United States foreign policy, but there is less agreement about the effectiveness of it. Nathan Glazer and Daniel Moynihan believe that "without too much exaggeration it could be stated that the immigration process is the single most important determinant of American foreign policy." These two scholars admitted that United States foreign policy "responds to other things as well, but probably first of all to the primal facts of ethnicity."[17] But has this been as detrimental to the United States, as some politicians have insisted?

Gabriel Almond has argued that the attempts of ethnic and linguistic groups to influence U.S. foreign policy have historically been "mainly directed toward traditional national aims such as the preservation or return of national territory, the achievement of national independence, or the protection of minority ethnic or religious groups in foreign countries from persecution by the dominant groups."[18] This being the case, Almond concluded that the attempts of U.S. minorities to raise questions about U.S. foreign policy are not really a threat to the national interest. It might only be a threat to those people and groups who resent any challenge to their definition of what the national interest ought to be.

EUROCENTRICITY AND THE PROBLEMS OF THE MODERN WORLD

The problem with the question of what is in the national interest is difficult to define and changes over time. Historically, the answer for the query about the national interest has been, "What the public or the electorate wants." As Charles Evan Hughes once remarked, "Public opinion in a democracy wields the scepter;" and Abraham Lincoln declared, "With Public sentiment on its side, everything succeeds; with public sentiment against it, nothing succeeds."[19] The problem, of course, is that public opinion is often awkward to describe, elusive to define, difficult to measure, and impossible to see, even though it may be felt. A far greater conundrum for our country is that, although equality is a basic political tenet, this always has been affected by the reality of socioeconomic ranking and stratification within the society. The White Anglo-Saxon Protestants (WASPs) have always believed that they have a better sense of what is in the national interest than do others among their fellow citizens.

So natural do the biases of the dominant American group appear that people do not often recognize their role in forming U.S. foreign policy and in determining what is in the national interest. For example, it has been remarked that the American Aid-to-Britain movement during the early stages of World War II was initiated not because Germany posed a threat to the United States but "simply because the vast masses of the dominant old-line American strain reacted instantly and passionately to England's sudden and extreme danger. England, the home of Magna Carta, of Shakespeare and of Milton and Keats and Shelley, of the King James version of the Bible; their imperishable home."[20] The special relationship of "old" Americans to England was no more clearly expressed than in February 1914, when New Hampshire Governor Robert O. Blood, an old-stock Yankee, presented the newly appointed U.S. ambassador to the Court of St. James to the state legislature as "the man who is going over to represent us in our fatherland." Seven members of the legislature, either conscious of their alien background, of the uproar caused by the activities of the German Americans, or simply because they were "American-firsters," protested that "England was not our fatherland," that "we Americans cannot have two fatherlands." But the governor offered no correction. He probably considered his detractors to be not only boors but "anti-American" to boot.[21]

If Vietnam and other recent U.S. foreign policy initiatives suggest that those responsible for our foreign policy were not the brightest and best, it should be clear that these people are inadequate to deal with the more complex foreign policy issues of the twenty-first century. Roger Morris called attention to the danger posed to the United States by having its foreign policy under the control of "a small, ingrown elite of men clustered in New York and Washington." He writes that these men "awaited the call from the White House to determine America's role in the world, or to judge the fitness of one of their colleagues who would. The call usually came."[22] Schooled in selected private academies and colleges and later employed in prestigious old law firms, major banks, corporations, and foundations, these people, usually white males, have generally been considered to be among the best and the brightest. Yet their position in the U.S. social hierarchy has frequently made them oblivious to, or contemptuous of, the views of other Americans and of most of the country. They also have been largely contemptuous of Congress and they believe that the general American public knows, or needs to know, little about foreign policy.

The rapid changes taking place in the global system make it dangerous to leave foreign policy formulation and execution to the present actors. It is clear that many members of this establishment seldom recognize the role of institutionalized and habitual interactions— and often unarticulated ideologies—in the making of foreign policy. They remain largely unaware of the established patterns of nondisclosure and noninteraction that support largely unconscious and unarticulated patterns of interaction, custom, and manners. They are unable to make new decisions that are adaptable to a rapidly changing world in which past notions are clearly inadequate for our nation's future.[23]

African Americans Can Strengthen U.S. Foreign Policy

African Americans and other racial/linguistic minorities who will compose one-third of the nation in the year 2000 can introduce new dimensions in the formulating and execution of U.S. foreign policy. By scrutinizing and raising questions about whether certain decisions are really in the national interest, this often-excluded one-third of the nation can raise the nation's level of consciousness—and force the establishment to articulate the basis of its judgment before actions are taken that could jeopardize the nation's interest. It is surprising to note that when challenged, those responsible for our foreign policy often claim "privileged information," "gut-feelings," and "superior experience" as rationalizations for being unable to explain their positions. Often not sharing these unarticulable or plain wrong sentiments, African Americans and others like them, can see the negative implications of U.S. foreign policy in ways that the established practitioners do not. Thus, simply by raising questions about U.S. foreign policy, African Americans can force a reexamination of it. In many cases, racial/linguistic minorities are better informed about conditions in many parts of the world, including their ancestral lands, than the majority of Americans. In the case of African Americans, it is unfortunate that until recently most Americans have either ignored or challenged their interest in U.S. foreign policy. Even the centuries-long interests of blacks in Africa were generally overlooked by most white Americans. Thomas Bailey, writing in *Man in the Street*—a criticism of the attempts of minority groups to shape American foreign relations—declared quite openly: "No mention has been made of the most numerous hyphenate group of all, the Afro-Americans, who constitute about one-tenth of our population. They are racial hyphenates rather than national hyphenates, for they have since lost any foreign nationality."[24]

Bailey did note that when Benito Mussolini attacked Ethiopia in 1935, some American blacks reacted; Hubert Fauntleroy Julian ("Harlem's Black Eagle") went to fight in Ethiopia. But in Bailey's view, Julian "was an outstanding exception." He asserted that as far as the Ethiopian war was concerned, "the sympathies of the American Negroes, in so far as they have any, were with their colored brethren."[25] Bailey was clearly convinced that blacks could have no possible interest in U.S. foreign policy. Their interest in the Ethiopian war was based not on the philosophically sophisticated notion of nationality, but on the more primordial sentiment of race.

Bailey is correct in suggesting that race is more primordial than the notion of nationality because this statement does reveal why African Americans have long been prevented from participating fully in American life, including its foreign policy. A bloody civil war freed the slaves but failed to transform them into people with full civil rights. After more than a century of protests and striving, the descendants of the Africans are still struggling to achieve full civil and economic equality with other Americans. And while it seemed—and still seems—quixotic to most white Americans (and even to some blacks) that Afro-Americans would seek to help anyone, including the Africans, many African American leaders have always realized that their fate was linked to those below the global color line, and that they had better involve themselves in foreign policy. Bailey rightly observed: "To most Americans, God is Nordic, and the black and yellow do not fit into our color scheme."[26] African Americans have to help destroy this notion if they would have equality in this land.

The dramatic event that took place on Thanksgiving Eve 1984, when prominent black Americans (a congressman, a member of the Commission on Civil Rights, and the leader of a black lobby known as TransAfrica) were arrested for sitting-in at the South African embassy in Washington, D.C., was a hallmark in the long and often ignored attempt of African Americans to influence U.S. policy, to the benefit of the nation and the world. These men and women decided to escalate black protest against South Africa's official policy of apartheid and the Reagan administration's policy of "constructive engagement," which was having detrimental effects in South Africa, in the rest of Africa, and in the world. They were determined to compel the United States to accept the almost worldwide consensus that it should cooperate with the rest of humanity in pressuring South Africa to abolish apartheid—a practice deemed repugnant to all civilized people.[27]

Despite increasing riots and civil disobedience in South Africa, the demonstrations and arrests of African Americans and their allies who created the Free South Africa Movement, the movement on university campuses and state and local institutions to secure divestment in companies doing business in South Africa, the hesitation of companies in South Africa to respect the Sullivan Principles, and the increasing activities in Congress to pass bills imposing sanctions against South Africa, the Reagan administration, claiming that it could not and should not take the side of the oppressed, stuck to its policy of "constructive engagement." When the Nobel Peace Prize Committee honored Bishop Desmond Tutu for his creative attempts to resolve the problems of his country peacefully, the president himself sought, but understandably failed, to convince Tutu that apartheid was not uncivilized and unchristian.[28]

Reluctant to change a mind-set that axiomatically placed the welfare of South African whites over that of the oppressed black majority, the United States refused to cooperate with those forces seeking peaceful resolution of the Southern African crisis. It took the callous attempt of South Africa to blow up American oil installations in Canada and to attack Botswana for Reagan to recall his ambassador. It took the deaths of almost seven hundred Africans, P. W. Botha's rejection of any but his own plans for political change, and the almost certain passage of relatively mild sanctions by the U.S. Congress for the president to issue an executive order applying even milder sanctions against South Africa. Nevertheless; on September 9, 1985, Reagan was forced to issue the following statement: "I, Ronald Reagan, President of the United States of America, find that the policies and actions of the Government of South Africa constitute an unusual and extraordinary threat to the foreign policy and economy of the United States and hereby declare a national emergency to deal with that threat."[29]

African Americans, using their political clout, were able to galvanize a process, the present activities of which may well bring majority rule in South Africa in the near future. Unfortunately, Reagan followed his announcement with remarks indicating that this order did not really represent his views and affirmed his support of the policy of constructive engagement by sending his ambassador back to Pretoria. An embarrassed White House staff and a saddened nation heard with disbelief the president's uninformed claim that Pretoria had abolished segregation and discrimination against blacks just as the United States had previously done. Whether it was cynicism or wisdom, Reagan did send Ambassador Edward Perkins as his representative to South Africa. This African American diplomat acquitted himself with distinction in that troubled land.

ENHANCING AFRICAN AMERICAN INFLUENCE IN FOREIGN POLICY

African Americans must support programs and create institutions or centers to enhance their ability to help the United States formulate and execute a successful policy. Institutions working in the foreign policy field (for example, TransAfrica, Africare, and the Association of Black American Ambassadors) must be saluted and supported. It is also imperative that African American institutions of higher education assume a leadership position in the establishment of first-rate programs in foreign relations. African Americans, Asian Americans, and Latinos must attempt to make a difference, for they will comprise one of every three Americans by the year 2000.

As indicated earlier, the United States is uneasy in the context of multiple power centers and multiple competitors, but that is what tomorrow will be. African Americans have as yet not been fully involved in the debate about the position of this nation within the world system as many profound changes take place. Whereas America's relative power might be decreasing as multipolar economic and political structures emerge, this country's power and impact will remain formidable and decisive in the affairs of this planet. The best recent example of this reality lay in the conduct and outcome of the Persian Gulf War in late 1990 and early 1991. The role played by blacks, from General Colin Powell to the 30 percent of all ground troops and 50 percent of all female troops, indicate that African Americans must and will play a meaningful role in America's future.

In preparing for the future, African Americans must accept axiomatically the reality of the cultural and linguistic diversity among the world's peoples. The assertion that to recognize the diversity of the world's populations means that the United States has lost power should be rejected; the United States can no longer force the world to be what it wants it to be. That was always an illusion. International affairs essentially involve dealing with foreigners, people with different cultural backgrounds and perceptions embodied in diverse languages and symbols. The cultures of people still largely provide them with necessary designs or models for living, indicating what is considered proper, or moral, or even sane; rules by which they relate to each other; a body of knowledge and tools by which they relate and adapt to their environments; and a veritable storehouse of knowledge, beliefs, and formulae through which they attempt to understand the universe and their place within it.[30]

The languages that people speak furnish their cognitive claim as to what is fact, or data, or reality, notions not readily available or easily explainable to outsiders who do not speak their languages. If, as the history of the last two hundred years has shown, Americans have difficulties dealing with Westerners whose cultures have a common Judeo-Greco-Roman root and whose languages almost all stem from an Indo-European base, how much more difficult it is for Americans to deal with the peoples, cultures, and languages of Asia and Africa. Thus, there is not only the need to learn the cultures and languages but also the humanities and different historical backgrounds of other nations and peoples. Despite the arrogance or idiocy of Trevor Roper, Regis Professor of History at Oxford, who still believes that other peoples had no histories before the arrival of Europeans, this view is not challenged. But what is not challenged is the view of many non-Western peoples that their contact with the West was cataclysmic. Many firmly believe that having been conquered, colonized, or otherwise dominated by the West and by its successor state, the United States, their own development stopped or was impaired. Therefore, these people are deeply disturbed by their economic dependence upon alien and remote powers that do not appear to appreciate their problems. These people believe that there are McLuhan-like M factors (psychological features that treasure traditional life) that cause them to remain underdeveloped. By knowing the histories of other people, Americans would be better prepared to understand, if not always to accept, the views of other peoples.

African Americans also need a thorough grounding in the economics of international trade and development as well as the cultural-historical and technological factors that influence these issues. Multinational corporations, many of which have sales that are larger than the GNP of all but the world's major powers, increasingly dominate this planet. Their statuses and their roles must be understood. Even though the United States lost its position as the world's leading exporter in 1986, American corporations still earn 30 percent of their profits from international trade. American farmers depend upon foreign markets for 40 percent of their income, and overseas credit contributes half of the combined incomes of this country's thirteen largest banks.

African Americans need to know how and why the United States shifted from being the world's largest creditor to the world's largest debtor nation and how to deal with this situation. Americans do have a yen for Japanese products, and although Japan has replaced the United States as the largest provider of "foreign aid," usually loans, it is important to know how to attempt to deal with the increasing debt and development crises in the Third and Fourth Worlds. Nixon and Kissinger rejected out of hand the Third World's proposal for a new international economic order; and the Brandt Report's call for development funds for the Third World was ignored. It is now, however, clear that economic problems are global. African Americans must be prepared to deal with the difficult issues of protectionism, monetary stability, and debt management, and how to bring remaining communist and socialist countries into the global economic system. This global economy will need to know how to distribute the resources that should be available to all humankind: the mineral and fish resources of the sea, those from space, and so forth.

African Americans must clearly understand the processes that have enabled this republic to survive for two hundred years and why some of its institutions are still being borrowed by other nations. The political changes taking place in Latin America, Asia, Africa, the Islands of the Sea, and Eastern Europe should be studied carefully and not viewed simply as the result of imitating the United States. American views about "human rights" are not shared by many of the world's peoples. The United States will almost certainly object when in time other nations attempt to impose certain universal rights on American society. The United States did not sign the League of Nations treaty, and it only recently signed the treaty on genocide, which forbids nations to enact laws whose purposes are to destroy ethnic groups or populations as took place in Nazi Germany. The United States government is also not convinced that one person, one vote is good for South Africa.

In summary, then, the time has come for African Americans to assert boldly that they have a perspective on foreign policy and international affairs that can help the United States deal with the problems of a new century that will affect the entire nation. Dr. W. E. B. Du Bois prophesied at the end of the last century that the problem of the twentieth century was going to be the problem of the color line and the unequal relations between the darker and lighter peoples of this earth in Africa, Asia, America, and the Islands of the Seas. As weak and disenfranchised as blacks were then, Du Bois was determined that they would help solve that problem. It is now clear that the problems of the twenty-first century will affect all of mankind, and that foreign policy is the key to dealing with them. African Americans have always attempted to help and have often pushed the United States to live up to ideals often only faintly glimpsed by its founders. More attention to, deeper understanding of, and greater participation in foreign policymaking on the part of African Americans should help the United States deal more effectively with all the world.

NOTES

1. Franklin Delano Roosevelt, cited in Henry W. Bragdon and Samuel R. McCutchen, *History of a Free People* (New York: Macmillan, 1967), 634.
2. U.S. Senate, *The War on Poverty: 1964*, 88th Cong. 2nd sess., 1964, S. Rept. 2642.
3. James Laxer, *Decline of the Super-Powers* (New York: Paragon House, 1989), 9.
4. Ibid., 13.
5. Alvin Toffler and Heidi Toffler, "Grand Designs," *World Monitor*, October 1988, 48–50.
6. Ibid.
7. Winthrop D. Jordan, *White Over Black: American Attitudes Toward the Negro, 1550–1812* (Baltimore: Penguin Books, Inc., 1968), 260ff.
8. James Madison in *The Federalist*, no. 10 (New York: Modern Library, 1941), p. 55.
9. George Washington in Burton I. Kaufman, ed., *Washington's Farewell Address: The View from the Twentieth Century* (Chicago: Quadrangle Books, 1969), p. 18.
10. Washington in Kaufman, *Washington's Farewell* Address, p. 18.

11. Quoted in Thomas A. Bailey, *Man in the Street: Impact of American Public Opinion on Foreign Policy* (New York: Macmillan, 1948), p. 16.

12. Quoted in Bailey, *Man in the Street,* p. 16.

13. Louis L. Gerson, "The Influence of Hyphenated Americans on U.S. Diplomacy," in *Ethnicity and U.S. Foreign Policy,* ed. Abdul Azez (New York: Praeger, 1981), 2 1ff.

14. Quoted in Stephen A. Garrett, "East European Ethnic Groups and American Foreign Policy," *Political Science Quarterly,* 93 (1978): 307.

15. George F. Kennan, *Memoirs, 1958–1963* (Boston: Little Brown, 1972), 286–87.

16. Charles McC. Mathias, Jr., "Ethnic Groups and Foreign Policy," *Foreign Affairs* 59 (1981): 997; Jimmy Carter, whose presidency witnessed enormous pressures from America's ethnic groups to influence his foreign policy, complained in his farewell address: "We are increasingly drawn to single-issue groups and special interest organizations to ensure whatever else happens, our own personal views and our own private interests are protected. This a disturbing factor in American political life." *Vital Speeches* 47 (February 1981): 226–28.

17. Nathan Glazer and Daniel P. Moynihan, eds., *Ethnicity: Theory and Experience* (Cambridge, Mass.: Harvard University Press, 1975), 23–24.

18. Gabriel A. Almond, *The American People and Foreign Policy* (New York: Harcourt Brace and Co., 1950), 183.

19. Quoted in Bailey, *Man in the Street*, 16.

20. Louis Adamic, *Two-Way Passage* (New York: Harper & Row, 1941), 59–61.

21. Ibid.

22. Roger Morris, *Uncertain Greatness: Henry Kissinger and American Foreign Policy* (New York: Harper & Row, 1977), 23.

23. Elliott P. Skinner, "Ethnicity and Race as Factors in American Foreign Policy," in *American Character and Foreign Policy,* Michael P. Hamilton, ed. (Grand Rapids, Mich.: Wm. Eerdmans Publishing Co., 1986).

24. Bailey, *Man in the Street*, 30.

25. Ibid.

26. Ibid.

27. Study Commission on U.S. Policy Toward South Africa, *South Africa: Time Running Out* (Berkeley: University of California Press, 1981).

28. See "Bush Meets Tuto and Vows to Press Pretoria," *The New York Times,* May 19, 1989, p. A8.

29. "Reagan Orders Sanctions on Pretoria," *The New York Times,* September 10, 1985, pp. 1, 12.

30. Edward B. Tylor, *Primitive Culture: Researches into the Development of Mythology, Philosophy, Religion, Languages, Art and Custom,* vol. 1 (New York: Morrow, 1889), 53; Margaret Mead, *New Lives for Old: Cultural Transformation—Manus* (New York: Morrow, 1956).

31. The very discourse used by Westerners to "manage," and even to "produce," the non-West, culturally, politically, ideologically, and imaginatively, has been the subject of criticism by Edward Said, *Orientalism* (New York: Pantheon Books, 1978), 3; Michel Foucault, *Power-Knowledge* (New York: Pantheon Books, 1980); Clifford Geertz, "Ritual and Social Change: A Japanese Example," *American Anthropologist* 59 (1957): 32–54; and Stephen A. Tyler, *Cognitive Anthropology* (New York: Holt, Rinehart, and Winston, 1969).

28

The African Growth and Opportunity Act

*Changing Foreign Policy Priorities
Toward Africa in a Conservative Political Culture*

RONALD WALTERS

In the era of Republican approaches to government, United States policy toward Africa has experienced a significant shift from an emphasis upon public sector-sponsored development assistance to private sector-driven trade and investment. One of the more interesting aspects of this shift is that it represents an example of "political convergence" between Republicans and a sector of the Democratic Party, but also involving many black Democrats as well. Nevertheless, the shift prompted a political conflict initiated by the difference of opinion between those who favored it, for whatever reasons, and many Africa-oriented groups and politicians who favored the maintenance of economic development strategies. We will examine the nature of this conflict, emphasizing the arguments of the opponents in an effort to understand why a "bipartisan" piece of legislation that ostensibly promised much to the continent of Africa, might instead be considered to be detrimental.

THE FIRST ITERATION: REAGAN'S TRADE AND INVESTMENT APPROACH

In 1985, when the American government was led by a Republican president and the Democratics controlled Congress, the Congress attempted to reduce the amount of foreign aid to Zaire from $6.4 million to $4.0 million, in order to discipline a government widely regarded as corrupt, both politically and economically. However, the secretary of state, George Shulz, nevertheless opposed it.[1] This was symptomatic of the Cold War framework in which American policy toward Africa was nuking use of the Zaire regime and the strategic positioning of this country in its anti-Soviet policies in Angola, South Africa, Mozambique, and Zimbabwe and in Eastern Africa as well.

Where the Reagan administration did support increases in African economic assistance and no immediate political interests were at stake, it was in an attempt to stimulate the emergence of private enterprise as markets for the sale of American goods. In fact, when the administration came into office, Africa was suffering from a famine and officials registered considerable dismay that in light of the economic assistance that the United States had previously provided, Africa was not strong enough to defend itself from the ravages of the drought. The answer, for them, was not to repeat the economic development assistance approach but to assert that private enterprise could help to pull Africa out of its economic morass. The program designed for this purpose would be called the Economic Policy Initiative, and it would be designed to act as further leverage with African countries for them to support the increasingly stringent private sector "conditionalities" (political or economic conditions constructed as requirements for eligibility to participate in a funding program) being implemented by the International Monetary Fund (IMF) and the World Bank. These international agencies had for some time supported an export orientation to African agriculture and desired stronger private market management to this sector of African economies in order that it might earn greater foreign exchange. The achievement of this objective required changing the attitude toward socialism resident in the political transition to independence of many African governments to that of capitalist-oriented economics. The administration selected the countries of Zaire, Senegal, Ghana, Mali, Uganda, Madagascar, Soma, and Zambia to participate in a five-year, $500 million program that is trumpeted as the "new" approach to African economic solvency.[2]

Some of those who opposed the United States dictating what the policies of African countries should be, such as well-known African American economist Robert Browne, a former Carter administration appointee as director of the Africa Development Bank, regarded this program as a "new form of colonialism."[3] Others, such as Congressman William Gray, head of the Congressional Black Caucus (CBC), felt that the amount of funds were insufficient in light of the commitment of $8.4 billion made to Central America. Indeed, by 1990, Central America received thirty-four times the per capita aid to Africa.[4] Moreover, Africa aid was later reduced in order to provide funds for former Soviet governments as, during the mid-1980s to late-1980s period, economic support funds, for example, were slashed from $452.8 million to $58.9 million.[5] These reductions in economic development funds and the underlying attitudes that fostered them were continued under George Bush.

THE SECOND ITERATION: CLINTON'S PRIVATE SECTOR INITIATIVES

The Setting

A major impetus for the thrust in the direction of private sector-led development strategies was the feeling among African officials that the declining economic assistance from the West together with their mounting debt contributed to a growing marginalization of Africa in world economic relations, as indicated by Michael Clough's work *Free at Last: U.S. Policy toward Africa and the End of the Cold War* (New York: Council on Foreign Relations, 1992). In fact, Carol Lancaster captured the sentiment of many African observers with her statement that "the 'marginalization of Africa' is not just speculation. Not only are foreign governments closing embassies and cutting back aid flows but Africa's role in the world economy is also shrinking." She went on to state that the percentage of African exports and imports of total world trade dropped significantly between 1965 to 1992, from 4 percent to 2 percent.[6]

What can be clearly seen above is the sharp difference in the aggregate resource flows to Africa in the period of the Cold War prior to 1993, especially in terms of net private capital. Then, as also indicated, net official capital flows fell sharply by 48 percent in 1996 alone.[7] Also, the advent of the Republican-controlled Congress in 1995 led to policy proposals for FY 1996 of deep cuts in African economic assistance. In fact, the Africa AID budget experienced: the loss of "earmarks" for the Development Funds for Africa and Reductions in the amounts; a 33 percent reduction in funds for the African Development Foundation; and a nearly 50 percent reduction in the U.S. International Development Assistance (IDA) replenishment, a major source of multilateral funding for Africa programs.[8]

Nevertheless, in the period after 1993, some countries began to experience significant levels of economic growth. Therefore, what made the sudden economic interest in Africa possible was not simply Republican ideology or past marginalization, but that the new signs that some parts of the continent were experiencing significant rates of economic growth and political progress made the plausibility of reasonable profits appear to change the former image of Africa as merely an aid case. Thus, the evidence of a new image presented itself in that twenty-five countries had experienced elections since 1990; and signs of an economic recovery were found in the rise in output for the fourth consecutive year since 1994. Africa grew by 2.6 percent in 1994, 3.2 percent in 1995, 4.4 percent in 1996, 3 percent in 1997, and was forecast to grow at 4 percent for 1998.[9] United Nations data on thirty-eight countries indicated that in 1997, fifteen of these countries achieved rates of at least 5 percent, among them eleven reached 6 percent, with several over 7 percent, such as Angola, Ethiopia, Rwanda, and Uganda. Moreover, the return on the rate of investment had reached 33.3 percent compared to 14 percent in Asia.

In this period, American export sales to Africa had increased by 13.5 percent between 1995 and 1997, reaching $6.1 billion, indeed achieving levels of trade with West Africa that were greater than those with the former states of the Soviet Union combined. The vaunted "Afro-pessimism" that saw the former European colonial powers withdrawing from Africa economically was represented in the declining terms of trade between them. The African Caribbean Pacific (ACP) countries' share of the European import market declined from a level greater than 7 percent in 1975 by half to 3.5 percent in 1995 and even then, 47 percent of ACP export to the European market originated in just twelve countries.[10] In fact, the serious decline of ACP trade preference has been the result of European countries expanding their global economic competition, courting markets in Asia, Latin America, and Central and Eastern Europe.

Thus, the stage was set for the presentation of the McDermott proposals with the release of a report on U.S. trade and investment policy for Africa in June 1996. McDermott, a Democrat, launched a bipartisan coalition on trade and investment that had three pillars: the accomplishment of a U.S.-Africa Free Trade Area by 2020; the creation of a U.S.-Africa Economic Cooperation Forum; and the establishment of a U.S.-Africa Trade and Investment Partnership modeled on APEC (the Asia Pacific Economic Cooperation association).

H.R. 1432: The African Growth and Opportunity Act

The idea of the "African Growth and Opportunity Act" was presented by Rep. Jim McDermott (D-Wash.) in the spring of 1996. The congressman noted that American policy toward Eastern Europe in the post-Soviet era was being shaped by fundamental economic directions and his observation was that similar planning for the African continent was not occurring. Furthermore, he held that Africa was adrift in this era and that the previous emphasis upon development assistance for Africa "did not constitute a policy."[11] This position was consistent with that of the Clinton administration, which had begun to link the national interest of the United States in this era closely to the economic security of the United States through its effective participation in global economic affairs, led by the private sector.

One year later, in the spring of 1997, the legislation H.R. 1432 was introduced by Rep. Charles Rangel, a member of the Congressional Black Caucus (CBC) and the ranking minority member on the House Ways and Means Committee, and a key Republican sponsor, Rep. Phillip Crane (R-Ill.). On April 29, 1997, the House Trade Subcommittee heard twenty witnesses, including an amazing array of supporters from both the right and left ideological spectrum, leading off with Rep. Newt Gingrich, Speaker of the House, followed by David Dinkins, former mayor of New York City and chairman of the Constituency for Africa, and Jack Kemp, former Republican vice presidential candidate and head co-chair of Empower America.[12]

Fully "fleshed out" by now, the bill contained the original three emphases of the McDermott proposals and added the following:

1. A $150 million equity fund and a $500 million infrastructure fund
2. An Export-Import Bank initiative to expand loans for private projects
3. The elimination of trade quotas on textiles
4. The renewal and expansion of GSP (General System of Prefrences) for trade to Africa and to allow an additional eighteen hundred products that are currently excluded to be traded from Africa for ten years.

The Development of Opposition

Opposition developed to H.R. 1432 in late 1997 and the spring of 1998, led by a coalition of forces represented by labor, humanitarian organizations headed by Public Citizen, progressive Africa-oriented organizations headed by TransAfrica, and some members of the Congressional Black Caucus, headed by Congressman Jesse Jackson Jr. The bill was initially also opposed by Rev. Jesse Jackson Sr., the president's special envoy to Africa, and Rep. Maxine Waters, head of the CBC, both of whom later supported it because of substantial pressures from the White House. There were a series of factors that came to represent the broad basis of objections to this bill as presented later.

The bill did not mandate debt reduction. There was strong feeling that African leaders could not provide the leadership or maintain significant participation in the trade and investment regime if their economic resources were devoted to serving the crushing level of debt. In 1997, total debt in sub-Sahara Africa was $223 billion, an amount that represented 90 percent of GNP of those countries. Of this amount, the U.S. proportion is relatively small at $4.5 billion; however, American leadership was felt to be important in creating a climate for movement on significant measures to reduce the debt by the European countries and multilateral financial institutions to whom most of the debt was owed.

The World Bank and the International Monetary Fund had created a strategy for highly indebted poor countries (HIPC) to pay down the debt of the most severely indebted countries, which also maintained the highest levels of poverty. But this did not take into consideration the fact that for moderately poor countries such as Zambia, serving the debt amounted to five times the health budget and thirty times the budget for education, or that in Zimbabwe, seven hundred people were dying from AIDS per week.[13]

The bill did not protect or mandate an increase in the Development Fund for Africa (DFA). The principle supported by many groups was that economic assistance was complimentary to trade and investment and that, given the poverty of Africa, the trade and investment thrust could not be successful without maintaining development assistance funding at significant, even enhanced levels. In this sense, Secretary General Rubens Ricupero, at the United Nations Conference on Trade and Development (UNCTAD), said that a report of his organization called for Official Development Assistance (ODA) to be "increased, as foreign direct investment (FDI) was not a substitute but only a complement to ODA."[14] Thus, the report called for significant increase in public investment in physical and human infrastructure" in order to "help lay the basis for recovery of private investment and a process of diversification."

Accordingly, there was language in the bill that stated that it recognized the importance of development assistance, but it did not go so far as to either increase levels of assistance or to explicitly recognize that higher level of development assistance was crucial to trade and investment objectives.

The bill continues the emphasis on "conditionalities." Opponents felt that the bill violated the political sovereignty of African countries by placing emphasis on so many critical conditions for eligibility, such as:

- No trade with Libya, Cuba, or Iraq
- Cuts in government spending, privatization of governmental services
- Eliminating barriers to trade such as government protection for national industries and reduction of business taxes and regulations
- Liberalization of trade and movement toward the WTO regime
- Movement toward democratic institutions and practices

Countries such as South Africa strongly objected to the political and economic conditions contained in the bill on the grounds that, should the South African government accede to such conditions, it would violate the confidence of countries such as those named in the bill, when they supported the Black South African struggle for majority rule and the United States government did not. Moreover, the UNCTAD report referred to above also indicated that those countries that liberalized their trade fastest showed the lowest levels of growth, while those that liberalized slowest maintained the protection of their fragile economies from the strong influences of global market forces such as prices and trading regimes.[15] This finding was supported by another expert observer:

> African societies typically lack a sizeable independent formal business sector with the capital and experience to seize quickly the new opportunities opened up by the reforms. Trade liberalization exposes them to foreign competition; removal of government regulations loosens their monopoly holds on domestic markets; and the reduction in government contracts and other public resources means a cut in revenues.[16]

At the same time, movement toward the WTO is fraught with difficulty, as African countries have resisted the economic conditionalities as well as their expansion to noneconomic sectors beyond trade issues.[17]

The bill did not mandate any labor or human rights standards. The UN Reports find that real wages on the continent are depressed to the point that further reductions are unlikely to stimulate competition. However, the current level of wages makes it attractive for some investors to build economic enterprises where they do not have to raise wages too far above the mean to attract workers and to do so without providing labor rights guarantees. For example, in Vietnam, workers in the Nike plant that manufactures tennis shoes earn $73 per month whereas the minimum wage is $40 per month.[18] Although this wage is nearly 100 percent greater than the average, because of its very low level, it provides manufacturers with a significant margin of profit, yet does not raise the average wage to levels that would allow for substantial changes in the conditions of life for workers. This fact leaves African workers open to considerable exploitation, given the distance between the sale price of the product and its manufacturing costs and the lack of social investments by the companies to provide "added value" to the workers' lives.

Accordingly, organized labor opposed a similar regime of trade expansion in NAFTA, which, together with the WTO, has relatively weak labor tights regimes to protect workers' right to organize in the plants for higher wages and to protect their jobs from foreign imports in selected industries.

Therefore, the AFL-CIO opposed H.R. 1432 on these grounds and also that the "African content" definition in the bill, at only 30 percent, may create an incentive for other countries such as China to provide the other 70 percent of content in textile apparel and tranship such goods through Africa bound for the U.S. market. The further importation of such goods would further depress the already devastated textile industry in the United States with lower priced goods, thus causing workers to lose remaining jobs in this industry. At present the level of textile trade from Africa to the United States is only 1 percent of total trade in textiles and the United States Trade Representative (USTR) data indicate that the level would have to reach 3 percent before any damage to U.S. jobs would occur.[19]

Without strong labor rights, it should be noted, the bill would have the same effect as the largely failed Caribbean Basin Initiative, which gave American firms access to the cheap labor of the Caribbean but gave American firms access to the cheap labor of the Caribbean but stimulated little economic development in the region. By contrast, it should be noted that some of the countries that have challenged the enhancement of labor rights most vigorously have been countries such as Egypt and Tanzania, feeling that they would lose their comparative advantage in the low-wage structure of the continent.[20]

Lacks any measures to assure African leadership and direction and to ensure that poor households benefit from investment. In order for Africans to exercise leadership and direction over the degree and focus of trade and investment, there needs to be expanded financial capability, business development and training centers, and effective instruments for international trade and investment. Indeed, Jennifer Whitaker concludes in her analysis of African economic development prospects that "further prospects for progress in Africa will depend upon infusions of technical assistance and training from the advanced nations."[21] Moreover, United Nations data indicates that only four countries in Africa are connected to the Internet, whereas about 120 cities have such facilities available. This means that there must be a substantial growth of communications technology in order to facilitate global transactions. Communications infrastructure conceived in relationship to the entry of Western firms into the former Soviet Union, are absent from Africa and where such regional economic organizations such as the Western African Common Market and the SADCC have sought to enhance their capability to promote private sector economic activity, funding for this purpose has been largely absent.

Therefore if African leadership does not have the human, financial, and technological capacity to lead this area, they would be subject to the much larger and much more sophisticated planning and financial capability and thus the leadership of large corporations.

The effect of shrinking the public sector. The above statement suggests that the lack of ability in governments, or in the private sector in most African countries, to lead in the trade and investment field, together with the requirement that government play less of a role, presents several problems for Africa's fragile economies and political systems.

One of these problems is the protection of consumers' economic interests and the reduction of poverty. Unregulated markets and private sector activity as the primary engine of economic growth has traditionally been unsuccessful at reducing widespread poverty. Some evidence for this is found in the fact that despite higher levels of aggregate GDP for the continent, it has had scant impact on the reduction of malnutrition. World Bank data finds that, for example, "Sub-Sahara Africa (SSA) has had an aggregate malnutrition rate of nearly 30 percent for the last decade. While malnutrition prevalence has decreased significantly in most other developing countries in the last decade, it has been nearly static for SSA."[22]

Market activity throughout the Third World often sets prices for goods at such a level that lower-income classes cannot participate and are often relegated to inferior goods. Indeed, World Bank economists indicate that growth rates of 6 to 7 percent per annum for a considerable period of time are necessary to reduce poverty and even then, "relying on aggregate income growth as the sole means for reducing poverty in Africa will effectively postpone significant poverty reduction for the poorest for up to 50 years."23

In addition, market deregulation reduces the ability of governments to continue to regulate the quality of goods, monitor prices, and adjust fiscal policy such that the fruits of economic activity are distributed to the poorer parts of the populations. By contrast, Mamadou Dia recognized that "the combination of the patrimonial state and the absence of the rule of law puts the average entrepreneur at the mercy of the political elite and bureaucracy. Property rights are not legally protected and wealth can be confiscated or reduced through selective manipulation of the formal rules and regulations."24 In any case, it is far from certain, given the role of the authoritarian governments in the evolution of private sector development in the "Asian Tiger" countries, that strong governmental leadership is not a necessary ingredient. The problem is not only strong leadership, but that which has entrepreneurial goals. Dia would suggest that a set of central tasks are: reconciling indigenous institutions with transplanted ones; developing accountable and skilled management; and funding what he regards as the "missing and skilled management, and funding what he regards as the "missing middle" of capital formation. All of this would appear to require strong state leadership and the outset if the Asian model is at all relevant.

Lobbying

The attack. The first significant opposition to the bill was that which TransAfrica transmitted to Rep. Rangel by letter in early February of 1997, containing the concerns of its president, Randall Robinson. In this letter, he asserted that provisions in the bill would: contain government's role in African economies; open African economies too much through the privatization of critical public facilities; and grant foreign investors new rights without the governments being able to effectively regulate such activity.25

Organized labor began to contact its allies in the black community to oppose the legislation and, in a repeat of the debate over the NAFTA legislation, urged Rep. Rangel to "include adherence to core labor standards (as defined under Section S02[a][4] of the 1974 Trade Act, as amended) among the eligibility requirement listed under section 4; provide for funding and enforcement for mechanisms to prevent illegal transhipment of goods through Africa; require that all workers employed producing goods granted market access under the bill be local citizens; and provide support for some of the nonlabor matters previously mentioned."26

Thus, in late February some members of the CBC began to follow the lead of labor and registered their concern over the legislation, as six members, led by Rep. Sanford Bishop, sent a letter to Congressman Rangel expressing their view that the legislation should be changed to protect American jobs. They pointed out that 50 percent of the nation's textile workers were minorities and that 80 percent of them were women.27

Rangel responded to organized labor and its allies by releasing a letter to Robinson on February 25, asserting that Robinson had "misread the bill," and that it did not mandate eligibility requirements, but merely established the preferences of the U.S. government, that in fact there would be separate negotiations with each country over the terms of the trade agreement and these would be governed by existing law. In any case, a key point of difference was over the shift in the strategy from development to private sector support and to this, Rangel responded: "You further assert that 'the bill's backers describe it as a radical shift in emphasis from sustainable development strategies to a private sector and market incentives approach.' I must admit that I have never heard the bill described this way by its supporters. Rather, they talk about a shift from dependence on foreign assistance to a private sector and market incentives approach so *as to create* a sustainable development strategy."[28]

One week later, Rangel answered the AFL-CIO, repeating essentially the points raised in his reply to Robinson, that many of the proposals in the bill would be administered flexibly and would be subject to the president's determination. However, with respect to the key concern on the transhipment of goods, he said only that, "I am pleased to report that in the full Ways and Means Committee markup of the bill on February 25, we were able through a Chairman's amendment to strengthen considerably the textile transhipment and enforcement provisions of the bill."[29] The lack of specificity, however, did not mollify labor.

An interesting coalition in opposition to the bill developed between Randall Robinson and Ralph Nader, head of Public Citizen, who published a joint commentary in the *Washington Times,* repeating many of the points of opposition presented above. However, they added: "The potential effect of the Crane Bill is ominous, particularly as we observe how the imposition of similar conditions by the IMF on Asia is resulting in growing instability, lower growth rates and the purchase at fire sale prices of natural resources and productive capacity by a few immense foreign corporations. Because economic and political pressure on subSahara Africa is enormous, some African governments have not made public their misgivings. We must not replace European colonialism that long burdened Africa with a new colonialism of servitude to external corporate interests."[30]

By early March, both TransAfrica and Public Citizen were in full revolt. Public Citizen posted a position on its "Global Trade Watch" Web site that was in full opposition to the bill, urging opponents to vote against it because it was a "job-killer" and comparing it to NAFTA.[31] The posted position was supported by a list of twenty organizations headed by TransAfrica, and others in the religious, environmental, social justice, and human rights community. The same day, TransAfrica released an open letter to "Members of Congress" calling the Crane Bill "lethal medicine for Africa," identifying specific changes in language focused on eliminating section 9(e) related to the "conditionalities" under which a country would be eligible to participate in the bill, requir ing binding labor rights and increasing the African content to 50 percent and African ownership of 55 percent of the economic activity, strengthening aid programs for Africa, and binding debt relief.[32]

The counterattack. The Clinton administration began its counterattack by distributing a list of talking points issued by assistant secretary of state for African affairs, Susan Rice.[33] The points were essentially an added defense of the points raised by Rangel and continued several others that placed a strong reliance on the view of African ambassadors and their countries in the following language: "Africans need this bill. They don't want a handout. They want the hand of a partner. And they've said so. The African Ambassadors to Washington have repeatedly urged Congress and the President to enact this legislation." The use of African legitimacy as a counter to various arguments was also a key staple of Rep. Rangel, who traveled to Africa as head of the Presidential Mission on Economic Cooperation to Africa from December 6 to 17, 1997. The Rangel mission, which contained five members of the CBC (Rep. Rangel, Rep. William Jefferson, Rep. Carrie Meek, Rep. Sheila Jackson-Lee, and Rep. Carolyn Kilpatrick), other congressional staff, nongovernmental organizations, private sector individuals, and executive branch representatives, visited Ethiopia, Eritrea, Uganda, Botswana, Mauritius, and Cote d'Ivoire. In his report to the president at the end of the mission, Rangel indicated that he had "received strong positive feedback from the countries we visited that they fully supported these new U.S. initiatives to move from a purely donor-donee relationship to one based more on economic cooperation and increased trade and investment. They had "received a strong message from every country [they] visited that enactment into law of H.R. 1432, the African Growth and Opportunity Act, will be a key catalyst in getting U.S. business to do business with viable countries in Africa and is therefore essential. Everything must be done to ensure passage of this legislation early next year."[34]

Thus, the African Diplomatic Corps in Washington was substantially supportive of the bill and spoke for itself in the lobbying process. For instance, in early March 1998, the ambassador of Djibouti, Roble Olhaye, who was also dean of the African Diplomatic Corps, wrote to Randall Robinson informing him that they had indeed been consulted on the details of H.R. 1432 and supported the legislation. Furthermore, he assured Robinson of his sensitivity to the fact that the bill was drafted to the advantage of large corporations and continued: "We believe that the legislation is drafted in such a way so as to allow African countries themselves to determine what should be the proper balance between foreign corporations and indigenous African economic interests and still be eligible to receive the benefits of the legislation."[35]

The point of assurance was a rejoinder to Robinson's concerns and that of others regarding whether African governments, ravaged by debt and declining resource flows from the major industrial countries, were in any credible position to reject the prospect of additional economic activity of either a public or private derivation.

Also in early March, the assistant secretary general of the Organization of African Unity, Ambassador Vijay S. Makhan, released a document boldly entitled, "Political Support for the African Growth and Opportunity Act, H.R. 1432 (Crane-McDermott-Rangel Bill)," which reaffirmed the support of the organization for the legislation. In addition, the communication contained a point-by-point refutation of the three issues raised in the original letter of concern from Randall Robinson to Rep. Rangel, indicating that with regard to the conditionalities, that thirty African countries had undergone reforms that had created sentiments against deficit financing of budgets; that privatization was not so much of an issue as most governments had already sold off many nonperforming parastatals; and that the bill itself would not establish new rights for corporations, because many countries had revised their investment codes to attract foreign investors.[36] Ambassador Makhan left no confusion as to the lobbying purpose of his letter as he said: "I trust that this letter would assist in securing the passage of this Bill as it is, in Congress."[37]

Finally, the role of some of the other Africa-oriented nongovernmental organizations was important as either supportive or appositive to the bill. For example, the Constituency for Africa (CFA), led by David Dinkins and Mel Foote, executive director, was the lead private organization promoting the bill. The CFA held a series of "town meetings" around the country and as a part of its regular program, provided grassroots education on the purposes of the bill. In fact, a major such town meeting held in Denver, Colorado, was hosted by Mayor Wellington Webb, the major purpose of which was to place the new emphasis on trade and investment as an agenda item on the table of the G-7 Summit meeting of heads of the major economic powers in the summer of 1997.

In the preparations for this meeting, it became clear that many of the nongovernmental organizations such as Amnesty International, the Washington Office on Africa, Bread for the World, and others opposed the bill. Nevertheless, the Denver town meeting was held June 13–14, the week before the G-7 meeting, and it touted the advantages of trade and investment with Africa. Then, a subsequent town hall meeting was held in July 1997 that also featured Mayor Webb and Rev. Jesse Jackson and that discussed essentially the same message.[38]

Passage

On March 11, H.R. 1432 passed the House, 233–186. The balance of the Democratic Party voted against it, but many Democrats voted for the bill, including twenty-four members of the CBC (twelve against). Rep. Jesse Jackson Jr. led the opposition on the floor. Earlier in the month, he also had joined the public opposition to the bill with the letter to Rep. Philip Crane that emphasized the strong provisions in the bill that, in his opinion, weighted the balance substantially in favor of foreign corporations doing business in Africa "unfettered" from the proper kinds of collateral investments in the social sector.[39] Direct social sector investment from private corporations was important to progressives, since it had constituted the critical conditionalities fought for as a requirement for American corporations electing to do business inside South Africa before Black majority rule.

Jackson also found that in attacking the bill on the floor, he confronted some of his own colleagues who were defending it, as the following exchange suggests:

> MR. JACKSON: I would ask the gentleman, is he aware in the bill of any African countries losing foreign aid they are now receiving unless they adopt the economic reforms dictated in this bill?
>
> MR. [DON] PAYNE: Mr. Chairman, I am glad the gentleman brought that question up. This bill is separate from aid. The Development Fund for Africa was an earmarked area that this year is funded for about $700 million, and $30 million has been allocated or recommended by the administration to go into the aid. Therefore, the answer is no. This is a separate entity, and it will not take aid from any country that does not conform to the bill.
>
> Second, I might say that a country that does not comply with governance and human rights, with transparency and basic human rights, will not be invited to be in the rounds, just as NATO expansion has been done.
>
> MR. JACKSON: Mr. Chairman, if the gentleman will continue to yield, is the gentleman aware of any African countries being forced to cut corporate taxes, privatize, and shrink their government services, or grant expanded rights to foreign investors under the bill?
>
> MR. PAYNE: To my knowledge, I know of none. If the gentleman knows of any information that I am not privy to, I would certainly appreciate it, but to my knowledge it does not negatively impact on what is going on in those countries. There will be IMF requirements which already are in many countries.[40]

This exchange was a delicate dialogue prompted by Jackson's challenge to the conditionalities in the bill, which were answered by Payne in a way that suggested that although some have interpreted them as advisory, they in fact were binding. Thus, Rep. Maxine Waters proposed to amend the bill to eliminate the necessity for countries to comply with all of the conditions.[41] As the amendment failed, her next attempt was to ensure that the $700 million appropriation for the DFA remained in force for the next nine years, accomplishing a form of earmarking.[42] This amendment too failed under the reasoning put forth by Rep. Royce (R-Calif.), that "since the bill does not require a cutoff of aid to Africa, the aid floor is unnecessary."[43] Rep. Waters then offered another amendment that proposed that the president had the discretion with respect to the issue of conditions of eligibility to participate in the bill. However, this, too, failed.

Therefore, the issue of the conditions of eligibility to participate remained rather firm as the bill was passed into law, opponents having lost measure after measure of "perfecting" elements that would make the bill acceptable for them to support. Nevertheless, twenty-four members of the CBC supported the bill and twelve finally opposed it.[44]

Next Steps: Senate Prospects

After H.R. 1432 passed the House, the focus of the process passed to the Senate and at this writing (April 1998), the Senate has not taken up the measure. However, the landscape of its politics is littered with the residue of both, the existing proposals offered by TransAfrica and Public Citizen. Bread for the World has drafted a bill to shore up Development Assistance, focusing on rural finance, agricultural research and extension, and food security, entitled, "Africa: Seeds of Hope"—H.R. 3636, which was introduced on April 1, 1998, by Reps. Douglass Bereuter (R-Neb.), Lee Hamilton (D-Ind.), Cynthia McKinney (D-Ga.), Eva Clayton (D-N.C.), Tony Hall (D-Ohio), and James Leach (R-Iowa).

Although the White House had based its policy direction on this thrust by making it the basic element in its five-nation Africa trip taken March 25–April 3, 1998, and is thereby heavily invested, it has offered no bill of its own, preferring to support the general direction of the House bill, monitor the debate, and weigh in at the appropriate time. That time would appear to be in Senate consideration of the bill, since in the Senate, S. 778 has attracted only four cosponsors and there is a stronger unified support base for the bill, all of which means that it could fail. Otherwise, the administration has already begun to implement aspects of the proposals within the capability of the executive, such as installing a Special Trade Representative for Africa in the USTR and committing the $150 million and the $500 million to OPIC to administer should the authorizing legislation pass.

An Integrated Approach

Whether or not H.R. 1432 becomes law, the route to a much stronger thrust in trade and investment is one that is balanced by a strong development assistance role. The concept of a balanced policy was not envisioned at first by the proponents of the bill, who touted it as "trade not aid," appearing to deprecate the role of economic assistance for development and the domestic version of a "handout" as "dependency." Rep. Sheila Jackson-Lee, for example, said that "this bill is not trade and not aid, it is trade and aid," in an attempt to reconcile the two approaches.[45]

We have referred earlier to the view of the UNCTAD that economic assistance is complimentary to trade and investment, because it provides the infrastructure within which the private sector can succeed. Indeed, even some of the most radical opponents of capitalist strategies recognize that "the public sector should be the *facilitator* while the private sector plays the central role of main actor."[46] And although the bill expresses the desire to support governments dedicated to eliminating poverty and establishing accountable government and calls for the continuance of development funding—things that opponents share—it does not go far enough. It does not mandate a balanced strategy that alone would achieve the goals of trade and investment; it does not mandate debt relief; it does not mandate labor standards that would spread the fruits of such economic activity to the common person. That is the critical evaluation that is at the heart of the opposition to the bill: does it seek to empower all Africans or merely create an African version of a small middle-class elite?

Here, there might be a recognition that given the persistent level of poverty, disease, and debt, and the lack of dynamic growth, which is the case with most African countries, perhaps the trade and development model will be relevant to only the handful of countries with which U.S. companies will ultimately seek to partner. For the others, the urgent necessity for measures to make them economically viable as partners must entail making greater economic resources available and lessening the entanglement of crushing levels of concessional debt. So, while one side of the policy seeks to take advantage of those already positioned to participate, the other side of a balanced policy would seek to enhance the position of others to do so.

CONCLUSION

One source of the dynamics that makes possible a "bipartisan" approach favoring the new shift to private sector-oriented policies toward African economic development is lodged in the larger political culture of conservatism. This has contributed to a "political convergence" not only over Africa policy but also over crime, welfare reform, and other issues in which the interest of African descendant peoples have been involved. In this sense, we have a typical political formulation: the president, the Republican Party, and a faction of the Democratic Party provides the winning coalition on an issue that has traditionally been defined by Republican interests.

In this case, the fact that the sector of the coalition within the Democratic Party also includes the majority of the CBC, which itself was split, constitutes a difference in the typical formulation. This might be explained by the difference within the black and progressive community over ideology as expressed in former conflicts over U.S. policy toward Angola or South Africa, where clear sides were drawn with respect to those who supported either the left or the right. This difference was expressed formerly as a "two-line struggle."[47]

The left in these cases supported the strongly people-oriented socialist regimes of the MPLA government of Angola or the African National Congress of South Africa, while the right supported the UNITA rebels in Angola and the white minority regime of South Africa. This mirrors and tends to explain the continuation of the ideological conflict at a time when American policy is focused globally on economic security, through the deployment of the conservative economic tools of the private sector.

The left, sensitive to the profound level of economic disadvantage on the continent, favors enhanced levels of economic assistance to Africa, debt forgiveness, policies that more equitably distribute the returns from economic activity, democracy, and human rights. The right, by contrast, favors free trade approaches and private direct investment from which it might benefit due to its position of economic advantage.

This abbreviated discussion using the symbolic terms of "left" and "right" also masks, however, other divisions of class and culture. Over time, a class of Africans and African American bureaucrats and business-oriented associates have emerged within the African policy debate, and they possess a much stronger business orientation to world and African affairs. Thus, the ideological divisions are also expressed, to some extent, by a generational divide about problem solving on the African continent and the collusion between the new African American business elite, desperate African politicians, and pragmatic African American politicians helps to legitimize this "new" approach in the eyes of U.S. foreign policy decisionmakers.

However, like the older aspects of what was considered to be two separate lines of strategy that were each righteous roads to the solution of African dependence, both were necessary then and are necessary now. In any case, the deep splits within the Democratic Party coalition with respect to the bill, assures that, given this environment, it would appear that the bill that emerges will carry a decidedly Republican stamp.

NOTES

1. Joanne Omang, "Shulz Cites 'Major Concerns' on Foreign Aid Bill," *The Washington Post*, March 26, 1985, p. 11.
2. Leon Dash, "New U.S. Plan Would Help Free-Market African States," *The Washington Post*, May 7, 1984, p. 1.
3. Ibid.
4. Peter J. Schraeder, *United States Foreign Policy toward Africa: Incrementalism, Crisis and Change* (Port Chester, N.Y.: Cambridge University Press, 1994), p. 251.

5. Ibid.

6. Carol Lancaster, "United States and Africa: Into the 21st Century," Policy Essay no. 7, Overseas Development Council, Washington, D.C.,1993, p. 11.

7. Christina Katsouris, "Sharp Fall in Resource Flows to Africa," *Africa Recovery*, vol. 11, no. 2 (October 1997), p. 1.

8. "US/Africa Assistance Falls; Additional Cuts Expected," The *Washington Notes on Africa, vol.* 21, no. 3 (Winter 1995–1996), p. 10.

9. Henk-Jan Brinkman and Carl Gray, "Fourth Year of Positive Growth in Africa," *United Nations Office of Communications and Public Information,* vol. 11, no. 3 (February 1998), p. 1.

10. "Trade in the New World Order," *The Courier, Journal of the Africa, Caribbean and Pacific Organization,* November–December 1997, p. 58.

11. Press Release, Remarks by Rep. Jim McDermott (D-WA), Overseas Development Council, Conference on African Economic Recovery, June 12, 1996, Washington, D.C.

12. *West Africa,* May 19–25, 1997, p. 800.

13. "AIDS Claims 700 Lives a Week in Zimbabwe," *Electronic Mail & Guardian,* March 21, 1998. References the *Sunday Standard of Zimbabwe,* Misa, March 16, 1998.

14. "UNCTAD Secretary-General Calls for Action to Sustain African Economic Recovery," UNCTAD, TAD/INF/2727, Press Release, October 21, 1997.

15. "UN Secretary General Calls for Action to Sustain African Economic Recovery," op. cit.

16. Lancaster, "United States and Africa," p. 40.

17. Tim Wall, "Africa Resist New Trade Conditionalities," *Africa Recovery,* January–April 1997, p. 9.

18. "Taking a Look inside Nike's Factories," *Time,* March 30, 1998, p. 52.

19. "Likely Impact of Providing Quota-Free and Duty-Free Entry to Textiles and Apparel From Sub-Saharan Africa," U.S. International Trade Commission, Publication 3056, September 1997.

20. Tim Wall, op. cit.

21. See Jennifer Seymour Whitaker, *How Can Africa Survive?* (New York: Council on Foreign Relations, 1988), p. 78.

22. "Nutritional Status and Poverty in Sub-Sahara Africa," *Findings,* Economic Management and Social Policy, No. 108, International Bank for Reconstruction and Development, April 1998, p. 1.

23. Peter Svarre, "Growth Alone Won't End Poverty, says World Bank," *Africa Recovery,* January–April 1997, p. 31.

24. Mamadou Dia, *Africa's Management in the 1990s and Beyond: Reconciling Indigenous and Transplanted Institutions* (Washington, D.C.: The World Bank, 1996), p. 44.

25. Letter, Randall Robinson, president, TransAfrica, to Rep. Charles B. Rangel, February 10, 1998.

26. Letter, Peggy Taylor, director, Department of Legislation, AFL-CIO, to Rep. Charles B. Rangel, February 24, 1998.

27. Lorraine Woellert, "Black Caucus Divided on Africa Trade," *The Washington: Times,* February 26, 1998, p. A4.

28. Letter, Rep. Charles B. Rangel, Committee on Ways and Means, to Randall Robinson, President, TransAfrica, February 25, 1998.

29. Letter, Rep. Charles B. Rangel, House Ways and Means Committee, to Ms. Peggy Taylor, Legislative Director, AFL-CIO, March 2, 1998.

30. "A Force March to Congress' Tune," *The Washington Times,* March 11, 1998, p. A11.

31. "Global Trade Watch," *Public Citizen,* March 4, 1998. Retrieved from <http://www.citizen.org/gtw>.

32. Letter, Randall Robinson, President, House, U.S. Congress, March 4, 1998.

33. AF/Fo, March 4, 1998.

34. Letter, Rep. Charles B. Rangel, Head of Presidential Mission on Economic Cooperation to Africa, to President Bill Clinton, December 17, 1997. This communication was followed by a more detailed report of January 17, 1998.

35. Ambassador Roble Olhaye, Republic of Djibouti and Dean of the African Diplomatic Corps, to Randall Robinson, President, TransAfrica, March 4, 1998, cc: The Honorable Congressman Charles B. Rangel.

36. Ambassador Vijay S. Makhan, Assistant Secretary General of the Organization of African Unity, to Rep. Charles B. Rangel, March 10, 1998. cc: Rep. Phil Crane, Rep. Jim McDermott, Mel Foote, Constituency for Africa, Mrs. Rosa Whitaker, Assistant U.S. Trade Representative for Africa.

37. Ibid.

38. The writer serves as Vice President of CFA and in March of 1998 made a public statement in opposition to the Bill. See "The Second Rape of Africa?," *The Washington Informer,* March 5–12, 1998.

39. Letter, Rep. Jesse Jackson Jr. to Rep. Philip Crane, March 10, 1998.

40. "African Growth and Opportunity Act, *Congressional Record,* House of Representatives, p. H1042.

41. Ibid., p. 1065.

42. Ibid., p. 1070.

43. Ibid., p. 1515.

44. See House of Representatives, Roll Call no. 47, March 11, 1998.

45. African Growth and Opportunity Act," *Congressional Record,* House of Representatives, March 11, 1998, p. H1052.

46. Tajudeen Abdul-Raheem, ed., *Pan Africanism: Politics, Economy and Social Change in the Twenty-First Century* (New York: New York University Press, 1996), p. 156.

47. See Ronald Walters, *Pan Africanism in the African Diaspora* (Detroit, Mich.: Wayne State University Press, 1993), p. 74.

Part 3

Section 10

Human Rights and Gender in U.S. Foreign Policy

The rapidly evolving agenda of international affairs at the start of the twenty-first century is captured in part by the two insightful contributions in Section 10, one on human rights, the other on gender. These selections underscore the reality that Double Diversity intersects in powerful ways with many substantive issues. Historically, domestic ethnic groups have been deeply concerned about gaining civil rights in the United States, and ensuring the safety and democratic protection of their cultural cousins in their ancestral homeland. The struggle of women to achieve equality in foreign affairs and the impact of greater gender integration certainly parallels the conditions of ethnic minorities. Furthermore, these essays show that the political struggles and alliances we see in Double Diversity also form around other topics. For example, the Larman C. Wilson piece demonstrates that policy issues don't get automatically placed on the foreign policy agenda, nor are they automatically institutionalized and sustained. Topics such as human rights must compete with other issues, and interest in them will rise and fall over time, even within the same administration.

29

Human Rights in U.S. Foreign Policy

The Rhetoric and the Practice

LARMAN C. WILSON

In applying the concepts of continuity and change, ends and means to U.S. foreign policy, the case can be made that the commitment to idealism in foreign Policy by U.S. administrations has for the most part been rhetorical. There has been some continuity in the rhetorical commitment to human rights, which were defined initially as inherent in democracy and representative government, with great importance assigned to elections.

There has been a large gap, however, between the commitment and efforts to translate it into policy; the commitment to human rights, whether as the end or as the means of foreign policy, like the commitment to other ideals, has usually been transcended by other policy considerations—namely, those having to do with national security. An early example of the difference between commitment and practice on ideals was the decision to create a national democratic society in the United States but to eschew giving aid to other threatened democratic governments or societies. A more recent example has been the use of the commitment to democracy as a rationalization to justify supporting nondemocratic regimes that are being threatened by communist subversion.

Several U.S. administrations, however, including those of Presidents Wilson, Roosevelt, Kennedy, and Carter, have made a particularly strong rhetorical commitment to representative government and human rights and have attempted to convert these ideals into principles of foreign policy. As a result of the efforts of these presidents to implement as policy what they advocated concerning human rights, they were faced with the dilemma of "the politico-moral balancing" of "what *ought* to be done with what can be done."[1] In the process of trying to resolve the dilemma, to balance the commitment to human rights with other policy considerations, their original rhetorical commitments to human rights had to be greatly modified and reduced in the crucible of foreign policy decisionmaking. In fact, the commitment of every president to human rights appeared to assume a decreasing priority.

President Carter's pronounced commitment to the place of human rights in his administration's approach, contrary to that of the Reagan administration, provides the most recent case. President Carter's public statements about human rights—that it would be the "soul" of his foreign policy, for example—appeared to have broken the so-called conspiracy of silence on the subject generally attributed to the Nixon and Ford administrations. And his ready acceptance of and zealous efforts to implement the human rights program mandated by the Congress in the early 1970s signified to some that "humanitarian concerns have moved from the wings to center stage in the foreign policy decisionmaking process."[2]

President Carter's statements and efforts on behalf of human rights provoked great controversy; his policy, in fact, renewed the debate about the national interest between idealists and realists.

There were three interesting aspects of President Carter's human rights approach involving both foreign and domestic policy. First, his high-intensity commitment to human rights and his earnest early efforts to translate the former into action were in response to a human rights program mandated by the Congress before he assumed office. Although he was happy to comply with the program of Congress, what was unique was that this was the first time that the Congress had legislated human rights policy. Second, the active pursuit of human rights as a goal of foreign policy—its institutionalization in the executive branch—indicated a departure in policy, one that could not be sustained. The third aspect was President Carter's unique rationale for human rights in foreign policy. Unlike his predecessors, he maintained that all members of the United Nations were bound under the 1945 Charter and the Universal Declaration of Human Rights of 1948 to respect human rights, which justified certain U.S. actions against countries that violated the human rights of their citizens. Related to this stance is the question whether human rights are now—or are becoming—a matter of public policy. That is, does there exist an international law of human rights, based upon both treaties and custom, that imposes legal duties upon all states in the treatment of their citizens and that justifies states in taking action against violators of human rights? This is a widely debated question.

The major purpose of this essay is to examine the place of human rights in U.S. foreign policy, with special emphasis on the relation between rhetoric and practice in the policy mandated by the Congress and pursued by recent administrations.[3] This will include an answer to the following question: Will humanitarian concerns in U.S. foreign policy move from center stage, as some believed in the late 1970s, back to the wings?

THE HUMAN RIGHTS INITIATIVE OF CONGRESS

Beginning in the late 1960s and continuing in the early 1970s, there was a mounting congressional challenge to limit the executive's prerogatives in matters concerning Vietnam. One manifestation of this challenge by the Congress was a growing concern about the place of human rights in U.S. foreign policy. This concern was initiated mainly by liberals but was soon supported by a conservative liberal coalition in which the former were opposed to leftist governments and the latter opposed to rightist governments.

The first legislative initiative occurred in 1973, when the House Foreign Affairs Subcommittee on International Organizations and Movements, of which Representative Donald M. Fraser (Democrat, Minnesota) was chairman, conducted a series of hearings on the international protection of human rights. From this beginning there flowed an extensive body of legislative restrictions, introduced by a group of Democratic congressmen—namely, Representatives Fraser and Tom Harkin (Iowa) and Senators James Abourezk (South Dakota), Alan Cranston (California), Hubert H. Humphrey (Minnesota), and Edward M. Kennedy (Massachusetts)—upon U.S. bilateral aid to states that were guilty of violating human rights. There was also a partially successful effort to apply these restrictions to the actions of the U.S. members of certain multilateral lending agencies—the World Bank and the IMF—and the regional development banks.

It was during Congressman Fraser's subcommittee hearings that one witness presented a widely accepted—and often quoted—characterization of human rights as "the stepchildren of United States foreign policy."[4] The subcommittee's report reflected this viewpoint in its conclusions: The human rights factor is not accorded the high priority it deserves in our country's foreign policy. . . . The State Department . . . has taken the position that human rights is a domestic matter. . . . Unfortunately, the prevailing attitude has led the United States into embracing governments which practice torture and unabashedly violate almost every human rights guarantee pronounced by the world community. . . . A higher priority for human rights in foreign policy is both morally imperative and practically necessary."[5]

The subcommittee's high priority for human rights contrasted sharply with the views expressed by Henry Kissinger at the 1973 hearings for his confirmation as secretary of state. He stated: I believe it is dangerous for us to make the domestic policy of countries around the world a direct objective of American foreign policy. . . . The protection of basic human rights is a very sensitive aspect of the domestic jurisdiction of . . . governments."[6]

Congress was more responsive to Congressman Fraser than to the new secretary of state, however, and initiated its "new directions in development aid" in the Foreign Assistance Act of 1973. This act, stressing basic human needs and the needs of the poor majorities in developing countries, sought to deny to some countries economic and military aid and funds for police training on the grounds that they had violated human rights and called upon the president to take action for the protection of human rights in Chile. A year later, the Congress added a new section—502B—to the Foreign Assistance Act. That section declared that "a principal goal of the foreign policy of the United States shall be to promote the increased observance of internationally recognized human rights by all countries" and set forth the following human rights formula for U.S. action: "The President shall substantially reduce or terminate security assistance to any government which engages in a *consistent pattern of gross violations of internationally recognized human rights.*"[7]

In late 1975, the Department of State indicated its reservations and preference for "quiet but forceful diplomacy" as the best means for promoting human rights. The department's report stated, among other things, the following:

> Experience demonstrated that the political, social, and cultural problems which cause seemingly intractable human rights abuses to occur need to be resolved *before* real improvements in human rights conditions can apparently take place—with or without bilateral or international pressure. . . . In view of the widespread nature of human rights violations in the world, we have found no adequately objective way to make distinctions of degree between nations. This fact leads us, therefore, to the conclusion that neither the U.S. security interest nor the human rights cause would be properly served by the public obloquy and impaired relations . . . that would follow the making of inherently subjective . . . determinations that "gross violations" do or do not exist or that a "consistent" pattern of such . . . does or does not exist in such countries.[8]

This report prompted a strong reaction by the Congress and the enactment of additional legislation, including the addition of Section 116, the Harkin amendment, to the Foreign Assistance Act by means of the International Development and Food Assistance Act of 1974. No longer setting forth the "sense of Congress," Congress in this section legally *prohibited* development assistance to a country that had "a consistent pattern of gross violations . . . *unless* such assistance will directly benefit the needy people in such country" (emphasis added). The president was required to submit an annual report to the Congress regarding compliance.

In 1976 the Congress extended the restrictions that applied to bilateral aid to two regional development banks. In Public Law 94–302, the U.S. executive directors of the African Development Fund and the Inter-American Development Bank were directed "to vote against any loan, any extension of financial assistance, or any technical assistance" to a country violating the human rights of its citizens. (This directive was relaxed the following year.) In the same year, Congress included extensive human rights directives in the International Security Assistance and Arms Export Control Act. This act included the creation of the position of coordinator for human rights and humanitarian affairs in the Department of State, to be appointed by the president and approved by the Senate,"[9] and the requirement of annual reports to the Congress by the secretary of state on human rights practices in each country receiving security assistance.

When the Arms Export Control Act was first passed, it permitted Congress by a concurrent resolution to end military assistance to a country because of violations of human rights. This led to President Ford's veto of the measure because he believed that such congressional authority intruded upon his prerogatives in the foreign policy field. At the same time he expressed the opinion that such restrictions

> would most likely be counterproductive as a means for eliminating discriminatory practices and promoting human rights. The likely result would be a selective disassociation of the United States from governments unpopular with the Congress, thereby diminishing our ability to advance the cause of human rights through diplomatic channels.[10]

He did accept the measure, however, when the Congress changed it to provide that a joint resolution was necessary in order to terminate aid.[11] Notwithstanding Secretary of State Kissinger's earlier statements about human rights in foreign policy and the low priority he assigned to them, he responded to the pressure from Congress. This was indicated by the change in his attitude and policy toward Africa and by his criticisms of the Pinochet government in Chile. At the 1976 meeting of the General Assembly of the Organization of American States (OAS), held in Chile, he gave an entire speech on the subject, entitled "Human Rights and the Western Hemisphere." He declared: "One of the most compelling issues of our time, and one which calls for the concerted action of all responsible peoples and nations, is the necessity to protect and extend the fundamental rights of humanity."[12]

THE CARTER ADMINISTRATION AND HUMAN RIGHTS

While he was campaigning for the presidency, former Governor Carter introduced the issue of human rights in foreign policy, and his effort seemed to evoke a favorable public response. He criticized the incumbent administration for its preoccupation with national security and lack of interest in human rights. Insisting that the pursuit of human rights was in the national interest, he promised that, if elected, he would place great stress upon human rights. Once he became president, he made it clear that human rights would be central to the foreign policy of his administration. This commitment was indicated in his inaugural address, when he declared:

> Because we are free we can never be indifferent to the fate of freedom elsewhere. Our moral sense dictates a clear-cut preference for those societies which share with us an abiding respect for individual human rights.... Our commitment to human rights must be absolute.[13]

Following this pledge and his statement four months later at the University of Notre Dame reaffirming "America's commitment to human rights as a fundamental tenet of our foreign policy,"[14] President Carter reiterated his commitment to human rights in a series of public addresses and press releases, and he stressed five points.[15] First, he rejected the domestic jurisdiction argument advanced by his predecessors and critics that the pursuit of human rights in U.S. foreign policy would violate the domestic jurisdiction and sovereignty of a foreign state, thus constituting intervention in its internal affairs. President Carter rejected this view as an invalid rationalization, maintaining that the United States, along with other members of the United Nations, had a responsibility and a "legal right" under the Charter and Universal Declaration of Human Rights to criticize violations of human rights. In his March 1977 speech at the United Nations, he declared:

> All the signatories of the UN Charter have pledged themselves to observe and to respect human rights. Thus, no member of the United Nations can claim that mistreatment of its citizens is solely its own business. Equally, no member can avoid its responsibilities to review and to speak when torture or unwarranted deprivation occurs in any part of the world.... The solemn commitments of the UN Charter, of the UN's Universal Declaration for Human Rights ... and of many other international instruments must be taken just as seriously as commercial or security agreements.[16]

There is considerable debate among experts in international law concerning the binding nature of the human rights articles of the United Nations Charter and of the Universal Declaration.[17] Two leading scholars have recently made a legal case rejecting the traditional domestic jurisdiction sovereignty obstacle to international protection of human rights and justifying humanitarian intervention in support of human rights.[18]

There is no debate, however, about a state's being legally bound if it has become a party to one of the human rights treaties drafted by the United Nations.[19] One reality involving these treaties, an embarrassing one to President Carter, is that the United States at the time of his United Nations speech had not even signed all of them and had not ratified the principal ones, such as the two United Nations covenants. This is why he also promised in his speech to sign the unsigned ones and to seek the approval of the Senate.[20] President Carter subsequently fulfilled his pledge to sign the unsigned treaties. Ironically, the reservations he proposed in his message transmitting the four human rights treaties to the Senate seriously undercut the significance of the signing by the United States. In fact, some states will surely object to the nature of the U.S. reservations.[21]

Second, President Carter denied the "linkage" concept of former Secretary of State Kissinger. In rejecting the view that the human rights goal would jeopardize more important goals, such as national security and world order, Carter emphasized that his administration would pursue objectives in human rights at the same time that it sought economic, military, and political goals. Third, President Carter declared that the United States would honor its pledge to human rights even if it strained bilateral relations.

Fourth, he rejected the claim that the efforts of the United States to draw world attention to human rights would cause an increase in the number of violations of human rights. He believed, instead, that such an approach by the United States would promote human rights and reduce violations in the long run.

And, fifth, President Carter maintained that concern with human rights was in and would serve the national interest. He also referred to this idea in his University of Notre Dame speech: "I believe that we can have a foreign policy that is democratic, that is based on fundamental values, and that uses power and influence which we have for humane purposes." And he further observed that there was a "trend" in behalf of the individual in the world and that "to lead it will be to regain the moral stature that we once had."[22]

Implementation. President Carter moved rapidly to translate into action his own commitment to human rights and to carry out the congressional program. He signed the two United Nations covenants on human rights and the American Convention on Human Rights and sent them to the Senate, along with the Convention on the Elimination of All Forms of Racial Discrimination, requesting that they be approved. The work of the Human Rights Commission of the Organization of American States was strongly supported, and at the 1977 meeting of the General Assembly Secretary of State Cyrus Vance made an important address on human rights and announced that the United States was increasing its financial contribution to the Human Rights Commission of the OAS. One of the most forceful actions taken was the announced cutoff by the administration of military aid to Argentina, Ethiopia, and Uruguay, a cutoff that was subsequently applied to other countries. This provoked a strong reaction, and the countries charged the United States with intervention in their internal affairs. The Carter administration also successfully lobbied for repeal of the 1972 Byrd amendment, which permitted U.S. imports of chrome from Rhodesia (now Zimbabwe) in violation of a resolution of the United Nations Security Council. These actions and others evoked criticism of the policy, and the president also had some difficulties with the Congress. Before turning to a discussion of the controversy and his problems, it may be helpful to examine the institutionalization of the human rights machinery in the executive branch.

An important aspect of President Carter's implementation of human rights was his prompt expansion and development of a human rights bureaucracy. He was interested in upgrading and broadening the functions of the Human Rights Office, created in 1975 as the Office of the Coordinator for Human Rights and Humanitarian Affairs. In order to pressure the Ford administration into paying greater attention to human rights, the Congress in 1976 elevated the position to that of an assistant secretary of state. To head this three-division bureau—Office of Human Rights, Office of Refugee and Migration Affairs—and section on Prisoners of War and Missing in Action, each headed by a deputy assistant secretary—President Carter appointed Patricia Derian, a former activist in the civil rights movement in Mississippi, as the first assistant secretary of state for human rights and humanitarian affairs.[23]

Another body was created by the National Security Council in early 1977 for the purpose of coordinating decisions—concerning human rights—the Interagency Committee on Human Rights and Foreign Assistance, commonly called the Christopher Committee because its chairman was Warren Christopher, the deputy secretary of state. The Christopher Committee was composed of representatives at the deputy assistant secretary level from the departments of Defense and the Treasury, the Agency for International Development (AID), and the National Security Council, plus representatives from all the functional and regional agencies, such as the departments of Agriculture and Commerce and the Export-Import Bank (EXIM) and the Overseas Private Investment Corporation (OPIC).

Despite the alacrity with which the Carter administration carried out the human rights program mandated by the Congress and institutionalized and developed its own initiatives, some conflicts with the Congress arose. One serious difference between the two branches that developed in 1977, and also involved differences between the House and Senate, concerned the role of the U.S. member in each of the multilateral lending agencies regarding questions of human rights. The approach of the House, reflected by the amendment of Congressman Herman Badillo (Democrat, New York), *required* the U.S. members in these international lending institutions to oppose loans to countries that violated human rights *unless* such loans directly served the basic needs of the citizens of the recipient countries.[24] The Senate, however, preferring a more moderate approach, wanted the U.S. members in these institutions to exert their influence in directing aid away from countries with poor records in human rights. The Foreign Relations Committee was opposed to mandating that the U.S. members vote against loans to countries that violated human rights. President Carter favored the approach of the Senate and obtained a compromise between the two houses, which instructed, but did not require, the U.S. members in the multilateral lending institutions to oppose loans *unless* the aid would serve basic human needs.[25] During the 1977 debate, the president of the World Bank, Robert S. McNamara, expressed his negative reaction to the U.S. approach. He stated:

> The Bank ... is helping large numbers of ... people to move out of absolute poverty towards a more decent life. What we are not capable of is action directly related to civil rights. Such action is prohibited by our Charter, it would require information and competence which we lack, and there is no agreement among our member governments on acceptable standards of civil rights.[26]

Mr. McNamara warned further that the bank "could not accept funds from the U.S. if they were not to be 'pooled' but 'tied' to prohibitions on loans to certain countries."[27]

Subsequently, the Congress placed additional restrictions on the executive concerning the multilateral lending institutions. In 1978, legislation on the Supplementary Financing Facility of the IMF required the secretary of the treasury, in consultation with the secretary of state, to submit an annual report to the Congress on the observance of human rights by countries taking advantage of the IMF facility. In addition, the Foreign Assistance and Related Programs Appropriations Act of 1970 required the president to direct the U.S. executive directors in the multilateral agencies to attempt to amend the Articles of Agreement of these agencies and to establish human rights criteria to be applied to loan decisions.[28]

Although during President Carter's first year in office Congress amended the Export-Import Act of 1945 (EXIM) to include provisions concerning human rights, the next year it limited the provisions applying to U.S. trade. This action reflected the belief that EXIM dealt with trade, not aid, and that its purpose was to promote U.S. exports, which positively contributed to the U.S. balance of payments and employment. Also in 1978, the Congress amended and added provisions concerning human rights to the statute of OPIC, which included exceptions upon the basis of national security and basic human needs.

Reaction to Carter's Human Rights Policy. The commitment and style of the Carter administration in carrying out the human rights program developed and mandated by the Congress provoked great controversy and renewed the idealist-realist debate of the 1950s about U.S. foreign policy. Much of the criticism was focused upon style and rhetoric rather than upon substance; some concentrated upon the problems of implementation. Related to the last point were problems of the Carter administration and the inherent difficulties for any government to "differentiate among the categories of the impossible, the desirable and the possible."[29] The bulk of the criticism directed at President Carter included both style and substance and revolved around charges of two specific sorts. The first was that the human rights policy was inconsistent and represented a double standard; the second was that it was counterproductive and ineffective.[30]

The problems of the relation between commitment to human rights and implementation of a policy concerning human rights confronting the Carter administration were indicated by the title of a critical article, "The Hell of Good Intentions,"[31] and a recent critical book, *American Dream, Global Nightmare: The Dilemma of U.S. Human Rights Policy.*[32] Another scholarly critic, one actually in favor of human rights in U.S. foreign policy, criticized President Carter's approach and style, in these words:

[The Carter administration] announced it with trumpets. It gave it a general and abstract statement in advance of particular issues and apart from specific controversies. It hung strong and unqualified words around its neck, and when, as was inevitable, it has had to soften or bend these words, it has been vulnerable to charges that it is irresolute.... The Carter Administration's initial pronouncements gave its policy the quality of a categorical imperative.[33]

This is a valid opinion, even though President Carter had rejected "rigid moral maxims" and had admitted the "limits of moral suasion" in his University of Notre Dame speech.[34] Only after the first eighteen months in office did the administration move away from the general approach and start to deal with problems of implementation case by case.

The presidential rhetoric that raised false and unreal expectations lent credence to charges of inconsistency and a double standard in American policy, especially when human rights seemed to clash with the goal of national security. An example often cited is the administration's action to cut off military assistance to Argentina, Chile, El Salvador, Ethiopia, and Uruguay because of violations of human rights, while continuing such assistance to Iran, the Philippines, and the Republic of Korea despite their violations of human rights. It was also argued that the human rights policy was being applied to small states, particularly in Latin America, in which the United States had no strategic interests.

Related to the charges of inconsistency and a double standard was the assertion that the human rights policy was both counterproductive and ineffective. Countries to whom aid was terminated did not appear to change their policies, but they refused any further U.S. assistance and, in some instances, expelled the U.S. military training missions and turned elsewhere for their purchases and aid. This had the effect of greatly reducing the influence of the United States in relation to that of other suppliers—from Asia, Europe, or the Soviet bloc—and causing a loss of business for American businessmen.

The efficacy of the human rights policy was challenged by a number of critics. One of the strongest charges of the ineffectiveness of the policy was presented by Ernst Haas, who believed that a human rights policy could not possibly succeed, given the heterogeneity and pluralism of the world and the nature of the international political system.

A consistent and energetic policy in the human rights field makes impossible the attainment of other, often more important, objectives of American policy. Once this was realized, something had to give. The human rights policy was the first victim of the realization that politics is the art of the possible, the practice of carefully considering the tradeoffs between competing but equally legitimate objectives ... What was understood by previous administrations also became clear to Carter: international politics is not like the politics of the American civil rights movement.[35]

These criticisms and views were persuasive and relevant. With regard to the conflict between individual and collective rights, the Carter administration's approach to human rights certainly reflected a minority position in the world. The emphasis upon individual, civil, and political rights was juxtaposed with the emphasis upon collective, economic, and social rights on the part of a majority of countries—the Third World, the Communist countries, and even some of the Western democracies. The perspective on individual rights was indicated by the Carter administration's official definition of human rights. Secretary of State Cyrus Vance set forth, in his April 1977 speech at the University of Georgia, three categories of rights: (1) "the right to be free from governmental violations of the integrity of the person"; (2) "the right to the fulfillment of such vital needs as food, shelter, health care, and education"; and (3) "the right to enjoy civil and political liberties."[36] Most of the emphasis was on the first and third categories; Secretary Vance stated in Georgia that the first category was assigned that priority because it was the first to be dealt with by U.S. diplomats.

The Carter administration discovered how easy it was to make public commitments to human rights in foreign policy and how difficult it was to carry them out. The gap between the two, commitment and implementation, steadily widened as the reality of balancing was accepted, although reluctantly. The following dilemma has been acknowledged by policy makers:

> The question is not human rights versus no human rights; instead it is human rights versus national security versus friendly relations with existing regimes versus economic benefits to the U.S. economy and U.S. investors versus humanitarian aid to impoverished people.[37]

The chief executive's personal relations with the generals heading three Latin American countries—Videla of Argentina, Pinochet of Chile, and Somoza of Nicaragua—also undercut his stress upon human rights.[38] At the time of the fall 1977 ceremonial signing of the Panama Canal treaties in Washington, President Carter met individually with each attending head of state, including those from Argentina and Chile (Somoza did not attend).

This conveyed the impression that the treaties were more important than human rights as an issue of hemispheric solidarity.[39] In the Summer of 1978, President Carter sent a letter to General Somoza, praising him for his improvements in human rights. This case of great praise for cosmetic improvements in one of Latin America's most unpopular dictatorial dynasties indicated the primacy given by the administration to maintaining political stability in this strategic area. During the 1978–1979 insurrection in Nicaragua, the principal concern of the United States was the possibility that the toppling of Somoza by the Sandinistas would bring into being "a second Cuba," and the United States pursued a variety of efforts, both in the OAS and outside it, to mediate and reconcile the differences between the two sides. The United States was slow to join the growing Latin American consensus that Somoza had to leave and that a Sandinista government would be an improvement from the standpoint of human rights. Finally, Secretary Vance introduced a resolution at an OAS meeting in June 1979, the month before the defeat of Somoza, calling upon General Somoza to step down and leave his country, the revised resolution passed with a two-thirds majority.[40]

These actions, even though limited to this hemisphere, communicated the general message, in the words of one observer, that human rights would have a significant place in nearly all decisions regarding U.S. foreign policy, but that the amount of significance would depend upon (1) the nature of other variables involved, (2) the type of human rights violations, and, therefore, (3) the countries involved.[41]

After the initiatives of 1977, the Carter administration used international organizations to advance the cause of human rights but only to a limited extent. President Carter preferred to rely on a bilateral approach rather than upon either the United Nations or the OAS. Following his policy statement delivered before the General Assembly in March 1977, as noted above, he decided to present inter-American issues to the regional forum, the OAS, where the United States could exercise considerable influence. The low priority assigned to the United Nations and its Human Rights Commission as useful forums was indicated in the Carter Administration's policy of appointing to the commission part-time representatives selected upon the basis of patronage rather than expertise.[42] In the first year, President Carter also considered the OAS to be important and used it significantly. Following Secretary Vance's address on human rights at the 1977 General Assembly of the OAS, however, and his announcement that the United States would increase its contribution to the budget of the OAS Human Rights Commission, the administration used the OAS only irregularly—for the signing of the Panama Canal treaties, efforts to resolve the Nicaraguan crisis, and so on. One exception was the continued strong U.S. support of the Human Rights Commission, which, although more effective than that of the United Nations, has quite limited powers.

Once the Carter administration had institutionalized and expanded the human rights machinery in the executive branch, particularly in the State Department, and had begun actively trying to implement a human rights policy, two aspects of the process emerged— the internal and the external. The former involved the bureaucratic struggle for influence among competing interests within the executive branch and between it and the legislative branch. The latter involved a human rights constituency outside the government that came to the fore in support of President Carter's commitments to human rights.

The first year of the Carter administration's efforts in behalf of human rights was characterized by factionalism and bitter debates. Many people in various agencies resented what they considered to be a single-minded approach on the part of those in the Human Rights Office. This brought about the formation of various coalitions. In the State Department, for example, there was usually a joining of forces by the Human Rights Office, the Office of Congressional Relations, and the Legal Adviser's Office in opposition to the Defense Department, certain regional bureaus of the Department of State, and such functional bureaus as Political-Military Affairs and Economic and Business Affairs. One serious estrangement developed between the Human Rights Bureau and the Bureau of East Asian Affairs over the Philippines and the Republic of Korea. There also was great tension between the Human Rights Bureau and the Bureau for Inter-American Affairs. The desk officers and regional officers in particular argued that the exponents of human rights were damaging relations with those countries with which the desk officers were concerned as well as with U.S. interests in general. Although many of the early debates and much of the tension were later moderated and dissipated, the Christopher Committee both brought out the strong disagreements and helped smooth them over. In the words of one report, however, "the costs in terms not only of confusion and disillusionment, but of sheer time and energy expended have been high."[43]

The efforts of the Congress first, and then of the Carter administration, were strongly supported by an emerging human rights constituency. Growing out of the civil rights movement and catalyzed by Vietnam and Watergate, this constituency consisted primarily of a coalition of liberals and minority groups. More specifically, the constituency included a vast array of religious, minority, women's, educational, service, and research organizations. A number of the organizations formed the Human Rights Working Group of the Coalition for a New Foreign and Military Policy. The coalition, along with other associations working independently or cooperating informally, applied pressure and made its position known in support of human rights by lobbying, testifying before congressional committees, publishing newsletters, using the mass media, and raising funds.[44]

HUMAN RIGHTS AS PUBLIC POLICY

In considering the human rights policy of the United States under international law, it is necessary to expand the discussion of President Carter's argument that the United States had both a legal duty and a legal right with respect to human rights because it was a party to the United Nations Charter.[45] I seriously doubt the validity of his argument. Instead, it is more reasonable to maintain upon the basis of the existing evidence, and particularly of the practice of the United States, that human rights have not yet achieved the status of international public policy. It is the case, however, that an international law of human rights is emerging. In legal parlance, such a body of law at present is *lex ferenda* (law that it is desired to establish), not *lex lata* (law that exists).

Richard Bilder, among others, has maintained that there exists a "law of human rights" in the form of "a body of international law, institutions, procedures and precedents."[46] He identifies two relevant sources of international law, treaties and custom, and cites the former as "the most important source of international human rights law for lawyers."[47] In considering treaties as a source of legal obligations of the United States, it should be remembered that the United States maintains an important distinction between self-executing and non-self-executing treaties and has placed the United Nations Charter in the latter category, which is a significant qualification of the provision in the U.S. Constitution (Article VI, Section 2) that treaties "shall be the supreme law of the land." In the classic *Fujii* case,[48] the court took the position that, because the United Nations Charter was a non-self-executing treaty and the human rights articles had not been implemented by special congressional legislation, the human rights provisions of the charter were not applicable as domestic law. This continues to be the U.S. approach, and President Carter, in recommending to the Senate reservations to the human rights treaties, maintained the non-self-executing distinction and consequently weakened the position of the United States on human rights.

Considerable debate surrounds custom as a source of legal obligation regarding human rights. A minority view of increasing popularity is that human rights and duties are now derived from principles of customary international law-that is, that the increasing number of legal documents dealing with human rights, both domestic and international, and with popular reaffirmations of human rights, have become a part of customary international law. The Universal Declaration of Human Rights is cited as an example of a source of customary international law and conceptually as legally binding on all states in the international community.[49] I find this argument to be unpersuasive, although at the same time this minority view does contribute to the incremental process that may lead to the future acceptance of duties toward human rights under custom. At present, however, the practice has not been broad enough or the consensus adequate to establish human rights obligations under customary international law. To cite one example, the two human rights covenants of the United Nations, derived from the Universal Declaration and completed in 1966, came into effect in 1976 and so far have some forty ratifications. This limited treaty participation in a United Nations with some 150 members is inadequate and cannot be employed as evidence of a custom that binds those nations, such as the United States, that have not ratified.

Interestingly, both the chief executive and the Congress have been inconsistent in their approaches to human rights under international law, whether from the perspective of treaties or customary rules. President Carter stressed customary rules, but at the same time undercut his approach to treaty approval by proposing damaging reservations to the U.N. covenants. The Congress, in legislating a human rights program, provided as one justification for its concern about human rights the international obligations of the United States as a member of the United Nations. The Senate, by contrast, has consistently refused both before and since the enactment of the human rights program to approve the human rights treaties for fear that they would prompt the United Nations to intervene in the domestic affairs of the United States. Until the United States becomes a full party to these treaties, or until many more years have elapsed and legal duties regarding human rights have been established under customary international law, the case of national duties concerning human rights as international public policy cannot be effectively made.

THE REAGAN ADMINISTRATION AND HUMAN RIGHTS

The 1980 presidential campaign raised once again the important question of balance in foreign policy—namely, the proper equilibrium between national security and human rights—and Governor Ronald Reagan indicated that he favored a shift in emphasis to the former. During the campaign he spoke in favor of human rights and did not challenge President Carter's call for improvements in human rights in foreign countries, but he did criticize the incumbent's inconsistent application of human rights in U.S. foreign policy. Governor Reagan attacked the Carter administration for neglecting U.S. national security, stressed that the Soviet Union was the principal threat to the United States—and human rights—and world peace, and made it clear that human rights in U.S. foreign policy would receive a lower priority as national security was given primary attention. It was indicated that "quiet diplomacy" would be the hallmark of the new administration in the field of human rights. These views were brought together and expressed by Governor Reagan during the late October presidential debate when he declared:

> Because someone didn't meet exactly our standards of human rights, even though they were an ally of ours, instead of trying patiently to persuade them to change their ways, we have, in a number of instances, aided a revolutionary overthrow which results in complete totalitarianism, instead, for these people. I think that this is a kind of a hypocritical policy when ... we're maintaining a detente with the one nation in the world where there are no human rights at all—the Soviet Union.[50]

Although Governor Reagan spoke in favor of human rights in an address on the eve of the election and assured the nation of his commitment as president-elect, he replied to a question on human rights at his first press conference as president-elect in these words:

> Yes. I think that all of us in this country are dedicated to the belief in human rights. But I think it must be a consistent policy. I don't think that you can turn away from some country because here and there they do not totally agree with our concept of human rights, and then ... maintain relations with other countries, or try to develop them where human rights are virtually nonexistent.[51]

The practice of the Reagan administration, in appointments, statements of officials, and changes in foreign policy, illustrates a new balance between national security and human rights. Three nominations to high office symbolized the stress upon national security and the Soviet Union. The first was that of Jeane Kirkpatrick, professor of government at Georgetown University, to be ambassador to the United Nations; the second was that of General Alexander Haig, former commander of the North Atlantic Treaty Organization, to be secretary of state; and the third was that of Ernest Lefever, a former senior fellow at the Brookings Institution and president of the Ethics and Public Policy Center, to be assistant secretary of state for human rights and humanitarian affairs.

Dr. Kirkpatrick's nomination as the only Democrat in the cabinet was not a controversial one, and the Senate Foreign Relations Committee supported it unanimously in mid-January. Certain of her views on human rights were expressed before her nomination and have been reiterated since, for they represent frequently expressed views of members of the Reagan administration, including the president himself. In 1979, she wrote an article, "Dictatorships and Double Standards," which was critical of the human rights policy of the Carter administration. In this article, which attracted Governor Reagan's attention, she expressed certain views that have become important in U.S. foreign policy. She insisted:

What makes the inconsistencies of the Carter administration noteworthy are, first, the administration's moralism—which renders it especially vulnerable to charges of hypocrisy; and second ... [its] predilection for policies that violate the strategic and economic interests of the United States.... The foreign policy of the Carter administration fails not for lack of good intentions but for lack of realism about the nature of traditional versus revolutionary autocracies and the relation of each to the American national interest. Only intellectual fashion and the tyranny of Right/Left thinking prevent intelligent men of good will from perceiving the facts that traditional authoritarian governments are less repressive than revolutionary autocracies, that they are more susceptible of liberalization, and that they are more compatible with the U.S. interests.[53]

Before her nomination had been approved, she said that she hoped that the foreign policy adopted by the Reagan administration would embody "a mixture of morality and power" and criticized the human rights policy of the Carter administration: "Ideals never exist in the abstract. If you try to apply it in that context, the result will be havoc." She also stated that if she had to choose between a "traditional autocrat" such as Nicaragua's Somoza or a "Cuban-backed dictatorship," she would select the former, for "there are degrees of repression."[54]

General Haig's nomination caused a certain amount of controversy, partly because of his past association with President Richard M. Nixon and Watergate and his being a career military man, but primarily because of his preoccupation with the Soviet Union and national defense. At his first press conference as secretary of state he expressed the following opinion concerning human rights: "The assurance of basic human liberties will not be improved by replacing friendly governments which incompletely satisfy our standards of democracy with hostile ones which are even less benign." He saw no need, however, to change the provisions in the Foreign Assistance Act that linked U.S. aid to human rights, for he believed that the law was "not overly restrictive."[55] In answering a question dealing with human rights and terrorism, he indicated the priorities of the new administration. After affirming that "human rights is an essential and fundamental aspect of American foreign policy and domestic policy," he declared:

And as such when you move it from the mainstream of fundamental policymaking and give it an extraordinary role in organizational terms, you frequently result in distortions that probably put in jeopardy the well-meaning objective you seek to achieve. So I would like to see some organizational change in the period ahead—no deemphasis; a change in priorities.

Now the greatest problem to me in the human rights area today is the area of *rampant international terrorism* on both sides of the Iron Curtain.[56]

The nomination of Dr. Lefever, however, provoked a great controversy that culminated in the rejection of his nomination in early June by the Senate Foreign Relations Committee and his subsequent withdrawal from consideration. His nomination by the Reagan administration to head the Bureau of Human Rights was surprising, for he was the most outspoken critic of President Carter's human rights policy in general and toward Chile, the Republic of Korea, Rhodesia (under Ian Smith), and South Africa in particular. He had published a number of articles and had testified in favor of abolishing the human rights machinery. He appeared to be the antithesis of the previous incumbent, Patricia Derian, who was a forceful and outspoken advocate of human rights in U.S. foreign policy. He had the strong support of Senator Jesse Helms (R-N.C.), chairman of the Subcommittee on Western Hemisphere Affairs of the Foreign Relations Committee, who supported him to the end.

In an article published in 1978, "The Trivialization of Human Rights," Dr. Lefever identified "Six Flaws in the Human Rights Policy" of the Carter administration, the second being "confusing totalitarianism with authoritarianism."[57] He believed that the national interest justified assisting authoritarian regimes (Chile, Iran, and the Republic of Korea) while totalitarian regimes (Cambodia, Cuba, North Korea, and the Soviet Union) were the real enemies of the United States. His distinction between totalitarianism and authoritarianism has become another hallmark of the new administration. In general he saw as limited what the United States should attempt to do in promoting human rights:

> In a formal and legal sense, the ... [U.S.] Government has no responsibility—and certainly no authority—to promote human rights in other sovereign states.... Beyond serving as a good example and maintaining our security commitments, there is little the ... [U.S.] Government can or should do to advance human rights, other than using quiet diplomatic channels at appropriate times and places.[58]

Before his nomination, he recommended that Congress repeal the human rights legislation. He proposed that the United States should remove from the statute books all clauses that establish a human rights standard or condition that must be met by another sovereign government before our government transacts normal business with it, unless specifically waived by the president.

> It shouldn't be necessary for any friendly state to pass a human rights test before we extend normal trade relations, before we sell arms or before we provide economic or security assistance. This approach I believe should be adopted toward adversary states like the Soviet Union.[59]

Following the vote of the Foreign Relations Committee against his confirmation in early June, he withdrew his name from consideration by the Senate.[60] The apparent failure of the Reagan administration to initiate a prompt search for another candidate suggested to some observers that the administration might leave vacant the position of assistant secretary for human rights.[61]

In late October, however, almost five months after Dr. Lefever withdrew his name, President Reagan nominated Elliot Abrams, assistant secretary of state for international organization affairs, for the position. Mr. Abrams's support of the president, for whom he had campaigned in 1980 by speaking to Jewish groups throughout the United States about Reagan's foreign policy, had come about in a way similar to that of Ambassador Kirkpatrick. Abrams had been a liberal Democrat during his law school days at Harvard University and later worked for two Democratic senators. He became disillusioned with President Carter's foreign policy, however, and switched to the Republican party.[62] His appointment was not controversial and received little press coverage. He was approved unanimously by the Senate Foreign Relations Committee in November.

The administration's stress upon national security and the apparent unlinking of human rights and foreign policy is demonstrated by a number of recent policy changes, especially concerning relations with Latin America. In keeping with the distinction between authoritarian and totalitarian governments, U.S. assistance, both economic and military, to certain military governments has been resumed. In February, the administration announced that Chile would be eligible for EXIM financing, which had been denied it since 1976. The next month President Reagan asked Congress to repeal a 1977 amend-ment to P.L. 95–148 that prohibited military aid and the sale of arms to Argentina. While agreeing to the request, the House Foreign Affairs Committee and the Senate Foreign Relations Committee specified that such aid should be contingent upon the president's certifying that "significant progress" in human rights had been made in Argentina.[63] Although the administration opposed this requirement, the Congress approved it. (The two committees and the Congress took a similar approach in April and May in response to the administration's $26 million military aid package to El Salvador in requiring pres-idential certification of progress in human rights. Secretary of State Haig presented a formal objection to these qualifications.[64]

Although military aid was to be resumed to Argentina, the outbreak of war in the spring of 1982 between England and Argentina over the control of the Falkland/Malvinas Islands and Argentina's strong reaction against the United States for siding with England post-poned indefinitely the resumption of aid."[65] Military aid was resumed, however, to Honduras and Uruguay and was strongly favored for Guatemala.

The Reagan administration's preoccupation with national security in Latin America has been especially apparent in El Salvador. The fighting between the left and the right, that is, the efforts of the Farabundo Marti Front for National Liberation to overthrow the government, has been presented as a cold war struggle in which the Soviet Union, Cuba, and the Sandinista government of Nicaragua are arming and helping the left. To docu-ment this view, the U.S. government released in February 1981 a White Paper on El Salvador, accompanied by a summary entitled Communist *Interferetice in El Salvador*, which was widely criticized.[66] This approach resulted in (1) the removal of President Carter's ambassador to the country, Robert White, who had stressed reform and urged the United States to pressure the government of El Salvador instead of providing it arms; (2) the denial of economic aid to Nicaragua on the ground that it was helping the left in El Salvador; and (3) an increase in military aid, training, and U.S. advisers to the Salvadoran government. Despite great controversy about the government's human rights record—and that of its rightist allies—the Reagan administration has made the required certifications that the government is "making a concerted and significant effort" concerning human rights and is "making continued progress" in the field of economic and political reforms.[67] Three certifications have been made so far—in January 1982, in July 1982, and in January 1983—and each has been widely debated and challenged by spokesmen of the human rights constituency, including Pat Derian, Elliot Abrams's predecessor.[68]

Another indication of the changing of past policies is in the development of President Reagan's arms-transfer policy. When the administration announced seven guidelines for conventional arms transfers to foreign countries, human rights was not one of them. In a speech in May 1981, James L. Buckley, deputy secretary of state for security affairs, while explaining the new arms policy, criticized President Carter's human rights and nuclear proliferation criteria as ones that had "substituted theology for a healthy sense of preservation."[69]

In early July, another policy change was announced, which involved the U.S. represen-tatives in the multilateral lending institutions. In a proposal to the chairman of the House Subcommittee on International Development Institutions and Finance (of the Committee on Banking and Finance), the assistant secretary of the treasury for legislative affairs proposed a change in P.L. 96–259. The change would free the U.S. representatives in the World Bank and in the InterAmerican Development Bank from voting against or abstaining on loans to states on grounds that they were violators of human rights, namely, on loans currently being considered to Argentina, Chile, Paraguay, and Uruguay.[70] The change in policy was justified because "there have been significant improvements in the human rights situations" in the four countries.[71] The new policy was implemented in late July 1981, thus reversing a four-year practice, when the U.S. representative to the World Bank voted in favor of two loans to Chile. A final example of change toward human rights in foreign policy is the Reagan administration's first annual report on human rights.[72] The report's introduction articulated an approach different from that in the four preceding annual reports of the Carter administration.[73] The report stressed civil and political rights and made no mention of economic and social rights. It stated that much more attention will be given to the human rights conduct of "opposition and terrorist groups" and that "Soviet bloc human rights violations" would be regularly exposed. It also made clear that among the "instruments" for pursuing human rights, "traditional diplomacy" will be stressed along with the "criterion of effectiveness." The introduction did refer to the problem of balance and consistency, in these words:

> Since the United States will continue to seek the redress of human rights abuses even in friendly countries, human rights policy will sometimes be very troubling. We will sometimes be forced to make hard choices between the need to answer human rights violations and other foreign policy interests, such as trade or security. In some cases we will have to accept the fact that bilateral relations with a friendly country may be damaged because of our human rights concern. This is the unavoidable price of a consistent policy.[74]

In addition to the 1981 annual report, the Reagan administration's expenditures and requests for funds for economic and military assistance also suggest a change in orientation. In relative terms, the amounts requested or expended for military aid have increased markedly, and requests and expenditures for economic development assistance and Food-for-Peace have declined.[75] Although the resignation of Secretary of State Haig in June 1981 and his replacement the next month by George P. Shultz, who was approved unanimously by the Senate Foreign Relations Committee, have resulted in a decline of cold war rhetoric, it is too early to note any shifts or to be able to characterize Secretary Shultz's approach. It does appear, however, that human rights concerns are being "factored in" more than previously. It has been reported that Secretary Shultz did visit the Human Rights Office shortly after his appointment and indicated his personal commitment to human rights; he has also increased Mr. Abrams's staff.[76]

CONCLUSION

In answering the question posed in the introduction, whether human rights would move from the center of the stage back to the wings, certain qualifications are necessary. First, the experience of the Carter administration revealed that human rights were at center stage primarily at the rhetorical level and that they remained there so far as attempts at policy implementation were concerned only during the first eighteen months of his incumbency. After 1978 the rhetoric and practice were greatly modified; the former was curtailed because it was increasingly difficult to translate it into policy. Second, human rights as a policy during the Carter administration moved from receiving great emphasis to being "factored into" the foreign policy decisionmaking process. The Reagan administration's comparatively limited rhetorical commitment to human rights in U.S. foreign policy and much greater stress upon national security and the threat posed by the Soviet Union suggest less concern with the former. In his first two years, President Reagan indicated certain changes in the U.S. stand on human rights, principally a preference for unlinking foreign assistance from human rights and for quiet diplomacy. These changes illustrate an important question of foreign policy, which came forth during the 1980 campaign: How should human rights be balanced with other considerations in U.S. foreign policy? What, for example, is the proper balance or equilibrium between human rights and national security in U.S. foreign policy? Is it possible to reconcile the two?

This is a difficult question to answer in practice, for the balance can never be fixed or permanent, but is a constantly shifting mixture of the many facets of a state's foreign policy, which respond to the changing needs of the state and the challenges confronting it. Obviously, there are priorities, and national security must transcend all others if the very existence and survival of a state is in jeopardy. If survival is not at stake, human rights have an important place, particularly in the foreign policy of a state that is a superpower, a world leader, and one that has a democratic and representative system of government. Because of the nature of foreign policy, the shifting priorities, and the constant balancing and tuning required, there can be no consistent policy for dealing with human rights according to a fixed priority. The particular balance is a function of the circumstances in each case. For this reason double standards are inevitable. Certainly the national interest can be harmed by a preoccupation with human rights or with national security (unless survival is at stake), and the problem for the United States as a democracy and a superpower is the proper foreign policy equilibrium. Finally, the proper balance between human rights and national security to be achieved and translated into foreign policy will continue to pose a constant dilemma for the United States. It is likely that human rights "will continue to be an element of future American foreign policy," one of varying and limited priority, but one that "will continue to receive [some] attention in the policymaking process."[77] But there will be a much more restrained public articulation of a commitment to human rights in U.S. foreign policy.

NOTES

1. Kenneth W. Thompson, ed., *The Moral Imperatives of Human Rights: A World Survey* (Washington, D.C.: University Press of America, 1980), p. 17.

2. Richard B. Lillich, "A United States Policy of Humanitarian Intervention and Intercession," in Human Rights and American Foreign Policy, ed. Donald T. Kommers and Gilburt D. Loescher (Notre Dame, Ind.: University of Notre Dame Press, 1979), p. 279.

3. There have been a number of recent books on human rights and U.S. foreign policy, some of them with identical titles. C. Beitz, *Human Rights and Foreign Policy: The Problem of Priorities* (College Park: University of Maryland, 1978); Tom J. Farer, ed., *Toward a Humanitarian Diplomacy: A Primer for Policy* (New York: New York University Press, 180); Kommers and Loescher, *Human Rights and American Foreign Policy*; Peter G. Brown and Douglas MacLean, eds., *Human Rights and U.S. Foreign Policy: Principles and Applications* (Lexington, Mass.: D.C. Heath & Company, 1979); Barry M. Rubin and Elizabeth P. Spiro, eds., *Human Rights and U.S. Foreign Policy* (Boulder, Colo.: Westview Press, 1979); and Sandy Vogelgesang, *American Dream, Global Nightmare: The Dilemma of U.S. Human Rights Policy* (New York: W. W. Norton & Company, 1980).

4. Statement by Professor Tom Farer quoted by Richard Lillich in "A U.S. Policy of Humanitarian Intervention," p. 278.

5. "Human Rights in the World Community: A Call for U.S. Leadership," 93d Cong., 2d sess. (1974), p. 13.

6. Quoted in Roberta Cohen, "Human Rights Decision-Making in the Executive Branch: Some Proposals for a Coordinated Strategy," in Kommers and Loescher, *Human Rights and American Foreign Policy*, p. 217.

7. Library of Congress, Congressional Research Service, *Human Rights and U.S. Foreign Assistance: Experiences and Issues in Policy Implementation (1977–1978),* Report prepared for the Committee on Foreign Relations, United States Senate, 06th Cong., Ist sess. (1979), p. 17 (emphasis added). For an excellent discussion of the legislation, see, in addition to the Library of Congress report, pp. 16–29, Tom Harkin, "Human Rights and Foreign Aid: Forging an Unbreakable Link," in Brown and MacLean, *Human Rights and U.S.*

Foreign Policy, pp. 15–26. For a list of all the pertinent legislation, see William Buckley, "Human Rights and Foreign Policy," *Foreign Affairs*, vol. 58 (Spring 1980), pp. 784–85.

8. Library of Congress, *Human Rights and U.S. Foreign Assistance*, p. 15.

9. In early 1974, there was only one full-time human rights officer in the executive branch—in the State Department's Bureau of International Organization Affairs. His duties involved the preparation of the government's position on human rights at the United Nations. The next officer added was in the legal adviser's office. For the background to the creation of the Human Rights Office, see John D. Martz and Lars Schoultz, eds., *Latin America, the United States, and the Inter-American System* (Boulder, Colo.: Westview Press, 1980), p. 187. For the expansion of the human rights machinery, *see* Cohen, "Human Rights Decision-Making," pp. 219–221.

10. Library of Congress, *Human Rights and U.S. Foreign Assistance*, p. 20.

11. A joint resolution is subject to the veto, which can be overridden by a two-thirds vote; a concurrent resolution requires a simple majority vote and is not subject to the veto.

12. Quoted in Martz and Schoultz, *Latin America, the United States, and the Inter-American System*, p. 176. Once Secretary Kissinger was out of office, however, he presented his original and preferred position. Ibid., p. 177.

13. Quoted in Cohen, "Human Rights Decision-Making," p. 222.

14. U.S. Department of State, "Humane Purposes in Foreign Policy," News Release, May 22, 1977, p. 2.

15. Cohen, "Human Rights Decision-Making," pp. 222–223.

16. U.S. Department of State, "Arms, Economic Prosperity, and Human Rights," News Release, March 17, 1977, pp. 3–4. The new Section 502B in the Foreign Assistance Act of 1974 included language regarding U.S. "international obligations as set forth in the Charter of the United Nations."

17. Two leading scholars in international law, the late Professor Hans Kelsen and Judge Philip Jessup, had opposing views about the legal status of Articles 55 and 56 of the United Nations Charter. While the former held that they were not legally binding, the latter held that they were. Hans Kelsen, *Principles of International Law*, 2nd ed. (New York: Holt, Rinehart and Winston, 1966), pp. 226, 237; Philip C. Jessup, *A Modern Law of Nations* (New York: Columbia University Press, 1948), p. 91, and the United States, applying its distinction between self-executing and nonself-executing treaties, maintains that the Charter is not a self-executing treaty, which means that the human rights provisions require implementing legislation by the Congress. Traditional international law provides that a "declaration" does not impose a legally binding duty; instead, it is a moral obligation.

18. Thomas Buergenthal, "Domestic Jurisdiction, Intervention, and Human Rights: The International Law Perspective," in Brown and MacLean, *Human Rights and U.S. Foreign Policy*, pp. 111–120; and Lillich, "A U.S. Policy of Humanitarian Intervention," pp. 278–298.

19. The treaties drafted by the United Nations in the 1950s and 1960s are the following: Convention on the Political Rights of Woman; Convention on the Abolition of Slavery; Convention on the Status of Refugees; Convention on the Elimination of All Forms of Racial Discrimination; Covenant on Civil and Political Rights; and Covenant on Economic, Social, and Cultural Rights. All these treaties are in effect; the United States has ratified the first three.

20. In addition to the Genocide Convention, which has been before the Senate since the early 1950s, President Carter asked the Senate to consider four additional treaties: the UN Covenant on Civil and Political Rights; the UN Covenant on Economic, Social, and Cultural Rights; the UN Convention on the Elimination of All Forms of Racial Discrimination; and the American Convention on Human Rights (this convention went into effect in 1978).

21. In his 1978 letter of transmittal of four treaties to the Senate—the convention on racial discrimination, the two covenants on human rights, and the American Convention on Human Rights—President Carter, who had signed the last three in 1977, stated the following: "It is increasingly anomalous that the list of parties [to the two covenants on human rights and the covenant on racial discrimination] does not include the United States, whose human rights record domestically and internationally has long served as an example to the world community." He proposed to the Senate that certain articles in the two covenants on human rights be classified as non-self -executing. U.S. Congress, Senate, Four Treaties Pertaining to Human Rights: Message from the President of the United States Transmitting. . . . 95th Cong., 2d sess. (1978), pp. v-vi, viii, x, xii, xv.

22. U.S. Department of State, Press Release, May 22, 1977, pp. 1, 3.

23. Concerning the development of the human rights bureaucracy, see Cohen, "Human Rights Decision-Making," pp. 226–36; and Library of Congress, *Human Rights and U.S. Foreign Assistance*, pp. 31–42.

24. Library of Congress, *Human Rights and U.S. Foreign Assistance*, p. 21.

25. Ibid., pp. 21–22. In carrying out the legislation applicable to the U.S. representatives to the multilateral

institutions, the administration interpreted the words "to oppose" to include abstentions. See Elizabeth P. Spiro, "Front Door or Back Stairs: U.S. Human Rights Policy in the International Financial Institutions," in Rubin and Spiro, *Human Rights and U.S. Foreign Policy*, p. 137.

26. Quoted in Rubin and Spiro, *Human Rights and U.S. Foreign Policy*, p. 136.

27. Ibid., p. 146.

28. Mr. McNamara's reference above to the "Charter" meant the bank's Articles of Agreement, which prohibit political considerations from being taken into account in extending loans (Article 4, Section 10); the bank relies upon economic and technical criteria.

29. Sandra Vogelgesang, "What Price Principle? U.S. Policy on Human Rights," *Foreign Affairs*, vol. 56, no. 4 (July 1978), p. 833.

30. See Ernst B. Haas, "Human Rights: To Act or Not to Act?" in *Eagle Entangled: U.S. Foreign Policy in a Complex World*, ed. Kenneth A. Oye, Donald Rothchild, and Robert J. Lieber (New York: Longman, 1979), pp. 182–92; Library of Congress, *Human Rights and U.S. Foreign Assistance*, pp. 47–67; Abraham M. Sirkin, "Can a Human Rights Policy Be Consistent?" in Brown and MacLean, *Human Rights and U.S. Foreign Policy*, pp. 199–213; and Cohen, "Human Rights Decision-Making," pp. 224–25.

31. Stanley Hoffman, *Foreign Policy* (Winter 1977), pp. 3–26. For another very critical article, see Buckley, "Human Rights and Foreign Policy," pp. 775–796.

32. Vogelgesang, *American Dream*.

33. Charles Frankel, "Human Rights and Foreign Policy," *Headline Series*, vol. 241 (October 1978), p. 54.

34. U.S. Department of State, News Release, May 22, 1977, pp. 2–3.

35. Haas, "Human Rights," pp. 169, 185, 193. See also Hoffmann, "Hell of Good Intentions."

36. U.S. Department of State, "The Secretary of State, Speech: Human Rights Policy," Press Release, April 30, 1977, p. 1. Secretary Vance stated later in his speech: "In pursuing a human rights policy, we must always keep in mind the limits of our power and of our wisdom. A sure formula for defeat of our goals would be a rigid, hubristic attempt to impose our values on others. A doctrinaire plan of action would be as damaging as indifference."

37. Lars Schoultz, "U.S. Diplomacy and Human Rights in Latin America," in Martz and Schoultz, Latin America, the U.S., and the Inter-American System, p. 174.

38. Most of these cases are drawn from ibid., pp. 181–183, 195–197.

39. Ibid., p. 182.

40. "OAS Votes for Ouster of Somoza," *Washington Post*, June 24, 1979.

41. Schoultz, "U.S. Diplomacy and Human Rights in Latin America," p. 183.

42. Ibid., p. 196.

43. Library of Congress, *Human Rights and U.S. Foreign Assistance*, p. 82. Concerning bureaucratic politics, see Spiro, "Front Door or Back Stairs," pp. 134–35.

44. Some of the groups in the coalition are the following: Americans for Democratic Action; American Friends Service Committee; Center for International Policy; Clergy and Laity Concerned; National Council of Churches; Washington Office on Africa; Washington Office on Latin America.

45. See earlier and footnotes 17, 18, and 19.

46. Richard B. Bilder, "The Status of International Human Rights Law: An Overview," in *International Human Rights Law and Practice: The Roles of the United Nations, the Private Sector, the Government, and Their Lawyers*, ed. James C. Tuttle (Philadelphia: American Bar Association, 1978), p. 3.

47. Ibid., p. 7.

48. Sei *Fujii v. State of California*, 1952; for text, see *American Journal of International Law*, vol. 46 (July 1952), pp. 559–73.

49. See, for example, Bilder, "Status of International Human Rights Law," pp. 3–8.

50. Congressional Quarterly Weekly Report, vol. 38 (October-December 1980), p. 3284.

51. Ibid., p. 3353.

52. Commentary (November 1979), p. 42.

53. Ibid., p. 44.

54. "Envoy-Designate Would Be Selective with Aid to U.N.," *Washington Post*, January 8, 1981.

56. "Excerpts from Haig's Remarks at First News Conference as Secretary of State," *New York Times*, January 20, 1981 (emphasis added).

57. Policy *Review*, no. 3 (Winter 1978), p. 16.

58. Ibid., pp. 23–24.

59. U.S. Congress, House of Representatives, Human Rights and U.S. Foreign Policy: Hearings before the

Subcommittee on International Organizations of the Committee on Foreign Affairs, 96th Cong., 1st sess., May 10, June 11, July 12, and August 2, 1979, p. 218.

60. "Panel Rejects Lefever by 13–4," *Washington Star,* June 5, 1981. The human rights constituency opposed him and influenced his rejection. See "Human Rights Community Expresses Concern over Lefever Nomination to State Department Post," Press Release of Ad-Hoc Committee of the Human Rights Community, February 24, 1981. In early July, it was announced that Dr. Lefever would serve as a consultant to Secretary Haig on terrorism, counterterrorism, and nuclear and nonproliferation issues. "Lefever Sworn In as Consultant to Haig," *Washington Post*, July 4, 1981.

61. "Demise of Human Rights Post May Result from Senate Panel's Rejection of Lefever," *Wall Street Journal,* June 8, 1981; "Reagan Weighs Plan to Abolish State Department Human Rights Office," *Washington Star,* July 7, 1981. Senator Howard Baker, the majority leader, and Senator Jesse Helms spoke in favor of abolishing the position.

62. *New York Times*, November 5, 1981; October 19, 1982.

63. Washington Office on Latin America, Latin America Update (May/June 1981), p. 1.

64. Ibid., pp. 3–4.

65. The war over the Falkland/Malvinas Islands was precipitated by Argentina's invasion and occupation in early April 1982 and by England's efforts to retake the islands. The United States announced its neutral position in the dispute, and Secretary of State Haig engaged in shuttle diplomacy in an effort to mediate. At the end of April, however, the United States sided with England. Argentina bitterly attacked the United States for this action and held it responsible for England's victory in June. Since that time the Reagan administration has been working to normalize and to improve relations with Argentina.

66. The summary was published by the Department of State, Bureau of Public Affairs, as Special Report No. 80, February 23, 1981. Critical evaluations of the validity of the White Paper were published June 8, 1981, in the *Wall Street Journal* and the *Washington Post*.

67. For the five criteria for certification, see U.S. Congress, House of Representatives, Presidential Certification on El Salvador (volume 1): Hearings before the Subcommittee on Inter-American Affairs of the Committee on Foreign Affairs, 97th Cong., 2d sess., February 2, 23, 25, and March 2, 1982 (1982), pp. 2–3.

68. The first two certifications prompted hearings before the Subcommittee on Inter-American Affairs in which both critics and defenders presented their views. Two volumes of hearings resulted; the testimony contained in ibid., volume 2, was presented in June, July, and August 1982.

69. "Administration Reiterates Aim of Scuttling Carter Rights Policies," *Washington Post,* July 10, 1981.

70. "U.S. Ends Opposition to Loans to Repressive Latin Regimes," *Washington Post,* July 9, 1981.

71. Ibid. In an eight-page "Press Guidance" paper prepared by the State Department, it was stated that "it is important to give a positive signal to Chile in terms of further improvement."

72. U.S. Congress, Country Reports on Human Rights Practices for 1981: Report Submitted to the Committee on Foreign Affairs, U.S. House of Representatives, and the Committee on Foreign Relations, U.S. Senate, by the Department of State, February 1982, 97th Cong., 2d sess. (1982). This report resulted in congressional hearings in which leading critics and defenders appeared, including Elliot Abrams. U.S. Congress, House of Representatives, Review of State Department Country Reports on Human Rights Practices for 1971: Hearing before the Subcommittee on Human Rights and International Organizations of the Committee on Foreign Affairs, 97th Cong., 2d sess., April 28, 1982.

73. U.S. Congress, Country Reports, pp. 1–11.

74. Ibid., p. 9.

75. For comparative figures and foreign aid charts for fiscal years 1978–1983, see Washington Office on Latin America, U.S. Assistance to Latin America, Occasional Paper no. 2 (May 1982).

76. *New York Times,* October 19, 1982.

77. Howard Warshowsky, "The Department of State and Human Rights Policy: A Case Study of the Human Rights Bureau," *World Affairs*, vol. 142, no. 3 (Winter 1980), p. 213.

Gender and the Foreign Policy Institutions

NANCY E. MCGLEN AND MEREDITH R. SARKEES

Relations among countries have frequently been called "high politics," because foreign policy choices can be some of the most momentous decisions a national government can make. The consequences, in terms of the benefits of peace or the costs of conflict, can be enormous. As a result, foreign policy decisions are usually taken at the highest level of government. However, in the American system, power to make foreign policy has never been specifically located.

Under the Constitution, the responsibility for foreign policy formulation has been divided between the President and the congress. Over time, the dominance of the president in this process grew, while the influence of Congress declined. In part, this was because of congressional willingness to abrogate responsibility for difficult decisions. Correspondingly, this also reflected the increased importance of the United States as a major actor in world politics and the resulting necessity for quick decisions and rapid actions for which the office of the presidency was best suited. This process peaked in the "Imperial Presidency" of the Johnson-Nixon era of 1963–1974. More recently, Congress has used a variety of its powers to reassert its role in foreign policy. Indeed, the current Republican majority in the Congress has proposed legislation that would in a major way strengthen the congressional role. A House bill would cut funding for many foreign programs and eliminate several agencies in the foreign policy establishment. Secretary of State Warren Christopher is quoted by *Congressional Quarterly* as saying the bill "wages an extraordinary assault on this and every future president's constitutional authority to manage foreign policy."

The shifting balance of power between the executive and congressional branches has also been mirrored in the changing power of the relevant governmental institutions. Throughout U.S. history, the institution that has almost exclusively controlled the foreign policy process has been the State Department. Organized around the Foreign Service and the nation's ambassadors, the State Department has been uniquely suited to formulate and implement foreign policy. However, recent developments have led to a decline in the department's influence and a corresponding rise in the power of the White House and the Pentagon. Much of this trend has been attributed to, the personalities of recent presidents, such as Richard M. Nixon, Jimmy Carter, Ronald Reagan, and George Bush. This shift can also be seen as a result of the function of the State Department itself, with its relatively passive role of observation, reporting, and negotiation, as compared with the Defense Department's primary function of action. Particularly during internationally activist administrations, the military has become the largest implementer of foreign policy decisions. Additionally, recent reorganizational measures, which have consolidated five of the nine intelligence agencies within the Department of Defense, have made the Pentagon into the largest gatherer and supplier of information for the formulation of foreign policy. Thus, today both executive-branch departments, State and Defense, are major foreign policy agents.

In addition to these two departments, recent presidents have increasingly relied on the staff of the National Security Council (NSC) to aid in the formulation and occasionally implementation of foreign policy. The NSC is a relatively recent innovation, having been created in 1947 as an institution that would allow presidents to avoid the bureaucratic quagmire often found in Foggy Bottom (a sobriquet for the State Department) and the Pentagon. Composed of the president and the vice president, the secretaries of State and Defense, and assisted by the chairman of the Joint Chiefs of Staff and the director of the Central Intelligence Agency, the NSC has become an important player in making foreign policy under recent presidents.

The Congress also has a constitutional role to play in determining the foreign policy of the nation. It alone can declare war. Additionally, all treaties and presidential appointments to executive agencies and, more specifically, ambassadorships must receive Senate approval. In recent years, Congress has voted to withhold monies to force a change in some presidents' foreign policies. Several congressional committees, as a result, have become prominent actors. The continuing influence of Congress is reflected not only in the traditionally powerful Senate Foreign Relations and House Armed Services (now National Security) committees but also in the intelligence committees and appropriations committees in both the Senate and House. Lawmakers have, on occasion, relied on their power of the purse to do battle with the president over the direction of foreign policy.

PAST AND CURRENT PRACTICES

The federal government has long recognized that women in its employ are treated unequally. A 1992 study by the U.S. Merit Systems Protection Board found that women are prevented from moving to the upper echelons of government service in large part because of the attitudes and stereotypes of supervisors who believe women are less committed to the workplace than men. The same study reports that women in the government are aware of this "glass ceiling": More than half agree with the statement that "a woman must perform better than a man to be promoted."

All four institutions, the departments of State and Defense, the NSC, and the relevant committees in Congress that form the core of the foreign policy structure, have a historical record of discrimination, direct or indirect, against women. The State and Defense departments went so far as to adopt specific policies to prohibit women from entering or to restrict the influence and opportunities of those women who were already employed. The State Department has been the target of lawsuits seeking to eliminate its discriminatory practices in hiring, promotions, and assignments of women. As a result of court orders, the State Department has been revising the Foreign Service exam, as well as its appointment, review, and promotion processes. Similarly, the Defense Department and its military branches virtually excluded women until very recently and are still wrestling with the implications of the policies that prohibit women from many combat positions. Although the NSC and Congress did not adopt specific policies prohibiting women from serving, indirect discrimination has meant that few women until recently have made it into the inner circle of either organization. In the NSC, at least, this is changing. In the Clinton

Administration, a number of women have been appointed to key positions, including the number three staff job.

A related problem for women employed by the federal government is sexual harassment. Societal stereotypes have created a climate in which women have become the targets of unacceptable behavior. A 1980 study by the U.S. Merit Systems Protection Board of over 20,000 federal employees discovered that 42 percent of female employees and 15 percent of male employees reported having been sexually harassed in the previous 24 months. Similarly, a 1989 survey by Government Executive Magazine of 941 of the highest-ranking women government executives reported that 40 percent felt they had been sexually harassed.

PAST PRACTICES AT STATE

Homer Calkin in his book on women in the State Department concluded that the field of foreign policy, and in particular the State Department, had been especially inhospitable to women. Calkin reported that it was 1922 before the department appointed Lucile Atcherson as its first woman FSO. The reason for the delay was, in part, tied to the late acceptance of women as full-fledged voting citizens, with all the rights of men to participate in politics (the Nineteenth Amendment had only become the law of the land in 1920). Even with enactment of the Nineteenth Amendment, however, the State Department was reluctant to hire women as FSOs because it felt they lacked the ability to do the job. The reasons given parallel the cultural stereotypes reviewed in the preceding chapter: Once women married they would leave their posts; women could not handle the unfavorable climatic conditions in various parts of the world; and cultural prejudices in other nations against women would make them unsuitable government representatives. In light of these rationales, the State Department Personnel Board even suggested applying for an executive order specifically excluding women from the department. As an alternative, it was proposed by Wilbur J. Carr, director of the Consular Service, that the department could use the entrance examination as a means of keeping women out. Although no such explicit policy was adopted, the results suggest just such a practice was followed. Between 1926 and 1929, only four women were appointed to the Foreign Service, and from 1930 to 1941, no women were admitted.

A major policy shift took place in 1946 with the passage of the Foreign Service Act, which established the goal of a Foreign Service broadly representative of the American people. As a result, during the 1950s and 1960s more women were admitted to the State Department. However, the department continued to discriminate against women. Indeed, from 1960 to 1970, the percentage of women Foreign Service Officers actually declined from 9.2 percent to 4.8 percent. In reaction to this lack of progress, in 1970 the Ad Hoc Committee to Improve the Status of Women in Foreign Affairs Agencies was created, with the goal of ending discrimination in the State Department, the U.S. Agency for International Development (AID), and the U.S. Information Agency (USIA). This committee later became known as the Women's Action Organization (WAO). The WAO was instrumental in urging the department to take steps to encourage the recruitment of qualified women and to provide more training for women. As an early organizer, Mary S. Olmsted explained:

> I think that in the beginning the WAO made people focus on what was really an appalling array of discriminatory attitudes and policies against women. A lot of people who were not in any way feminists had to admit that women were getting a very raw deal.... Assignments to positions illustrate the point ...

It used to be that women were not assigned to certain posts, Moscow for instance. It was very, very race to have a woman on a selection board up until the time WAO started protesting about that issue. It was hard for a woman to get university training. 117e broke down the ban against women Foreign Service Officers being married. Another problem WAO tackled was cone assignments, or assignments to functional specialties.... Traditionally, women officers were concentrated in the consular and administrative cones, although a limited number, myself included, spent their careers in the economic or political cones.... WAO also worked to improve the status of secretaries. Further, WAO pressed for better housing overseas and improved shipping allowances for single people (mostly women).

Throughout the 1970s, the State Department professed a willingness to help women, with Secretary of State Cyrus Vance in particular urging the department to make a special effort to hire qualified women. Vance created a committee, the Executive Level Task Force on Affirmative Action, with Ambassador Philip C. Habib as chairman, to review the recruitment and examination procedures in the State Department. The committee made recommendations designed to ensure that the service become "truly representative of American diversity." Yet, in its report on conditions in the department, the Commission on Civil Rights found that "what some identify as traditional elitist attitudes have combined to limit severely employment opportunities for women and minorities in the Foreign Service."

Dissatisfied with State's progress toward the goal of diversity, Congress passed the Foreign Service Act of 1980, which required the Department of State to take steps to increase equal opportunities for women and minorities. Mary Olmsted and her colleagues reported that this legislation represented the first time Congress had required affirmative action steps of a specific federal department. As a result of this legislation, there has been some movement toward increasing the number of women at State. However, Olmsted et al. concluded in their review that "the progress in the improvement in the status of women in the [State] Department continues to be agonizingly slow. If this rate should continue, it will be decades into the twenty-first century before women can expect to be represented equitably and to play a significant role in foreign affairs." Two 1989 studies (one by a five-member commission authorized by Congress, the other an internal State Department study) both concluded that the department was still failing to recruit sufficient women and minorities. While the Clinton Administration has made efforts to rectify this by appointing more women to the State Department, the president has placed many fewer women in high positions in State than he has in several other departments.

CURRENT PRACTICES AT STATE

Not surprisingly, given the historical treatment of women in the department, State has been the target of legal challenges. Two early lawsuits were particularly important in this litigation effort to reform the department. In August 1971, the first major sex discrimination case filed against the State Department was decided in favor of Foreign Service Officer Alison Palmer. An expert on African affairs, Palmer was the subject of repeated acts of sexism from her initial appointment to the Foreign Service in 1958. However, unlike many of her contemporaries, she did not lightly dismiss the behavior of her male superiors. She claimed that she was denied appointment as a political officer by the U.S. ambassadors in Ethiopia, Tanzania, and Uganda because she was a woman. One ambassador told her "the savages in Ethiopia would not be receptive to a woman, except maybe to her form." In compensation, Palmer was awarded a promotion, back pay, and a desired assignment to the National War College. State conceded that there had been discrimination, but promised that changes would be made so that diplomats could no longer request that women be excluded from certain assignments. However, in 1976 Palmer was compelled to file her second lawsuit, a class action suit joined by the WAO.

This suit was combined with another class action, *Cooper v. Baker*, and in toto they alleged that the State Department discriminated in hiring, assignments, performance ratings, and awards. The State Department was found to have violated Title VII of the Civil Rights Act of 1964 and to have engaged in gender discrimination in a wide range of activities, including the Foreign Service exam, assignments, evaluations, and awards. As a result of this case, two independent experts were to examine department processes and suggest modifications in its personnel system. The department canceled the 1989 Foreign Service exam, because it had been found to be unfair to women and minority candidates. In May 1990 the U.S. Court of Appeals concluded that women were hampered in promotions because of fewer honor awards, service in less prestigious assignments, and discriminatory evaluations. As a result of the ruling in *Palmer v. Baker*, twenty-six superior honor awards were conferred upon women who had been initially passed over. The State Department also notified 601 women that they might be entitled to compensation. As of May 1994, compensatory relief measures had been provided to over two hundred women. In a subsequent case, the Voice of America and its parent organization, USIA, were likewise found to have been guilty of sex discrimination and ordered to compensate the victims.

In many ways Palmer deserves the major credit for forcing State to face up to its discriminatory treatment of women. It has not been easy for her, and the rewards have been few. Indeed, she left the Foreign Service feeling that her prospects had been irretrievably damaged. Throughout it all, she has had little support from the other women in State, a phenomenon she is at a loss to understand. But as she explains: "If I hadn't fought it, widespread discrimination would have continued forever. I would have been ashamed."

Unfortunately discriminatory practices seem to have continued. The department has been the target of an increasing number of Equal Employment Opportunity (EEO) complaints in the last decade: twenty-five in 1983; thirty-two in 1987; fifty-five in 1988; and in 1989, '5 informal leading to forty-two formal. The pace has not abated: from 1989 to 1993, there was a 40 percent increase in the number of normal complaints. The most frequently cited issues in dispute were reprisal actions, conditions of employment, promotions, and performance levels.

Similarly, nearly one-third of the women interviewees at State felt they had been discriminated against while working there. Several interviewees cited the former rule that all women had to resign from the Foreign Service when they got married. That practice stopped in the 1970s and some returned to work. Many more women undoubtedly left State permanently because of the marriage rule. Perhaps still others postponed or never married because of the ban.

Women with long careers in the State Department also recalled that when they were first in the Foreign Service, efforts were made to limit their rotation or early training to the traditional women's fields of consular affairs and administration. Typical is the response of a woman in her seventies when questioned as to whether she had ever faced discrimination (although often the older women did not recognize these practices at the time as sex discrimination):

I found as I was coming up in the ranks that I usually had to accept a position at a grade lower than my personal grade, whereas men usually did not have to. When I went out to India as a Class 3 officer, I had to take a Class 4 officer's job, but while I was there, I worked myself up into a Class 2 officer's job. I once asked for an assignment as economic counselor in Beirut. This was back when Beirut was still a lovely city, and assignments there were sought after. The person who was handling Lebanese affairs in the geographic bureau at the time said that over his dead body would the department send a woman to Beirut. Hence I did not get the assignment. My name was put forward as ambassador to Bangladesh, and there was considerable objection to that, although a woman got the job several years later. I am sure that I was the first woman ever proposed for that position and I was turned down cold....

The stereotype that other cultures will not accept women FSOs has been a problem for many females in the State Department. Because success in overseas assignments in key missions is so important for progressing up through the ranks, the inhospitable (or perceived inhospitable) environment in other nations for women in positions of authority can be and has been a problem.

In the same vein, sexual harassment has also been an issue for women at State. The department issued its first policy statement prohibiting sexual harassment and establishing procedures for the filing of formal complaints in 1981. Despite such policies, sexual harassment remains widespread. Indeed, as reported in *USA Today*, 52 percent of women employees claimed to have experienced sexual harassment while working in the State Department, the largest proportion of women employees in any government agency.

In general, however, women at State interviewed by the authors were positive about their status. When asked to evaluate the level of discrimination in their department on a seven-point scale (with one as severe discrimination and seven as equal treatment), the women at State gave an average score of 5.0. This was only slightly lower than their ranking for the government as a whole and better than the ranking they gave the country. A few, however, were quick to point out that the department was not exactly a leading government agency in improving women's status. "Only when forced does State do better.... Except when a Court tells them to do something, they wouldn't do it on their own." However, the women at State were in general agreement with the proposition that things for women were improving. The intractable nature of the problems for women can be seen in the fact that in 1993 a group of female FSOs accused the department and Secretary of State Christopher of violating the previous antidiscrimination ruling, and they sought a five-year extension of the court's injunction prohibiting discrimination.

As of 1995 the Clinton Administration has decided to enter into global-settlement negotiations in an attempt to resolve all of the discrimination issues of *Palmer v. Baker* (now *Palmer v. Christopher*) in one consent decree. The settlement would include both specific relief for women officers as well as overall changes in the department's evaluation process in an attempt to make it more objective. The department has created a new diversity training program for all officers. However, as one of the lawyers involved in the litigation noted, the women in the department are facing an increased backlash from male colleagues, and a number of women have refused to accept court-ordered promotions due to the perception among fellow officers that they might not have deserved them.

PAST PRACTICES AT DEFENSE

As Maj. Gen. Jeanne Holm, USAF (Ret.), described in her comprehensive history of women in the military, the barriers placed in the way of women who wanted to enter the military side of the foreign policy establishment have been even steeper than those faced by women at the State Department. She concluded: "The story of women's progress is a marvelous tale of persistence, courage and foresight in the face of repeated frustrations and the built-in institutional resistance of the tradition bound military subculture."

Women first began to play a recognized role in the nation's military during the Civil and Spanish-American wars as nurses. But nurses had no regular organizational structure until 1901, when Congress established the Nurse Corps as an auxiliary of the U.S. Army. The nurses, however, had no military rank, nor did they receive any of the military benefits.

The War Department initially resisted employing civilian women in any positions other than nurses. Only after suffering severe personnel shortages during World War I were the commanders able to convince the War Department to employ civilian women in clerical positions and other support roles. However, the War Department still rejected the concept of women serving permanently in the military, and it deactivated the women at the end of World War I. In fact, in 1925 the Naval Reserve Act of 1916 was even altered to require the employment of male citizens, so that the Navy could not even enlist Yeomanettes again.

Needless to say, this rejection of women, despite their contributions, was not popular with many women's groups. In an attempt to pacify them, the War Department in 1920 established a Director of Women's Programs, U.S. Army, with the limited purpose of serving as a liaison between the War Department and women's organizations. Instead, the director used the position to demand that the Army give greater recognition to women and began organizing the Women's Service Corps as an agency with full military status.

Even though World War II saw a large expansion of roles for women, the War Department was still unwilling to include women in the regular services. The compromise proposal was for the creation of an auxiliary of highly educated women. Thus, in the early 1940s, the Women's Army Corps (WAC), the Navy women's reserve (WAVES), the Coast Guard women's reserve (SPARS), the Marine Corps women's reserve, and the Air Force civilian Women's Air Service Pilots (WASPs) were established. Yet, women faced continued hostility for invading male preserves. Commented General Holm:

> Reception by the men ranged from enthusiasm through amused condescension to open hostility. Each found that she had to prove herself each time she went to a new job or had a change in supervisors. Whereas a man was accepted immediately at face value and was assumed to be competent at his job, a woman was always regarded with suspicion. Because it was considered unnatural for a woman to join the military, she was often considered a deviate of some sort.

Even though the standards for women officers and enlisted women were higher than those for men, military men in general believed that most jobs in their professions were inherently masculine, and they would not accept the possibility that they could be performed by women. Holm reported, "Like the male Marine Corps office clerks in World War I who estimated it would take two women to replace one male marine at a desk, most men genuinely believed the masculine mythology of the military world."

The War Department's treatment of black women was even worse. Most commanders refused to accept African American women in their units, and those who did often employed them in stereotypical positions. For example, sixty black medical technicians in the WAC were put to work cleaning, rather than in practicing their medical specialties. When they began a sitdown strike, they were told that " 'black girls' are 'fit only to do the dirtiest type of work' because that's what 'Negro women are used to doing.' "

By the end of World War II, acceptance of women was still limited. Even the wartime directors of the WACs, WAVES, SPARS, and women marines did not ask for the retention of the women's units. However, in 1948, perhaps in response to the cold war, Congress passed the Women's Armed Services Integration Act, opening up the military services to women, but only in a very limited way. Women were to remain segregated in their own divisions, they were not to constitute more than 2 percent of the military, and women officers could not be promoted beyond the rank of lieutenant colonel/commander, except for the colonel/captain director of each women's branch. Not until the Vietnam War was there any major change in women's role in the military. In November 1967, President Lyndon B. Johnson signed Public Law 90–130, which removed restrictions on the careers of female officers in the Army, Navy, Air Force, and Marine Corps by repealing the limits on the percentage of women in the services and barriers to their promotion. The traditional "slotting" of women into certain positions was also eased, although the resistance of male military officers and enlisted men persisted.

Throughout the 1970s, women's progress in the military was relatively rapid as many of the old barriers were eliminated as a result of court decisions, the threat of legal action or executive initiatives. The adoption in 1973 of the All Volunteer Force also expedited the progress of women. The results of these changes were dramatic. By 1985, women's share of all active-duty military positions had increased to almost 10 percent.

The election of President Reagan brought a temporary halt to women's advancement, partially as a result of a review of women in the military conducted at Defense Secretary Caspar W. Weinberger's request. The study reflected the earlier philosophy that it was preferable to have men rather than women in the services. However, it soon became clear that the Administration could not achieve its policy of expanding the military without women. The Defense Advisory Committee on Women in the Services continued to push for changes to improve the status and opportunities of women, and in January 1988 the Task Force on Women in the Military recommended policies that would reduce sexual harassment and increase career opportunities. As noted earlier, the Clinton Administration took one step toward the latter by eliminating the ban on women serving as combat pilots and on combat ships. This is an important change because from the perspective of women in the military the combat exclusion has had a very detrimental influence. As Retired Brig. Gen. Evelyn P. Foote noted:

> As long as women are operationally excluded, they will never acquire the experience that leads to their acquiring rank of more than one star. Unless they get the operational experience, they will never be in a position to have a significant impact on national defense policy. . . .
>
> The women absolutely hate combat exclusion, because it is an artificial barrier. . . . The women who serve the combat forces forward are not given credit for being in combat. They are in combat, and if they are attacked, they will attack back.

Civilian women at Defense frequently cite the organizational bias against women and their consequent lack of military, especially combat, experience as reasons for the difficulties they face working for the department. A woman in the naval weapons area outlined the problem:

> The military themselves have discrimination against civilians, whether they're male or female, because most civilians have not been in operations. So there is that bias or perception that civilians don't know what they're talking about. Then when you put the women on top of that, it makes it even a little worse. Department of Defense is a very macho world. . . . If the military stays male, women will always be less effec-

tive because they have not had to demonstrate to peers, to male peers, that they know what they are talking about because they have not been "under fire." Put it in quotes because there's a lot of men who have not been under fire either.

CURRENT PRACTICES AT DEFENSE

The Defense Department has faced a significant number of EEO complaints but only a few lawsuits. However, the level of discrimination in the Navy was revealed in November 1991 with the resolution of an eighteen-year-old lawsuit for sex discrimination in hiring and promotions. In finding for the plaintiffs, Judge Harold Green complained that "the government has sought to prolong this litigation by every means possible, both fair and foul."

Discrimination has also been a problem for civilian employees. More than half of the women interviewed at Defense (69 percent of those in career positions) stated that they had experienced sex discrimination. They complained about slow promotions or a failure to be moved up in rank. Others discussed experiences where their orders were challenged or senior colleagues refused to deal with a woman. The slow effort to build credibility, moreover, was frequently negated when women had to deal with men outside of their circle of associates. One woman's experience is typical. "If they know your expertise, they will listen to you. They will ask your advice. Often if you walk into a room of strangers, however, they merely will just assume you are a secretary."

In a study reported in the *Washington Post* in 1989, of 941 of the highest ranking women in the military, nearly 70 percent said their views were not as respected as men's. The problem is further exacerbated for the women civilian policymakers who do not have military credentials. Indeed, the failure to let women serve in equal numbers and positions with men in the military presents a double burden for women civilians. The women who discussed this problem indicated that as a result of their lack of "surface" credibility, they had a hard time proving themselves to their colleagues.

Perceived or anticipated sexual discrimination by male foreign nationals, a problem at State, was also identified by the women at Defense as a problem. For instance, a woman told the following story:

When I first started in this area, some stupid man got a hold of my boss and said, "Oh the Japanese won't deal with a woman." I had already been there several times and the ambassador and his deputy had asked me to come back because I was negotiating something for the Japanese they hadn't been able to get done. I had to overcome that silly stuff.

Older men or those whose backgrounds did not involve working with women were a source of complaints for some women. As one woman described the situation:

A lot of our political appointees now, because of the restrictions on going to work for companies afterward and ethics, and the "revolving door" tend to be retired people. Now retired people in their sixties, let's say, have not worked with many women in industry in responsible positions. They're not very much used to it. They tend not to take you seriously.

Surprisingly, the civilian women at Defense rated the overall position of women at Defense as virtually identical to the position of women at State. Moreover, the women at

Defense gave their department higher ratings than they gave government as a whole. Looking toward the future, women at Defense were only marginally less optimistic than women at State.

However, in the uniformed services, sexual harassment remains one of the major problems. The military has had a long history of sexual harassment. For example, during World War II, women were subjected to dirty jokes, slander campaigns, and obscene cartoons. Similarly, a 1990 report by the Defense Manpower Data Center indicated that close to two thirds of women on active duty had been subject to "uninitiated and unwanted sexual attention." Moreover, the report found women were reluctant to report the incidents because they feared reprisals or thought nothing would be done.

In 1992, disclosure of the Tailhook incident by Lt. Paula Coughlin focused public awareness on sexual harassment in the military. Lt. Coughlin had been the victim, along with approximately ninety other women, of a sexual attack by a group of male Navy aviators at their annual convention in September 1991. After being groped by the pilots while trying to walk down a hall, Lt. Coughlin reported the incident, but the investigating officers took virtually no action and the pilots stonewalled. Coughlin finally was forced to go public. The resulting investigation of the Navy's handling of the incident resulted in the resignations of the secretary of the navy and the chief of naval operations. Although 117 officers were implicated, virtually all charges were dismissed. Coughlin resigned her position in February 1994, claiming that the attack and the reaction to her going public had stripped her of her ability to serve. Several of those who testified at the hearing linked sexual harassment in the military to the exclusion of women from combat positions, arguing that until that policy is reversed women can never expect to be treated as equals.

In fact, sexual harassment within the military seems to be increasing. A General Accounting Office (GAO) report released in March 1995 compared sexual harassment at the three service academies in 1993–1994 with that in 1990–1991 and found significant increases, particularly at the Naval and Air Force academies. Such harassment led to the resignation of Elizabeth Saum from the Air Force Academy after she was subjected to a mock rape staged as part of a sexual exploitation scenario that had been added to the survival training program in 1993. (This phase of the training was only discontinued this year.)

A male with responsibility in personnel matters whom the authors interviewed at Defense indicated that sexual harassment is not a problem limited to the military side of the department. Although the incidents he described were of a less serious nature, his attitude toward them suggests that complaints by civilian women also may be ignored or downplayed:

> There is sexual abuse—but not the kind you could ever pin down. I think harassment is everywhere—I don't mean the real kind you would do anything about—I mean the innuendos, the comments all done in jest and those kinds of things [done] with the nicest motives but having the most terrible effect.... There is a generation who believes when a woman is attractive, they should pay her a compliment no matter what. So they, even during the course of a business meeting, might make a compliment not done maliciously, but it's done. It is a part of stereotypes those people have.

The Clinton Administration has made efforts to improve the status of women. For example, in the Office of the Secretary of Defense, the special assistant to the secretary, the directors of defense research and engineering, reserve affairs and legislative affairs, and three deputy under-secretaries are all women. In addition, the Administration appointed the first woman as Air Force Secretary, Sheila Widnall. Women also hold two of the top positions in the Army and two in the Navy.

NATIONAL SECURITY COUNCIL

Since the NSC came of age during a time of somewhat more enlightened attitudes toward women, it has avoided the overt discriminatory policies against women of the State and Defense departments. However, because of the council's composition, there has been a virtual exclusion of women's participation. The first woman to break the barrier to the inner sanctum of this important center of foreign policy formulation was U.S. Ambassador to the U.N. Kirkpatrick, whom President Reagan invited to sit on the NSC. President Clinton has continued the practice of including the representative to the U.N. on the NSC, resulting in a second woman, Madeleine K. Albright, serving there.

Although only two women have been members of the actual council, the staff, which is largely composed of political appointees, has been more open to women. In the Clinton Administration, several women have held important staff positions. Because other government agencies, notably State and Defense, are the other major source of advisers for the NSC staff, the prospects for more women serving depend heavily on the promotion and recognition of women in those departments.

CONGRESS

Congress, too, has barriers to women's entry. However, most of the hurdles exist outside the institution and as a result few women are elected. For example, the Senate, the most important of the two houses in influencing foreign policy (due to its authority to ratify treaties and approve presidential appointments), has only had twenty-three women members, six of whom have been elected since 1992. The number of women elected to the House of Representatives is only somewhat better. Yet it was not until 1992 (the Year of the Woman) that women held 14 percent of House seats.

If one looks at the committees in the Senate and the House responsible for reviewing foreign policy issues, one sees the impact of internal rules on women's status. Party committees responsible for assigning new members to standing committees have tended to operate under traditional stereotypes about women's interests and abilities. Consequently, they have given few women positions on the "foreign policy" committees. Moreover, for the few women who have achieved such appointments, their limited time in Congress (nearly half of the women who have served in the Senate remained in office less than a year) has meant that none, to date, has acquired the seniority to move into the position of chair or ranking-minority member. Thus, the few women who have been, or are currently, serving on the foreign policy committees have generally not taken very influential or visible roles. The one possible exception is Representative Schroeder, who is currently the third-ranking Democrat on the National Security Committee. Schroeder has been a leading advocate for expanding opportunities for women in the military, including sponsoring legislation to remove combat restrictions on women.

The absence of women committee and subcommittee chairs has contributed to the limited movement of women into important staff positions. Not until 1995 was Congress under any obligation to avoid discrimination in hiring staff or to report on how many women it employs or in what positions they serve. An examination of recent staff members finds that only one woman, Marilyn A. Elrod, has ever been a top aide to a foreign policy committee. She was staff director for the House Armed Services Committee in the 103rd Congress.

Section 11
The Impact of 9-11

The terrorist attacks of September 11, 2001, raised difficult and contentious issues of national identity, citizenship, and the role of immigration in America's security. Commentators sifted through the most immediate horrific facts in search of longer lasting trends and issues of national government.

Robert Putman of Harvard's Kennedy School of Government reports on opinion polls he commissioned prior to and after the attacks, indicating an increase in interracial, interethnic trust and solidarity. Putnam then asks himself whether the changes in American attitudes are merely temporary or permanent. Some, including Putnam, found at least the makings of longer lasting changes in attitudes and behavior. He believes that for these shifts to be sustained, national leaders must make strong political commitments that emphasize the positive interpretations over other negative interpretations of minority status.

In his contribution to this section, John Fonte begins from a position skeptical of the collectivist claims by intellectuals and activists (including some represented in this volume). He sees in the poll numbers and the public debates since 9–11 a return to greater commitment to individual rights and responsibilities. Barone argues that Americans are thinking of themselves as citizens under attack, not as members of ethnically distinct or oppressed subgroups.

The author situates Domestic Diversity in the context of the political divisions that have marked American electoral coalitions for the past several presidential and congressional elections. These contests have turned on cultural distinctions broadly defined (abortion, prayer, etc.). September 11, he believes, has pushed sectarianism and cultural cleavages back toward "One Nation—Indivisible." Interestingly, he draws parallels between the ethnic assimilation patterns of the Irish and those of African Americans; between earlier assimilation of Italians and the Hispanics of today; and between Asians and Jews.

While the author places the intersection of 9-11 and ethnicity in the context of basic American values in a changing world, by drawing distinctions so sharply, he misses the evolutionary, historical context provided by people like Michael Lind. In his volume, Lind reminds us that such debates are rooted in past patterns of exclusion and discrimination

339

as well as inclusion and citizenship. Individuals from excluded groups typically must claim group prerogatives in order to claim their individual rights as Americans.

Although there is disagreement over the precise role of ethnic claims, Putnam and Barone recognize that these are genuinely significant and weighty issues whose resolution will shape America's national destiny at home and abroad.

31

Bowling Together

ROBERT D. PUTNAM

The closing decades of the twentieth century found Americans growing ever less connected with one another and with collective life. We voted less, joined less, gave less, trusted less, invested less time in public affairs, and engaged less with our friends, our neighbors, and even our families.

Our "we" steadily shriveled.

The unspeakable tragedy of September 11 dramatically interrupted that trend. Almost instantly, we rediscovered our friends, our neighbors, our public institutions, and our shared fate. Nearly two years ago, I wrote in my book *Bowling Alone* that restoring civic engagement in America "would be eased by a palpable national crisis, like war or depression or natural disaster, but for better and for worse, America at the dawn of the new century faces no such galvanizing crisis."

Now we do.

But is September 11 a period that puts a full stop to one era and opens a new, more community-minded chapter in our history? Or is it merely a comma, a brief pause during which we looked up for a moment and then returned to our solitary pursuits? In short, how thoroughly and how enduringly have American values and civic habits been transformed by the terrorist attacks of last fall?

During the Summer and Fall of 2000, my colleagues and I conducted a nationwide survey of civic attitudes and behaviors, asking about everything from voting to choral singing, newspaper readership to interracial marriage. Recently, we returned to many of the same people and posed the same questions. Our survey period extended from mid-October to mid-November 2001, encompassing the anthrax crisis and the start of the Afghan War. Emerging from the immediate trauma of unspeakable death and destruction, these five hundred Americans were adjusting to a changed world and a changed nation.

Although the immediate effect of the attacks was clearly devastating, most Americans' personal lives returned to normal relatively quickly. For example, despite anecdotal reports of increased religious observance in the immediate aftermath of the tragedy, we found no evidence of any change in religiosity or in reported church attendance. Our primary concern, however, was not with change in the private lives of Americans but with the implications of the attacks and their aftermath for American civic life. And in those domains, we found unmistakable evidence of change.

The levels of political consciousness and engagement are substantially higher than they were a year ago in the United States. In fact, they are probably higher now than they have been in at least three decades. Trust in government, trust in the police, and interest in poli-tics are all up. Compared with a year ago, Americans are somewhat more likely to have attended a political meeting or to have worked on a community project. Conversely, we are less likely to agree that "the people running my community do not really care what I think." This is no doubt partly the result of a spurt of patriotism and "rally round the flag" sentiment, but it also reflects a sharper appreciation of public institutions' role in addressing not just terrorism but other urgent national issues. The result?

A dramatic and probably unprecedented burst of enthusiasm for the federal govern-ment.

Using a standard question ("How much can you trust the government in Washington to do what is right—all of the time, most of the time, some of the time, or none of the time?"), we found that 51 percent of our respondents expressed greater confidence in the federal government in 2001 than they had a year earlier. No doubt the identity of the commander in chief has something to do with the somewhat greater increase in confidence among Republicans, southerners, and whites; even before September 11, the advent of a Republican administration probably changed the partisan polarity of this question. Never-theless, the bipartisan, nationwide effect of the terrorist attacks and their aftermath is clear.

Although we found most of the changes in civic attitudes to be relatively uniform across ethnic groups, social classes, and regions, some registered more sharply among younger Americans (those aged 35 and under) than among their elders. Interest in public affairs, for example, grew by 27 percent among younger people, as compared with 8 percent among older respondents. Trust in "the people running your community" grew by 19 percent among younger people, as compared with 4 percent among older ones.

Nonetheless, Americans from all walks of life expressed greater interest in public affairs than they had during the national political campaign of 2000. This spike in political aware-ness has not, however, led most Americans to run out and join community organizations or to show up for club meetings that they used to shun. Generally speaking, attitudes (such as trust and concern) have shifted more than behavior has. Will behavior follow attitudes? It's an important question. And if the answer is no, then the blossom of civic-mindedness after September 11 may be short-lived.

Americans don't only trust political institutions more: We also trust one another more, from neighbors and co-workers to shop clerks and perfect strangers. More Americans now express confidence that people in their community would cooperate, for example, with voluntary conservation measures in an energy or water shortage. In fact, in the wake of the terrorist attacks, more Americans reported having cooperated with their neighbors to resolve common problems. Fewer of us feel completely isolated socially, in the sense of having no one to turn to in a personal crisis. At the same time, we are now less likely to have friends over to visit. Television viewing increased from about 2.9 hours to 3.4 hours a day. In that sense, whether because of fear or because of the recession, Americans are cocooning more now than a year ago.

We were especially surprised and pleased to find evidence of enhanced trust across ethnic and other social divisions. Whites trust blacks more, Asians trust Latinos more, and so on, than these very same people did a year ago. An identical pattern appears in response to classic questions measuring social distance: Americans in the fall of 2001 expressed greater open-mindedness toward intermarriage across ethnic and racial lines, even within their own families, than they did a year earlier.

To be sure, trust toward Arab Americans is now about 10 percent below the level expressed toward other ethnic minorities. We had not had the foresight to ask about trust in Arab Americans a year ago, so we cannot be certain that it has declined, but it seems likely that it has. Similarly, we find that Americans are somewhat more hostile to immigrant rights. Other surveys have shown that public skepticism about immigration increased during 2001, but that trend may reflect the recession as much as it does the terrorist attacks. Yet, despite signs of public support for antiterrorist law-enforcement techniques that may intrude on civil liberties, our survey found that Americans are in some respects more tolerant of cultural diversity now than they were a year ago. Opposition to the exclusion of "unpopular" books from public libraries actually rose from 64 percent to 71 percent. In short—with the important but partial and delimited exception of attitudes toward immigrants and Arab Americans—our results suggest that Americans feel both more united and more comfortable with the nation's diversity.

We also found that Americans have become somewhat more generous, though the changes in this domain are more limited than anecdotal reports have suggested. More people in 2001 than in 2000 reported working on a community project or donating money or blood. Occasional volunteering is up slightly, but regular volunteering (at least twice a month) remains unchanged at one in every seven Americans. Compared with figures from immediately after the tragedy, our data suggest that much of the measurable increase in generosity spent itself within a few weeks.

As 2001 ended, Americans were more united, readier for collective sacrifice, and more attuned to public purpose than we have been for several decades. Indeed, we have a more capacious sense of "we" than we have had in the adult experience of most Americans now alive. The images of shared suffering that followed the terrorist attacks on New York and Washington suggested a powerful idea of cross-class, cross-ethnic solidarity. Americans also confronted a clear foreign enemy, an experience that both drew us closer to one another and provided an obvious rationale for public action.

In the aftermath of September's tragedy, a window of opportunity has opened for a sort of civic renewal that occurs only once or twice a century. And yet, although the crisis revealed and replenished the wells of solidarity in American communities, those wells so far remain untapped. At least, this is what that gap between attitudes and behavior suggests. Civic solidarity is what Albert Hirschman called a "moral resource"—distinctive in that, unlike a material resource, it increases with use and diminishes with disuse. Changes in attitude alone, no matter how promising, do not constitute civic renewal.

Americans who came of age just before and during World War II were enduringly molded by that crisis. All their lives, these Americans have voted more, joined more, given more. But the so-called Greatest Generation forged not merely moods and symbols, as important as those were; it also produced great national policies and institutions (such as the GI Bill) and community-minded personal practices (such as scrap drives and victory gardens). So far, however, America's new mood has expressed itself largely through images—of the attacks themselves, for instance, or the Ad Council's "I am an American" campaign, which powerfully depicts our multicultural society—and gestures, such as the president's visit to a mosque.

Images matter. What a powerful lesson in inclusive citizenship would have been imparted had FDR visited a Shinto shrine in January 1942! But images alone do not create turning points in a nation's history. That requires institutionalized change. To help foster a new "greatest generation," the Bush administration should endorse the bill offered by Senators John McCain and Evan Bayh to quintuple funds for the AmeriCorps program of national youth service. And given that young Americans are more open to political participation than they have been in many years, educational and political leaders should seize this moment to encourage youths' engagement in political and social movements. The grassroots movement to restore the Pledge of Allegiance in American classrooms advocates

344 • Robert D. Putnam

fine symbolism; but the time is right to introduce a new, more activist civics education in our schools as well.

Finally, activists should recognize that wartime mobilization can also spark progress toward social justice and racial integration, much as the experiences of World War II helped to generate the civil-rights movement of the 1950s. Americans today, our surveys suggest, are more open than ever to the idea that people of all backgrounds should be full members of our national community. Progressives should work to translate that national mood into concrete policy initiatives that bridge the ethnic and class cleavages in our increasingly multicultural society.

32

Politics After September 11

MICHAEL BARONE

"Everything has changed since September 11." How often have we heard that or thought it? And yet it seems to me that, at least in the field that I cover, American politics, September 11 has not changed everything. Of course, the war on terrorism has introduced a new focus on public affairs, one on which both major parties and almost all articulate opinion are in agreement. But the disputes and disagreements on other issues continue pretty much unchanged. Support for the two major parties continues at about the same levels, with the most even division between the two parties since the 1880s. But when I look beyond or beneath partisan politics, I think the war has in fact made major changes that are likely to be of enduring importance. I think it has strengthened two powerful and underlying trends in American society, trends that are often unnoticed or unremarked upon but that have been changing American politics and government in the past two decades and are likely to change them even more in the years ahead. And I think both of those trends have been moving—and will continue to move—in the opposite direction from that which elite liberal opinion believes. Elite liberal opinion takes the view that this war, like all other wars, will move America toward a bigger, more centralized government. I believe that the war will strengthen the existing tendency away from bureaucracy and toward markets, toward more decentralized government. Elite liberal opinion has also been trumpeting that we are becoming for the first time a multicultural, multiracial society. I believe the war will increase the idea of a common citizenship and the awareness that our differences in ethnic and racial origins and in cultural attitudes are less important than our common citizenship. Let me take both points in turn.

BIG GOVERNMENT KEEPS GETTING SMALLER

I start by examining whether this war, like others (most notably World War II), will increase the demand for big government. I think it will not because government tends to take on the character of the larger society. And the larger society is becoming more, not less, decentralized: a society that is moving toward markets and away from bureaucracy, toward decentralized choice and accountability and away from centralized command and control. In this respect, America is returning to its basic character. For it's my contention that current postindustrial America more closely resembles Tocqueville's preindustrial America than the industrial America in which most of us grew up. Industrial America was Big Unit America, a nation dominated by Big Government, Big Business, and Big Labor. The leaders of these big units made decisions and deals among themselves and then gave orders to the millions of Americans in the ranks below them. This was a nation in which economic production was increasingly governed by the time-motion studies of Frederick W. Taylor, who saw workers as unskilled, interchangeable parts whose job was to perform their tasks as required by experts in charge of the centralized big units. People took pride in being small cogs in large machines. This was an America of people in uniform, in which almost all young men spent years in the service; it was an America in which people were conformists, organization men, average guys and gals. It was Big Unit America that won World War II. This was a war won by twelve million Americans under arms—one-quarter of the number of Americans employed the year before Pearl Harbor—and by the mass production of relatively simple machines. It was a war in which the government absorbed 45 percent of the gross domestic product (with 80 percent of that spent on defense). It was a war in which the government rationed coffee and sugar, gasoline and rubber; in which the government ordered factories converted to defense production; in which the government set wage and price controls. This was a triumph of industrial Big Unit America, a triumph produced by large organizations operating under centralized command and control. It was a triumph that gave Americans an appetite for bigger government, and politicians of the postwar period gave us bigger and bigger government—bigger by far than the government of the New Deal.

For some years Big Unit America performed well, winning the war and building a prosperous postwar America. But after a time the big units started performing poorly. Big government gave us urban riots, the Vietnam War, and inflation. Big business gave us planned obsolescence and blundering corporations. Big labor stopped growing and began to shrink into a few industrial redoubts and the public sector. In response, America changed. During the 1970s and 1980s and 1990s we became a nation more like Tocqueville's America: decentralized, individualistic, culturally various, property-loving, religious. We have moved from bureaucracy to markets, from regulation to competition, from centralized command and control to decentralized choice and accountability. This change was not immediately recognized or everywhere welcomed. Twenty years ago, elite opinion held that history was progress from small organizations to large organizations, from small government to big government, and that this movement was inevitable; it could be delayed but never reversed. And if the big units produced stagflation—low economic growth and high inflation—and an America that was beleaguered and in retreat abroad, then the public should just grow up and be pleased with the best the centralized experts could produce and accept that in this complex world nothing better was possible. But in the meantime the economy was being revived by cuts in taxation, by the deregulation of transportation (advocated by the young Ralph Nader and initiated by Democrats such as Jimmy Carter and Edward Kennedy) and of communications and finance. Private sector innovations such as leveraged buyouts and junk bonds made the managers of large corporations far more accountable and responsive to the marketplace. Small businesses created innovative products and services and displaced lumbering corporate dinosaurs, in which workers made their own deals with employers rather than rely on the leaders of big labor unions.

Defined-benefit pension plans, which assumed that workers would stay with one employer over a lifetime and would depend on it for retirement income, were replaced by defined-contribution plans, which assumed workers would move from employer to employer and could be trusted to make choices on their own. Small, flexible, supple organizations outperformed and were more creative than large, inflexible, lumbering organizations.

Over time, government tends to take on the character of the society; the public sector comes to resemble the private sector. So, over the last twenty years, we have seen movement, some of it still nascent, toward substituting decentralized choice and accountability for command and control. The great public policy successes of the 1990s—reducing welfare dependency and reducing crime—were the result of initiatives taken locally, starting with Tommy Thompson's welfare reform in Wisconsin in 1987 and Rudolph Giuliani's crime control in New York City in 1994, which were then initiated and adapted in other states and cities. Both policies involved giving individuals a wider array of choices and holding them accountable for results in ways they hadn't been before. Similarly, in education we find that localities and states have pioneered in giving individuals more choice and holding them accountable; George W. Bush's education reform, passed late in 2001, is an extension of those policies to the federal level. Health care has been reformed not by the centralized command-and-control model advocated by Hillary Rodham Clinton— roundly rejected in the political marketplace—but by a variety of initiatives in the private and public sectors that give people more choices and hold them accountable. And now the military has responded in the same way.

Since September 11, many commentators have speculated—some gleefully, some with dismay—that the war would strengthen support for big government. Historically, war has indeed been the great friend of the state. But consider how this war so far is being won. It is being won not by lumbering infantry but by high-tech machines and high-skill special forces. Precision bombing and real-time communication have been far better in Afghanistan than they were even in the Gulf War. The military has incorporated the high-tech revolution that has been the work primarily of the private sector. Special forces or CIA agents on the ground, with skills every bit as impressive as those of private sector techno geeks, were able to relay, via global positioning satellites, the coordinates of enemy troops and equipment to fliers of forty-year-old B-52s, who were able to rain bombs in exactly the right place. Old cargo planes and navy fighters were adapted to be used as bombers. B-2 bombers flew round trips from Missouri to bring American power to bear in Afghanistan. The military has shown the kind of adaptability and expertise we have seen in the private sector over the last twenty years, and all this has been done at a relatively low cost.

The military in World War II absorbed 36 percent of GDP. The military in 2001 absorbed just 2.9 percent of GDP. Assume this rises in years ahead to 4 or 5 percent; that will still be below the percentage of GDP absorbed by the military in the peacetime years in the middle 1980s or the early 1960s. The American triumph in World War II was a triumph of industrial America—a military of twelve million men and mass production of relatively simple machines. The American triumph in the war against terrorism is the triumph of postindustrial America, a triumph of high-tech machines and high-skill individuals, people acting with a wide array of choices and initiative and a high degree of accountability.

It seems to me exceedingly unlikely that the American people will conclude from our success in this war that we should return to a public sector characterized by centralized command and control. Rather, I think it likely they will conclude that we should continue to move toward a public sector characterized by choice and accountability. George W. Bush seems to understand this. His domestic policies—on taxes, education, Social Security, medical care—are all policies that increase the amount of choice and accountability in our society. And he understands, as his father in 1991 and 1992 did not, how to make a connection in the public's mind between the way we have won a war and how we should govern ourselves in peace. We have seen a diminishing demand in postindustrial America for the big government initiatives for which there was a big political demand in industrial

America. We have not seen major increases in the percentage of the private economy devoted to government. We have seen the Republican Party win most of the presidential elections since 1968; the only Democrats elected (Jimmy Carter and Bill Clinton) ran as "new Democrats" sympathetic to the changing character of the country. We have seen Republicans finally triumph over the Democrats' institutional advantage and win control of Congress in the 1990s. I do not believe that the war against terrorism will prompt a change in the direction of this trend. I think it will continue and perhaps apace.

ONE NATION—INDIVISIBLE

America in recent years has been very sharply and very evenly divided politically, primarily along cultural lines. Look at the numbers. In 1996 Bill Clinton was reelected with 49 percent of the vote; the Republicans held the House with a popular vote of 49 to 48.5 percent. In 1998 the Republicans held the House with a popular vote of 49 to 48 percent. In 2000 George W. Bush and Al Gore each won 48 percent of the vote; the Republicans held the House with a popular vote of 49 to 48 percent. We have had three straight presidential elections and three straight House elections in which neither party has won 50 percent of the vote. This hasn't happened since the 1880s. And the divisions today, as in the 1880s, are along cultural lines. In the 1880s the Democratic Party was supported chiefly by southerners and Catholics. The Republican Party was supported by northern Protestants. You voted as you fought or according to where you came from. Today, the deepest divisions are along the lines of religion. Evangelical Protestants and Mormons voted overwhelmingly for George W. Bush; Jews and those with no religion, overwhelmingly for Al Gore. People who attend religious services at least weekly gave Bush a considerably larger margin than did the wealthy. People who attend religious services less often or not at all gave Al Gore a similar margin. The issues that really divide people are abortion and gun control, not tax cuts. And those divisions were exacerbated by the controversy over Florida's electoral vote because the arguments were congruent with the bedrock attitudes of both parties' constituencies. The Republicans in Florida argued that you should obey the rules, not change them in the middle of the game. The Democrats in Florida argued that you should change the rules because they were unfair to certain people in certain circumstances. No wonder the debate was so bitter: Neither party had to argue (as both surely would have, had it helped their cause) against the grain of its underlying attitudes. Since September 11, despite George W. Bush's continuously high job ratings, there has been very little if any change in the narrow electoral margin between the two parties. The special elections held this fall and winter and the November elections in New Jersey and Virginia pretty closely tracked the 2000 election results. Multiple polls taken at the beginning of the year suggest that Republicans are just slightly stronger today (by one to three percentage points) than on September 10. But this change, if it is a change, is not necessarily permanent. I think it's prudent to conclude that the country remains closely divided along partisan lines, as it has been for the last half-dozen years.

But something did happen on September 11. Democrats and Republicans, red states and blue states, Christian conservatives and cultural liberals (with just a few exceptions, mostly in isolated corners of university campuses) reacted the same: WE have been attacked. Republican and Democratic leaders of the House of Representatives, men who had barely been speaking to each other, watched the September 11 attacks on television together and could see that we were all reacting the same way: WE have been attacked, and WE must respond. The nearly unanimous support Democratic and Republican politicians have been giving to George W. Bush's conduct of the war against terrorism is, I believe, sincere and deeply felt. And that feeling has prevailed among Americans of different races and national origins. This is important to understand, for in recent years many have been saying that we are at a whole new place in our history, that America is becoming for the first time a multiracial, multicultural nation in which people will live in separate boxes—whites, blacks, Latinos, Asians—a nation in which, some people hope, so-called minorities will take an adversarial attitude toward what has been the larger society. I think this view misses a very large part of American history; in fact, I feel this so strongly that I went to the trouble of writing a book, *The New Americans* (published in May 2001). My thesis is that minority groups of today resemble immigrant groups of one hundred years ago— blacks resemble the Irish, Latinos resemble Italians, and Asians resemble Jews. A hundred years ago, many people said these races—they called the Irish, Italians, and Jews different "races"—could never be interwoven into the American fabric, could never be Americans. Today we know those predictions turned out to be false. Today we hear predictions that these new Americans—blacks (whom I call "new" Americans only because they did not get their full rights as citizens until the 1960s), Latinos, and Asians—can never be interwoven into the American fabric, can never become Americans. I believe that those predictions too will prove to be false, if we learn intelligently from the lessons of the past. We are not doomed to be a nation in which people live in separated racial boxes, snarling at each other. We are a nation that more than any other has the capacity to take new people in and make them part of an America that is stronger for their presence.

And I believe we can see that from what has happened in America since September 11.

The attacks on America have produced an enhanced sense of common citizenship. We recognized instantly that for all our differences on cultural issues—and they are differences based on deep-seated moral values in many cases—we also share a common belief in basic American freedoms and in the decency of American life. Take a look at the obituaries in the *New York Times* of the people who died in the attacks on the World Trade Center, or of those who died at the Pentagon or on United flight 93. These were all kinds of people, from all kinds of backgrounds, with all kinds of cultural and political values. But they were also Americans. And remember September 14, when George W. Bush came to Ground Zero in New York. Someone shouted, "I can't hear you." Bush grabbed a bullhorn and said, "I can hear you. The whole world can hear you. And the people who knocked down those buildings will hear from all of us soon." And immediately the rescue workers began chanting, "USA! USA! USA!" Look at their faces on videotape. They come from different backgrounds and are members of what we call different "races" (though we know from history that what people consider different races changes over time). Their responses and the responses of those of us who were watching on television were the same. We recognized instantly that our differences bind us together; they make us the same. Those who would keep us apart, in separate boxes, have this country all wrong. However different our backgrounds and attitudes, we are more than ever one nation, a proud and free postindustrial America, more productive and more tolerant, more creative and more welcoming of newcomers, than any nation that has ever before existed.

33

Liberal Democracy
vs. Transnational Progressivism

The Ideological War Within the West

JOHN FONTE

Nearly a year before the September 11 attacks, news stories provided a preview of the transnational politics of the future. In October 2000, in preparation for the U.N. Conference Against Racism, about fifty American NGOs called on the U.N. "to hold the United States accountable for the intractable and persistent problem of discrimination."

The NGOs included Amnesty International-U.S.A. (AI-U.S.A.), Human Rights Watch (HRW), the ArabAmerican Institute, National Council of Churches, the NAACP, the American Legal Defense and Educational Fund, and others. Their spokesman stated that their demands "had been repeatedly raised with federal and state officials [in the United States] but to little effect. In frustration we now turn to the United Nations." In other words, the NGOs, unable to enact the policies they favored through the normal processes of American constitutional democracy—the Congress, state governments, even the federal courts—appealed to authority outside of American democracy and its Constitution.

At the UN Conference against Racism, which was held in Durban two weeks before September 11, American NGOs supported "reparations" from Western nations for the historic transatlantic slave trade and developed resolutions that condemned only the West, without mentioning the larger traffic in African slaves sent to Islamic lands. The NGOs even endorsed a resolution denouncing free market capitalism as a "fundamentally flawed system."

The NGOs also insisted that the U.S. ratify all major UN human rights treaties and drop legal reservations to treaties already ratified. For example, in 1994 the U.S. ratified the UN Convention on the Elimination of Racial Discrimination (CERD), but attached reservations on treaty requirements restricting free speech that were "incompatible with the Constitution." Yet, leading NGOs demanded that the United States drop all reservations and "comply" with the CERD treaty by accepting UN definitions of "free speech" and eliminating the "vast racial disparities in every aspect of American life" (housing, health, welfare, justice, etc.).

HRW complained that the United States offered "no remedies" for these disparities but "simply supported equality of opportunity" and indicated "no willingness to comply" with CERD. Of course, to "comply" with the NGO interpretation of the CERD treaty, the United States would have to abandon the Constitution's free speech guarantees, bypass federalism, and ignore the concept of majority rule—because practically nothing in the NGO agenda is supported by the American electorate.

All of this suggests that we have not reached the final triumph of liberal democracy proclaimed by Francis Fukuyama in his groundbreaking 1989 essay.

POST-SEPTEMBER 11

In October 2001, Fukuyama stated that his "end of history" thesis remained valid: that after the defeat of communism and fascism, no serious ideological competitor to Western-style liberal democracy was likely to emerge in the future. Thus, in terms of political philosophy, liberal democracy is the end of the evolutionary process. There will be wars and terrorism, but no alternative ideology with a universal appeal will seriously challenge the principles of Western liberal democracy on a global scale.

The 9-11 attacks notwithstanding, there is nothing beyond liberal democracy "towards which we could expect to evolve." Fukuyama concluded that there will be challenges from those who resist progress, "but time and resources are on the side of modernity."

Indeed, but is "modernity" on the side of liberal democracy? Fukuyama is very likely right that the current crisis with radical Islam will be overcome and that there will be no serious ideological challenge originating outside of Western civilization. However, the activities of the NGOs suggest that there already is an alternative ideology to liberal democracy within the West that has been steadily evolving for years.

Thus, it is entirely possible that modernity—thirty or forty years hence—will witness not the final triumph of liberal democracy, but the emergence of a new transnational hybrid regime that is postliberal democratic, and in the American context, post-Constitutional and post-American. This alternative ideology, "transnational progressivism," constitutes a universal and modern worldview that challenges both the liberal democratic nation-state in general and the American regime in particular.

TRANSNATIONAL PROGRESSIVISM

The key concepts of transnational progressivism could be described as follows:

The ascribed group over the individual citizen. The key political unit is not the individual citizen, who forms voluntary associations and works with fellow citizens regardless of race, sex, or national origin, but the ascriptive group (racial, ethnic, or gender) into which one is born.

A dichotomy of groups: Oppressor versus victim groups, with immigrant groups designated as victims. Transnational ideologists have incorporated the essentially Hegelian Marxist "privileged versus marginalized" dichotomy.

Group proportionalism as the goal of "fairness." Transnational progressivism assumes that "victim" groups should be represented in all professions roughly proportionate to their percentage of the population. If not, there is a problem of "underrepresentation."

The values of all dominant institutions to be changed to reflect the perspectives of the victim groups. Transnational progressives insist that it is not enough to have proportional representation of minorities in major institutions if these institutions continue to reflect the worldview of the "dominant" culture. Instead, the distinct worldviews of ethnic, gender, and linguistic minorities must be represented within these institutions.

The "demographic imperative" tells us that major demographic changes are occurring in the United States as millions of new immigrants from non-Western cultures enter American life. The traditional paradigm based on the assimilation of immigrants into an existing American civic culture is obsolete and must be changed to a framework that promotes "diversity," defined as group proportionalism.

The redefinition of democracy and "democratic ideals." Transnational progressives have been altering the definition of "democracy" from that of a system of majority rule among equal citizens to one of power sharing among ethnic groups composed of both citizens and non-citizens. James Banks, one of American education's leading textbook writers, noted in 1994 that "to create an authentic democratic Unum with moral authority and perceived legitimacy, the pluribus (diverse peoples) must negotiate and share power." Hence, American democracy is not authentic; real democracy will come when the different "peoples" that live within America "share power" as groups.

Deconstruction of national narratives and national symbols of democratic nation-states in the West. In October 2000, a U.K. government report denounced the concept of "Britishness" and declared that British history needed to be "revised, rethought, or jettisoned." In the United States, the proposed "National History Standards," recommended altering the traditional historical narrative. Instead of emphasizing the story of European settlers, American civilization would be redefined as a multicultural "convergence" of three civilizations-Amerindian, West African, and European. In Israel, a "post-Zionist" intelligentsia has proposed that Israel consider itself multicultural and deconstruct its identity as a Jewish state. Even Israeli foreign minister Shimon Peres sounded the post-Zionist trumpet in his 1993 book, in which he deemphasized "sovereignty" and called for regional "elected central bodies," a type of Middle Eastern European Union (EU).

Promotion of the concept of postnational citizenship. In an important academic paper, Rutgers law professor Linda Bosniak asks hopefully "Can advocates of postnational citizenship ultimately succeed in decoupling the concept of citizenship from the nation-state in prevailing political thought?"

The idea of transnationalism as a major conceptual tool. Transnationalism is the next stage of multicultural ideology. Like multiculturalism, transnationalism is a concept that provides elites with both an empirical tool (a plausible analysis of what is) and an ideological framework (a vision of what should be). Transnational advocates argue that globalization requires some form of "global governance" because they believe that the nation-state and the idea of national citizenship are ill suited to deal with the global problems of the future.

The same scholars who touted multiculturalism now herald the coming transnational age. Thus, Alejandro Portes of Princeton University argues that transnationalism, combined with large-scale immigration, will redefine the meaning of American citizenship.

The promotion of transnationalism is an attempt to shape this crucial intellectual struggle over globalization. Its adherents imply that one is either in step with globalization, and thus forward-looking, or one is a backward antiglobalist. Liberal democrats (who are internationalists and support free trade and market economics) must reply that this is a false dichotomy—that the critical argument is not between globalists and antiglobalists, but instead over the form global engagement should take in the coming decades: Will it be transnationalist or internationalist?

TRANSNATIONAL PROGRESSIVISM'S SOCIAL BASE: A POSTNATIONAL INTELLIGENTSIA

The social base of transnational progressivism constitutes a rising postnational intelligentsia (international law professors, NGO activists, foundation officers, U.N. bureaucrats, EU administrators, corporate executives, and politicians). When social movements such as "transnationalism" and "global governance" are depicted as the result of social forces or the movement of history, a certain impersonal inevitability is implied. However, in the twentieth century the Bolshevik Revolution, the National Socialist revolution, the New Deal, the Reagan Revolution, the Gaullist national reconstruction in France, and the creation of the EU were not inevitable, but were the result of the exercise of political will by elites.

Similarly, transnationalism, multiculturalism, and global governance, like "diversity," are ideological tools championed by activist elites, not impersonal forces of history. The success or failure of these values-laden concepts will ultimately depend upon the political will and effectiveness of these elites.

HUMAN RIGHTS ACTIVISTS

A good part of the energy for transnational progressivism is provided by human rights activists, who consistently evoke "evolving norms of international law." The main legal conflict between traditional American liberal democrats and transnational progressives is ultimately the question of whether the U.S. Constitution trumps international law or vice versa.

Before the mid-twentieth century, traditional international law referred to relations among nation-states. The "new international law" has increasingly penetrated the sovereignty of democratic nation-states. It is in reality "transnational law." Human rights activists work to establish norms for this "new international [i.e., transnational] law" and then attempt to bring the United States into conformity with a legal regime whose reach often extends beyond democratic politics.

Transnational progressives excoriate American political and legal practices in virulent language, as if the American liberal democratic nation-state was an illegitimate authoritarian regime. Thus, AI-U.S.A. charged the United States in a 1998 report with "a persistent and widespread pattern of human rights violations," naming the United States the "world leader in high tech repression." Meanwhile, HRW issued a 450-page report excoriating the United States for all types of "human rights violations," even complaining that "the U.S. Border Patrol continued to grow at an alarming pace."

ANTI-ASSIMILATION ON THE HOME FRONT

Many of the same lawyers who advocate transnational legal concepts are active in U.S. immigration law. Louis Henkin, one of the most prominent scholars of international law, calls for largely eliminating "the difference between a citizen and a non-citizen permanent resident." Washington University international law professor Stephen Legomsky argues that dual nationals holding should not be required to give "greater weight to U.S. interests, in the event of a conflict" between the United States and the other country in which the American citizen is also a dual national.

Two leading law professors (Peter Spiro from Hofstra and Peter Schuck from Yale) complain that immigrants seeking American citizenship are required to "renounce all allegiance" to their old nations." Spiro and Schuck even reject the concept of the hyphenated American and endorse what they call the "ampersand" citizen. Thus, instead of traditional "Mexican-Americans" who are loyal citizens but proud of their ethnic roots, they prefer postnational citizens, who are both "Mexican & American," who retain "loyalties" to their "original homeland" and vote in both countries.

University professor Robert Bach authored a major Ford Foundation report on new and "established residents" (the word "citizen" was assiduously avoided) that advocated the "maintenance" of ethnic immigrant identities and attacked assimilation as the "problem in America." Bach later became deputy director for policy at the INS in the Clinton administration.

The financial backing for this anti-assimilationist campaign has come primarily from the Ford Foundation, which made a conscious decision to fund a Latino rights movement based on advocacy-litigation and group rights. The global progressives have been aided—if not always consciously, certainly in objective terms—by a "transnational right." It was a determined Right-Left coalition led by libertarian Stuart Anderson, who currently holds Bach's old position at the INS, that killed a high-tech tracking system for foreign students that might have saved lives on September 11. Whatever their ideological or commercial motives, the demand for "open borders" (not simply free trade, which is a different matter altogether) by the libertarian right has strengthened the Left's anti-assimilationist agenda.

THE EU AS A STRONGHOLD OF TRANSNATIONAL PROGRESSIVISM

The EU is a large supranational macro organization that embodies transnational progressivism. Its governmental structure is postdemocratic. Power in the EU principally resides in the European Commission (EC) and to a lesser extent the European Court of Justice (ECJ). The EC, the EU's executive body, initiates legislative action, implements common policy, and controls a large bureaucracy. It is composed of a rotating presidency and nineteen commissioners chosen by the member-states and approved by the European Parliament. It is unelected and, for the most part, unaccountable.

A white paper issued by the EC suggests that this unaccountability is one reason for its success: "[the] essential source of the success of European integration is that [it] is independent from national, sectoral, or other influences." This "democracy deficit" represents a moral challenge to EU legitimacy.

The substantive polices advanced by EU leaders on issues such as "hate speech," "hate crimes," "comparable worth" for women's pay, and group preferences are considerably more "progressive" in the EU than in the United States. The ECJ has overruled national parliaments and public opinion in nation-states by ordering the British to incorporate gays and the Germans to incorporate women in combat units in their respective military services. The ECJ even struck down a British law on corporal punishment, declaring that parental spanking is internationally recognized as an abuse of human rights.

Two Washington lawyers, Lee Casey and David Rivkin, have argued that the EU ideology that "denies the ultimate authority of the nation-state" and transfers policymaking from elected representatives to bureaucrats "suggests a dramatic divergence" with "basic principles of popular sovereignty once shared by both Europe's democracies and the United States."

In international politics, in the period immediately prior to 9-11, the EU opposed the U.S. on some of the most important global issues, including the ICC, the Comprehensive Test Ban Treaty, the Land Mine Treaty, the Kyoto Global Warming Treaty, and policy toward missile defense, Iran, Iraq, Israel, China, Cuba, North Korea, and the death penalty. On most of these issues, transnational progressives in the United States—including politicians—supported the EU position and attempted to leverage this transnational influence in the domestic debate. At the same, the Bush administration on some of these issues has support in Europe, particularly from parts of the British political class and public, and elements of European popular opinion (e.g., on the death penalty.)

After 9-11, while some European nation-states sent forces to support the United States in Afghanistan, many European leaders have continued to snipe at American policies and hamper American interests in the war on terrorism. In December 2001, the European Parliament condemned the U.S. Patriot Act (the bipartisan antiterrorist legislation that passed the U.S. Congress overwhelmingly) as "contrary to the principles" of human rights because the legislation "discriminates" against noncitizens. Leading European politicians have opposed extraditing terrorist suspects to the United States if those terrorists would be subjected to the death penalty. Even a longtime Atlanticist, like the Berlin Aspin Institute's Jeffrey Gedmin, questions the "basis for a functioning alliance" between the United States and Western Europe.

Both realists and neoconservatives have argued that some EU, UN, and NGO thinking threatens to limit both American democracy at home and American power overseas. As Jeanne Kirkpatrick puts it, "Foreign governments and their leaders, and more than a few activists here at home, seek to constrain and control American power by means of elaborate multilateral processes, global arrangements, and UN treaties that limit both our capacity to govern ourselves and act abroad."

CONCLUSION

Talk in the West of a "culture war" is somewhat misleading, because the arguments over transnational versus national citizenship, multiculturalism versus assimilation, and global governance versus national sovereignty are not simply cultural but also ideological and philosophical. They pose Aristotle's question: "What kind of government is best?"

In America, there is an elemental argument about whether to preserve, improve, and transmit the American regime to future generations or to transform it into a new and different type of polity. We are arguing about "regime maintenance" versus "regime transformation."

The challenge from transnational progressivism to traditional American concepts of citizenship, patriotism, assimilation, and the meaning of democracy itself is fundamental. If our system is based not on individual rights (as defined by the U.S. Constitution) but on group consciousness (as defined by international law); not on equality of citizenship but on group preferences for non-citizens (including illegal immigrants) and for certain categories of citizens; not on majority rule within constitutional limits but on power-sharing by different ethnic, racial, gender, and linguistic groups; not on constitutional law, but on transnational law; not on immigrants becoming Americans, but on migrants linked between transnational communities; then the regime will cease to be "constitutional," "liberal," "democratic," and "American," in the understood sense of those terms, but will become in reality a new hybrid system that is "postconstitutional," "postliberal," "postdemocratic," and "post-American."

This intracivilizational Western conflict between liberal democracy and transnational progressivism accelerated after the Cold War and should continue well into the twenty-first century. Indeed, from the fall of the Berlin Wall until the attacks of September 11, the transnational progressives were on the offensive.

Since September 11, however, the forces supporting the liberal-democratic nation state have rallied throughout the West. In the post–9-11 milieu there is a window of opportunity for those who favor a reaffirmation of the traditional norms of liberal-democratic patriotism. It is unclear whether that segment of the American intelligentsia committed to liberal democracy as it has been practiced on these shores has the political will to seize this opportunity. In Europe, given elite opinion, the case for liberal democracy will be harder to make. Key areas to watch in both the U.S. and Europe include immigration-assimilation policy; arguments over international law; and the influence of a civic-patriotic narrative in public schools and popular culture.

FOURTH DIMENSION?

I suggest that we add a fourth dimension to a conceptual framework of international politics. Three dimensions are currently recognizable. First, there is traditional realpolitik, the competition and conflict among nation-states (and supranational states such as the EU). Second is the competition of civilizations, conceptualized by Samuel Huntington. Third, there is the conflict between the democratic world and the undemocratic world. My suggested fourth dimension is the conflict within the democratic world between the forces of liberal democracy and the forces of transnational progressivism, between democrats and postdemocrats.

The conflicts and tensions within each of these four dimensions of international politics are unfolding simultaneously and affected by each other, and so they all belong in a comprehensive understanding of the world of the twenty-first century. In hindsight, Fukuyama is wrong to suggest that liberal democracy is inevitably the final form of political governance, the evolutionary endpoint of political philosophy, because it has become unclear that liberal democracy will defeat transnational progressivism. During the twentieth century, Western liberal democracy finally triumphed militarily and ideologically over National Socialism and communism, powerful antidemocratic forces, that were, in a sense, Western ideological heresies. After defeating its current antidemocratic, non-Western enemy in what will essentially be a material-physical struggle, it will continue to face an ideological-metaphysical challenge from powerful post-liberal democratic forces, whose origins are Western, but that could be, in the words of James Kurth, called "post-Western."

NOTE

John Fonte is a senior fellow at the Hudson Institute. This piece is adapted from his article "Liberal Democracy vs. Transnational Progressivism" in the Summer 2002 issue of Orbis, and is based on a presentation made to FPRI's Study Group on America and the West, chaired by James Kurth.

Section 12

Conclusion

As we read these essays on multiculturalism, Double Diversity, and foreign affairs, several questions remain for future writers directly relevant to the future design and conduct of international relations in America. One is the extent to which the separate groups described in these essays will or will not cooperate with one another in the future. Is there any evidence that African Americans, Asian Americans, and Latinos are cooperating in the broader substantive goals they may share, such as increased foreign assistance, a more assertive trade policy, and wider and more effective minority participation in the design and conduct of U.S. foreign policy?

For example, one can envision a scenario of greater common efforts to increase the overall aid budgets and to promote more foreign trade to Africa, Latin America, and Asia. However, one can also envision conflicts across groups fighting for their "fair share" of the foreign affairs budget for their ancestral homelands. It is most likely we will see both occur simultaneously.[1]

A second question is how the growing differentiation within ethnic communities will affect the goals they pursue and the means they employ to achieve these goals. As the middle classes grow, will we see the common fronts of ethnic solidarity hold or break open on foreign policy? Will we witness more breaches such as the one that occurred in the African American elite over the African trade bill debates, described by Walters in this volume? We see this in another way in the Cuban American community as generational change and employment differentiation proceed.

Little noted thus far is the possible intersection of the digital Information Revolution and the growing diasporas spreading out from developing nations. At the heart of the Information Revolution is a distributed architecture capable of linking far-flung populations into new patterns of communications. Ethnic diasporas are always seeking ways to remain in better touch with their traditional homelands and with other fellow émigrés. The intersection of these twin developments is likely to create a new phenomenon—the Digital Diaspora—that may have a profound effect on all the issues described in this volume. AnnaLee Saxenian's work on Chinese and Indian immigrants in Silicon Valley and their continuing ties to their ethnic homelands suggests that the Digital Diaspora dynamic is already under way.[2]

Another question is how the evolution of U.S. external relations with countries like China, India, and Iran will affect the domestic populations with roots in those countries. If relations sour with China, what impact will it have on domestic Chinese American attitudes?

Also, will Huntington's ethnic particularism swamp the design and conduct of American foreign policy and thereby undercut the coherence of our relations with the world? Or, following Shain, will ethnic identities and their newly robust civic values revitalize American international leadership? A third likelihood proposes that both Shain and Huntington will be proven wrong, and Americans of color will continue to be excluded from anything more than token positions in senior American foreign policy positions, thereby rendering the impacts of ethnicity minimal. This "more of the same" scenario will simply mean less U.S. capacity to conduct a fully credible and effective foreign policy. Will some of the traditional cultural values of some groups undercut core American values that have contributed to the economic, political, and social successes of the country, even if they improve foreign relations?

Uncertainties remain about the ultimate impact of Double Diversity. Will the impact be great or small, positive or negative? Visionary leadership, commitments to traditional American values of fair play, openness, and human rights, as well as the play of politics, will ultimately shape the answers to these questions.

Notes

1. It is interesting to note that on college campuses today more and more younger Americans are now studying and traveling to areas outside their ancestral homeland, as African-Americans journey to China and learn Chinese, and Asian students spend a year in Brazil and speak Portuguese, while Latinos study French culture and politics.
2. AnnaLee Saxenian, "The Bangalore Boom: From Brain Drain to Brain Circulation." Revised paper prepared for Working Group on Equity, Diversity, and Information Technology, National Institute of Advanced Study, Bangalore, India, Dec. 3–4, 1999.

Double Diversity

*The Intersection of Big Changes
at Home and Abroad*

ERNEST J. WILSON III

INTRODUCTION

The United States now faces an unusual and difficult political challenge, the resolution and consequences of which will reach well into the next century and significantly affect our leadership position in the world. This challenge can be simply stated, although not simply resolved, as responding to and creatively managing the intersection of domestic diversity with international diversity and pluralism.

The world beyond our borders is changing radically. The once stable architecture of postwar world power has shifted from rigidly bipolar to multipolar. Political and economic power is less concentrated. Simultaneously, within our borders, American society also has shifted radically, experiencing dramatic changes in the structure of the economy and the distribution of political and economic power across regions and classes. Overlaying these important shifts are equally substantial demographic and cultural changes, as the United States becomes more black, more brown, more yellow, and less white.

The *intersection* between these twin changes—growing domestic pluralism and diversity, bumping against growing global pluralism and diversity—is prompting often fractious debates among American intellectuals over the meaning and value of multiculturalism, standards of excellence, and how to provide greater gender and ethnic equity. Simultaneously, journals debate the place of U.S. power in a post-Cold War world, and how best to achieve U.S. economic and strategic security. These parallel debates are now conducted separately. This chapter will try to join them, for it is the interaction of domestic and world pluralism that will exert powerful pressures on the design and implementation of U.S. foreign policy. How will those with responsibility for managing international transactions—government officials, corporate managers and strategists, interest group leaders, and political leaders—respond to this new challenge?

From World War II onward, U.S. foreign policy was based on the old organizing principle that U.S. national security rested on containment and anticommunism. The anchor to this policy was the actions of the U.S.S.R. The stakes of the struggle were the European heartland, the richest region outside the United States. This political and economic strategy was buttressed by the cultural origins and orientations of the overwhelmingly white, Anglo-Saxon, and Protestant U.S. foreign policy elite. A well-educated and relatively outward looking cadre of internationalists nurtured the vision of a prosperous and democratic Euro-centered world.[1]

With Europe the other main source of world power, it was not surprising that the Euro-centered policy was the product of children of Europe. It is unlikely that such a culturally and strategically unified vision will be carried into the next century. The countries—and its elites—are more heterogeneous. Indeed, the thesis of this chapter is that too much carry-over of the old vision will poorly serve our national interests. Instead, a new world at home and abroad requires a broader and more inclusive vision of what the United States and the world can become. Making such a vision reality requires opening up U.S. foreign policy-making to new groups. The reinvented government called for by President Clinton needs new and better channels through which to listen to what all Americans are saying about their interests and concerns. Foreign policymaking must be democratized at home, espe-cially where new local and international forces intersect. Labor unions, chambers of commerce, the League of Women Voters, and city councils insist on playing larger roles in international transactions.

The intersection of domestic and global diversity may prove especially volatile in the years ahead because it touches not only objective conditions of national income and economic well-being but also the more subjective, equally important side of political life as lived by individual men and women. This means issues of values, people's sense of iden-tity and culture, profound matters of race and blood, indeed, of what it means to be an American. As such, "Double Diversity" presents nearly unprecedented challenges to foreign policymakers and all Americans.

In part, these changes and our responses to them reflect the blurred dividing line between foreign and domestic policy. Driven by the expansion of so many transitional ties, private organizations on the local level are reaching out to their counterparts in other countries and are busily creating their own mini-foreign policies. NGOs in South Carolina deal directly with NGOs in South Africa or South America, bypassing the U.S. Department of State. American business people insist that the investment climate in dozens of "foreign" coun-tries will make or break their businesses. What then is "foreign policy"? What is domestic politics?

As significant as these trends are, we do not claim that they are completely unique and without historical precedent. After all, the decade of the 1980s was not the first time that immigration accelerated and helped to reshape American society at the same time as the international environment changed as well. From 1900 to 1910, the United States was flooded with immigrants, who added about 1 percent to the population each year. In addi-tion, in the late 1800s and early 1900s old empires crumbled as new ones were created. We need only remember the unsettling internal consequence of those "distant" global changes to realize that growing Double Diversity will be a challenge to our foreign policy, espe-cially at a time when global interdependence is greater.

Support for U.S. foreign policy following the Cold War has been significantly shaped by the expansion of interests of African Americans, Asian Americans, and Latinos, as well as women, in the design and implementation of foreign policy.

Because the changes in the international arena and those here at home have been widely described, analyzed, and evaluated, I will not repeat them in detail here, although I will sketch their most important outlines. Instead, this chapter concentrates on the intersec-tions of the international and the domestic changes, as they have received far less attention. These intersections are multidimensional, and operate through channels that are social and demographic as well as explicitly political and economic.

THE INTERNATIONAL CHANGES

U.S. policymakers now confront a world grown more disorderly and unpredictable. There are far more global players, both state and nonstate, and they are tied to one another in more complex and crosscutting ways. Once-weak states in Asia and Latin America now possess undreamed of economic and political clout. In this sense, the globe has become more politically plural, and economically and technologically integrated. Financial and other markets operate literally around the clock. The international game also has become more culturally diverse, as many of these new actors lie outside the familiar North Atlantic Euro-American core. Once, the commonalities of a shared Judeo-Christian, largely Anglo-Saxon culture, and its attendant ease of communication helped smooth our manifold relations with Europe. Arguably, the same automatic ease will be missing in our relations with Japan, Korea, and China, countries with cultures very different from our own. The opportunities for misunderstanding grow apace. It is the simultaneous expansion of new patterns of economic power, backed up by greater political and cultural pluralism, that is at the heart of the Double Diversity challenge. Because the international changes of the past several years have been widely described in journals such as *Foreign Affairs* and *Foreign Policy,* I will not go into great detail here. In summary, they include:

1. The breakup of the Soviet Union into a loose collection of newly independent states, with Russia at the core.
2. The shift from a bipolar to a multipolar (or nonpolar) structure of global political power.
3. The growing economic influence of countries with non-Western cultures, especially in East Asia, as economic dynamism there contrasts with sluggishness in Europe and America.
4. The eruption of latent nationalism and ethnic conflicts in virtually every part of the globe, but especially in the ex-Soviet Union and Central and Eastern Europe.
5. The ongoing globalization of technology and markets. The net effect of these changes is a new world system more politically plural and culturally diverse than its predecessor.

A number of particularly challenging global issues have forced themselves onto our foreign policy agenda. They include immigration, drug smuggling and use, population, the environment, and health concerns (such as AIDS): issues in which many minority groups have a special interest. Overriding all these is the imperative of dramatically improving aggregate U.S. economic performance.

Are these foreign or domestic policy issues? It is increasingly difficult to distinguish between them, as all spill over between the two arenas. The links from the outside to the inside can be as direct as the challenges to U.S. citizens posed by Columbian drug smugglers or Japanese automakers. Or, they can be as indirect as the collapse of the Soviet Union and the reduced need to maintain military spending at historical levels, freeing resources to be allocated to other domestic uses. Whether indirect or direct, these international transactions are likely to have differential impacts on different groups of the population.

THE DOMESTIC CHANGES

I will devote more attention to domestic conditions than international ones, given the focus of this chapter. After describing recent domestic demographic and socioeconomic changes, I will turn to their intersections with the global system.

We must interpret the recent explosive changes in U.S. demographic patterns against the background of our recent past, when immigration was relatively low. One expert reminds us that following World War II and continuing through the McCarthy era, the share of the population that was foreign-born declined. As those who entered the United States in earlier years aged, and immigration restrictions excluded entire regions of the world, the proportion of foreign-born dropped from almost 9 percent to 5 percent in the 1950s. In the 1960s, before the immigration policy reforms, the share fell again to historical lows; less than 5 percent of the total population was foreign-born.[2]

The greatest wave of immigration since the early 1900s found 7.3 million people coming to the United States between 1981 and 1990. As distinct from earlier immigration waves that were predominantly European, fully 85 percent of recent immigrants came from Latin America, Asia, and the Caribbean (35 percent, 38 percent, and 12 percent, respectively). Over 2.5 million Latin Americans and almost nine hundred thousand immigrants from the Caribbean came to the United States during this period. Almost three million Asians immigrated as the Asian population in the United States nearly doubled. The Latino population also increased 53 percent over the ten-year period. These changes in the number and origins of immigrants pose tremendous challenges to the United States. For example, some employers are now struggling to adapt to the now-common situation in which their employees and customers do not speak English. In Los Angeles, for example, 30 to 40 percent of the population speaks a language other than English at home.

Perhaps the single most striking development of the current domestic wave of growing diversity is the increasing differentiation *within* the population of nonwhites. This new differentiation greatly complicates the domestic sources of U.S. foreign policy. The great American divide between black and white is being blurred and complicated by a mosaic of cultures and colors. Americans are no longer just "black" or "white," minority or majority, with the latter usually richer and the former almost always poorer. For example, within the Asian population, Koreans, Chinese, and Japanese Americans are enjoying considerable economic success, and, along many welfare indicators, are ahead of white Americans on average. Within the Latino community, education and income rates also differ substantially.

There are also important differences in residential and work patterns. Since 1900, the United States has reversed its percentages of urban and rural residents. At the turn of the twentieth century, only 39.9 percent of Americans lived in cities; by 1990 fully 75 percent did. These changes also complicate the conduct of foreign policy, as urban populations more than rural ones are typically more directly involved in foreign affairs.

The most recent of these demographic and societal changes come in a difficult economic environment. In brief, the American economic pie is growing only slowly, and the distribution of the shares has become much more skewed. For the working population as a whole, real average weekly earnings have actually declined in recent years.[3] For African Americans, these figures are compounded by a tremendous racial maldistribution of income, as the black-white median gap has remained steady over the past several decades—African American median income is only around half that of whites. The intersection of slow growth, less economic equality, and increased ethnic differentiation gives the current period its peculiar character.

These economic changes will greatly shape the subjective meanings that different groups give to raw demographic changes. Groups that feel themselves losing economically will respond differently to demographic upheavals than groups that win. There is no longer a neat black-white divide, as different nonwhite groups are winning and losing at different rates. The differing sentiments that result will, in turn, translate into debates over foreign as well as domestic policy.

Areas of Intersection

The global-domestic intersections that interest us are just barely visible, and their future shape almost unimaginable. They are each composed of complex economic, political, and cultural elements. Trying to predict their future would not be especially fruitful. Therefore, we will assume that there are not one but several plausible scenarios that can flow from these complex intersections. For each of three dimensions—economic, political, and cultural—we suggest a utopian and dystopian view of what the future may hold. This chapter makes the alternative futures as stark as possible by drawing out alternative "good news"/"bad news" scenarios of the intersection of Double Diversity. The *utopian* scenarios assume constructive and positive-sum gains, with favorable impacts on U.S. foreign policy. The *dystopian* scenarios assume zero-sum conflicts and negative impacts on foreign policy. These scenarios are not predictions but an exercise in imagining alternative paths of where our current ethnic conditions could lead us. By so doing, we can alert policymakers to the kinds of emerging diversity issues that will confront them.

Both views, "good news" as well as "bad news," can be found in our society. On the bad news side, for example, a 1993 report on the relationship between immigrants and established residents concluded that "the current transformation of the American political economy [through immigration] has rekindled fears of social disorder, disorganization, conflict among newcomer and established groups, and fragmentation of the entire social fabric."[4] Will there be many more Los Angeleses in our future, or will the rise of intergroup competition, mistrust, and hostility give way to more effective integration and cooperation, and ultimately to an innovative and improved foreign policy?

Economic Issues

What major economic issues are raised by Double Diversity? A central one is the way that changes in the demographic composition of the United States affect domestic processes such as savings, investment, and productivity, in an international environment that has grown sharply more competitive and threatening. For example, will the demographic changes just described affect savings rates, capital investment, and labor force quality? A separate issue is how recent demographic changes will affect economic management at the level of the firm, and microeconomic efficiency. Especially important is how the changes will affect our capacity to shift more resources to investment and away from current consumption.

Diversity will affect international transactions as well. Diversity may help or hinder our trade relations with other parts of the world. Will the U.S. international competitive position be enhanced by the presence in Miami and Los Angeles of millions of people of Central and South American origins? Or overseas Chinese with China and East Asia? African Americans with oil-rich Nigeria and Angola?

Conversely, to what extent will overseas "cousins" seek deliberately to link up with their local cousins for business purposes? Some now argue that overseas Chinese or Indians constitute a distinct, qualitatively new subsystem of the world economy, with its own rules and structures. A related question: at the margins will these populations find the United States a more attractive and hospitable place for investment and flight capital because of the presence of a culture or subculture with which they feel more comfortable? The flip side of this issue is that overseas economic changes will increasingly affect local ethnic relations, influencing such issues as China's control of Hong Kong.

UTOPIAN-DYSTOPIAN VISIONS OF ECONOMIC INTERSECTIONS

Let us take simply one or two of these economic issues, and briefly explore their more positive utopian, and more negative dystopian, possibilities.

A *utopian* vision of U.S. demographic changes and their impact on future economic relations is that growing diversity will help U.S. competitiveness as entrepreneurially minded immigrant Americans enhance the quality of our services and manufactures at home, and develop strong and advantageous commercial ties with their homelands in Latin America, Asia, or Africa. Also, immigration provides a pool of poor and ambitious workers willing to accept lower wage rates than native-born Americans, thereby holding down labor costs. American consumers will benefit from lower prices, and employers from a lower wage bill, the savings from which they can plough back into expanding their businesses. Language skills and enhanced sensitivity to other cultures could also help make U.S. firms more competitive in overseas markets.

A *dystopian* view of our future concentrates on the inefficiencies that might arise from a workforce that, increasingly, speaks less English, knows less math, and reads and writes less well. Management for the foreseeable future will be mainly white and male; employees are increasingly female and brown, black, or yellow. Management-employee relations will be more strained when the latter are culturally distinct from the former. Efficiency and competitiveness will suffer. This is exacerbated when, as Robert Reich writes, white collar-blue collar gaps are growing in terms of income and technological sophistication.[5]

The difficulties in a diverse workforce are compounded, arguably, in an international marketplace where the competition in Japan, Korea, or China is unencumbered by the historical legacy of a multiethnic population. Cultural homogeneity makes stable economic growth easier. Orders are given, trust is developed, skills are imparted more quickly and with greater acceptance. In this dystopian view, productivity declines, and competitiveness weakens. More and more income is shifted to consumption. The economy spirals downward.

POLITICAL INTERSECTIONS: UTOPIAN AND DYSTOPIAN VIEWS

Economic dystopia could be reinforced by political dystopia. Certainly the post-1960 political mobilization of African Americans and other ethnic groups wrought enormous changes in the U.S. political system, from the election of black mayors and members of Congress to Richard Nixon's crafting of a conservative, mainly white political coalition. This coalition, hostile to further African American advances, was further nurtured by Reagan and Bush with Willie Horton-type appeals, playing into a national politics of racial resentment. In such a climate, the next several years could bring ultrachauvinist appeals to racial and ethnic solidarity and memories of ethnic homelands, the risk of rising terrorism, and continuing policy gridlock that could further balkanize and disable U.S. foreign policymaking.

In the dystopian vision, the political antipathies between suburban and urban voters in cities such as Detroit and Los Angeles will heighten as the suburban areas become more culturally white and economically strong, and the inner cities further deteriorate into black, brown, and yellow ghettos without jobs and without hope. Television and movies show the urban ethnics what they cannot hope to have, as they show suburbanites what they do not want. The result is the politics of resentment between city and suburbs, between the poor and the rich, between white communities and communities of color.

Dytopians argue that urban ethnics may turn for solace and support to their ethnic homelands in Latin America, Africa, or Asia. The dispossessed will look back toward their regions of origin instead of forward to their American future. They risk falsely glorifying their past achievements and using past glories to justify further self-segregation. In an extreme dystopian future, immigrant chauvinism and sympathies for the "homeland" may merge with resentment toward white America, producing violence and terrorism against U.S. foreign policy in the Middle East or elsewhere.

Ethnic foreign policy goals (say, ending apartheid) can serve as a rallying cry for community mobilization. But the deliberate mobilization of ethnicity for political ends is not unambiguously or equally good for all members of the group. Not only will *different groups* have different interests but also different strata within one group will have different interests—African American members of Congress and African American garbage collectors, Latino businesspeople and Latino fruit pickers. Business people and fruit pickers will be affected quite differently, for example, by NAFTA. Middle-class ethnic mobilizers may press their own narrow interest under the guise of a universal ethnic good. Working-class ethnics may get diverted from bread and butter issues by international campaigns.

Another dystopian view is that, in substantive areas of domestic and foreign policy, the further mobilization of ethnic groups in foreign policy could lead to even more policy gridlock, as groups with narrow but well-articulated interests grab and capture very small pieces of turf in the policy process. We are already familiar with the intensity with which Irish Americans promote Ireland (and sometimes the IRA), Cuban Americans oppose Castro's regime, and Jewish Americans lobby for Israel. Will we find that African Americans gain a de facto veto over U.S. policy toward Africa and the Caribbean, while Latinos get to veto policy toward Latin America? If so, then U.S. foreign policy will lose any hope for the coherence it needs to engage properly with Third World societies.

The political risk is whether the inevitable jockeying and bumping together of different groups in a democracy will help produce a more perfect union for our time, or whether culture will be so politicized and highly contentious that ultimately it disrupts the health of the body politic. Certainly the opponents of "multiculturalism" see this dystopian future ahead.[6] Other dystopians predict that race riots and mutual intolerance will produce a United States of America more like the violent and gritty film *Mad Max* than the "city on the hill" imagined by the Puritans.

A more utopian political picture sees the melting pot metaphor as driving the eventual assimilation of Cambodians and Nigerians just as it did the successful earlier integration of Irish, Italians, and Jews, groups also shunned and despised by earlier generations of WASPs. The creative energies of new immigrants will reinvigorate the political process and American democracy, bringing it new creativity and new ways of mobilizing all Americans. Latino and Asian leaders will follow African Americans into the traditional political process. Also, despite what the dystopians predict, the mobilization of groups of color into the foreign policy process may not contribute to gridlock, as hyphenated Americans from poor countries, whose own U.S. communities are poor, will be less inclined to hammer away at foreign policy than to focus on immediate domestic economic and welfare imperatives. Divisive conflicts over the details of regional policy are less likely than generalized pressures to do something in the region, including appointing ethnic representatives to regional positions. Therefore, the direct impact of these groups on foreign policy may be modest. Still, as groups become more middle class, they eventually become more directly concerned with foreign policy issues and diversify their concerns beyond the strictly bread-and-butter issues of jobs and services. We can anticipate, therefore, growing interest in foreign policy among these groups.

Utopians would argue that increased U.S. engagement in new regions is positive. For example, U.S. policy toward Israel has certainly been strengthened by Jewish leadership on Middle East issues. This has given the United States a strong presence in the region that it might not have otherwise had.

However, the position that any particular ethnic group takes on a substantive foreign policy issue is far from obvious. The NAFTA treaty is a case in point, especially among Latino Americans for whom there exists no formal consensus over the treaty's impact on the American Spanish-speaking communities. Chicanos and Cuban Americans hold different positions, and the anticipated impacts will differ by industry and for those close to or far from the U.S.-Mexican border. Many Latinos agree that they would likely be the first to suffer job loss, as half of Latino Americans live in states that border Mexico and many work in low wage positions that risk moving south. But this fear does not prevent many Latinos from conditionally supporting some form of free trade agreement. Views range from advocating renegotiating of the treaty to inserting safeguards in the implementing legislation. The expected costs in job loss and environmental quality are tempered for some by the belief that as the image of Mexico improves in the United States, so will the image of Latino Americans. In their eyes, Mexico for the first time has been treated as an equal partner with the United States.

Across the border, the Mexican government has begun to reach out to Latino Americans in novel ways, pushing greater economic and cultural integration between Mexicans and Americans of Mexican origin. For example, in July 1992, the Mexican government established a cooperative agreement with U.S. Latino organizations to establish a $20 million loan program for joint ventures between Mexico and Latino-Americans. The Mexican government has also opened an office in its embassy to work solely with Latino Americans to foster interaction and exchange. There are parallel efforts by African governments to reach out to African Americans through economic ties as well as through cultural links. For example, there have been annual African American summits in 1992 and 1993 at which African heads of state and political leaders have met leading African American politicians and business people.

CULTURAL INTERSECTIONS: UTOPIAN AND DYSTOPIAN VISIONS

This is probably the most obvious and yet the most difficult area on which to comment. Cultural intersections are obvious in material manifestations like spicy restaurant menus and exotic clothing styles. Equally important are the less immediately obvious aspects of culture. Ethnic groups and races are not simply collections of people who happen to be the same color. They have cultural particularities as well that give deepest meaning to our lives and actions.

Utopians would argue that America's unique mosaic of immigrant cultures creates its own national supraculture that fosters greater cross-cultural understanding. Our many cultures nurture interpersonal skills that enable Americans to navigate with aplomb the difficult waters of ethnic neighborhoods and racial boundaries in the United States and, by extension, internationally. Many commentators point to the optimism and openness of Americans overseas, and to the greater ability of American firms to incorporate local people as workers and managers.

Furthermore, the growing mix of cultures might help to complicate the historically diffi-cult and defining fault line of black and white, muting this basic, binary conflict and channeling some of those energies into considerations of "multiculturalism."

Cultural clashes are the flip side of cultural sharing and learning. America's capacity to coopt and incorporate may break down under the pressure of new immigrants. We have described some of these possibilities under the political dystopian vision, and need not repeat them here.

DIRECT AND INDIRECT FOREIGN POLICY IMPACTS

This chapter is ultimately concerned with United States foreign policy. We know that Double Diversity will bring changes, but we do not know whether they will be modest or monumental. Nor can we know the precise foreign policy areas they will most affect. In other words, we know neither the magnitude nor the direction of the impacts that will surely come.

There are at least two ways to think about these impacts. The more conventional way traces the direct influence of interested and mobilized ethnic elites on foreign policy. This can range from the influence of Polish Americans on U.S. policy toward Poland, to the influence of Jewish Americans on U.S. policy toward the Middle East. This classic "foreign policy" paradigm poses the issue in terms of direct "politics in/foreign policy out." In these terms the new Double Diversity impacts are likely to be modest on the design of overall U.S. foreign policy but will have greater effect on U.S. regional policies.

Under the last two Republican administrations, African American interest groups were almost entirely frozen out of any serious foreign policy channels (with the excep-tion perhaps of the development oriented AfriCare). African foreign policy experts were apparently made to feel less than welcome in the foreign service; witness the Republi-cans' serious reductions in senior African American officers and the lawsuits and administrative actions brought by African Americans against the Department of State. By the end of the first Bush administration, African Americans were appointed to only seven out of 170-odd ambassadorial posts, and only one of the top fifty positions in the State Department. Organized African American leverage over substantive foreign policy matters was comparably low. Latino figures and effective influence were even lower. There was no indication that African American input was seriously considered under the Republicans.

Ethnic Americans with Third World roots will expand their lobbying for more favorable policies across the board toward their home regions whether Africa, Latin America, or Asia. This could certainly involve more liberal immigration policies. Groups also press for more foreign assistance to "their" areas, more state visits by presidents from these areas, and probably greater support from the Export-Import Bank and other agencies for more private investments. There may be less pressure for military intervention in these areas. Some of the new attention will remain in the relatively neutral arena of culture—museums and visiting dance troupes. These are the specific substantive areas that will be most affected by the diversification or "ethnicization" of foreign policy. In general, these indi-viduals and groups will seek more high-level attention to developing areas as a whole, irrespective of their country of origin.

However, foreign policy has historically been the domain of elite or upper-middle-class politics. The Latino and African American middle classes are still relatively small, and their attention more attuned to domestic socioeconomic issues. Foreign policy is unlikely to be a major preoccupation. But with Latino and African American and Asian middle classes growing, we will see greater international interest and more attempts to exercise direct influence. They are likely to seek most radical policy changes as much as more attention (conventionally defined) to these parts of the world. Perhaps there may be greater emphasis on direct "people-to-people" exchanges among NGOs. Certainly the history of CBC interest in Africa is instructive, as the CBC was largely responsible for the regular increases in U.S. Agency for International Development funding for the continent, and provided backing to create the African Development Foundation. Also, African American support for sanctions against South Africa had an important influence on Congress's decisions to impose them on that country. In 1993, the number of African American members of Congress increased to thirty-nine, and since the administration will need those votes on other issues, their views on Africa carry more weight. (The number of Latino members also rose in 1993—to a total of nineteen.)

In a general sense, more direct lobbying and public agitation by these groups is likely to introduce into U.S. foreign policy greater sensitivities to their home areas and the people who live there. Americans (policy officials as well as the average citizen) might gain a more nuanced appreciation for non-European countries and peoples.

However, there is potentially a far more important, if indirect, link between the behavior of black, yellow, and brown citizens and U.S. foreign policy. These links are more structural in nature. It is certainly no secret that the most wretched, rejected, and rebellious elements of American society are disproportionately black and brown in number. The poorest of the poor are disproportionately concentrated in our inner cities, and they are people of color. Observers from progressives such as Professor William Wilson to conservatives such as Charles Murray agree on this point. As the Kerner Commission reported twenty-five years ago, the United States is still a society divided between black and white.

Black-white economic and spatial segregation is reflected in black-white attitude differences. Survey research polls show substantial gaps between black and white opinions along important political dimensions. Although there is certainly ample evidence of black-white cultural homogenization and ethnic crossover, there also is evidence that many younger African Americans remain enclosed in an angry, antiestablishment urban culture that scorns standard "white" notions of economic and political success. This is especially true for young African American males. The ladders of upward mobility, those well-paid, low-skilled positions that once let earlier ethnics climb out of Italian or Irish ghettos, have themselves been pulled up and tossed away. Unlike some of its European counterparts—and here is the critical point for public policy—the U.S. economy has been unable to provide new ladders of upward mobility to its lowermost citizens, especially through apprenticeship programs. African Americans are especially hurt here, but the Latino communities are affected as well. Recent books by Studs Terkel, E. J. Dionne, and Thomas and Mary Edsall demonstrate the ways that race and ethnicity risk paralyzing our polity and economy, as some whites are reluctant to support policies they feel would benefit African Americans disproportionately and give them something for nothing.

U.S. foreign policy in the 1990s and beyond will be decisively affected, however indirectly, if there is further consolidation of an American underclass disproportionately black and brown. A growing underclass will be a terrible weight on the economic recovery of America. Sharp divisions of race and wealth will stunt the possibilities for a full and creative foreign policy. In the short term, as well as the long, we need to allocate scarce and expensive capital, and scarce and expensive leadership attention to domestic priorities to ensure that America does not select this dystopian path to the future. Reallocations from consumption to investment, and from less directly productive investments to other more productive ones, will be difficult politically and financially. Yet, it is becoming painfully obvious to more and more Americans that the growing inequalities and disaffection has become unacceptably expensive for them, in societal, moral, and economic terms. Deteriorating racial relations, and a stagnant economy partially stalled by racially motivated policy paralysis, will spill into our international relations as well, both diplomatic and economic. As the international economist Robert Hormats and others ask, can a great nation with great ambitions abroad meet those ambitions, and its obligations, if it contains within itself a terrible drain on its moral standing and its economic strength?

CONCLUSION

In this chapter I have analyzed and described the new differentiation within and between ethnic groups and races in the United States, and how this domestic differentiation intersects political pluralism and cultural diversity internationally. I also speculated on how the intersection of domestic and global change (Double Diversity) might evolve along economic, political, and social dimensions, and how over the coming years these might be expressed through utopian or dystopian paths.

Diversity—both domestic and foreign—is not something we can ignore. It is not a choice but a condition of life at home and abroad, and we ignore it at our peril.

In this period of profound domestic and international structural changes, the role of leadership becomes especially important. These are rare historical moments when more possibilities open up than are usually available under more "normal" times. With our choices greater in number, progressive leadership plays an important role in shaping future paths, especially in setting new agendas for action.

For America to retain its international leadership position, our political and civic leaders must grasp the full implications of the two scenarios. They can lead by telling the American people that these two potential futures are before us. They can lead by pointing out the terrible costs of the dystopian future. They can lead by insisting that Americans need to pursue the positive scenario, while doing everything possible to avoid the dystopian "bad news" scenario. They can lead by drawing on traditional American democratic values of inclusion and openness. Diversity must be defined by the leadership as opportunities to be seized, not as terrible burdens to be shed, or intractable problems to be avoided.

To make progress in this area, the leadership needs to catch up conceptually to our increasingly diverse social realities. The Clinton administration pursued gender, racial, and ethnic diversity in its appointments, including those in the foreign policy area. Longer to develop are changes in the content of policy, aimed at reflecting these different forces of diversity in a post–Cold War foreign policy framework more cognizant of the changed structures of domestic and international politics.

For new leadership to emerge, the traditional foreign policy establishment must open up and become more representative of the new diversity of gender, ethnicity, and race. Foreign policy appointments should reflect the growing interest in global issues found beyond the Boston–New York–Washington corridor, in the Far West, the Midwest, and the South. The State Department as much as the Labor Department should have a leadership team that in President Clinton's words "looks like America." The ultimate purpose is not a bean-counting exercise of meeting affirmative action numbers. Instead, embracing diversity means drawing on the talents of all Americans, especially those who may bring different perspectives of global change than the traditional foreign policy elite. Those with responsibility for making foreign policy should consult more frequently with nongovernmental organizations and groups that are primarily domestic but have international potential. Similarly, new ways must be found to listen to new international voices. Presidents and prime ministers have views,—but, in Zaire and Burma and elsewhere, so do democratic NGOs. Their views are likely to be the views of the future.

It is not only the federal government that must respond to these major domestic and international changes. Other large American institutions (universities, foundations, corporations, and so on) also need to develop new strategies to benefit from this Double Diversity as well.

At this critical point in our history, where utopian and dystopian paths lie ahead, the country badly needs to concentrate on commonalities and the points that unite us, even as we explore the cultural and other differences between groups or individuals that distinguish us from one another. Indeed, it is precisely the search itself that is so uniquely American. Groups of color need to devote energy to strengthening and enriching the common bonds that link all Americans, just as Anglo-Americans need a more sympathetic understanding of the perspective of the outsiders and the underdogs. The theme of Americans reinventing themselves is, after all, a dominant one in the literature and intellectual history of America, from the colonists reinventing themselves as a people separate from the British, to individuals such as Ben Franklin reinventing himself several times, to the recent enormous popularity of the film *Malcolm X,* whose hero, like so many quintessentially American characters before him, worked hard at continual self-transformation. Here at the intersection of dual diversity, in a post–Cold War world, never was the need greater for such transformation.

NOTES

1. See Destler, Gelb, and Lake (1984) and Michael Clough, "Global Changes and Institutional Transformation: Restructuring the Foreign Policymaking Process," The Stanley Foundation, October 22–24, 1992.
2. Robert Bach, *Changing Relations: Newcomers and Established Residents in U.S. Communities,* A report to the Ford Foundation by The National Board of the Changing Relations Project, 1993, p. 3.
3. Average U.S. wages in private industry fell (in constant 1977 dollars) from $184 per week in 1975 to $169 per week in 1987. See Wright (1990), p. 298. The total income of the wealthiest 20 percent of Americans increased from 41.5 percent to 43.7 percent of total U.S. income between 1977 and 1987. In contrast, the income of the poorest 20 percent decreased from 5.2 percent to 4.6 percent. See Burtless (1990), p. 1.
4. See Robert Bach, cited above, p. 29.
5. Reich, Robert (1991). What Is Nation? *Political Science Quarterly* 106(2), Summer.
6. Schlesinger (1992).

Credits

Telhami, Shibley, "Arab and Muslim America: A Snapshot," *Brookings Review*, Winter 2002, pp. 14–15. Reprinted by permission of the publisher.

Stanford, Karin L., "Citizen Diplomacy and Jesse Jackson: A Case Study for Influencing U.S. Foreign Policy Toward Southern Africa," *The Western Journal of Black Studies*, 19(1), 1995, pp. 19–29.

Skinner, Elliott P., "African-American Perspectives on Foreign Policy," in Ralph C. Gomes and Linda Faye Williams, eds., *From Exclusion to Inclusion: The Long Struggle for African-American Political Power* (New York: Greenwood Press, 1992), pp. 173–185. Reprinted by permission of the publisher.

Walters, Ronald, "The African Growth and Opportunity Act: Changing Foreign Policy Priorities Toward Africa in a Conservative Political Culture," in Charles P. Henry, ed., *Foreign Policy and the Black (Inter)National Interest*, Albany, State University of New York Press, 2000, pp. 17–36.

Wilson, Larman C., "Human Rights and American Foreign Policy: The Rhetoric and the Practice," in Don C. Piper and Ronald J. Terchek, eds., *Interaction: Foreign Policy and Public Policy* (Washington, D.C.: American Enterprise Institute, 1983). Reprinted by permission of The American Enterprise Institute for Public Policy Research, Washington, D.C.

McGlen, Nancy E. and Meredith R. Sarkees, "Gender and the Foreign Policy Institutions," Excerpted from Headline Series No. 307, *The Status of Women in Foreign Policy*. Reprinted with permission of Foreign Policy Association, New York. www.fpa.org.

Putnam, Robert D., "Bowling Together." Reprinted with permission from *The American Prospect*, 13(3), February 11, 2002. The American Prospect, 11 Beacon Street, Suite 1120, Boston, MA 02108. All rights reserved.

Barone, Michael, "Politics After September 11," *Hoover Digest*, 2002, No. 2. Reprinted by permission of the publisher and Michael Barone.

Fonte, John, "Liberal Democracy vs. Transnational Progressivism: The Ideological War Within the West," *Orbis*, 46(3), Summer 2002.

Wilson, Ernest J., III, "Double Diversity: The Intersection of Big Changes at Home and Abroad," in D. Yankelovich and I.M. Destler, eds., *Beyond the Beltway* (New York: W.W. Norton and Co., 1994), pp. 155–174.

Index